Communication in Question

Competing Perspectives on Controversial Issues in Communication Studies

Josh Greenberg
Carleton University

Charlene D. Elliott
Carleton University

THOMSON

NELSON

Australia   Canadá   Mexico   Singapore   Spain   United Kingdom   United States

THOMSON

NELSON

Communication in Question:
Competing Perspectives on Controversial Issues in Communication Studies

by Josh Greenberg and Charlene D. Elliott

Associate Vice President, Editorial Director:
Evelyn Veitch

Editor-in-Chief, Higher Education:
Anne Williams

Executive Editor:
Laura Macleod

Marketing Manager:
Shelley Collacutt Miller

Developmental Editor:
Theresa Fitzgerald

Permissions Coordinator:
Daniela Glass

Content Production Manager:
Carrie McGregor

Production Service:
GEX Publishing Services

Copy Editor:
Marcia Gallego

Proofreader:
GEX Publishing Services

Manufacturing Coordinator:
Ferial Suleman

Design Director:
Ken Phipps

Interior Design:
Dianna Little

Cover Design:
Peter Papayanakis

Cover Image:
Photos.com/Jupiter Images

Compositor:
GEX Publishing Services

Printer:
Thomson/West

Library and Archives Canada Cataloguing in Publication Data

Main entry under title:

Communication in question: Competing perspectives on controversial issues in communication studies/ Joshua Greenberg, Charlene Elliott, [editors].

Includes bibliographical references.
ISBN 978-0-17-610422-1

1. Mass media--Textbooks. I. Greenberg, Joshua II. Elliott, Charlene

P91.25.C64 2007   302.23
C2007-903376-8

ISBN-13: 978-0-17-610422-1
ISBN-10: 0-17-610422-4

TABLE OF CONTENTS

Postscript 335

Communication Studies through the Prism of Everyday Life

In a seminal essay, communications theorist John Durham Peters (1986) provocatively asks why the discipline of communication studies has failed to offer a coherent vision of itself in relation to other social sciences. To encourage debate about the field's past, present, and future, Peters suggests that as an institution, communication studies suffers from an identity crisis borne out of the myriad "conceptual confusions" regarding its central intellectual tasks. Twenty years have passed since Peters' influential paper, although his argument continues to resonate and it remains questionable whether we are, today, any further along. Book-length studies (Katz, Peters, Liebes, & Orloff, 2002) and conferences have been devoted to the questions of what makes up communication's vision and central intellectual tasks, but no definitive answers yet exist. It is disputable whether there are definitive answers at all, and whether all the hand-wringing that sometimes accompanies these debates is worth it. Self-reflective exercises such as those Peters advocates are not unique to communication studies—similar debates remain unresolved within the more traditional social science disciplines as well, particularly sociology (see, for example, Brady, 2004; Burawoy, 2004; and Gans, 1989). In the end, Peters modestly proposes that the task of communication studies should be to create the "conditions that help foster a higher quality of mind" (1986, p. 552).

We agree with this objective, but a fundamental question for us remains: In what ways might communication studies actually go about doing this? Or, more to the point, what pedagogical strategies might communication scholars use to encourage their students to think differently about the centrality of communication in their lives and to reflect critically about how it informs their actions in the world? Peters does not identify which steps ought to be taken, preferring instead to offer "novel insights," to "pose questions that need to be asked," and to provide "a sense of how to answer them" (1986, p. 528). His questions are thorough: What is the position of communication within the broader university structure? What is the status of communication as a profession? What are the intellectual consequences of not taking these questions seriously? To Peters' list we might also add the question of the "public turn" in our work, or the ways in which we can mobilize our knowledge and understanding of communication to inspire hope in our students to make their own lives and the lives of other citizens better.[1] Might we promote such a fundamental "public turn" in our work by encouraging students to apply communication theories and methods to solving the key public problems of our time? Although no singular answer or approach exists to deal with these questions, we suggest there is opportunity to forge a vision for communication by presenting the field as an open, fluid assemblage of approaches that allow us to explore both the extraordinary and the mundane aspects of everyday life.

American sociologist C. Wright Mills, an important figure in the history of critical communication studies, offers much insight into the current functioning and the future of the field. Mills was the most widely read social scientist in North America at the time of his death in 1962 (Keen, 1999). Without question he was a visionary, an uncompromising dissenter and a renegade intellectual who believed that critique was a fundamental prerequisite to the development of a truly democratic society.[2] Drawing inspiration from a number of classical thinkers (including Karl Marx, Max Weber, Thorstein Veblen, and John Dewey), Mills believed that academic work should be seen not as a science per se, which invites all kinds of allusions to what he called "abstract empiricism" (i.e., the tendency of researchers to reduce complex configurations of self, history, and society to quantitative indicators generated by statistical methods), but as an intellectual craft. The intellectual should endeavour not to separate her life from her work, but rather to integrate personal experience with professional interest in order to enrich understanding of both. As a craft or an art of scholarship, communication research should be critical and reflexive, as well as dealing with the substantive problems and experiences of everyday life.

In *The Sociological Imagination* (1959), arguably his most influential book, Mills proposes that scholars should seek to illuminate the distinctions and relationships among history, biography, and social structure. "Troubles occur within the character of the individual and within the range of his immediate relations with others," he writes, while "issues have to do with matters that transcend these local environments of the individual and the range of his inner life" (p. 8). Part of the difficulty individuals have with establishing the connections between their personal troubles and public issues is that they become overwhelmed with information that potentially limits their capacity to understand the complexity of what is happening around them. In what Mills calls the "Age of Fact" (and what social scientists have since referred to as the "information society" or "media society"), individuals struggle to acquire this insight and understanding. Ultimately, however, they become inured to the social forces that constitute their lives (and which they, in turn, help constitute) as a result of being inundated with too much information. A culture of indifference, Mills argues, is the "signal feature of our period"[2](p. 12). In terms that anticipate Peters' argument almost thirty years later, Mills suggests that what is needed "is a *quality of mind* that will help [citizens] use information and to develop reason in order to achieve lucid summations of what is going on in the world and what may be happening within themselves" (p. 6).

We find much value in Mills' vision for research and argue that it is as crucial for students in communication and other social sciences today as it was for students in the post–World War II era. Mills was a social democrat who believed that all individuals have the capacity to be intellectuals, whether they are professors, students, or people living and working outside of the formal institutions of higher learning. He positioned the "sociological imagination" as a concept that could apply well beyond the discipline that bore its name to encourage within citizens a capacity for critical social analysis of the personal problems and public issues that constitute their everyday lives. We heed Mills' wisdom and encourage our students to develop a *communicative imagination* to establish connections between their everyday experiences and encounters with communications media and the broader policies, social structures, and historical forces that condition their emergence, the ways in which these media are used, and the ways they transform our lives.

Key Controversies in Communication

Envisaging the relationship between critical inquiry and everyday life is the coordinating theme for *Communication in Question*. Indeed, the book's genesis came from our informal conversations about the challenges we face in inspiring undergraduate students about the richness of issues and topics they can pursue within the field of communication, or of the communicative dimensions of issues and topics with which they are already familiar. Our university (like others, we assume) boasts no shortage of students who enroll in communication courses because they want to learn about the latest applications in new media technology. Yet, when it comes to establishing connections between, for example, the rising popularity of blogs or podcasting with the policies that enable the growth of new media technologies and the increasing tendency toward the privatization of information dissemination, retrieval, and storage, the interest meter always seems to dip. To illustrate, one of the editor's introductory communication seminars deals with the emerging popularity of podcasting as a medium for delivering university lectures. After discussing all the benefits of the technology, the professor typically introduces some of the policy implications of popularizing this form of privatized learning (e.g., funding for instructional resources, the development of new communication technologies). What often begins as a lively, enthusiastic discussion about media usage quickly transmogrifies into a collective groan: "Why do we have to reduce *everything* to policy?" the students complain. "Can't we just accept this new, more convenient way of accessing information as progress?" Many of us have also no doubt encountered more than a handful of requests from students wanting to learn in their communication courses what it takes to succeed in the world of advertising or public relations. The challenge, for those of us who don't *do* advertising or PR in the strict instrumental or commercial sense, is to harness this interest by introducing students to the social, historical, and economic conditions from which their favourite ads or PR campaigns for iPod, Volkswagen, the GAP, or Greenpeace have emerged.

Our goal with this book is to confront this pedagogical challenge head on. The approach we take here is novel, we believe, both in terms of content and style. Featuring short, engaging position papers by leading Canadian academics, journalists, and policy advocates, *Communication in Question* is designed foremost as a tool for generating small-group discussions and debates. The book presents twenty topics, with each topic comprising two essays. The topics are organized to address a cross-section of five key themes, ranging from the general to the particular: Communication and Canadian Society, Media and Social Issues, Technology and Everyday Life, Regulation and Cultural Industries, and Entertainment and Popular Culture. While these themes and their related topics are not exhaustive, we feel they represent a broad spectrum of interests and capture the diversity of research projects and programs that are ongoing within the field.

Communication in Question presents students with an issue-oriented, topical reader that can serve as a locus for small-group discussion and debate and generate points of departure that can help students develop their own research ideas. We hope that the engaging prose of the papers and their connections to everyday life will motivate students to formulate informed perspectives on topics with which they have either limited familiarity (e.g., media ownership, telecommunications regulation) or for which they may lack sufficient critical distance (e.g., the relationship between media representation and body image). The "competing perspectives" format of the reader also provides material for students to chew on and consider in relation to the more general overview of the field their instructor or other communication textbooks can provide. Even if they disagree with one or both perspectives, students can use each essay as a starting position for asking more probing questions and challenging the assumptions and arguments they have been presented. The book illustrates that there are always at least two clear and reasonable positions to take regarding a contentious question about communication, through which students can develop their own perspectives.

Finally, the book is designed to provide an alternative to the innumerable American readers of this sort on the market. We have used many of these books in our courses before and are excited to provide an option that doesn't require the student to spend time unpacking why, for example, Canadian media companies are not bound by FCC regulations, and instead focus on discussing and debating actual issues in Canadian media regulation. With this in mind, *Communication in Question* provides valuable Canadian content that we hope will expose readers to the richness and diversity of issues and perspectives that inform communication studies in this country and encourage them to think and act in a more reflexive, critically informed way in their everyday lives. The fact that all of the contributors are Canadian or currently working in a Canadian university also reveals the wealth of domestic expertise on issues that arguably transcend national borders and concerns.

Given our interest in encouraging our students to develop a communicative imagination, it seems appropriate to return to the sage advice of C. Wright Mills. A firm believer in the importance of education, Mills suggested that in a classroom the teacher ought to try to show others how men and women think, and at the same time reveal what a fine feeling she gets when she does it well. As professors of communication we strive to inspire in our students an interest in and commitment to seeing their everyday lives not as manifestations of individual will or as the effects of powers acting on them from above, but as complex configurations of biography, history, and social structures that they have the capacity not only to understand but also to change. We hope this book embodies this critical ethos.

Josh Greenberg
Charlene D. Elliott

References

Baudrillard, J. (1983). *In the shadow of the silent majorities.* New York: Semiotexte.

Brady, D. (2004). Why public sociology may fail. *Social Forces, 82*(4), 1629–1638.

Burawoy, M. (2004). Public sociologies: Contradictions, dilemmas, and possibilities. *Social Forces, 82*(4), 1603–1618.

Gans, H. (1989). Sociology in America: The discipline and the public. *American Sociological Review, 54*, 1–16.

Katz, E., Peters, J. D., Liebes, T., & Orloff, A. (Eds.). (2002). *Canonical texts in media research: Are there any? Should there be any? How about these?* Cambridge: Polity Press.

Keen, M. F. (1999). *Stalking the sociological imagination: J. Edgar Hoover's FBI surveillance of American sociology.* Westport, CT: Greenwood Press.

Mathieu, P. (2005). *Tactics of hope: The public turn in English composition.* Portsmouth, NH: Boynton/Cook.

Mills, C. W. (1959). *The sociological imagination.* New York: Oxford University Press.

Peters, J. D. (1986). Institutional sources of intellectual poverty. *Communication Research, 13*(4), 527–560.

Sterne, J. (2005). C. Wright Mills, the Bureau for Applied Social Research, and the meaning of critical scholarship. *Cultural Studies—Critical Methodologies, 5*(1), 65–94.

Notes

[1] Paula Mathieu (2005) advocates a similar pedagogical strategy for students in English.

[2] Mills was especially critical of the "abstract empiricism" that defined both social science and communication research in the early post–World War II era, represented in the works of communication scholars such as Paul Lazarsfeld and Robert K. Merton. However, Mills' own involvement with the Bureau for Social Research (the locus of abstract, empirical scholarship to which he pithily refers) and his proclivity for survey and quantitative methods where it suited him suggest a contradiction at the heart of Mills' radicalism. Jonathan Sterne (2005) has recently published an important article that speaks to these points.

[3] Jean Baudrillard (1983) presents a more contemporary, nihilistic variation of this theme of the relationship between media saturation and public indifference in his book *In the Shadow of the Silent Majorities*. However, where Mills laments the effects of information overload on citizens' ability to think critically about the world, Baudrillard argues that the indifference produced by excessive media consumption and information is an "explicit and positive counter-strategy … a collective retaliation and of a refusal to participate in the recommended ideals, however enlightened" (p. 14).

ACKNOWLEDGMENTS

The genesis of this text was a conversation between the coeditors about the challenges of encouraging undergraduate students to become excited about communication theories, policies, technologies, and practices. While each of us has created patchworks of readings and assembled pedagogical materials to make communication meaningful in a way that registers with the everyday lives of our students, we wondered why a reader that could meet this need had not yet been produced. Our hope is that this volume will help to fill this gap.

We are grateful to our colleague Paul Attallah for his enthusiastic response to the idea of this book and for his ongoing support and advice. We also wish to thank Theresa Fitzgerald at Thomson Nelson, who was an excellent developmental editor. Many thanks also go to our authors, whose intellectual contributions made this book a reality.

The comments and feedback from the following reviewers were very much appreciated: Dale A. Bradley, Brock University, Alexandre Sévigny, McMaster University, and Nicole Neverson, Trent University.

Josh Greenberg
Charlene D. Elliott

PART 1 Communication and Canadian Society

The mass media play an important role in the construction of national identity and, under ideal conditions, help to spread and promote democratic discussion and debate. Yet fundamental questions remain. What is Canadian identity? Do Canadian media help to construct and preserve it? And is a public media system the best guarantor for promoting democracy in Canada?

The issues in this section deal with these questions, albeit in slightly different ways. The section begins with a debate over whether Canadians need a national public broadcaster to enhance democracy. According to David Taras, public service broadcasters such as the CBC reflect and foster democratic discussion by engaging citizens in the life of their communities in a way that the private broadcasters do not. However, he argues that while demand for public broadcasting seems to be growing in other parts of the world, recent federal governments in Canada have sought to restrict rather than enlarge the capacity of the CBC. This has created a downward spiral in the range of programming choices the CBC can offer and has led to increased commercialization of its content. Nevertheless, the CBC continues to enjoy levels of public trust and confidence that far outstrip the commercial broadcast media. It regularly provides more detailed and in-depth analysis of the pressing issues of the day because of its mandate to promote the public interest. Any further reduction of this mandate, Taras argues, will have an indelible negative impact on Canadian democracy.

Paul Attallah, conversely, argues that democratic development has proceeded for millennia without the aid of public broadcasting. Indeed, broadcasting (especially television) has been so vilified by cultural critics that it is remarkable anyone would expect a broadcaster to contribute to democratic development or renewal at all. Challenging the belief that public broadcasting serves the public interest ipso facto, Attallah argues that public broadcasting operates on the basis of ensuring "simultaneous exposure of all people to the same news, entertainment, drama, sports, and so on." Yet, he claims, not everyone agrees on the topics that should be on the public agenda. In a country as diverse as Canada, there is a danger that decision making about what is in the public interest will be left to people who are inherently distrustful of popular tastes and preferences. Rather, as Attallah contends, "an unrepresentative elite" has become the primary beneficiary of "a public subsidy in pursuit of its particularistic interests." This situation, he argues, is not democratic at all.

The second issue considers the impact of American news on Canadians. James H. Wittebols argues that "seismic shifts" in the American media-scape during the past few decades have resulted in the promotion of a narrow range of business perspectives and interests that prove incompatible with the democratic values Canadians espouse. Wittebols acknowledges that Canadian news has always had a different look and feel than news south of the border. However, under the American-led pressures of globalization, Canadian news appears to be taking on some of the aesthetic characteristics of U.S. news programming. "News tickers crawling across the bottom of the screen, the musical and graphical flourishes designed for ongoing stories, the increasing lack of depth in reporting … are fast becoming features of the Canadian TV news land-scape." Wittebols suggests that "Canadian news media are beginning to suffer increasingly from many of the same ills that transformed American news giants from at least occasional defenders of civic virtue into faithful advocates for economic and political power." These are worrisome trends, he notes, to which Canadians ought to attend soon, before it's too late.

Christopher Dornan, on the other hand, argues that no evidence supports the contention that American media programming has a negative effect on Canadians. In fact, he suggests that Canadian mythology rather than reality is revealed in this belief. Dornan argues that the fear of American cultural imperialism is a "decidedly Canadian anxiety" that is "as old as Canada itself." Like children who enjoy being "frightened by stories of monsters in the basement they know are not real," Canadians also know deep down that they are not so easily manipulated by the pervasiveness of American culture. Where Wittebols speaks of the similarities between entertainment and news programming, Dornan considers the distinction between them important because Canadians overwhelmingly turn to national news broadcasters over their American equivalents, even when they can't get enough of *Desperate Housewives*. Thus, while offensive broadcasters like Fox TV News and Rush Limbaugh are popular in the United States, Canadians simply do not enjoy or take very seriously this type of American news programming. And Canadian broad-casters, for their part, are perfectly aware of this and are in no rush to emulate that model.

The third debate speaks less to the effects of foreign media content than to the patterns and principles of ownership. Richard Schultz argues that existing policies that prevent foreign corporations from owning Canadian media properties "are based on a misreading of Canadian history, on an undocu-mented claim that foreign ownership is intrinsi-cally bad, and on simplistic assumptions." More importantly, these restrictions are "dangerously contagious for other sectors" of the economy, such as telecommunications, where massive capital infu-sion will be necessary in the not-too-distant future. The problem with the foreign ownership policy restrictions, Schultz argues, has to do ultimately with the spurious claims of its advocates. Schultz sees in the "cultural nationalist" project "a gloomy, undefined foreboding of the unknown" that fails to appreciate the strengths of the Canadian media industry because it is based on an assumption of weakness. More importantly, this assumption is getting in the way of economic progress. Ultimately, it does not and should not matter whether the owners of Canadian media come from Canada or abroad. Canadian audiences, Schultz's analysis suggests, will ultimately determine the flavour of media programming, and no corporate executives worth their salt would ignore this.

Valerie Scatamburlo-D'Annibale and Kyle Asquith argue against this perspective, claiming that limits to foreign ownership of Canadian media are not only necessary but should be strengthened. In their view, "the current debate over owner-ship restrictions on Canadian media is, at its very core, a debate about competing interests" between the Canadian public and mostly American media corporations. They conceptualize communication as culture and argue that, unlike other commodities, culture should not be left to the vagaries of market competition but should be vigorously protected by legislation. Scatamburlo-D'Annibale and Asquith argue that loosening the restrictions of existing ownership rules will create an environment in which fewer owners will prosper as the more powerful foreign companies buy up and push out the weaker Canadian ones. In this scenario, powerful foreign media corporations will be provided more opportunity to amass more wealth, and when profit motives become paramount, "democratic communicative principles" and the promotion of Canadian culture ultimately suffer.

The final debate examines the popular metaphor of the "media diet" and asks whether Canadians have balance in their access to news and information. According to Lydia Miljan, Canadians possess a rich variety of media fare. While Canada's heavily concentrated news environment might suggest that at the macro level we do not enjoy a great variety of options, she indicates that the CBC provides an important alternative to the private sector news broadcasters. Miljan also argues that we need to distinguish "old media" from "new media" and suggests that news and information from the Internet also enrich our media diet. Importantly, new media provides social movements and other resource-poor groups that have been traditionally shut out from the conventional mass media with a means of reaching and directly influencing the public. Despite the myriad choices available to Canadians, however, Miljan laments that we do not take advantage of these choices, concluding "it is up to us to seek out the rich variety of information at our disposal and to ensure we achieve maximum balance in our media diets."

Robert Hackett and Yuezhi Zhao bring a critical perspective to the debate about media balance. Their task is to interrogate the very notion of balance because "the rhetoric, concept, and practices of balance are part of journalism's occupational culture and its claim to be serving important democratic functions." This interrogation of the concept of balance is important, they argue, because "a seemingly balanced media diet may help to sustain and legitimate profound imbalances in the media system and its connections with the dominant political, economic, social, and cultural power structure." It does so, they demonstrate, in three ways. First, it simplifies complex issues (e.g., abortion) to portray two different, normally institutional perspectives when far more points of view could and should be represented. Second, it fails to consider how some matters or events become defined as "issues of public importance" while others are ignored altogether. And third, the notion of balance operates only in relation to issues of so-called legitimate controversy rather than to issues where there is a normative consensus. Thus, news can unintentionally reinforce dominant ideological perspectives by taking for granted that some perspectives and value systems (e.g., capitalism) are embraced by everyone. Hackett and Zhao also argue that suggestions of consumer sovereignty are too simplistic because the mainstream media "do not simply 'give people what they want.' " Rather, they give us programming that is "economical and convenient to offer, that is generally compatible with a consumerist stance, and that affluent and/or mass consumers … are prepared to accept as a reward for joining the audience."

ISSUE **1**

Constructing Canada: Do we need a public broadcaster to enhance democracy?

✔ YES

The CBC and the New Wave of Public Broadcasting
David Taras

David Taras is professor in the Faculty of Communication and Culture at the University of Calgary and director of the Alberta Global Forum. He is author of *The Newsmakers: The Media's Influence on Canadian Politics* and *Power and Betrayal in the Canadian Media,* and coauthor of *The Last Word: Media Coverage of the Supreme Court in Canada.* He has also published numerous journal articles and book chapters on Canadian politics and communication. He appears regularly as a political commentator on Global TV's morning edition in Calgary.

Public service broadcasters play a vital role in ensuring democratic dialogue and in engaging citizens in the life of their communities. Indeed, support for public service broadcasting (PSB) is part of a new wave of thinking about democratic institutions that is sweeping much of the democratic world. Canada is the exception to the rule. Canadian governments have lacked both the will and the vision needed to refashion public service broadcasting into a more effective instrument for building communities. But this doesn't take away from the great possibilities that exist. This essay will begin by recounting a day in the life of Canadian broadcasting in order to describe the role played by the Canadian Broadcasting Corporation/Radio Canada (the CBC). I will then review the new vision of PSB that has emerged in recent years and the forces that have created the renewed interest in public service broadcasting. A third section will describe the challenges faced by the CBC, Canada's largest PSB, and some of the ways that it can be reimagined and reinvigorated. Finally, I will make the case for the importance of PSB in maintaining the checks and balances that are crucial in a democracy.

A DAY IN THE LIFE OF CANADIAN BROADCASTING

June 7, 2006, was in some ways a typical day in Canadian broadcasting. *CBC Newsworld* broadcast the internment ceremony at the National Military Cemetery for Nichola Goddard, a young Canadian Forces officer killed in a firefight with the Taliban in Afghanistan. Goddard was the first Canadian woman soldier ever killed in combat. The broadcast was poignant and heartrending. But it was also controversial. Weeks before, Stephen Harper's Conservative government had banned journalists from covering the arrival ceremonies for Canadian soldiers killed in Afghanistan. Although the government claimed that the decision was designed to protect the privacy of the families, the families had not been consulted. Some suspected that the real reason for the ban was that the government anticipated a large number of casualties in Afghanistan, and that the future of the mission depended on shielding Canadians from learning about the high costs in lives that were going to be paid. By broadcasting the internment ceremony, the CBC undoubtedly strained its relations with the Harper government, a government that has been deeply suspicious of the media.

On that same day, Global television announced its fall TV lineup. The network unveiled what can be described as a star-spangled schedule of American programs. New shows included *Friday Night Lights*, about Texas high-school football; *Standoff*, which focuses on the high stakes encounters of an FBI crisis negotiator; *Shark*, a courtroom drama featuring a shrewd win-at-all costs lawyer; and *Six Degrees*, about six people whose lives somehow become interconnected. These new shows were to be added to Global's existing stable of Hollywood hits—*Survivor*, *The Apprentice*, *Las Vegas*, *Prison Break*, and *24*, to name but a few. The network also announced a handful of Canadian programs, but none of these were being highly touted or promoted outside of news broadcasts. Private broadcasters maintain only the smallest Canadian beachhead in their prime-time schedules. Indeed, for all types of programming in 2005, the amount that private broadcasters spent on American shows surpassed the amount spent on all of their Canadian programming.

Also on June 7, all of the major Canadian news programs gave extensive coverage to an alleged plot by Islamic extremists to take over the Parliament buildings, behead Prime Minister Harper, and blow up national landmarks, including the Peace Tower, the Toronto Stock exchange, and the CBC headquarters (ironically, even the alleged terrorists seemed to understand the significant role the public broadcaster plays in Canadian life). Coverage by CBC's flagship newscast, *The National*, was extensive. In addition to multiple reports, the newscast featured a panel discussion on the future of Canadian multiculturalism, and editorialist Rex Murphy provided his usual erudite and pungent commentary on the impact that the terrorist plot might have on Canadian society. On the previous night, *The National* had aired a documentary on Islamic extremism in Europe and the social divides that Moslem immigration had created. People who watched *The National* could not avoid the message that the country had reached a crossroads in terms of its laws, its immigration policies, and, most painfully, even its image of itself.

On June 6, *The National* had an audience at 10 p.m. of 810,000, while *CTV Evening News* had an audience at 11 p.m. of 693,000. On June 7, although pre-empted in much of the country by the final round of the NHL playoffs, *The National* still attracted 582,000 viewers versus 693,000 (curiously, exactly the same numbers as the night before) for *CTV Evening News*. *Global National*, which airs at 5:30 p.m., competes primarily against local supper-hour news shows.

To some degree, June 7 mirrored the dilemmas faced by the CBC: its uneasy and often tense relationships with governments; the difficulty of having to compete against private networks that are sometimes little more than rebroadcasters of American TV shows; and the serious and sometimes disturbing nature of its information and educational programming, shows that may be of great value but are unable to compete in the popularity sweepstakes.

PUBLIC BROADCASTING AND THE DEMOCRATIC IMPERATIVE

Although the CBC is the most prominent PSB in Canada, there are a host of other important public broadcasting services. They include Vision TV, an often inspiring religious broadcaster that produces a stock of its own original programming and offers airtime to as many as 75 different faith groups, and the Aboriginal People's Television Network (APTN), which has become the engine fuelling a myriad of independent Aboriginal TV production companies. There are also educational broadcasters such as TV Ontario, Tele-Quebec, and the Knowledge Network, and not-for-profit broadcasters such as the Cable Public Affairs Channel (CPAC), a service supported by the cable industry.

Public service broadcasting originally had a paternalistic, top-down quality. The early mandates of the CBC and more famously of the BBC in the United Kingdom, ARD and ADF in Germany, and the NOS in the Netherlands, to name some of the more prominent examples, all stressed the need to defend national sovereignty and traditional values. A stern broadcasting father used radio and eventually TV to teach high culture and social responsibility to the masses.

Today the spirit that guides public service broadcasting is entirely different. In the wake of what is seen as the failure of private broadcasters to produce anything but commercial products, the new goal of **public broadcasting** is to build social capital by "bridging," "bonding," and "witnessing," but most of all by treating audience members as citizens rather than as consumers (Lowe & Jauert, 2005). Scholars argue that the health of a society depends on the degree to which citizens are involved in the life of their communities—the greater the degree of involvement, the greater the stock of social capital that a society has at its disposal. Philosopher John Ralston Saul has spoken about the new wave of support for public broadcasting that is now sweeping Western democracies. According to Saul, "Everybody who is smart in bureaucracies and governments around the Western world now knows that public broadcasting is one of the most important remaining levers that a nation state has to communicate with itself" (Cobb, 2001, p. A10).

Much of this new realization is predicated on two great fears. The first is the fear that giant media conglomerates have become so large and all-encompassing that they threaten to smother small independent voices and local and even national cultures. The second is what many observers see as the failure of the media giants to instill a spirit of community, build trust, or stir citizen participation. Saul sees the great media conglomerates such as Disney and Time Warner as aging dinosaurs, bloated and slow moving, driven only by their own gargantuan appetites. He sees their failure as being all but complete as they devour each other in corporate takeovers and produce ever more sensational programming and the soft candy of soft news. In this context, PSBs become the great guardians of the public sphere, ensuring at the very least that alternative voices and minority perspectives can be heard.

Robert Putnam (2000) has gone the furthest among so-called media malaise theorists in arguing that commercial broadcasting has played a major role in eroding social capital. In a more comprehensive study, Thomas Patterson (2002) also found that the endless patter of ever more sensational and shocking programs, the relentless obsession with crime and celebrity news, and the loosening of journalistic standards and budgets had diminished community life. On the other hand, scholars such as Pippa Norris believe that the trend line is not as clear. She contends (2000) that a "virtuous circle" exists linking the viewing of TV news and the reading of newspapers with increased **civic engagement**. In her examination of European audiences, she found a strong relationship between watching public broadcasting and an increase in social capital. More knowledgeable viewers turned more often to PSBs for news and information (Holtz-Bacha & Norris, 2000).

PSBs are by any standard a resounding success in most advanced democracies. They attract the largest audiences and set the agenda for public debate (Hallin & Mancini, 2004). The reasons behind this success are hardly a mystery. First, there is a strong correlation between levels of funding and audience numbers. The simple reality is that the higher the level of funding, the greater the investment in programming, the larger the audiences. The reverse is also true. Public service broadcasters in Canada, the United States, and Greece have the lowest audience numbers among PSBs. Not surprisingly, funding levels per capita are the lowest in these countries.

Second, PSBs that depend on licence fees for their financing (each TV owner has to pay an annual fee), as is the case in Germany, the Netherlands, and the United Kingdom, are more successful than public broadcasters that depend on annual allocations from governments. Stable funding, and hence the ability to undertake long-term planning, allows broadcasters to take risks and be far more creative. Moving from the germ of a first idea, to putting financing in place, to preparing scripts, to hiring staff and going into production, and then finally going to air can take three or four years or longer. Not knowing what their allocations will be from year to year handicaps broadcasters in extraordinary ways. PSBs that are in this dependent position are also less willing to offend their political masters. The CBC may be the example par excellence of a PBS that has been kept on a short and precarious financial leash.

THE CBC AND THE CANADIAN PUBLIC SPHERE

Any discussion about the future of public service broadcasting in Canada must deal with the plight of the CBC. Beginning in the early 1990s, the CBC has suffered a series of harsh blows. Most dramatically, its parliamentary appropriation has been cut by approximately 50 percent since 1990. The corporation was also denied access to lucrative cable TV licences and due to budgetary reasons had to stage a dramatic retreat from local programming, which is essential in building audience loyalties. Without access to cable channels that it desperately needed and unable to strongly compete at a local level, the CBC has been caught in a pincher movement that has left it deeply wounded. Arguably, some of these wounds were self-inflicted. Layers of bureaucracy, endless and sometimes pointless revisioning exercises, and poor programming decisions have made matters worse.

Unfortunately for the CBC, the downward spiral seems difficult to stop. The broadcaster lost the rights to broadcast the 2010 Vancouver Olympic Games to CTV; it also lost the rights to curling, one of the mainstays of its sports programming. And it has taken many bows to commercialism. In summer 2006, over protests from its news managers, it bumped *The National* to 11 p.m. on Tuesdays to make way for *The One: Making a Movie Star*, an American reality show that aired on ABC at the same time, and which soon plummeted in the ratings.

Despite setbacks, the CBC has had many triumphs. The corporation simply does a number of things better than anyone else; it is a leader in children's programming, it produces and airs long-form documentaries and news stories that are often outstanding, and it inevitably provides live coverage of the great events of public life—the swearing in of a new government, the handing down of a budget, remembrance day ceremonies, etc.—something that private broadcasters are reluctant to do.

Most critically perhaps, aside from *La Presse*, which has a business reporter in Toronto, the CBC is the only news organization in the country that has French-language journalists stationed in English-speaking Canada (excluding Ottawa). Its Northern service does Herculean work in covering vast expanses, its radio audience remains deeply devoted, and its téléromans continue to captivate audiences in Quebec. Moreover, the country's independent production industry has been significantly bolstered by the CBC's willingness to take chances on new talent and ideas. In fact, Catherine Murray (2001) contends that CBC licence fees played a pivotal role in "bridging" some of the country's major independent companies until they could go to Bay Street with their first public offerings. In addition, the corporation's website is one of the most visited Canadian sources for news. Online, the public service broadcaster strongly outdistances many of its rivals.

What is perhaps most interesting is that despite its many trials and tribulations, the CBC retains the loyalty and affections of a large majority of Canadians. In the last major survey conducted on public attitudes toward the national broadcaster, in 2004, the CBC enjoyed a far higher level of trust than did commercial broadcasters, federal and provincial governments, consumer groups, and telephone, cable, and satellite providers (Raboy & Taras, 2005). Interestingly, a survey published in a 2006 Senate report (Standing Senate Committee on Transport and Communications, p. 67) found that Canadians trusted CBC television news more than those of CTV or Global. Public attitudes, however, can be complex. People's natural tendency is to judge the CBC by what they watch and listen to today, rather than by what the broadcaster could be if it were given greater resources and a new and bolder mandate.

With hindsight it is easy to envision steps that could have been taken to strengthen and reposition the CBC. First, the CBC could have been given a significant place in the cable universe. Canadian television has long since gone from being financed mainly by advertising to being based largely on cable subscriptions. The most coveted spaces on the cable and now the digital landscape are the licences for sports, music, and children's channels now held by private broadcasters. Whereas in Europe PSBs such as the BBC and ARD and ZDF in Germany have gained valuable footholds in cable and digital TV, the CBC, aside from its two news channels, Newsworld and the French-language Réseau de l'information de Radio-Canada (RDI), has been cut out of the action. Had the CBC been allowed to obtain even one or two of the more lucrative licences, it would have enjoyed increased and more dependable revenue and greater economies of scale. The new promised land of Canadian TV has, in effect, been handed over almost lock, stock, and barrel to private broadcasters.

A 1996 task force headed by former CBC president Pierre Juneau recommended that the annual parliamentary appropriation be replaced by a tax on the sale of communication services that would be the equivalent of the GST (Mandate Review Committee, 1996). In one bold step, the CBC would have been given the ability to dispense entirely with advertising and would have been free from the budgetary grip of its political masters.

Similarly, the Lincoln Report, the product of a two-year review of Canadian broadcasting undertaken by the House of Commons Standing Committee on Canadian Heritage (2003), made a number of recommendations that would have strengthened the CBC. The report envisioned an asymmetrical model that would have allowed the CBC to take on different shapes and responsibilities in different parts of the country. It might dispense with local news shows in Toronto, a market well served by private broadcasters and indeed by TV Ontario, but play a large role in Regina, in the Canadian North, or in Newfoundland, where citizens have fewer choices.

There were also proposals for multi-year funding and for a special matching fund to encourage more local and regional programming. Although available to all broadcasters, this program would have allowed the CBC to jump back into local programming in a significant way. The

Lincoln Report also recommended changes in the way the president and the board of governors are selected in order to make them more representative and responsible. But the report, like others of its kind, including a report issued in June 2006 by the Standing Senate Committee on Transport and Communications that recommended more funding for the CBC, has been left to gather dust on government bookshelves.

CREATING CHECKS AND BALANCES

The goal of most democratic constitutions is to create checks and balances in order to ensure democratic deliberation and to prevent the arbitrary use of power. The press is part of this series of counterweights. The power of a prime minister, for instance, is challenged and limited to varying degrees by the Opposition parties, the provincial premiers, and the Charter and Supreme Court, among other forces and institutions. Prime ministers are also locked into "frame wars" with the press over whose interpretation of events will be conveyed to the public.

But checks and balances also have to exist within the media system. Andrew Graham and Gavyn Davies have argued that PSBs are needed as a counterweight to the growing size and strength of media conglomerates and as a way of widening the range of choice available to viewers and listeners. Although some observers seem unconcerned about the power of media conglomerates in Canada, others are frightened by the grip that single media organizations have over entire areas of the country. It is crucial to note that most democracies, including France, the United Kingdom, Germany, Australia, and interestingly enough, the United States, have imposed tight ownership restrictions. Canada has not.

Some scholars argue that hyperconcentration of newspapers and television is of little consequence because citizens now have access to an endless sea of websites, blogs, news sources, and e-mail messages. Studies show, however, that much of what we see and discuss in the **new media** (the blogosphere, cellphones, iPods, etc.) is the product of what we watch on TV and read in the newspapers. The **old media** (newspapers, films, etc.) still dominate and set the agenda for the new (Schudson, 2004). In this context, it is hard to argue that Canadians do not benefit from having the alternative voices that are provided by public service broadcasters. In some markets, the CBC stands as a lone counterweight to giant media monopolies.

Graham and Davies (1997) also argue that PSBs provide a counterweight to the "socially dis-integrative" effects of the new media. Much of what takes place online has little to do with creating or shaping communities—which is, in essence, what PSBs are all about.

CONCLUSION: A TIME FOR REFORM

There is much that is wrong with PSBs, but there is also much that is right. Without question, the CBC in particular is drifting precariously from crisis to crisis. There is no shortage of reports, recommendations, and ideas. and the pressures for innovation are dramatic—not the least of which is the need to rethink broadcasting in light of the high waves of technological change that threaten to sweep away all of the current broadcasting models, including those of the private broadcasters. To rephrase an ancient dictum, if we are not for ourselves who shall be for us? And being for ourselves, who are we? And if not now, when?

References

Cobb, C. (2001, January 30). Saul enters CBC debate. *National Post*, p. A10.

Graham, A., & Davies, G. (1997). *Broadcasting, society and policy in the multimedia age.* Luton, UK: John Libbey Media/University of Luton Press.

Holtz-Bacha, C., & Norris, P. (2000). *"To entertain, inform and educate." Still the role of public television in the 1990s?* Cambridge, MA: Joan Shorenstein Center on the Press, Politics and Public Policy, Harvard University.

Lowe, G. F., & Jauert, T. (2005). Public service broadcasting for social and cultural citizenship. In G. Lowe & P. Jauert (Eds.), *Cultural dilemmas in public service broadcasting* (pp. 13–33). Goteborg, Sweden: Nordicom.

Mandate Review Committee [Juneau Committee]. (1996). *Making our voices heard: Canadian broadcasting and film for the 21st century. Report of the Mandate Review Committee—CBC, NFB, Telefilm.* Ottawa: Ministry of Supply and Services.

Murray, C. (2001). Wellsprings of knowledge: Beyond the CBC policy trap. *Canadian Journal of Communication, 12*(1), 1–31.

Norris, P. (2000). *A virtuous circle: Political communication in post-industrial societies.* Cambridge, UK: Cambridge University Press.

Patterson, T. (2002). *The vanishing voter.* New York: Knopf.

Putnam, R. (2000). *Bowling alone: The collapse and revival of American community.* New York: Simon & Schuster.

Raboy, M., & Taras, D. (2005). The trial by fire of the Canadian Broadcasting Corporation: Lessons for public broadcasting. In G. Lowe & P. Jauert (Eds.), *Cultural dilemmas in public service broadcasting* (pp. 263–265). Goteborg, Sweden: Nordicom.

Schudson, M. (2004). Click here for democracy: A history and critique of an information-based model of citizenship. In H. Jenkins & D. Thorburn (Eds.), *Democracy and new media* (pp. 49–60). Cambridge: MIT Press.

Standing Committee on Canadian Heritage, House of Commons. (2003). *Our cultural sovereignty: The second century of Canadian broadcasting.* Available at http://cmte.parl.gc.ca/cmte/committeepublication .aspx?sourceid=37522

Standing Senate Committee on Transport and Communications, Senate of Canada. (2006, June). *Final report on the Canadian news media.* Available at http://www.senate-senat.ca/transcom.asp

ISSUE 1

Constructing Canada: Do we need a public broadcaster to enhance democracy?

✗ NO

What Is the Public in Public Broadcasting?
Paul Attallah

Paul Attallah teaches in the School of Journalism and Communication at Carleton University. He taught formerly at l'Université de Montréal and l'Université du Québec. He is the author of several books and articles on communication history and theory.

Public broadcasting serves many excellent purposes. This, however, does not link it intrinsically to democracy any more than to the promotion of industry, world peace, or healthy diets. We must distinguish between *how we use* public broadcasting and *what it is* in itself.

Indeed, most observers agree that democracy predates all forms of broadcasting by approximately 2500 years. Of course, the democratic forms of the past were not always consistent with our contemporary version. Nonetheless, the notion of a self-reflexive, normative structure rooted in a civil society engaged in rational reflection flowered and evolved for millennia entirely without the aid of public broadcasting. Democracy needed free speech, a public sphere, confidence in human reason, articulate individuals, respect for an independent judiciary, deliberative bodies, and so on. But it didn't need broadcasting, public or otherwise.

The alleged benefits of public broadcasting are suspiciously recent.

Furthermore, the very idea that public broadcasting enhances democracy marks a breathtaking shift in attitudes toward the media. Indeed, ever since their first broadcasts to the public, radio and television have been the object of an unending stream of invective and vilification.

Television, in particular, stands accused of numerous crimes. First, it is accused of having ushered in the age of image politics, which displaced substantive political debate with image management, spin doctoring, photo ops, and manipulation. Second, it denatured political discourse by reducing everything to glib sound bites. Third, it transformed election coverage into horse races, thereby replacing knowledge of arguments with the mere spectacle of jockeying for advantage. Fourth, television inserted *itself* into the political process such that much news coverage now concerns the performance of the media in covering politics. Fifth, and most damagingly, television turned all politics into entertainment. Politicians became actors upon its stage and eventually adopted the tricks of the actor's trade. They sought to please rather than to lead. They became consumed by the trivialities of appearance, the cut of their clothes, or the sound of their voice. Worse yet, they began to parade across the small screen pouring out their emotions instead of their ideas.

Television, then, according to the accusations, forces politics to conform to its own peculiar rhythms (the scheduling of press conferences, important announcements, meetings, etc.), to its need for striking images and facile commentary, to its inexhaustible appetite for engaging personalities, and its unerring instinct for entertainment. The end result is the 24-hour news channel, which, precisely because it needs to fill 24 hours every day, elevates the private lives of politicians to the same status as news about war or terrorism. It flattens everything into triviality and congratulates itself for being so friendly.

It is remarkable, therefore, that we should now call upon broadcasting, the very technology that has debased and corrupted democracy, to enhance it. Furthermore, it is often those who most vociferously denounce broadcasting who also clamour most loudly for public broadcasting.

However, if broadcasting is so bad for democratic life, why is public broadcasting so beneficial? The argument runs as follows. Private or corporate broadcasting is driven by commercial or industrial interests, not by the public interest. These interests draw it ineluctably toward the entertaining, the conventional, the uncontroversial, the mildly amusing, and the slightly bland. Hence, private broadcasting neglects the substantive concerns of citizenship and drives out all noncommercial, unprofitable, or unconventional voices. Therefore, we need public broadcasting, which alone can represent the entire range of public opinion. Only public broadcasting can air unconventional, controversial, or challenging material. Only public broadcasting can speak for those who are disenfranchised, marginalized, or ignored by private broadcasting. Only public broadcasting can treat viewers as citizens rather than as consumers, because only public broadcasting is committed to the public interest rather than the corporate interest.

It's a noble argument, and no one would want a broadcasting system devoid of such sentiments. Unfortunately, it's also inaccurate.

WHY ONLY BROADCASTING?

Public broadcasting rests on the notion that in all societies there exists a general or collective interest that is superior to all private or individual interests and can never be fully or adequately expressed by private media. However, if such an interest really does exist, why should broadcasting **alone** be required to give it voice? If it is so important, why not have *public* newspapers, *public* novels, *public* movies, *public* magazines and songs, *public* stage plays and nursery rhymes, *public* pamphlets, *public* billboards, and *public* websites?

It would of course be laughable—indeed dangerous—to propose that newspapers be required to express the overarching public interest. However, newspapers *are* unregulated and owned by private interests. Should the state, therefore, intervene to regulate them or launch its own newspaper that would achieve in print what public broadcasting does electronically?

Such a course of action seems ill-advised and should incite us to reconsider the flawed notion that public broadcasting is required to enhance democracy.

WHAT IS THE PUBLIC INTEREST?

But this raises the most difficult question of all. What *is* the public interest, and how does public broadcasting defend it? Broadcasting basically ensures the simultaneous exposure of all people to the same news, entertainment, drama, sports, and so on. Should *that* be our definition of public interest? One might have thought that public interest consisted not in narrowing the range of information and entertainment but in guaranteeing its maximum diversity; not in ensuring uniformity of exposure but in multiplying the opportunities for unique and individualized thought; not in ensuring the centralized production and dissemination of unitary content but in maximizing the possibilities for decentralized production and distribution.

Nonetheless, if we assume that the public interest is best served through the type of homogeneous exposure that broadcasting favours, then another uncomfortable question arises. Who gets to decide the nature of the programming, who gets to choose the specific news, sports, drama, and entertainment to which all will be exposed? After all, our differences in age, sex, income level, general interests, life experience, and so on, might lead us to make very different choices. And that's a problem with the notion of a *public* interest. The definition always emanates from a particular point of view and only pretends to be a general, universal, public interest.

The main reason for simultaneous mass exposure to content is to ensure collective orientation, meaning everyone agrees that the same topics are important and should be on the public agenda. Unfortunately, different people from different backgrounds often disagree. Some think the public agenda should focus on the decriminalization of drugs, others on universal daycare, and still others on increased military expenditure. Who gets to decide which of those, which mixture of those, which emphasis upon those is right? In the world of newspapers, each newspaper decides for itself and seeks out whatever readers it can. In the world of public broadcasting, we view such plurality of viewpoints with suspicion and seek instead to create consensus.

So far, we've examined the problem of public interest in relationship to news. But what happens if we look at entertainment? Typically, public broadcasting has viewed mass appeal entertainment as an opportunity to circulate content that exhibits approved social norms and attitudes; that highlights issues and attitudes deemed politically or socially relevant; that is most aesthetic, challenging, or difficult; and that speaks to minority audiences.

Again, none of these goals is hateful in itself. The issue is whether such goals can lay claim to the enhancement of democracy. They cannot because they assume that even entertainment should serve a consensus-building function by circulating the approved views of those who get to define public interest.

Public broadcasting, therefore, is distrustful of public taste, fearing that if left to their own devices, people will choose unapproved content. Consequently, public broadcasting has long insisted that we aspire to something higher, that public taste in itself is unworthy and in need of improvement. It seeks, therefore, to elevate and educate public taste. Indeed, the world's first public broadcaster, the BBC, was specifically intended to wean its audience from the merely popular content of BBC One toward the loftier and more valuable content of BBC Two. It was, quite simply, based on a deep prejudice against popular taste and the enduring conviction that only the higher tastes of the higher classes were truly worthy of mass dissemination.

CBC television was constructed on a similar paternalistic pattern. It looked down upon American broadcasting as merely popular and set itself the task of enlightenment and education. Now, such a task can be accomplished with greater or lesser talent, and, in all fairness, the CBC has enjoyed some notable successes. But the point is not to attack the CBC for the mere fact of being a public broadcaster or to anoint private broadcasters for the mere fact of *not* being public broadcasters. It is to highlight the fact that prejudices against public taste eventually undermine the very rationale for public broadcasting by digging a chasm between the broadcaster and its audience. To be truly public, broadcasting should have the same regard for all tastes. It cannot be content with just a fraction of the audience. However, by condemning popular taste, it alienates large segments of the public. As a result, CBC television shares have dwindled to approximately 5 percent of the total population, and CBC radio is smaller yet. These low numbers in turn generate demands for the dismantling of the CBC on the grounds that serves not the public interest but only an unrepresentative elite, which enjoys a public subsidy in pursuit of its particularistic interests.

There are no easy answers to these problems. But it might be useful to acknowledge that the shaping of collective attitudes and the enforcement of cultural choices are not the expression of public interest; they are the expression of particular interests masquerading as public.

THE FUNCTIONS OF PUBLIC BROADCASTING

We also need to challenge the notion that public broadcasting accomplishes important social functions that private broadcasters can never meet. Private channels such as the Discovery Channel, the History Channel, and National Geographic clearly fulfill a classic public broadcasting agenda. There has never been so much educational and documentary programming, and most of it emanates from private broadcasters.

The same is true of such private outlets as the Independent Film Channel, Bravo, ARTV, and CoolTV. As for minority audiences, private specialty channels cater to gays and lesbians, science fiction fans, lovers of drive-in movies, NFL aficionados, game show fans, book lovers, news junkies, horror fans, cartoon watchers, and so on.

Consequently, if the claim is that public broadcasting enhances democracy by serving marginalized or disenfranchised audiences, by airing unconventional or aesthetically important content, by treating viewers as citizens with appetites for information, knowledge, and opinion, then we must conclude that private broadcasters also accomplish virtually all of these goals.

Public broadcasting has no monopoly on the enhancement of democracy, just as private broadcasting has no monopoly on mass appeal programming. Indeed, internationally, several large private broadcasters—Channel 4 in Britain, STV in Sweden, SBS in Australia—act for all intents and purposes just like public broadcasters. And the audiovisual landscape of North America is littered with private specialty channels that serve the same function.

Conversely, in Canada, the national public broadcaster, the CBC, provides some services—Newsworld, Sirius radio—available only on a private pay-model. Indeed, the public BBC is available in Canada only to paying cable and satellite subscribers. Hence, in our impure reality, private broadcasters espouse public objectives and public broadcasters use classically private business models. This underscores the need to unlink notions of public interest and democracy from the structures that we are accustomed to and that may prevent us from thinking anew.

Perhaps, then, the public interest is better served not by creating a public broadcaster, with its attendant bureaucracy and internecine struggles, but by encouraging the development of numerous voices from all sectors of society. But to do so requires us to abandon the illusion that only public broadcasting can enhance democracy.

If we look only to Canada, who can argue that *Corner Gas*, which airs on the private CTV network, is less successful, less Canadian, and less important than any of the sitcoms that have aired on the public CBC? Would it be useful to argue that the privately produced *W5* is less of a news program than the publicly produced *the fifth estate*? Can it be claimed that sports coverage on a private network lacks some essential quality that it would suddenly possess if only it were aired on a public network?

Of course, this does not mean that in the absence of public broadcasting, private broadcasters would suddenly be more respectful of the public interest. It means that the public interest can assert itself in unanticipated ways and that neither public nor private broadcasting has an intrinsic link to democracy.

CIVIL SOCIETY

Democracy is more robust than just public broadcasting. Furthermore, numerous other institutions and social factors such as laws, an independent judiciary, literacy, relative social stability and wealth, free speech, and deliberative assemblies play an infinitely more important role in enhancing democracy. And to them may be added sociocultural habits such as individualism, reason, and the transmission of our heritage to the future. All of these factors hugely predate and will outlast the transitory phenomenon of public broadcasting.

The desperate urgency with which so many in Canada pine for public broadcasting really has nothing to do with the imaginary virtues of public broadcasting. It has to do with their uneasy sense that Canadian civil society is weak and incapable of shouldering its burden. Historically, **civil society** has been the realm of spontaneous or elective social relations ungoverned by the authority of the state. It is the social space that gives rise to aspirations of autonomy and democracy, that allows rational discourse to be exercised and honed, that fosters spontaneous and humane social and individual arrangements. The impulses of civil society—the civil rights movement, the women's movement, the movement of gays and lesbians, the antiwar movement, the environmental movement, the antiglobalization movement—can certainly cross over into the political sphere, but they do not depend on it and are not driven by it. Indeed, civil society frequently stands opposed to the political order and has fought it in the name of norms and values that have been only slowly accepted. On the other hand, some civil society phenomena—bowling leagues, a preference for white over red wine, dog owners' associations—are extremely unlikely ever to cross over into the political realm but nonetheless contribute to the texture of our collective life.

Alas, as innumerable observers have noted, Canadian civil society is weak. Spontaneous citizens' organizations are just as likely to turn to the state for funding or official sanction as they are to stand opposed to it. Indeed, many civil society groups—dance groups, legal reform associations, various rights-seekers—would barely exist without direct government subsidy.

The hope, therefore, is that public broadcasting will somehow stand in for our weak civil society, somehow strengthen it by finally putting us all in touch with each other. That is where the linking of public broadcasting to democracy comes from: public broadcasting will somehow play the role that civil society cannot. Unfortunately, we can neither rescue nor repair civil society through public broadcasting. Its problems need to be addressed in civil society itself. This does not mean that public broadcasting can never make a contribution to civil society; it means that public broadcasting has no privileged link to the defence of democracy. Civil society is made up of the vastest possible range of groups and interests and associative forms. Public broadcasting is only one among them—not the most important, not the singular focus of our hopes and aspirations, not the thing that should absorb all of our energies.

Indeed, as the Canadian example shows, public broadcasting very easily falls prey to special interests rather than to the public interest. For example, when was the last time public broadcasting offered a program that you looked forward to with fevered anticipation? Or that captured perfectly the mood of your time or generation? That generated a star whose name was on everyone's lips? The point is not that these absolutely never happen but that they happen so infrequently as to be almost invisible. If the public interest means that, occasionally, the public is interested, then our implementation of public broadcasting has not been very successful, as evidenced by the modesty of audiences, the lacklustre performance of programming, and the overwhelming preference for American television.

A NEW DISPOSITION

We now stand at the brink of the biggest media shakeup since broadcasting itself. Traditional over-the-air network broadcasting in which the flow of content is centrally produced and disseminated is disappearing before our very eyes. It is being replaced by file sharing and downloading, online streaming, video blogging, location-free viewing, and so on. People increasingly watch TV over the Internet via Bittorrent or YouTube.com, on DVRs and DVDs. Indeed, networks now deliberately make their content available online. And user-generated content is at least as compelling as centrally produced programming. Broadcasting is yesterday's technology.

These new technologies detach individuals from network programming and encourage them to associate based on their elective affinities. Any one of them is closer to civil society than broadcasting ever was, and any one of them is as likely to generate autonomous feelings of citizenship or selfhood as public broadcasting ever could.

In this context, the argument over public broadcasting is simply quaint. Not just because of new technologies but also because the technological shift points to a new definition of the public interest. The public interest is no longer the synthesized culture and opinion shaping of the past—it is the interest of individuals to make their own culture as they wish, to sample and use collective culture on their own terms, to be heard above and beyond the structures and strictures of existing media. This does not mean that the future is a nirvana in which all will turn out well. There will be mistakes, abuses, and false starts. But it does point to a fundamentally **new media disposition** in which the production and dissemination of content are no longer the exclusive purview of centralized producers and distributors.

In an age of increasingly decentralized technologies that disconnect citizens from uniform schedules and program menus, democracy is no longer coterminous with broadcasting's mass transmission of uniform content. Democracy comes instead from freedom of speech and mutual respect and the attendant institutional arrangements that enshrine and honour those values. Of course, public broadcasting can contribute to democracy, but it is only one contributor among many. Indeed, the sensible approach might be to look beyond the media altogether and toward a reinvigorated public sphere.

Discussion Questions

1. What are the main arguments usually made against broadcasting?

2. What argument is usually made in favour of public broadcasting specifically, despite the arguments against broadcasting generally?

3. What is "the public," and how is it defined by (a) the defenders of public broadcasting and (b) those who point to new television technologies? How are debates about the value of public broadcasting essentially debates about the concept of the public and the public interest?

4. What is civil society, how does it manifest itself, who can participate in it, and why is it weak in Canada?

5. If you could turn back the clock and were given the chance to construct the Canadian broadcasting system from scratch, what would you keep, what would you change, and how would you build a better system than the one that exists today?

6. Do you think the CBC is doomed to extinction? Why or why not?

7. Some observers believe that the old broadcasting models are breaking down. Describe the forces that are bringing about this change. Do you agree with their predictions?

ISSUE 2

Not neighbourly: Is American news bad for Canadians?

✔ YES

Not Necessarily the News: U.S. Television News Routines and What They Mean for Canadians
James H. Wittebols

James H. Wittebols is professor of communication studies at the University of Windsor. He has taught at Canadian and American universities for over 20 years. His research comparing U.S. and Canadian television news coverage of terrorism and human rights has been published in the journals *Political Communication* and the *Canadian Journal of Communication*. His most recent book, *The Soap Opera Paradigm: Television Programming and Corporate Priorities*, addresses how network news operations have adapted soap opera storytelling techniques in presenting news. Currently he is researching how media interests (public relations, advertising, and publicity) try to project authenticity to audiences.

There is an oft-cited quote from Thomas Jefferson that given an option between a government without newspapers or newspapers without government, he would choose the latter. The subtext to that argument—that democracy is not possible without a free, vibrant press—is truer than ever today.

Given the nature of today's news media, dominated by large corporations with substantial links to other powerful sectors of the economy (technology, defence, and finance, to name a few), the contrast might be better framed today as the increasingly quaint notion of the press as a beacon of public interest and democratic deliberation versus the ascending reality of the news media as fully ensconced in the arms of economic power.

For over two decades there have been seismic shifts in the values that guide the production of American news. The growing concentration of ownership has meant that network news divisions, once seen as a public service and not expected to be profitable for networks, are now major contributors to a corporate parent's bottom line. Therefore the worldview the American news media presents is carefully bounded by business and **commercial values** that have not only changed what is considered news but have also narrowed the frames within which issues are presented and debated to serve the interest of profit over citizen education. The result is a number of implications for the kind of news presented in the United States: a turn away from public service values and hard hitting investigative reports toward a greater emphasis on entertainment over information;[1] a cozy, mutually beneficial relationship with the U.S. government; and an emphasis on visual over intellectual stimulation.

But this issue is about more than just American news and its effects on American policy and public opinion. A glance at any cable or satellite television lineup in Canada will reveal that there are many "American" options when it comes to getting news. Beyond the 24/7 cable news operations, Canadians can also get the flavour of local news outlets in the United States by turning to the traditional broadcast networks' local affiliates, usually from border cities such as Buffalo, Detroit, and Seattle.[2] Indeed, Canadians have far more access to U.S. news outlets than vice versa. And while such access may enhance Canadians' understanding of their southern neighbours, when it comes to a better understanding of the world, American news outlets are increasingly poor sources—especially of news that questions government and corporate power. The only real benefit for Canadians in accessing American news media is to better understand how American public opinion is formed.

However, Canadian citizens who stick to Canadian media can justifiably claim they are at least indirectly affected by the pervasive influence of U.S. news outlets, as their features are increasingly being imitated by their Canadian counterparts. While it used to be the case that Canadian news "looked" and "felt" different from American news—and while there are still American news channels (e.g., FOX News) whose content many Canadians no doubt find alienating and are not likely to look for or find north of the 49th parallel—the style and aesthetics of Canadian news are increasingly looking like a trimmed-down version of American news. News tickers crawling across the bottom of the screen, the musical and graphical flourishes designed for ongoing stories, the increasing lack of depth in reporting—to name a few—are fast becoming features of the Canadian TV news landscape. Such "me too-ism" demonstrates a way in which American news is "bad" not only for Americans but for the majority of Canadians, who turn to U.S. news channels to complement their own news fare.

LOWERING COSTS BY LETTING OTHERS DO THE WORK

For many years the traditional American broadcast networks looked at their news operations as part of the public service obligations that came with obtaining a licence to operate from the U.S. media regulator, the Federal Communications Commission (FCC). Indeed, as late as the early 1970s, news shows contained only two minutes of advertising in a half-hour. As networks were bought by larger corporate interests in the 1980s, news operations were mandated to create profit—commercial time was increased to over seven minutes per half-hour and news staff was slashed, compelling those left to run the news divisions to focus on news that could be gathered cheaply (Wittebols, 2004, p. 93). One way news operations would cope with these changes was to focus on routine news events (press conferences, news briefings, public relations–generated events) staged by government and corporate interests. Fewer and fewer investigative or enterprise reports can be supported when news budgets are focused on corporate profitability instead of public service (Just & Rosenstiel, 2005).

Public relations (PR) interests have become much more influential largely through the phenomenal growth of **video news releases (VNRs)** over the last decade. VNRs are pieces contracted or produced by powerful interests and then sent over the airwaves to television news outlets in the United States (most of the companies distributing this type of work also "serve" Canadian television news outlets as well). They are meant to provide a means for stations to present cheaply assembled stories, thus saving on staff resources while providing the free coverage PR operations so highly covet.

As a recent analysis by the Center for Media and Democracy demonstrated, far too often local stations will assemble news stories using only the resources provided by those doing the promoting and without seeking any contrasting perspectives. The Center tracked the use of 36 VNRs released over a 10-month period and found 64 of the 77 stations monitored for the study used those VNRs in 98 instances. The high percentage of stations using VNRs indicates the pervasiveness of this kind of disguised news. Given that this is only a small fraction of the VNRs produced in a year, the success rate for VNR producers is stunning and illustrates the increasing influence of PR on television news production in the United States (Farsetta, 2006; Farsetta & Price, 2006).

The Center found many stations actively disguised the VNRs as locally produced news stories and failed to include any independent reporting on the issue. A third of the time, these VNRs were aired without any alteration, the ultimate coup for corporate propaganda. In some instances, news anchors actually read setup pieces written by the VNR producer verbatim (Farsetta & Price, 2006).

While the vast majority of VNRs in this study were produced for corporate clients, the Bush Administration was actively contracting with PR firms to produce them on behalf of a diverse number of government agencies (on such topics as education, health care for children, prescription drugs for seniors, the Iraq war). Some of these VNRs went beyond reasonable definitions of public service and swam in the waters of advocacy for the administration's frequently controversial policies. The Government Accountability Office, an independent investigative arm of the U.S. Congress, investigated these VNRs and found they violated laws prohibiting use of taxpayer funds to propagandize the public (Bartstow & Stein, 2005).

Coupled with more traditional concerns such as advertiser pressure, the interests and influence of media owners, and pressure from government sources (Hollar, Jackson, & Goldstein, 2006), the rise in the number of VNRs coupled with newsroom pressure to cut costs probably means these kinds of disguised news stories will be seen even more frequently in the future. This has certainly been the American experience, but Canadian research paints a similar picture by noting the steady decline of journalistic independence, reductions of news-gathering resources, growth of a sophisticated corporate and government PR apparatus, and ideological convergence between news values and neoconservative values (Hackett, Gruneau, Gutstein, Gibson, & Newswatch Canada, 2000; Patriquin, 2004). Canadians would do well, therefore, to sit up and take notice of the American experience so that they can better understand and appreciate the changes taking place in their own media system.

CITIZENS AS CONSUMERS

Commercial values also are expressed in what can be charitably called consumer news, though more accurately it can be seen as embedded advertising posing as news. "News you can use" segments focused on finding the right car seat for infants or, more lately, the best prices for gasoline in your neighbourhood are more innocuous examples of this type of news. But local television news also regularly promotes shopping and the joys of consumerism.

Holiday shopping season finds "news" programs sending reporters to shopping malls to identify good buys and stage shopping competitions between reporters. In what are probably paid arrangements, journalists will go into separate stores to point out special deals. While holiday season may be a good time for the media to talk about important consumer issues (e.g., the use of child labour by American corporations operating overseas to produce the clothing we give our friends and families as gifts), the purpose much of the time is to encourage more shopping rather than incite us to think reflexively and act ethically.

At other times, store openings are celebrated as community events and examples of local economic development. So it was with the spring 2006 opening of an IKEA store in suburban Detroit, when stations aired a series of celebratory stories during their news shows to promote commercial interests that years ago would have been seen only during advertising breaks. Gushing reports about the deals to be found in IKEA stores, with reporters exclaiming they no longer had to go to Chicago to shop at IKEA, were the staples of such stories. In the guise of news, however, viewers are more likely to see the story as a legitimate news story. But the more important question is, what does this kind of reporting displace in the newscast, what issues of substance and public value are sacrificed in the name of promoting good old-fashioned American consumerism?

While the breakdown of the traditional wall between the editorial and financial interests at news organizations is troubling on its own, media acquiescence to the powerful institutions they are supposed to watchdog has immediate concerns for those who see the education of citizens as the key to a healthy democracy. On that question, there is much to be concerned about with respect to the American news media.

COVERING POWER

It should come as no surprise that as fully integrated members of global media companies, U.S. media tend to share the worldview of the transnational corporations that own them. The linkage of U.S. foreign policy interests to U.S. media results in coverage that sees American power as a benefit to the entire world and generally assumes the inherent rightness and goodness of the world's dominant superpower.

The war in Iraq provides only the most recent examples of how the news media took the official line and failed the American people as watchdog of the powerful. Media subservience to the Bush administration as it manufactured the arguments for the 2003 invasion, as well as a largely spineless opposition Democratic Party that accepted the administration's premises used to scare people into war, enabled the invasion and occupation of Iraq. Among other assertions, this war was premised on:

- A connection between al-Qaeda and Saddam Hussein.

- The certainty that Iraq had weapons of mass destruction (WMD) and was "close" to developing nuclear weapons.

- The belief that Saddam was a source of terrorism outside Iraq.

These arguments were not critically examined by the press and became shared assumptions by the media. Even prestigious American and international media such as the *New York Times* were at the forefront of this **manufacturing of consent**, serving as a rationalization machine and reporting almost stenographically the information that questionable sources put forth to advance these arguments.

Judith Miller's reporting at the *Times* stands out as the most egregious form of subservience in this war (Foer, 2004; Mayer, 2004; Massing, 2004). Miller is best known for her involvement in the story surrounding the outing of undercover CIA agent Valerie Plame, whose husband, Joseph Wilson, exposed the "uranium from Africa" part of the Iraq nuclear weapons charade.[3] But it was Miller's cozy relationship with Lewis "Scooter" Libby, who was the vice president's chief-of-staff, and other administration officials in the Defense Department which was a major factor in her reportage and resulted in the discrediting of much of it.

While some agencies of the U.S. government, most notably the CIA, had long disdained Iraqi exile Ahmed Chalabi as unreliable, he was revived by a Bush administration seeking a rationale for war, which used his exile sources as the primary sources for the WMD claims in Iraq (Mayer, 2004). Within the Pentagon's Office of Special Plans, set up to bypass the CIA, Chalabi's credibility issues were put aside as staff cherry-picked evidence supporting the administration's position (Massing, 2004). One of Chalabi's fellow exiles, nicknamed "Curveball" by skeptical CIA analysts, was a primary source for Miller, though she was never allowed to meet or interview him about his claims. Nonetheless, this sourcing provided Miller with several front-page stories in the *Times* hyping the WMD claims. While some other media, most notably Knight Ridder newspapers, brought more skepticism to their reporting (Rendall, 2006), it was the vaunted *Times* that set the agenda for much of the rest of the press. Miller's own role in this journalistic charade resulted in her leaving the paper and leaving the *Times* with substantial egg on its face for being manipulated by an administration that was determined to invade Iraq. This subservience is not exceptional for the *Times* or other elite media. Much-heralded stories like the Pentagon Papers or the Watergate and CIA investigations are anomalies. Far too often, the elite press is willing to give the president the benefit of the doubt. The use of the atomic weapons in Japan, the Bay of Pigs invasion of Cuba, the Gulf of Tonkin incident, which spurred U.S. intervention in Vietnam, and the invasion of Grenada in 1983 are just a few historical examples of a lack of skepticism by U.S. elite press (Solomon, 2005).

Pre-invasion public opinion polling bears out the fact that what you believed to be true depended on your source for news. Well after the existence of WMD in Iraq was shown to be false, well after the links between Saddam and al-Qaeda were shattered by lack of any evidence, substantial portions of the American public still believed these to be true.

A 2003 study by Steven Kull, director of the University of Maryland's Program on International Policy Attitudes, showed many Americans got basic facts about the war wrong, largely a result of the news media they consumed (Kull, Ramsay, & Lewis, 2003–2004). Knowledge about three basic facts was tested: the lack of a Saddam Hussein–al-Qaeda connection, the failure to discover WMD, and the lack of international support for the war. Answers to these questions were then matched to the news sources respondents said they relied on the most. The fact that such misperceptions were prevalent among those who self-identified as paying close attention demonstrates the press failed to adequately educate U.S. citizens. Viewers of CNN, FOX, and the three traditional networks (NBC, ABC, and CBS) were more likely to have at least one of the misperceptions. Only those who identified "print media" or PBS/NPR (public television news and radio, respectively) as their primary sources of news had fewer than 50 percent of members with one misperception. Viewers of FOX were the most likely (80 percent) to get at least one of the answers to the three basic facts wrong. Of respondents who relied on FOX, 45 percent got all three facts wrong and were more likely to get them wrong if they said they were following events closely, while only 9 and 4 percent of those relying on print media or public broadcast media got all three facts wrong.

As an indicator that Americans' news diets are creating a political Tower of Babel, the study also found that Bush supporters who viewed FOX news were far more likely to have one or more misperceptions about the war than Bush supporters who used public media as their primary source, even when accounting for how closely both were following news about the war.

As the war and President Bush have become unpopular with the American public, some media are now beginning to take off the gloves and provide a more intimate view of how the president operates. The fact that the press is unwilling to pull back the curtain and reveal behaviour by a "nice guy" president which belies his public demeanour until polling shows he has lost popularity is telling in terms of how subservient the press behaves with respect to the executive branch (Froomkin, 2005). When polling guides reporting, the press is demonstrating its timidity in serving as a watchdog on power. And given Americans' reliance on TV news as their primary source of news, none of this bodes well for American democracy. Furthermore, I would argue that since what occurs in the United States has implications for nearly every part of the world, it doesn't bode well for global democracy, either. The Iraq war is just the latest example of what happens when elite media teams up with government power to create support for policies that are unlikely to gain the consent of the public on their own merits.[4]

Finally, the American media's symbiotic relationship with power is most obvious in the area of electoral political coverage. Coverage of political campaigns in news programs has shrunk so dramatically that there is now more politics in the advertising during news show breaks. Political advertising focuses increasingly on a candidate's personality or charisma; thus it is no surprise that candidates are elected despite substantial opposition to the policies they advocate. This is because people are largely unaware of specific policy positions that candidates take. Voters who rely on television news come to see politics as personality contests—as beauty pageants for government officials (Wittebols, 2004). Coverage of personality issues is easier, and cheaper, than coverage of issues, particularly for television. But American news media can be rightfully criticized for decreasing news coverage of politics, especially at the local level. That's because media companies, both big networks like FOX or CNN and local network affiliates benefit immensely from the massive amounts of money raised for politics. Collecting two-thousand-dollar cheques from wealthy contributors, candidates raise money feverishly, which by and large ends up in the pockets of the media as paid advertising. While periodically "reforms" are introduced to limit contributions and expenditures, the amount of money spent on media aspects of campaigns continues to skyrocket. Thus the news media actually devote less time to coverage of election campaigns during the news program itself.

Reports about the conduct of campaigns in Canada indicate that the ability to market candidates like consumer commodities means Canadian politics is heading down a path well worn in the United States. "Branding" of candidates (Cobb, 2005a) and the use of negative attack ads (Cobb, 2005b; Okalou, 2003) have been staples of American politics, and criticized by good government advocates, for decades. Negative advertising in Canada is thought to have started during the 1993 election when what is called the "face ad"—an ad mocking Jean Chrétien's facial paralysis—was produced by his conservative opponent's campaign (Yaffe, 2004). And given that

Canadian media, particularly television, stand to benefit from the ad wars begun by panicked candidates who must respond to attacks and counterattacks, it will be hard to put the genie back into the bottle. Thus media actually benefit from contributing to the poisonous atmosphere created by political advertising campaigns.

CONCLUSION

There is no doubt that having access to American news sources helps Canadians better understand their often puzzling neighbours to the south. But to go so far as to rely exclusively on the U.S. news media or to argue that U.S. news is superior in quality to that produced by Canadian outlets can hardly be supported by any comparison of the two countries' media on issues of international importance. It is commonly argued that Canadian and American news are entirely different beasts—American news organizations value style over substance and prioritize private over public interests, while Canadian media (particularly the much lauded CBC) operate in a more socially responsible manner. Indeed, this is why so many Canadians still turn to domestic news as their first source of information about themselves and the world in which they live (particularly at important moments such as elections or after major events like a terrorist attack). That Canada did not join the U.S.-led war in Iraq can be explained in part by the unwillingness of Canadian politicians at that time to climb aboard the Bush administration's war train and of the nation's media to report on that decision with considerable favour. Yet, there should still be a reason to pause and think critically about the effects of American news on the Canadian media industry and, by extension, Canadian values. As mentioned, Canadian news media are beginning to suffer increasingly from many of the same ills that transformed American news giants from at least occasional defenders of civic virtue into faithful advocates for economic and political power—increasing concentration of ownership, greater commercialization pressures, and the same use of VNRs directed at television news operations.

As fully integrated members of the corporate order, American media offer narrowly framed debates on the viability and direction of the economy. Given power brokers in both the Republican and Democratic parties are enthusiastic for so-called free trade regimes, it is not surprising that critiques of free trade agreements are lacking. Taken-for-granted perspectives on globalization and neoliberal economics exclude serious consideration of alternative perspectives on world trade.

Such perspectives, when taken on by an increasingly corporate-dominated Canadian media system, have the strong potential of resulting in a similar narrowing of the boundaries in which Canadian public opinion takes shape and Canadian government economic policies are formed. The recent shift in federal political power in Canada has also shifted Canada's foreign policy from a state of relative independence to nearly full-fledged support for the American-led "global war on terror." Canada's active involvement in Afghanistan, for example, which aids the United States in its involvement in Iraq, seems to be benefiting from the very same media that only a few years earlier lauded the country's independent foreign policy vis-à-vis the United States. Increasingly, Canadians are getting news about the mission in Afghanistan that sheds more light on the personal stories of soldiers and their families than the divisive nature of the reasons for war in the first place. While it would be misleading to suggest that Canadian media have kowtowed to the Harper administration's militaristic involvement in Afghanistan, the critical tone that previously characterized its coverage of U.S. intervention overseas has softened dramatically.

As long as Canadian television news continues to adopt trends developed in the United States (wire service crawls, use of music and graphical flourishes, increasingly shorter stories, use of VNRs) and so long as style and presentation inform the development of content and substance, Canadian citizens will become less knowledgeable about the world, and, ultimately, democratic decision making in Canada will suffer.

In brief, if you want theatre, watch U.S. television news. Consult Canadian news sources for news about Canada, but do so with increased skepticism and an eye to the shift toward American-style reporting. If you truly want to learn about what's going on in the rest of the world, go online and read the world's press.

Resources

Barstow, D., & Stein, R. (2005, March 13). Under Bush, a new age of prepackaged TV news. *The New York Times*. Retrieved March 16, 2005, from http://www.nytimes.com

Cobb, C. (2005a, September 20). Branding is the name of the game. *Ottawa Citizen*, p. A3. Retrieved December 5, 2005, from ProQuest database: http://proquest.com

Cobb, C. (2005b, September 20). When ads attack. *Ottawa Citizen*, p. B1. Retrieved December 5, 2005, from ProQuest database: http.proquest.com

Eggerton, J. (2005, March 20). DOD's big flack attack. *Broadcasting and Cable*. Retrieved March 21, 2005, from http://www.broadcastingcable.com

Farsetta, D. (2006, May 2). News fakers respond. Retrieved May 2, 2006, from http://www.alternet.org/mediaculture/35719/

Farsetta, D., & Price, D. (2006, April 6). Fake TV news: Widespread and undisclosed. Center for Media and Democracy. Retrieved April 6, 2006, from http://www.prwatch.org/fakenews/execsummary

Foer, F. (2004, June 7). The source of the trouble. *New York Magazine*. Retrieved June 7, 2007, from http://nymag.com

Froomkin, D. (2005, September 12). Now they tell us. *The Washington Post*. Retrieved September 13, 2005, from http://www.washingtonpost.com

Hackett, R. A., Gruneau, R., Gutstein, D., Gibson, T. A., & Newswatch Canada. (2000). *The missing news: Filters and blind spots in Canada's press*. Aurora, ON: Garamond Press and the Canadian Centre for Policy Alternatives.

Hollar, J., Jackson, J., & Goldstein, H. (2006, April). *Fear and favor 2005: FAIR's sixth annual report. Outside (and inside) influence on the news*. Retrieved April 3, 2006, from http://www.fair.org

Just, M., & Rosenstiel, T. (2005, March 3). All the news that's Fed. *The New York Times*. Retrieved March 26, 2005, from http://nytimes.com

Kull, S, Ramsay, C., & Lewis, E. (2003–2004, winter). Misperceptions, the media and the Iraq war. *Political Science Quarterly, 118*(4), 569–598. Retrieved October 10, 2003, from http://pipa.org

Leonnig, C. D. (2005, September 17). Jailed reporter is distanced from news, not elite visitors. *The Washington Post*, p. A1.

Massing, M. (2004, February 26). Now they tell us. *New York Review of Books*. Retrieved June 6, 2006, from http://www.nybooks.com/

Mayer, J. (2004, June 7). The manipulator. *The New Yorker*. Retrieved June 8, 2006, from http://www.newyorker.com/

Okalou, S. (2003, October 6). Issues and attack ads: The strategy's behind Ontario's election campaigns. *Strategy Magazine*. Retrieved September 20, 2006, from http://www.strategymag.com

Patriquin, L. (2004). *Inventing tax rage: Misinformation in the National Post*. Halifax, NS: Fernwood Books.

Project for Excellence in Journalism. (2006). *2006 annual report on the state of the news media.* Washington, DC: Author.

Rendall, S. (2006, March/April). Wrong on Iraq? Not everyone. *Extra!* Retrieved April 3, 2006, from http://fair.org

Solomon, N. (2005). *War made easy: How presidents and pundits are spinning us to death.* Hoboken, NJ: John Wiley & Sons.

Wittebols, J. H. (2004). *The soap opera paradigm: Television programming and corporate priorities.* Lanham, MD: Rowman & Littlefield.

Yaffe, B. (2004, Ocober 30). Negative political advertising works, when done right. *The Vancouver Sun*, p. C9. Retrieved September 20, 2006, from http://www.proquest.com

Notes

[1] The Project for Excellence in Journalism, part of the Columbia University graduate program in journalism, produces annual reports on the state of the news media. The 2006 report quotes an editor of "one of the country's major papers": "If you argue about the public trust today, you will be dismissed as an obstructionist and a romantic" (Project for Excellence, 2006, p. 4).

[2] Readers will note I focus on television news in the United States. I do so because TV news from the United States is more accessible to Canadians than print or radio news. Increasingly, people look to television to get their news and are reading newspapers less regularly.

[3] Miller's connections to those she covered became obvious when she was jailed for refusing to reveal the name of the Administration official who had leaked Plame's identity as a CIA agent in an effort to discredit Wilson's report that a Nigerian uranium deal supposedly sought by Iraq was false. She was visited in jail not only by fellow journalists but by administration officials as well, including Lewis Libby and eventual UN ambassador John Bolton (Leonnig, 2005).

[4] While far less a life-and-death matter, more mundane examples of government efforts to shape the news occur almost daily. Beyond the considerable press relations efforts of government departments and agencies, spring 2005 revealed the existence of government contracts given to newspaper columnists to plug administrative legislative initiatives, such as the "No Child Left Behind" education legislation. Conservative columnist and talk show host Armstrong Williams was found to have received $250,000 from the Bush Administration for just this purpose. Congressional outrage purportedly shut the program down after Armstrong and several other "journalists" were found to be on the take (Eggerton, 2005).

ISSUE 2

Not neighbourly: Is American news bad for Canadians?

✗ NO

America in Our Midst: U.S. News and Entertainment in Canada—An Object Lesson
Christopher Dornan

Christopher Dornan is director of the Arthur Kroeger College of Public Affairs at Carleton University and an associate professor in the School of Journalism and Communication. He is the co-editor of *The Canadian Federal Election of 2006*, along with two previous volumes in this series.

Is American news bad for Canada? Well, if it is, presumably we should want less of it. By that reasoning, ideally we should want none of it at all. We should want a border impermeably sealed against reportage from our nearest neighbour, a country walled off from journalism issuing from the most powerful nation on the planet. The Canadian Radio-television and Telecommunications Commission (CRTC) could electronically jam Jim Lehrer and Tucker Carlson, Internet firewalls could be erected to block access to Boing Boing and the *Sports Illustrated* website, vigilant Canada Customs officials could impound truckloads of the *New York Times* like so much contraband, citizens in Toronto could inform on their neighbours illicitly tuning in to Buffalo's Channel 7 *Eyewitness News*. At last we would be safe from the noxious, corrosive influence of America's running accounts of its own affairs. We would be free to pursue our national destiny in a climate of smug ignorance.

Absurd and grotesque as it may be, there are actually countries in the world that have pursued just such policies, but you would not want to live there. Know where they don't get much American news? North Korea, that barrel of laughs. Even in Castro's Cuba, the locals may be discouraged from watching signals drifting over the Caribbean from Miami, but CNN, Fox News, and MSNBC are in-room viewing options in any hotel with a swimming pool. The mullahs of Tehran may despise American journalism as much as they despise American geopolitics, but they do not make the mistake of ignoring either, because the first is the fastest way to keep up with the second. To be attentive to the world at all is necessarily to be attentive to the United States.

The result is that, apart from isolated pockets of despotism, the world is awash in American news, both news *about* the United States and news *from* the United States. It's all one big swimming pool, from Helsinki to the Honduras.

There are those who argue that this amounts to a form of information imperialism, a means by which the United States forces itself on the rest of the globe. The worldwide prominence of

American news is said to be a means by which the United States imposes its values, its perspective, and its interests on an unwilling planet through a process of **cultural imperialism**—the ideological arm of what some describe as "Coca-colonization" (e.g., Kuisel, 1991). This is a nice theory, and for a while there, back in the 1960s and 1970s, it was very popular among those on the receiving end of U.S. information exports, and even among many Americans themselves, or at least the ones who owned Che Guevara T-shirts. It had a neat symmetry to it, too. The nation that gave us *The Outer Limits* ("We control the horizontal. We control the vertical.") was literally manipulating our thoughts through our televisions. Do not adjust your set.

It got to the point where the well-intentioned folks at UNESCO—the United Nations Educational, Scientific and Cultural Organization—insisted that what was necessary was precisely a massive readjustment of the global television set. What it saw as the international information imbalance—in which the rest of the world was subject to torrents of U.S. news while the United States itself ethnocentrically ignored the world beyond its borders—was so pernicious that it simply had to be redressed. UNESCO called for a grandiose **New World Information and Communication Order (NWICO)**, in which the global news diet would be bureaucratically reengineered so as to wean the world off the killer carbs of American content.[1] How exactly this was to be accomplished was murky at best, especially since it was proposed at about the same time as entire families from Antigua to Zimbabwe were transfixed by the same primetime soap opera, all wondering who shot J.R. The world might well resent the brash American dominance of the airwaves, but if pulling the plug means no more *Dallas* or *Desperate Housewives*, it is always going to be a hard sell.

The proposals for a NWICO came to nothing, not because they were unworkable and not because the U.S. government and big media corporations became apoplectic at the mere suggestion. The NWICO faltered and died because the premise on which it was founded was simply false. The NWICO doctrine held that the hypnotic lure of American media content was a sure route to the extermination of other forms of nationalism and identity. Drenched in Hollywood sitcoms and locked into a news agenda dictated by New York and Washington, the world could not help but become vassal to the United States. It would lose the ability to think outside a box stamped "Made in the U.S.A." But if that were so, then the NWICO itself should have been a heterodoxy impossible to imagine.

One might riposte that what American media content promotes is not so much specific U.S. policies—which are easily contrasted against one's own self-interest and therefore easily contested—as a broad set of values by which worth and purpose come to be judged: rampant consumer materialism, say. But while it is no doubt true that U.S. news and entertainment giddily celebrate material comfort, the United States did not invent consumerism any more than it invented capitalism. It just happens to be very good at both. But other countries are just as good at them in their own way and have been at them just as long, perhaps longer. Well before there was Bud Light there was the Czech Budweiser Pils brewery. IKEA makes better, more affordable, and considerably more stylish furniture than La-Z-Boy. And to anyone who thinks it was the Americans who elevated conspicuous consumption to a gleaming ideal, I have one word: Lamborghini.

In any case, history has refuted the NWICO doctrine. U.S. media content did not extinguish other nationalisms or identities, it stoked them. It made American priorities vivid and palpable, something to embrace or resist as one chose. Even something to detest. What it did not do is narcotize the world into thinking like Americans. The Palestinians who cheered in the streets when the World Trade Center towers collapsed had been reared on *Friends* and *Frasier*, pulling them in on the satellite dishes that carpet the ghettoes of the Third World. They liked the sitcoms just fine, but this did not make them love America.

Canada is likely the global citizen that has the greatest affection for the United States. Nestled against it for as long as both countries have existed and sharing a common language, we know America best. We admire its virtues, are impressed by its strengths, imitate its finest features, and do all we can to avoid its faults. We are also the country that has had the longest experience with exposure to U.S. cultural products and therefore the country that has been longest troubled by it.

Blessed by safety, prosperity, and civility, Canada is by any measure an enviable dominion. But it is also a nation whose political preoccupation, and particular neurosis, is whether it can continue to exist as a nation. The United States, as we well know, has no such self-doubt. It has a different set of neuroses.

We have always been taught to believe that Canadian sovereignty is a fragile thing perpetually threatened on two fronts, the first of which is internal—the aspirations of those Quebecers who would rather go it alone under their own flag—and the second of which runs along the 49th parallel. The danger in the second instance is no longer annexation but assimilation. Foreign and domestic policy might become so attuned to that of our muscular neighbour as to become indistinguishable. The two economies could become so integrated that Canada risks ending up as a mere comprador subsidiary of America, Inc. Were that to happen, the nation of Canada would cease to exist in all but name. We might keep our own flag, but it would not amount to much beyond a separate team at the Olympics and a vote at the United Nations which would be handily in the pocket of the United States.

The fifth column that would supposedly soften our resistance and ease the way for assimilation was something as seemingly innocuous as information. They would come with their wire services and their network news divisions, their glossy magazines and their dazzling celebrity culture. Slavishly attentive to all things American, even our own television channels and newspapers would be little more than conduits for U.S. content—so cheap to acquire and so much more tantalizing than the drab domestic equivalent.[2] After a while, we would simply forget who we were. We would be welcomed into the hive.

This decidedly Canadian anxiety is as old as Canada itself. It is as though we need to tell ourselves this cautionary tale even though, deep down, no one truly believes it, the way children like to be frightened by stories of monsters in the basement they know are not real. In 1902 Sir Sanford Fleming, then the chancellor of Queen's University, became so alarmed at what he saw as the unsavoury influence of the then-newfangled mass-circulation newspaper that he commissioned a $250-prize essay competition on the subject "How can Canadian universities best benefit the profession of journalism as a means of moulding and elevating public opinion?" The following year the winning entries were anthologized by the editors of *Queen's Quarterly* in a volume published by Copp press. One by one, they itemized the by-now familiar sins of a populist press: the undue influence of advertising, the unseemly invasions of privacy, the literary bankruptcy of journalistic prose, and the pursuit of sensation at the expense of civic duty. Prominent among these was the complaint that Canadian newspapers featured all too much news from and about the United States.

Almost 70 years later, the complaint was still extant and even more inflamed. In 1970 a special Senate committee, under the chairmanship of Keith Davey, delivered a report on the mass media, ruefully concluding in its very first pages that Canada had become "a cultural as well as economic satellite of the United States. And nowhere is this trend more pronounced than in the media" (Senate, 1970, p. 11). The fifth column was in our midst, and our own media corporations had become its eager quislings. "What we *are* suggesting," the report continued, "is that the Canadian media—especially the broadcast media—have an interest and obligation to promote our *apartness* from the American reality. For all our similarities, for all our sharing, for all our friendships, we *are* somebody else" (p. 11).

It has therefore all but established itself as a given in Canada that a nation that laps up another's media products imperils itself as a nation. The only problem with this axiom is that, like the NWICO doctrine, it is manifestly false. And the proof of that is all around us. Anyone who believes that Canada is a pale excuse for a nation, a junior doppelganger of the United States, simply has not lived in the United States for any length of time, or anywhere else for that matter. The bleating about how Canadian identity is smothered by U.S. cultural exports—as though a nation's sense of what it is about can be expressed only through situation comedies and junk journalism—is as tiresome, misplaced, and mystifying to an outsider as the equivalent Australian "cultural cringe" toward Britain, the mother country half a world away. (And even the Australians, happily, have dropped the cultural cringe, correctly surmising that it was irrelevant, and indeed detrimental, to the ongoing project of building a just and vibrant society.)

Sometimes it takes an outsider to state plainly what should be evident to all. In 1990 a British academic, Richard Collins, published *Culture, Communication and National Identity: The Case of Canadian Television*, in which he demolished the argument that Canada was diminished as a nation by its appetite for American media content. The book was not well received in those circles that have made a veritable industry of hand-wringing over the viability of Canadian culture in the face of the American threat—in the upper echelons of the federal Department of Canadian Heritage it was seen as something akin to *The Satanic Verses*—but it deserves an audience among those who are genuinely interested in the issue and who haven't already been fitted with blinkers. Collins makes the simple and devastating point that it is more than possible to foster a separate society while still gorging on Oprah, Dr. Phil, Howard Stern, and Charlie Rose, because a nation's sense of purpose and its centre of gravity depend on robust civic institutions that transcend the ephemera of the media. Put it this way, if you like: Canada has its problems, no question, but it remains a less violent society than the United States by a truly remarkable margin. If the two nations share essentially the same media content, why should this be so? Perhaps it has nothing to do with what's on television.

To argue, then, that American news is bad for Canada, one would have to show that Canadians attend to American news at the expense of the affairs of their own community; or that the practices of American journalism have somehow sullied a purer Canadian strain; or that Canadians are simply poorer for the wealth of choice of American journalism we have at our disposal. But all of these contentions are, in a word, nonsense.

First of all, Canadians do not ignore their own news in preference for American news. Far from it. They might seek out U.S. news *in addition to* news of Canada, but not instead of it. There may have been a time when the U.S. network anchors were household names in anglophone

Canada—Jennings, Rather, Brokaw—but how many of us can name the U.S. anchors today? They have become the answers to trivia questions. They are no match for Mansbridge, Robertson, and Newman, who together draw more than 3 million viewers a night. A 2004 study by the Canadian Media Research Consortium (CMRC) found that almost 80 percent of Canadians watch their country's national TV newscasts either daily or a few times per week. A mere 35 percent say they watch U.S. news either daily or frequently—and many of these are likely the same people. It is possible to buy *USA Today* in Canada, but it sells in negligible numbers and even then largely to U.S. businesspeople passing through, as opposed to the more than 5 million copies of Canadian daily newspapers sold each day. In 2006 the Canadian edition of *Time* magazine closed up shop, its parent company judging that it was no longer worth the expense of maintaining it.

Second, while the United States produces forms of journalism that leave one aghast, the Canadian media have shown no impulse to emulate them. For decades now, local U.S. television news has been a parade of grisly car crashes, blood-soaked murder scenes, nightly drug busts, and smoking arson sites. If it bleeds, it leads, goes the cliché in U.S. local newsrooms. Canadian local newscasts will pay attention to crime and catastrophe, certainly, but it is not their raison d'être. They are just as likely to report on hundredth birthdays and diamond wedding anniversaries, school science fairs and ethnic community festivals. It may be hokey, but better the benign than the malign.

And there is simply no Canadian equivalent of the abrasive bombast of Rush Limbaugh and his ilk. We have our blowhard radio call-in hosts, but they are opinionated, not vindictive. Fox News, similarly, that minaret for "America first" prejudice, finds no counterpart in Canada. It is not Fox's tub-thumping for a specific waveband on the political spectrum that grates on the nerves—lord knows, CBC Radio is a transmitter tower for a squishy left-of-centre sensibility—but the mean-spiritedness with which it does so. On Fox News, opposing viewpoints are entertained not to debate but only to bray at, mock, and vilify. The network has the Neanderthal personality of the schoolyard bully—personified by its most prominent host, Bill O'Reilly—and though we may watch it in Canada with an eye-popping fascination, Canadian media companies have not been tempted to even try to ape its ugly, discursive style.

By the same token, the United States has given us a range of splendid journalistic outlets we should count ourselves lucky to have: the *New Yorker*, the *New Republic*, *Harper's*, the *Atlantic Monthly*, *Scientific American*, the *Smithsonian*, PBS's *Frontline* and *Nova* documentary series, *Wired*, *Esquire*, the *Utne Reader*, *Forbes*, *Fortune*, and even (perhaps especially) the *Daily Show* and the *Colbert Report*. The availability of all of these and more are a boon to Canada, not a liability.

That is one of Canada's singular advantages over the United States: we have the full range of their media content and our own besides. They, by contrast, pay almost no attention to any media content other than their own. In that regard, ironically, they have something in common with North Korea.

References

Babe, R. (1990). *Telecommunications in Canada: Technology, industry and government*. Toronto: University of Toronto Press.

Canadian Media Research Consortium. (2004). *Canadians watch Canadian news. Report Card on Canadian News Media*. 2004. Retrieved September 2006 from http://cmrcccrm.ca/english/reportcard2004/01.html

Collins, R. (1990). *Culture, communication and national identity: The case of Canadian television.* Toronto: University of Toronto Press.

Hardin, H. (1986). *Closed circuits: The sellout of Canadian television.* Vancouver: Douglas & McIntyre.

Kuisel, R. F. (1991). Coca-Cola and the Cold War: The French face Americanization, 1948–1953. *French Historical Studies, 17*(1), 96–116.

Moore, M. (2005, October 21). UN body endorses cultural protection; US objections are turned aside. *The Washington Post.* Retrieved September 2006 from Global Policy Forum website, http://www.globalpolicy. org/globaliz/cultural/2005/1021body.htm

Queen's Quarterly (Ed.). (1903). *How can Canadian universities best benefit the profession of journalism as a means of moulding and elevating public opinion?* Toronto: Copp.

Rothkop, D. (1997, June 22). In praise of cultural imperialism? Effects of globalization on culture. *Foreign Policy.* Retrieved September 2006 from Global Policy Forum website, http://www.globalpolicy.org/ globaliz/cultural/globcult.htm

Senate of Canada. (1970). *Special Senate Committee on the Mass Media: The Davey Committee report.* Ottawa: Queen's Printer.

Smith, A. (1980). *The geopolitics of information: How Western culture dominates the world.* New York: Faber & Faber.

UNESCO. (1980). *Many voices, one world: The MacBride report.* Paris.

Notes

[1] The United States, the United Kingdom, and the major Western news agencies such as Reuters and the Associated Press saw the NWICO proposals as a pretext to infringe on the free flow of information. Authoritarian governments, they argued, would use the provisions to control what information their populations might have access to. In the wake of the MacBride Report, the UNESCO (1980) document that first proposed a New World Information and Communication Order, both the United States and the United Kingdom withdrew from UNESCO in protest—the former in 1984 and the latter in 1985. Britain rejoined in 1997 and the United States in 2003.

For a clear, contemporaneous account of the NWICO debate, see Anthony Smith (1980). Most academic studies have taken the side of UNESCO against Western "cultural imperialism," but there have been those who unapologetically champion U.S. dominance of global culture. See, for example, David Rothkop (1997), who argues that "globalization is a vital step toward both a more stable world and better lives for the people in it. Furthermore, these issues have serious implications for American foreign policy. For the United States, a central objective of an Information Age foreign policy must be to win the battle of the world's information flows, dominating the airwaves as Great Britain once ruled the seas."

The current version of the NWICO debate involves measures to protect local cultural expression in the face of the Hollywood juggernaut. In late 2005, UNESCO voted 148 to 2 (with 4 abstentions) to ratify an international treaty designed to do just that. The United States saw the treaty as an attempt to impede the sales of its cultural products around the world and argued that it "could be used to unfairly obstruct the flow of ideas, goods and services across borders" (Moore, 2005). In a clear echo of objections to NWICO a quarter of a century ago, the U.S. ambassador to UNESCO, Louise Oliver, suggested that dictators could potentially use the treaty to control what their citizens read. Interestingly, even some of the United States' closest allies, such as Britain and Canada, voted with the majority. Only Israel sided with the United States.

[2] This is an argument that has long enjoyed currency in Canadian academic circles. While the national mythos invites Canadians to be proud of our innovations in communication (the world's first domestic communication satellite, a robust continent-wide telecommunications system, etc.) because these have helped to stitch together a sparse population spread over a vast geographic expanse, contrarians have been at pains to point out that this elaborate technical apparatus has actually been an aqueduct system sluicing American content into Canadian households. See, for example, Hardin (1986) and Babe (1990).

Discussion Questions

1. If the world loves U.S. entertainment, why does the world not love America?

2. Most American media products are freely available to Canadian consumers, from *Newsweek* to *Hustler*. A few, however, are prohibited. One can receive CNN in Canada but not HBO, FOX News but not Nickelodeon. On what grounds? Compile a list of U.S. media outlets and products that cannot be legally purchased in Canada. Why have these been banned to us? Argue either in favour or against.

3. Canadians overwhelmingly watch American movies, read American magazines, listen to American music, and prefer American TV dramas and comedies. But they pay far more attention to Canadian journalism in all its guises than to U.S. news. Canadians read Canadian newspapers, watch Canadian nightly news, listen to Canadian call-in shows. Why should this be so? What are the implications?

4. Although Canadians largely rely on Canadian sources of news, how are they still affected by U.S. news styles and techniques?

5. How were American attitudes about going to war in Iraq reflective of the kind of news Americans choose to believe?

6. What kinds of interests do local TV stations have in ad-driven U.S. political campaigns?

ISSUE 3

Evil empires: Should limits to foreign ownership of Canadian media be lifted?

✔ YES

Evil Empires? Nonsense—A Case for Eliminating Restrictions on Foreign Ownership of Canadian Media Properties
Richard Schultz

Richard Schultz is James McGill Professor and chair of the Department of Political Science at McGill University. He is the author or coeditor of eight books and more than fifty articles and book chapters, including *Changing the Rules: Canadian Regulatory Regimes and Institutions,* "From Master to Partner to Bit Player: The Diminishing Role of Government Policy in Communications," and "Canadian Communications and the Spectre of Globalization: Just Another Word … " His current project is a co-authored book entitled *Contested Networks: The Bureaucratic Transformation of Canadian Telecommunications 1976–1993.* In 2005 he was a Visiting Fellow at the Shorenstein Center on Press, Politics and Public Policy at the Kennedy School of Government at Harvard University, where his research concentrated on the links among media diversity, concentration, and cross-ownership.

INTRODUCTION

In the garden of Canadian media policy there are many sacred totems. These include the notions embedded in the *Broadcasting Act, 1991,* that broadcasting is a "single system"; that broadcasting is "a public service essential to the maintenance and enhancement of national identity and **cultural sovereignty**"; that "the Canadian broadcasting system should serve to safeguard, enrich, and strengthen the cultural, political, social, and economic fabric of Canada;" and that "the programming … should be of high standard." Undoubtedly the most sacred, and consequently the most powerful, totem is that the Canadian broadcasting system, and arguably the media system more generally, "shall be effectively owned and controlled by Canadians."[1]

Anyone who dares challenge these totems, especially that of Canadian ownership, risks being branded a heretic, or worse, a follower of a false god—the market—or a member of the "economic right" with a "crabbed critique of cultural products" (Grant & Wood, 2004, p. 8). There is no question that government can play an important role, through the use of tax and subsidy policies and especially a well-funded public broadcaster, in supporting Canadian media to further cultural, as opposed to industrial, policy objectives. However, the existing mix of foreign ownership restrictions is neither necessary nor helpful in pursuing these objectives. Canada's current media foreign ownership policies are based on a misreading of Canadian history, on an undocumented claim that foreign ownership is intrinsically bad, and on simplistic assumptions. These policies have resulted in unintended yet profoundly negative consequences for media ownership and are proving to be dangerously contagious for other sectors. And although they will shortly become irrelevant, their continuance will prove to be costly without any demonstrable benefit.

Before developing these arguments, it is important that we understand what the current foreign ownership policies are and the assumptions upon which they are based. In the following section, I provide a summary overview of the policies for both broadcasting and media generally. In the subsequent sections I will discuss the assumptions and the rationale for such policies and then go on to my critique of them and why I think they should be eliminated.

CANADA'S MEDIA FOREIGN OWNERSHIP POLICIES

There are two types of foreign ownership restrictions. The first, found in both the broadcasting and telecommunications sectors, limits direct foreign ownership to 20 percent and indirect ownership by a holding company to 33 percent. This limitation is combined with a requirement in both sectors that non-Canadians cannot exercise control over either a licensed broadcaster, including cable companies, or a telecommunications company. Moreover, 80 percent of the directors of broadcasting licensees and telecommunications carriers must be Canadian.

A number of commentators, including the House of Commons Standing Committee on Canadian Heritage in its 2003 report, *Our Cultural Sovereignty*, defend the restrictions on the grounds that the actual limitations are not 20 percent and 33 percent respectively but combined amount to 46.7 percent (p. 389). This is accounting hocus-pocus. There is not, and has not been, a single case since the restrictions were introduced of a non-Canadian interest owning 46.7 percent of a Canadian broadcasting licensee. It simply would not make economic sense for a non-Canadian interest to invest this heavily in a company where it could not exercise any degree of control. Given the large number of family-controlled corporations in the broadcasting sector (e.g., Rogers, CHUM, and Shaw), where differential shareholder voting rights are common, why would any foreign shareholder consider making a large investment if it knew that a single Canadian shareholder with perhaps a minority of preferred shares could exercise near total control? It is quite simply intellectually dishonest to claim that 46.7 percent is the upper limit of foreign ownership when the actual effective percentage is only 20 percent.

The second form of ownership restrictions applies to various publishing media. The *Income Tax Act* is employed as an indirect means of keeping publishing firms Canadian-owned by limiting deductions for advertising expenses to newspapers and magazines that are 75 percent or more Canadian-owned. In the 1990s Canada also attempted to supplement this form of restriction by imposing an 80 percent excise tax on foreign periodicals that contained advertisements directed at Canadians.[2] The conflict that this caused, and the subsequent setback for Canada's policies, played a major role in the Canadian push for an international treaty to restrict the impact of international trade agreements on cultural products.

RATIONALE FOR CURRENT OWNERSHIP RESTRICTIONS

Before critiquing the current restrictions it is worthwhile to spend some time on the major arguments and reasons advanced in their defence. Defenders of the status quo have a much distorted understanding of the history of Canadian policies. The Heritage Committee, for example, claims that "the philosophy of Canadian ownership and control has always been central to Canada's cultural industries" (2003, p. 385). The fact is these policies, and their underlying philosophy, are of relatively recent vintage, dating primarily from the 1960s and 1970s. Prior to these years, and it is worth remembering that broadcasting dates from the 1920s, there were no foreign ownership restrictions in the individual media sectors. More importantly, when the prohibitions on foreign ownership were introduced in the broadcasting sector in 1969, no attempt was made to justify the new policy on the grounds that foreign owners had acted against Canadian public policy interests or that their behaviour had somehow been deleterious compared to that of Canadian owners.[3]

In the 1993 *Telecommunications Act*, the current restrictions were established for telecommunications companies. Again, no specific explanation was provided justifying the restrictions. This was indeed unfortunate because for most of the last century, the Canadian telecommunications sector was a laboratory that could have been used to establish if foreign ownership truly poses a public policy problem. From the 1920s, the second-largest telephone company in Canada, BC Telephone, as well as a regional operator in Quebec, had been foreign controlled by the same American parent. At no time in the history of that ownership was a credible case made that BC Telephone's service record was deficient because of its foreign ownership.

In terms of specific arguments invoked to justify foreign ownership restrictions, most are not particularly persuasive. One, in fact, is risible. In their submission to the Commons Heritage Committee, the Canadian Conference of the Arts claimed that television program scheduling would be negatively affected. They argued that "the creation of a program schedule should be based on appealing to a Canadian audience—not as an afterthought to an international schedule but as the primary focus" (2002, p. 4) As anyone who can read a television schedule will know, since the advent of simultaneous substitution 30 years ago, Canadian private television schedules in prime time are largely based on American schedules so that broadcasters can capture the substantial indirect subsidy in advertising revenues that results. Of course, given the popularity of these shows, their placing does satisfy the premise of the Conference of the Arts argument: appealing to a Canadian audience.

A second argument, which has been advanced by Raboy and Taras (2004), is that foreign-owned as opposed to Canadian-owned companies would either not respect Canadian laws and regulations or introduce serious obstacles to their implementation. Surely this argument cannot be taken seriously. In almost every sector of the Canadian economy there are major non-Canadian firms. Yet no one would argue that these firms violate applicable Canadian laws, such as those dealing with occupational health and safety, consumer protection, or environmental standards. Nor could they argue that these firms act with impunity or impose extra costs and delays through foot-dragging, legal action, or American government lobbying sufficient to eviscerate Canadian public policies. If the Canadian media industry is somehow different from other industrial sectors and the state and its regulators are so weak that, without ownership prohibitions and stringent restrictions of the kind now in place, non-Canadian firms will operate untrammelled by public laws, then our national problems go much deeper than simply protecting Canada's cultural industries.

Raboy and Taras also argue that "to imagine that Viacom, or News Corporation or Sony would become major producers of Canadian programming is to live in a fantasy world" (p. 64). This is undoubtedly true, but as every official study since the 1970s has shown, it is fantasy to imagine that Canadian broadcast companies have or will become major producers of Canadian programming. As Grant and Wood have noted, "strict caps on local ownership would seem to ensure local control. But do they? Experience suggests that in this, as in the evasion of content and spending requirements, much ingenuity can be expended to make this reality depart from the experience" (2004, p. 242). They go on to argue that the proposition that domestic broadcasters "will reliably support local expression … cannot be relied upon" (p. 260). Anyone with the slightest familiarity with the history of Canadian content rules can only agree. This should be obvious because, notwithstanding the totem of the public service role that is assigned to broadcasting, Canadian private broadcasting is, as the editor of *Canadian Business* has noted, "a business first and foremost" (Chidley, 2003, p. 8).

If the preceding arguments can be debated on factual grounds, the larger overarching reason for Canada's foreign ownership restrictions is much more difficult to debate or refute—not because it is a particularly strong argument based on persuasive facts and logic, but just the opposite. It is a quasi-religious, almost apocalyptic argument for which no rational evidence, as opposed to fears, can be adduced. Most of the defence of current ownership restrictions is based on deep-seated, long-standing emotional fears and/or dislike of American popular culture. Defenders of the current policies have always been consumed by what I would describe as a "gloomy, undefined foreboding of the unknown" (Stewart, 1975, p. 1813), and they appear to believe that just invoking the presumed threat is a sufficient defence.

Defenders of the restrictions routinely point to the size of the American market and its cultural industries and the economies of scale that characterize them, compared to the small Canadian market and industries. They contend that removing the restrictions would lead to the swamping of the Canadian cultural sectors by imported products. From these arguments, they then go on to argue that, absent foreign ownership restrictions, Canada's cultural space would be eradicated, and ultimately Canadian culture in all its manifestations would be lost (White, 2005). While the first part of these arguments is true, there is no way of assessing the conclusion since we cannot prove a negative.

Canadian cultural nationalists in many respects are the mirror image of Quebec language nationalists. They invoke similar arguments about the need to protect their identity from a menacing sea of foreign challengers. They have little confidence in the vibrancy of their communities—linguistic or cultural—but see them as fragile, intrinsically weak, and constantly threatened. In the case of the cultural nationalists, they are not prepared to concede, or even recognize, that their fears may be grossly exaggerated or that the restrictions they support may be unnecessary. Two arguments can be advanced to support this assessment.

The first, that foreign ownership restrictions fail to serve their putative purposes, is offered by Grant and Wood. They conclude their review of such policies by arguing that "statutory limits on foreign ownership *may* be of value to the extent that they preserve a greater number of local gatekeepers able to bring new cultural expression before their domestic publics. But in contrast to other available measures … they are surely not the sharpest or surest tools in the kit" (2004, p. 262).

The second, that the Canadian cultural character is stronger than the cultural nationalists would have us believe, is argued by Michael Adams in his book *Fire and Ice: The United States, Canada and the Myth of Converging Values* (2003). Adams finds strong and growing cultural divergence rather than the unidirectional convergence called Americanization that the nationalists fear most. Using longitudinal public opinion studies, Adams concludes that "at the most basic level—the level of our values, the feelings and beliefs that inform our understanding of and interaction with the world around us—Canadians and Americans are markedly different, and becoming more so" (p. 4). In short, Canadians are not what they watch or read, and therefore the threatened loss of Canadian culture is grossly exaggerated.

The fact that cultural nationalists have been unable to make a strong, empirically based case that Americanization is occurring suggests that they exhibit what has been labelled the "third-person effect."[4] This hypothesis was first formulated in 1983 by W. Phillips Davison, a professor of journalism and sociology, who noted,

> In its broadest formulation, this hypothesis predicts that people will tend to overestimate the influence mass communications have on the attitudes and behavior of others. More specifically, individuals who are members of an audience that is exposed to a persuasive communication (whether or not this communication is intended to be persuasive) will expect the communication to have a greater effect on others than on themselves. (p. 3)

Cultural nationalists, sophisticates that they are, of course, do not consider themselves to be susceptible to Americanization but worry about the rest of us, who presumably do not have sufficient defensive skills. Therefore, we must be protected through such measures as foreign ownership restrictions.

THE CASE FOR REMOVAL

Although the rationales for the current restrictions are weak, the case for their removal is stronger when one considers three significant arguments against them. The first is the impact of the restrictions on media concentration; the second is the unfortunate and costly contagion the current restrictions may have on a related sector, telecommunications; and the third is the growing irrelevance of the restrictions in the face of technological changes that may result in an excessively costly burden being imposed without any commensurate benefits. We shall examine each in turn.

One of the great ironies in the current debate over foreign ownership restrictions is the widespread failure to appreciate the fundamental link between those restrictions and the degree of concentrated media ownership in Canada. The House of Commons Heritage Committee, for example, devoted a chapter of its report *Our Cultural Sovereignty*, to two ownership issues: **media concentration** (both within and across different forms of media) and foreign ownership. The conclusion—debatable, in my opinion—of the committee is that Canadian media are concentrated and something should be done about it. Yet in its report the committee appears to be completely unaware that the high degree of media ownership concentration in Canada is a direct consequence of the foreign ownership restrictions.

The size of Canada's media conglomerates is a product of our foreign ownership policies. Who were the alternative purchasers when CanWest Global bought Southam from Hollinger? Who were the alternative purchasers of CHUM? According to newspaper accounts, the only possible alternatives in the latter case were other, already large, Canadian media conglomerates. Had the restrictions on foreign ownership not been in place, a much wider pool of potential purchasers could have been found. This is simple common sense: widen the pool of potential buyers and you decrease concentration; narrow it, as we inevitably do with our restrictions, and you encourage greater concentration.

The second reason for removing the restrictions is that they risk infecting the telecommunications sector, where large infusions of investment are required if Canada is to establish the necessary infrastructure to enjoy the promises of the information age. The contagion from the cultural sector was exemplified after the Industry, Science and Technology Committee of the House of Commons concluded that the existing restrictions in the telecommunications sector "compromise, among other important economic contributions, the diffusion of new communications technologies and Canadians' access to modern telecommunications services" (2003, p. 55). Consequently, the committee recommended the complete removal of foreign ownership restrictions for telecommunications carriers.

For the cultural nationalists, as well as some of the companies that benefit from the existing restrictions, the Industry Committee's recommendations were sacrilege. The House Heritage Committee stated that it "strongly disagrees" with its Industry counterpart. It rejected Industry's emphasis on economic factors and called its recommendations "extremely simplistic … to a complex set of issues" (2003, p. 421). It consequently recommended that the existing foreign ownership restrictions in both the broadcasting and telecommunications sectors be maintained without change.

Raboy and Taras (2004) described the Heritage Committee's recommendation as a "no-brainer," and although they did not mean it this way, it certainly was that: a mindless, knee-jerk reaction that, if acted upon, could have serious negative consequences for the Canadian telecommunications sector and consequently for Canadian society and economy. No industrial sector has flourished in this country without access to considerable foreign capital. No sector has gone through the profound transformation that telecommunications is experiencing. We simply do not have enough domestic capital to finance the growth and technological changes that are required. While the larger companies have adequate access to meet their capital needs under the current regime, it is the small, newer companies, the future Research in Motions (the makers of the BlackBerry) of this world who need access. Regrettably, the domestic venture capital sector in Canada is neither large enough nor adventurous enough to satisfy their needs.

Although it may appear initially to contradict the second, the third reason for removing restrictions is that increasingly, with technological changes that are currently underway, foreign ownership restrictions will become irrelevant. The reason that this argument is *not* contradictory is that the restrictions will impose significant costs without any commensurate benefits on domestic companies.

In the United States, where there is significantly less media concentration and cross-ownership than in Canada, a ferocious debate has been waged over the past few years over attempts by the FCC to relax existing ownership rules and restrictions. As a result of court challenges, opponents of the new rules successfully derailed the original proposals, and the FCC is currently holding a new proceeding to develop regulatory changes. Unlike the earlier period when communications companies were driving the move for relaxation of the rules, in the current debates the media companies, according to one report, "may take little advantage of changes this time" (Ahrens, 2006, p. D1). Why? Because they have found ways through technology, if not to reinvent themselves, to get around the barriers that exist between them and their potential audiences.

"Big media" in the United States are exploiting the rollout of higher broadband speeds and the Internet as well as handheld devices such as iPods and cellular telephones to download video signals, to attain "greater reach and potentially more influence, than it would have had, were companies allowed to buy a few more television stations" (Ahrens, 2006, p. D1). Ahrens notes in the case of CBS, "the company sees its future not in owning more television stations but in expanding a revenue stream that was an afterthought in 2003: the Internet and its various iterations of digital downloading and streaming, channels that give CBS a far bigger footprint than local television stations" (p. D1). Various American industry players, from NewsCorp to Clear Channel, are also reducing their stakes in traditional broadcasting, both television and radio, and substituting Internet companies, such as MySpace, to gain direct, immediate, and financially rewarding access to consumers.

Notice the use of the word "consumers." Just as the concept of a "telephone subscriber" has disappeared to be replaced by "telecommunications consumer," the technological wave is having the same consequences for the concept of broadcasting audiences. What is most important in this wave is the empowering of the consumer of the broadcasting service at the expense, but not the fortune, of the service provider. Canada's "old media," now "protected" by regulation and foreign ownership, risk being deregulated not by the wish of corporations or the decisions of state regulators but by those who are the real deregulators—customers exercising choice. What transformed the Canadian rail and air sectors and is now underway in telecommunications is about to hit, like a tsunami, the broadcasting sector (Schultz, 1995). In the words of Jerry Brown, PriceWaterhouseCoopers executive responsible for the firm's Canadian entertainment and media advisory practice, "media consumption is being driven more and more by consumers' desire to have access to the news, music, TV and videos they want, when they want it, and in a format that suits the situation they are in at the time" (Adams, 2006, p. R3).

CONCLUSION

In 1999 President Bill Clinton, speaking to a conference on federalism, turned from his text to address a number of Quebec separatists who were in the audience, including then-premier Lucien Bouchard, and urged them to set aside their "fear of the other." His admonition, I believe, can be justly directed at Canada's cultural nationalists and in particular their support for the current foreign ownership restrictions. These policies have never been rationally based but are premised on a fear that, notwithstanding its potency among certain elite circles, simply does not resonate with the Canadian public. The current policies are costly, are not particularly effective in promoting the ends desired, and are becoming irrelevant in the new media world. The Canadian government has many other instruments, from subsidies to the public broadcaster, to foster Canadian voices and to ensure that Canadian stories are told. Foreign ownership restrictions are a tool best discarded.

References

Acheson, K., & Maule, C. (1999). *Much ado about culture: North American trade disputes.* Ann Arbor: University of Michigan Press.

Adams, A. (2006, July 25). A good news, bad news issue. *The Globe and Mail*, p. R3.

Adams, M. (2003). *Fire and ice: The United States, Canada and the myth of converging values.* Toronto: Penguin.

Ahrens, F. (2006, June 29). As FCC digs into ownership, big media no longer cares. *The Washington Post*, p. D1.

Canadian Conference of the Arts. (2002, December 10). *Safeguard, strengthen and enrich: Review of the Canadian broadcasting system, cross-media ownership and foreign ownership.* Available at http://www. ccarts.ca/en/advocacy/publications

Chidley, J. (2003, October 26). What made Izzy so smart. *Canadian Business*, p. 8.

Grant, P., & Wood, C. (2004). *Blockbusters and trade wars: Popular culture in a globalized world.* Vancouver: Douglas & McIntyre.

Phillips Davison, W. (1983). The third-person effect in communication. *Public Opinion Quarterly, 47*(1), 1–16.

Raboy, M., & Taras, D. (2004, March). The politics of neglect of Canadian broadcasting policy. *Policy Options*, 64.

Schultz, R. (1995). Paradigm lost: Explaining the politics of deregulation. In C. E. S. Franks, J. E. Hodgetts, O. P. Dwivedi, D. Williams, & V. S. Wilson (Eds.), *Governance in a mature society.* Montreal: McGill-Queen's University Press.

Standing Committee on Canadian Heritage, House of Commons. (2003). *Our cultural sovereignty.* Ottawa: House of Commons.

Standing Committee on Industry, Science and Technology, House of Commons. (2003). *Opening Canadian communications to the world.* Ottawa: House of Commons.

Stewart, A., & Hull, W.H.N. (2004). *Canadian television policy and the Board of Broadcast Governors.* Edmonton: University of Alberta Press.

Stewart, R.B. (1975). The reformation of American administrative law, 88, 1667-1813.

White, J. (2005, October 31). Losing Canadian culture. *Briefing Paper: Trade and Investment Series* (Vol. 6, No. 3). Ottawa: Canadian Centre for Policy Alternatives.

Notes

[1] These are all extracts from the statement of broadcasting policy in Section 3 of the *Broadcasting Act, 1991*.

[2] See Acheson & Maule, 1999, pp. 186–205.

[3] There was no claim, for example, that foreign owners had ignored long-standing regulatory prohibitions on the formation of radio networks other than that allowed by the CBC. Nor was there evidence adduced to support the claim that foreign owners were worse than Canadian owners in respecting and fulfilling the first attempts by the Board of Broadcast Governors to impose Canadian content regulations. See Stewart and Hull, 2004.

[4] I am grateful to Adam Thierer, author of *Media Myths: Making Sense of the Debate over Media Ownership* (Progress and Freedom Foundation, 2005) for drawing this hypothesis to my attention.

ISSUE 3

Evil empires: Should limits to foreign ownership of Canadian media be lifted?

✗ NO

Opening the Floodgates: Foreign Ownership, Neoliberal Ideology, and the Threat to Democratic Media Culture
Valerie Scatamburlo-D'Annibale and Kyle Asquith

Dr. Valerie Scatamburlo-D'Annibale, an award-winning author and educator, is associate professor of communication studies at the University of Windsor and the former chair of the Graduate Program in Communication and Social Justice. She is currently at work on a book that explores the phenomenon of "patriotic correctness" in American higher education and media culture.

Kyle Asquith is a graduate student in the Master's Program in Communication and Social Justice at the University of Windsor. His thesis confronts neoliberal discourses in CRTC "new media" rulings.

INTRODUCTION

[Canadians] are indeed fighting for our lives.... We can only survive by taking persistent action at strategic points against American imperialism in all its attractive guises ... [b]y attempting constructive efforts to expose the cultural possibilities of various media of communication and to develop them along lines free from commercialism. (Innis, 1952, pp. 19–20)

Let the air remain as the prerogative of commercial interests and subject to commercial control, and how free will be the voice, the heart of democracy. The maintenance, the enlargement of freedom, the progress, the purity of education, require the responsibility of broadcasting to the popular will. There can be no liberty complete, no democracy supreme, if the commercial interests dominate the vast, majestic resource of broadcasting. (Spry, cited in Raboy, 1990, p. 36)

In their unique ways, both Innis and Spry acknowledged the fundamental tensions that existed between an ostensibly democratic society and a completely corporate-driven media system. Both recognized the centrality of cultural politics in policy discourses and were wary of relying on market forces as a proxy for serving the public good. Both understood that communication in the public interest was a cornerstone of active citizenship and informed democratic participation. Today, the ghosts of Innis and Spry hover over the contemporary Canadian landscape as "new" debates unfold about media regulation in the age of "globalization."

At the current historical juncture, dominated as it is by talk of "technological revolution," "media **convergence**," and a "borderless world," Innis and Spry's concerns may appear to some as anachronistic, as quaint remnants of a bygone era. We beg to differ. In fact, we contend that they are even more important given that the Canadian federal government is contemplating greater trade liberalization in the telecommunications and broadcasting industries, with implications for ownership of our media systems. Raboy and Taras argue that "it is precisely in the current context of transnational corporate convergence ... that a country's sovereignty over its media becomes essential" (2004, p. 64). As such the sentiments that animate the above quotations—concerns about American imperialism in its various forms, profit imperatives undermining the public good, and democracy imperilled by commercial ideologies—inform our response to the question about limitations on foreign ownership of Canadian media.

We believe that the current debate over ownership restrictions on Canadian media is, at its very core, a debate about competing interests—the interests of the Canadian public and those of a few media corporations, including Canadian cable and telecommunications empires and other global media (mainly American) conglomerates. It is a struggle that highlights the "historic tension between commerce and culture that has marked the development of communications in Canada" (Raboy, 2005, p. 6). It is also a struggle between the values of **neoliberalism**—the "free market" ideology espoused by corporate entities and international organizations like the World Trade Organization (WTO)[1] at the behest of the United States—and what Giroux (2004) refers to as a substantive and viable "critical democracy."

We contend that democratic imperatives and the interests of the broader Canadian public would be ill-served if greater foreign ownership of our media and communications systems were allowed. Hence, in what follows, we argue against removing foreign ownership restrictions through our discussion of (1) neoliberal ideology and its undemocratic underpinnings, (2) the perils associated with concentrated transnational media markets and foreign (especially American) control of Canadian media, and (3) the problem of viewing communications and culture as commodities rather than as public goods.

NEOLIBERALISM AND THE PUBLIC INTEREST

In April 2003, the House of Commons Standing Committee on Industry, Science and Technology (SCIST) released a report entitled *Opening Canadian Communications to the World*. Of particular importance for our purposes here is the report's advocacy of what it dubbed the "free entry" approach (2003, p. 34), which would entail the complete removal of foreign ownership restrictions for both telecommunications common carriers and broadcasting distribution, including cable, wireless, and satellite distributors. Given the fact that Canadian media and telecommunications companies, the United States government, American media firms, and Industry Canada have all been ardent proponents of greater trade liberalization, it is necessary to comprehend the major arguments used to buttress their promotion of the free entry approach.

The SCIST report cited a number of reasons for eliminating existing restrictions, among them the emergence of a "global knowledge-based, networked economy," technological convergence, and international agreements brokered by the WTO. The document doesn't explicitly identify its underlying neoliberal assumptions, yet the imprint of that ideology permeates its pages through references to the imperatives of globalization and its conceptual partner, "free trade" (Herman, 1999). Like globalization, free trade has an aura of virtue, and both concepts connote a certain sense of internationalism and an air of inevitability. For that reason, we believe neoliberalism is a far superior term in describing the politico-economic paradigm that tacitly informs the report. Whereas the term "globalization" tends to signify some uncontrollable and unchallengeable world order devoid of human agency and presumably engendered by the aforementioned "technological revolution," neoliberalism better epitomizes the deliberate, calculated promulgation of a corporate-controlled agenda. After all, the economic systems and structures that shape the global systems of production and distribution are human made, as are the institutions that make the rules governing the world economy. Thus, neoliberalism is neither uncontrollable nor unchallengeable; rather, it is best understood as "the set of national and international policies that call for business domination of all social affairs with minimal countervailing force" (McChesney, 2001, p. 2). The basic rules of neoliberal ideology are to "liberalize trade and finance" and abolish "outdated" government regulation (Chomsky, 1999, p. 20). In the arena of communications, the centrepiece of neoliberal policies is invariably a call for markets to be deregulated, which, in practice, means that they are "re-regulated to serve corporate interests" (McChesney, 2001, p. 2).

A free entry approach would, according to the SCIST report, "make Canada more attractive to international capital" and "would permit capital markets themselves to determine the most efficient allocation of resources" (2003, pp. 34–35). The assumption is that "the market," unfettered by "pesky" government restrictions, is the panacea for whatever may ail Canadian communications. The report maintains that markets should not be "constrained by outdated legislation" (p. 22). A truly competitive market, we are told, "offers the promise of the best combination of product selection, service quality and prices" (p. 32). Hence, doing away with foreign ownership restrictions would allegedly allow ambitious entrepreneurs ("new entrants") to compete as never before. In turn, consumers would presumably be offered a treasure trove of exciting possibilities in a new communications nirvana. Such arguments must be carefully dissected.

McChesney (2000b, p. 8) reminds us that the claim that the "market is a fair, just, and rational allocator" of resources is premised on the notion that "the market is based on competition." Yet the rhetoric doesn't coincide with the reality. The global media/cultural environment is currently dominated by five transnational corporate behemoths—Disney, Bertelsmann, Time Warner, Viacom, and News Corp. In Canada, the concentration of ownership is unparalleled in any country of similar social, political, and economic standing. The Canadian mediascape, which is one of the most consolidated media systems in the world, is dominated by four major players—Bell Globe Media (BCE), CanWest Global, Quebecor, and Rogers (Shade, 2006, p. 355). Moreover, there is a great deal of cross-ownership, where one firm often has holdings in two or more kinds of media.[2]

Such concentrated control amounts to an oligopolistic communications regime in Canada. And, removing the barriers to foreign capital, as the SCIST report suggests doing, is unlikely to ameliorate the situation. The notion that eliminating ownership regulations would benefit upstart companies, increase competition, and offer more choices to consumers is the sort of rhetoric that is served up to disguise what is really at issue—the increasing consolidation of media power in fewer and fewer hands to the detriment of democratic communicative principles. As Skinner (2006, p. 46) notes, "while opening the floodgate to foreign investment in Canada's media seems a sure way to raise share prices, history illustrates that it will *not* [italics added] increase the range of diversity in media" so necessary to healthy and functioning democracies.

In an ostensibly democratic society, the media must serve a role beyond generating greater returns for corporate shareholders. Within democratic theory, the media have two important "public good" functions: to act as watchdogs for those in power and those who want to be in power and to provide a forum for accurate information and informed analysis on important social issues (McChesney, 2000a, p. 2). Democracy therefore requires an open communication system in which information derived from a *diversity* of sources circulates freely. This requirement cannot be met by the notion of consumer choice that is promulgated by corporate interests lobbying for more consolidation of media ownership and control. This illusory notion of consumer choice mistakenly equates quantity with diversity—but having access to more channels or media outlets doesn't ensure diversity when those very outlets are all owned and controlled by a handful of media conglomerates. Rather than consumer choice, media consolidation actually leads to more homogenization of informational and entertainment output (McChesney, 2004), and the free expression of a diverse range of views is threatened when ownership of the most influential media is concentrated in the hands of a few. The likelihood of media fulfilling their public good functions is greater when there are more rather than fewer players in the mediascape. A diversity of perspectives and voices can be realized only in an environment where media ownership itself is diverse.

Moreover, despite all the talk about increased competition, history also demonstrates that new firms are ill-equipped to challenge giant firms in oligopolistic market environments. In this regard, "oligopolistic markets are far closer to being monopolistic markets than they are the competitive markets described" in free market folklore (McChesney, 2000a, p. 8). Indeed, in neoliberal economic regimes, "competition often results in monopoly or oligopoly, as stronger firms drive out weaker" ones (Harvey, 2005, p. 67). And that is precisely the scenario coveted by large media conglomerates (McChesney, 2001).

It is also vital to consider the ramifications of greater foreign control of Canadian media should existing limits be eliminated. For if one is concerned about "concentration of media within Canadian controlled companies, it follows that one must, by extension, be concerned by an excessive concentration of Canadian media assets in foreign hands" (Communications, Energy and Paperworkers Union of Canada, 2003, p. 6). Across the spectrum of industries, "some 64% of foreign direct investments have been attributed to American firms" since Investment Canada began keeping track of them in 1985 (Hurtig, 2006, pp. 2–3). Therefore, in the Canadian context, "talk about foreign ownership and control" essentially means American control (Hurtig, 2006, pp. 2–3). Eliminating restrictions would likely place all media in Canada in "direct danger of being bought out by big American conglomerates" that have little "interest in telling Canadian stories" (Barlow, 2005, p. 19). The SCIST report noted that the United States would "likely" place "significant value" on a less restrictive regime in Canada (2003, p. 9), as though it would be wise to simply capitulate to the demands of American media empires. Although corporations like AOL/Time Warner insist that neoliberal free trade is a step toward a more developed and diverse media environment in Canada, the fact is that free trade, as embodied by the WTO, stands to benefit American corporations the most (Chomsky, 1999; White, 2005).

Chomsky (1999, p. 65) cautions us that the United States views the WTO as the "most effective instrument for bringing America's passion for deregulation and for the free market generally" and "American values" to the world. These American values are illustrated "most dramatically" within the realm of telecommunications and other so-called new media. One of the welcome effects of the WTO agreement on telecommunications is that it provides "Washington with a new tool of foreign policy." As an instrument of American imperialism, this "new tool" would allow the "United States to intervene profoundly in the internal affairs of others, compelling them to change their laws and practices."

An American media giant could conceivably swallow up a Canadian broadcast distribution or telecommunications company and "efficiently" expand its corporate reach by engulfing all of Canada as a "new market." Owing to close geography and similar cultural and economic landscapes, Canada is an enticing market for takeover, and the policies put in place to ensure a Canadian presence would likely come under siege (Standing Committee on Canadian Heritage, 2003). Of course, the authors of the SCIST report and their corporate collaborators would have us believe that such concerns are the products of an old-fashioned and thus outdated nationalistic mindset. Citing a representative of CanWest Global, the report suggests that the "nationality of the owner of a programming undertaking has no measurable impact on the programming that the undertaking carries" (2003, p. 50). However, the report's argument that "carriage and content are distinct entities, and that distribution can be separated from programming undertakings" (p. 52) is naïve and misleading.

> [The] system and structure of media distribution has everything to do with what gets produced and circulated—especially when … the same companies own subsidiaries in virtually every corner of the media industry.… [T]here is no longer a sharp divide between broadcasting and telecommunications, hardware and content. (Raboy & Taras, 2004, p. 64)

What is even more disturbing is the tendency to treat media as just another industry. The authors of the report suggest that "many other industries in Canada are wholly or partially foreign-owned and controlled" (SCIST, 2003, p. 51). They further argue that just as those other industries are subject to regulation by provincial and federal governments, so too would be foreign-owned media through bodies like the CRTC and provisions in the *Investment Canada Act* (ICA). Three points are worth making in response to such assertions.

First, despite the CRTC's presumed commitment to the public interest, its track record in this respect has been dismal in recent years. Far from being a cultural watchdog, the CRTC has, for the most part, become nothing more than a handmaiden to big business interests. It alone opened the floodgates to more and more cross-media ownership and greater consolidation of media power in Canada.

Second, the very idea that we should place our faith in the ICA to protect the public interest and Canadian media from foreign takeover is laughable. Are we to believe that legislation *put in place* to appease foreign investors and advance the neoliberal corporate agenda can be trusted to protect the interests of Canadian citizens? Additionally, since the ICA is managed by the Ministry of Trade, public interests are likely to be marginalized if they are inconsistent with market imperatives. Already, the vast majority—close to 95 percent—of so-called investments in Canadian companies since the ICA was implemented were complete takeovers (Hurtig, 2002). We are hard-pressed to believe that the situation would be different if media companies were involved.

Finally, there is an inherent danger in viewing communications and culture as mere commodities, as the Industry Committee is prone to do. Chomsky reminds us that "communications are not quite the same as uranium. Concentration of communications in any hands (particularly foreign hands) raises some rather serious questions about meaningful democracy" (1999, p. 71). At the political level, the media play a vital role in the functioning of democracies. Historically, they have provided the forums where issues of importance to the public are discussed and debated and where information that is essential to active citizen participation in community life is presented. This role is crucial since democratic societies depend on "an informed populace making political choices," and ideally the media should be independent "of the state and society's dominant economic forces" (Herman & McChesney, 1997, p. 3). However, consolidated media power (in both domestic *and* foreign hands) has negative implications for the exercise of political democracy, as it enables commercial interests to exercise a powerful influence over media content.

In a similar vein, subjecting culture to the whims of the market is problematic because it is not a commodity. Culture is the sum of the stories we tell about ourselves—stories that inform who we are and how we describe the world. Existing restrictions do help to ensure at least some diversity within the media and provide Canada with a role beyond that of a "drainage basin" for the American communications industry (Siegel, 1996, p. 4). They are also designed, on some level, to ensure that Canadians have "access to cultural products that reflect their diverse cultural experiences and give voice to their aspirations and imaginations" (Canadian Conference of the Arts, 2003, p. 6). Culture plays a central role in producing narratives, metaphors, images, and symbols. It goes beyond the narrow pursuit of economic self-interest and extends to celebrate a community with a unique character forged from a multifaceted matrix of factors, including shared experiences and values. It is also an important terrain in the struggle against the antidemocratic tendencies of neoliberalism. As Giroux argues,

> as the forces of neoliberalism dissolve public issues into utterly privatized and individualistic concerns [and] … [a]gainst the neoliberal attack on all things social, culture must be defended as the site where exchange and dialogue become crucial affirmations of a democratically configured space of the social in which the political is actually taken up and lived out.…Culture is the public space where common matters, shared solidarities, and public engagements provide the fundamental elements of democracy. (2004, p. 112)

Culture must be protected against those who would insist that it is just another commodity subject to the vagaries of the market—this includes nations like the United States, which was one of only two governments that voted against the adoption of an international Convention of Cultural Diversity in 2005. That initiative was designed to ensure that governments could continue to make cultural policies in the national interest, regardless of the international trade arrangements they may have signed. In its refusal to adopt the measure, the American government reaffirmed its view of culture as commodity. This defiant gesture was both a symbol of American "power and hubris" (Raboy, 2005, p. 6).

A single North American media market—a realistic outcome if ownership restrictions are removed—has significant consequences for both democracy and cultural sovereignty in Canada. It is naïve to think that mammoth media corporations functioning in any market economy can or would benevolently serve the public interest, since that would betray the very nature of capitalist enterprises in which the rules of profit maximization reign supreme (McChesney, 2004; Schiller, 1989). It is equally naïve to think that American ownership of Canadian media enterprises would have no effect on our social and cultural landscape. If existing barriers to foreign media control are eliminated, the chances of Canadians ever reclaiming this vital cultural space will be small indeed. In fact, "once in foreign hands, this crucial high ground may be lost forever" (Raboy & Taras, 2004, p. 64).

CONCLUSION

In democratic societies, the way in which the media landscape is structured and regulated is of paramount political importance. Control over, and access to, the means of communication is a fundamental aspect of economic, social, and cultural power. As such, the debates over media policies require informed and spirited public input.

The rhetoric of consumer choice so central to the larger discourse of neoliberalism is, undoubtedly, seductive. On the surface, the promises of more products, new and improved services, and so forth, made by those advocating for the elimination of foreign ownership restrictions may sound appealing. But the "democracy of goods" (available, of course, only to consumers with purchasing power) they are offering should not be confused with the principles of political democracy in general. A properly functioning democracy requires an informed citizenry with access to a variety of informational and media sources. Concentrated control of media (particularly by foreign entities) undermines this democratic tenet. And this is something that most Canadians seem to understand. Decima (2003) polling conducted only a few months prior to the release of the SCIST report found that a significant majority (72 percent) of Canadians opposed policy changes that would allow for greater foreign ownership of Canadian media and telecommunication companies. Decima's senior vice president noted that the results of the poll clearly indicate that the general public is "increasingly uncomfortable with the idea of foreign control of the country's communications industry" (Decima, 2003, p. 2).

It appears as though individual Canadians overwhelmingly support current restrictions on foreign ownership as do various unions, artistic communities, and cultural producers. Why then is the federal government poised to relax such restrictions? The answer is disturbingly simple: in an era of corporate power run amok, there is often "a gap between public preferences and public policy" (Chomsky, 1999, p. 55). Too often, governments and politicians are beholden to moneyed corporate interests at the expense of citizens' interests. Currently, those vigorously pushing for the elimination of restrictions are large American corporations and the cartel of wealthy families that own Canadian communications empires. Canadian citizens must push back. At a time when regulating the media in order to nourish a diversity of viewpoints is being undermined by the profit motive, we must listen to the ghosts of Innis and Spry. We must demand that our government representatives uphold their obligation to the public interest. For years, that obligation meant promoting the aims of localism, diversity, domestic cultural production, and national identity. Those goals should not be abandoned.

We now stand at the precipice of what is perhaps one of the most critical moments in the history of communications policymaking in Canada. The people's interests have been pitted against corporate interests, and the shaping of public policy is increasingly left in the hands of the powerful in ways that "privilege the prosperous over the populace" (Moll & Shade, 2004, p. 8). Neoliberal capitalists are subverting democratic imperatives, for they well understand that "controlling" democracy, as opposed to nurturing it, is intrinsically related to controlling the media (Roy, 2004). Those of us committed to democratic principles would do well to remind ourselves that neoliberalism is "profoundly suspicious of democracy" (Harvey, 2005, p. 66). In turn, we should be equally suspicious of the neoliberalism being operationalized within the realm of communication policy and regulation. We must first reject the attempt to eliminate foreign ownership restriction of Canadian media and then struggle to make our domestic media less subservient to commercial interests.

In democratic societies, the way in which the media landscape is structured and regulated is of paramount political importance. Control over, and access to, the means of communication is a fundamental aspect of economic, social, and cultural power. As such, debates over media policies require informed and spirited public input. They should not be left to the machinations of corporate moguls, their political bedfellows, and academic cheerleaders of neoliberal ideology.

References

Barlow, M. (2005). *The Canada we want: A citizens' alternative to deep integration.* Retrieved May 4, 2006, from http://www.canadians.org/documents/TCWW.revJan05v2.pdf

Canadian Conference of the Arts. (2003). *Ownership by Canadians: To enrich the social, political and cultural fabric of Canada.* Retrieved April 24, 2006, from http://www.ccarts.ca/en/advocacy/publications/documents/ForeignOwnReport.pdf

Chomsky, N. (1999). *Profit over people: Neoliberalism and the global order.* New York: Seven Stories Press.

Communications, Energy and Paperworkers Union of Canada. (2003). *A trade union analysis of trade issues at the World Trade Organization: Telecommunications, broadcasting, forestry.* Retrieved April 22, 2006, from http://www.cep.ca/campaigns/wto/thaking_away_e.pdf

Decima Research Inc. (2003, January 27). *Canadians continue to oppose foreign controls of media and telecommunications companies.* Retrieved May 12, 2006, from http://www.decima.ca/research/WhatsNew/whatsnew.asp?ID=75

Giroux, H. (2004). *The terror of neoliberalism: Authoritarianism and the eclipse of democracy.* Boulder, CO: Paradigm.

Harvey, D. (2005). *A brief history of neoliberalism.* Oxford: Oxford University Press.

Herman, E. (1999). The threat of globalization. *New Politics, 7*(2). Retrieved May 2, 2006, from http://www.globalpolicy.org/globaliz/define/hermantk.htm

Herman, E., & McChesney, R. (1997). *The global media: The new missionaries of corporate capitalism.* London & Washington: Cassell.

Hurtig, M. (2002). *The vanishing country: Is it too late to save Canada?* Toronto: McClelland & Stewart.

Hurtig, M. (2006). *Selling off our country: Takeovers place key Canadian industries in foreign hands.* Ottawa: Canadian Centre for Policy Alternatives. Retrieved June 2, 2006, from http://www.policyalternatives.ca/MonitorIssues/2006/04/MonitorIssue1353/index.cfm?pa=7AC00557

Innis, H. (1952). *Changing concepts of time.* Toronto: University of Toronto Press.

McChesney, R. (2000a). Journalism, democracy … class struggle. *Monthly Review, 52*(6), 1–15.

McChesney, R. (2000b). So much for the magic of technology and the free market. In A. Herman & T. Swiss (Eds.), *The World Wide Web and contemporary cultural theory* (pp. 5–35). New York & London: Routledge.

McChesney, R. (2001). Global media, neoliberalism, and imperialism. *Monthly Review, 52*(10), 1–19.

McChesney, R. (2004). *The problem of the media: U.S. communication politics in the 21st century*. New York: Monthly Review Press.

Moll, M., & Shade, L. (Eds.). (2004). Preface. In *Seeking convergence in policy and practice: Communications in the public interest* (Vol. 2, pp. 7–12). Ottawa: Canadian Centre for Policy Alternatives.

Raboy, M. (1990). *Missed opportunities: The story of Canada's broadcasting policy*. Toronto: University of Toronto Press.

Raboy, M. (2005, November 10). *Making media: Creating the conditions for communication in the public good*. The 2005 Spry Memorial Lecture, Vancouver, BC. Retrieved May 2, 2006, from http://www.com. umontreal.ca/spry/spry-e.html

Raboy, M., & Taras, D. (2004, March). The politics of neglect of Canadian broadcasting policy. *Policy Options, 25*(3), 63–68.

Roy, A. (2004). *An Ordinary Person's Guide to Empire*. Cambridge, MA: South End Press.

Schiller, H. (1989). *Culture, Inc.: The corporate takeover of public expression*. New York: Oxford University Press.

Shade, L. (2006). O Canada: Media (de)convergence, concentration, and culture. In P. Attallah & L. Shade (Eds.), *Mediascapes: New patterns in Canadian communication* (pp. 346–364). Toronto: Thomson Nelson.

Skinner, D. (2006). Media democracy in Canada. *Culture Front, Relay #11*, 44–46. Retrieved June 3, 2006, from http://www.socialistproject.ca/relay/r11_media.pdf

Siegel, A. (1996). *Politics and the media in Canada* (2nd ed.). Toronto: McGraw-Hill Ryerson.

Standing Committee on Canadian Heritage, House of Commons. (2003). *Our cultural sovereignty: The second century of Canadian broadcasting*. Ottawa: Communications Canada.

Standing Committee on Industry, Science and Technology, House of Commons. (2003). *Opening Canadian communications to the world*. Ottawa: Communications Canada.

White, J. (2005). Losing Canadian culture: The danger of foreign ownership of telecom. *Canadian Centre for Policy Alternatives, 6*(3), pp. 1–11.

Notes

[1] The WTO as a purveyor of "American values" is discussed later in this article.

[2] For example, some telecommunications companies in Canada are owners of cable companies, television networks, and newspapers. BCE is a case in point. BCE, the owner of Bell Canada, took an interest in television and print content industries in 2000 and 2001 with the acquisitions of the *Globe and Mail*, and CTV.

Discussion Questions

1. Identify the competing interests that emerge in debates over the foreign ownership of Canadian media corporations.

2. Why are media markets fundamentally undemocratic, according to the authors of this chapter?

3. What is problematic about Industry Canada's attempt to separate "carriage" and "content"?

4. Why should we fear foreign ownership in the media sector?

5. What are the implications of technological changes for media ownership policies?

6. Are there alternative public policy instruments that could be employed to better meet the objectives of our foreign ownership policies?

ISSUE 4

Media fare: Do Canadians have a balanced media diet?

✔ YES

Balance Is in the Eye of the Beholder
Lydia Miljan

Lydia Miljan is an associate professor at the University of Windsor. She teaches in the areas of Canadian public policy, research methodology, politics, and the media. Her main research interests include how journalists' personal views are reflected in news content, and public opinion formation. She has published two books, the fourth edition of *Public Policy in Canada*, with Stephen Brooks, and *Hidden Agendas: How Journalists Influence the News*, with Barry Cooper. *Hidden Agendas* was shortlisted for the Donner Prize for the best book in public policy 2003/2004.

The title for this essay is enigmatic. Nutritionists have clear ideas about how to achieve balance in food diets. Although nutritional guidelines have changed over the years, it is generally agreed that a balanced diet should include a combination of protein, carbohydrates, vegetables, fruits, and dairy, while fats and refined sugars are to be used in moderation. The benefits of a balanced diet are typically understood to be good overall body weight, muscle tone, and reduced levels of risk for developing food-related illnesses such as diabetes, heart disease, or cancer. When considering the usefulness of the diet metaphor for assessing the media offerings to Canadians, balance could be understood to entail a variety of things. A healthy media diet may include regularly reading news rich in public interest—politics, economics, and international relations—while celebrity and entertainment news, like fats and refined sugars, should be consumed in moderation. Balance could also refer to taking in a variety of different types of news stories, in other words, ensuring we have a reasonable daily intake of so-called hard news, perspective pieces (e.g., editorials, columns) and human-interest or soft news stories. Finally, a balanced media diet might also entail exposure to so-called left-wing and right-wing publications and/or arguments in relation to a range of specific issues.

The desirable outcome of a balanced media diet should be an interested and informed citizenry that is actively engaged in the life of the community and nation. Good indicators of a balanced media diet might include high voter turnout at election time or increased citizen participation in voluntary activity. But voter turnout numbers continue to slide, and Canadians are spending fewer hours than ever before participating in organized charitable work. It might be high time, then, to think hard about and assess the quality of our media diet.

To do so, we first need to examine the question of balance by reviewing the current state of media ownership in Canada, and, second, look at what media choices Canadians have available to them in terms of election coverage. Examining media offerings at election time is particularly relevant since this is when crucial public decisions about the nation's political future are made. As will be argued here, Canadians do enjoy a balanced media diet—but whether they are willing or able to take advantage of the variety of options available to them may be another matter entirely.

CORPORATE OWNERSHIP

The production of news, like food, tends to now fall within the purview of large corporations; and the larger the operation, the greater the output of information. It is reasonable to say that we have reached the point that local or small presses, like family farms, are increasingly being taken over by those with the means to invest in the infrastructure necessary for mass production. While we often lament the decline of the small, local family farm and family-run media organizations, there is insufficient evidence to conclude that mass production in either case is as unfortunate or problematic as we have been led to believe. Canadians now have ready access to more news and information than ever before.

There are many different ways of determining or measuring the balance Canadians have in their media diet. The most common method examines balance at the macro level, by considering patterns of media ownership. When examined this way, the answer to the question of whether Canadians enjoy a balanced media diet seems at first blush to be an unequivocal "no." As in most Western countries, few owners in Canada control a multitude of the nation's media properties. For example, only eight English-language markets in Canada have more than one daily newspaper, and even within those markets, one corporation commonly owns all or most of the papers. In Vancouver, for example, one company owns both the tabloid (the *Vancouver Province*) and the daily broadsheet (the *Vancouver Sun*). In New Brunswick, the Irving family owns all of the English-language daily and weekly newspapers.

The largest media chain in Canada is CanWest Global. It is estimated that CanWest controls 30 percent of the country's media market, including 11 major metropolitan daily newspapers (e.g., the *Vancouver Sun*, the *Calgary Herald*, the *Ottawa Citizen*, and the *Montreal Gazette*), 16 smaller-circulating community papers, and 16 television stations across the country (part of the Global and CH networks). The remaining media properties in Canada are controlled by four other conglomerates: Quebecor (which owns the Sun chain of newspapers), Bell Globemedia (which owns the Bell telecommunications network as well as the *Globe and Mail*, CTV, and several specialty channels such as TSN and Outdoor Life Network), Rogers Communications (which is Bell's chief competitor for home cable, phone, Internet, and wireless service, and also owns several radio stations and specialty channels, such as OMNI, Sportsnet, Tech TV, and the Shopping Channel), and Torstar (which owns the *Toronto Star* newspaper and other regional dailies in southwestern Ontario) (Raudsepp, 2002). In radio, large corporate ownership is the norm. CHUM Limited owns and operates 33 radio stations, 12 local television stations, and 21 specialty channels, as well as an environmental music distribution division. At the time of writing, CanWest is poised to take over CHUM and thus extend its dominance and control of the Canadian media market.

To balance the influence of the private corporate media empires, Canadians are offered a national public broadcaster as an alternative. The CBC developed out of a sense of urgency to protect Canadian interests from American competition and to construct a sense of nationhood.

Just as Sir John A. Macdonald argued that the Canadian National Railway was necessary to keep Americans at bay and to foster a national economy, Prime Minister Mackenzie King, and later R. B. Bennett, saw the need for a national radio policy to insulate Canadians from the influence of American culture and to foster a national identity (Nesbitt-Larking, 2001, p. 59). Today, the CBC is mandated to provide national and local radio and television broadcasts in English and French. As part of its mandate, it is required to reflect the regions to each other and to give balanced coverage on the pressing public issues of the day.

VARIETY OF CHOICES

Over the course of any given day and from every part of the country, Canadians consume and have access to various types of news and information from numerous sources. In addition to "old media," such as the daily press, private and public broadcasters, and more recently the 24-hour cable television networks (e.g., CBC Newsworld), Canadians can access news and information from "new media," such as the Internet, blogs, and chat rooms, and can do so on their computers or via personal communication devices like cellphones and iPods. Indeed, the reach and flexibility of new media not only enable Canadians to get news and information as soon as they want it, but also provide advocacy groups on all sides of the political spectrum with a new means of bypassing the structural barriers to conventional media in order to reach and influence the public directly (Earl, 2006). Canadians also have easy access to international news and public affairs programming by way of CNN, CNBC, BBC, Al-Jazeera, and even the maligned Fox News, among countless others, thanks in large part to the greater accessibility of satellite and digital cable packages provided by the large private media corporations.

It is too easy, therefore, to dismiss this diversity of media content available to Canadians by looking only at the macro level of ownership. The typical argument against concentrated media ownership stems from the fear that the owners' self-interests and ideologies will infiltrate the editorial decisions in the newsrooms (Hackett & Gruneau, 2000, pp. 49–54). During the era when Conrad Black's Hollinger Corporation was the majority shareholder of the Southam chain of newspapers, many feared that Black's conservative political views would be foisted on an unsuspecting Canadian public (Patriquin, 2004). Later, when CanWest Global obtained the Southam chain, some feared that the papers would more favourably reflect the policies of the Liberal Party because of then-chairman Israel Asper's association with the party. In addition, the chain's coverage of the Israel/Palestinian dispute was called into question when Asper attacked the coverage of the issue by other news agencies in the country (Everton, 2005).

CHANGING VALUES

It is very difficult to measure empirically the direct influence of media owners on editorial decision making. However, it is one thing to argue that ownership has occasion to influence newsroom decisions, and another thing entirely to say that it does so regularly. It is important to note, in this context, that while media empires were expanding throughout the latter part of the 20th century, a massive change was also occurring in social values associated with the rise of

postmaterialism (Abramson & Inglehart, 1995). This period witnessed rapid social and political changes in relation to widespread demands for respect of human rights and a greater acceptance of minority group differences, as concerns about cultural recognition for different group and individual identities displaced concerns about access to material resources. For example, since the 1980s and 1990s, there has been increased recognition for the rights of marginalized groups such as gays and lesbians, and changes in public policy in Canada reflect this. Six years ago the Liberal government passed a resolution in the House of Commons that reaffirmed the definition of marriage as "the union of one man and one woman to the exclusion of all others" (House of Commons, 1999). Five years later the federal government, still under Liberal rule, passed the *Civil Marriage Act*, providing gays and lesbians access to the institution of marriage. Today, a majority of Canadians (62 percent) think that the matter is settled, and 64 percent believe that "same-sex couples should have the same right to civil marriage as opposite-sex couples" (Canadians for Equal Marriage, 2006). The speed at which both politicians and the public have accepted new ideas can, in part, be attributed to the positive media coverage granted to those ideas and arguments because journalists are more socially liberal than the general public and often lead public opinion on social change (Miljan & Cooper, 2003).

Notwithstanding the evidence that media ownership has a limited if not weak effect on content, critics claim that news coverage of important social and political issues is often lacking in topic and source diversity, and that news stories provide unbalanced or one-sided portraits of the issue or event in question. For example, according to Peter Hart, the "media environment [is] dominated by official sources and establishment elites" (2005, p. 51). As Ericson, Baranek, and Chan note, "the media élite is not separate from the élites who control many of the government and corporate bureaucracies that are reported on" (1989, p. 5). The institutional bias of news media favours government officials, business leaders, and interest groups and tends to limit access to marginalized groups such as workers, visible minorities, and the so-called average Canadian. For example, in a study on the homeless in America, Rebecca Ann Linn and James Danowski found that the electronic media gave little attention to this specific cultural group. Because of the scant attention to the issue, they argue, "the homeless continue to be extensively stigmatized in news and information programming" (1999, p. 118). Whenever you have limited number of stories on marginalized groups, the tendency is for the media to use stereotypes and limited narratives. The extent to which this is true is in part determined by the story, in part by the ease of accessing certain groups, and in part by the proactive efforts of sources to influence the news-making process.

As a result of social change discussed above, some previously marginalized groups have become part of the new power elite. Evidence of this is the relationship between the media and gay and lesbian groups. Rather than censoring social change, corporate owners have embraced change. For example, the 2006 Pride Week in Toronto had four media sponsors: CTV News, Rogers Communications, Sirius Satellite Radio, and the *Toronto Star* (Pride Toronto, 2006). During Pride Week, CTV News provided not only sponsorship but also interviews on their newscasts with organizers and individuals participating in the event. The ability of formerly marginalized groups to obtain media sponsorship as well as interviews indicates that some diversity is reflected in the daily news.

ASSESSING BALANCE IN ELECTION STUDIES

The other concern of journalism is related to this notion of imbalanced or one-sided presentation of issues. In other words, even if we do balance our media diet with private and public news outlets and have diversity in the type of media we consume—television, newspapers, and radio—are we just getting the same nutritional value in different mass-produced packages? In their analysis of major Canadian newspaper coverage of the 2006 election, Stuart Soroka and Antonia Maioni, of McGill University's Observatory on Media and Public Policy (OMPP), concluded that there was "little sign of bias in news coverage" (Soroka & Maioni, 2006, p. 17). Similarly, ERIN Research (2006) found that CBC television's coverage of the campaign was "appropriately balanced" (p. 4) and that this result was consistent with newspaper coverage of the election conducted by the McGill group (p. 40). The measures ERIN Research used for balance were "the amount of exposure that party members received, the amount of discussion that journalists and others devoted to each party, and the positive-negative direction of that discussion" (p. 4).

While overall the Canadian media balanced their coverage of the political parties, bias was still detected within individual programs. In terms of the editorial content examined, there were differences in the tone of the coverage across the country. In addition to measuring how much airtime the leaders received, the OMPP measured the type of attention each party and leader got by assessing whether the story was positive, negative, or neutral. They then took the negative stories and subtracted them from the positive ones to obtain what they called "net tone." Based on their analysis of net tone, Soroka and Maioni concluded, "*Calgary Herald* columnists clearly did not like the Liberals so much. Nor did *National Post* columnists" (2006, p. 17). They argued, based on editorial and opinion pieces, that "the *Herald* and *Post* were pro-Conservative, the *Toronto Star* was pro-Liberal, the *Globe* a little less so" (p. 17). They also noted that while the *Globe and Mail* endorsed the Conservatives, overall, their columnists were pro-Liberal.

ERIN Research concluded that when all the newspapers were combined, the CBC was consistent with other news agencies in giving balanced attention to spokespeople for each of the major parties. However, the problem with reaching measurements of balance by using aggregated data is that Canadians rarely seek out the competing perspectives of different types of newspapers. So while the CBC and CTV may have been similar to the all the newspapers, they probably showed many differences when compared directly to individual newspapers. While, overall, the CBC may have been balanced over the coverage of five different programs, this does not mean that viewers of only *The National* received the same balance as viewers who watch only the CBC News Sunday Night program. Although the Internet ensures that Canadians have easy access to any nearly all of the nation's major papers, the typical *Calgary Herald* reader is unlikely to seek out the *Toronto Star*'s alternative editorial position on an issue like private healthcare. While ERIN Research found that television gave more negative coverage to the Liberals than the Conservatives or the NDP, is it accurate to say that the coverage was appropriately balanced?

While the net score card is the measurement that political parties are most interested in, it is not a good indicator of balance. This is because party coverage includes the attention media give to both policy and campaign tactics, and because the latter are based on cunning, strategy, backroom dealings, and gamesmanship, they tend to attract the most media attention. This is problematic because it primes the public to judge parties based on their appearance in media photo ops and how pundits assess their campaign tactics rather than on their policy platforms and ideas. Here the OMPP data offer some interesting cumulative results. Five issues dominated the 2006 electoral campaign: national unity, taxes, government corruption, social issues, and health care. In each of these issues, the Liberals were judged more harshly than the other parties (OMPP, 2006). What we cannot conclude from these results, however, is whether individual papers had the same proportions in their assessments of the specific party platform positions versus coverage of strategy. Examining individual newspapers may show that the *Calgary Herald* was far more critical of the Liberal Party platform than of the Conservative platform. The *Toronto Star*, by contrast, may have provided far more favourable coverage to Liberal and NDP positions than to the policy ideas of the Conservatives. In neither case would we conclude that the papers were not balanced. And this is important precisely because the electoral map is so regionally polarized. Was the *Toronto Star* appealing to its urban, ideologically left-of-centre readers when it provided positive assessments of the Liberals and negative assessments of the Conservatives? Alternatively, did the coverage help sway or consolidate votes for the Liberals and NDP in the Toronto area? The same question could be asked of the *Calgary Herald* in trying to appeal to the apparent support of readers in that region of the country for Conservative politics and politicians.

CONCLUSION

The moral of the OMPP research story is that Canadians have on offer the ingredients for a balanced media diet, but just as with their food choices, it is important to also seek out and consume a variety of media products. In the same way that some individuals must choose to eat a healthy diet of nutritious foods, others are perfectly content with eating pre-packaged food with little variety and questionable nutritional content. Canadians are fortunate to have a bounty of quality foods as well as quality media; but just as we have staggering levels of obesity, diabetes, and other food-related illness, so too is the populace characterized by a lack of political participation, over-reliance on entertainment media, and a sense of hyperindividualism. In the final analysis, it is up to us to seek out the rich variety of information at our disposal and to ensure we achieve maximum balance in our media diets.

We have examined the question of balance in the media diet on a number of levels. At the macro level, while there are few owners of the media in Canada, a number of different types of media are offered to Canadians. From traditional media such as newspapers and television to new media such as iPods and the Internet, Canadians have a bounty of sources to consume information. However, while we might have our media shelves packed with different sources, there is no guarantee that we will seek out and consume this variety. Regional tastes tend to dominate; so on the whole individual Canadians may not be balancing their media with alternative perspectives. It is up to us as individuals not only to be critical of the media we consume, but also to seek out the different sources of news and information available to us.

References

Abramson, P. R., & Inglehart, R. (1995). *Value change in global perspective*. Ann Arbor: University of Michigan Press.

Canadians for Equal Marriage. (2006, June 19). *Environics poll: Opposition to equal marriage falls sharply* [News release]. Retrieved June 8, 2007, from http://www.equal-marriage.ca

Earl, J. (2006, fall). Pursuing social change online: The use of four protest tactics on the Internet. *Social Science Computer Review, 24*(3), 362–377.

Ericson, R. V., Baranek, P. M., & Chan, J. B. L. (1989). Negotiating Control: A study of news sources. Toronto: University of Toronto Press.

ERIN Research. (2006). Balance in news coverage of the 2006 election campaign. *Final Report November 29, 2005–January 22, 2006, for the Canadian Broadcasting Corporation.* Retrieved February 29, 2006, from http://www.cbc.ca/news/about/burman/pdf/ERIN_report-2006.pdf

Everton, R. (2005). Israel Asper and Israeli propaganda. In J. Klaehn (Ed.), *Filtering the news: Essays on Herman and Chomsky's propaganda model* (pp. 63–94). Montreal: Black Rose Books.

Hackett, R. A., & Gruneau, R. (Eds.) (with D. Gutstein & T. A. Gilbson). (2000). *The missing news: Filters and blind spots in Canada's press.* Ottawa: Canadian Centre for Policy Alternatives; Aurora: Garamond Press.

Hart, P. (2005). Media bias: How to spot it—and how to fight it. In R. McChesney, R. Newman, & B. Scott (Eds.), *The future of media: Resistance and reform in the 21st century* (pp. 51–61). New York: Seven Stories Press.

House of Commons. (1999, June 8). *Journals (Hansard),* 36th Parl, 1st Sess., No. 240.

Linn, R. A., & Danowski, J. (1999). The representation of the homeless in U.S. electronic media: A computational linguistic analysis. In E. Min (Ed.), *Reading the homeless: The media's image of homeless culture* (pp. 109–120). Westport: Praeger.

Miljan, L., & Cooper, B. (2003). *Hidden agendas: How journalists influence the news.* Vancouver: UBC Press.

Nesbitt-Larking, P. (2001). *Politics, Society and the Media: Canadian Perspectives.* Peterborough: Broadview Press.

Observatory on Media and Public Policy. (2006, January 22). *Cumulative Report: 2006 Federal Election Newspaper Content Analysis.* Retrieved December 17, 2006, from http://www.ompp.mcgill.ca/pages/reports/OMPPElection2006(06-01-22).pdf

Patriquin, L. (2004). *Inventing tax rage: Misinformation in the National Post.* Halifax: Fernwood.

Pride Toronto. (2006). *Sponsors.* Retrieved June 21, 2006, from http://www.pridetoronto.com/sponsors/index.htm

Raudsepp, E. (2002, June). The daily newspaper industry under the microscope: Monopolies, concentration, conglomeration and convergence. *Canadian Issues, 25.*

Soroka, S., & Maioni, A. (2006, February 1). Little sign of bias in news coverage. *Toronto Star,* p. A17.

ISSUE 4

Media fare: Do Canadians have a balanced media diet?

✗ NO

The Supposed Criteria of Balance are Themselves Biased
Robert A. Hackett and Yuezhi Zhao

Robert A. Hackett is professor of Communication at Simon Fraser University and codirector since 1993 of NewsWatch Canada. He has written, coauthored, or coedited several articles, books, and monographs on journalism, political communication, and media representation, most recently *Democratizing Global Media: One World, Many Struggles* (coedited with Yuezhi Zhao) and *Remaking Media: The Struggle to Democratize Public Communication* (cowritten with William Carroll). He has also been involved for over 20 years in community-based media education and advocacy projects and groups, including Vancouver's annual Media Democracy Day, the Union for Democratic Communications, and Canadians for Democratic Media.

Yuezhi Zhao is associate professor and Canada Research Chair in the Political Economy of Global Communication, as well as director of the Global Media Monitoring and Analysis Laboratory in the School of Communication at Simon Fraser University. In addition to more than 30 journal articles and book chapters dealing with issues in the media, telecommunications, and democratic governance in North American, Chinese, and global contexts, she is the author of *Media, Market, and Democracy in China: Between the Party Line and the Bottom Line*, coauthor of *Sustaining Democracy? Journalism and the Politics of Objectivity*, and coeditor of *Democratizing Global Media? One World, Many Struggles*. Her forthcoming books include *Communication in China: Market Reforms and Social Contestation* and *Global Communications: Toward a Transcultural Political Economy*.

Are Canadians served with a balanced media diet? The answer depends on how one defines and measures "balance." Moreover, an apparently balanced media diet in one sense may help to conceal profound imbalances in another. We will first outline and assess several perspectives on media balance, then scrutinize the very concept of balance and its related practices in Canada's media system, with special attention to the news media.

BALANCE: THE CONVENTIONAL CRITICISMS

In some ways, Canadian media fare is consciously and carefully balanced. In broadcasting, balance is an explicit legal requirement. The 1991 *Broadcasting Act* mandates that programming "be varied and comprehensive, providing a balance of information, enlightenment, and entertainment for men, women and children of all ages, interests and tastes." Furthermore, the Act requires the system to "provide a reasonable opportunity for the public to be exposed to the expression of differing views on matters of public concern." Thus, the Act mandates balance in two senses—among different program genres and among different views.

Even though it is not regulated, Canada's press typically follows conventions of balance, for example by quoting both sides of controversial issues and by providing equal access for candidates and parties during elections. Consumers have the opportunity to read an apparently balanced range of increasingly multilingual newspapers, from human-interest-oriented tabloids to "serious" or "quality" broadsheets, reflecting editorial viewpoints from the centre-left *Toronto Star* to the archly conservative *National Post*. Yet notwithstanding such apparent guarantees of balance, critics continue to question whether Canadian journalism is truly balanced. For instance, echoing conservative attacks in the United States on the allegedly "left-liberal media" for their perceived anti-authority, anti-business, anti-Christian, and/or anti-Republican biases, a Vancouver-based neoliberal think tank, the Fraser Institute, has since 1988 published a newsletter called *On Balance*. Based on content analysis of selected issues, its underlying thrust is that journalists' political values and opinions skew the selection and presentation of news to the left. Such is the theme of a recent book by Fraser Institute associates Lydia Miljan and Barry Cooper (2003), who argue that anglo-Canadian journalists in major urban media are better educated, less religious, older, and more often male than the general population; that they may have "materialist," procapitalist values on economic issues but relatively liberal or "postmaterialist" views on social issues such as gay or women's rights—and that news coverage reflects these orientations.

An opposing critique derives from academics and activists on the left, the best known being Herman and Chomsky's "propaganda model" of the U.S. media. Far from being a product of journalists, they argue, news is typically subordinate to the perspectives and interests of the political and economic elites that own and finance the media and dominate the media as sources (1988). In their view, news media "manufacture consent" to repressive state and corporate policies that generate poverty and inequality at home, and wars and human rights violations abroad. In Canada, James Winter (1997) has similarly regarded news as a "management product" tied to vested corporate interests and perspectives.

In distinct but related left/progressive critiques, feminists, anti-racist activists, and other media critics have documented systematic stereotyping, underrepresentation, and other inappropriate and unacceptable portrayals of women, ethnic, racial, and other cultural minorities in the media. Feminist media studies, for example, have long demonstrated imbalances in the roles of men and women as interviewees in news reports (e.g., experts and authorities are disproportionately male) and in TV drama (e.g., women are often associated with home and family roles while men assume employment roles), as well as imbalances in the participation rate of men and women in media production (Strutt & Hissey, 1992, p. 66). Similarly, contrary to the conservative critique of the media's alleged cultural relativism, much has been written about racism in the Canadian media system and its underrepresentation or misrepresentation of immigrants, refugees, racial and religious minorities, and the non-Western "other" in the exclusionary construction of the imagined community of "Canada" and of "Canadian culture" (Greenberg, 2000; Henry & Tator, 2002; Karim, 2000; Murray, in press).

What should we make of these seemingly opposed views? Should we simply take a balanced approach and assume that the truth is somewhere in between? Journalists themselves often argue that because they are criticized from both sides, they must be "playing it down the middle." Yet such a self-serving conclusion is misleading. It is quite possible that one side has a better critique than the other, or that they are examining somewhat different questions and are thus not entirely mutually contradictory. Right-wing critiques of news media tend to focus on media bias toward particular candidates, issues, or parties, whereas left-wing critics are more interested in how broader patterns of news place limits on public discourse and legitimize elite power and the social order as a whole. For example, while conservatives highlight the media's liberal attitude toward the specific issue of abortion, feminists are more concerned with broader gender relations and the socioeconomic status of women.

Briefly, we offer this assessment of the more explicitly polarized arguments about media imbalance, especially as it relates to journalism. The right-wing critique of "left-liberal media" misleadingly focuses on newsworkers' personal political values rather than their professional self-conceptions. It also underplays the institutional constraints within which they work— everyday routines (such as the use of news agencies and "beats" that enable journalists to process information predictably and efficiently), the broader imperatives of media organizations (such as commercial media's need to attract audiences whose attention can be profitably sold to advertisers), extra-media influences (such as governments, market structures, and technology), and ideology (including the cultural "maps" of the world that help journalists to construct narratives that make sense to their audiences) (Shoemaker & Reese, 1996). Moreover, conservative critics offer relatively little evidence that journalists' presumed liberal attitudes influence actual media content; and indeed they ignore the heavy influence on news of the "right-wing information infrastructure" (Taras, 2001, p. 210) of conservative think tanks, media pundits, and media owners like Conrad Black in the 1990s and the Asper family in the 2000s. Finally, conservative critics exaggerate the "radicalism" of journalists' actual values. American studies (Croteau, 1998) found elite journalists to be liberal on social issues but more conservative than the general public on economic issues such as taxation and free trade. Miljan and Cooper's survey of Canadian journalists suggests a similar pattern. Arguably, the left-liberal media thesis persists not because of its intellectual merit, but rather as a result of its usefulness in a right-wing ideological campaign against threats to the legitimacy of corporate capitalism in general, and against public service broadcasting specifically.

Still, the conservative critique has a grain of truth to the extent that news coverage manifests

> an uneasy accommodation between the secular, largely urban, "liberal" views of many journalists and the economically-conservative interests of media owners.... [J]ournalists are often "permitted" to express liberal views on social or moral questions so long as they do not fundamentally or repeatedly challenge the core political and economic interests of media owners and the rest of the corporate elite. (Hackett & Gruneau, 2000, p. 225)

As for the left-wing critique, it usefully calls attention to the importance of media ownership and the political economic structure of the media in shaping news coverage, factors largely ignored by conservative critics. NewsWatch Canada's content analyses of the daily press suggest many patterns that are most plausibly explained by the power (whether consciously exercised or not) of media owners or advertisers, including the *Vancouver Sun*'s retreat from critical coverage of leaky condos built by real estate developers in the 1990s, and the more favourable treatment of each newspaper's parent corporation compared to coverage of "unrelated" media corporations (Hackett & Gruneau, 2000; Hackett & Uzelman, 2003).

But the standard left-wing critique of the media pays insufficient attention to what happens inside the "black box" of newsroom production and to the extent of diversity and dissent still possible even within corporate media empires. If right-wingers overemphasize the beliefs and autonomy of journalists, left-leaning critics overemphasize the determination of journalism by external forces. We need to understand both that journalism is connected to and influenced by other social institutions and practices, particularly relations of inequality and power, and that it has a certain institutional weight of its own. News does not simply reflect or express external forces. Indeed, the very concept of balance is an aspect of what we have elsewhere called North American journalism's "regime of objectivity," a set of practices and beliefs that help to define journalism as a cultural and political institution. Briefly, this multifaceted regime implies a normative ideal (journalists should seek to tell publicly relevant truths, devoid of vested interest or personal bias); an epistemology, or a set of assumptions about knowledge and reality (e.g., that it is possible to separate facts from values); a set of news-gathering and presentation practices (such as reporting opinions and facts only when they can be attributed to credible and relevant sources); institutional relationships (such as the independence of newsrooms not only from governments, but from media's own advertising departments); and a way of talking about news and evaluating it (using concepts like fairness, accuracy, bias—and balance) (Hackett & Zhao, 1998, pp. 83–86).

EVALUATING THE MEDIA: THE BIASES OF BALANCE

The rhetoric, concept, and practices of balance are part of journalism's occupational culture and its claim to be serving important democratic functions. And yet, a seemingly balanced media diet may help to sustain and legitimate profound imbalances in the media system and its connections with the dominant political, economic, social, and cultural power structure. How so?

First, balance as it is practised in journalism typically reduces "issues" to just two sides defined by a handful of institutionalized and centralized sources (usually political parties, officials, interest group leaders). Other voices, including people affected by government policies, and other possible ways of defining the issue are often sidelined. At the same time, the either/or approach to issues like abortion risks overaccessing the most extreme views, intensifying the polarization of debate, while oversimplifying complex issues and conflating different positions within the women's movement, for example, into a singular, unitary voice of "feminism" (Strutt & Hissey, 1992, p. 73).

Second, the conventional practice of balance typically calls for fair representation of "both sides" of "issues" whose existence is taken for granted. But it fails to consider how some matters become defined as issues, or matters of public concern, in the first place, while others are ignored. A case in point is Canada's military role in Afghanistan. In April 2006, the media were caught in a debate over access to the funerals of Canadian soldiers and whether the Canadian flag should be lowered in their honour. Media carefully balanced pro and con views on these questions, but ignored other vital issues: What really is Canada's mission? Who is "the enemy" (the Taliban or disaffected Afghanis)? How effective or productive is Canadian military intervention? What have been the costs as well as benefits to Afghan civilians? Such questions are generally confined to the margins—such as letters to the editor, or brief discrepant facts buried within lengthy news reports celebrating Canadian heroism and sacrifice. In short, the concept and practice of balance generally applies to "legitimate controversies," not to the broader and more fundamental aspects of power and established policies. In this way, the media's practice of balance helps to maintain the appearance of openness, while closing off more fundamental debate.

Third, precisely because the practice of balance applies only to issues of "legitimate controversy," not to matters of consensus or deviance (Hackett & Zhao, 1998, pp. 147–150; Hallin, 1989, pp. 116–117), it unintentionally reinforces deeply rooted dominant ideological perspectives that have been constructed and sustained as consensual, as part of what "everybody" understands and supports, be it patriarchy, capitalism as a social economic system, or the myth of Canada as a tolerant, racism-free, multicultural society. For example, constructed within broad racist and imperialist ideological frameworks, more "balanced" ethnic representations in the media in the form of increased attention to Muslim women and their victimization by their own cultures, including in some instances content produced by Canadian women journalists and human right activists, could contribute to mobilization for a war that perpetuates profound imbalances in global political, economic, and cultural power relations (Thobani, in press).

Indeed, concepts like balance are often the political smokescreen behind which struggles over media content are fought out. There is no objective measure of balance, and interest groups often use the notion to try to shift the goalposts, so that their positions become defined as centrist, and their opponents' as extremist. In such struggles, the best-resourced interest groups have the upper hand (Hackett & Zhao, 1998, p. 90).

Consequently, if we are interested in the role of media in promoting democratic communication and governance—that is, the ability of people to participate equally in shaping the rules that bind all citizens—we need to think about balance in broader ways. We should question whether the "normal" media standards such as balance actually reflect or contribute to broader imbalances of wealth, power, and cultural capital in the social and political system.

In that light, we should enquire critically into imbalances in the media agenda. What issues receive media attention in the first place? Do white-collar and corporate crime, which cost Canadians billions per year, receive as much attention as violent or street crime? Are government scandals offset by coverage of corporate corruption? Are the extensive business sections of daily papers matched by news of workers' struggles and unions' contributions to Canadian society? Do media promote environmental sustainability or spirituality with the same wall-to-wall intensity that they advertise consumer products and lifestyles? Do progressive and social democratic approaches to economic and fiscal policy receive a fair shake, compared to "free market" neoliberal approaches? Do the concerns of lower-income Canadians (such as social programs to reduce poverty and homelessness) weigh as heavily in the media as the preoccupations of the affluent (from tax cuts to luxury vacations)? Preliminary research points to blind spots and imbalances in the press on such dimensions as these (Hackett & Gruneau, 2000, pp. 165–217).

Another line of critique suggests that conventional journalism typically favours war over peace. The dependence on official and government sources, the presentation of conflicts as two-sided rather than multidimensional, the newsworthiness of "our" heroism and "the enemy's" evil, the focus on military strategy over civilian suffering, and much else, mean that journalism too often exacerbates conflict and undermines public support for its peaceful resolution (Lynch & McGoldrick, 2005).

Such imbalances in journalism point toward structural and ideological imbalances in Canada's media system, more broadly. For example, the CBC was created to help offset the structural biases of corporate-owned, profit-oriented commercial broadcasters. But ongoing cutbacks to CBC funding and sustained right-wing attacks on its legitimacy are tilting the system's balance away from public service broadcasting and toward commercialism. In this context, the provision of staged "reality" programming, infotainment, spectacle, celebrity journalism, consumer tips, and homogenized and commercialized music fare (even though it increasingly appropriates minority genres and elements to broaden its market appeal) threaten to eclipse the provision of serious journalism, civic information, public forums, and local and community-based art and music that are needed for a vibrant democracy and a thriving culture. Finally, despite the spread of digital media with interactive capacities, one-way media consumption still greatly outweighs participatory communication.

It would be unfair to blame media consumers for such imbalances. Notwithstanding this chapter's metaphor of a media diet, the setting of the media menu is much more complex than that of an individually catered restaurant dinner. From ownership politics to advertiser needs to economies of scale, pressures other than consumer choice influence media production. Within the media marketplace, affluent Canadians have more "votes" than others as a result of their particular attractiveness to advertisers. Other forms of social and cultural status also translate into media influence. Moreover, consumer choices are shaped as much by habit and availability as by consumers' "real" preferences. The commercial media do not simply "give people what they want"; they "give some of the people part of what they think they want—programming that media corporations find economical and convenient to offer, that is generally compatible with a consumerist stance, and that affluent and/or mass consumers (who lack ready access to the full range of potential alternatives) are prepared to accept as a reward for joining the audience" (Hackett & Zhao, 1998, p. 188; see also McChesney, 2004, pp. 138–209). Even if the media could more directly and fairly reflect our choices as consumers, there is no guarantee that such media would generate the kind of civic forums we want and need as citizens. Marketplace purchases are not the only way that Canadians' values should be measured in a democratic media system.

CONCLUSION

We are not rejecting the concept of balance. There have to be gatekeepers of public communication, and limits to legitimate controversy, if we are not to be overwhelmed by cacophony. News reports of orbiting spacecraft require no rebuttal from the Flat Earth Society. Similarly, if election debates are to be useful to voters, the media do not need to provide equal access to parties with no hope of electing a single MP alongside those with a meaningful chance of forming a government. Rather, we are problematizing the conventional concept and practices of balance, and suggesting that they need to be broadened in a democratic system of public communication.

References

Croteau, D. (1998). Challenging the "liberal media" claim. *Extra! 11*(4), 4–9.

Greenberg, J. (2000). Opinion discourse and Canadian newspapers: The case of the Chinese "boat people." *Canadian Journal of Communication, 25*, 517–537.

Hackett, R. A., & Gruneau, R. (with Gutstein, D., Gibson, T. A., & NewsWatch Canada). (2000). *The missing news: Filters and blind spots in Canada's press.* Toronto: Garamond Press; Ottawa: CCPA.

Hackett, R. A., & Uzelman, S. (2003). Tracing corporate influences on press content: A summary of recent NewsWatch Canada research. *Journalism Studies, 4*(3), 331–346.

Hackett, R. A., & Zhao, Y. (1998). *Sustaining democracy? Journalism and the politics of objectivity.* Toronto: Garamond Press.

Hallin, D. C. (1989). *The "uncensored war": The media and Vietnam.* Berkeley: University of California Press.

Henry, F., & Tator, C. (2002). *Discourses of domination: Racial bias in the Canadian English-language press.* Toronto: University of Toronto Press.

Herman, E. S., & Chomsky, N. (1988). *Manufacturing consent: The political economy of the mass media.* New York: Pantheon.

Karim, K. H. (2000). *Islamic peril: Media and global violence.* Montreal: Black Rose Books.

Lynch, J., & McGoldrick, A. (2005). *Peace journalism.* Stroud, UK: Hawthorn Press.

McChesney, R. W. (2004). *The problem of the media.* New York: Monthly Review Press.

Miljan, L., & Cooper, B. (2003). *Hidden agendas: How journalists influence the news.* Vancouver: UBC Press.

Murray, C. (in press). Designing policy monitoring to promote cultural diversification in TV. In K. Karim (Ed.), *Race in policy and media discourses.* Waterloo: Wilfrid Laurier University Press.

Shoemaker, P., & Reese, S. (1996). *Mediating the message: Theories of influences on mass media content* (2nd ed.). White Plains, NY: Longman.

Strutt, S., & Hissey, L. (1992). Feminisms and balance. *Canadian Journal of Communication, 17*, 61–74.

Taras, D. (2001). *Power and betrayal in the Canadian media* (2nd ed.). Peterborough, ON: Broadview Press.

Thobani, S. (in press). Gender and empire: Veilomentaries and the War on Terror. In P. Chakravartty & Yuezhi Zhao (Eds.), *Global communications: Toward a transcultural political economy.* Lanham: Rowman & Littlefield.

Winter, J. (1997). *Democracy's oxygen: How corporations control the news.* Montreal: Black Rose Books.

Discussion Questions

1. If the loudest critiques of media imbalance come from right-wing claims of "left liberal bias," on what grounds do Hackett and Zhao challenge it? Why is it a limited and misleading claim, in their view?

2. What kinds of imbalance may exist in a media system, apart from political bias?

3. Why do the authors say that "news reports of orbiting spacecraft require no rebuttal from the Flat Earth Society?" What are the limits to legitimate controversy in a democratic society? What kinds of information and viewpoints, if any, can ethically be excluded by news media or even censored by governments?

4. Are patterns of media ownership a good way to measure balance in news content?

5. How much control do you think individual Canadian journalists have in the presentation of news stories?

6. What role have the media played in the rapid social change seen in the last century?

PART 2 Media and Social Issues

Some of the most debated topics in communication studies have to do with the relationship between the media and contemporary social issues. While we are surrounded by media in various forms— blogs, podcasts, video games, television, newspapers, etc.—myriad questions arise about the impact of media on society. What is the relationship between food advertising and obesity? Do violent media create violent children? Do advertisements really influence social perceptions of beauty? Do news media perpetuate racist perspectives?

Such questions have to do with a spectrum of media—from advertising to video games—but also speak to a variety of audiences. Indeed, the social issues bound up with media are not focused solely on the "vulnerable" audience of children. They also have to do with adults, with questions of gender, race, and Canadian citizenship more generally. Starting with childhood obesity and concluding with representations of race, the issues tackled in this section illustrate the wide span of key controversies pertinent to students of communication.

Childhood obesity is a widespread and growing problem in Canada, which has prompted researchers to consider how the social environment contributes to being overweight. A core part of this environment, of course, is the media. The first debate addresses the question of whether banning advertisements to children is the best solution for combating childhood obesity in Canada. Bill Jeffery argues that such a ban is essential to combating the obesity problem, since it is "virtually beyond dispute" that television advertising of junk food to children leads to poor diets. He contends that children are vulnerable to media messages and are not media savvy—that is, they are unable to understand commercial intent. Given this, televised advertising to children should be illegal throughout Canada.

Charlene Elliott, on the other hand, argues that a singular focus on television advertising to children misses the point—that we need, instead, to recognize that children's food has become an advertisement in itself. The expanding category of "fun food" found in the Canadian supermarket— from glow-in-the-dark yogurt tubes to bug-shaped pasta—encourages children to value the artificial in food and to treat food as sport, entertainment, and distraction. Elliott argues that researchers interested in childhood obesity should consider what fun food communicates and how it advocates to children a certain relationship with food that is particularly unhealthy.

The second debate pivots on the connection between violent video games and childhood aggression. Rose Dyson frames violent video games as "essentially murder simulators" that reward children with points for making "heads roll and blood splatter." The consequences of such video games, she explains, play out on both an individual and social level—and she questions the appropriateness of indiscriminately socializing "an entire generation of young people into thinking that killing is fun."

Stephen Kline and Benjamin Woo challenge this stance, asserting that we must approach the presumption that violent video games equal violent children more cautiously. Even though there are risks associated with excessive video game use, the authors argue that video games do not make children aggressive. Media researchers should instead focus on lifestyle risk factors that emerge from living in a commercial environment.

The third issue under consideration shifts the focus from children to adults. It questions the relationship between media images and social perceptions of beauty. This debate pivots on the case of the Dove Campaign for Real Beauty, which purports to sell a healthy and more democratic image of female beauty along with its skincare products. This campaign can be classified as a form of corporate social responsibility, and Karen Blotnicky affirms that Dove's advertising has effectively prompted a "shift in our society's concept of beauty." Blotnicky contends that the "beauty prototype" pushed by marketers is unrealistic and unattainable, but that the more realistic images of women portrayed in the Dove campaign have a positive and direct impact on how women feel about themselves. She also believes that the publicity surrounding the campaign—from coverage on talk shows to personal blogs—is evidence of its ability to evoke change on a broader level.

Eileen Saunders, however, views Dove's campaign as just another means of selling soap. Certainly, the campaign has garnered attention, but it will likely have little long-term effect on the way our society thinks about beauty. Saunders

observes that the use of "real" people as models is merely an extension of the reality television trend, and that several other advertising campaigns have moved toward featuring nonprofessional models. Furthermore, she questions the underlying message of the campaign, which is still prefaced on the need to purchase beauty products in order to be beautiful. As such, consumers should remain skeptical of Dove's rhetoric, since it also preys on women's insecurities and promotes the idea that beauty, at any size, still needs to be purchased.

The final debate moves from advertising to news coverage. It explores the ways that race is depicted in Canadian news. Minelle Mahtani, Frances Henry, and Carol Tator affirm that the Canadian news media both articulates and sustains racist discourse. They use critical discourse analysis to unpack the ideological messages found in a single newspaper article—this close reading, they claim, provides insight into how journalists employ language to stigmatize racial communities.

Sean Hier suggests that the case study approach (which Mahtani, Henry, and Tator employ) proves extremely limited in its ability to provide a complete understanding of media representations of racial and ethnic diversity. Needed is "analysis of what does *not* appear in media coverage"—namely, patterns of misrepresentation, underrepresentation, and silence. Part of the problem arising from studies on racism in media, Hier affirms, is that analysts "tend to seek out explicit examples of stereotypical, sensational, and spectacular media coverage" at the expense of coverage that contributes to ethno-racial harmony and acceptance in Canada. Greater empirical data is required before claims can be made regarding the overall representation of race in Canadian news coverage. Hier also draws attention to the need to probe the impact of other digital media on perceptions of race and recognize the transformations that have taken place in Canada, which demands a much more complex reading of the situation.

ISSUE 1

Childhood obesity: Is banning advertisements to children the "best" solution?

✔ YES

Exhorting Gen-XS to XL, Cheating at Child's Play: Their Health, Our Laws
Bill Jeffery

Bill Jeffery, B.A., LL.B., is the national coordinator of the Centre for Science in the Public Interest in Canada. CSPI is a nonprofit health advocacy organization specializing in nutrition and food safety with staff in Toronto and offices in Ottawa and Washington, D.C. CSPI's Canadian advocacy is funded primarily by more than 100,000 subscribers to the Canadian edition of its *Nutrition Action Healthletter*, which does not carry advertisements. CSPI does not accept funding from industry or government.

INTRODUCTION

Banning advertising and other forms of marketing to children is an essential component of any effective strategy to combat rising childhood obesity and other diet-related diseases. Advertising directly to children contributes to poor diets (and probably sedentary play), ultimately leading to preventable chronic disease and premature death in adulthood. And, because children are simply not savvy consumers, they are uniquely vulnerable to the enticements of commercial advertising. If advertising to children does not already actually violate untested Canadian federal and provincial consumer protection statutes (and it might), those laws should be amended to explicitly ban such exploitative marketing practices.

THE TOLL OF POOR DIET AND PHYSICAL INACTIVITY

Diet-related disease wreaks a terrible toll on Canadian society. According to World Health Organization (WHO) figures, an average of nearly five years of healthy life expectancy is lost in countries like Canada mainly as a result of four diet-related risk factors: high blood pressure, unhealthy cholesterol levels, overweight, and low fruit and vegetable intake (2002). Health Canada reports that $6.6 billion per year is lost from the national economy owing to health care costs and lost productivity associated with preventable diet-related cases of cardiovascular disease, diabetes, and certain forms of cancer (Health Canada, 2003, 2004). Every year in Canada, an estimated 25,000 premature deaths are caused by diet-related diseases (Centre for Science in the Public Interest [CSPI], 2006, p. 5). This says nothing of the equally grim death and economic tolls of inactivity-related diseases (Katzmarzyk, Gledhill, & Shephard, 2000; Katzmarzyk & Janssen, 2004), which are also promoted by a barrage of child-directed advertisements for toys, video games, and entertainment products that promote sedentary play. Some researchers have even predicted that we are witnessing the first generation of children to have shorter life expectancies than their parents (Ontario Medical Association, 2005; Standing Committee on Health, 2007, p. 1). Considering that dietary practices begun during childhood often produce lifelong patterns that can cause adult diseases (e.g., Institute of Medicine [IOM], 2006a, p. 18; Kelder, Perry, & Klepp, 1994; Nader et al., 2006), we must be especially vigilant about threats to childhood nutritional status.

DOES MARKETING TO CHILDREN ACTUALLY MATTER?

It is virtually beyond dispute that at least television advertising of food to children leads to poor diets. Enormous resources are poured worldwide into advertising aimed at children for foods that are generally calorie-dense and nutrient-poor, presumably on the realistic expectation that such ads achieve the intended result: increased sales and profits (American Psychological Association [APA], 2004; Hastings et al., 2003, pp. 7–8; Schor, 2004, p. 21). In the United States, total marketing expenditures directed at children for food now exceeds $10 billion (IOM, 2004, p. 169). McDonald's restaurants alone now spend approximately $500 million annually on advertising worldwide, 40 percent of which is targeted at children (Schor, 2004, p. 122). And there has been a staggering 150-fold increase in spending (from $100 million to $15 billion) on child-directed marketing for food and other products in the United States during the same two and a half decades when obesity rates have also risen (Schor, 2004, p. 21)—a sobering reality to any grown-ups who still believed they ran similar gauntlets as children with no ill-effects.

In Canada, more than $720 million was spent in traditional advertising media (print, radio/TV, and billboard) to promote restaurants, food, and alcohol to children and adults in 1998 (McElgunn, 1999). But, this figure likely grossly underestimates total marketing expenditures—perhaps by more than 10-fold—which, for kids, includes promotional contests, package design, kids' clubs, child-oriented food product development, Internet and viral marketing, product placement (on store shelves and in programs), event- and school-based marketing, and so on. While there are no good estimates for Canada, some estimate that the average American child sees more than 95,000 TV commercials before turning 18, and spends nearly as much time watching TV as attending classes (e.g., Gentile & Walsh, 2002; Henry J. Kaiser Family Foundation, 2007, p. 3).

Presumably, confidential company evaluations of the effectiveness of their own food and toy advertisements show that advertising is worth the money they continue to spend on it. In fact, critics say that companies should make such research available to independent researchers because of its obvious implications for public health (IOM, 2006a, p. 387). But, two recent systematic reviews of studies published worldwide in English concerning (mostly television) advertising to children also confirmed what any sentient parent already knows to be true: advertising works (Hastings et al., 2003, p. 182; IOM, 2006a, p. 379).

Gerald Hastings and his coauthors (2003) were commissioned by the U.K. government's Food Standards Authority to examine the extent of commercial advertising of food to children and its impact on their diet. Hastings conducted two systematic reviews of the scientific literature involving, first, 50 methodologically sound studies assessing the nature and extent of food advertising directed at children, and second, 51 rigorous studies examining the effect of food promotion on children's food knowledge, preferences, and behaviour. Hastings demonstrated that foods marketed to children in the United States and elsewhere tend to be of very low nutritional value (p. 84). Though recent Canadian data are limited, Hastings's findings are consistent with a 1991 survey of Canadian television programming, which found that, for instance, only 3 percent of television food commercials promoted vegetables or fruit (excluding french fries), and approximately 40 percent promoted low-nutrient beverages, butter, margarine, salty snacks, sweets/candy, and chewing gum (Ostbye et al., 1993). Hastings also concluded that there is reasonably strong evidence that food promotion affects children's food brand and category preferences, as well as purchasing and purchase-related behaviour (pp. 19, 138).

Also in 2003, an expert report of the World Health Organization and Food and Agriculture Organization concluded that "heavy marketing of fast food outlets and energy-dense micronutrient-poor foods" is a probable cause of obesity (pp. 65, 148). The report stated,

> the huge expenditure on marketing fast foods and other "eat least" choices (US$11 billion in the United States alone in 1997) was considered to be a key factor in the increased consumption of food prepared outside the home in general and of energy-dense, micronutrient-poor foods in particular.... The Consultation considered that there is sufficient indirect evidence to warrant this practice being placed in the "probable" category and thus becoming a potential target for interventions. (p. 65)

The following year, the World Health Assembly passed a resolution, which states, "Food advertising affects food choices and influences dietary habits. Food and beverage advertisements should not exploit children's inexperience or credulity. Messages that encourage unhealthy dietary practices or physical inactivity should be discouraged, and positive, healthy messages encouraged" (2004, Article 16[3]).

Again, in 2004, the U.S. Henry J. Kaiser Family Foundation's report on the role of media in childhood obesity, though lamenting the absence of *definitive* evidence, concluded that food advertising is the most likely mechanism by which media use contributes to childhood obesity. The foundation concluded,

> It appears likely that the main mechanism by which media use contributes to childhood obesity may well be through children's exposure to billions of dollars worth of food advertising and cross-promotional marketing year after year, starting at the very youngest ages, with children's favorite media characters often enlisted in the sales pitch. Research indicates that children's food choices—and parents' food purchases—are significantly impacted by the advertising they see. (p. 10)

In April 2006, the U.S. Institute of Medicine of the National Academy of Sciences—a respected scientific review body whose advice Health Canada often relies upon—released a report entitled *Food Marketing to Children and Youth: Threat or Opportunity?* The report examined the influence of food and beverage marketing on the diets of U.S. children and youth. The study, the most comprehensive report on the influence of food marketing and children's health conducted in the United States in 25 years, was funded by the U.S. Centers for Disease Control and Prevention in response to a Congressional directive. The report corroborates the findings of Hastings et al. and recommends, among other things, that

- the food and beverage industries be urged to develop, promote, and enforce (with government and the scientific and public health communities) expanded industry self-regulatory codes on marketing practices that also apply to new forms of marketing

- Congress regulate broadcast and cable TV ads if the industry does not voluntarily shift emphasis from high-calorie, low-nutrient foods and beverages to healthful ones within two years

Then in May 2006, the U.S. Federal Trade Commission and the U.S. Department of Health and Human Services published their own report concluding that food advertising aimed at children is inadequately regulated by industry bodies, and calling for more rigorous and transparent self-regulation and greater government oversight.

WHAT IS EASIER (AND LESS ETHICAL) THAN TAKING CANDY FROM A BABY?

Concern about the adverse health effects of promoting junk food to children has animated calls for legislative or regulatory restrictions on such advertising.[1] But the ban on advertising to children (for all products, including food and toys) in Quebec came into effect in 1980, long before childhood obesity became a cause célèbre[2] (WHO, 2004a, p. 20). The primary justification for the ban was to address the unique vulnerability of children to deception. In the 1989 decision in *Attorney General of Québec v. Irwin Toy*, the Supreme Court of Canada accepted the following explanation of the objective of the legislation: "The concern is for the protection of a group which is particularly vulnerable to the techniques of seduction and manipulation abundant in advertising" (p. 987).

However, now, more than ever before, child development experts are helping advertisers translate the "desire for love into concrete objects, shapes, music, and themes for ads" (Schor, 2004, p. 46)—at least outside Quebec. Based on extensive interviews with U.S. marketing executives, Schor observes that the formula for advertising children's products from the 1920s through the postwar era was to convince mothers (the "gatekeepers") that the advertised product was beneficial for the child (p. 16). However, Schor notes that marketers began to abandon the gatekeeper approach in the 1980s and, instead, promote the idea of "kid power." Advertisers that once depicted mothers as loving and wise now depict parents as "neglectful, incompetent, abusive, invisible, or embarrassing" (Schor, 2004, pp. 54–55, 180). A Toronto-based children's marketing company recently characterized the new marketing strategy for targeting the "tweens" market cohort as "gate crashing" (Valiquette & Farrell, 2005).

Since the 1980s, gate crashing became even easier for marketers as commercial cable television channels devoted mainly or exclusively to youth audiences (like MuchMusic, YTV, and Teletoon) were launched and more households purchased second television sets; for example, according to a recent survey of nearly 6,000 Canadian students in grades three through ten, nearly half had their own television (Canadian Teachers' Federation, 2003, p. 52). The American Psychological Association's Task Force on Children and Advertising (2004, p. 21) noted that, in the days of fewer channels, the amount of television programming targeted to children was limited and relegated to time slots unpopular with adults, such as Saturday mornings. Now, according to the Task Force, children can be exposed to child-oriented advertisements all day, every day. While part of this effort will lead to children making their own purchases at the urging of marketers, it also prompts them to pester their parents to make purchases for them—a process marketers term **pester power**. For instance, a 2002 U.S. poll indicated that 83 percent of children aged 12 to 13 reported asking their parents to buy or let them buy something they had seen advertised; of those, 71 percent repeated the request an average of 8 times, and 11 percent repeated the request more than 50 times (Schor, 2004, p. 62). By contrast, a randomized, controlled trial of third- and fourth-grade students demonstrated that reductions in TV viewing led to a 70 percent reduction in children's requests for toy purchases (Robinson, 2001, pp. 179–182).

IF ADVERTISING TO CHILDREN IS NOT ALREADY ILLEGAL ELSEWHERE IN CANADA, IT SHOULD BE

Like most countries, Canadian laws prohibit false, misleading, and deceptive advertising, as well as unconscionable business practices. For example, the federal *Competition Act* prohibits such advertising:[3]

> 52(1) No person shall, for the purpose of promoting, directly or indirectly, the supply or use of a product or for the purpose of promoting, directly or indirectly, any business interest, by any means whatever, knowingly or recklessly make a representation to the public that is false or misleading in a material respect.

Similarly, most provincial governments have enacted some form of consumer protection legislation prohibiting misleading advertising or unconscionable trade practices.[4]

And Canadian appeal court rulings on "misleading advertising" have established two principles that may be relevant to the issue of advertising directed at children. First, the Ontario Court of Appeal held that courts must consider what is "misleading" from the vantage point of the advertisement's intended recipient (*R. v. International Vacations*, 1980, p. 284). Second, the Alberta and British Columbia courts of appeal ruled that courts should assume the advertisement will be interpreted by persons of "average" abilities appropriate to the circumstances and not by well-informed or sophisticated persons (*R. v. Cunningham Drug Stores*, 1973; *R. v. Imperial Tobacco*, 1971). These authorities make it plain that a court should *not* apply the same analysis to an ad aimed at a child as one aimed at an adult, which could, for example, include a literal analysis of its logical structure (*R. v. Suntours*, 1974, p. 181).

To respect these appeal court rulings, it seems plain that courts should consider developmental psychology research demonstrating the unique vulnerability of children to commercial advertising. In *Attorney General of Québec v. Irwin Toy* (1989, p. 1000), the Supreme Court of Canada examined the constitutionality of the near-total statutory ban on commercial advertising directed at children in Quebec and concluded that the ban was a permissible limit on commercial freedom of expression under the *Charter of Rights and Freedoms*. The law had been challenged by a toy company. The court relied heavily on the 1981 United States Federal Trade Commission's report entitled *Final Staff Report and Recommendation: In the Matter of Children's Advertising*. The report concluded that

> the specific cognitive abilities of young children lead to their inability to fully understand child-oriented television advertising, even if they grasp some aspects of it. They place indiscriminate trust in the selling message. They do not correctly perceive persuasive bias in advertising, and their life experience is insufficient to help them counter-argue.... As a result, children are not able to evaluate adequately child-oriented advertising. (*Irwin Toy,* 1989, p. 988)

Even though Congress ultimately prevented the FTC from issuing a ban (APA, 2004), the Supreme Court of Canada concluded that "the Report ... provides a sound basis on which to conclude that television advertising directed at young children is *per se* manipulative. Such advertising aims to promote products by convincing those who will always believe" (*Irwin Toy,* 1989, p. 988).

Since 1989, scientific evidence of children's incapacity to interpret commercial advertising has become even more compelling. In 2004, the American Psychological Association's *Report of the Task Force on Advertising and Children* concluded that

> the ability to recognize persuasive intent does not develop for most children before 8 years of age. Even at that age, such capability tends to emerge in only rudimentary form, with youngsters recognizing that commercials intend to sell, but not necessarily that they are biased messages which warrant some degree of skepticism. (p. 9)

The report also noted that "further investigation is needed to establish the upper age boundary of children who are uniquely vulnerable to televised commercial persuasion" (p. 5). Similarly, the Hastings report found that at around age 8, children are just "beginning to respond to advertising in a more sophisticated way" and that children's ability to retrieve and process information is still developing between the ages of 8 and 12 (2004, pp. 35–36). Children, because they are still maturing, have very poor cognitive defences against commercial advertisements (APA, 2004, pp. 36–37).

Courts are accustomed to creating and applying legal norms that recognize the vulnerability of young people. The Toronto-based nongovernmental organization Justice for Children and Youth (JCY) published a list of age-delimited legal milestones (both rights and responsibilities) specific to federal and provincial statutes and common law (judge-made law) affecting children in Ontario (2005). Of the nearly six dozen milestones, only two vest rights or responsibilities in children under age 12: the statutory duty to attend school from age 6, and the power to withhold consent to be adopted at age 7. In fact, most rights and responsibilities do not accrue to children until they reach the age of 18 or 19, depending on the province (Tasse & Lemieux, 1998, p. 49). Accordingly, the age of reason adopted by the Quebec legislature and accepted by the Supreme Court in *Irwin Toy* (1989, pp. 989–990) is comparatively lenient.

The Supreme Court of Canada also noted the relevance of the common law by stating,

> In sum, the objective of regulating commercial advertising directed at children accords with a general goal of consumer protection legislation, *viz.* to protect a group that is most vulnerable to commercial manipulation ... [as] reflected in general contract doctrine.... *Children are not as equipped as adults to evaluate the persuasive force of advertising and advertisements directed at children would take advantage of this* [italics added]. (*Irwin Toy*, 1989, p. 990)

Ironically, given the contribution of its marketing to the diets of youngsters, McDonald's once even argued (unsuccessfully) that lack of legal capacity to enter contracts (just like contracts for the sale of food) should disallow some of its teenage employees from joining labour unions (Wilson, 1994).

Furthermore, even subsection 9(1) of the *Competition Act* itself requires citizens to be at least 18 years old to petition for an investigation of misleading advertising. And section 16 of the *Canada Evidence Act* creates a presumption that children under the age of 14 are not reliable witnesses. As the Supreme Court of Canada stated in 1962, "the difficulty is fourfold: 1. His capacity of observation. 2. His capacity of recollection. 3. His capacity to understand questions put and frame intelligent answers. 4. His moral responsibility" (*Kendall v. The Queen*, 1962).

Finally, three Canadian national bodies representing marketers—though they do not provide adequate protection for children[5]—prescribe several general age-delimited controls on advertising directed at children, including preschoolers, children under age 16 and (depending on the province) 18 or 19 (Advertising Standards Canada, 2004; CBC, 2006; Canadian Marketing Association, 2004).

WHAT IS NEXT IN THE COURTS AND LEGISLATURES?

Child development evidence demonstrates that commercial advertising is inherently misleading to children. As such, this marketing information obstructs rather than supports informed economic choices and sends misleading market signals to sellers, to say nothing of the adverse health effects of flogging disease-promoting foods to impressionable children. Certainly, Parliament and provincial legislatures could not have intended that misleading advertising provisions of the *Competition Act*, the *Food and Drugs Act*, and other consumer protection statutes be interpreted in a manner that protects adults (and even older teenagers), but not children under the age of 13. In interpreting the scope of restrictions on advertising in those statutes, one must be mindful of the unique vulnerability of children in order to ensure that they receive more, not less, protection than experienced, intellectually mature adults though, plainly, even sophisticated adults are not impervious to the effects of advertising.[6] If those laws are deficient, it is incumbent on legislators to fix them to protect children from economic exploitation and to safeguard their health.

Cases (Generally available on the World Wide Web at http://www.canlii.org)

Attorney General of Québec v. Irwin Toy, [1989] 1 S.C.R. 927.

General Motors of Canada Ltd. v. City National Leasing, [1989] S.C.R. 641. Available at http://www.lexum .umontreal.ca/csc-scc/en/pub/1989/vol1/html/1989scr1_0641.html

International Accountants Society Inc. v. Montgomery, [1935] O.W.N. 364, 365 (Ont. C.A.).

Kendall v. The Queen, [1962] S.C.R. 469.

Miller v. Smith & Co., [1925] 2 W.W.R. 360.

Purolator Courier Ltd. v. United Parcel Service Canada Ltd., [1995] 60 C.P.R. (3d) 473 (Ont. Ct. Gen. Div.).

R. v. Cunningham Drug Stores, [1973] 13 C.P.R. (2d) 244, 248 (B.C. C.A.).

R. v. Imperial Tobacco Prods., [1971] 3 C.P.R. (2d) 178, 195 (Alta. C.A.).

R. v. International Vacations, [1980] 56 C.P.R. (2d) 255–56 (Ont. C.A.).

R. v. Viceroy Construction Co. Ltd., [1975] 23 C.P.R. (2d) 281, 284 (Ont. C.A.).

R. v. Suntours Ltd., [1974] 20 C.P.R. (2d) 179, 181 (Ont. Prov. Ct.).

Statutes(Generally available on the World Wide Web at http://www.canlii.org1)

Age of Majority and Accountability Act, R.S.O. 1990, c. A-7.

Business Practices Act, R.S.P.E.I. 1988, c. B 7.

Business Practices Act, S.M. 1990-1, c. 6.

Business Practices and Consumer Protection Act, S.B.C., c. 2 (2004).

Canada Evidence Act, R.S.C. 1985, c. E-10, as am. by An Act to Amend the Criminal Code (Protection of Children and Other Vulnerable Persons) and the *Canada Evidence Act*, S.C. 2005, c. 32, s 16.1(1) (assented to July 20, 2005). Retrieved June 13, 2007, from http://www.parl.gc.ca/PDF/38/1/parlbus/chambus/house/ bills/government/C-2_4.PDF in force January 2, 2006, per P.C. 2005-1817, C. Gaz. 2005.II.2550, SI/2005- 104 (available at page 2550 at http://gazetteducanada.gc.ca/partII/2005/20051116/pdf/g2-13923.pdf).

Competition Act, R.S.C. 1985, c. C-34.

Consumer Protection Act, S.S., c. C 30.1, (1996).

Fair Trading Act, R.S.A. 2000, c. F 2.

Food and Drugs Act, R.S.C. 1985, c. F-27.

Ontario Consumer Protection Act, S.O. 2002, c. 30.

Trade Practices Act, R.S.N.L. 1990, c. T 7.

Trade Practices Inquiry Act, C.C.S.M. 2006, c. T110.

Secondary Sources

Advertising Standards Canada. (2004). *Broadcast code for advertising to children*. Retrieved June 13, 2007, from http://www.adstandards.com/en/clearance/clearanceAreas/broadcastCodeForAdvertisingToChildren.asp

American Academy of Pediatrics Committee on Nutrition. (2003). Policy statement: Prevention of pediatric overweight and obesity. *Pediatrics, 112*(2), 424–430.

American Psychological Association. (2004). *Report of the APA Task Force on Advertising and Children*. Washington, DC: Author. Retrieved June 13, 2007, from http://www.apa.org/pi/cyf/ advertisingandchildren.pdf

American Public Health Association. (2004). 2003-17 food marketing and advertising directed at children and adolescents: Implications for overweight. *Association News, 31*(2). Retrieved June 13, 2007, from http://www.apha.org/advocacy/policy/policysearch/default.htm?id=1255

Canadian Broadcast Corporation. (2006). *Summary of CBC advertising standards.* Retrieved June 13, 2007, from http://cbc.radio-canada.ca/docs/policies/advertising.shtml

Canadian Marketing Association. (2004). *Code of ethics & standards of practice.* Retrieved June 13, 2007, from http://www.the-cma.org/regulatory/codeofethics.cfm

Canadian Teachers' Federation. (2003). *Kids' take on media.* Retrieved June 13, 2007, from http://www.ctf-fce .ca/bilingual/pubs/ctfreport/kidsenglish.pdf

Carr, S. (2004). *Overweight in Canadian children: Mapping the geographic variation.* Unpublished master's thesis, London School of Hygiene and Tropical Medicine, University of London, UK.

Centre for Science in the Public Interest (Canada). (2005). "Canada's Food Guide"—Promoting health or protecting wealth? Notes for a speech at the Canada Millennium Scholarship Foundation conference Think Again, Parliament Hill, Ottawa, September 16, 2005. Retrieved June 13, 2007, from http://www .cspinet.org/canada/

Centre for Science in the Public Interest (Canada). (2006). Testimony of Bill Jeffery before the House of Commons Standing Committee on Finance, October 5, 2006, Ottawa. Retrieved June 13, 2007, from http://cspinet.org/canada/pdf/financecttee_oct2006_en.pdf

Centre for Science in the Public Interest (United States). (2003). *Pestering parents.* Washington, DC: Author. Retrieved June 13, 2007, from http://cspinet.org/new/pdf/pestering_parents_final_part_1.pdf (Part 1) and http://cspinet.org/new/pdf/pestering_parents_final_part_2.pdf (Part 2).

Centre for Science in the Public Interest (United States). (2005). *Guidelines for responsible food marketing to children.* Washington, DC: Author. Retrieved June 13, 2007, from http://cspinet.org/ marketingguidelines.pdf

Chief Medical Officer of Health of Ontario (S. Basrur). (2004). *2004 Chief Medical Officer of Health report: Healthy weights, healthy lives.* Toronto: CMOH. Retrieved June 13, 2007, from http://www.health.gov .on.ca/english/public/pub/ministry_reports/cmoh04_report/healthy_weights_112404.pdf

Commercial Alert. (1998, September 8). *Nader starts group to oppose the excesses of marketing, advertising and commercialism* [News release]. Retrieved June 13, 2007, from http://www.commercialalert.org/ news/news-releases/1998/09/nader-starts-group-to-oppose-the-excesses-of-marketing-advertising-and-commercialism

Department of Justice Canada. (2006). *The federal child support guidelines: Step-by-step.* Retrieved June 13, 2007, from http://www.justice.gc.ca/en/ps/sup/pub/guide/guide.pdf

Federal-Provincial Committee on Advertising Intended for Children. (1986). *The effects of Quebec's legislation prohibiting advertising intended for children.* Ottawa: Minister of Supply and Services Canada.

Food Commission. (2000). *Children's food examined: An analysis of 358 products targeted at children.* London: Author. Retrieved June 13, 2007, from http://www.foodcomm.org.uk/PDF%20files/Childrens_Food_ Examined.pdf

Gentile, D. A., & Walsh, D. A. (2002). A normative study of family media habits. *Journal of Applied Developmental Psychology, 23,* 157–178.

Hastings, G., Stead, M., McDermott, L., Forsyth, A., MacKintosh, A. M., & Rayner, M., et al. (2003). *Review of research on the effects of food promotion to children.* London: Food Standards Agency; Glasgow, Scotland: Centre for Social Marketing, University of Strathclyde. Retrieved June 13, 2007, from http://www.food .gov.uk/multimedia/pdfs/foodpromotiontochildren1.pdf

Health Canada. (2003, January 2). *Health Canada announces new mandatory nutrition labelling* [News release]. Retrieved June 13, 2007, from http://www.hc-sc.gc.ca/ahc-asc/media/nr-cp/2003/2003_01_e.html

Health Canada. (2004, January 20). Speech by Diane Gorman, Assistant Deputy Minister of Health, at stake-holder meeting on review of Canada's Food Guide to Healthy Eating, Ottawa.

Heart and Stroke Foundation of Canada. (2004). *Heart and Stroke Foundation warns fat is the new tobacco* [News release]. Retrieved June 13, 2007, from http://ww1.heartandstroke.ca/Page.asp?PageID=33&ArticleID=2913&Src=news

Henry J. Kaiser Family Foundation. (2004, February). *Issue brief: The role of media in childhood obesity.* Washington, DC: Author. Retrieved June 13, 2007, from http://www.kff.org/entmedia/upload/The-Role-Of-Media-in-Childhood-Obesity.pdf

Henry J. Kaiser Family Foundation. (2007). *Food for Thought: Television food advertising to children in the United States.* Washington, DC: Author. Retrieved June 13, 2007, from http://www.kff.org/entmedia/upload/7618.pdf

Institute of Medicine. (2004, September). *Fact sheet: Advertising, Marketing and the media: Improving messages.* Retrieved June 13, 2007, from http://www.iom.edu/Object.File/Master/22/609/0.pdf

Institute of Medicine. Committee on Food Marketing and the Diets of Children and Youth. (2006a). *Food marketing to children and youth: Threat or opportunity?* Washington, DC: National Academies Press. Retrieved June 13, 2007, from http://www.nap.edu/catalog/11514.html

Institute of Medicine. Committee on Food Marketing and the Diets of Children and Youth. (2006b). *Progress in preventing childhood obesity: How do we measure up?* Washington, DC: National Academies Press.

Institute of Medicine. Committee on Prevention of Obesity in Children and Youth. (2005). *Preventing childhood obesity: Health in the balance.* Washington, DC: National Academies Press.

International Association of Consumer Food Organisations. (2003). *Broadcasting bad health.* London: Author. Retrieved June 13, 2007, from http://www.foodcomm.org.uk/Broadcasting_bad_health.pdf

Jeffery, B. (2006). The Supreme Court of Canada's appraisal of the 1980 ban on advertising to children in Québec: Implications for "misleading" advertising elsewhere. *Loyola of Los Angeles Law Review, 39*(1), 237–276. Retrieved June 13, 2007, from http://llr.lls.edu/volumes/v39-issue1/docs/jeffery.pdf

Justice for Children and Youth. (2005). Summary of age-based legal milestones for youth in Ontario. Retrieved June 13, 2007, from http://www.jfcy.org/agebased.html

Katzmarzyk, P. T., Gledhill, N., & Shephard, R. J. (2000). The economic burden of physical inactivity in Canada [Electronic version].*Canadian Medical Association Journal, 163*(11), 1435–1440. Retrieved June 13, 2007, from http://www.cmaj.ca/cgi/reprint/163/11/1435.pdf

Katzmarzyk, P. T., & Janssen, I. (2004). The economic costs of physical inactivity and obesity in Canada: An update. *Canadian Journal of Applied Physiology, 29*(1), 90–115.

Kelder, S., Perry, C., & Klepp, K. (1994). Longitudinal tracing of adolescent smoking, physical activity and food choice behaviors. *American Journal of Public Health, 84,* 1121–1126.

McElgunn J. (1999, September 27). Canada's top 25 advertising categories. *Marketing Magazine,* 44.

Nader, P. R., O'Brien, M., Houts, R., Bradley, B., Belsky, J., & Crosnoe, R. (2006). Identifying risk for obesity in early childhood. *Pediatrics, 118,* 594–601.

National Institute of Media and the Family. (n.d.). *Fact sheet: Media use—did you know?* Retrieved September 30, 2006, from http://www.mediafamily.org/facts/facts_mediause.shtml

Note, The elephant in the room: Evolution, behavioralism, and counteradvertising in the coming war against obesity. (2003). *Harvard Law Review, 116,* 1161, 1168–1170.

Ontario Medical Association. (2005). *An ounce of prevention or a ton of trouble: Is there an epidemic of obesity in children?* Toronto: Author.

Ostbye, T. J., Pomerleau, J., White, M., Coolich, M., & McWinney, J. (1993). Food and nutrition in Canadian "prime time" television commercials. *Canadian Journal of Public Health, 84*(6), 370–374.

Raine, K. (2004). Overweight and obesity in Canada: A population health perspective. Ottawa: Canadian Population Health Initiative of the Canadian Institute for Health Information. Retrieved June 13, 2007, from http://secure.cihi.ca/cihiweb/dispPage.jsp?cw_page=GR_1130_E

Robinson, T. N. (2001). Effects of reducing television viewing on children's requests for toys: A randomized controlled trial. *Journal of Development and Behavioral Pediatrics, 22,* 179–182.

Schor, J. (2004). *Born to buy*. New York: Scribner.

Standing Committee on Health, House of Commons. (2007, March). *Healthy weights for healthy kids*. Ottawa: Author. Retrieved June 13, 2007, from http://cmte.parl.gc.ca/Content/HOC/committee/391/hesa/reports/rp2795145/hesarp07/hesarp07-e.pdf

Statistics Canada. (2003). *Dietary practices, by sex, household population aged 12 and over, Canada, provinces, territories, health regions and peer groups, 2003*. Retrieved June 13, 2007, from http://www.statcan.ca/english/freepub/82-221-XIE/00604/tables/html/2188_03.htm

Sustain. (2005). *The Children's Food Bill: Why we need a law, not more voluntary approaches*. Retrieved June 13, 2007, from http://www.sustainweb.org/pdf/CFB_MpReport.pdf

Tasse, R., & Lemieux, K. (1998). *Consumer protection rights in Canada in the context of electronic commerce: A report to the Office of Consumer Affairs Industry Canada*. Retrieved June 13, 2007, from http://strategis.ic.gc.ca/epic/internet/inoca-bc.nsf/vwapj/Full_e.pdf/$FILE/Full_e.pdf

Thompson, S. (2005, January 31). Ronald McD the next Joe Camel? Europe slams icons as food fights back. *Advertising Age*, 1.

Trans Atlantic Consumer Dialogue. (2004, January). *Resolution on food advertising and marketing to children*. Retrieved June 13, 2007, from http://www.tacd.org/db_files/files/files-288-filetag.doc

United States Federal Trade Commission. (1981). *Final staff report and recommendation: In the matter of children's advertising*. Washington, DC: Author.

United States Federal Trade Commission and the Department of Health and Human Services. (2006). *Perspectives on marketing, self-regulation and childhood obesity*. Washington, DC: Author. Retrieved June 13, 2007, from http://ftc.gov/opa/2006/05/childhoodobesity.htm

Valiquette, M., & Farrell, M. (2005, December 7). Marketing to young Canadians in 2006 (PowerPoint slides 35–36). *Youth access*. Marketing Magazine seminar, Montreal, QC.

Wilson, J. (1994). *Wilson on children and the law* (3rd ed.). [Current loose-leaf service]

World Health Assembly. (2004). Resolution 57.17 of the 57th session of the World Health Assembly, passed May 22, 2004, adopting the Global Strategy on Diet, Physical Activity and Health. Retrieved June 13, 2007, from http://www.who.int/gb/ebwha/pdf_files/WHA57/A57_R17-en.pdf

World Health Organization. (2002). *World health report* (Annex tables 4, 9, & 10). Retrieved June 13, 2007, from http://www.who.int/entity/whr/2002/en/whr02_en.pdf

World Health Organization. (2004a). *Marketing food to children: The global regulatory environment*. Geneva: Author. Retrieved June 13, 2007, from http://whqlibdoc.who.int/publications/2004/9241591579.pdf

World Health Organization. (2004b, November 30). Speech by Dr. Catherine Le Galès-Camus, assistant director-general noncommunicable diseases and mental health of the World Health Organization, at the 4th Global Advertising Summit of the World Federation of Advertisers, New York.

World Health Organization and the Food and Agriculture Organization. (2003). *The report of the joint WHO/FAO expert consultation on diet, nutrition and the prevention of chronic diseases* (Technical rep. 916). Geneva: World Health Organization. Retrieved June 13, 2007, from http://www.who.int/hpr/NPH/docs/who_fao_expert_report.pdf

Notes

[1] By the summer of 2007, Centre for Science in the Public Interest's "Proposal for an Effective Pan-Canadian Healthy Living Strategy" (at http://cspinet.org/canada/pdf/PanCdn_EffectiveStrat.pdf) was supported by about two dozen Canadian health and citizens' groups.

See also Commercial Alert (1998), the United Kingdom's Food Commission (2000), Sustain (2005), the International Association of Consumer Food Organisations (2003), the American Academy of Paediatrics Committee on Nutrition (2003), the American Public Health Association (2004), the Trans Atlantic Consumer Dialogue (2004), the Chief Medical Officer of Health for Ontario (Basrur, 2004), Raine (2004), the Heart and Stroke Foundation of Canada (2004), and the European Commissioner of Health and Consumer Affairs, Markos Kyprianou (cited in Thompson, 2005).

[2] It is difficult to assess whether the restrictions on advertising actually improved Quebec children's diets, partly because Canadian governments have never conducted regular dietary intake surveys. But it is worth noting that overall obesity rates have generally been lower in Quebec than in nearly every other province, and per capita soft drink consumption has become lower in Quebec than the rest of Canada since the ban came into effect (Carr, 2004). Likewise, Quebec fruit and vegetable consumption rates are among the highest in Canada (Statistics Canada, 2003). Norway and Sweden have also established broad restrictions on advertising to children within the scope of their legislative competence, and other European countries have issued narrower restrictions (WHO, 2004a).

[3] See also section 74.01 of the Act.

[4] For example, *Ontario Consumer Protection Act*, R.S.O. 2002, c. 30, ss. 14(1), 14(2)(14-15), 15(1-2); *Trade Practices Act*, R.S.N.L. 1990, c. T 7, ss. 5(w), 6(f), 7; *Business Practices Act*, R.S.P.E.I. 1988, c. B 7, ss. 2(a)(xiii), 2(b)(i), 3(1); *Business Practices Act*, S.M. 1990-1, c. 6, s. 3; *Trade Practices Inquiry Act*, C.C.S.M. 2006, c. T110, ss. 2(a)(v), 2(a)(viii); *Consumer Protection Act*, S.S. 1996, c. C 30.1, ss. 5, 6(o), 7; *Fair Trading Act*, R.S.A. 2000, c. F 2, ss. 6(2)(b), 4(a), 4(b), 7; *Business Practices and Consumer Protection Act*, S.B.C. 2004, c. 2, ss. 4(1), 4(3)(b)(vi), 8(3)(b), 9 (2004). See also, the federal *Food and Drugs Act*, R.S.C. 1985, c. F-27, s. 5.

[5] One should be circumspect about the value of voluntary codes written and "enforced" by the same industry sectors that they purport to control, and doubly circumspect when the mission and unique talent of that industry is marketing, such as promoting the message that voluntary codes are actually ruthlessly tough regulations. A thorough analysis of the limitations of industry self-regulation of advertising is beyond the scope of this article. Instead, see Jeffery, 2006.

[6] Adults are not immune to manipulation. A recent note in the *Harvard Law Review* argued that advertising contributes to the development of unhealthy diets (in adults) by distorting consumers' ability to evaluate products, especially about credence attributes like nutritional features that cannot be evaluated without expert assistance. See Note, The elephant in the room: Evolution, behavioralism, and counteradvertising in the coming war against obesity. (2003). *Harvard Law Review, 116,* 1161, 1168–1170.

ISSUE 1

Childhood obesity: Is banning advertisements to children the "best" solution?

✗ NO

The Strange, the Bizarre, and the Edible: Communicating Fun in the World of Children's Food
Charlene D. Elliott

Charlene Elliott is an assistant professor in the Communication Studies at Carleton University. She researches and publishes in the areas of obesity and public health, marketing communication, intellectual property, and sensorial communication. Research grants include funding for studies on children's food advertising and on how children interpret food messages.

What a difference a decade (or so) makes! When, in 1994, Joel Best published *Troubling Children*—an edited volume on children and social problems—it made nary a mention of obesity. Now the World Health Organization has deemed obesity a pandemic and childhood obesity a major social crisis in the developed nations of the world.

Childhood obesity is not only a social problem, it is a problem linked to communication studies as well.[1] Researchers have traced the relationship between television *exposure* and childhood obesity (Lumeng, Rahnama, Appugliese, Kaciroti, & Bradley, 2006),[2] and the ways in which food-related media messages encourage the consumption of high fat, high sugar foods (Brownell & Horgen, 2004; Chamberlain, Wang, & Robinson, 2006; Horgen, Choate, & Brownell, 2001; IOM, 2006; Schwartz & Puhl, 2003; Wadden, Brownell, & Foster, 2002). Typically, these studies focus on television advertising targeted at children (Byrd-Brenner & Grasso, 2000; Hastings et al., 2003; Hill & Radimer, 1997; Kotz & Story, 1993; Story & Faulkner, 1990) and the dire consequences of such messages. Indeed, the belief in the effectiveness of televised food advertising is so strong that in January 2006, the U.S.-based Centre for Science in the Public Interest (CSPI), along with the Campaign for a Commercial-Free Childhood, threatened to sue Kellogg Co. and Viacom Inc.[3] for $2 billion for marketing foods "of poor nutritional quality to children under 8 years old" (CSPI, 2006). While CSPI was concerned about all junk food advertising to children,[4] the intended litigation focused primarily on television advertisements and children's programming, as well as the supporting food ads found on the Internet. CSPI's letter of intent to sue explains that "young children spend considerable time watching television and using other media, resulting in high exposure to food marketing" (2006, p. 4). And so, Tony the Tiger and SpongeBob SquarePants were (rightfully) blasted for promoting nutritionally poor food over the cable network.

In Canada, focus on advertising directed at children is equally strong. Quebec has a legal ban on advertising aimed at children under age 13, and CSPI Canada, along with Ontario's Chief Medical Officer of Health (Basrur, 2004), advocates that this ban be extended to the rest of the country. Along the same lines, the flagship report published by the Canadian Population Health Initiative of the Canadian Institute for Health Information (CIHI), titled *Overweight and Obesity in Canada: A Population Health Perspective*, recommended that children's media restrict "advertising of 'junk' foods during peak viewing times for children" (Raine, 2004, p. 55). It seems, then, that when it comes to questions of communication, banning television (or mass media) advertisements to children is the "best" solution for combating childhood obesity. But is it?

In a word, no. Certainly, it makes sense to limit televised junk food advertising to kids; but the most recent CIHI report acknowledges that "we do not know the impact on weight status of regulations that ban advertising to children" (2006, p. 83). So while the push to ban junk food advertisements to children is one strategy, this intense focus on both junk food and television/mass media can lead researchers to overlook other critical "spaces" and food messages targeted at children. Perhaps communication researchers should also be scrutinizing the *supermarket*, not only television, and, more importantly, the messages communicated through food packaging and the foods themselves. How, and what, food communicates is central to understanding children's relationship to food. As will be illustrated, this is highly significant to the question of childhood obesity.

SUPERMARKET FOOD AND THE PACKAGING OF FUN

The problem, in a nutshell, is that there's too much focus placed on junk food and mass media messages and not enough attention given to the marketing of so-called regular foods to children in the grocery store. Childhood obesity is not merely a consequence of consuming Pepsi and Pringles, and parents who trash the family television/computer in the quest to save their child from tempting junk food advertising still have to contend with the kid-oriented packaging found on the supermarket shelves. Most children make their first purchasing decisions in a food store—and they wield tremendous influence over product selection. Children can influence up to 80 percent of a family's food budget (Hunter, 2002; Roy, 2004),[5] so it is important to consider the types of appeals being directed to them.

The most striking part about children's food and food packaging is that kids' food is **fun food**—it is created and marketed to children primarily in terms of its play factor, its interactivity, and, strangely, its artificiality. When most people think of children's food in the supermarket, they think first of the cereal aisle, where cartoon characters grace boxes of colourful Froot Loops, Lucky Charms, or Mickey's Magix and the fun consists of watching one's cereal milk turn blue. But children's food has moved beyond the cereal aisle, and the play is becoming much more elaborate. A recent study on the marketing of children's food in the Canadian supermarket revealed that almost 90 percent of fun foods coded fell outside of the breakfast foods category (Elliott, 2006). Fun foods populate the dairy, beverage, and frozen foods categories; they can be found in packaged meals, fruit snacks, boxed crackers, and so on. Fun foods grab the attention of children with the use of colourful packages, funky product names, and cartoon iconography: they are strangely shaped and wildly coloured and may transform in shape, size, or hue. In the Canadian supermarket, children (and parents) do not merely select between Tony the Tiger and Toucan Sam, they are wooed by Chocolate Splat pudding, Strawberry Blasted Honeycomb cereal, Sourz Vortex yogurt, and Bug-a-licious pasta. They select from pink bug-shaped noodles, alphabet-shaped fries, and diamond-shaped "gushing" fruit snacks. And even more, they encounter packages that stress magical themes or bizarrely interactive qualities. For instance, the label on Kool-Aid Magic Switchin' Secret drink crystals explains that the beverage magically changes colour as it is stirred (plus it has a "secret" flavour). Quaker Instant Oatmeal Dinosaur Eggs contains mini dinosaur eggs in the oatmeal that "hatch" into coloured sugar dinosaurs with the addition of boiling water. Betty Crocker's Tongue Talk Tattoo Fruit Roll-Ups have "tattoos" painted right on the fruit snack (which kids can dye their tongues with), and Betty Crocker's Fruit Gushers are to be used as game pieces for the game printed on the back of the box. Even yogurt has entered the world of both magic and fun. Yoplait's Kosmo Koolberry tubes of flavoured yogurt glow in the dark—and the package instructs children to hold the tubes up to the light for two minutes and then "go into the dark to watch the tubes glow."

"FUN FOOD" IN QUESTION

Glow-in-the-dark yogurt, tattooing fruit snacks, and dino-hatching oatmeal. It is important to scrutinize these "regular" foods turned "fun" because the semiotics of fun foods—that is, what the food communicates—has significant implications for childhood obesity. These implications extend far beyond what is communicated about the food by television advertising or marketing. Two of the most important issues to consider include how the creation, promotion, and overall meaning of fun food has a negative impact on (1) children's overall relationship to food and (2) the ability to create reasonable nutrition plans for children. Note that neither of these issues pertains to television advertising or the use of cartoon characters found on Nickelodeon's cable network.

Children's Relationship to Food: When Fun Is a Problem

It is quite clear that, within the supermarket, many of the foods targeted at children and symbolically positioned as children's fare are defined in terms of their opposition to "regular" or adult food. Regular food looks like food—it does not come cut into stars or castles, it isn't wildly coloured, and it doesn't magically change hue or shape. Children's fare, in contrast, is fun—by definition, it is edible entertainment, to be consumed for reasons that have little to do with sustenance or nutrition. The whole point of fun food is its fun factor—whether it is yogurt that one eats in the dark or cheese strings designed to be peeled. The clear message is that food is primarily about play. Parkay's Fun Squeeze margarine (launched in 2001) expresses this beautifully—from the name (Fun Squeeze) to the colours ("electric blue" and "shocking pink") to the special bottle designed to allow children to draw blue or pink margarine happy faces on their pancakes, mashed potatoes, etc. (Who knew edible oil products could hold so much creative potential?)

What's obviously problematic is that the relationship presented to food is one that naturalizes the unnatural and is premised almost solely on entertainment. It is certainly strange that artificiality in food—generally considered to be a bad thing—is actually framed as a selling feature within children's food. And it is equally troubling that the behaviours believed to cause or support obesity in adults—using food as a distraction, eating for entertainment or sport—are precisely the behaviours encouraged by fun foods and fun food marketing. Appreciating the hyperartificial and eating primarily for fun certainly does not work to set the stage for a healthy relationship to food.

What about Healthy Fun?

Don't misunderstand: I'm not arguing that food should be dull. But the degree to which this food has pervaded the supermarket means that fun food can characterize every eating experience for a child. Marketers such as James McNeal, who penned *The Kids Market* (1999), or Martin Lindstrom, who co-wrote *BrandChild* (2004), would likely frame this as a triumph in kids' marketing. Scholars focusing on cultural studies of children's culture, conversely, might reasonably argue that fun food's interactivity and transgressiveness underscore the agency of the child. And as Seiter (1993) points out in her rich analysis of children's consumer culture, there is often something rebellious about the "children's world" marketed to kids. Purple ketchup underscores this rebellion (and affirms the world of the child) by its very difference from normal adult fare. But for those concerned about food and obesity, the fact that fun food is no longer reserved for special occasions creates some notable difficulties. Junk food aside, today's supermarket offerings mean that every negotiation with food can be fun: a breakfast of Lucky Charms and bright blue Kool-Aid Jammers fruit drink; a lunch of SpongeBob SquarePants pasta and Schneiders Cookie Kid Lunch Mate Fun Kit; and dinner, perhaps, of Buzz Lightyear-shaped chicken nuggets with Yoplait's Blu Arktik yogurt (which contains, as Yoplait's package emphasizes, "colour sparkles inside tubes!").

Clearly, not all of this food is bad for you. But a further problem is that, while fun food now spans the nutritional spectrum—from healthy to decidedly unhealthy—identical marketing techniques are used to cue children's foods to children and their parents. Squeeze-and-go yogurt tubes are great; squeeze-and-go pudding tubes (which employ the exact same marketing techniques) prove less than optimal. In the fruit snacks aisle, President's Choice Mini Chefs sour apple Zippy Fruit! (made solely of apples and concentrated apple and lemon juice) sits right next to Betty Crocker's Mystery Fruit Gushers (whose top four ingredients are sugar, fruit ingredients, corn syrup solids, and corn syrup). Both use the same techniques to attract children's attention—colourful packaging, cartoon images, bubble font—yet one product is definitely healthy, whereas the other contains (among other things) sugars, hydrogenated cottonseed oil, artificial flavours, and maltodextrin. Moreover, the names of healthier products—such as PC Mini Chefs Bug-a-licious! pasta, Zookies animal crackers, Funshines biscuits, and Wheelie Dealies pasta with meat—prove equally as fun as, and not particularly different from, the names of less nutritious products. (Why should children be able to distinguish that Funshines biscuits are good but Fun Squeeze margarine is a pass?) And while healthy food *can* be fun, if one cannot actually *distinguish* between healthy or unhealthy, then how, presumably, are healthy choices to be made in the first place? Bill Jeffery, National Coordinator for CSPI (Canada), argues that "nutrition is a credence attribute of food; it cannot be accurately estimated by consumers" (2006). If it cannot be estimated by parents (who also use packaging cues to select foods for their children), it most certainly cannot be accurately estimated by children.

Even the brands that make a pointed effort to develop healthy foods for children tend to reinforce an unnatural rapport with food. Does Yoplait *intend* kids to eat their glow-in-the-dark yogurt tubes in the closet? Or consider Loblaw's President's Choice Mini Chefs brand, which is to be lauded for its excellent selection of healthy foods targeted at children aged 5 to 10: it not only uses the "food as distraction" theme, but also prints a magnifying glass icon on the front of select packages to tell parents that the product "contains hidden vegetables". Here is a product that contains natural ingredients and good-for-you vegetables, and yet every effort is made to hide the natural and emphasize the strange—bug-shaped pink pasta, food recreated as mini-wheels, giraffes, or alligators. One might reasonably wonder why vegetables should be hidden, as well as the point at which one should break down and inform children that vegetables do indeed exist (and might actually be consumed on purpose rather than by accident).

The Confusing Nature of "Ethical Marketing"

Despite some excellent steps being taken in the battle against childhood obesity,[6] certain strategies may be of little help in winning the fat war. *Sesame Street*'s Cookie Monster, for instance, now sings "A Cookie Is a Sometimes Food," and in January 2005 Kraft Foods (U.S.) declared that it would

> shift the mix of products it advertises in television, ratio, and print media viewed primarily by children ages 6–11, such as many popular cartoon programs, toward products that qualify for the [Sensible Solutions] flag, and phase out advertising in these media for products that don't. (CSPI, 2006, p. 5)

In practical terms, this meant that advertising for products like Oreos, regular Kool-Aid, some cereals, and varieties of Lunchables were phased out of the American television, radio, and print media identified. And this step, along with the fact that Kraft offers healthy alternatives, is what management professor Karl Moore would classify as **ethical marketing** (2004). But the problem with this approach is also flagged when we consider the semiotics of packaging and the arena of the supermarket. While regular Kool-Aid, some cereals, and certain Lunchables don't qualify for the Sensible Solutions icon, sugar-free Kool-Aid, Alpha-Bits cereal, and white-meat chicken Lunchables do. Kool-Aid Jammers (made with sugar) aren't advertised, but Kool-Aid Jammers 10 (made with aspartame) are. Both packages prove virtually identical and, like PC Mini Chefs and Betty Crocker fruit snacks, Jammers and Jammers 10 sit next to each other on the grocery store shelves. But unlike the fruit snacks, Kool-Aid presents subtle variances *within* the brand. Brand awareness is for Kool-Aid writ large, and the meaning of Kool-Aid Jammers does not change with the addition of "10" (for 10 calories). Similarly, there is little meaningful difference between Lunchables Chicken Dunks (which qualify for a Sensible Solutions flag) and Lunchables Maxed Out Chicken Strips (which don't qualify). Children will be drawn to both. So although Kraft's senior vice president explained that "we want to help kids, as well as adults, make better food choices" through their revamped advertising policy (Mishra, 2005, p. A1), it remains unclear how the choice between Jammers and Jammers 10 creates a healthier rapport with food.

Examining the fun food messages found within the Canadian supermarket provides a more complete understanding of the social environment contributing to childhood obesity. It sets the groundwork for unravelling some of the more complex issues pertaining to children's foods, while remaining focused on important food "messages"—those of food packaging and the foods themselves. Raising questions about what children's food communicates draws attention to the unique ways in which play and artificiality have become selling points and key identifiers of children's fare, and suggests that the framing of food as hyperartificial entertainment and distraction creates problems for children's relationship with food. While the advertising of SpongeBob SquarePants Cheez-Its on Nickelodeon might catalyze a U.S. lawsuit in the aim to protect children from harm, a much larger problem simmers within the very meaning of children's food, which collapses both healthy and unhealthy under the same category of "fun" and treats every meal or snack time as an entertainment experience.

As Claude Levi Strauss famously affirmed, food is "good to think." When it comes to children's food, we certainly have much to think about.

References

Best, J. (1994). *Troubling children: Studies of children and social problems*. New York: Aldine de Gruyter.

Brownell, K., & Horgen, K. B. (2004). *Food fight: The inside story of the food industry, America's obesity crisis and what we can do about it*. New York: Contemporary Books.

Byrd-Brenner, C., & Grasso, D. (2000). Health, medicine, and food messages in television commercials during 1992 and 1998. *Journal of School Health, 70*(2), 61–65.

Canadian Population Health Initiative. (2006). *Improving the Health of Canadians: Promoting Healthy Weights*. Ottawa: Canadian Population Health Initiative of the Canadian Institute for Health Information.

Centre for Science in the Public Interest. (2006, January 18). Letter of intent to sue. Available at http://cspinet.org/new/pdf/viacom_kellogg.pdf

Chamberlain, L., Wang, Y., & Robinson, T. (2006). Does children's screen time predict requests for advertised products? Cross-sectional and prospective analyses. *Archives of Pediatric and Adolescent Medicine, 160*(4), 363–368.

Chief Medical Officer of Health of Ontario (S. Basrur). (2004). *2004 Chief Medical Officer of Health report: Healthy weights, healthy lives*. Toronto: CMOH. Available at http://www.health.gov.on.ca/english/public/pub/ministry_reports/cmoh04_report/healthy_weights_112404.pdf

Elliott, C. (2006, April 27–28). Marketing fun foods: A content analysis of food messages targeted at children. Paper presented at Child and Teen Consumption 2006, Copenhagen Business School, Denmark.

Harris Interactive Poll. (2003). Kid-fluence, the "nag-factor" and "pester power." *Trends & Tudes, 2*(8), 1–2. Available at http://www.harrisinteractive.com/news/newsletters/k12news/HI_trends&tudesnews2003_v2_iss8.pdf

Hastings, G., et al. (2003). *Review of research on the effects of food promotion to children*. [Prepared for the UK Food Standards Authority.] London: UK FSA; Glasgow, Scotland: Centre for Social Marketing, University of Strathclyde.

Hill, J. M., & Radimer, K. L. (1997). A content analysis of food advertisements in television for Australian children. *Australian Journal of Nutrition & Dietetics, 54*(4). 174–192.

Horgen, K. B., Choate, M., & Brownell, K. D. (2001). Television food advertising: Targeting children in a toxic environment. In D. G. Singer & J. L. Singer (Eds.), *Handbook of children and the media* (pp. 447–461). Thousand Oaks, CA: Sage.

Hunter, B. T. (2002). Marketing food to kids: Using fun to sell. *Consumers' Research, 85*(3), 16–20.

Institute of Medicine. (2006). *Food marketing to children: Threat or opportunity?* Washington, DC: National Academies Press.

Jeffery, B. (2006, March 6). Commercializing kids (PowerPoint slide 22). Lecture given at Carleton University, Ottawa.

Kotz, K., & Story, M. (1993). Food advertisements during children's Saturday morning television programming. *Journal of the American Dietetic Association, 94*(11), 1296–1300.

Lindstrom, M., & Seybold, P. (2004). BrandChild. London: Kogan Page.

Lumeng, J., Rahnama, S., Appugliese, D., Kaciroti, N., & Bradley, R. (2006). *Television exposure and overweight risk in preschoolers*. Archives of Pediatric and Adolescent Medicine, 160(4), 417–422.

McNeal, J. (1999). *The kids market: Myths and realities*. New York: James Madden.

Mishra, R. (2005, April 18). Push grows to limit food ads to children. *The Boston Globe*, p. A1.

Moore, K. (2004, June 7). Demise of the super size. *Marketing, 109*(20), 8.

Raine, K. (2004). *Overweight and obesity in Canada: A population health perspective*. Ottawa: Canadian Population Health Initiative of the Canadian Institute for Health Information.

Roy, S. (2004). *The littlest consumers*. Display & Design Ideas, 16(7), 18.

Schwartz, M. B., & Puhl, R. (2003). Childhood obesity: A societal problem to solve. *Obesity Reviews, 4*, 57–71.

Seiter, E. (1993). *Sold separately*. New Brunswick, NJ: Rutgers University Press.

Story, M., & Faulkner, P. (1990). The prime time diet: A content analysis of eating behaviour and food messages in television programmes and commercials. *American Journal of Public Health, 80*(6), 738–740.

Wadden, T. A., Brownell, K. D., & Foster, G. D. (2002). Obesity: Responding to the global epidemic. *Journal of Consulting and Clinical Psychology, 70*(3), 510–525.

Notes

Funding for this project was provided by Canadian Institutes of Health Research (CIHR).

[1] The point I'm trying to convey here is that the solution to childhood obesity isn't simply to place these children on a treadmill. One might intuitively respond, "what does communication have to do with the problem of obesity? Do words make people fat?" Words do not make children fat, but communication (as this chapter will reveal) has *much* to do with the problem of childhood obesity.

[2] Strangely, this study focused on the number of hours the television was on in a preschooler's room, regardless of whether it was being watched or not.

[3] Viacom operates the Nickelodeon children's cable television network.

[4] CSPI's letter of intent to sue defines advertising as "all forms of marketing in all forms of media and venues, including without limitation print advertisements, television and radio commercials, product labels, magazines, use of licensed characters, use of celebrities, viral marketing, websites, contests, premiums, incentives, toys and other merchandise, games, advergaming, sponsorships, school-based marketing (such as book covers and sponsored educational material), and kids clubs" (2006, pp. 1–2).

[5] Also see Harris Interactive Poll, 2003 (p. 2), which indicates that 84 percent of children surveyed (aged 8 to 12) claimed to "have an influence" on what groceries their parents buy.

[6] Banning the sale of soda pop at elementary schools provides one good example, along with the re-evaluation of school lunch programs.

Discussion Questions

1. What are the implications (positive and negative) of banning advertisements to children as a strategy to combat obesity?

2. Describe the marketing and advertising strategies used to identify children's food to both children and their parents. Are these strategies manipulative, as CSPI might argue, or does the world of "fun food" offer something positive to children that might be overlooked in the childhood obesity debate?

3. Researchers focusing on childhood obesity frequently point to our "toxic" food environment, which prompts unhealthy eating behaviours and contributes to obesity/ being overweight. Beyond televised advertisements and food packaging, what other questions should communication scholars consider to properly address the problem of childhood obesity?

4. Opponents of legal restrictions on marketing to children often cite the importance of protecting freedom of expression (of advertisers) and instead emphasize parental responsibilities to resist the effects of such marketing. Do food, toy, and entertainment companies have any responsibilities for the health or other consequences of their marketing practices?

5. Some people argue that media literacy training for children just lets marketers off the hook by urging children and parents to "learn" to resist commercial pressures. What is the potential for media literacy in dealing with social problems such as childhood obesity?

ISSUE 2

Toxic gaming: Do violent video games make children aggressive?

✔ YES

Teaching Children that Killing Is Fun
Rose Dyson

Rose A. Dyson, Ed.D., is a consultant in media education and president of Canadians Concerned About Violence in Entertainment (http://www.C-CAVE.com). She was also a co-founder of the Cultural Environment Movement at Webster University, St. Louis, Missouri, in 1996. She is an external research associate at the LaMarsh Centre for Research on Violence and Conflict Resolution at York University, Toronto; vice president of Media Council on Global Issues, Ryerson University, Toronto; chair of the Media Working Group, Science for Peace, University of Toronto; and a member of the executive board for the International Holistic Tourism Education Centre (http://www.ihtec.on.ca). She is author of *Mind Abuse: Media Violence in an Information Age* (http://www.blackrosebooks.net); coauthor of numerous other books, peer-reviewed articles, and book reviews; and editor of *The Learning Edge* (http://www.oise.utoronto.ca/CASAE). She has given numerous lectures and speeches, both nationally and internationally. Her expertise is widely sought by the media.

Countless studies have dealt with the impact on audience behaviour of exposure to media. Many have demonstrated that popular culture such as film, television, music lyrics, video, computer games, print, and the Internet coalesce into a seamless, pervasive, and increasingly centralized, globalized cultural environment that is drifting out of democratic reach. Medical and mental health experts agree that the voluminous data on television violence immediately transfers to violent video games. This chapter will assess the current debate over harmful effects from video games specifically and their impact both from an individual and a social perspective.

INTRODUCTION

Boundaries are disappearing between various forms of media. Advertising messages now surface regularly as product placements in print media, films, television programs, and video games. Yet, too often, each new innovation for our amusement brings ever more graphic violence and gruesome images of racism, misogyny, and other messages of depravity that are the antithesis of morals and values most educators would regard as appropriate for socializing the young.

Converging technologies, as well as content, fuel the billion-dollar video game industry, which has now overtaken film and television production in annual revenues. Last year, the two biggest video game companies, Nintendo and Sony, earned US$14 billion (Cameron, 2006). Financial analysts predict that, with the player base for them widening, video games will lead all entertainment sectors in growth over the next four years (Colbourne, 2005). Meanwhile, violence is increasingly being used as a cheap commercial ingredient because it sells well on a global market and translates easily into any language.

The ways in which these affect our health, community safety, foreign policy, and ecological sustainability are a growing concern. Fortunately, the message is spreading beyond the medical community and websites for professional organizations such as the American Psychological Association, American Psychiatric Association, Canadian Pediatric Society, and the U.S. Center for Disease Control and Prevention. As Andre Picard, reporter for the *Globe and Mail*, pointed out recently, the greatest public health challenges in this century involve slowly developing chronic illnesses such as cardiovascular disease, cancer, and diabetes. These are all lifestyle related and, in turn, profoundly influenced by media. What we see, hear, and read in the media influences how we live, what we eat, how we think, and how we act. Picard points out, "There are now, in Canadian homes, more TVs than toilets, and violent, sexually charged images are as readily accessible in most homes as clean water" (2006, p. A19).

But while there may be growing consensus that the topic of media is the major issue of our time, any moves to restrict the avalanche of advertising targeting children or the violent, blood-drenched thrillers marketed as video games to teens and young adults tend to be countered with cries of censorship, moral intolerance, religious fundamentalism, or all of the above. The popular assumption is that media literacy taught in schools will help students decode and deconstruct messages, enabling them to read between the lines and navigate their way toward responsible citizenship and self-sufficiency—together, that is, with input from vigilant parents, who are expected to provide round-the-clock protection if necessary, supervising the media diets of their children.

VIOLENT VIDEO GAMES

If, from a physiological point of view, we are what we eat, then from a psychological and emotional standpoint, we are also what we read, see, and hear in the media. Indeed, there is growing evidence of long-lasting physiological responses from ingestion of media violence, in addition to the host of better-known harmful effects such as desensitization, aggression, fear, anxiety, and attention deficit disorder, among others. New magnetic resonance imaging (MRI) techniques, employed for medical diagnostic purposes, have yielded evidence that when video game players participate in simulated violence, the heart rate and blood pressure rise, and brain cells that normally counsel empathy are shut down. Furthermore, these images are burned into the long-term memory, like posttraumatic stress disorders from real life events (Atkinson, 2004, p. F8; Linn, 2004).

Given this evidence, consider the potential impact of a video game like Manhunt. Any 12-year-old can easily assume the persona of James Earl Cash in this game, cast as the ultimate killing machine, with no clear indication of whether he is the good guy or the bad guy. Operant conditioning takes place when young people play these games, in which they are frequently rewarded with points for making heads roll and blood splatter. This conditioning is leading to what U.S. Lieutenant-Colonel David Grossman (2004) calls acquired violence immune deficiency syndrome. So far, we have tended to overlook the powerful educational impact of such interactive communications technology.

Occasionally, reports surface that video games help develop good eye-hand coordination and can even delay the aging process. But at what cost? And for what purpose? These techniques may be extremely effective and useful for military training and recruitment purposes, but is it appropriate to indiscriminately socialize an entire generation of young people into thinking that killing is fun? And to enjoy playing games such as 25 to Life, where one gains points for killing police officers and other law enforcement officers?

Indeed, evidence suggests that aggressive global marketing of American popular culture is starting to backfire. It appears that the makers of combat video games have unwittingly become part of a global propaganda campaign by Islamic militants to exhort Muslim youths to take up arms against the United States. According to American Defense Department officials and contractors reporting to Congress, tech-savvy militants from al-Qaeda and other groups have modified video war games so that U.S. troops play the role of bad guys in running gunfights against heavily armed Islamic radical heroes ("Islamists are hijacking video games," 2006). These officials have discovered that such games appear on militant websites, where youths as young as seven can play at being troop-killing urban guerrillas after registering with the site's sponsors. Despite such evidence, now available both from researchers and military personnel themselves, that popular culture is fuelling terrorism, in the dream factory, it is still business as usual (Defleurs & Defleurs, 2004; Dyson, 2003).

There are other indications that harmful effects from action-packed video games are spilling over into the community at large. One only has to consider the unfortunate death of a taxicab driver in downtown Toronto in January 2006 after being hit by two young college kids who were speeding along a city road, a copy of the video game Need for Speed Street Racing Death in their back seat. This tragic incident rekindled news coverage on the extent to which such games fuel the problem of illegal street car racing.

ANXIETY IN THE TEACHING COMMUNITY

In 2003 the Canadian Teachers' Federation published findings that one of the most popular games for boys in the younger grades was Grand Theft Auto; a series of violent, action-filled video games involving murder and prostitution. More than half the students among the 5700 interviewed said they had seen an aggressive act emanating from television, the movies, or computer games carried out in the playground.

The Federation also found distressing indications that children receive little or no parental restrictions when it comes to what they watch on television and which video games they can play. With this evidence in mind, it should come as no surprise to anyone that "baby-faced bicycle bandits" in upscale neighbourhoods are holding up gas stations using fake rifles and handguns or fatally stabbing each other over differences at house parties (Brieger, 2006; Freeze, 2004, p. A1), or that youth gang violence is escalating with gun shootings among poor, urban, black youth who taunt each other with trivial demands for respect.

Schools and community centres are now expected to fill the supervisory gaps left in the lives of children as parents work long hours to make ends meet. At home, parents increasingly rely on television, computers, and video games as electronic babysitters. As a society, we have largely abdicated our responsibility to shape the value systems of the young to large, profit-driven media conglomerates, yet we continue to blame the increasingly beleaguered and underfunded public education system for mushrooming problems. Meanwhile, evidence accumulates that violent, action-filled stories in video games and other cultural commodities are causing young boys, in particular, to show less and less interest in the gentle narratives stressed in schools (Fine, 2000, p. A1).

The results yielded by one teacher's initiative to address the problem speak for themselves. In 2004, Principal Mike Smajda at the Lemmer Elementary School in Escanaba, Michigan, launched an antiviolence program that has since been copied by other schools throughout the state. Administrators and teachers found that students who did without TV and all other screen entertainment for 10 days, and then limited their exposure to seven hours a week, displayed less aggressive behaviour and ended up with better standardized test scores. Some parents also noted an improvement in reading skills (Flesher, 2006).

COMMERCIALLY EXPLOITING KIDS

Children, in particular, are increasingly being targeted by aggressive, profit-driven marketing interests. Selling of lifestyle is now a central construct in the strategies of advertising industries. Themes in popular culture commodities often go far beyond the production of a film, television show, or video game itself. The result is that children form attitudes and values from a very early age, regardless of whether these involve sedentary activity, poor eating habits, or an inclination to resort to violence as a form of conflict resolution. Cereals, cookies, T-shirts, bubble bath, lunch boxes, toy guns, army tanks, swords, and laser zappers are examples of spin-offs from popular children's electronic entertainment. In fact, many children's television programs are little more than half-hour advertisements for these commodities. Infants, themselves, are now targeted by a growing market developed for Baby Videos. To date, sales of videos for children under the age of two are estimated at more than US$1 billion.

Professionals and activists have challenged this development, pointing to a lack of evidence that screen media is beneficial for babies and growing concern that it may be harmful (CCFC, 2007a). In the United States, a complaint has been filed with the Federal Trade Commission against the marketers of the videos *Baby Einstein* and *Brainy Baby* for violating section 5 of the *Federal Trade Commission Act* by promoting their videos as educational for babies. An appeal is also being made to the FTC to require that advertisements, packaging, and websites for all baby videos prominently display the American Academy of Pediatrics' (AAP) recommendation of no screen time at all for children under two years of age.

Susan Linn, founder of Campaign for a Commercial-Free Childhood (CCFC), instructor at the Harvard Medical School, and associate director of the Judge Baker Children's Center, says, "As corporations vie more and more aggressively for young consumers, popular culture—which traditionally evolves from creative self-expression that captures and informs shared experience—is being smothered by commercial culture relentlessly sold to children by people who value them for their consumption, not their creativity" (2004, p. 7). In her book *Consuming Kids: The Hostile Takeover of Childhood*, she provides countless examples of how consumerism as a value is marketed to children, and also how schools, themselves, are being modelled after corporations as marketers conclude that all roads eventually lead to the classroom. In-school advertising, which began to escalate in the 1990s, now includes, among other things, corporate-sponsored newscasts, field trips, classroom materials, vending machines, gymnasiums, walls, and whole buildings.

These trends are undermining the very qualities we rely on to ensure a healthy democratic citizenry. They promote materialism, impulsiveness, entitlement, unexamined brand loyalty, disengagement, and cynicism toward parents and other authority figures. Materialistic values are harmful, not just to individual health and happiness and sustainable democracies, but to the well-being of our planet. In this context, advocacy for responsible stewardship and care of our cultural environment is every bit as critical to our long-term survival as a species as old growth forests, clean air, and water.

THE VALUES DEBATE

The use of MRI techniques is by no means confined to the medical field. Anthropologists, sociologists, and neurologists, who study how we shop and why we choose one product over another, have helped spawn the controversial field of neuromarketing (Scrivener, 2006). Elaborate and expensive MRI equipment is now used to reveal subconscious thoughts and find the "sweet spot" in the brain that leads us to buy one thing but not another.

Clearly, marketers are becoming increasingly effective at zeroing in on our greatest vulnerabilities and exploiting them from a very early age. But it is not only the latest MRI techniques that are enhancing marketing expertise. The principles of child development, pioneered by Jean Piaget, Erik Erikson, and Lawrence Kohlberg, are now also applied to marketing and product development as industrial psychologists help the industry target children. Ways in which their cognitive, social, emotional, and physical development influence decision making, their likes, dislikes, activities, and insecurities are carefully examined in the cutthroat competition for market share.

The unscrupulousness of these predatory tendencies is underscored when one considers the implications of violent video games—essentially murder simulators—being sold to children. In Lieutenant-Colonel David Grossman words, "Remember that old point-and-shoot Nintendo video game called *Duck Hunt*? It was such a good marksmanship trainer that the United States Army bought several thousand of them" (2004, p. 79). Grossman, who has trained military personnel himself, is convinced that the extraordinary marksmanship skills demonstrated by teen and preteen perpetrators of high school massacres in recent years have been honed by playing violent video games.

Despite occasional court challenges and committee hearings involving the gaming industry, there is little evidence of change in their marketing practices. Referring recently to Sony's jealously guarded trade secrets at the 2006 video game trade show in Los Angeles, Scott Colbourne focused on plans for ever more pervasive appeal and influence in the world of entertainment. According to Colbourne, "It will have an integrated network service modeled on Microsoft's Xbox Live, which allows players to access content over broadband internet connections and communicate with each other. Sony showed families holding their own video conferences using the device" (2006, p. R1). Leading-edge new games promised for such family entertainment hold titles such as Stranglehold and Final Fantasy XIII.

Fortunately, these trends have spawned, among psychologists themselves, concern over erosion of their own ethics and governing principles, which are meant to encourage "contribution of their knowledge for the good of human welfare" (Ruskin, 1999, p. 1). A coalition of over 60 psychiatrists, psychologists, and other health professionals has asked the U.S. Congress for restrictions on "children-oriented advertising" (Teinowitz, 2004). A similar proposal is also before the entire European Union (Dyson, 2000; Linn, 2004). Such legislation already exists in many parts of the world, including the Scandinavian countries, the United Kingdom, and New Zealand. But legislation banning advertising directed to children 13 years and under in the province of Quebec has yet to be adopted in the rest of Canada.

The usual response from the media industries when criticized for excesses is a promise of self-regulation. But it is clear that self-regulation is not working. Instead, the trend is toward false and deceptive advertising with seductive claims that programming is educational for children (CCFC, 2007a). North Americans overwhelmingly believe that marketing in general harms children, and favour restrictions to protect them.

In the state of Massachusetts, lawmakers are weighing a bill that would ban virtually all advertising in schools, creating commercial-free zones from kindergarten through high school (CCFC, 2007b). Industry critics tend to be misled with promises of band-aid measures that do virtually nothing to restrict the growing proliferation of pollutants in the cultural environment. The perennial promise and adoption of classification criteria, for example, has little positive effect and may actually do more harm than good because the young tend to be attracted to products labelled "restricted." Once a product is released on the market, even if it is rated "mature," "restricted," or "brutal violence," it eventually ends up in the hands of those whom these labels are designed to protect.

Criticisms of media violence production and distribution are usually followed by industry-subsidized studies with methodology carefully developed to demonstrate that evidence of harmful effects is inconclusive. Consider the case of leading Japanese brain specialist Ryuta Kawashima following his release of findings that playing Nintendo games renders parts of the brain inert. He was not threatened with legal action but, instead, bought off by Nintendo, which became the leading donor to his research institute. In 2001 he told the *Observer* in Britain that a subdued prefrontal cortex caused weakness in the neurons, halting brain development and restricting a child's ability to control antisocial behaviour. Now, with Nintendo as a patron, he is not so certain and feels there is a need for more research (Cameron, 2006).

This familiar scenario ensures that the pendulum of public debate never gets beyond the issue of proof of harm and into policy. The onus of responsibility and accountability for supervising media consumption habits of the young is put on parents, but industry, itself, is exempt. In the past, we have observed these same trends on the issue of tobacco smoking and cancer. The result is a fertile climate for unbridled capitalism, nurtured by assumptions that nothing can be done to restrict ruthless, profit-driven marketing campaigns that target children, because of dangers posed to freedom of expression for us all. Politicians, paralyzed with fear of being branded as censors or prudish conservatives, tend to avoid the issue entirely.

One of the first lessons in media education ought to be that better distinctions must be made between individual freedom of expression and corporate freedom of enterprise. Diversity of opinion, a cornerstone of any healthy democracy, involves conflict in the form of competing ideas.

Now, in our information-overloaded, postmodern, global village, what we tend to end up with instead is fragmentation of ideas, with half-truths and propaganda slogans. These get framed in media spin that seldom leads to meaningful consensus, conclusions, or sound policy.

Addressing the toxic learning environment that violent video games foster and reinforce is long overdue. These interactive approaches to electronic entertainment have been with us for several decades. Many children who played them years ago are now in their mid-teens to early 20s, exactly the age group of the average crime perpetrator facing our law enforcement officers on the streets. Because of the ways in which violent video games make killing a conditional reflex through repeated stimulus and response, they are especially lethal. Play is children's work from a very early age, yet today we allow our children to immerse themselves in an environment where they repeatedly blow their virtual, hyper-realistic playmates' heads off in explosions of blood and gore. Instead of getting into trouble, they are rewarded with points. This is dangerous, pathological, and dysfunctional play.

CONCLUSION

The perils and rewards of modern life have been heightened both because of and in spite of new communication technologies. On issues involving freedom of expression and civil liberties, there is a pressing need for tradeoffs as these values impinge upon health care delivery, crime prevention, and the protection of children. Ironically, we subsidize the abuses of corporate media, not only by our direct purchase of these toxic games, but through tax shelters, privileges, credits, and production permits given out by the governments we elect. Ideological child abuse is now an integral part of our information-based, global economy because of the bizarre synergies inherent in the self-governing incoherence of free market forces. That needs to change.

The popular myth that complete freedom for the media means democracy and freedom for everyone else as well serves ever more powerful and fewer media moguls best. It helps to fuel global media monopolization, ensuring for them, alone, the privilege of deciding what the rest of us see, hear, and read and how we amuse ourselves.

References

Atkinson, W. I. (2004, March 13). Video mind games. *The Globe and Mail*, p. F8.

Brieger, P. (2006, April 20). Teen who fought Tanner tells court he didn't kill him. *National Post*, p. A14.

Cameron, D. (2006, May 13). Moving to the dark side of the screen. *Sydney Morning Herald*. Available at http://www.smh.com.auHome

Campaign for a Commercial-Free Childhood. (2007a, May 15). *CCFC urges cable companies to tune out baby first TV* [News release]. Available at http://www.commercialfreechildhood.org

Campaign for a Commercial-Free Childhood. (2007b, June 13). *Mass. lawmakers weigh ban on all marketing in schools* [News release]. Available at http://www.commercialfreechildhood.org

Canadian Teachers' Federation. (2003). *Kids' Take on Media: What 5,700 Canadian kids say about TV, movies, video and computer games and more*. Ottawa: Author.

Colbourne, S. (2005, November 22). Approach of new consoles has game makers drooling. *The Globe and Mail*, p. R1.

Colbourne, S. (2006, May 10). Gamers get set to break a sweat. *The Globe and Mail*, p. R1.

Defleurs, M., & Defleurs, M. (2003). *Learning to hate Americans*. Spokane, WA: Marquette Books.

Dyson, R. (2000). *Mind abuse: Media violence in an information age.* Montreal: Black Rose Books.

Dyson, R. (2003). Missing discourse on global media and terrorism. In D. Demers (Ed.), *Terrorism, globalization and mass communication.* Spokane, WA: Marquette Books.

Fine, S. (2000, September 5). Are schools failing boys? *The Globe and Mail*, p. A9.

Flesher, J. (2006, February 28). Michigan kids urged to kick the TV habit. *Associated Press.*

Freeze, C. (2004, May 25). Baby-faced bicycle bandits go down. *The Globe and Mail*, p. A1.

Gerbner, G., Morgan, M., & Sigorielli, N. (1994). *Cultural indicators.* Philadelphia: University of Pennsylvania.

Grossman, D. (2004). *On combat.* Millstadt, IL: PPCT Research Publications.

Islamists are hijacking video games, U.S. warns. (2006, May 5). *The Globe and Mail*, p. A11.

Linn, S. (2004). *Consuming kids: the hostile takeover of childhood.* New York: The New Press.

Picard, A. (2006, April 6). Media diet can affect your children's health. *The Globe and Mail*, p. A19.

Ruskin, G. (1999, September 30). *Commercial alert: Psychologists, psychiatrists call for limits on the use of psychology to influence or exploit children for commercial purposes.* [Press release].

Scrivener, L. (2006, May 7). The scientist in aisle 3. *Toronto Star*, p. D1.

Teinowitz, I. (2004, February, 24). *Report hits commercialization of childhood.* Washington, DC: AdAge.com.

ISSUE 2

Toxic gaming: Do violent video games make children aggressive?

✘ NO

Toxic Gaming? On the Problems of Regulating Play
Stephen Kline and Benjamin Woo

Stephen Kline is a professor in the School of Communication and director of the Media Analysis Laboratory at Simon Fraser University. In the last five years he has coauthored *Social Communication in Advertising* (revised edition), *Researching Audiences*, and *Digital Play*. He has also written 19 research articles and book chapters on a variety of topics, including studies of children's media and video games, family dynamics surrounding sedentary lifestyles, advertising and the consumer culture, children's consumer competence and media literacy, and videographic methods of audience research. His research grants include funding for projects on community media education, pharmaceutical advertising, video game policy debates, and studies of children's food advertising and sedentary lifestyles.

Benjamin Woo is a doctoral student in the School of Communication at Simon Fraser University. His master's thesis was on Canadian comic books and graphic novels, and he is currently researching subcultures associated with the consumption of "geek" media and cultural commodities.

INTRODUCTION: VIDEO GAMES GET THE ST. LOUIS BLUES

In 2000 the county of St. Louis, Missouri, passed an ordinance prohibiting the sale or rental of graphically violent video games to minors without the consent of their parents or guardians. Even though the ordinance would use the industry's own Electronic Software Ratings Board (ESRB) guidelines to judge a game's violent content, the video game industry considered it a form of censorship and a threat to its "right" to commercial free expression. The Interactive Digital Software Association (IDSA) challenged the constitutionality of the ordinance on the industry's behalf, turning the case into a minor *cause célèbre* for the video game industry. The subsequent court case considered two issues concerning children's use of media. First, are video games a form of commercial entertainment that qualifies for free speech protection under the U.S. Constitution? And second, since children are legally considered developmentally inadequate subjects, is there evidence of harm done to children from exposure to or excessive use of violent games?

Judge Stephen Limbaugh's decision recognized the need to establish whether video games constituted a medium of communication, like films or TV:

> It appears to the Court if an entirely new "medium" is being given First ... Amendment protection, there does need to be at least some type of communication of ideas in that medium. It has to be designed to express or inform, and there has to be a likelihood that others will understand that there has been some type of expression. (*IDSA v. St. Louis*, 2002)

But Judge Limbaugh was rather dismissive of the industry's claim to free speech, stating that the creative labour that produces video games is insufficient to qualify them as any more expressive than a game of bingo. The court also determined that there was sufficient evidence of harm to justify the county's interest in restricting the access of children under age 17 to violent video games. The ordinance was upheld based on the interests of parents who wished to control their young children's access to violent games.

However, a subsequent appellate court reversed both decisions. Judge Morris Sheppard Arnold's finding stated that, given existing precedents protecting other forms of entertainment, there is "no reason why ... video games are not entitled to a similar protection" (*IDSA v. St. Louis*, 2003). Furthermore, because "content-based restriction on speech is presumptively invalid," this judge shifted the burden of proof of harm to the county. While sympathetic to the concerns of the county with respect to "the right of parents to control their children's exposure to graphically violent materials," the court's view was that the evidence of video games' harmfulness was still not sufficiently convincing. According to the court, "The County's conclusion that there is a strong likelihood that minors who play violent video games will suffer a deleterious effect on their psychological health is simply unsupported in the record." Judge Arnold therefore determined not to limit the free expression of this new medium without more definitive evidence of video games' psychological harm. The video game industry thus remains free to make and sell violent games to children until there is definitive proof of harm, an issue that is still being argued in the U.S. Congress at the time of writing (Sinclair, 2006).

The question of whether violent video games cause violence in children is a topic of considerable public debate because these courtroom struggles reveal policy confusion about how to deal with the unintended risks of mass-mediated pleasures for young people. However, we find the intervention of a group of "Thirty-Three Media Scholars" who filed a brief as amici curiae (friends of the court) on behalf of the video game industry, arguing against the social scientists, the most interesting facet of the St. Louis case. In unpacking their critiques below, we seek to explore the methodological assumptions separating cultural studies and social sciences positions on the putative role of entertainment media in socializing youth and fostering aggressive behaviour. We do so by examining the amici curiae's critiques of the behaviouralist approach to the social scientific study of media violence, opposing it to the more complex multifactors risk analysis favoured by most contemporary researchers. We submit in conclusion that in Canadian courts, based on albeit incomplete scientific evidence, the precautionary risk reduction principle should be considered along with the rights of commercial speech in regulating the sale and circulation of violent video games—particularly in the case of very young children.

SOCIAL SCIENCE AND PANIC CULTURE

The growing controversy over **media effects** on children is often viewed as only the latest in a series of moral panics dating from Plato's injunction against youth reading poetry (Barker & Petley, 2001). Yet after World War II, children's growing fascination with comic books and then television drew increasing public attention from both cultural critics lamenting the loss of "high culture" and social scientists studying the effects of media on children. Because in most modern countries children are legally protected owing to their "developmental inadequacy" (Kunkel & Gantz, 1992), policymakers have turned to social scientists to help understand the potential harmful effects violent media may have upon youth.

Over the last half-century, sociologists and psychologists have wrestled with the complex questions of how children use and respond to entertainment media. In deliberating these questions, aggression has been a core issue, and considerable social scientific research addresses the question of youth media effects (Anderson, Huston, Schmitt, Linebarger, & Wright, 2001; Huesmann, Moise-Titus, Podolski, & Eron, 2003; Johnson, Cohen, Smailes, Kasen, & Brook, 2002). The majority of researchers have cautiously concluded that a "limited effects" model explains the evidence best. But according to the entertainment industries, this body of research provides no firm grounds for government regulation in the public interest (Minow & LaMay, 1995; Murray, 1995).

In spite of the industry's position and lobby efforts, protests about violent entertainment have not disappeared. If anything, pressure for legislative intervention has increased alongside rising popularity of realistic fighting, combat, and shooting video games. With bloody finishing moves and realistic graphics, games like *Mortal Kombat* galvanized public fears about the rising toxicity of children's media culture. Witnessing the mounting pressure on legislators, video game makers decided to create the ESRB self-regulatory code in 1994, which purported to make governmental regulation of the industry unnecessary by empowering parents to make informed decisions about which games are appropriate for their children. Yet, in the wake of a spate of schoolyard murders in the United States in the late 1990s, public alarm about media violence grew, seemingly in step with children's enthusiasm for digital entertainment. Researchers quickly proclaimed that the newer video games like *Quake* and *Soldier of Fortune* involve gratuitously graphic and gory representations of killing that position their players as active perpetrators rather than simply voyeurs (Anderson & Bushman, 2001; Dill & Dill, 1998). These mounting public anxieties prompted the U.S. Senate Commerce Committee to hold more hearings on the gaming industry and violent children's media in general. David Grossman, a media critic and retired U.S. Army officer, testified to his belief that violent video games, like the simulations used by the military, are desensitizing children to violence and breaking down the psychological barriers that prevent killing. Psychologists Craig A. Anderson (2000) and Jeanne B. Funk (2000) also testified that the scientific evidence supporting the concern that violent entertainment contributes to aggressive and antisocial behaviour. Once again defending their industry, IDSA president Doug Lowenstein (2000) and psychologist Jeffrey Goldstein (2000) both submitted comments for the record explaining that there is very little empirical evidence to support the claim that video games, in and of themselves, are harmful to children.

MEDIA EFFECTS GOES COURTING

Given the symbolic and legal role children occupy in contemporary society as "vulnerable subjects," it seems inevitable that children's fascination with simulated combat would become a focal point of struggle between media corporations and parents, teachers, activists, and researchers (Kline, 2005a). Yet breaking with social science consensus, in the St. Louis case 33 academics (including prominent media studies scholars like Henry Jenkins, Jib Fowles, Todd Gitlin, Martin Barker, and David Buckingham) took the stand in support of the gaming industry's *legal* position to dispute the claims that "there is a causal connection between viewing violent movies and TV programs and violent acts" and that video games "provide a complete learning environment for aggression" (Brief *Amici Curiae*, 2002, p. 2). Summarizing critiques of the experimental literature on media violence (Freedman, 2002; Goldstein, 2001), they argued that social scientists have "failed to prove that it causes—or is even a 'risk factor' for—actual violent behavior" (Brief *Amici Curiae*, 2002, p. 2).

Although the amici brief draws attention to the problematic assumptions of certain behaviouralist studies of media effects, it also confounds rather than clarifies the methodological and policy debates about violent games' impact on children. Without supporting the behaviouralists' claim that a causal connection between media violence and youth violence exists, we find the amici's methodological arguments about "scientific evidence" disingenuous. First, because social scientific research operates on the principle of falsifiability, most social scientists do not claim that the evidence *proves* the causal hypothesis but, rather, cautiously *reject* the null hypothesis, which states that there are "no effects." This methodological oversight is compounded because in preparing their brief, the amici relied upon critics from *within* the radical behaviouralist tradition who have argued that aggressive behaviour, not learning, is the only criterion for evaluating the causal hypothesis. If a child has more aggressive thoughts or feelings or plays more aggressively after viewing violent entertainment, this, in their view, is not evidence of "real" aggression. Moreover, if the effects of exposure to violence interact with other dispositional and situational factors, social background, neighbourhood, and family dysfunction, then such evidence is dismissed as confounded. This is curious, given the espoused opposition of the amici scholars to the quantitative methods used by many social scientists to evaluate long-term learning (and media) effects as simplifying and decontextualizing (Buckingham, 2000).

No doubt the early experimental media effects studies conducted in labs and lecture halls with adult psychology students during the 1980s are indeed highly problematic and outdated. For example, the observed effects of a 10-minute exposure to *Space Invaders* tell us very little about playing *America's Army* for 25 hours a week. The operationalization of violent content and aggressive behaviour that characterized much of this work is crude and often confusing, and experimental studies can provide only limited understanding of the complex attitudinal and affective processes that take place while engaging in imaginary conflict.

It is important to put this skepticism about research design into perspective. The Youth Risk Behavior Surveillance data for 2001 found that 33 percent of teenagers reported getting in a physical fight during the previous year (Grunbaum et al., 2002). Using estimates that 10 percent of aggression can be accounted for by violent media consumption (Freedman, 2002), this would suggest that there are roughly 1.34 million more fights each year in the United States than would happen without television's influence. The risk factors model acknowledges the many environmental and dispositional factors besides media that contribute to the socialization of aggression. It is interested

100

in both the circumstances that can lead some children to prefer violent entertainment as well as the circumstances, such as family mediation and peer groups, that can influence the way children use and interpret media. The causal hypothesis railed against in the *amici curiae* brief is, ultimately, a straw man argument derived from a legal rather than scientific evaluation of the evidence.

Perhaps most importantly, the risk factors model suggests that something can be done about youth violence. A natural experiment conducted by Tom Robinson in San Jose, California, shows the potential of this model. Robinson reasoned that if media use is a factor in aggression, then reducing media consumption should reduce the risk (Robinson, Wilde, Navacruz, Haydel, & Varady, 2001). He tested this hypothesis, finding that schools that received the experimental treatment—a media education program—not only reduced their media consumption by 25 percent but also enjoyed a significant reduction in playground aggression. Kline (2005b) has since replicated Robinson's findings in a Canadian study, indicating there are ways of countering risks of heavy media use through positive interventions in children's lives as well as by regulating their media consumption. Voluntary reduction of TV and video game use was found to reduce peer aggression and hostility in the classroom and to encourage more social play.

REGIMES OF TRUTH: TOWARD CULTURAL SCIENCE

No one will dispute the claim that the relationship between violent media and behaviour is "multi-faceted and complex" (Brief *Amici Curiae*, 2002, p. 1). Yet those interested in changing social policy must recognize that "in societies like ours, the 'political economy' of truth ... is subject to constant economic and political incitement" (Foucault, 1980, p. 131). In examining the amici's intervention in this case, it is important to remember that however well-intentioned, our quests for truth remain social discourses deeply embedded in the broader struggles over power in a politicized world. This is true of media effects researchers, and especially so when scholarly conflict spills from one " regime of truth"—the academy—into another—the courts.

The amici brief's conflation of legal and scientific notions of proof is particularly problematic. We particularly find that the rhetoric of censorship with which they and the IDSA defend gaming's special status among media industries is a red herring. After all, the county ordinance would neither prevent the industry from publishing any games nor restrict any adult's choice among these games; the only people actually constrained would be those children whose taste in video games significantly diverges from their parents'. So who is being censored here? It is important to recognize that not every instance of cultural regulation is tantamount to censorship. And more importantly, at least in Canada, children still have a protected status as "developmentally incomplete subjects."

Indeed, by focusing on the proof of harm that is required for restriction of rights in the public interest, the U.S. courts have completely ignored the legal issues concerning the vulnerability of children and the need for precautionary approaches. Video games, after all, are not political speech acts pure and simple, but cultural commodities sold in the marketplace. They therefore have characteristics of both speech acts and products. Whether a child has a right to fully participate in the marketplace that overrides his or her parents' interest in controlling that child's upbringing is an issue that has already been determined in the Canadian Supreme Court in relationship to cigarettes and advertising. Given Canadian laws restricting the choices that children, especially those under 12, may make in the marketplace for reasons of developmental inadequacy, precautions may be appropriate when drafting regulations of the rights of cultural consumption. Otherwise, we would have no standing to prevent children from smoking, drinking beer, and engaging in consenting sexual activities.

The 33 scholars themselves state that their opposition to the St. Louis ordinance "does not mean that youth violence is not a serious problem—or for that matter, that media messages do not have powerful effects" (Brief *Amici Curiae*, 2002, p. 3). Indeed, thinking about media effects is among the most difficult issues confronting communication scholars (Williams, 1974). Williams recognized important differences underlying approaches to communication studies. Although affiliated with the humanities tradition, he worried that scholars within the qualitative tradition were becoming overtly hostile and dismissive of the empiricist findings of quantitatively oriented social scientists. He warned that an ever-widening methodological divide stymied cross-fertilization of ideas. Williams instead argued for a hybrid perspective that would help address questions of social structure and determinant relationships while still acknowledging the diversity and agency of audiences who consume media in diverse social contexts and circumstances.

Unfortunately, the field remains split by the competing regimes of truth offered by the social scientific and humanistic approaches. The risk factors approach we have introduced has the benefit of allowing us to look for pragmatic ways to mitigate the worst excesses of heavy media use without requiring us to completely banish media from our lives or, in most cases, condemn children's taste choices. *Video games do not make children aggressive*, but there is evidence of risks associated with excessive use that Canadian governments must adjudicate. We suggest that prevention of aggression and bullying rather than censorship of media should be the central question media researchers pursue. This approach will help us to identify and manage those lifestyle risk factors that accompany so many of the market's pleasures—from tobacco and alcohol use to driving fast and playing violent video games. We hope that, moving beyond the straw man of the behaviouralist causal hypothesis, we will be able to reconceptualize how children learn with and about media in a broader social and cultural context. Only then will we truly be in a position to recognize the myriad ways that media affect the lives and social relations of children and us all.

References
Cases

Interactive Digital Software Ass'n v. St. Louis County, 200 F. Supp. 2d 1126 (E.D. Mo. 2002).

Interactive Digital Software Ass'n v. St. Louis County, 329 F. 3d 954 (8th Cir. 2003).

Irwin Toy Ltd. v. Quebec (A.G.) [1989], 1 S.C.R. 927.

Secondary Sources

Anderson, C. A. (2000). *Violent video games increase aggression and violence*. Available at http://commerce
.senate.gov/hearings/0321and.pdf

Anderson, C. A., & Bushman, B. J. (2001). Effects of violent video games on aggressive behavior, aggressive cognition, aggressive affect, physiological arousal, and prosocial behavior: A meta-analytic review of the scientific literature. *Psychological Science, 12*(5), 353–359.

Anderson, D. R., Huston, A. C., Schmitt, K. L., Linebarger, D. L., & Wright, J. C. (2001). Early childhood television viewing and adolescent behavior: The recontact study. *Monographs of the Society for Research in Child Development, 66*(1, Serial No. 264).

Barker, M., & Petley, J. (Eds.). (2001). *Ill effects: The media/violence debate* (2nd ed.). New York: Routledge.

Brief amici curiae of thirty-three media scholars in support of appellants, and supporting reversal. (2002). Retrieved June 25, 2006, from http://www.fepproject.org/courtbriefs/stlouis.html

Buckingham, D. (2000). *After the Death of Childhood.* London: Polity.

Dill, K. E., & Dill, J. C. (1998). Video game violence: A review of the empirical literature. *Aggression and Violent Behavior, 3*(4), 407–428.

Foucault, M. (1980). Truth and power. In C. Gordon (Ed.), *Power/knowledge: Selected interviews & other writings, 1972–1977.* New York: Pantheon Books.

Freedman, J. L. (2002). *Media violence and its effect on aggression: Assessing the scientific evidence.* Toronto: University of Toronto Press.

Funk, J. (2000, March 21). Testimony of Jeanne B. Funk, Ph.D., Department of Psychology, University of Toledo, regarding the impact of interactive violence on children before the United States Senate Commerce Committee. Available at http://commerce.senate.gov/hearings/0321fun.pdf

Goldstein, J. (2000). *Effects of electronic games on children.* Available at http://commerce.senate.gov/hearings/0321gol.pdf

Goldstein, J. (2001, October 27). *Does playing violent video games cause aggressive behavior?* Paper presented at the Playing by the Rules Conference, University of Chicago.

Grossman, D. (1999). Testimony of Col. Dave Grossman, author, *On Killing,* before the U.S. Senate Commerce Committee hearing on Marketing Violence to Children. Available at http://www.senate.gov/~commerce/hearings/0504gro.pdf

Grunbaum, J. A., Kann, L., Kinchen, S. A., Williams, B., Ross, J. G., Lowry, R., et al. (2002). *Youth risk behavior surveillance—United States, 2001.* Retrieved June 30, 2006, from http://www.cdc.gov/mmwr/preview/mmwrhtml/ss5302a1.htm

Huesmann, L. R., Moise-Titus, J., Podolski, C.-L., & Eron, L. D. (2003). Longitudinal relations between children's exposure to TV violence and their aggressive and violent behavior in young adulthood: 1977–1992. *Developmental Psychology, 39*(2), 201–221.

Johnson, J. G., Cohen, P., Smailes, E. M., Kasen, S., & Brook, J. S. (2002). Television viewing and aggressive behavior during adolescence and adulthood. *Science, 295*(5564), 2468–2471.

Kline, S (2005a). *A becoming subject: Consumer socialization in the mediated marketplace.* In F. Trentmann (Ed.), *The making of the consumer* (pp. 199–223). Oxford: Berg.

Kline, S. (2005b). Countering children's sedentary lifestyles: An evaluative study of a media-risk education approach. *Childhood, 12*(2), 239–258.

Kunkel, D., & Gantz, W. (1992). Children's television advertising in the multi-channel environment. *Journal of Communication, 42*(3), 134–152.

Lowenstein, D. (2000). Testimony of Douglas Lowenstein, President International Digital Software Association before the Senate Committee on Commerce on the Effects of Interactive Violence on Children. Available from http://commerce.senate.gov/hearings/0321low.pdf

Minow, N. N., & LaMay, C. L. (1995). *Abandoned in the wasteland: Children, television, and the First Amendment.* New York: Hill & Wang.

Murray, J. P. (1995). Children and television violence. *Kansas Journal of Law and Public Policy, 4*(3), 7–14.

Robinson, T. N., Wilde, M. L., Navacruz, L. C., Haydel, K. F., & Varady, A. (2001). Effects of reducing children's television and video game use on aggressive behavior: A randomized controlled trial. *Archives of Pediatrics & Adolescent Medicine, 155*(1), 17–23.

Sinclair, B. (2006, June 14). Congress holds at-times-contentious game hearing. *Gamespot News.* Retrieved April 12, 2006, from http://www.gamespot.com/news/6152736.html

Williams, R. (1974). Communications as cultural science. *Journal of Communication, 24*(3), 17–25.

Discussion Questions

1. Children are often at the centre of debates regarding media violence. Should children be treated as a separate category (distinct from adults) in such debates? Why or why not?

2. In your opinion, how successful is the Canadian approach to media regulation?

3. Explain the difference between "action-filled" and "violence-filled" entertainment. Is this distinction significant to the debate surrounding media violence?

4. Does the debate over video game violence bring new and interesting questions on how we might understand the role of the audience? Why or why not?

5. Identify and explain some creative solutions for dealing with excessive media violence.

ISSUE 3

Real beauty? Can advertising credibly promote social change?

✔ YES

Creating Social Change through Advertising
Karen Blotnicky

Karen Blotnicky, a professor in the Department of Business Administration and Tourism and Hospitality Management at Mount Saint Vincent University in Halifax, specializes in marketing. Karen is the Eastern Canada business columnist for CBC Radio One and the small business columnist for Halifax's *Sunday Herald* newspaper. She is the president of the Marketing Clinic, a family-owned marketing research and consulting company based in Bedford, Nova Scotia. Karen holds an M.B.A. from Saint Mary's University in Halifax. She is completing a doctorate degree in International Business at Northcentral University in Prescott, Arizona.

Can advertising credibly promote social change? It can. In fact, advertising, if skillfully employed, can be a powerful agent of social change. Dove's Campaign for Real Beauty is a leading example of a socially responsible yet highly effective advertising campaign that has facilitated a shift in our society's concept of beauty while also successfully selling product.

To begin, we will discuss of the impact of advertising on popular culture messages. Then, we will consider the notion of a beauty prototype, as well as how modern-day advertisers have defined beauty in advertising images. Finally, we will address the impact of advertising on body image, along with the need for social change agents to provide a more realistic and attainable beauty prototype, and examine the Dove Campaign for Real Beauty as an example of how a strong advertising campaign can effectively promote social change.

ADVERTISING, CULTURE, AND BEAUTY

In North America the media does influence popular culture. In some ways, it is a two-way street. Advertisers use cultural symbols and ideals to communicate with their audience, while trying to create a competitive edge. This competitive edge also involves defining beauty, giving it a corporate brand that is distinctive and compelling. In fact, to some extent, defining modern beauty has become a battle of the brands.

Modern beauty branding has always been within accepted parameters, or "narrow, stifling stereotypes" (Traister, 2006, p. 1). Those parameters may be framed as a beauty prototype. A prototype may be described as an ideal type used to categorize people or objects (de Casanova, 2004, p. 288). The North American beauty prototype has generally been youth focused, emphasizing physical attractiveness, and above all, thinness. The notorious Barbie doll serves as an icon to the typical standard of beauty. A U.K. study revealed that if the fashion doll were a real woman, standing 5 foot 6, her measurements in inches would be 39-21-33. In reality, women have only a one in one hundred thousand chance of ever achieving such a figure (Solomon, 2002, p. 8). American fashion models, often held up as examples of feminine beauty, are thinner than 98 percent of American women (Eating Disorders Awareness and Prevention, 2000).

In addition, this definition of beauty has been racially driven (de Casanova, 2004, p. 288; Redmond, 2003 p. 1), as Caucasian models outnumber Black, Indian, Asian, or Hispanic models ("Fashion Magazines," 2005, p. 2). A U.K. study revealed that many beauty magazines employ thin white women to represent various lines of beauty products; the whiteness of the model's skin is related to overall feminine beauty, and "lean, pure, radiant images of white women are imagined to be natural sources of light, beauty, (and an) entry point to a higher state of female grace" (Redmond, 2003, p. 1).

Studies have shown how the image of modern woman is tightly connected to the current standard of beauty. In order to identify how products advertised during commercials were related to the program audience, and in particular, an audience of postfeminist women, researchers studied commercials aired during episodes of the sitcom *Ally McBeal*. The sitcom was chosen for the study as an example of "television's treatment of feminism," which researchers asserted provided insight into "mass-mediated cultural attitudes towards feminism" (Crouse-Dick, 2003, p. 19). **Postfeminism** is the belief that while feminism was needed in the past, the battle has since been won, and that feminism is no longer required, or desirable, for women to achieve their goals (Hall & Rodriguez, 2003, p. 878). The study revealed that the ideal postfeminist woman presented in the advertisements had three distinct qualities: they were sexy, intelligent, and powerful. Sexy women were shown to be "thin, flawlessly beautiful, sexually ready, and sexually available. The ideal woman was also supposed to be like other ideal women: looking, acting, and owning the same items" (Crouse-Dick, 2003, p. 18). This advertising media sent a clear message: successful women are both thin and beautiful.

The beauty prototype that pervades modern media and most of today's ads is what makes Dove's campaign so compelling. In 2004 Dove launched what turned out to be a critical campaign for women's products in North America: the Dove Campaign for Real Beauty. Dove set out to be "socially responsible" by sharing a different view of beauty: one grounded in real women. Their bold move to sell a product, while also being socially responsible, has turned heads and has also had a ripple effect across the industry ("Fashion Magazines," 2005, p. 1; Thomaselli, 2005, pp. 1–2).

MEDIA'S IMPACT ON BODY IMAGE

Clearly there is a standard for female beauty that has been promoted in the media, and that both feeds and supports modern culture. But has this image had an impact on how women view themselves? If such images have had an impact on how women view themselves, what has been the outcome of that viewpoint? Advertising is designed to sell products. Can it sell products if the images create a negative viewpoint? The evidence indicates that not only do such ads sell products, but they sell products because they evoke negative self-images among women and girls.

Marketers insist that their advertising works. If advertising works, and if advertising focuses on the ideal woman with ideal beauty, then it should affect how women see themselves relative to that ideal. Criticisms of advertising have rested primarily on the belief that its impact on consumers limits their ability to think and act as independent creatures in the vastness of a consumer society (Miejer, 1998, p. 235).

One study revealed that women's moods and body images were negatively affected after viewing idealized body parts or full body images in advertising (Tiggeman & McGill, 2004, p. 40). Yet when presented with views of average-size or plus-size women, according to Halliwell, Dittmar, and Howe (2005, p. 410), female viewers actually experienced a drop in their levels of anxiety. Studies have also demonstrated that women automatically and spontaneously compare their own body image to those ads, and that when they do so, images of extremely thin women in ads have negative effects on a women's self-esteem, while images of less-thin women have positive impacts on self-esteem (Smeesters & Mandel, 2003, p. 6).

Studies have documented, as well, the critical impact that advertising has on girls because 42 percent of teens look to advertising for guidance about beauty and appearance, compared to 45 percent who look to their friends for advice (Comiteau, 2005, p. 31). In other words, advertising is pervasive and is seen as an authority on appearance. Experts maintain that "young people's sense of self and sense of societal norms are influenced by the media they consume, and that includes advertising" (Comiteau, 2005, p. 30).

DOVE'S CAMPAIGN FOR REAL BEAUTY

Unilever, parent company for Dove, conducted a study of more than three thousand women in 10 nations. The study revealed that over 90 percent of women were unhappy with their body image. An American study showed that 30 percent of 10-year-old children are afraid of becoming fat. The average model (the closest example we have of packaged beauty) has a body mass index of 16.3, which is considered underweight (Eating Disorders Awareness and Prevention, 2000, p. 2).

Dove set out to sell product through its ads, but with a twist. They embarked upon a campaign to establish a more democratic view of beauty, with a goal to expand society's beauty stereotype away from its thin, flawlessly beautiful, white, sanitized image. In Dove's own words, the campaign had social as well as sales goals:

> For too long, beauty has been defined by narrow, stifling stereotypes. Women have told us it's time to change all that. Dove agrees. We believe real beauty comes in many shapes, sizes and ages. That is why Dove is launching the Campaign for Real Beauty.

> Dove's global Campaign for Real Beauty aims to change the status quo and offer in its place a broader, healthier, more democratic view of beauty. A view of beauty that all women can own and enjoy everyday. ("Dove Launches Campaign," 2006, p. 1)

Creating the Dove campaign was a unique experience for advertising consultants at Ogilvy in New York. A creative team with a strong female contingent was instrumental in helping their male co-workers begin to understand what it is like to be made to feel self-conscious every day. Daryl Fielding, Ogilvy's global category partner, confessed that unlike their female counterparts, men are not bombarded every day with media images designed to make them insecure. The Dove Campaign for Real Beauty used a multimedia approach to communicate what healthy women really look like. Television ads, billboards, and the Internet showed photos of real women, not models, whom Dove scouted out in major cities. The photos showed real women in their underwear, wearing no makeup. Their bodies were not well trained or toned. They didn't even sport a sun-kissed glow. The ads also featured older women, awash with wrinkles and grey hair. The ad campaign flew in the face of modern beauty advertising by showing the real thing—a gutsy step for Dove. If the campaign failed, they would lose sales. If the campaign had a lasting negative impact, their brand might become associated with an undesirable female body type.

Is it possible to sell reality? One could argue that women don't want their real selves, that they are motivated to buy products to enhance themselves. They are buying hope, an illusion, a promise. Some critics felt that showing real women with rolls, cellulite, and the odd blemish would do little to sell a product that is intended to create the illusion that women can be something they are not.

Dove also came under fire for featuring body-firming cream as part of their beauty line during the campaign. Critics argued that focusing on such products was in stark opposition to Dove's real beauty message. Dove contended that such products can make women feel happy and healthy, whether or not they wear a size 2.

Marketing consultant Mary Lou Quinlan felt good about the ads from a personal viewpoint, but her professional side made her question Dove's ability to actually sell the product (Daniel, 2005, p. 1). Her concerns were echoed by Gerald Celente, another marketing consultant, who argued that "using the average person won't sell anything.… Do you want to see the floppy Big Mac that the fast food worker … hands to you, or the perfect airbrushed billboard version?" (Daniel, 2005, p. 1).

To ensure that their message reached a broad market, Dove combined ads with a multimedia message platform. They launched the Dove Self-Esteem Fund, a fund that supports programs to raise the self-esteem of women and girls. They also hosted panels in the United States to discuss the meaning of "real beauty."

Real Beauty: Success or Failure?

The campaign appears to have been successful. This success may be measured by focusing on several key areas of advertising impact: social acceptance, social impact, sales impact, and future use.

The most critical factor in advertising success is its acceptance by the target market. Arguably, a firm could have benevolent motives, but if those fall flat in the court of customer opinion, even the noblest of intentions will have little impact socially or economically. The social acceptance of Dove's Campaign for Real Beauty was mixed. In some ways, it was divided on gender lines. Women seemed to like what they saw, while men seemed to dislike it (Verma et al., 2005, pp. 8–9).

Social impact from the Dove multimedia campaign has been considerable. The campaign provides validation for women who do not meet the stringent criteria associated with accepted norms for beauty. It also affects educators and counsellors. The campaign has been noted and debated on blogs worldwide, and it has received press coverage in Canada, the United States, and Latin America (Lagnado, 2004, p. 20). The publicity given to the campaign provides a measure of its overall influence. The use of blogs, a popular form of expression among young men and women, illustrates that the advertising campaign had effects that reached beyond the popular press.

Over a million women have gone to the Campaign for Real Beauty website and voted on the images of the non-models. Hundreds of thousands have given the campaign a firm thumbs-up (Jeffers, 2005, p. 35).

Canada's watchdog site, the Media Awareness Network, has constructed lesson plans for teachers of various grades focusing on body image and the impact of the Dove campaign. This kind of activity is an important indicator of the impact such an advertising campaign has on modern culture, and in particular, on the educational establishment.

Other advertisers are also taking notice. Magazines are featuring more average-size and plus-size women in their ads and on their covers ("Fashion Magazines," 2005, p. 1). Nike also started using real women in its ads to attract women to their fitness apparel and the NikeWomen.com website (Thomaselli, 2005, pp. 1–2).

Fashion photographer Gabrielle Revere, whose photos have graced the pages of such hit magazines as *Glamour* and *Vanity Fair*, has received funding from the Campaign for Real Beauty in order to expand the North American beauty ideal. Revere is travelling worldwide to photograph real women from nations with living conditions far removed from our own. She has photographed women from China and Bangladesh who have had facial surgery. She is also seeking to photograph women who have survived the sex trade in South America and children orphaned by AIDS in South Africa. The proceeds of her work will go to support two charities: World Vision and Noah Orphans (Fuller, 2006, p. 1).

The overall impact of the Dove Campaign for Real Beauty in the United States was acknowledged June 7, 2006, when Ogilvy and Mather of New York were awarded the Effie, the industry's premier award for effectiveness in advertising. Ty Montague, chief creative officer and co-president of JWT, New York, keynote speaker and chair of the judging panel for the prestigious award, stated,

> The Dove campaign was the clear Grand EFFIE winner. It is a successful campaign rooted in a powerful human and cultural insight: that beauty has heretofore been defined by the media and is actually defined much differently by real women. (Lee, 2006, p. 1)

Future Use

The time has come to challenge traditional views of beauty and to introduce more diversity into promoting beauty products. Quinlan concedes that such real beauty campaigns may be necessary as the baby boomers mature and immigration changes the complexion of Canada and the United States (Daniel, 2005, p. 3).

This sentiment was echoed by Faith Popcorn, trend-marketing guru in the United States, who attributes such changes in part to greater social acceptance of ethnic diversity in advertising. Popcorn argues that greater acceptance of Blacks and Hispanics also led to the acceptance of larger buttocks and more facial hair, helping to dispel the sanitized white image of beauty (Thomaselli, 2005, p. 3).

In 2005 Dove expanded the Campaign for Real Beauty into Canada, recruiting non-models from Vancouver, Edmonton, Calgary, Toronto, Ottawa, Montreal, and Halifax to star in their ad campaign (Dobson, 2006, p. 4). They launched a Canadian companion website at http://www.campaignforrealbeauty.ca, as well as a Canada-based Self-Esteem Fund. The fund supports two organizations that assist those who suffer from such eating disorders as anorexia and bulimia, including the National Eating Disorder Information Centre and a Quebec-based association (Halpern, 2005).

Dove ratcheted up its advertising blitz by airing the first female-oriented ad during the Super Bowl and shelling out over $2 million for the promotion (Crawford, 2006, p. 1; Garfield, 2006, p.1; Lippert, 2006, p. 23; Thompson, 2006, p. 4; Wasserman, 2005, p. 16). The ad featured a young girl expressing her concerns about her looks and her image. It cut through the clutter of beer ads and male-focused media messages to make an impact. The impact was such that even Anheuser-Busch decided it was time to start focusing some of its splashy ads on women (Thompson, 2006, p. 4).

Dove celebrated its success by launching a similar campaign, using the same format, down under. The Australian Campaign for Real Beauty features various forms of advertising, a companion website, and the support of the Dove Self-Esteem Fund in Australia ("Dove Launches Campaign," 2006, p. 1).

According to Deb Boyda, managing partner of Oglivy, the firm that created the campaign, Dove's focus on real beauty has more than made its mark. Says Boyda, "We hoped it would draw attention, but it's been a lot better than we expected. The traffic and the comments on the website and the depth and connection to the idea that comes through in consumers' reactions makes it clear that we have touched a chord with people" (Jeffers, 2005, p. 35).

CONCLUSION

The Dove Campaign for Real Beauty exceeded all expectations. Not only did it increase sales, brand recognition, and brand loyalty, it has stimulated an international discussion of what real beauty is. And that was Unilever's ultimate goal behind the campaign. Dove continues to try to make this change a reality, and they are committed to the longer term:

> We know that working to change the traditional view of beauty is a monumental undertaking, and that it will take some time. We hope other leaders in the beauty industry will join us on this path. We hope that, five or 10 years from now, mainstream images of beauty will look and feel different. We hope that girls will grow up with a more self-accepting perceptive, less focused on trying to emulate an impossible model and more able to appreciate and enjoy who they already are. (Lagnado, 2004, p. 20)

So can advertising credibly promote social change? Clearly, if an ad campaign can create social change, Dove's Campaign for Real Beauty is doing it on a global scale, proving once and for all that advertising, if skillfully employed, can be a powerful agent of social change.

References

Comiteau, J. (2005). From Rosie to real. *Adweek, 46*(35), 30–32, 45.

Crawford, K. (2005, February 4). Sanitizing the Super Bowl. *CNNMoney.com.* Retrieved June 26, 2006, from http://money.cnn.com/2005/01/20/news/fortune500/superbowl_ads/

Crouse-Dick, C. E. (2003). She designed: Deciphering messages targeting women in commercials aired during *Ally McBeal. Women and Language,15*(1), 18–28.

Daniel, D. (2005, November 8). Real beauty = Real sales? *CMO Magazine.* Retrieved March 1, 2006, from http://www.cmomagazine.com/read/current/real_beauty.html

de Casanova, E. (2004, June). No ugly women: Concepts of race and beauty among adolescent women in Ecuador. *Gender & Society, 18*(3), 287–308.

Dobson, S. (2006, May 8). Dove still keeping it real. *Marketing. 111*(17), 4.

Dove launches campaign for real beauty in Australia. (2006, June 26). Retrieved June 26, 2006, from http://www.femail.com.au/dove-campaign-for-real-beauty.htm

Fashion magazines showing more body types. (2005, August 9). *USA Today.* Retrieved June 26, 2006, from http://www.usatoday.com/news/health/2005-08-09-magazines-real-curves_x.htm

Eating Disorders Awareness and Prevention, Inc. (2000). *From body image to eating disorders: An information package for health professionals* [Brochure]. Seattle, WA: Author.

Fuller. W. (2006, April). Moving images. *O: The Oprah Magazine, 7*(4), 62.

Garfield, B. (2006, February 6). The sell-out Bowl. *Advertising Age, 77*(6), 1–3.

Halliwell, E., Dittmar, H., & Howe, J. (2005). The impact of advertisements featuring ultra-thin or average-size models on women with a history of eating disorders. *Journal of Community & Applied Social Psychology. 15*, 406–413.

Halpern, M. (2005, February 14). Dove boosts girls' self-image. *Marketing, 110*(6), 3.

Jeffers, M. (2005). Behind Dove's "Real Beauty." *Adweek, 46*(35), 34–35.

Lagnado, S. (2004). Getting real about beauty. *Advertising Age, 75*(49), 20.

Lee, T. (2006, June 8). Ogilvy wins Grand Effie for Dove's "Campaign-for-Real-Beauty. Retrieved June 26, 2006, from http://www.ogilvy.com/press/

Lippert, B. (2006, January 30). Cleavage-free zone. *Adweek, 47*(5), 23.

Miejer, I. C. (1998). Advertising citizenship: An essay on the performative power of consumer culture. *Media, Culture & Society, 20*, 235–249.

Redmond, S. (2003). Think white women in advertising: Deathly corporeality. *Journal of Consumer Culture, 3*(2), 170–171.

Smeesters, D., & Mandel, N. (2003, March). Positive and negative media image effects on the self. *Journal of Consumer Research, 32*, 1–7.

Solomon, N. (2002, July/August). Still not good enough—from Barbie to Botox. *The Humanist*, 7–8.

Thomaselli, R. (2005). Beauty's new, er, face. *Advertising Age, 76*(33), 1.

Thompson, S. (2006, January 30). Marketers realize big game isn't a boy's club, soften up Super Bowl. *Advertising Age, 77*(5), 4–5.

Tiggemann, M., & McGill, B. (2004). The role of social comparison in the effect of magazine advertisements on women's mood and body dissatisfaction. *Journal of Social and Clinical Psychology, 23*(1), 23–44.

Traister, R. (2005 July 22). Real beauty—or really smart marketing? *Salon.com.* Retrieved June 8, 2006, from http://dir.salon.com/story/mwt/feature/2005/07/22/dove/index.html

Verma, P., Schoenleber, S., Douglas, C. A., Pleatman, R., Mainville, J., Chapman, A., et al. (2005). United States: "Campaign for Real Beauty." *Off Our Backs, 35*(7–8), 8–9.

Wasserman, T. (2005, December 19–26). Getting comfy in their own skin. *Brandweek. 46*(46), 16.

ISSUE 3

Real beauty? Can advertising credibly promote social change?

✗ NO *A message from Unilever*

Real Curves: Democratizing Beauty or Selling Soap?
Eileen Saunders

Eileen Saunders is the founding director of the Arthur Kroeger College of Public Affairs at Carleton University and has served as the associate dean of the Faculty of Public Affairs since 1997. Her research interests are in the field of social inequality and gender, children and the media, and media institutions and policies. She is the author of numerous publications concerning such topics as regulatory guidelines on questions of gender representation in the media, the role of violence in the media, public opinion and social inequality, and access of visible minority groups to news media.

We have become accustomed in Western cultures to the idealized images of wafer-thin supermodels and celebrities, much maligned by medical professionals and feminist critics alike. One need not look far to find these role models for the chronically malnourished: Kate Moss, the Olsen twins, Victoria Beckham, Paris Hilton, and Nicole Richie all easily spring to mind. But what happens when these images are seemingly turned upside down; when the images we see on the screen are of "normal" women: women with curves, women carrying extra pounds, women with wrinkles? Women, in short, who do not conform to the standard stereotypes of models found in advertising campaigns. Conventional wisdom in mainstream beauty advertising suggests that to be effective, ads for beauty products need to be aspirational; in other words, they motivate women consumers by holding out ideal images for them to desire. As one advertising executive notes, "The purpose of advertising is to create desire beyond what the product can actually deliver.... People are living lives of desperation; they don't want to be themselves" (Daniel, 2005).

If this is true, how does one make sense of a campaign that eschews the super-thin and airbrushed models and features "real women with real bodies and real curves"? In the following discussion we consider the case of one headline-inducing campaign that has done just that—the Dove Campaign for Real Beauty. Launched in 2004 with the promise to promote a more "democratic" view of beauty, the Dove campaign has spawned imitators and garnered extensive media attention. It has won industry awards for its marketing campaign and been hailed by both industry insiders and feminist critics. The obvious question that springs to mind is how effective the campaign is as social advocacy. Can advertising that challenges the traditional ideals of beauty serve as a catalyst for long-term cultural shifts in how we think of beauty? Or is this just another marketing gimmick with no real impact on the cultural standards by which women are judged and by which they judge themselves?

THE CAMPAIGN

The Campaign for Real Beauty was first launched in Europe in February 2004 and soon moved to Canada, the United States, and Latin America the following September. In 2005 the Asian leg of the campaign began, followed by Unilever Arabia's announcement in February 2006 that they were launching the Dove campaign in the Middle East. This self-described global campaign was initiated on the basis of a 10-country study commissioned by Dove and its parent company, Unilever, surveying 3200 women on their attitudes about beauty, appearance, and self-esteem.[1] The final report, *The Real Truth about Beauty: A Global Report,* argued that "authentic beauty is a concept lodged in women's hearts and minds and seldom articulated in popular culture or affirmed in the mass media. As such it remains unrealized and unclaimed" (Dove, 2004, p. 47). Dismayed that only 2 percent of the women surveyed saw themselves as beautiful, the report clearly blamed the media as a big part of the problem. According to the campaign website, Dove sees itself as a "starting point for social change" and intends to offer a "broader, healthier, more democratic view of beauty" (Dove, 2005). The other motivation for the new approach was more pragmatic—the need to re-brand Dove as something other than just a soap brand. This goal was tied to Dove's move into hair and skincare product lines, a move that required a significant corporate repositioning. According to a Dove marketing manager, "as soon as your product mix includes moisturizers that sell for $16 and toners and shampoos, it can't be this boring brand that lives in your shower that you don't think about. We really needed to make it a beauty brand" (cited in Okalow, 2004, p. 1). And so Dove as the champion of "real beauty" was born.

The first phase of the campaign involved attention-getting billboards and print ads featuring women who challenged conventional notions of beauty. Viewers were invited to cast their votes on whether these women were "oversized or outstanding," "wrinkled or wonderful," "fat or fab." The strategy seemed to work; according to the company, sales of Dove products advertised in the first two months of this campaign increased 600 percent (Daniel, 2005). Additionally, a Dove executive, citing company figures, noted that awareness of Dove as a beauty brand was up between 35 and 50 percent in the first year of the campaign (cited in Okalow, 2004).

These ads were supplemented by online panel discussions, interactive website programming, a travelling photo exhibit of nontraditional beauty images by women photographers, and the promotion of the previously established Dove Self-Esteem Fund, which partners with schools and organizations such as the Girl Scouts of America to promote educational initiatives aimed at girls and young women.

The second phase of the campaign began in the United States and Canada in June 2005 with the unveiling of a new line of "firming" products. Launched with a massive blitz of billboard, print, and television ads featuring six nonprofessional models of different size, shape, and skin colour dressed only in their underwear, the campaign generated instantaneous media buzz. These "real women with real curves" appeared on a variety of talk shows and were featured in press interviews sharing their thoughts on beauty; biographies of each were posted on the Dove website and they became overnight celebrities. The slogan "Stand Firm to Celebrate Your Curves" encouraged women to see their natural body curves as beautiful. In the United Kingdom, a national search, using the regional press, sought groups of so-called firm friends; in the end, Dove chose five friends from Portsmouth as their models (Unilever, 2006). The strategy of using ordinary women to sell beauty products proved so popular that Dove expanded the concept. In 2005 they launched a new line of skincare products and found a new crop of "real women" to sell their slogan that "all skin is beautiful when it is beautifully moisturized" (Clegg, 2005).

A third phase to the Campaign for Real Beauty was launched in early 2006 with the focus on self-esteem, especially for girls and young women. Bolstered by another commissioned survey, this one involving 11 countries and focusing on attitudes about self-worth and their link to unrealistic beauty ideals, Dove claimed it was now time to "walk the talk" and seek solutions to the self-esteem problems they found among young women (Dove, 2006). Dove chose Super Bowl XL as its venue for launching their new self-esteem initiative, with a specially produced heart-tugging spot featuring a series of young girls thinking about their self-perceived flaws over a soundtrack of a Girl Scouts chorus singing Cyndi Lauper's "True Colors." The intent, according to Dove, was to draw attention to the self-esteem problems girls and young women face and encourage viewers to get involved. This involvement apparently takes place by going to the Dove Campaign for Real Beauty website and visiting one of the numerous sites available to girls and interested adults: "Share your self-esteem building story," "Ask a self-esteem expert," or "Free our girls from beauty stereotypes" (which, if one follows the links, is done by ordering a free tote bag filled with Dove beauty products).

REALITY ADVERTISING?

If advertising is about grabbing attention, then the Dove Campaign for Real Beauty has been a major success. Their billboards had people talking, their "real beauties" were the célèbres du jour on talk shows in the United States, and most importantly, awareness of Dove as a concerned corporate citizen was enhanced. As one Dove executive described the company's intentions, "we really want to be *thought leaders* in this area" (quoted in Okalow, 2004; emphasis added). But is the campaign having any effect on the way we think about beauty? According to Silvia Lagnado, Dove's global brand director, the campaign will soon lead to that goal: "We hope that, five or ten years from now, mainstream images of beauty will look and feel different" (2004, p. 20).

In trying to look at the long-term effects of the Unilever Dove campaign, it is important to point out that they are not the first, or only, company to try the "real versus ideal" route. What some industry watchers see as the natural offshoot of the reality television trend has meant more campaigns that feature nonprofessional models chosen to represent the Everywoman.[2] Nike, for example, has its recent print ads celebrating "Big Butts, Thunder Thighs and Tomboy Knees," while Levi Strauss ran a multimillion-dollar print campaign spotlighting people from all walks of life, with the theme "A style for every story." Not everyone, however, is sold on "reality advertising," and some see it as risky. As marketing consultant Mary Lou Quinlan notes, in order to motivate consumers to buy beauty products, there needs to be some assurance of transformation offered: "If we're all fine the way we are, we don't need to buy anything. That's not what marketing is about" (quoted in Daniel, 2005). Adds another critic, more pointedly, "They'll come to think of Dove as the brand for fat girls. Talk about 'real beauty' all you want—once you're the brand for fat girls, you're toast" (Stevenson, 2005). It is equally true that not all companies are as likely to use a "real beauty" strategy; this choice depends partially on your target audience and your brand image. It is hard to imagine, for example, that Dior would launch a new skincare product with "Jenny the cashier" as their model. Their corporate positioning as a beauty brand relies on creating an aura of privilege and class that elevates the product out of the realm of the everyday.

Then again, we might ask, how unconventional or reality-based are these supposed new images of beauty? Dove claims to be challenging societal and media norms about beauty, but is it? We might begin to question their commitment to a healthier and more realistic definition of beauty by noting that Unilever is also the parent company of Slim-Fast, a diet product that clearly preys upon and reproduces the very anxieties about body image that Dove seeks to dispel. There is also the question of the nonprofessional models chosen to represent the average woman. Long before the Campaign for Real Beauty began, Dove had used nonprofessional models to sell their product lines; the novelty here was to make their ordinariness the focus and the selling point. The women, according to the company, range in size from 4 to 12, which, while closer to the norm, is still smaller than the average size 14 for women in the United States (Corbett, 2006). More importantly, with professional makeup, hair styling, and photography, they still represent conventional beauty norms. As one ad industry critic commented, "Sizes 6 and 8 notwithstanding, they're still head-turners, with straight white teeth, no visible pores and not a cell of cellulite" (Garfield, 2005, p. 53). These women look glamorous and, in the end, that is what they offer to Everywoman—the promise and the potential to look glamorous. It is the assurance of transformation that still draws us in, and in that sense the campaign has more in common with the premise of reality makeover shows such as *Extreme Makeover*, *The Swan*, and recent entrant *Cover Shot*, all which transform plain Janes into glamour queens. Ordinary women can be beautiful, yes, but only through the magical powers of cosmetic surgery, professional makeovers, or, in the case of Dove, beauty products like firming creams. As noted by one observer, "Just as reality TV turns ordinary Joes into stars for a day, so Dove's campaign elevates ordinary women into honorary beauties" (Clegg, 2005). This irony becomes even sharper when you consider that the beauty products launched with this campaign were a range of firming products designed to make those curves more pleasing to the eye. Dove's message is contradictory; if we are beautiful the way we are, why do we need to firm those curves? Well, apparently curves are fine, just so long as they don't jiggle and the cellulite doesn't show. Cultural critic Susan Bordo identified the significance of the firm body when she noted, "It is perfectly permissible in our culture (even for women) to have substantial weight and bulk—so long as it is tightly managed. Simply to be slim is not enough—the flesh must not wiggle" (Bordo, 1993, p. 191).

Media are often a convenient scapegoat for a range of social ills, and self-esteem related to body image is no exception. We know that all media are dominated by unrealistic body shapes and unattainable images of female beauty; the prevalence of these stereotypes is not the question. We also know that women of all ages in Western cultures express dissatisfaction with their own bodies and physical appearance. But, despite a series of studies attempting to measure body satisfaction, or more accurately, dissatisfaction, following media exposure to thin, attractive models, the empirical evidence supporting a direct correlation remains in question. In a review of the psychological research conducted in this area, Sarah Grogan (1999) found studies that pointed to a drop in self-esteem after viewing thin models, studies that measured no difference, and one that concluded body satisfaction had increased following exposure. In this last study, researchers found that the female subjects, who overall tended to overestimate their own body size, actually reported they felt thinner and less depressed following exposure to advertising that emphasized a thin body ideal (Myers & Biocca, 1992). Despite this, women have long been critical of media images of beauty, particularly in advertising, and demanded more realistic representations. But what evidence exists to indicate that more realistic models, even if they were to appear, would have a positive effect on self-image and self-esteem—the claim that underscores this campaign? One recent study (Smeesters & Mandel, 2006) had surprising results on this score. In an article published in the *Journal of Consumer Research*, the authors tested the impact on self-esteem of model size in four categories: extremely thin, moderately thin, moderately heavy, and extremely heavy. Contrary to conventional wisdom, they found that the participants in the study reported *lower* self-esteem after looking at moderately heavy (i.e., realistic) models, while self-esteem improved after looking at ads with moderately thin women. Apparently, reality—despite the hype—is not quite as inspirational as promised.

BEAUTY, THE BODY, AND SOCIAL CONTEXT

If it is true that "real beauty" does not win when matched against the ideal, how are we to understand this? Are women simply passive dupes of an oppressive beauty culture that they are incapable of escaping, despite the good intentions of sympathetic advertisers? The meaning of beauty in the everyday lives of women has long plagued feminist scholarship, which alternates between those who see women as victims of an oppressive beauty machine (see, for example, Chapkis, 1986) and those who describe the personal pleasures to be found in the pursuit of beauty ideals (see Davis, 1997).

Advertising to sell beauty products does not operate in a cultural vacuum; rather, it takes place in a cultural context that attaches a variety of social meanings and values to the body. This is not to deny that the economic stakes in maintaining a cycle of insecurity regarding one's body and appearance are considerable. The U.S. diet industry, for example, is worth $100 billion per year (Media Awareness Network, 2006), and its lifeblood is the reproduction of ideal images of beauty that nourish a sense of dissatisfaction and low self-esteem.

But that economic imperative alone is not sufficient explanation for the tenacity of these unrealistic and unhealthy ideals. Rather, we need to recognize that our ideas about beauty are tied into a set of cultural understandings that reach beyond media advertising. Therefore, to talk about beauty, body image, and self-esteem, we need to situate the discussion in reference to ideals that are attached to the slim, firm body, recognizing that these ideals shift culturally and historically. We are all aware of the oft-cited studies showing that as North American women have been increasing in average weight and dress size in recent years, the average weight of models has decreased (see Media Awareness Network, 2006).[3] In other words, the ideal is actually becoming more unreachable for the average woman. Nevertheless the rewards—social and economic—remain considerable for the slim and beautiful body in contemporary culture, fuelling a continuing incentive to strive for that ideal. "In affluent Western societies, slenderness is generally associated with happiness, success, youthfulness and social acceptability.... People who do not conform to the slender ideal face prejudice throughout their lifespan" (Grogan, 1999, pp. 6–7). In the face of continuing judgment of our character based on our appearance, our body becomes a project, a work in progress, with its look and form open to redesign and renovation. Even age is seen as something to be transcended in the quest for perfection, as an unending stream of age-defying products appears on the market. We become willing—indeed, enthusiastic—participants in the consumption of goods and services that will bring us closer to the ideal. "The more people attach value to how we look and what we do with our bodies, the greater are the pressures for people's self-identities to become wrapped up with their bodies" (Shilling, 2003, pp. 109–110). It is important to recognize, as well, the class undertones to this project. As Bordo notes, as early as the mid-1800s, "the gracefully slender body" was a mark of upper-class status for women (1993, p. 191), and it continues to be integral to the maintenance of social class distinctions and the aspirations toward social mobility.

We live in an era where individual choice and personal pleasure are trumpeted as the path to female empowerment. Described as "postfeminist" by critics, this position links a rhetoric of female strength and liberation to a strategy of consumption, celebration of the body, and personal transformation (Banet-Weiser & Portwood-Stacer, 2006). Describing this rhetoric, Bordo notes, "We're encouraged to believe that we can have at least the bodies, if not the lifestyles, of the rich and famous" (1997, p. 8).

So while the supermodel may have been displaced by the "real woman" in the Dove campaign, the beauty ideal she represents has not been displaced. We need to be skeptical of the seductive rhetoric of profound social change that we are being sold here. What is masked in the spin about "democratizing beauty" is that it continues to rely on a message of transformation through consumption, because "in the end, you simply can't sell a beauty product without somehow playing on women's insecurities" (Stevenson, 2005). Sure, Dove gains by positioning itself as a socially aware company whose feel-good values we can applaud, but it will not change how women perceive and experience their bodies. The premise of democratization obscures the fact that we are being invited to vote with our dollar. This is not a case of "celebrating real beauty" so much as telling us where we can purchase it.

References

Banet-Weiser, S., & Portwood-Stacer, L. (2006). "I just want to be me again!" Beauty pageants, reality television and post-feminism. *Feminist Theory, 7*(2), 255–272.

Bordo, S. (1993). *Unbearable weight: Feminism, Western culture and the body.* Berkeley: University of California Press.

Bordo, S. (1997). *Twilight zones: The hidden life of cultural images from Plato to O.J.* Berkeley: University of California Press.

Chapkis, W. (1986). *Beauty secrets.* Boston: South End Press.

Clegg, A. (2005, April 18). Dove gets real. *brandchannel.com.* Retrieved May 9, 2006, from http://www.brandchannel.com/features_effect.asp

Corbett, R. (2006, January 29). Dove's larger models spur sales and attention. *Women's eNews.* Retrieved July 13, 2006, from http://www.womensenews.org/article.cfm/dyn/aid/2617

Daniel, D. (2005, November 8). Real beauty = Real sales? *CMO Magazine.* Retrieved June 14, 2006, from http://www.cmomagazine.com/read/current/real_beauty.html

Davis, K. (1997). Embody-ing theory: Beyond modernist and postmodernist readings of the body. In K. Davis (Ed.), *Embodied practices: Feminist perspectives on the body* (pp. 1–26). London: Sage.

Dove. (2004, September). *The real truth about beauty: A global report.* Retrieved May 3, 2006, from http://www.campaignforrealbeauty.com/supports.asp?id=92&length=short&section=campaign

Dove. (2005). *Why the Campaign for Real Beauty?* Retrieved May 3, 2006, from http://www.campaignforrealbeauty .com/supports.asp?id=94&length=short&section=campaign&src=InsideCampaign_whythecampain

Dove. (2006, February). *Beyond stereotypes: Rebuilding the foundations of beauty beliefs.* Retrieved May 3, 2006, from http://www.campaignforrealbeauty.com/DoveBeyondStereotypesWhitePaper.pdf

Garfield, B. (2005). Garfield's ad review. *Advertising Age, 76*(30), 53.

Grogan, S. (1999). *Body image: Understanding body dissatisfaction in men, women and children.* London: Routledge.

Kellogg USA. (1998). New Kellogg's Special K cereal campaign speaks honestly about body image. *About-Face.* Retrieved May 25, 2006, from http://www.about-face.org/r/press/kellog020298.shtml

Lagnado, S. (2004). Getting real about beauty. *Advertising Age, 75*(49), 20.

Media Awareness Network. (2006). *Beauty and body image in the media.* Retrieved July 11, 2006, from http:// www.media-awareness.ca/english/issues/stereotyping/women_and_girls/

Myers, P., & Biocca, F. (1992, summer). The elastic body image: The effect of television advertising and programming on body image distortions in young women. *Journal of Communication, 42*(3), 108–134.

Okalow, S. (2004, November). Dove: A clean slate. *Strategy Magazine.* Retrieved May 17, 2006, from http:// www.strategymag.com/articles/magazine/20041112/dove.html

Shilling, C. (2003). *The body and social theory* (2nd ed.). London: Sage.

Smeesters, D., & Mandel, N. (2006, March). Positive and negative media image effects on the self. *Journal of Consumer Research, 32,* 576–582.

Stevenson, S. (2005, August 5). When tush comes to Dove. *Slate.* Retrieved July 13, 2006, from http://www .slate.com/id/2123659/

Tjepkema, M. (2006). Adult obesity in Canada: Measured height and weight. Retrieved August 1, 2006, from Statistics Canada website, http://www.statcan.ca/english/research/82-620-MIE/2005001/articles/adults/ aobesity.htm#1

Unilever. (2006). *Clever PR boosts Dove "Real Women" campaign.* Retrieved May 9, 2006, from http://www .unilver.co.uk/ourbrands/casestudies/dove_casestudy.asp

Notes

[1] The claim to be a global survey of women's attitudes is somewhat misleading. Of the 10 countries included in the study (Canada, the United States, Great Britain, France, Italy, Portugal, the Netherlands, Brazil, Argentina, and Japan), there is a decidedly Western focus. There is no representation, for example, from China, India, Africa, or the Middle East.

[2] An earlier campaign launched by the Body Shop in 1997, known as the Ruby Campaign, featured a robust doll named Ruby and the slogan "There are 3 billion women in the world who don't look like supermodels and only 8 who do." In 1998, in a campaign with language very similar to that used later by Dove, Kellogg's Special K brand initiated its "Reshape Your Attitude" ads. A spokesperson for Kellogg at the time noted, "Real beauty is being strong and healthy and accepting yourself the way you are—goals that every woman can achieve" (Kellogg, 1998).

[3] Overall, obesity rates have increased fairly dramatically. A recent Statistics Canada report noted that in 2004, almost a quarter of adult Canadians, 23.1 percent, were obese, compared to just 13.8 percent in 1974. In addition, another 36 percent of Canadians were found to be overweight (Tjepkema, 2006).

Discussion Questions

1. Both articles conceptualize a slightly different standard of beauty. Identify the two visions, and argue for the one you find the most convincing.

2. Identify recent examples of "reality advertising" campaigns. Do they offer a more realistic or socially responsible alternative to traditional advertising?

3. The Dove campaign is clearly targeted toward women. Do advertisers have a distinct strategy for targeting men when attempting to market products? How might this inform our understanding of gender?

4. Some observers argue that the Dove campaign is not really new or innovative—other brands (e.g., the Body Shop, Kellogg's Special K, Nike) have launched similar campaigns. Why do you think the Dove Real Beauty campaign has achieved more prominent success?

5. Dove's entire campaign concept would be moot if body images in advertising did not affect women's self-perceptions. Do you believe the campaign is a step in the right direction? Why or why not?

ISSUE 4

Representing race: Are Canadian news media racist?

✔ YES

Discourse, Ideology, and Constructions of Racial Inequality
Minelle Mahtani, Frances Henry, and Carol Tator

Minelle Mahtani is an assistant professor in the Department of Geography and Planning and the Programme in Journalism at University of Toronto. Her areas of research include critical "mixed race" theory, media and minority representation, immigrant audience reception of English-language television news in Canada, and the challenges facing women of colour in the academy. Her research has appeared in *Social Identities, Gender Place and Culture, Society and Space, Progress in Planning,* and *Ethnicities,* among other international journals. Dr. Mahtani was an associate television producer at CBC's *Canada: A People's History* and *The National.* She is currently completing a book about the racialized and gendered experiences of self-identified "mixed race" women in Toronto.

Frances Henry is one of Canada's leading experts in the study of racism and antiracism. She recently coauthored the first, second, and third editions of *The Colour of Democracy: Racism in Canadian Society* and coauthored (with Carol Tator) *Challenging Racism in the Arts* and *Discourses of Domination: Racial Bias in the Canadian English Language Press.* Her most recent book, cowritten with Carol Tator, is *Racial Profiling in Canada: Challenging the Myth of a "Few Bad Apples."* Professor Henry also maintains her active interest in Caribbean anthropology and has recently authored *Reclaiming African Religions in Trinidad: The Socio-political Legitimation of the Orisha and Spiritual Baptist Faiths.* Now retired as a professor emerita from York University, Dr. Henry continues an active research and writing career both here and in the Caribbean. Dr. Henry has been a member of the prestigious Royal Society of Canada since 1989.

Carol Tator has worked on the frontlines of the antiracism and equity movement for over three decades as an advocate, educator, and scholar. She teaches antiracism and equity in the Department of Anthropology at York University. Carol has published widely on the subject of racism and has coauthored four books with Frances Henry, including *The Colour of Democracy: Racism in Canadian Society; Racial Profiling in Canada: Challenging the Myth of a "Few Bad Apples;" Discourses of Domination: Racism in the English Canadian Print Media;* and *Challenging Racism in the Arts: Case Studies of Controversy and Conflict.* Carol's research focuses on analyzing the impact of racialized ideologies, discourses, policies, and practices across a wide range of institutional sectors.

INTRODUCTION

As this chapter will reveal, the Canadian news media construct and sustain racist discourse. As students of communication know, the media do not report facts and figures about the social world in an entirely fair or balanced manner (despite claims from some media organizations to the contrary!). We show in this chapter how **racism** is articulated through media discourse in a way that can initially go unnoticed but nevertheless must be questioned and challenged. We start with a discussion about the key concepts of ideology and discourse and then go on to closely analyze two cases of racist media discourse that illustrate our arguments. Volumes of research and the lived experiences of numerous racialized communities in Canada indicate that racism remains a systemic problem. The issue of racism in the media is particularly important because if we hope to develop effective strategies and mechanisms for contesting and controlling racism in Canadian society, we need a better understanding of how a society's dominant cultural images, ideas, and symbols are produced and maintained.

A significant body of literature documents media **bias** in the press (e.g., Fleras & Kunz, 2001; Henry & Tator, 2002; Mahtani, 2001). This research demonstrates that mainstream news media often characterize or *frame* **racialized** communities as "problem people" who pose a clear and present danger or threat to the dominant culture. Media representations of racialized people tend to focus on conflictual and confrontational aspects of ethno-cultural relations and social issues (e.g., so-called illegal immigration, crime in minority neighbourhoods, terrorism) rather than the historical and social contexts underpinning these issues (Fleras & Kunz, 2002). Racialized communities frequently suffer from both misrepresentation (i.e., they are described as threats to social order and well-being) and underrepresentation (i.e., their contributions to democracy are ignored).

IDEOLOGY AND DISCOURSE

Two key concepts in communication studies are ideology and discourse, and it is oftentimes difficult if not impossible to speak of one without the other (Purvis & Hunt, 1993). "Ideology" is a contested term, but it generally refers to the attempt to understand how social relations of dominance and subordination are reproduced in society. According to Hall, ideology is best understood as comprising a number of overlapping "mental frameworks—the languages, the concepts, categories, imagery of thought, and the systems of representation—which different classes and social groups deploy in order to make sense of, figure out and render intelligible the way society works" (1996, p. 26). We would push this definition of ideology one step further by noting that ideology not only helps us *think about* everyday social life in particular ways, but it also regulates social order by constituting the framework according to which individuals and groups *act on* the world, and how these thoughts and actions reproduce unequal relations of power and domination.

At the most basic level, the meanings we create about the world can be generated from abstract systems of language, and while we can make sense of the world only through language, the ways in which words are used and the manner by which arguments are constructed have always resulted from historical changes and social conflicts (O'Sullivan, Hartley, Saunders, Montgomery, & Fiske, 1994, pp. 92–95). For example, we no longer use racially pejorative terms to describe certain ethno-cultural groups because those groups have effectively mobilized to argue and convince others that these terms are inappropriate and offensive. **Discourse**, which entail forms of language that express ideological values and beliefs, not only articulates the social and cultural experiences of people but actually defines and helps construct public attitudes and experiences in specific ways. In this regard, our use of discourse is informed by an interest in understanding how the values and beliefs we normalize as just, rational, and acceptable are formed and justified by and through the media.

It is important to examine the discursive dimensions of ideology because discourse is oftentimes politicized in the sense that it expresses concepts of power that reflect the interests of ruling authorities. Journalists and other opinion shapers and cultural producers use words and phrases in ways that often conceal or naturalize particular ideological perspectives, presenting the interests of ruling groups as the interests of all. For example, using the word "riot" to describe unrest or a political demonstration often justifies violent responses from police to otherwise nonviolent protests, and the almost ubiquitous use of the term "terrorist" when "freedom fighter" might be more accurate can help justify oppressive state policies that unfairly target certain minority groups for intensified surveillance. As these examples and the analyses we present below illustrate, words are not innocent—rather, they are loaded with meanings and histories that hold and reproduce inequalities in power.

Our approach to the study of ideology and discourse draws on a framework known as **critical discourse analysis (CDA)**, a research strategy that explores the way social power, dominance, and inequality are produced, reproduced, and resisted in our everyday text and talk. CDA not only attempts to reveal or deconstruct the ideological messages contained in discourse, but it also emphasizes the specific linguistic techniques writers use to help make their case. CDA is helpful, according to van Dijk (1998), because it allows us to see how the historical, cultural, and political contexts of language use and communication affect the content, meanings, and structures of a particular text (e.g., a news report). Most importantly, CDA is a strategy that allows the researcher to advance a change-oriented agenda (Kress, 1990). Many critical discourse analysts (including the authors of this chapter) are motivated by a desire to challenge dominant ways of interpreting and understanding the social world and to articulate new possibilities and more democratic ways of thinking and acting.

RACIALIZATION IN THE NEWS

Our research on racialization in the news has demonstrated over and again that the images of ethno-racial communities portrayed in the news and other cultural products are not the kinds of images these groups would use to portray themselves. Whereas individuals and groups from the dominant white Euro-Canadian culture tend to feel secure in how images of their communities are represented, racialized communities do not have a similar luxury. Rather, as a result of their all-too-real experiences of marginalization and exclusion, members of these social groups are often sensitive to these negative portrayals of their appearances, values, and belief systems, and they are acutely aware of how these representations reproduce symbolic and material inequalities. The cases we discuss here illustrate the power of their discontentment and frustration.

Case 1: Parliamentarian/RCMP Officer Assaults First Nations Woman

This case is about Jack Ramsay, who, while serving as a member of Parliament under the Reform Party of Canada in 1999, was accused by a Native woman of having assaulted her 30 years earlier when he was an RCMP officer in rural Saskatchewan near the reserve where she lived. It is a particularly compelling case not only because Ramsay was eventually indicted on the charges, but also because the news media covering the accusations, the trial, and its aftermath relied heavily on and helped to construct a racialized discourse.

The *Globe and Mail* dispatched reporter Erin Anderssen to cover the case at the outset of the trial. The first story, which appeared on the front page on November 22, 1999, began like this,

> The native reserve of Pelican Narrows was no dream posting for a veteran in 1969. The 600 Crees who lived there, crammed into log shacks on the rocky brush sloping up from the lake, made do without running water or telephones.
>
> The Roman Catholics lived on the west side, the Anglicans on the east; at one time, they would meet in the middle to fight with slingshots.
>
> A gravel road had reached the village two years earlier, but the nearest town, Flin Flon, was 120 kilometres away.
>
> White trappers had named the town after the pelicans that flocked to the bay in summer. The Crees call it "Narrows of Fear," after an old battle.
>
> Ramsay arrived in 1969 to be the RCMP corporal in charge of a two-man detachment. He was 32 years old, still a year away from marrying his wife, Glenna, two decades from his first run at politics.
>
> He'd been a Mountie for 12 years, lured off his father's Alberta farm by the "fair and square" postcard image of the red serge. He'd served in about a dozen small communities across Manitoba and Saskatchewan.

To the casual reader a racialized discourse is difficult to detect, but a closer reading reveals some important lessons about the nature of ideology, discourse, and racialization. First, the trial was about an alleged sexual assault by Ramsay, yet the first four paragraphs of the front-page article in the country's premier daily newspaper focus primarily on the problems in the Native community where the accused was stationed. In other words, the article is *fronted* with a description of the community that relies heavily on a series of stereotypes about Native communities.

Most obviously, poverty is presented graphically in the phrase "crammed into log shacks." The presence of the verb "crammed" suggests a shortage of housing space, and the noun "shack" is used instead of "house" or "building." That the villagers also made do without "running water or telephones" highlights further their level of economic deprivation and lack of technological sophistication.

The hostility between Catholics and Protestants is also present: they lived in separate parts of the village, and "at one time, they would meet in the middle to fight with slingshots." No attribution or source is offered for this putative historical fact, making the assertion practically incontrovertible. The next paragraph reinforces the isolation of the village, and the subsequent paragraph, which indicates the Cree name of the village, "Narrows of Fear," suggests the presence of aggression and violence. Thus, within a few lead paragraphs, the *Globe* writer has stereotyped the Native community of Pelican Narrows as impoverished, isolated, given to religious factionalism, and prone to violence. The only stereotype missing is that of the "drunken Indian," but that would come later in the article.

Presumably, the writer is making these points to establish that Pelican Narrows is "no dream post'" for a Mountie. The hardship of the social and physical environment is beginning to emerge as the context (some may say the excuse) for Ramsay's behaviour, which, after all, is what was really on trial.

After discussing Ramsay's arrival and describing something about his personal life, the writer then details how Ramsay would later become a strong critic of the RCMP, eventually leaving the force. The paragraph that continues on the article overleaf (A2) notes, "He would later write publicly about the Mounties who walked into reserve homes without knocking, who used drunken Indians to pad their arrest statistics." The writer is making the point here that Ramsay would become a critic of the RCMP, but she still manages to slip the "drunken Indian" into the report without questioning or contextualizing it at all (such as with the use of quotation marks). The full complement of commonly held stereotypes against Native people is now complete.

It is worth noting that toward the end of this very long lead story, Ramsay's article condemning the RCMP (published by *Maclean's* in 1972) is cited at length. In the original article, Ramsay offered several reasons for leaving the force, but the parts reproduced in the *Globe* highlight one particular criticism that is especially noteworthy. As the *Globe* writer notes, Ramsay wrote "about a close friend who was prosecuted internally for having an extra marital affair with a 16-year-old native girl" (an act he "could not condone"), and then he also recalled "a similar story about a native constable accused of getting a white girl pregnant—charges he says were hushed up "because if an Indian was discharged, people might think the force was prejudiced." In citing this particular incident, the article reinforces Ramsay's ideological perspective that Native constables were treated better because the Mounties feared being labelled prejudiced in an era marked by political correctness.

This lead story about accusations of sexual violence committed by a Canadian political official was saturated with stereotypes of Native people and counterposed with personal insights into the "life of the man" accused. In addition to starting on the front page and covering *all* of page A2, the article included two photos of Ramsay (the first in full colour as a young RCMP constable, and the second showing him in the present day) and documented in great detail his long history of service to his country as both a law-and-order official and a parliamentarian. While it is also true that the coverage did not necessarily celebrate Ramsay or condone the actions he was accused of having committed, not a single positive image of Native life was presented in any of the reporting.

We have discussed just the opening story of this topic for illustrative purposes. However, the body of coverage about the Ramsay affair by the *Globe and Mail* drew on a common stock of Native stereotypes that helped construct and reproduce a negative image of Native people as drunken, poor, drug addicted, violent, and hostile. In this regard, the discourse conformed to previous research that has found most coverage in the mainstream news media constructs images of Aboriginal people as a significant threat to social order (e.g., Roth, Nelson, & Kasennahaw, 1995). Nowhere in any of the articles was the context for the deprivation of life in Native communities, which is the legacy of Euro-Canadian colonialism (i.e., the enforced reserve system, residential schools), discussed, nor were the contributions First Nations people have made to the development of Canadian democracy.

Case 2: Globe Columnist Frames Muslims as Terrorists

In June 2006, shortly after the RCMP announced they had uncovered an alleged terrorist plot to attack targets in Southern Ontario involving several Canadian-born Muslim youths, *Globe and Mail* columnist Christie Blatchford wrote a contentious column that in effect painted peaceful, law-abiding Muslims in Canada with the now common brush of terrorism (see Appendix, page 129). As a columnist, it is Blatchford's job to write provocative pieces that will generate discussion and debate. In this regard, it can be argued that while many journalists attempt to hide or bracket their own ideological perspectives (through such strategies as quoting competing sources, attempting to be fair and balanced), columnists write from an explicitly ideological perspective. As Greenberg argues, news columnists produce overtly biased viewpoints that not only take sides by evaluating events, but also explain events in ways that have to do first and foremost with the attribution of responsibility: "they are primarily, but not exclusively blame-oriented and, as such, they attempt to mobilize and enrol newsreaders around particular ideological positions by resonating in ways that will connect with their ethics and emotions" (2000, p. 521).

In her column, provocatively titled "Ignoring the Biggest Elephant in the Room," Blatchford presents a negative portrayal of Muslims in Canada and draws the seemingly inevitable conclusion that Muslims are terrorists with no place in our society. It is an ideology based on a process of "othering," where Muslims ("they") are envisioned as a foreign threat that should not be permitted or encouraged to join the rest of "us" in Canadian society. The events of September 11 have cast Muslims as both aggressors and victims, and on the whole they have been universally demonized (Poole, 2002). The "us/them" dichotomy not only inferiorizes Muslims as a homogeneous social group, but it also places them at the borders of criminality (Karim, 2000).

The first paragraph begins with a strong insult by describing what was said at the news conference at the Islamic Foundation of Toronto as "horse manure" on which she might have floated home. She then describes the "bald reassurances" offered by those present at the conference that faith and religion had nothing to do with the arrest of the men. By including the descriptor "bald," the writer uses the linguistic technique of *reversing* to make the point that these are thin or transparent assurances, implying that those who made them did so only for the sake of appearances. The *repetition* of the word "nothing" adds evens more emphasis to their insincerity. This paragraph also contains *hyperbolic* language, in that the plot was "busted open" by police. The last sentence makes use of heavy *irony* when the writer wonders if the mainstream media had lied or whether she has a demented brain, because the men were "all, well, Muslims." By the intervening interjection of "well" she focuses attention on the noun "Muslim." She continues with *irony*, noting that she checked and "they are all Muslims," which allows her to again *emphasize* the identification of the men. In describing the 15 arrested men, she notes with deliberate *irony* again that two were "conveniently … in the joint on gun charges." Thus, she alerts the reader to the fact that at least two of them were familiar with the technology of violence by identifying the nature of their previous offence.

Ponderous *hyperbole* is used to describe the reaction to their arrest, when she writes of "the great Canadian self-delusion machine." The writer's aim here is to inform the reader that although the young men had the materials—described in detail—to make bombs, and thus posed a threat, the delusion machine (a thinly veiled snipe at official multicultural policy and the judicial system) tells us that it is really the system that is at fault. Here, "blame the victim"–type thinking is *reversed*. They are "innocent until proved otherwise and probably innocent and, if convicted" demonstrates a torturous illogicality, the aim of which is to blame the justice system, the only legitimate institution in society developed to deal with illegal behaviour.

The writer does not pursue this "logic" but moves on to describe the breaking of windows that took place at a mosque after the arrest of the men. These "vandals" whom she facetiously describes as "crazed right-wing conservatives, or maybe the Jews" present the real danger to society. Again, a *blame the victim in reverse schema* is used to denigrate what the police chief and others mentioned at the press conference. *Stereotypic* thinking is evident in her choice of suspects because it could only be right-wingers or Jews who would have broken the windows of a mosque. And when Chief Blair is quoted as saying that hatred, violence, and property damage will not be tolerated, the writer *demeans and mocks* his statement, asserting that windows everywhere will be safe and "the war on windows will be won." This demonstrates a well-known linguistic strategy of *trivialization*. Important incidents are thus minimized and mocked (who wages wars on windows?) to the point where they become material for inappropriate humour.

This tactic is again used in the following paragraphs where she quotes the description of the arrested men given by police ("students, employed, unemployed") as "running the gamut from A to, oh C" and ends with "blah, blah, blah." And in case the reader has missed the point, the interjection "oh" is used. The writer reverts back to *irony* when she writes that she already knew them to be Muslims, perhaps because she is a trained observer, "or you know, because I have eyes." This implies, of course, that only a fool could not see the truth about what's really going on.

In the next paragraph, the writer moves back to the arrested men and takes her argument to a new level, invoking *cultural* arguments to support her contention that the police and others should have clearly identified them as Muslims. The main tactic here is *mockery* and the cultural presentation of them as the "other." In describing the men, she ridicules the frequent use of Mohamed for their first, middle, and last names. She notes that their female relatives wore black head-to-toe burkas and editorializes that "there's a sight to gladden the Canadian female heart—homegrown burka-wearers darting about just as they do in Afghanistan." Bringing in the reaction of Canadian women is irrelevant to the discussion. The use of the verb "darting" to describe the movements of the female relatives suggests that they are incapable of walking like normal human beings by giving the reader the erroneous impression that the burka prohibits a normal walking pattern. It is also a loaded word insinuating sinister or conspiratorial behaviour.

In the next few paragraphs Blatchford uses the well-known linguistic strategy of *disclaiming*. She notes that Chief Blair, "who is a wonderful guy," was right in going out to the press conference in Scarborough; that he told the Muslims their places of worship will get extra protection and if anyone wearing a beard or hijab is hassled, the police will treat that seriously. She is trying to reassure the reader that he made important statements that she agreed with. Finally, the major *disclaimer* is brought out into the open—that this whole business is as distressing "to the vast majority of good, peaceable Canadian Muslims" as it is to everyone else. This is tantamount to saying that "some of my best friends are ..." Thus while maintaining that the majority of Muslims are peace-loving, good people, she quickly moves on to condemn the conduct of peaceable Canadian Muslims at the press conference. She says that many of the people asking questions at the conference and those who answered them were more interested in an anti-Muslim backlash to the arrests than a "whole whack of their young people ... bent on blowing something up in the city" (again using *hyperbolic* language). They were also "worked up" about Canadian soldiers in Afghanistan and Americans in Iraq, and she concludes that although the people maintain that Islam is a "religion of peace, they do not sound or appear particularly peaceable," this kind of argumentation resorts to the use of *generalizations* applied to specific events. The American presence in Iraq and Canadians in Afghanistan is not the focus of this article, so generalizations about their role in the Middle East is irrelevant to the discussion about arrested Muslims in Toronto or the vandalism of a mosque. It is brought in merely to make the point that Muslims are not a peaceable people, despite their claims to the contrary. The same argument is used again by the writer when she evaluates the statement made by Sheikh Husain Patel in answer to a question from a member of the audience: "The politics of overseas should not be addressed in a violent manner in Canada." But this did not "ring in my ears as a renunciation of violence per, but as a renunciation of violence in this country." Needless to say, violence in this country was the subject of the press conference and presumably the focus of the writer's article. The piece ends with a facetious trivializing comment that the "war on windows" goes well.

CONCLUSION

Racism in the Canadian media may not always be visible, and rarely does it take the explicit form most of us are familiar with when we talk about racism. Nevertheless, racist discourse is pervasive and systemic. We have talked about only two cases in this chapter, but numerous others could be cited to show how the media articulate and transmit powerful and negative messages about ethno-racial groups, which in turn pass into the collective psyche of Canadian society (Henry & Tator, 2002; Poole, 2002; van Dijk, 1991). Not only do journalists have enormous power to inferiorize and stigmatize the perspectives of marginalized groups, but racist news discourse also makes it incredibly difficult to develop an equitable society. The cases we have discussed here—a front-page story about a politician's secret past and a column with hateful and derogatory language about Muslims—provide a close-up view into how the everyday words, ideas, and images of journalists construct "imperfect mirrors" of racialized communities (Miller, 1998). Using the tools of critical discourse analysis, we have identified some common rhetorical strategies used by mass media to produce negative stereotypes that reinforce the "otherness" of Native peoples and Muslims. More importantly, in doing so, we hope to have mobilized the reader to take up the tools of academic scholarship to show how the social world may be represented differently in the interests of all citizens.

References

Fleras, A., & Kunz, J. (2001). *Media and minorities: Representing diversity in a multicultural Canada*. Toronto: Thomson Nelson.

Greenberg, J. (2000). Opinion discourse and Canadian newspapers: The case of the Chinese "boat people." *Canadian Journal of Communication, 25*(4), 517–537.

Hall, S. (1996). The problem of ideology: Marxism without guarantees. In S. Hall, D. Morley, & Q.-H. Chen (Eds.), *Critical dialogues in cultural studies*. London: Routledge.

Henry, F., & Tator, C. (2002). *Discourses of domination: Racial bias in the Canadian English-language press*. Toronto: University of Toronto Press.

Karim, K. (2000). *Islamic peril: Media and global violence*. Montreal: Black Rose Books.

Kress, G. (1990). Critical discourse analysis. In R. Kaplan (Ed.), *Annual review of applied linguistics: Vol. 2*. New York: Cambridge University Press.

Mahtani, M. (2001). Representing minorities: Canadian media and minority identities. *Canadian Ethnic Studies, XXXIII*, 99–133.

Miller, J. (1998). *Yesterday's news: Why Canada's daily newspapers are failing us.* Halifax: Fernwood.

O'Sullivan, T., Hartley, J., Saunders, D., Montgomery, M., & Fiske, J. (1994). *Key concepts in communication and cultural studies.* London: Routledge.

Poole, E. (2002). *Reporting Islam: Media representations of British Muslims.* London: Palgrave.

Purvis, T., & Hunt, A. (1993, September). Discourse, ideology, discourse, ideology, discourse, ideology. *British Journal of Sociology, 44*(3), 473–499.

Roth, L., Nelson, B., & Kasennahaw, M. D. (1995). Three women, a mouse, a microphone and a telephone: Information (mis)management during the Mohawk/Canadian governments' conflict of 1990. In A. N. Valdivia (Ed.), *Feminism, multiculturalism and the media: Global perspectives.* London: Sage.

van Dijk, T. (1991). *Racism and the press.* London: Routledge.

van Dijk, T. (1998). *Ideology: A multidisciplinary approach.* London: Sage.

Appendix

Ignoring the Biggest Elephant in the Room
CHRISTIE BLATCHFORD

I drove back from yesterday's news conference at the Islamic Foundation of Toronto in the north-eastern part of the city, but honestly, I could have just as easily floated home in the sea of horse manure emanating from the building.

So frequent were the bald reassurances that faith and religion had nothing—*nothing*, you understand—to do with the alleged homegrown terrorist plot recently busted open by Canadian police and security forces, that for a few minutes afterward, I wondered if perhaps it was a vile lie of the mainstream press or a fiction of my own demented brain that the 17 accused young men are all, well, Muslims.

But no. I have checked. They are all Muslims.

Barely two days after the nighttime raids that saw 15 of the accused arrested (the remaining two, in Kingston, conveniently were already in the joint on gun charges), the great Canadian self-delusion machine was up and running at full throttle.

Why, it's not those young men—with their three tonnes of ammonium nitrate and all the little doohickeys of the bomb-making trade—who posed the threat. No sir: They, thank you so much, are innocent until proved otherwise and probably innocent and, if convicted, it's because of the justice system.

It's those bastard vandals (probably crazed right-wing conservatives, or maybe the Jews) who yesterday morning broke windows at a west-end mosque who stand before us as the greatest danger to Canadian society.

As Toronto Police Chief Bill Blair, who came to the building to offer his assurances that Muslims and Muslim institutions will be protected, said at one point: "Hatred in any form and certainly in its expression in violence and damage to property will not be tolerated."

Thank God: Windows everywhere in Canada's largest city are safe, especially windows in mosques. The war on windows will be won, whatever the cost.

Such is the state of ignoring the biggest, fattest elephant in the room in this country that at one point Chief Blair actually bragged—this in answer to a question from the floor—"I would remind you that there was not one single reference made by law enforcement to Muslim or Muslim community" at the big post-arrest news conference on Saturday.

Indeed, law-enforcement types there took enormous pains to say just the opposite: The arrested men are from a diverse variety of backgrounds ("They're students, they're employed, they're unemployed" one official said, which is akin to running the gamut from A to oh, C); they come from all parts of Canadian society; blah, blah, blah.

Even before I knew for sure that they're all Muslims, I suspected as much from what I saw on the tube, perhaps because I am a trained observer, or you know, because I have eyes.

The accused men are mostly young and mostly bearded in the Taliban fashion. They have first names like Mohamed, middle names like Mohamed and last names like Mohamed. Some of their female relatives at the Brampton courthouse who were there in their support wore black head-to-toe *burkas* (now there's a sight to gladden the Canadian female heart: homegrown *burka*-wearers darting about just as they do in Afghanistan), which is not a getup I have ever seen on anyone but Muslim women.

And from far outside the courthouse, if the Muslim question wasn't settled, there was the likes of Scarborough Imam Aly Hindy telling the *Toronto Star* that: "Because they are young people and they are Muslims, they are saying it is terrorism."

Now look, of course it is a good thing that Chief Blair, who is a wonderful guy, made the trek out to Scarborough yesterday.

It's even good that he told local Muslims that their places of worship will get extra patrols and that if anyone wearing traditional beards or the *hijab* is hassled, the police will investigate and treat it seriously.

The chief is right that now, as in the aftermath of 911 (talk about property damage), all of us have to be particularly tolerant of one another.

And he is also right that there is a distinction, though in my view it may be a distinction without a difference, between terrorism motivated purely by religious zealotry, and terrorism, as was the alleged case with these 17 mostly young men, motivated by political ideology—even if the ideology seems to have been nothing more than the ideology of rage fuelled by overseas conflicts.

And it should go without saying—but it never, ever can in this country, and must be shrieked at every turn—that this whole business is as at least as distressing to the vast majority of good, peaceable Canadian Muslims as it is to everyone else.

But what came clear at that meeting yesterday, which was an odd mix of community venting and news conference, is that many of those people who went to the microphone to ask questions, and some of those who answered them from the podium, are far more concerned about a possible anti-Muslim backlash to the arrests than they are about the allegations that a whole whack of their young people were bent on blowing something up in the city; that they are generally worked up about Canadian soldiers in Afghanistan and the Americans in Iraq, and that even as they talk about Islam being a religion of peace, they do not sound or appear particularly peaceable.

Only one question from the floor, this from a young man, really dared to depart from the convention of deploring the supposed coming anti-Muslim backlash and the idea of Muslim as victim.

He asked what the imams were doing to ensure that the sort of violent views that allegedly motivated the homegrown terrorists were not allowed to "become entrenched in our community."

Sheikh Husain Patel answered him. "It is important we educate our young brothers," he said.

He mentioned a series of conflicts overseas, including Iraq and Palestine, then said: "You cannot justify a legal goal by using illegal means. The politics of overseas should not be addressed in a violent manner in Canada."

That did not ring in my ears as a renunciation of violence per se, but as a renunciation of violence in this country.

I wondered if the answer had satisfied the young man who asked the question, but I lost him in the crowd afterward.

The war on windows, though—that goes well.

ISSUE 4

Representing race: Are Canadian news media racist?

✗ NO

Racism, Media, and Analytical Balance
Sean P. Hier

Sean P. Hier is assistant professor of sociology at the University of Victoria. His areas of research interest and expertise are race and ethnicity, surveillance, and media studies. His recent and forthcoming books include *Contemporary Sociological Thought: Themes and Theories, Identity and Belonging: Rethinking Race and Ethnicity in Canadian Society; The Surveillance Studies Reader, Race and Racism in 21st Century Canada: Continuity, Complexity and Change, Surveillance and Social Problems in Canada; and Contested Barriers: Racism and the Complexity of Social Change.*

In their critique of racial bias in the Canadian English-language press, Frances Henry and Carol Tator (2002) provide six case studies to explain how journalists (re)produce "discursive spaces" (p. 6) that contribute to the denigration and marginalization of people of colour, First Nations communities, and other minorities. They argue that white Canadian journalists and editors unconsciously reproduce and transmit "discourses of domination" that pass as everyday, commonsense truths about the social world. They also argue that white journalists and editors reaffirm and propagate racist ideologies that legitimize and reinforce patterns of social inequality in the country (Henry & Tator, 2006). For Henry and Tator, it is not necessarily that individual journalists and editors are racists, but rather that news production and journalistic activity take place in a cultural-ideological system that normalizes and naturalizes Euro-Canadian beliefs, values, and ways of life.

Henry and Tator's argument about racism, ideology, and the cultural production of meaning is representative of studies concerned with racism and media generally (see, for example, Mahtani, 2001, pp. 99–109). The general point that Henry and Tator make is an important one, namely, that the production of media discourse takes place in a wider cultural-ideological system of meaning (see also Henry, Tator, & Mattis, 1997). Their case studies effectively debunk the notion of journalism as a neutral or objective exercise that is free of cultural biases and stereotypical imagery. Their argument about the cultural production of media discourse is also important because it reminds us of the dangers of relying on actual media content (what appears on the evening television news, for example) or on specific media outlets (such as mainstream newspapers) to understand the complexity of relations involved in systems of cultural representation.

In this commentary, I do not wish to contest Henry and Tator's important case study findings. The relationship between media and racism, however, will require more analytical attention than their analyses permit. In studies of racism and media available in Canada, it is commonly argued that analyzing and understanding what appears in media reporting is insufficient for gaining a complete understanding of media representations of diversity. What is additionally required to fully understand the relationship between racism and media is analysis of what does *not* appear in media coverage. In identifying this problem, studies tend to foreground one of three mutually reinforcing arguments: first, slanted or stereotypical representations in media coverage narrowly represent the complexity of ethno-racial minority achievements, thereby presenting a distorted view (misrepresentation); second, an insufficient amount of coverage highlighting the positive achievements of ethno-racial minorities inhibits complete appreciation of difference in the country (underrepresentation); and third, significant ethno-racial minority achievements are not addressed in media coverage at all (silence). These three foregrounded arguments are commonly situated in the context of a fourth "foundational" argument about Euro-Canadian cultural hegemony appearing in the background of analysis. The latter is used to provide rhetorical credibility for the foregrounded arguments—that is, taken-for-granted claims about Canadian culture and institutional life that are asserted rather than demonstrated (Alford, 1999).

Addressing interrelated patterns of misrepresentation, underrepresentation, and silence is crucial for gaining a complete understanding of the cultural production of knowledge generally, and the relationship between racism and media particularly. The same kinds of arguments, however, can also be applied to scholars who study racism and media. Regardless of the good intentions motivating research, racism and media studies misrepresent the diversity of coverage in the **mainstream media** available in Canada, underrepresent the diversity of media outlets, and remain silent on important patterns of coverage in mainstream and other media pertaining to equity, social justice, and human rights. They also fail to address (or simply ignore) important changes taking place in Canadian culture over the past three decades. By reproducing patterns of misrepresentation, underrepresentation, and silence, and by ignoring changes to Canadian cultural life, analysts fail to assess the potential influence that media have on patterns of ethno-racial harmony, acceptance, and incorporation in the country.

In examining the first foregrounded pattern of misrepresentation in the mainstream media, analysts commonly use case studies to generalize about the nature of racism in the media specifically, and about racism in the country generally. Case studies take one of two forms: they either involve investigations of particular events (e.g., news coverage of editorial diversity during times of war), or they focus on certain groups (e.g., representations of Black men in the mainstream press or the scripting of visible minority characters on television). Studying media representations in this manner, analysts select media coverage over certain periods of time or select coverage pertaining to certain events, thereby ignoring other periods of time and other events.

Given that almost all analysts have a self-avowed commitment to exposing racism in all its forms and manifestations, they tend to seek out explicit examples of stereotypical, sensational, and spectacular media coverage (after all, they often get their information from mainstream media). Studies of this nature are important because they help us to understand how ethno-racial signifiers can be invoked to produce negative or stereotypical portrayals of groups of human beings (e.g., post-9/11 representations of Arabs), but they cannot be presented independently of positive coverage on antiracism, anti-oppression, and social justice. Why, for example, is there a dearth of studies on Canada mainstream media coverage of antiracism or reparation/redress politics? Has there been no mainstream media coverage that contributes to ethno-racial harmony and acceptance in Canada? What about the increasing presence of visible minority characters occupying influential social positions on primetime television shows (e.g., as lawyers, doctors, and news anchors)? Or changes in ethno-racial diversity in women's magazines? Is it empirically and analytically sound to draw from a limited number of studies in the 1980s and 1990s to generalize about misrepresentation in mainstream magazines in 2007? And consider the growing number of popular films that deal with cultural and generational complexity (e.g., *Bollywood/Hollywood*) and explicit racism (e.g., *Higher Learning*), or that portray same-sex interracial couples in a positive light (e.g., *The Family Stone*) or a charismatic, authoritative Black American President (e.g., *Deep Impact*). Do the positive social messages transmitted in these films fail to resonate with "white" Canadian viewers? Do we have sufficient data to decide? I am not suggesting that analysts' misrepresentation of racialized discourses in the mainstream media is insidious or underhanded. The point, rather, is that we require a greater amount of empirical data before we can accept the all-encompassing claim that mainstream media available in Canada only misrepresent minorities and reinforce white Euro-Canadian hegemony.

Related to patterns of misrepresentation of the diversity of coverage in the mainstream media consumed by Canadians is the underrepresentation of the diversity of Canadian and, necessarily, international media outlets. It is understandable that analysts take a special interest in media discourse appearing in mainstream media outlets, but it is difficult to find current investigations that include media other than mainstream newspapers and television (the latter is less common than the former). Considering the proliferation of online media over the last 10 years, this is indeed a curious oversight. New media have a profound influence on the ways that people make sense of, communicate, and live in the world, and any comprehensive understanding of racism and antiracism must attend to the significance of these global communication technologies.

While a few studies investigate organized racism on the Internet (see Hier, 2000, for an examination of Canadian racist groups), there has been no systematic attempt to understand the diversity of representations about race that are transmitted through other digital media (e.g., blogs, chat rooms, message boards, online communities). Additionally, analyses of ethnic press or non-English-, non-French-language newspapers are rare (see, however, Bright et al., 1999); studies of the significance of racism in music have focused primarily on hate rock (see Futrell, Simi, & Gottschalk, 2006), showing little interest in antiracist messages in popular music; and analyses of the significance of changing representations in comics, local street papers (e.g., Vancouver's *Georgia Straight*), billboards, street advertisements, flyers, micro media (e.g., buttons and stickers), e-mail distribution lists, indy media, and popular books are almost nonexistent. In all likelihood, students will be able to recall sitting in a class where a Euro-Canadian (a.k.a. white) peer raised questions about imperialism and racism. Where did that information come from? Did the student conduct primary research and draw these conclusions herself? Is this student a unique white individual who is able to stand outside dominant racist ideologies? Again, my point is not to qualify the significance of studies that demonstrate underrepresentation of ethno-racial diversity in mainstream Canadian and international media. My point, rather, is that studies of racism and media underrepresent the diversity of media outlets, and thereby misrepresent media coverage on diversity.

The third pattern that is reproduced in racism and media studies is silence. Silence can take many forms, including failure to analyze the significance of minority media profiles or experiences and the impact of antiracist education in the niche or micro media. Given that analysts usually set out to examine racism in mainstream media coverage, it is not surprising that they remain silent on antiracism and social justice discourses in **alternative media**. To illustrate the diversity of media discourse that has been hitherto ignored by analysts, I will offer three examples drawn from the mainstream press, government-sponsored niche media, and the Internet. While I do not argue that these three examples buttress claims that Canadian and international media transmit racist images and information, they do complicate generalizing claims about the Canadian and international media as strictly and unequivocally racist.

The first example concerns two stories drawn from the *Globe and Mail*. In the wake of the devastation left in New Orleans after Hurricane Katrina hit the United States in August 2005, claims of Katrina's unequal "racial toll" proliferated in the international press. Despite evidence revealed later that year that age rather than race was the biggest factor in the deaths associated with the catastrophe—of the 623 bodies identified by December, 293 were black, 262 were white, and two-thirds were over age 60—the front-page headline of the *Globe and Mail's* Saturday, September 3, 2005, edition read: "KATRINA'S UNEQUAL TOLL: Disaster bares divisions of race and class across the Gulf States." In the ensuing story (surrounding a half-page photograph of a crowd of African-Americans appearing frustrated and tired), *Globe* columnist Christie Blatchford argues that race and class intersected in New Orleans to produce a racially stratified society that was reflected in the unequal toll of natural disaster. It is not my purpose to dispute Blatchford's claims, but rather to reflect on the significance of one of Canada's major newspapers running a front-page story of this nature. Is it fair to assume that this an example of Euro-Canadian racism? Can we simply infer that it is a "discourse of domination" (Henry & Tator, 2002)? Is covert "othering" at work? And is it fair to assume that the majority of white Canadian readers of this Saturday edition believed on some level of consciousness that Black Americans deserve to suffer in this way? Or is this instead an example of a mainstream Canadian newspaper addressing openly an important social issue in our world? Is it possible that news coverage of this kind could motivate Canadians of all backgrounds to consider the relationship between race and class? And is it beyond the pale of imagination that thousands of white Canadians endorsed Blatchford's discourse? I do not wish to minimize the significance of race and representation in the press, but this story is not an isolated example of explicit engagement with debates about social inequality and race in the Canadian press.

Consider another, substantively different example from the *Globe and Mail*. On June 26, 2006, the newspaper ran a front-page story profiling the Maxwell sisters of New Brunswick—five sisters who all earned degrees from Harvard University. The significance of the article, articulated in part by a large photograph appearing on page A1, is that they are Black Canadians. The article detailed how their father, a medical doctor (now deceased), experienced blatant racism in Canada in the 1940s and 1950s, and it contrasted his experiences with those of his five daughters (two doctors, two lawyers, and a law student at McGill University), who thrived at Harvard, "an unprecedented feat at a 370-year-old institution long seen as a bastion of white privilege" (p. A1). Critics of the article will charge that the story is either an example of counterposing the sisters' "otherness" to the Canadian norm of whiteness (which in this case would be not attending an Ivy League University and not achieving remarkable intergenerational, familial, cultural accomplishment) or that it is a case of using the few to minimize, rationalize, and distort the plight of the many. The ideological effects of the story are conceivably consistent with the latter claim, but the story can also be read as a positive, affirming discourse on how a family overcame, but still lives with, racial adversity. In the latter vein, it might also serve to remind "white" Canadians that racism in any form is unacceptable, and that race is still a factor in patterns of social incorporation and mobility.

The second example of silence on antiracism discourse in Canadian media pertains to films produced and funded by the National Film Board (NFB). Over the past 25 years, the NFB has produced a number of films dealing with Aboriginal inequality, racism, immigration, and the enduring legacy of hardship. In films including, but not limited to, *Sisters in the Struggle, Speak It! From the Heart of Black Nova Scotia, The Road Taken, Moving the Mountain, In the Shadow of Gold Mountain*, and *The War Between Us*, the NFB critiques racism in Canada's past and present. Despite the significant impact these films could have on students, there is not a single study of the significance of these or related films in the literature. Indeed, I have used many of these titles in my university courses on racism and antiracism in Canada for years. The films never fail to bring students to tears and to evoke strong interest in antiracism and social justice—among white students and students of colour alike. My experiences might very well be unique and nonrepresentative, but they suggest that the ideological effects of the films are profoundly antiracist and inspirational.

The third example is perhaps the most obvious to younger readers: antiracist discourse on the Internet. A quick Google search of Canadian sites using the terms "antiracism and Canada" yields dozens of hits. Websites including the National Anti-Racism Council of Canada, the Canadian Council of Churches' Charter for Racial Justice, and Anti-Racism Links provide a wealth of information on antiracism activism, the history of racism, and equity politics. The presence of these sites on the Web implies neither a lack of engagement with racism nor a "discourse of domination." There might very well be productive debate to be staged on the specific antiracist strategies these individuals and organizations endorse. And there might be important debates to stage about how effective the sites are in raising consciousness and invoking change. Both of these potential debates are issues for empirical research, and the fact remains that there is a plethora of antiracist material online (from around the world) that the academic literature does not engage.

The three main patterns of misrepresentation, underrepresentation, and silence highlighted above find support in a fourth, mutually reinforcing background argument that the extent of racism in Canada is not as pervasive as many analysts suggest. I am not arguing here that racism does not exist in Canadian society; however, it behooves a serious analyst to note that there have been important changes in Canada, particularly in the past three decades, which partially explain the growing complexity of media coverage today. While Canadian history is fraught with explicit forms of institutional racism, demographic changes since 1970 profoundly influenced Canadian culture, as well as Canadian political and social institutions. Although racism persists in Canadian institutions and in everyday life, there have been significant changes to levels of institutional participation among and within Canada's diverse ethnic, racial, cultural, and religious populations. These progressive, albeit uneven, changes can be observed in institutional domains, including immigration practices, educational attainment rates, labour market participation, and patterns of civic-democratic participation. Advances in educational attainment rates, labour market returns, and occupational distribution for Canadian-born members of visible minority groups, in particular, have been comparable if not in excess of Canadians of Western European ancestry. It is important to realize, too, that the changes taking place in Canada are not simply outcomes of interrelated social-structural transformations underway since the 1960s; they are, importantly, also catalysts for interrelated changes that continue to transform the country (see Hier & Bolaria, 2006; Hier & Walby, 2006). In fact, scholarly interest has recently come to focus on the emergence of "Canadian" as an ethno-racial identity among English-speaking, non-Aboriginal Canadians (Howard-Hassmann, 1999). While many researchers offer important studies laying claim to institutional or systemic forms of racism in Canada, a significant body of evidence also contests the extent to which the social categories of race and ethnicity function as *categorical determinants* for the inequitable distribution of services and resources in the country (Hier, 2007).

The four mutually reinforcing patterns in studies of racism and media that have been highlighted above are not presented with the intention of dismissing arguments that media misrepresent, under-represent, and remain silent on issues of significance to ethno-racial minority groups in Canada and elsewhere. They are presented, rather, with the intention to open debate about the diversity of media representation in Canada, and to contest totalizing claims that the media (as an institution) in Canada are racist. That analysts persist in misrepresenting the diversity of coverage in the mainstream media, underrepresenting the diversity of media outlets, and remaining silent on the diversity of antiracism and social justice media discourses probably says more about the structure of the production of academic knowledge about race and racism than it does about the empirical world. Of course, this argument may inspire outrage among those who believe that the media are unequivocally racist. My purpose here is not to undermine or debunk the research of these analysts, but to encourage them to strive for greater analytical balance and more proportional representation of media coverage in Canada.

To conclude, students interested in seeking greater analytical balance in their research on media and racism will want to ensure they adhere to principles of sound research design where matters of sampling and generalization are concerned. To put this differently, it is incumbent on researchers to formulate hypotheses, design empirically rigorous research strategies, and minimize bias or preconceived assumptions about how things "really are." As I argue above, one way to do so is to begin to balance media reporting on racism and antiracism, analyze a variety of media outlets, and avoid the pervasive tendency to remain silent on progressive media activity in the area of racism and social change. Concomitantly, analytical balance also involves taking seriously progressive social changes in Canadian society and avoiding polemical argumentation that frames the question of racism and the media in either/or terms: racism is either there or it is not. By striving for analytical balance, it is conceivable and entirely possible that we will conclude that media coverage of racism and antiracism is much more complicated than the existing literature suggests.

References

Alford, R. (1999). *The craft of inquiry*. Oxford: Oxford University Press.

Bright, R., Coburn, E., Faye, J., Gafijczuk, D., Hollander, K., Jung, J., & Srymbos, H. (1999). Mainstream and marginal newspaper coverage of the 1995 Quebec referendum: An inquiry into the functioning of the Canadian public sphere. *Canadian Review of Sociology and Anthropology, 36*(3), 313–330.

Futrell, R., Simi, P., & Gottschalk, S. (2006). Understanding music in movements: The white power music scene. *Sociological Quarterly, 47*(2), 275–304.

Henry, F., & Tator, C. (2002). *Discourses of domination: Racial bias in the Canadian English language press.* Toronto: University of Toronto Press.

Henry, F., & Tator, C. (2006). *The colour of democracy.* Toronto: Harcourt Brace.

Henry, F., Tator, C., & Mattis, W. (1997). *Challenging racism in the arts.* Toronto: University of Toronto Press.

Hier, S. P. (2000). The contemporary structure of Canadian racial supremacism: Networks, strategies, and new technologies. *Canadian Journal of Sociology, 25*(4), 471–493.

Hier, S. (2007). Researching race and racism in 21st century Canada. In S. Hier & S. Bolaria (Eds.), *Race and racism in 21st century Canada: Continuity, complexity, and change* (pp. 19–33). Peterborough, ON: Broadview Press.

Hier, S., & Bolaria, S. (2006). *Identity and belonging: Rethinking race and ethnicity in Canadian society.* Toronto: Canadian Scholars' Press.

Hier, S., & Walby, K. (2006). Competing analytical paradigms in the sociological study of racism in Canada. *Canadian Ethnic Studies, 26*(1), 83–104.

Howard-Hassman, R. (1999) "Canadian" as an ethnic category. *Canadian Public Policy, 25*(4), 523–537.

Mahtani, M. (2001). Representing minorities: Canadian media and minority identities. *Canadian Ethnic Studies, 33*(3), 99–133.

Discussion Questions

1. On the basis of the arguments and evidence presented in these chapters, can we reach a definitive conclusion that Canadian media are racist? Explain how you have been persuaded to your position.

2. How can the existing literature on racism and Canadian media be understood as a place to *begin* social analyses and not as a place to *end* them?

3. What does Hier mean when he calls for analytical balance to the study of racism and the media? How would an analytically balanced approach change how we understand the role of the media in sustaining or challenging racism in Canadian society?

4. Why is it important to examine the discursive dimensions of ideology in the media?

5. Apply CDA (critical discourse analysis) by examining another newspaper column. What explicit and implicit coded messages did you find in this column? What challenges and opportunities arose from employing this method to analyze the text?

PART 3 Technology and Everyday Life

ISSUE 1 — Cell in the city: Has cellphone use eroded the distinction between the public and the private sphere?

ISSUE 2 — The big blog: Have blogs decentred traditional news media?

ISSUE 3 — Big Brother society: Can video surveillance protect us from terror?

ISSUE 4 — Technological fixes: Can new communications technology save democracy?

Henry Ford II, grandson to the eminent American industrialist, famously stated that "the technological triumphs of the past few years have not solved as many problems as we thought they would, and, in fact, have brought us new problems we did not foresee." Ford, writing in the post–World War II era during his tenure at the helm of his family's automotive company, was speaking about the polluting effects of industrialization. Ford's remarks suggest that technology can be a double-edged sword. While offering what are seemingly unlimited conveniences that promise to make our lives easier, technology also produces consequences—consequences that may create problems in social relations and actually make our lives more complicated and difficult to manage.

This section offers competing perspectives on some of the key communication technology issues of our time. It begins with a look at the cellphone, asking if new developments in mobile communications have eroded the barriers between public and private space. Kim Sawchuk and Barbara Crow argue that the advent of the cellphone has disturbed and transformed conventional models of individual and collective behaviour in public space. While the emergence of cellphones has not caused these changes, the technology illustrates an emergent

privatization of everyday life. Importantly, Sawchuk and Crow link the relationship between the rise of the cellphone with the erosion of public space to broader changes in communication policy that favour the deregulation of public utilities and valorize consumerism over citizenship.

Richard Smith offers a different perspective. He acknowledges that cellphones and other personalized communication devices (e.g., iPods, BlackBerries) encourage "people to turn inward and at the same time push the inward outward" by violating social norms about how to communicate in public. There is no doubt, Smith concedes, that the ever-presence of the cellular phone is a "potentially caustic ingredient to civil discourse." However, he also encourages us to think about the creative potential of mobile technology as a vehicle for enlivening and democratizing both communication and everyday life. Smith points to instances when the cellphone was used as a catalyst for debate on public behaviour and communication standards, as a means for constructing a virtual public sphere (e.g., the creation of free, community Wi-Fi networks) and a medium for encouraging young people to participate in the political process. He suggests that when we focus on questions of agency, or what people actually do with technology, rather than questions of the structural conditions in which technologies emerge, we see far more possibilities for enhancing rather than constraining democratic expression.

The second issue considers the emergence of the blogosphere and asks if blogging has challenged the authority and legitimacy of more conventional news media. Journalist Gwen Preston argues that websites and blogs became central tools in the 2006 defeat of veteran politician and one-time vice-presidential candidate Joseph Lieberman by millionaire candidate Ned Lamont in Connecticut's Democratic senatorial nomination. Citing unnamed "political analysts," Preston argues "that the candidates and parties are no longer in control of politics." Lest readers think this is a uniquely American phenomenon, Preston points to the ways in which bloggers influenced the 2006 Liberal Party leadership race as well. Where campaign managers used to worry incessantly about what the press and broadcast media reported, they are now paying "close attention to the blogging world." Moreover, she suggests that blogs may be eclipsing the power of conventional media because bloggers are able to monitor newspapers, television, and radio in search of errors and to hold journalists to account.

Mary Francoli argues that the optimism surrounding the impact of blogs on politics and the media is probably inflated. Rather than seeing the growth of the blogosphere as indicative of the blogger influencing a world that once operated beyond the reach of most citizens (as citizen-journalist), she writes that blogs may be "having the opposite effect … reinforcing the dominance and continued health of mainstream media at a time when pundits are lamenting its declining relevance." The conventional media still have the trust and financial support of major advertisers, and while citizens are *modifying* how they seek out and use information, Francoli argues they "do not appear to be abandoning their traditional news consumption habits," particularly with respect to political and policy issues. Rather, by incorporating blogs into the broader platform of news delivery, the mainstream media is able to extend its appeal to an audience in search of the

bombastic, opinion-based discourse that is characteristic of blogs, "while becoming increasingly accountable for its work and actions."

Debate number three considers the increased use of closed-circuit television (CCTV) surveillance cameras for security and policing of public space. Joe Scanlon reflects on the case of Britain, where citizens have their facial images captured by a remote-operated camera at least five times per day. Scanlon argues that the "seemingly never-ending threats" of terrorism in the United Kingdom helps to explain why the public so willingly accepts more surveillance over their everyday lives. However, he also notes that while CCTV may not prevent terrorism or other violent crimes, it does help the public to feel safer. Fear of crime can be as debilitating to a community as actual crime itself, and Scanlon's paper suggests that we should not dismiss the widespread public support for surveillance even if the evidence of its efficacy is contradictory and inconclusive.

Peter Simpson challenges the argument that camera surveillance improves public safety and security. According to Simpson, the rhetoric of camera advocates suggests that video surveillance is an effective tool for looking at a set of problems (e.g., panhandling) in order to solve them. He argues, however, that the technology actually causes us to *look away* from the underlying reasons for these problems in the first place. Rather than looking to communication technology to solve the safety and security issues that arise in city centres, Simpson claims we are better off investing in social programs that provide marginalized people with education and job employment opportunities.

The final issue moves from the specific to the general and asks whether new communication technology, particularly the Internet, can help us to solve what many political commentators and activists describe as a "democratic deficit." Journalist Mary Gooderham argues that the Internet has modernized the town hall meeting and reinvigorated the participatory dimension of democracy that conventional politics has long forgotten. Drawing on examples from Canada and the United States, Gooderham illustrates how the Internet is democratizing democracy itself. Whereas the political process for too long kept citizens on the sidelines of decision making, new media networks are now making society more democratic "by encouraging discussions and debates about issues."

Catherine Frost acknowledges the Internet's potential as a tool for invigorating democracy, but she also argues that the very technology that provides access to a virtual sea of information can be restricting and work against the principles of democratic renewal. The example of Google China aptly demonstrates how vast networks of search engines filter citizen access to important information in a way that limits the development of an informed citizenry. And while the Internet provides incredible opportunities for progressive, resource-poor communities to 'get their message out' to a broader constituency, it affords antidemocratic organizations such as white supremacists equal opportunities. Frost also points to the fact that since "we can now pick and choose the sites and content that will receive our attention," rather than exposing us to *more* information from a *diversity* of sources, the Internet may actually be contributing to a *narrowing* of discussion and debate. If we use new media technology as consumers rather than citizens, her paper suggests, we will "no longer have to encounter opinions [we] don't like, topics that don't appeal to [us], or issues that don't concern [us]." In this context of "narrowed social and political awareness," Frost argues, "democracy is unlikely to thrive." Ultimately, the potential for the Internet to revive democracy will come down to human decisions and policies about how new technology should be used, rather than anything intrinsic to the technology itself.

ISSUE 1

Cell in the city: Has cellphone use eroded the distinction between the public and the private sphere?

✔ YES

A Tale of Two Beavers: Cellphones and Shifting Notions of Public and Private Space
Kim Sawchuk and Barbara Crow

Kim Sawchuk is an associate professor in the Department of Communication Studies at Concordia University in Montreal, where she teaches courses in research methodologies, communications theory, and feminist media studies. For the past two years she has been a member of the Mobile Digital Commons Network, a research consortium investigating and inventing wireless mobile technologies for artistic practices and public usage. She is a founding editor of *Wi: A Journal of Mobile Digital Culture* and is the current editor of the *Canadian Journal of Communication*.

Barbara Crow is an associate professor and Director of the Graduate Programme in Communication and Culture at York University. Her research interests include digital technologies, feminist theory, social movements, and the political economy of communication.

INTRODUCTION

Canadians have a long history and symbolic connection to technologies for talking (phone) at a distance (tele). The telephone's inventor, Alexander Graham Bell, has been immortalized in a television Canadian Heritage moment. The first geostationary domestic telecommunications satellite, Anik-A1, is now a star attraction at the Canadian Museum of Civilization in Ottawa.[1] One of our national icons, *Castor canadensis*, is used in Bell Mobility's most recent cellphone advertisements. Frank and Gordon, two animated cartoon images of middle-aged beavers from La Tuque and Winnipeg, have lots of time on their tails. Hence their mission: to demonstrate to consumers the reasons to upgrade their high-speed Internet and cellular phone services.

Cellphones have had the fastest diffusion of any consumer technology (Townsend, 2002, p. 63). While its origins are in the military walkie talkie, commercial mobile telephony was provided by AT&T in the United States as early as 1947. These early models proved uneconomical and were abandoned except for limited use in the oil and gas industries. Cellular telephones, or cellphones as they are known in North America, made their first widespread public appearance in 1973. Early cellphone units provided a half-hour of talk time, weighed in at two pounds, and cost approximately US$4000 (see a photo at http://www.lumenelle.com/about/ken_larson.html). Despite these prohibitive costs, thousands of people (mostly those in business) immediately put themselves on waiting lists.

In the last decade, the use of cellphones has increased fourfold in Canada. In 1985, there were 6000 subscribers to cellular telephone services, in 1995 there were 2,584,387, and by 2005 this number had skyrocketed to 16,809,988.[2] The industry predicts an increase of 20 percent in the cellphone market in the next year alone. Today the lightest handset weighs six ounces, and there are thousands of styles of handsets and services to choose from.

The sheer number of cellular telephones in Canada, indeed in the world, signals a remarkable shift in person-to-person communications within the broader media environment (Brown, Green & Harper, 2002; Katz, 2006; Katz & Aakhus, 2002; Ling, 2004). The ubiquitous presence of the cellphone is changing the notions of private persons and interactions within public space. This change is visible in the growing presence of microwave towers atop office buildings and audible in the one-way conversations held in public places such as buses and on the street. In this paper, we explore and expose some consequences of the introduction of the cellphone in the telecommunications landscape to highlight the erosion of the traditional borders of what we commonly call the public and private spheres.

We examine two locations where these erosions have taken place. First, we consider the practices of private individuals within public spaces. Noticeable here is the consolidation of individual people into *individuated* consumers. Second, we detail the policies, regulations, and laws governing cellular communications that subtend the surface patterns in the everyday. Here we note how the cellphone has played a role in the ceding of public space to private corporate interests, which, ironically, has led to the erosion of individual privacy protection within public policy.

PRIVATE PRACTICES IN PUBLIC SPACES

The current version of the cellphone is a complex technological object that does much more than allow individual users to talk from anywhere, anytime. The introduction of these multifaceted instruments into our lives is deterritorializing and reterritorializing (Deleuze & Guattari, 1983) the traditionally understood relationship between the public and the private in the mobile, wireless digital world we increasingly inhabit. What is important here is that the cellphone is displacing the traditional landline, which had a singular function and operated from a singular location. By the end of 2006, a global survey of subscribers predicted that 58 percent of users would rely on a mobile phone as their primary telephone instead of a landline (A. T. Kearney & Judge Business School, 2005). The cellphone is a multifunctional communications device that can be used anywhere, anytime, and anyplace.

As a multi-use instrument, the cellphone is a prime example of the technological convergence that has usurped the traditional locale or setting of telecommunications in the private home and paid work (Katz, 2006; Ling, 2004). Unlike the traditional telephone, which had one primary function, cellphones are simultaneously cameras, MP3 players, PDAs (e.g., BlackBerries), and televisions. In addition to being a way of talking, cellphones can upload and download text images and sound, have broadcast capabilities, and allow access to the Internet. Moreover, industry predicts that cellular telephones will be transformed into mobile devices offering telecommunications, location-based services, and remote sensors. These uses, of course, vary with how much the consumer spends on these services.

The cellphone has become a status object, a way of displaying an individual, private style in public space. Advertisements encourage this privatization and individuation of use, such as the recent Motorazr ads, which highlight the cool lifestyle of the ultra-thin fashionable users whose body types mirror the attributes of the phone itself. Commercials push not just the cellphone but the many accessories that can customize it. Cellphones, unlike home-based landline phones, are a personal accessory carried close to the body.

The cellphone, unlike the traditional landline telephone, is not located in a private home but on the individual person. The advertisements selling the new status object are supported by packages that ascribe a single phone and number to a single person; a consumer who purchases a cellphone is actually purchasing a number. Individual handsets come with a "subscriber identity module" (SIM) or "smart" card and a discrete number, which is locked into the phone by the service provider. This number is not linked to a household but rather to the individual who signs the contract agreement.

Cellular phones are part of an emergent "user-pay" culture, in which time is transformed into a commodity, unlike landlines, which are location or space based and are paid for on a monthly rate. The cellphone is also different from using a telephone in a booth, which, for 25 cents gave you as much time as you wanted, as long as the call was local. In North America cellphone time is calculated according to minutes, which can be expensive. The cellphone reinforces individuation because of the predominance of pay-per-use rather than a flat-rate system that guarantees minimum access at a reasonable cost, as we shall discuss in the next section.

With the rising use of cellphones (and the concomitant demise of above-ground public-use phones), conversations no longer take place in circumscribed areas, such as a room, a house, or a booth. As private individuals carrying cellphones enter into public space they engage in new forms of behaviour, develop new codes of social interaction, and face new demands for etiquette. It is becoming common to see people at a table in public space engaged in conversation with someone at the other end of the line rather than with the person across the table. Individuals walking on the streets engage in intimate private conversations, often oblivious to the volume in which they speak and oblivious to the world around them as they become absorbed by what they hear on the other end of the line. Drivers, encased in their vehicles but travelling through public space, may be further sequestrated in a bubble of private conversation as they meander down the street. This has prompted new studies about the cellphone's effects on driving, a very public activity, and the cost of this activity on the public health system. These new practices have prompted demands for both new public policies and rules of personal decorum in corporate and public space. Some countries have begun to consider prohibiting talking on a hand-held cellphone while driving.[3] Advertisements for cinemas routinely remind moviegoers to turn off their cells.

The advent of the cellphone has eroded older patterns of individual social behaviours in public space in North America, and in Canada specifically. As we have argued in this section, one of the primary reasons for these patterns of behaviour, usage, and new concerns is the articulation of the cellphone to the private individual rather than to a specific locale such as a house or the public phone booth.

But as we have suggested, broader forces are shifting the surface of the media landscape. Like the movement of tectonic plates affecting the earth—causing earthquakes, upheavals, or new formations of hills and valleys—these forces are largely unseen, but their effects on the erosion of public space are very real. In the section that follows we examine in detail the erosions within communications policy contributing to these tendencies.

PUBLIC POLICIES, PRIVATE CORPORATIONS, AND INDIVIDUAL CONSUMERS

Canada has had some of the most extensive coverage and lowest costs of telephone landlines in the world. This is not the result of a benevolent state policy, as Dwayne Winseck points out, but rather of hard-fought battles to ensure that the principles of public access are enshrined in telecommunications policy (Babe, 1990; Barney, 2005; Raboy, 1990; Winseck, 1995). No matter where you lived or how much you earned, communications were deemed essential. With the introduction of landline telephone services in 1931, there was a public commitment to the fair provision and access of communications, guaranteeing low rates and a regional distribution of services. These ideals were reflected in the language enshrined in Canadian telecommunications policy, from the *Railway Act* to the *Telecommunications Act* (Winseck, 1995), which stipulated that services should be provided with "just and reasonable" pricing that is "not unjustly discriminatory or unduly preferential" (*Railway Act*, 1979, c.R-2).

These principles of economic justice to serve the public good, not just individual consumers, are being eroded as we move into the epoch of mobile telecommunications. As we argued previously, the cellular telephone is not *the* cause, but one of the causes and indications of a larger climate change that favours the deregulation of public utilities. Private companies in a competitive market setting are increasingly carrying out the provision of formerly public services for private financial gain. Within this scenario individual citizens, previously conceptualized as part of a shared public space, are addressed principally as private consumers in a free market.

When we buy a cellphone we are not accessing just an individual object, but are given access to a territory and to a band in the spectrum. Like other natural resources, such as water, the air we live and breathe is being transformed into a privatized commodity by the state, which is supposed to work first and foremost in defence of the public interest. Cellphones, like all forms of wireless communications such as radio, radiopaging, satellite communication, and over-the-air broadcasting, use radio frequencies to transmit a signal. Radio frequency Hertzian waves are not, as many of us might think, an infinite resource. They are divisible and they must be allocated. The provision of cellphone services is predicated on this allocation of spectrum.

Here we note a shift in the territory of public policy and legislation governing communications. Spectrum is not distributed or regulated by the mechanisms or principles enshrined in the *Telecommunications Act* or in any of the four broadcasting acts. Rather, spectrum is allocated by Industry Canada and is governed by international agreements established by the International Telecommunications Union (ITU) and the Radiocommunication Committee of the Inter-American Telecommunication Commission (CITEL). On the basis of these international regulations and reviews of telecommunications needs, Industry Canada auctions licences to the spectrum at various times. The most recent auction of spectrum resulted in the granting of 306 licences to 12 companies for a total of $56 million—hardly a price that nonprofit groups or most individuals can afford, yet also not a great deal considering the value of spectrum.

These competitive rounds and expensive licences over the invisible territories that we literally walk through and breathe have public implications for private cellphone users. As consumers we may not be aware of how a network operates or know about spectrum as our phone seamlessly "hands over" our connection between the territories controlled by service providers. Indeed, it is the cellular structure of these spaces that gives the "cellphone" its North American name. It is only when we don't have a signal that we realize that we have cause to think about frequency and worry. Yet as we walk down a street, or move through any public space, we enter and pass through different zones of spectrum coverage.

As industry battles to buy up spectrum allocation, it is service providers rather than citizens and community groups who determine what kind of access, cost, and distribution should be fundamental to the delivery of these kinds of services. Indeed, only a small band of spectrum and wireless fidelity (Wi-Fi) networks are currently being made available to community groups, which may offer alternative information over the airwaves that connect the new cellphone as a multi-use technology to the broader world. The control of spectrum by Industry Canada is all the more troubling since the state (and thus public money) has been subsidizing the research and development and delivery of satellites. Ironically, most cellphone Internet access also relies on public and private investment in fibre-optic, underground, and often invisible cable. ̄

While the discourse of deregulation is often used to convince consumers that more competition will benefit them by leading to lower costs, the policy effect has resulted in fewer avenues for citizens to raise concerns about telecommunication services and provisions. The policy-making process is now driven by a branch of the government committed to the instantiation of market principles, rather than the public provision of services. The idea that all consumers are equal in the eyes of industry, and marketers, is also being shown to be a fallacy. Indeed, marketers are responsive to those with the highest incomes or those deemed most likely to purchase their services (Sawchuk, 1995).[4]

In the current impetus of reform governing telecommunications, cellphone users are constructed as consumers. Yet what protects the individual consumer? Interestingly, the prominent policy issue pertaining to cellphones has not been about costs, but about protection of privacy. How is the consumer protected from invasions of privacy?

Sympatico, Canada's largest Internet service provider, recently announced a change to its privacy position, stating that they

> reserve the right to review any materials or Content sent through the Service, and to remove any such materials or Content in their sole discretion.
>
> [and]
>
> reserve the right at all times to disclose any information as they, in their sole discretion, deem necessary to satisfy any applicable law, regulation, legal process or governmental request. (Sympatico, 2006)

If, as a consumer, you are concerned about privacy issues pertaining to your cellphone, you are directed to your service provider's agreement and the Privacy Commission of Canada,[5] which regulates and administers issues pertaining to privacy.

Two Acts, the *Privacy Act* and the *Personal Information Protection and Electronic Documents Act* (PIPEDA), are important. The first Act pertains to the regulation of your personal information held by federal government organizations. The second one refers to personal information held by private sector organizations and more specifically attends to how technologies have changed the collection and dissemination of this information. The remedies for seeking personal information in each of these contexts are quite different and generally require individuals to opt out of services.

As Kerr, Barrigar, Burkell, and Black (2006, p. 3) contend, PIPEDA requires a "higher threshold of consent," and the significant terms of "knowledge" and "consent" in relation to personal information are not defined in the Act. For example, consider all of the privacy protection statements we are required to read as we navigate the Internet and that cellphone providers make available in our service agreements and online. How many of us understand them? Moreover, while there is legislation to protect the collection and dissemination of personal information, the onus is on individuals to control the circulation of this content. This issue is particularly relevant in a digital context, where telecommunication companies own what we send, say, and write on our cellphones.

CONCLUSION

Scholars, such as Manuel Castells (1996), argue that we no longer live in a world where the public and private spheres are useful to understanding the global world, but rather, we live in a more fluid, nodal, and networked society. While we agree in general with Castell's observation, it is important to map this ongoing reconfiguration of the public and the private as *discursive* and thus socially constructed terms with enormous power. It is also important, therefore, that we see the emergence of the cellular telephone and its impacts on society within a broader context of practices and policies.

In the last two decades, Canada has undergone a political and cultural shift (often called neoliberalism) that favours private corporations and the free market in developing social and communications policies. This shift has been accompanied by a loosening of labour market rigidities, an increased mobility of production and capital, and the globalization of trade and financial markets (Crow & Longford, 2000). As this change occurs, workers and citizens have been *individuated* as private subjects who are constructed in terms of their consumer and private relations with the state and market. Arguably, questions of the public good are being superseded by a concern with finding the best deal on airtime and value-added service. The cellphone, of course, has not caused this shift, but it is playing an integral role in recent reconfigurations of the relationship of private individuals to public space and in the ceding of public policy to private corporate interests.

And thus we return to Frank and Gordon, depicted in a recent advertisement lounging in limos like wanna-be rock stars with 'deluxe green rooms'. They offer the image not of the busy beaver, but of the couch potato. Is this how the telecommunications industry imagines us? Is this who we want to be?

References

A. T. Kearney & Judge Business School (University of Cambridge). (2005, October). *Mobinet 2005: Raising the Stakes.* Retrieved August 8, 2006, from http://www.atkearney.com/shared_res/pdf/Mobinet_2005_ Detailed_Results.pdf

Babe, R. E. (1990). *Telecommunications in Canada: Technology, industry, and government.* Toronto: University of Toronto Press.

Barney, D. (2005). *Communication technology: Democratic audit.* Vancouver: University of British Columbia Press.

Brown, B., Green, N., & Harper, R. (Eds.). (2002). *Wireless world: Social and interactional aspects of the mobile age.* London: Springer-Verlag.

Castells, M. (1996). *The rise of the network society.* London: Blackwell.

Crow, B., & Longford, G. (2000). Digital restructuring, gender, class, and citizenship in the information society in Canada. *Citizenship Studies, 4*(2), 207–230.

Delueze, G., & Guattari, F. (1983). *Anti-Oedipus: Capitalism and schizophrenia.* Minneapolis: University of Minnesota Press.

Katz, J. (2006). *Magic in the air: Mobile communication and the transformation of social life.* New Brunswick, NJ: Transaction.

Katz, J., & Aakhus, M. (Eds.). (2002). *Perpetual contact: Mobile communication, private talk, public performance.* Cambridge: Cambridge University Press.

Kerr, I., Barrigar, J., Burkell, J., & Black, K. (2006). Soft surveillance, hard consent. *Personally Yours, 6,* 1–14.

Ling, R. (2004). *The mobile connection: The cellphone's impact on society.* San Francisco, CA: Morgan Kaufman.

Raboy, M. (1990). *Missed opportunities: The story of 'Canada's broadcasting policy.* Montreal & Kingston: McGill-Queen's University Press.

Sawchuk, K. (1995). From gloom to boom: Aging, identity and target markets. In A. Wernick & M. Featherstone (Eds.), *Images of aging* (pp. 173–188). London: Routledge.

Statistics Canada. (2005, December 12). Survey of household spending. *The Daily.* Retrieved August 7, 2006, from http://www.statcan.ca/Daily/English/051212/d051212a.htm

Sympatico. (2006, June 1). *Sympatico high speed unplugged service—acceptable use policy.* Retrieved August 6, 2006, from http://www.highspeedunplugged.sympatico.ca/CustomerPreSales/Agreements/ AcceptableUsagePolicy.aspx

Townsend, A. (2002). Mobile communications in the twenty-first century. In B. Brown, N. Green, & R. Harper (Eds.), *Wireless world: Social and interactional aspects of the mobile age* (pp. 62–77). London: Springer-Verlag.

Winseck, D. (1995). A social history of Canadian telecommunications. *Canadian Journal of Communication, 20*(2). Retrieved June 11, 2007, from http://www.cjc-online.ca/viewarticle.php?id=286

Notes

[1] Listen to Heritage's Alexander Graham Bell radio minute at http://www.histori.ca/minutes/minute .do?id=13750.

[2] According to Statistics Canada (2005), "About 30% of households with the lowest incomes had a cellphone in 2004—triple the proportion of only 10% just five years earlier. Among households with the highest incomes, the vast majority, or 85%, had at least one cellphone, up from 60% five years earlier."

[3] For an interesting website that keeps track of countries that have regulations pertaining to cellphones and driving, check out http://www.cellular-news.com/car_bans/.

[4] For example, the Mobile Digital Commons Network, primarily funded by Heritage Canada, has been developing mobile games to engage both consumers and citizens with this technology in urban and national parks. See http://www.mdcn.ca.

[5] See Office of the Privacy Commissioner of Canada at http://www.privcom.gc.ca/index_e.asp. For interesting work in this area, check out two Canadian sites, Michael Geist's homepage, http://www.michaelgeist.ca/, and "On the Identity Trail," http://idtrail.org/component/option,com_frontpage/Itemid,1.

ISSUE 1

Cell in the city: Has cellphone use eroded the distinction between the public and the private sphere?

✘ NO

Cellphones, Civility, and Civic Engagement
Richard Smith

Richard Smith is a professor in the School of Communication at Simon Fraser University. His research focus is social inclusion (and exclusion) brought on by the introduction of new media. He has an ongoing interest in technology for education, privacy, and surveillance in public spaces, online communities, and the wireless information society. He is the publisher of the *Canadian Journal of Communication* and is coauthor of *Mobile and Wireless Communications*.

civility |sə vil'ə tē|

ORIGIN late Middle English: from Old French *civilite*, from Latin *civilitas*, from *civilis* 'relating to citizens' (see **civil**). In early use the term denoted the state of being a citizen and hence good citizenship or orderly behavior. The sense [politeness] arose in the mid 16th cent.

I don't want to sound like Pollyanna—endlessly optimistic about technology in our society—but neither do I wish to let the easy critique of mobile devices ("they are leading to iPod zombies, cellphone boors, and crackberry dropouts!") stand unchallenged. To do so is to deny the active decision making and creativity of the people who buy and use these gadgets. In other words, it denies their **agency**.

In the context of mobile phones and iPods, agency suggests uses for the devices beyond anything dreamed up by the designers and sometimes with entirely unanticipated results. As we shall see in the examples in this chapter, user-driven creativity often results in situations and outcomes that the companies that build these gizmos did not predict.

In the case of mobile phones, iPods, and mobile e-mail devices such as BlackBerries, Palm Treos, and, for that matter, laptops with wireless Internet connections, the hue and cry has gone out that these things are not just annoying but are harming our society by pushing the private and the public worlds together in ways that are damaging to public discussion and debate (in other words, they are contributing to the degradation of the **public sphere**).

There are several ways in which these gadgets do damage. One way is that they allow us to retreat into our private sphere when we are in public. This can take the form of zoning out with wireless e-mail on the bus, surfing on a laptop in a café, or just listening to (or watching) your iPod on the street. You are actively partaking of media and messages of your own choosing, and in so doing neglecting those around you in the immediate physical world.

Another impact of using gadgets to turn inward is the potential narrowing of perspective. By selecting your own news sources, perhaps attending only to a particular set of blogs and podcasts, you can develop a very idiosyncratic view of the world and be unwilling to accept the compromises or accommodations that make democratic politics possible in a diverse and rapidly changing country such as Canada. Some political commentators have pointed to the rise of specialty news sources as a factor in the increase in special interest politics.

The other way gadgets can harm civil society, and the aspect that is more familiar to people these days, is the extent to which they push the private sphere out into the public sphere. This is what we might associate with the annoying person who speaks loudly on the phone or who has his iPod turned up so loud that you can hear the music, too.

The annoyance factor is not the only way in which the private sphere invading the public sphere is deleterious, however. There is another, possibly more insidious, impact in the way in which topics of conversation can become hijacked or diverted by the invasion of personal life into the public arena. For many of us, snippets of conversation are too tantalizing to ignore. We can't help ourselves, and we become unwilling participants in a one-sided conversation about someone's latest sexual exploits or medical trauma. We are unable to block it out, it seems.

The combination of gadgets allowing people to turn inward and at the same time push the inward outward to others is a potentially caustic ingredient to civil discourse, various commentators have claimed (Rosen, 2004, p. 1). And, it would be foolish, I think, to deny that these things are happening. We can see them all around us. I recently spent 90 minutes listening to a blow-by-blow account of someone's pregnancy, during a ferry trip from Nanaimo to Vancouver, that was being showered upon all and sundry in a way that was completely inescapable. As a teacher I endure both the interruptions of ringtones (no longer even just a ring, but a song) and the blank faces of students otherwise engaged in laptop explorations. It goes beyond rudeness and into declines in workplace productivity: Etiquette consultants are doing a booming business in North America, advising office workers of how to use their phones and BlackBerries appropriately. And many jurisdictions in Canada and the United States have moved to limit or ban altogether the use of mobile phones while driving, citing safety hazards.

And yet, I would like to see that something else is possible with this technology. With this in mind, I have a few illustrations of alternative outcomes for mobile technology in public space. I hope they will provide hope and inspiration to others who might take them and build on these initiatives.

BUS UNCLE

The first example I would like to point to is the (currently) notorious case of the "Bus Uncle." This situation occurred in Hong Kong in the spring of 2006, when a young man, speaking on his mobile phone on the bus, tapped an older man—also speaking on his phone—on the shoulder to ask him if he could speak a little more quietly. The older man was insulted by this request and reacted strongly, heaping abuse on the young man. A bystander recorded the whole scene on a mobile phone video camera and later uploaded the video to the Internet site YouTube.com.[1] In the weeks that followed, millions of people downloaded and watched the video, remixes with added music and subtitles were uploaded, and endless debates took place in the mainstream and online media.

It would be easy to see this as a case of cellphone rage, but could it be that there is something more afoot here? I have viewed the video and lurked in some of the online discussions going on, and I would like to suggest that we should look behind the obscene language of the Bus Uncle and what it bespeaks about the degradation of social etiquette to consider for a moment the fact that at least two positive contributions to civil society have come of this.

First, in the specific situation, the mobile phone acts as a catalyst for debate (however intemperate) on public behaviour and communication standards between these two men and acted out for all the people on the bus to hear. This is—in some ways—a more positive climate for public sphere engagement with issues than a bunch of people sitting on the bus doing Sudoku or reading comic books in isolation. At least they are talking to each other!

Second, and more important, the cellphone video captured by the bystander across the aisle and uploaded to the Internet has become the germ for an explosion of debate within Hong Kong and around the world about the nature of public behaviour. Bus Uncle inadvertently serves as a lightning rod for public discussion about respect for elders, the importance of standing up for one's opinions and rights, and even the seed for creativity in countless remix versions. Songs have even been written using looped segments of the Bus Uncle's diatribe.

PLACE SITE

When wireless local area networks (WLANs) based on the 802.11x standard—sometimes known as "Wi-Fi"—first began popping up in businesses and homes, they seemed to offer a simple solution for people needing freedom from wires in the workplace. It was a convenient way to get an Internet connection on your laptop without having to locate a plug, carry around a cable, and mess with your configuration. Pretty soon these connections began popping up in public places, most notably in cafés and parks. The café owners saw it as a way to attract customers to their establishments, and many travellers found it a convenient way to connect to the office or home while having coffee and biscotti.

Some places made the connection available for free, as an amenity, like sugar for the coffee or air conditioning. Other places charged for the connections, although these establishments, as you might expect, were not as popular. Regardless of the business model, the common feature seemed to be the tendency for people to sit down, log in, and zero in on what was on the screen while ignoring what was going on around them. At one time, coffee shops were important places where citizens gathered to engage in face-to-face discussion and debate about the pressing public issues of the day (Habermas, 1989). Nowadays, café owners and non-wireless-toting patrons are beginning to talk and bemoan the increased presence of "laptop zombies" who don't talk to the other patrons and are proving to be a negative influence on the social structure of the coffee-consuming environment.

Rather than take this lying down, however, a group of students from the University of California's Berkeley campus set out to build something to counteract this "trend." They called their software PlaceSite[2] and built it on top of the Wi-Fi Dog software created by Montreal's Îsle Sans Fil project.[3] The software brings local and community networking features (a chat room, an events listing, a bulletin board, a classified ads section) to the log-in screen that everyone receives when they use the network. So far the software has been deployed in only a few trial locations in California, but the concept has been taken up by wireless networking enthusiasts in other cities, most notably in Toronto.

Wireless Toronto, a nonprofit community group offering free wireless Internet through partnerships with local citizens and businesses across the city, has put in place several of the community networking features found in PlaceSite when they set up a node in a new location. The jury is out on the impact of these features, as echoed in this quote from the newsletter of a Toronto park and new hotspot:

> The park is now a free wireless "hotspot," thanks to Wireless Toronto and Kijiji—a free, local, community classifieds site (http://www.kijiji.ca). There are still some bugs to get out, so the hotspot is not always hot. Hopefully it will soon be completely reliable. Park staff has moved some tables under the trees into the centre of the park, south of the bake oven and west of the playground. For people who work in a hot apartment, the park can be a cooler office. And people with young kids can catch up on extra work at the park while their kids dig rivers in the sandpit. It's not conducive to conversation, but that's modern life. ("Wireless Internet," 2006)

The effort these folks are making—implementing new technologies but configuring them in ways that make sense for local situations and community needs—is commendable, but it would be difficult to describe this as the rule, rather than the exception, in wireless access procedures.

IMPROVEVERYWHERE

Another group taking an "alternative" approach to mobile technologies in society, ImprovEverywhere, has tackled the "iPod problem" head-on in their work. For this group of New York–based improvisational performance artists, the portable MP3 player—most commonly the iPod, but any MP3 player will do—represents a potential tool for public involvement rather than individual withdrawal.

ImprovEverywhere has put on a number of different "missions" since its founding in 2001, but one of the most famous involved MP3 players and a staged event in New York City's Central Park in the fall of 2005. The organizers first created a "script" and recorded it as an MP3 file that could be downloaded from their website. People who signed up to participate in the mission were asked to register on the website, download the instructions file and copy it to their MP3 player, and then arrive at a certain time and day to the park and wait for instructions. They were also asked to not listen to the instructions until told to do so.

Unbeknownst to the participants, the organizers had prepared four versions of the instructions, so pretty soon the large mass of people began to separate into groups and slowly, gradually, a story began to emerge with different group "actors." Photos and a video clip of the event are available at the ImprovEverywhere website (http://www.improveverywhere.com). The point of all of this is that a technology thought to separate and cut people off from each other became a catalyst for camaraderie and joy. This is another example of people who purposefully take charge of a technology, adapt it to their needs, and see how they can make it enhance rather than detract from their existence.

GET YOUR VOTE ON

Many people believe that personal media will undo years of cultural and national consolidation begun in the era of the first national newspapers and continuing through radio and television broadcasting right to the end of the twentieth century. In those earlier eras commentators observed that political sensibilities, and in particular the sense of nationalism, grew as a result of common information provided through national media. This kind of common base of information would seem to be eroded in an era of personal media—people can pick and choose their media content and can be expected to attend to the sources that support their existing biases and interests.

As we have already observed, personal portable media also can be seen as a means of dropping out and avoiding contact with other human beings, as vividly portrayed in the comic strip *Way Off Main*, which appears in Vancouver's alternative newspaper the *Georgia Straight* and presents ironic perspectives on daily life in the urban jungle (a particularly poignant cartoon shows people using their phones to avoid social contact—see http://www.straight.com/article/way-off-main-119). These concerns are not unprecedented. Previously considerable controversy arose about teenagers' use of the transistor radio, as documented in Susan Douglas's excellent book *Listening In* (2004).

Dropping out of casual conversations is one thing, however, when people drop out of the larger political process there is a graver danger. Formal political participation is falling in some Western democracies, especially among young people. Although it would be difficult to prove a link between personal portable media and political participation, the potential is there. More importantly, the mobile phone presents a possibility of action in the form of initiatives designed to engage and interest young people in the democratic process. This is exactly what the organizers of Get Your Vote On did, in the spring of 2005.

Get Your Vote On (GYVO) is a nonpartisan organization focused on getting young people to vote. They began before the 2005 federal election in Canada, had a major presence around the 2005 B.C. election, and were active in the most recent (January 23, 2006) federal election in Canada. One of their major tools for outreach is the mobile phone.

The mobile phone is an interesting tool for activists, especially those who have concerns about political participation, because it is interactive and personal. The organization can use it—like any other form of mass media—to send out messages, but more importantly they can use it to elicit contributions and opinions. Young people, raised on the interactivity of computer games, are not sufficiently engaged by a medium or a process that does not encourage, honour, and showcase their contributions, as is the case with traditional broadcast and print media.

One of the ways that GYVO was able to both familiarize young people with the voting process and excite them with the results of participation was through text message–based polling. Five times during the campaign around the B.C. election, the organizers sent out messages that asked for a response, or a vote. This approach is similar to the text message voting for *American Idol*—which in the 2005–2006 season attracted 64 million "votes" in the last round, by the way—except in this case both the question and the response went out and came back by cellphone text message. The results were tallied immediately and displayed on the GYVO website.

The organization didn't rely on texting for their whole campaign, however. They also had advertising, sticker and leaflet drops, and events with bands and speakers. At least 20,000 young people signed up to vote at these events, and countless others participated in other ways. They also planned to integrate texting with the live events by having the results of spontaneous voting flashed onto big screens at concerts and rallies. The objective was to create familiarity with the process of voting and show how participation could have a direct and local impact. Early feedback suggests that the program was enormously successful, albeit local and limited in scope. The mobile phone, however, has had a major impact on global politics, as we see in the next section.

SMART MOBS

The GYVO initiative is a subset of a wider phenomenon first described in the groundbreaking 2002 book *Smart Mobs*. In that book, technology pundit and commentator Howard Rheingold brought to wider public attention a social and technological phenomenon that was spreading across the globe, namely activism enabled by the mobile phone. In countries ranging from the Philippines to Nepal we've seen significant political changes brought about or hastened by mass political participation through widespread access to mobile phones and, in particular, text messages ("texting").

The use of mobile phones in activist campaigns is becoming more organized these days, and there is even a website dedicated to promoting this use, MobileActive.org (see http://mobileactive. org/). The organization came together in September 2005 and issued a "Toronto Declaration," which includes this statement: "Mobile technology offers the opportunity for reflecting an inclusive, democratic and compassionate voice for social justice. Put in the hands of the people and social movements, mobile phones and SMS can produce positive results for the common good" (MobileActive, 2005).

Rheingold provides several examples in his book, ranging from the anarchic and largely whimsical "flash mobs" to the concerted and impassioned campaigns waged through phone messages to unseat corrupt and despotic governments. The power of these messages is sufficiently potent that the government of Nepal recently took the extreme step of shutting down the nation's phone system rather than endure endless activism facilitated through the phone networks ("People Defy Curfew," 2006).

What these phenomena have in common, however, is the way in which a personal portable communication device—the mobile phone—becomes a catalyst for local, regional, and even national political activism. Text messages typically come from your friends—it is much less common to receive the kind of "spam" that e-mail does—and so they may be more likely to spur the recipient to action. Whatever the reason, the cellphone is now a potent tool in the hands of the activist and a key feature of political campaigns worldwide.

CONCLUSION

Although the technology is more than 20 years old, the mobile phone is relatively new as a mass phenomenon in Canadian society. With growth rates generally exceeding 10 percent in recent years, it is not uncommon for most of the people with phones around you to have had them only a short time. As such it is not surprising that there is no shortage of annoying and undesirable actions related to mobile phones. And it isn't surprising that people like to project other larger issues in society onto the new phenomenon in their midst. Rudeness, political apathy, even narrow-mindedness have all be ascribed to mobile phone use.

But that isn't the whole story. Rather, as the case studies above illustrate, mobile phones can also be used toward prosocial ends. More importantly, these examples show that in order to chart a different course for mobile technology—or any technology, for that matter—it is necessary to think consciously and proactively. It is also necessary to create the type of use pattern and habits that you think are desirable and not merely accept the default path of least resistance, which is too often the path of commercialization.

Finally, I hope these examples illustrate something very important about the public sphere or the current "hot topic," civil society. Civility is not a thing that exists in the world apart from people. Instead, it is the ongoing creation of people who care about the world around them. Civility—in the broadest sense of the term as defined at the start of this chapter—doesn't exist apart from the actions of everyday people in their everyday lives. It is, instead, the creation of activists, citizens, and just common people with uncommon aspirations and actions. That is what agency means in this context, and it is up to us to use our communication technology in a way that enhances our world and doesn't detract from it.

References

Douglas, S. J. (2004). *Listening in: Radio and the American imagination.* Minneapolis: University of Minnesota Press.

Habermas, J. (1989). *The structural transformation of the public sphere: An inquiry into a category of Bourgeois society* (T. Burger with F. Lawrence, Trans.). Cambridge, MA: MIT Press; Cambridge, UK: Polity Press.

MobileActive. (2005). *Toronto declaration.* Retrieved June 6, 2007, from http://mobileactive.org/Toronto_Declaration

People defy curfew orders on Saturday; police, protestors clash nationwide. (2006, April 9). *Nepalnews.com.* Retrieved June 10, 2006, from http://www.nepalnews.com/archive/2006/apr/apr09/news04.php

Rheingold, H. (2002). *Smart mobs: The next social revolution.* Cambridge, MA: Perseus.

Rosen, C. (2004, summer). Our cellphones, ourselves. *The New Atlantis, 6,* 26–45.

Wireless Internet. (2006, June 9). *Friends of Dufferin Grove Park Newsletter,* 7(6). Retrieved June 9, 2006, from http://www.dufferinpark.ca/newsletter/wiki/wiki.php/June2006.WirelessInternet

Notes

[1] See http://www.youtube.com/watch?v=gVpgBUXaNbM.

[2] See http://www.placesite.com for more information and examples.

[3] Îsle Sans Fil is a nonprofit community group devoted to providing free public wireless Internet access to mobile users in public spaces throughout Montreal.

Discussion Questions

1. Using examples from your own experience with mobile technology, discuss ways in which users demonstrate agency in their use of cellphones or iPods.

2. Do you agree that rudeness is not on the increase because of mobile phones and portable media players? How do you respond when you observe or are affected by rude behaviour involving mobile technology?

3. If you could organize a "flash mob" around a theme, what would it be? Do you think this is a viable or useful form of social or political action?

ISSUE 2

The big blog: Have blogs decentred traditional news media?

✔ YES

Netroots as Crucial Now as Grassroots to Political Campaigns: Websites and Blogs Helped Defeat Democrat in U.S., Are Tools in Liberal Leadership Race in Canada
Gwen Preston (Vancouver Sun)

The power of the Internet and online activism was demonstrated this week in Connecticut when a cable TV businessman used an Internet-based campaign to defeat veteran politician Joseph Lieberman to become the state's Democratic nominee for Senate. Political operatives on both sides of the border are no strangers to Internet politics, but if anything, Lieberman's defeat is causing them to sharpen their Web-based strategies and take notice of netroots activists.

Ned Lamont, millionaire great-grandson of former J. P. Morgan & Co. chairman Thomas Lamont, used bloggers and activist networks to channel anger against Lieberman for his staunch support of the Iraq war into support for Lamont's bid.

Numerous Democrat websites and blogs got behind Lamont and touted him as the anti-war alternative to Lieberman. Activist websites across the U.S., such as MoveOn.org, recruited volunteers and provided links for campaign donations.

Lamont's tactic worked and he came from near-anonymity to defeat Lieberman, taking 52 percent of Tuesday's vote.

U.S. political analysts are calling this a fundamental shift in the distribution of political power: that the candidates and parties are no longer in control of politics.

And the lesson isn't being lost in Canada.

Liberal leadership contenders are treating bloggers like mainstream journalists, and politicians and activists are using networks such as MySpace.com to connect with supporters spread far and wide.

Campaign websites are expected but people now want more from a site than just information.

"Five years ago you could treat your website like a brochure for the candidate, but now it's far more important to treat it as a two-way dialogue," said Mark Marrissen, campaign manager for Stephane Dion's Liberal leadership bid.

"We don't edit the feedback, so there can be negative stuff about the candidate. It's really important to give people the opportunity to voice their opinions."

Gerald Brier, assistant professor of political science at the University of B.C., said campaign websites have given the voter a chance to be more active in their decision.

"If I was a smart voter in 1984 and wanted to make an informed decision, I would have relied on my candidate to come to my door with a copy of his platform," he said. "Now I can just go to Conservatives.ca or Liberals.ca and get it there."

Brier also noted the essential role websites now play in fundraising.

"With the rules now about small campaign donations you have to find efficient ways to find and collect from multiple donors," Brier said. "The Internet has been very helpful in that way, much like direct mail advertising was in the 1920's."

Denise Brundston has worked on a number of provincial and federal Liberal campaigns. She says fundraising capacity is the Internet's biggest impact on campaign politics.

"With the new campaign finance regulations, our bread and butter is no longer the corporate world but the grassroots Liberals," she said. "With e-mail and Internet networking we can reach out to those people."

E-mail has altered communication of all types, campaigning included.

"Twenty years ago campaigns relied on a team of people stuffing envelopes," Marrissen said. "It may seem obvious, but e-mailing is a pretty fundamental change."

Brundston said e-mail contact not only allows the campaign team to get information out but also to get feedback.

So websites and e-mail have changed the way campaigns connect directly with voters.

Beyond direct connections, campaign information has always been filtered by the media.

Bloggers are changing that.

Campaign managers now pay close attention to the blogging world. Marrissen said bloggers play a particularly important role in leadership races, where the voters are political party members.

"The blogs are only read by a small segment of the population," he said. "But they are likely people who are or want to be delegates at the leadership convention. And they're reading the blogs because bloggers are independent and because the leadership race is not yet being followed by the news media."

To that end, Marrissen has tailored Dion's campaign towards bloggers.

"We try to engage with bloggers," he said. "We have a blog campaign chair and vice-chair, and they set up interviews between independent bloggers and Stephane, much like we would with the media."

Stephen Taylor is the founder of ConservativeBloggers.ca, the host site for conservative bloggers. He said, during the 2006 federal election, his blog got thousands of hits.

"In blogs, you get a voice that isn't usually represented," Taylor said. "People come to the blogs looking for specific or new information or a different perspective on an issue—things they can't find in the news."

Taylor thinks blogs also play an important role in impacting and monitoring the media.

"During the [federal] election, a lot of blogs broke issues before the news picked it up," he said. "A lot of journalists were coming to the blogs to find out what was going on."

Taylor said bloggers inspect the mainstream media closely for errors. For example, some bloggers noticed a Reuters picture from Lebanon with smoke much thicker and darker than other photographs of the same scene showed.

"They wrote, 'Hey, that looks like Photoshop work,' " Taylor said. "The next day Reuters pulled the picture."

Bloggers then inspected other photos by the same photographer, Adnan Hajj, and found more tampering. One was a picture claiming to show an Israeli fighter jet dropping three missiles when in fact it was dropping one flare, which Hajj cloned twice.

Reuters subsequently ended their association with Hajj and pulled all of his 920 pictures from their database.

Brier agreed blogs that provide real-time commentary from average people are playing a new role in the distribution of power.

"During election debates there are now all kinds of running commentaries," Brier said. "This can influence how the media portrays the outcome of the debate—who won, who lost—or how people think about what happened. That's a powerful tool."

The Internet has certainly influenced the pace of politics. "What used to happen in a week in a campaign now happens in a couple of hours," Marrissen said.

And Web-based networking is making it possible for politicians and activists to reach out to people beyond their usual support base.

Marc Emery, leader of the B.C. Marijuana party, said he uses Internet networking daily to guide people interested in politics, but unsure how to get involved.

"We're on MySpace.com, which now has over 100 million users," Emery said. "Most of them are young people, 16- to 30-year-olds, looking for guidance and leadership. It's a massive pool of people waiting to be harnessed."

Emery, who spends three to five hours a day on MySpace, said people contact him daily asking for advice on political involvement.

"First I ask for their postal code, then I look up their House representative or MP and tell them what they can do," he said.

"It's people from all over the world who come to me and say, 'I want to help but I don't know how.' I've gotten thousands of people involved in the democratic process."

Emery said Internet networking of this sort has allowed him to connect with demographics normally hard to touch.

"I've talked to people or groups I've never had contact with," he said. "I've been able to get them to join campaigns throughout the States."

ISSUE 2

The big blog: Have blogs decentred traditional news media?

✗ NO

Death by Blog? An Examination of the Relevance of Mainstream Media in the Era of Citizen Journalism
Mary Francoli

Mary Francoli received her Ph.D. in political science from the University of Western Ontario. She has taught at Carleton University and is currently the Leverhulme Visiting Fellow in New Media and Internet Politics at Royal Holloway, University of London. She is interested in the impact of new media on governance, the state, and society. Her research is largely focused on the idea of the "digital commons" and how new forms of "e-participation" affect the relationship between citizens and their elected representatives. She has also been looking at how governments, particularly the Canadian government, are adopting "e-government" strategies, and researching the institutional and policy changes that are required for these strategies to be realized.

In 2002 the outspoken Republican Trent Lott resigned from the U.S. Senate after racist remarks he made at a colleague's birthday party caught the attention of the media and were widely publicized. *Meet the Press*, NBC's weekly talk show, was the first of literally hundreds of mainstream news outlets to discuss the comments (Kline & Burstein, 2005, p. 11); however, the story originated on the Internet and had been circulating for quite some time before the mainstream media picked it up. This was perhaps the first real, and very public, instance of weblogs, or **blogs**, breaking a political story. Blogs are websites that resemble personal diaries where the author posts thoughts, opinions, and comments, usually focused on a specific topic. Many blogs are arranged in reverse chronological order and contain numerous hyperlinks to other websites (Blood, 2002; Frost, 2004). The blogging public, on the other hand, are often known as bloggers and the most popular bloggers as the "bloggerati." They, along with other technophiles, were sent into frenzy over the Lott affair. Heaps of praise were given for this new citizen-driven communication tool and its promise for enhancing democracy. Indeed, it was one of the crowning achievements of blogs and marked the introduction of the **blogosphere** as a new arena for political debate and citizen engagement.

The Lott incident gave rise to what has become a seemingly endless debate over the actual impact and utility of blogs and the blogosphere. Some have gone so far as to argue that blogs are replacing, or decentring, the mainstream media when it comes to delivering news and political affairs and informing policymaking. In a new book dedicated to the issue, technological guru and cultural icon Adam Curry argues that blogging represents "the liberation of the news and information we read, watch or hear from the constraints of Big Media Control" (quoted in Kline & Burstein, 2005, p. 271). Many academics have agreed. According to Jay Rosen at New York University, "professional journalism has entered a period of declining sovereignty in news, politics and the provision of facts to public debate" (quoted in Kline & Burstein, 2005, p. 319). Given this, one can't help but feel that the communication landscape is changing, perhaps irrevocably, with reports that forty thousand new blogs are created every day, or one new blog each second. However, a closer look at the state of the blogosphere and an examination of its relationship to mainstream media like television and the press suggests that this initial Pollyannaism about the place and impact of the citizen-journalist may have been somewhat inflated. Rather, the growth and development of the blogosphere seems to be having the opposite effect, by reinforcing the dominance and continued health of mainstream media at a time when pundits are lamenting its declining relevance.

Despite the emergence of new technologies and new media applications like blogs, the mainstream media is adapting and will not be relinquishing to the bloggerati its privileged role as the dominant arena for discussion and debate about the daily affairs of the community, nation, and global society. I will demonstrate this by first examining the growth and composition of the blogosphere, as well as the current state of mainstream media. Next, interviews I conducted with members of the mainstream media will highlight the positive impact that blogs are having on traditional media. Finally, I will illustrate some of the fundamental problems with blogs that purport to deliver news and political affairs, pointing to advantages the mainstream media has in the delivery of such information.

GROWTH AND COMPOSITION OF THE BLOGOSPHERE

Let's begin by reviewing what we know about blogs. Thanks to sites such as technorati.com, we know that the blogosphere is growing by leaps and bounds. While it is impossible to ascertain the total number of blogs, it is estimated that there are over 50 million (technorati.com, 2006). Growth has been rapid, and it is argued that the blogosphere doubles in size approximately every six months. Today, it is estimated that the blogosphere is a hundred times bigger than it was just three years ago (technorati.com).

Blogs spring up on any topic you can imagine. For example, Bloggers Blog is a blog for bloggers with news and trends related to blogging (bloggersblog.com). Cute Overload is a blog that collects and posts cute images, primarily of animals (cuteoverload.com). This site was a 2006 winner of the Webby Awards in the People's Voice category. There is Crazy-ass Family, a blog created and updated by a mother blogging about her family. As she says, "you just can't make this stuff up" (crazyassfamily.blogspot.com). For a list of some award-winning blogs from around the world, one can visit the weblog awards site (weblogawards.org). This is just a glimpse into the diverse content found in the blogosphere.

News and political affairs constitute only one small category of blog in the expansive blogosphere; but this doesn't mean people will turn to blogs instead of television, newspapers, or even online alternative news sites for the information they need to participate meaningfully in society. Many blogs are not kept up-to-date. According to technorati.com, only 55 percent of new blogs remain active after their first three months of existence. This means that almost half of new blogs become virtually useless as a means of gathering news and information within a very short time. Of those more diligent bloggers, 11 percent update their blogs weekly (technorati.com, 2006). Yet, again, a weekly update is problematic for news and political junkies who have become used to and demand the instantaneous stream of information that 24-hour cable networks like CBC Newsworld or CNN provide.

THE STATE OF MAINSTREAM MEDIA

Individuals appear to be aware that blogs might not be an ideal place to find reliable news and information, and there are signs that they not yet ready to abandon their more trusted news sources. The number of visits made to even the most popular blogs still tends to fall far short of the number of viewers that tune in to the evening television news (Kline & Burstein, 2005, p. 5). In fact, more traditional media such as television and newspapers have been doing fairly well. Statistics Canada (2005) tells us that newspaper and advertising revenue has been on the rise. More significantly, the industry enjoyed a boost in circulation revenue between 2003 and 2004, a time when blogs were supposed to be rapidly growing in popularity. Other evidence indicates that over half of all adults read a newspaper every day, and the amount of time they spend doing this has remained stable in spite of the competition of blogs (Canadian Newspaper Association, 2006). Perhaps this is because newspapers remain accessible and more tactile, portable, and easily shared, and they are often available in coffee shops and other public places where citizens tend to congregate and discuss the news of the day.

Canadian and foreign news and public affairs programs, on both conventional and specialty pay television, have also enjoyed increased popularity during the time that blogs are supposed to have been stealing a significant share of the media audience. People are just not turning away from the familiar, and they aren't as comfortable using blogs as some of the most ardent advocates might have us believe. In March 2005, the Pew Internet and American Life Project reported that 62 percent of Americans who regularly go online didn't even really know what a blog was (Beeson, 2005, p. 18). The situation hasn't improved with time. A Gallup poll in February 2006 showed reading blogs at the bottom of a list of 13 popular online activities, with 60 percent of respondents stating that they never read blogs (Bowman, 2006, p. 88).

THE POSITIVE IMPACT OF BLOGS ON THE MAINSTREAM MEDIA

Despite this rather bleak picture of the blogosphere, blogs have had a very important role and significant impact on how mainstream media conducts its business. Interviews with editors, reporters, and producers with some of Canada's most recognized mainstream media outlets, such as the *Globe and Mail*, the *National Post*, the *Toronto Star*, *CBC*, and *CTV* reveal some interesting results. Counter to criticism that blogs may be encouraging laziness among journalists by enabling them to gather information via blogs, many journalists suggest that blogs make them more accountable and force them to work harder. Raj Ahluwalia, a producer at the CBC, explains the situation this way: "For everything you do someone is watching. People are able to critique and have an outlet to critique. It makes you more conscious of what you say … you double or even triple check your facts" (personal communication, May 2006). Members of the mainstream media may be right to feel concerned, as bloggers are aware of their power. Indeed, some early bloggers in discussing their relationship with mainstream media stated, "It's 2001 and we can Fact Check your ass" (Matheson, 2004, p. 452).

Blogs are not only pressuring the mainstream media to do its job better, but they are also bolstering its relevance. Blogs don't exist in a vacuum. The mainstream media feeds the blogging public by keeping people informed and providing them material on which to offer their opinions or comments. And almost all blogs—particularly those focused on news and political affairs—link to existing mainstream media sites. The number of bloggers (excepting mainstream journalists who blog) who actually gather and report their own news is negligible. For the most part they tend to comment on the work done by the mainstream media (Kline & Burstein, 2005, p. 241).

The argument that blogs may be decentring mainstream media also neglects the fact that the mainstream media has been embracing the blogosphere. Blogs provide journalists with access to a wealth of ideas and viewpoints of people from all walks of life and communities, ensuring that more voices are heard in mainstream sources (Kline & Burstein, 2005, p. xv). By surfing community- or issue-specific blogs, journalists can get an idea of what members of the public are saying about any number of issues. However, while awareness of public sentiment is important, journalists have shown a reluctance to rely on information gathered solely from blogs, pointing to their increased need to fact check, as noted above.

Mainstream media outlets have also embraced the blogosphere by becoming active participants as journalists establish their own websites and blogs. Websites constructed by the mainstream media are doing exceptionally well. CNN's site attracts over 22 million users a month, and the *New York Times* more than 10 million a month (Kline & Burstein, 2005, p. 241). This is far beyond what most popular political news blogs receive. A quick search of sites such as cyberjournalist.net shows how quickly journalists and mainstream media institutions have been to set up their own blogs. In October 2003, cyberjournalist.net linked to 77 institutional blogs (Matheson, 2004, p. 450). Three years later, it showed 180 institutional blogs, a further 82 blogs set up by mainstream media for a limited period (usually during a specific event), and a further 94 blogs written by journalists, but not hosted on their affiliated news sites (cyberjournalist.net, 2006). Taken together, this represents growth of close to 400 percent over a three-year period. And it's not just the American media going online. *Maclean's* popular columnist Paul Wells writes one of the most widely read Canadian political blogs, and there are at least eleven blogs by various columnists at the *Toronto Star*. The *National Post* is home to seven blogs while the *Globe and Mail* hosts eight. Television is not getting left behind. The CTV website has a blog for Kris Abel called Tech Life. Kevin Newman, Global television's national anchor, has been hosting a blog with posts going back to May 2005. The CBC has an official blog appropriately titled Inside the CBC. Its Radio 3 website is also home to a blog.

Institutional and professional blogs differ from the main news organization's website. Typically, information and opinions are intertwined with existing biases that are presented up front. Blogs show utility here as they solicit feedback and allow for interactivity in a way that is difficult for the news organization to do, given its duty to uphold traditional professional norms such as objectivity and balance. Many blogs offer a comments feature where anyone can go to submit a comment or to provide further information (MacKinnon, 2004). The tendency to provide hyperlinks to a plethora of other sources, including other media outlets and blogs, also lends to uniqueness. In general, however, news organization websites tend to shy away from linking to competing media for fear of losing their audience.

INSTITUTIONALIZATION OF THE MEDIA AND THE WEAKNESS OF BLOGS

It is important to remember that mainstream media has the advantages of institutional establishment and resources for delivering news and political affairs. Members of the Press Gallery are given a pass that allows them access to the Parliamentary precinct without needing to constantly clear security; this pass provides access to the scrums, where media have the unique opportunity to regularly question politicians. It is a time and place that is specially reserved for accredited journalists. The average citizen and even many Hill staffers are not allowed access to the scrum area at that time. Election campaigns are another prime example. In Canada, various members of the mainstream media are usually assigned to follow a particular party during the campaign. This means going on tours with them—a rather costly venture that isn't open to everyone. In short, journalists have the privilege of access; bloggers, for the most part, do not.

The institutional organization of mainstream media also means that it is supposed to be an unbiased, objective source of information. Bloggers, on the other hand, are not subject to the same professional standards or obligations. This typically leads one to question the veracity of information they might read on a blog. As Tyler Hamilton, an Internet reporter and blogger with the *Toronto Star* argues, "It's the fact journalists working for media outlets are paid that keeps us unbiased, because we are in the business of providing quality journalism to readers. But how do I know, reading a blog, that the person behind it isn't being paid behind the scenes by an organization to say certain things? We don't. But if I get caught in the same situation at work, I get in trouble. I can't take junkets. Bloggers can" (personal communication, April 27, 2006). It's not just the inability to accept junkets that differentiates bloggers from mainstream journalists. Blogs by their very nature are opinion oriented. Susan Delacourt, bureau chief at the *Toronto Star*, explains the nature of journalism well: "It's only real journalism when it aspires to fairness, balance and dispassionate observation" (personal communication, April 27, 2006). According to Gloria Galloway at the *Globe and Mail*, this issue of fairness and balance contributes to questions regarding the credibility of blogs: "Many operate under assumed names and most are heavily slanted—as is their right. So I would never just quote from a blog." Others, such as Norris McDonald at the *Toronto Star*, express similar sentiments: "Blogging to me is done (in the main) by a bunch of egotistical know-it-alls with (mostly) axes to grind. Much of what is presented as 'fact' is rumour or twisted. There is next to no credibility" (personal communication, April 27, 2006).

Technophiles like to point out that in spite of their lack of access to institutionalized news-gathering resources, bloggers have managed to break stories, such as the aforementioned comments made by Senator Lott that led to his resignation. In the United States, bloggers are credited with exposing broadcasting stalwart Dan Rather and questioning the documents he used on the CBS evening news to discredit President Bush's military record. Blogactive.com broke a major story when it published audio of Republican Congressman Edward Schrock, a well known opponent to gay rights in the United States, soliciting men for sex (Kline & Burstein, 2005, p. 12).

But perhaps the best known, or most memorable, example of a blog breaking a story was in 1998 when Matt Drudge, author of the infamous Drudge Report, wrote about former President Clinton's affair with Monica Lewinsky (BBC, 1998).

However, it is important to note that what happens in the United States doesn't always ring true in Canada, particularly when it comes to the relationship between news and politics. In a 2005 article, "Are Canadian Bloggers Pussies?" Siri Agrell found that "in a year when American bloggers led major stories on both sides of the border and Canadian politics reached new levels of intrigue and animosity, political blogs in this country made little—if any—impact." Agrell attributes this ambivalence about the blog to the "polite, self-deprecating modus operandi" and a fear of being accused of libel that is so often described as typically Canadian. Bloggers themselves blame the public and lack of interest in the political process. "It's not that we're pussies or afraid," Catherine McMillan, author of Small Dead Animals, one of Canada's political blogs, told Agrell. "The key difference, I think, is that our traffic levels need to build and the network itself needs to build." However, as *National Post* editor Mick Higgins remarked, even in those few cases in the United States where bloggers have managed to break stories, "it does seem that it took the mainstream media to highlight the work of the bloggers to get it to a wider audience" (personal communication, April 27, 2007). This is well illustrated by the *Meet the Press* coverage of the Lott scandal.

In speaking to Agrell, Catherine McMillan laments that lack of credibility is contributing to the low flow of traffic on blog sites. Again, the question of credibility surfaces in relation to the blogosphere, where rumour and innuendo have tended to be favoured over facts. Remembering the words of its longest-serving former editor, C. P. Scott, who once stated, "Comment is free, but facts are sacred," the *Guardian* in the United Kingdom launched a new blog titled Comment is Free, or CiF. It exhibits the problem of the blog as a means of news delivery and issues related to credibility well. CiF was meant to be a forum where anyone could comment and columnists could engage directly with readers. Georgina Henry of the *Guardian* describes the result of this experiment as a "rude shock." There are days, she says, "when I have spent hours removing the anti-semitism and Islamophobia that dances round any piece about Israel/Palestine, and the incoherent abuse, swearing, the false statements, the ill-disguised misogyny, the intimidation, and the downright nastiness that fuels so many comments, I wonder whether Guardian values—free comment, but fair comment too—are in danger of being drowned out in an anarchic, unmoderated medium" (Henry, 2006). Such statements are common on blogs and are evidence that many are simply electronic diaries of a sort that are used as an outlet for rants and extremism as opposed to the more balanced work that the mainstream media is supposed to provide.

The long and short of it is that while blogs are in no way going to replace or even displace traditional media, they do serve a very useful function and purpose. They are helping the mainstream media do its job better by providing access to people who might not otherwise be able to reach a large audience, and also by serving as a system of checks and balances to ensure facts really do remain sacred. However, the mainstream media is not under any great threat when it comes to its command over the production of news and political affairs. Its institutionalization and wealth of resources provide access to political players in a way that the average blogger could never hope to obtain. Mainstream media outlets have also demonstrated an ability to adapt to new media applications such as blogs and are still well received by audiences. Broadcast news, and to a lesser extent newspapers, continue to be the dominant sources of information for citizens on the pressing news and information of the day. Given the proclivity of bloggers to substitute gossip and innuendo for facts and figures, it is questionable whether they will ever receive the same level of credibility as more conventional and trusted news formats.

Before worrying that traditional media will become obsolete, we should also remember that similar claims have been made in the past. The emergence of television sent many people into a tizzy about from the future of books and radio (Keith, 2000, p. 11). Likewise, the emergence of the Internet led many others to doubt the survival of television (Tapscott, 1998), and it was rumoured that shopping malls might disappear with the growth of e-commerce. New technologies don't always mean the death of old technologies; instead, we should question how they are changing and even, as we've seen here, strengthening more established media institutions.

CONCLUSION

While this chapter has demonstrated the growth of the blogosphere, it has argued that the mainstream media retains its dominance when it comes to the delivery of news and political affairs. A look at the state of the mainstream media shows that advertisers continue to place their trust and money there, and citizens do not appear to be abandoning their traditional news consumption habits (although they are certainly modifying them). Indeed, citizens are using the Internet only rarely to find news, and the audience that tunes in to the evening television news continues to surpass the traffic on even the most popular blogs. An examination of the benefits enjoyed by mainstream media organizations and their willingness, and ability, to adapt to new media have also pointed toward an inflated sense of euphoria on the part of those arguing their displacement in favour of the citizen-blogger. Rather, mainstream media's embrace and awareness of the blogosphere is allowing it to serve democracy better. It can better understand public sentiment, it has an increased capacity for interactivity, and it provides material for the blogging public while becoming increasingly accountable for its work and actions.

References

Agrell, S. (2005, October 6). Are Canadian bloggers pussies? Why Canadian bloggers have yet to break a major political scandal. *Maisonneuve*. Available at http://www.maisonneuve.org/index.php?&page_id=12&article_id=1830

BBC. (1998, January 25). Scandalous scoop breaks online. *BBC news*. Retrieved August 30, 2006, from http://news.bbc.co.uk/2/hi/special_report/1998/clinton_scandal/50031.stm

Beeson, P. (2005, March). Blogging: What is it? And how has it affected the media? *Quill*, 16–19.

Blood, R. (2002). *The weblog handbook: Practical advice on creating and maintaining your blog.* Cambridge, MA: Perseus.

Bowman, J. (2006, March). 2006—year of the blog. *Policy Options*, 88–90.

Canadian Newspaper Association. (2006). *The ultimate online guide to Canadian newspapers.* Retrieved June 5, 2006, from http://www.cna-acj.ca/client/cna/cna.nsf/web/FactsReadership

Cyberjournalist.net. (2006). Retrieved June 2, 2006, from http://www.cyberjournalist.net

Frost, G. (2004, November 30). "Blog" tops U.S. dictionary's words of the year. *Reuters.com*. Available at http://www.reuters.com/

Henry, G. (2006, May 29). The anarchy and the ecstasy. *The Guardian*. Available at http://www.guardian.co.uk

Keith, M. (2000). *Talking radio: An oral history of American radio in the television age*. New York: M. E. Sharpe.

Kline, D., & Burstein, D. (2005). *Blog! How the newest media revolution is changing politics, business, and culture*. CDS Books: New York.

MacKinnon, R. (2004). *The world-wide conversation: Online participatory media and international news*. Retrieved August 31, 2006, from http://cyber.law.harvard.edu/blogs/gems/techjournalism/WORLDWIDECONVERSATION.pdf

Matheson, D. (2004). Weblogs and the epistemology of the news: Some trends in online journalism. *New Media & Society, 6*(4), 443–468.

Statistics Canada. (2005, December 8). Newspaper publishers. *The Daily*. Retrieved August 20, 2006, from http://www.statcan.ca/Daily/English/051208/d051208c.htm

Tapscott, D. (1998). *Growing up digital: The rise of the net generation*. New York: McGraw-Hill.

Technorati.com. (2006). Retrieved June 2, 2006, from http://www.technorati.com/

Discussion Questions

1. How do you receive information about current affairs and politics? Do you use blogs? Why do you use certain forms of media and not others?

2. Are weblogs and journalism fundamentally different? If so, how?

3. One blogger has stated: "Blogging ain't journalism, but more of it should be, if we're serious about 'advancing' this form." Do you agree, and how might blogs be "advanced" as a form of journalism?

ISSUE 3

Big Brother society: Can video surveillance protect us from terror?

✔ YES

CCTV in the United Kingdom: Britons Apparently Like Big Brother Watching Them
Joseph Scanlon

Joseph Scanlon is professor emeritus and director of the Emergency Communications Research Unit at Carleton University. After a career in journalism he joined the faculty of the Carleton School of Journalism, serving as the school's second director. His interest in the study of rumours led to his current research in the sociology of disaster. He has written more than two hundred book chapters and academic and professional articles in his field. He now lives part of the year in London, England, which helps explain his interest in CCTV in the United Kingdom.

When a music fan in Texas was looking for information about the Beatles, he logged onto a website that linked him to a webcam in Liverpool, which he hoped would show him visuals of the Cavern Club where the Beatles got their start. As he was watching, he saw three men using a ladder to climb up and smash a window and break into a building near the club. He phoned the Merseyside police, who were astonished to receive his call but responded in time to arrest three men as they left the crime scene in their car ("Fab Four Fan," 2006).

No one in the United Kingdom would have been surprised to learn about that incident, because closed-circuit television (CCTV) is everywhere in the United Kingdom. The London Underground has cameras in station entrances, stairs, escalators, platforms, and train cars. Throughout the U.K. there are cameras in shopping malls, public and private buildings, restaurants, city centres, and residential neighbourhoods. Cameras in hospitals support covert surveillance of parents suspected of abusing their children, and cameras are being installed to help traffic wardens issue parking tickets. In Bradford, CCTV is linked to the Automatic Number Plate Recognition (ANPR) system. If police type a licence plate into the system, when the camera picks up the vehicle with that plate number it pings. There are so many cameras in the United Kingdom that in 1999 the BBC estimated citizens could expect to be caught on camera every five minutes (Duffy, 1999), and in 2004, a Home Office study estimated Britain had 10 percent of the world's CCTV cameras (Sharpe Research, 2004).

Time and time again, CCTV has been used in the aftermath of major incidents. For example, at 8:50 a.m., July 7, 2005, three suicide bombers blew themselves up on the London Underground. An hour later, a fourth detonated a bomb on a bus in Tavistock Square. The bombings left 52 dead and 700 injured. Immediately, scores of police started watching hundreds of hours of videotape. Five days later, the assistant commissioner of the Metropolitan Police announced police had retrieved CCTV footage showing the four bombers at King's Cross Station shortly before the attacks. Later, police found more tapes showing the four en route to their deadly mission and tapes of a practice run.

When CCTV cameras were initially installed, they were used for surveillance of public areas. That use did not raise concern: it was accepted that people could not expect privacy walking along the street. CCTV has expanded enormously since then and in recent years has come under some statutory control and a few guidelines. However, these measures have done little to restrain its use, and its application has never been seriously challenged in the courts. Despite the steadily expanding use of CCTV and despite a review that suggested CCTV has minimal impact on reducing crime (Welsh & Farrington, 2002), public support for CCTV in Britain still appears to be extremely high. Britons are well aware Big Brother is watching and seem to like it that way.

Why is CCTV so readily accepted in the United Kingdom? Perhaps it is because for well over a century, persons in the U.K. have been the targets of terrorism, initially by anarchists, then by the Irish Republican Army, now by Islamic suicide bombers. [1] Though this chapter does not take a stand for or against CCTV and its obvious invasion of privacy, it is perhaps not surprising that these seemingly never-ending threats should lead to public acceptance of invasive measures to combat them. It also seems clear that acceptance was bolstered by the fact that CCTV videos have played a widely publicized role in solving high-profile cases and providing evidence related to terrorist attacks.

CCTV EVERYWHERE

In the U.K., public use of images caught on CCTV cameras is normal. For example, the London Metropolitan Police released photos of men who failed in a second attempt to bomb the Underground. They also released visuals of a man leaving a Citibank cash machine who, they said, was using a pinhole camera to copy card information and PINs (Singh, 2006). They use camera to focus on the leaders of protests, gathering visual evidence in case they decide to make an arrest. All police publicize the CCTV camera success: when new cameras were installed in Surrey, the police issued a news release announcing two arrests within the first two days (Surrey Police, 2002).

Does all this help reduce crime? After reviewing dozens of studies of CCTV's effectiveness, David Welsh and Brandon Farrington (2002) concluded, "Overall the best current evidence suggests that CCCTV reduces crime to a small degree. CCTV is most effective in reducing vehicle crime in car parks, but it had little or no effect on public transit and city centre settings." However, Welsh and Farrington said they found problems with 24 of the 46 studies they reviewed: more than half had no second area as a control. Some that were rigorous were done not just after CCTV was installed but after other innovations as well, making it difficult to determine what exactly caused shifts in levels of crime. For example, in one case special patrols were added just before the cameras were put in place (Burrows, 1979).

Nevertheless, public support for CCTV appears strong. The Home Office commissioned two studies of public attitudes toward CCTV. One, based on focus groups, found that people perceived CCTV as an anticrime measure that helps deter criminal and antisocial behaviour: "People generally claim they feel safer where CCTV is installed, and express unquestioning faith in its crime prevention effectiveness" (Sharpe Research, 2004, p. 7). Those in the focus groups did not perceive CCTV as an invasion of personal privacy. They saw being watched by a camera as little different from being watched by passers-by. They also had faith in British criminal justice: "People frequently quote the maxim 'innocent until proved guilty' and genuinely believed that this prevails in the British system of law enforcement and criminal justice. They expect citizens to be fairly and benignly treated" (p. 7).

The other study, a survey in three high-crime areas, found that 82 percent favoured CCTV—with 57.3 percent very happy. Only 4 percent were unhappy, and 14 percent declined to express an opinion. Those interviewed had clear ideas about the impact of CCTV: crime rates would fall, people would report more incidents, fewer people would be hanging around, and the police would respond more quickly. They also said installation of CCTV would affect their behaviour,

> Overall, 15 percent said they would go to places they currently avoided once CCTV was installed. Of those who actually avoided places in daylight 30 percent said that they would go to places once CCTV were installed. Of those who avoid places after dark, 25 percent said they would go to new places if CCTV were installed. (Welsh & Farrington, 2002, p. 38)

Two similar studies were conducted in Scotland. One found CCTV had no impact on reducing crime (Central Research Unit, 1999). The other found some reduction (Short & Ditton, 1996).

Why the Support?

Why is there such strong public support with so little solid evidence? It seems likely this comes from CCTV's role in a number of high-profile incidents

- On December 17, 1983, IRA terrorists placed a bomb outside Harrods department store in Knightsbridge, killing 6 people and wounding 90. The bombers were arrested because their video images were caught on camera.

- On February 12, 1993, two adolescent boys kidnapped and later killed a youngster named Jamie Bulger. BBC's *Crimewatch* showed viewers computer-enhanced still pictures of the boys, created from tapes from cameras in the Bootle Strand Shopping Centre near Liverpool. The kidnappers were identified.

- In 1999, a man set off mail bombs in three separate incidents. Police watched 26,000 hours of tape before spotting him entering a food store.

- In 1992, a man kidnapped a real estate agent and held her in a makeshift grave. When police released an audio tape, the man's ex-wife heard it and called her son. Both recognized the voice. The man was convicted not only of the kidnapping but also of the murder of another woman.

The massive publicity given these incidents confirmed the impression that CCTV is effective in catching criminals.

THE LEGAL BASIS OF CCTV

Initially, CCTV was largely unrestricted. However, the issue was discussed in a 1997–98 report by the Select Committee of Science and Technology of the House of Lords. The committee noted that some witnesses said such systems "intrude on individual privacy and civil rights." But it also gained public acceptance and approval because CCTV cameras "help deter crime and assist the authorities to catch and prosecute criminals" (p. 4.1).

That year Britain passed the *Data Protection Act 1998*, and two years after that the Data Protection Commissioner issued a code of practice for CCTV. In the introduction, the commissioner stated,

> Closed circuit television (CCTV) surveillance is an increasing feature of our daily lives. There is an ongoing debate over how effective CCTV is in reducing and preventing crime, but one thing is certain, its deployment is commonplace.... We might be caught on camera while walking down the high street, visiting a shop or bank or travelling through a railway station or airport....

> There does seem to be public support for the widespread deployment of this surveillance technology, but public confidence has to be earned and maintained. (France, 2000, pp. 2–3)

The code of practice made clear that someone must be legally responsible for a CCTV system—and provided examples of proper use. It suggested, for example, that ATM machines must not be monitored in such a way as to catch PINs. The code also stressed people have a right to know CCTV is being used. As a result, municipalities advise the people about their rights. Wolverhampton, for example, published a form that people requesting images can fill out. It emphasizes in boldface type "Your Right to Know" and tells people what information to provide if they want to request images of themselves:

> The date, time and location of when your image was captured, together with a description of what you were wearing and a photograph will enable us to locate the footage. If you would like a particular incident searched for, please supply additional details. (Wolverhampton City Council, n.d., p. 1)

There are now four other statutes that cover various aspects of CCTV in Britain: the Human Rights Act 1998, the Regulation of Investigatory Powers Act 2000, the Freedom of Information Act 2000, and the Private Security Industry Act 2000. None place much restraint on its use.

While the Human Rights Act 1998 states that everyone has a qualified right to privacy, the Act also makes it clear that this right can be abrogated as necessary "in a democratic society in the interests of national security, public safety or the economic well-being of the country, for the prevention of disorder or crime, for the protection of health or morals, or for the protection of the rights and freedoms of others." This in effect exempts CCTV. The Regulation of Investigatory Powers Act 2000 deals only with cases where covert surveillance is involved, such as targeting of specific individuals. The Freedom of Information Act 2000 deals with CCTV only in the sense that access to information includes statistics on its use. Finally, the Private Security Industry Act 2000 empowers the Security Industry Authority to impose regulations and standards on sectors of the security industry and includes training requirements. This has no relevance to the use of CCTV for public surveillance.

A 1995 article by Colin Hay in Social and Legal Studies argued that incidents like the Bulger case—where CCTV was used to identify teenage criminals—created a moral panic. Hay also argued that the wide use of CCTV tapes constituted trial by the media and that the guilt of those spotted on tape was assured. It is certainly true that CCTV tapes are proving decisive evidence in criminal cases usually because they lead to a plea, but there is no evidence to suggest that the Bulger case or any other incident captured on CCTV has altered the public view of crime. Only time will show the total impact, just as time will show whether DNA, which is now being used mainly to proclaim innocence rather than guilt (when it does nothing of the kind), will persevere.[2]

Court Decisions Involving CCTV

Even those limited restraints on CCTV were reviewed as a result of a case now being appealed to the European Court of Human Rights (*Durant v. Financial Services Authority*, 2003). The case began when a customer of Barclays Bank sued and lost. He subsequently sued the Financial Services Authority (which regulates banks), citing the *Data Protection Act 1998* in hopes of acquiring some of the bank's documents. The British courts ruled that the fact that someone is mentioned in a document does not necessarily mean that document contains personal data. To be personal, a document has to focus on the person named. The decision means many privately owned surveillance cameras are not covered by the *Data Protection Act 1998*. For example, if a camera in a store is used merely to record on tape what goes on and images were retrieved only after a police request, they are not covered under the Act.

Two other legal cases specifically related to CCTV but did not challenge its use in a public area. In the first, a man was awarded damages by the European Court of Human Rights, which ruled that Brentwood Council had acted illegally when they passed images of his suicide attempt to television without making sure his identity was masked. The court stated specifically that Brentwood Council had violated Article 8 of the European Convention on Human Rights which guarantees a right to privacy.

The man had been walking along Brentwood High Street when he used a kitchen knife to cut his wrists. CCTV operators spotted his actions and called police. Later, the images were released to the media. Friends told the man they recognized him in advertising for a network television show called *Crime Beat*. He complained to Brentwood Council, who contacted the program and received assurances the images were masked. Yet when the program was run, friends and family recognized the man. He complained directly to the companies and received an apology, but nothing more. Not satisfied, he asked the British courts for permission to appeal but was refused. He then went to the European Court of Human Rights. It was argued he had surrendered his rights because his suicide attempt took place in public. The court rejected this argument. It said the earlier decisions that the television program had acted improperly and given apologies were insufficient: "Everyone whose rights and freedoms as set forth in this Convention [on Human Rights] ... shall have an effective remedy ... notwithstanding that the violation has been committed by persons acting in an official capacity" (*Peck v. UK*, 2003). The court said that an apology was not an effective remedy. It awarded 11,800 pounds in damages plus costs.

In the second case, a judge found two Liverpool men guilty of redirecting a council CCTV camera so they could spy on a woman in her home. The men had trained a camera on a woman's flat and watched her as she disrobed.

These cases to some extent restrict the use of CCTV images and the use of cameras to catch images outside their defined areas, but they do not inhibit the use of CCTV cameras for surveillance—as long as someone takes responsibility for this and notices are posted advising people CCTV is being used.

CONCLUSION

Overall, though the United Kingdom has more CCTV cameras than any other country in the world, the public seems to like this—and that support has remained even though there is little evidence that CCTV cameras have much impact on crime. Even when surveillance cameras are covered by legislation or subjected to court review, the constraints imposed on them, especially in public areas, are minuscule.

It is clear that CCTV can be used effectively if someone commits an overt act in a public place and that act is observed by a CCTV camera operator. That is one way it is used on the London Underground: when a criminal act is observed, the police are notified. They watch and record what is happening then move in and make an arrest. That is also what happens in most communities: the operators spot some untoward behaviour and notify police, who move in to investigate and, if necessary, make an arrest. Once that happens, a conviction is guaranteed—the tapes are accepted in court as convincing proof of guilt.

However, although CCTV tapes have played a crucial role in identifying those involved in major crimes such as the 2005 attacks on the London Underground, the Bulger kidnapping, or the mail bombings, CCTV has done little to prevent such occurrences. They are useful only after the fact, and the investment in time and personnel involved in using them was enormous. It seems likely that only in a high-profile case would it be possible to have police deploy the resources required to review all the available tape—and in the U.K. there is now an enormous amount of tape recorded every day.

When it comes to preventing serious crime, CCTV has serious limitations. It is of little value, for example, when no physical violence is visible as the crime is being committed. Jamie Bulger, for example, was led away by the two boys who kidnapped him. No one watching—even watching closely—would have observed anything untoward. It was only after the fact, when the little boy's disappearance had been reported, that he was observed leaving with the boys who kidnapped him. The same problem would arise when someone plants an explosive device. Bags, parcels, suitcases, and briefcases are misplaced too often for even the most dedicated tape watcher to notice this in time to prevent an explosion. It is also doubtful CCTV could help prevent suicide attacks. The Underground is full of people carrying various kinds of parcels and backpacks: suicide bombers would probably not be spotted unless they were already under police surveillance; and if that were the case, police would have to act without waiting for CCTV images to bolster any subsequent prosecution.

CCTV, in short, would appear to be of relatively little value in stopping terrorist attacks and of little value in stopping other serious crimes that do not involve visible physical violence. It is definitely of value after the fact—if it is deemed important enough to make the necessary commitment of time and personnel. Yet despite its limited value in reducing crime—except in car parks—CCTV is increasingly used in Britain, and the public seems to like that.

References
Cases

Durant v. Financial Services Authority (2003). E.W.C.A. Civ. 1746 (C.A.).

Peck v. UK (2003), App. No. 00044647/98) Eur. Ct. H.R.

Legislation

Human Rights Act 1998 (U.K.), 1998, c. 42, art. 8.

Secondary Sources

Burrows, J. N. (1979). The impact of closed circuit television on crime in the London Underground. In P. Mayhew, R. V. G. Clarke, J. N. Burrows, J. M. Hough, & S. W. C. Winchester (Eds.), *Crime in public view* (Home Office Research Study No. 49, pp. 21–29). London: Her Majesty's Stationary Office.

Central Research Unit, Scottish Office. (1999). *The effect of closed circuit television on recorded crime rates and public concern about crime in Glasgow.* Edinburgh: Home Office for Scotland.

Duffy, J. (1999, May 4). Something to watch over us. *BBC News.* Available at http://news.bbc.co.uk/

Fab Four fan in Texas nabs thieving three in Liverpool. (2006, August 26). *Daily Mail,* p. 9.

France, E. (2000). *CCTV code of practice.* London: Information Commissioner.

Hay, C. (1995). Mobilization through interpellation: James Bulger, juvenile crime and the construction of moral panic. *Social and Legal Studies, 4,* 197–223.

House of Lords. United Kingdom Parliament. (1997–98). *Select Committee on Science and Technology fifth report.* London: The Queen's Printer.

Sharpe Research Limited. (2004). *Public attitudes to the deployment of surveillance techniques in public places.* London: Information Commissioner's Office.

Short, E., & Ditton, J. (1996). *Does closed circuit television prevent crime? An evaluation of the use of CCTV surveillance cameras in Airdrie Town Centre.* Edinburgh: Central Research Unit, Scottish Office.

Singh, A. (2006, April 3). He just took a picture of your PIN. *Evening Standard,* p. 18.

Surrey Police. (2002, September 17). New cameras bring instant success [News release].

Welsh, B. C., & Farrington, D. P. (2002). *Crime prevention effects of closed circuit television: A systematic review.* London: Home Office Development and Statistics Division.

Wolverhampton City Council. (n.d.). *Data Protection Act 1998: CCTV images and you.* Wolverhampton, UK: Data Protection Adviser.

Notes

[1] The first terrorist attack against the London Underground occurred on October 30, 1881, at 8:13 a.m., just 20 years after the first line was built. A device planted by anarchists exploded between Charing Cross and Westminster and left 62 people dead, more than died in the most recent terrorist attacks.

[2] DNA can verify that blood or semen stains belong to a particular individual. They do not prove that someone was not involved in a crime, only that the samples obtained are not from that person.

ISSUE 3

Big Brother society: Can video surveillance protect us from terror?

✗ NO

Looking Away: The Problems of CCTV Surveillance Systems
Peter Simpson

Peter Simpson taught philosophy in three universities before he joined the Canadian Association of University Teachers (CAUT) as an assistant executive director. His responsibilities include developing policy and collective bargaining language on such topics as academic freedom and security and surveillance on university campuses.

In the mid-1990s I became involved in a grassroots challenge to the installation of a public CCTV surveillance system in Sudbury, Ontario. Like many older and smaller cities in Ontario, Sudbury had experienced enormous residential and commercial expansion outside of the city centre. Major subdivisions and so-called box stores were draining life and money from the downtown core, and this was having a negative impact on both the residents and the merchants who lived and worked downtown. With a grassroots group called Citizens for a Better Downtown, I participated in organizing community meetings to address the issue of urban decay and appealed to local politicians to respond to our concerns.

At the time, I was a professor in the Department of Philosophy at Laurentian University. A significant part of my interest in the issue of urban revitalization came from research I was conducting on the nature and control of social space. Within the context of our community activism, I raised the argument that downtown Sudbury required increased residential density—the city centre could thrive and develop only if there were more people living in it who could take it upon themselves to reclaim the space as their own. Part of my argument concerned the fairly common assumption that this area was dominated by the sort of visible criminal element that was making it unsafe for tourists and residents. Only by growing the residential community downtown, we maintained, could the city centre space be reclaimed and revitalized for everyone to enjoy. This, and not increased policing and heightened security, would lead to the development of the kinds of commercial activities (grocery stores, hardware stores, bookstores, bakeries, restaurants, and so on) that encourage and sustain a growing population.

While we engaged these issues in public meetings, other discussions were going on behind closed doors. Several key figures in the city, under the rubric of a volunteer civic organization, had been meeting with the Sudbury Regional Police. These discussions led to the phasing in of a rudimentary video surveillance system comprising 16 closed-circuit television cameras to monitor the entire downtown core. The arguments presented to support this system were more or less bound up with the notion of community safety: the cameras would both help police respond to crimes and deter the criminal element from committing them. This surveillance would, in turn, make it safer for people to visit and shop in the downtown, and, voilà, the revitalization of the city would be complete.

This broader context is important for at least two reasons: first, because my sense of the issues at stake in any constructive debate over CCTV systems, and about the dangers of surveillance in general, is irreducibly material. This is to say that the cameras at the centre of these systems are always placed somewhere, at some time, and, as I will argue below, coming to terms with the "somewhere, at some time" is essential to understanding the destructive impact of surveillance. Second, I want it to be clear that from the beginning my interest in this issue was situated in a dispute over how best to reverse the decay of urban social space, and to reclaim the "publicness" of the community. It was not bound up with some notion of protecting personal privacy and thus valorizing the primacy of individual rights.

In the weeks and months that followed the announcement of the surveillance camera system implementation, my work in advocating for increased residential life downtown was being supplanted by a critical engagement of the CCTV model being proposed as a solution to the problems facing the city. In effect, my challenge took the form of asking about the efficacy of the CCTV system: does it work? What is its work? And, to the consternation of many people in the media who interviewed me or reported on the debates I was engaged in with those arguing the other side, these questions presupposed an analytically prior question: what is it? What exactly is a CCTV system?

The obvious answer to this question is that a CCTV system is a network of cameras that display and record, from a remote location, the comings and goings of all people who move within the range of the cameras' vision. But what else is it besides this obvious, taken-for-granted definition? I am going to assume that the reader will understand that the question of efficacy cannot be answered by the sort of statistical data often cited in support of such systems. That is, surveillance systems cannot be demonstrated to reduce or eliminate crime since you cannot prove why something did not happen. More important still is the fact that no data were ever produced to support the installation of the camera system in Sudbury, despite claims by advocates of the system to the efficacy of cameras in deterring or reducing crime.

This paper is partly analytical and partly reflective. Similar programs to the CCTV system in Sudbury have been established elsewhere in Canada, many more have been established in the United States, and many, many more are in place and have been so for some time in the United Kingdom. As such, the arguments we were up against in Sudbury have been advanced elsewhere, and our criticisms will no doubt resonate with the experiences of activists and academics who have opposed surveillance of public space in other jurisdictions.

Further, the goal of this paper is to alert students of communications to the insidious claims-making that often lies hidden in the background when appeals are made about the importance of CCTV security systems. We all need to remain aware of the ways in which CCTV systems function as paradigms of the promise that news media make to their consumers: that what we see on the news is a neutrally and passively recorded real event, something so self-evidently "real" as to require no interpretation or analysis. This illusory appeal is precisely the sort of thing to which students of communication need to become critically attuned.

The paper engages three aspects of the CCTV system, and of camera surveillance in general: first, the peculiar nature of the cameras' supposedly neutral and objective placement and gaze—the way they do not *look at* particular problems but, rather, *look away*; second, the weakness of the notion that a surveillance camera can act as a deterrent, and ultimately as a preemptive remedy for crime; and third, the concession such cameras make to the notion of alienated, criminalized social space. I will argue that the cameras are not a solution to a specific problem, but rather, they make the problem they purport to address and solve worse by looking away from the root cause.

When the 16 cameras were introduced in Sudbury, the primary objective of their sponsors (a coalition of police and community groups, including the Lion's Club) was to achieve a more tangible sense of safety and security, which, they argued, would make citizens feel more comfortable shopping downtown. It is important to flesh out the notion of safety that we are working with here: it means, in effect, the protection of my body and my private property as I move through the public space. I am likely to feel unsafe if I am fearful of being robbed, raped, or beaten, or of having my personal space (in public) disturbed by unpleasant behaviour such as panhandling or squeegeeing by homeless people or other disaffected social groups.

Two points need to be made here. First, the fears may not be empirically supported. It may be the case that violent crimes like robberies, rapes, or random beatings (which citizens report fearing most about going into downtown city centres) do not happen, or that they do not happen any more often than elsewhere in the city. In fact, in nearly every major city in Canada and the United States, violent crimes have been declining steadily. Second, there may in fact be no absolute danger, but rather specific targets for specific crimes. To say that there are "specific targets for specific crimes" is not to assign to criminal behaviour a sense of rationality in selecting victims, either. Rather, it is the case that women, and not men, are most often victims of rape, and persons of apparent means, and not homeless people, targets of robbery.

The installation of cameras to monitor downtown areas does not depend on investigating and resolving either of these questions about the nature of risk in city centres. The cameras ignore rather than respond to questions about the legitimacy of fear, by posing as a deterrent to those whose actions, whether they happen or not, would be a cause for fear. Furthermore, the insensitivity of the cameras to class or gender (real features of victims of crimes) is held up as a strength: by recording all that happens, by being incapable of discriminating according to the very real categories that shape one's vulnerability to the sorts of assaults (whose likelihood is assumed by the fear), the cameras act as a comprehensive deterrent.

But worse, the cameras may actually incite fear. As Colin Hay (1995) has argued, in certain crucial ways, the presence of CCTV systems actually feeds these very fears. The installation of a CCTV system and the training of the cameras on the specific locations in a city amount to a definitive declaration that the areas being filmed are "crime scenes." Indeed, Hay argues that the installation both concedes the criminalization of the spaces recorded and, further, feeds the general fear that space in our world is lost to criminality. To enter such areas is, in effect, to become an actor in a media spectacle, an actor in the reality crime dramas we are familiar with through television. This is why we often feel a sense of mounting anxiety or menace whenever we see CCTV footage, a fact not lost on the producers of popular crime dramas.

People familiar with criminological research will know that crimes tend to happen in certain places, and they tend to be committed by certain people for reasons that are more or less known.

Spousal assault, rape, child abductions, and other violent crimes are likely to be committed by people we know or to whom we are related, and they are much more likely to happen in homes or in places where alcohol is consumed, such as bars. As such, these kinds of crimes are likely to go unrecorded by cameras capturing merely a panoramic view of downtown public space. Not only are so-called stranger crimes unlikely to occur, but surveillance cameras are also not likely going to be placed where more serious crimes take place.[1]

As solutions, then, CCTV systems are ineffective precisely because of their seemingly comprehensive scope. Indeed, they are far from comprehensive in the double sense of neither capturing "all crime" nor addressing any of the underlying reasons for crime. At best, they are tools for dealing insufficiently with the effects of material and cultural deprivation that is germane to modern society. Indeed, this is the lie of public CCTV surveillance systems: they do not *look at* all, but rather *look away* from the real bases of urban crime and violence.

When crimes do occur in downtown districts, they are more likely to be property crimes like petty theft or nuisance crimes such as so-called aggressive panhandling. Here too the indiscriminate nature of the cameras must be exposed for their fallacious underpinnings since the public spaces they monitor are neither neutral nor indiscriminate, but tend to be located on the streets and neighbourhoods of the poorest sections of the city, places where the lives and life chances of citizens are hardened and sharpened by poverty and other structural inequalities. If the desire to achieve greater security or safety in these areas is the primary goal, this would surely be better provided by the state if it put more money into providing opportunities for work, housing, health care, education, and other basic necessities for creating a truly civil society. Instead, terms like "security" and "safety" are being differentially promised only to those with the means to travel in and out of downtown, to shop, or to drink in bars. Thus, the indiscriminate nature and use of surveillance systems may provide security to those with property to protect in a space where the dangers are political and more broadly social in nature—dangers that arise from the failure of capitalist systems to achieve an equitable distribution of wealth. Again, the security of a camera network is not a way of addressing the specific problems of poverty and desperation that are often causes of crimes that happen downtown, but rather is a way of looking away and pretending either these problems don't exist or can't be resolved at their core.

Instead, surveillance systems offer a different and arguably false form of security. They assume public spaces like Main Street or the local park and playground are the kinds of places where citizens need to be protected. The security they provide is thus not tailored to specific problems and the places where these problems are likely to occur. The cameras, advocates argue, are intended to help solve any problem that might arise, not by recording criminal behaviour per se, but by threatening or actually doing so. Surely, nobody will feel safe knowing that if they are assaulted the crime against them will be recorded. People support the use of cameras because they want to know that the prospective assault will be prevented before it occurs. But, as I have already noted, what they ignore is the ways in which a space designated as worthy of CCTV surveillance is defined as functionally lawless, a zone of crime, real or potential.

One of the most serious crimes that occurred during my time in Sudbury and following the implementation of the CCTV system was the beating of a young man by two other young men. This was a particularly savage beating administered with a pool cue, and it occurred on the pretext that the one of the young men had looked at one of the other two, and a young woman with them, in an offensive way.

At the trial, the role of the CCTV system became an issue not because it was entered into the prosecution's evidence (as is so often the case in TV crime dramas like *Law & Order*), but because it failed to deliver on the promises that had been advanced to promote it. Although the various players in this crime had all passed through the system's gaze at one moment or another, the beating itself, and the events that led up to it, were not captured but occurred off camera. This notion of "off camera" space is vital for recognizing the limitations of the system's claim to deterrence. There is always an edge or a seam beyond or between which the cameras record nothing at all. As I attempted to argue in the Sudbury debates at the time, this means that while the cameras might at some point or another capture some types of crime, far more often their crime-prevention "success" is measured in how many crimes they merely displace by pushing them out of view.

Most important is the fact that if we are to take the issue of deterrence seriously, we must recognize that when people decide against committing a crime because they are afraid of being caught, they are doing so entirely based on rational calculation. And if someone wants to commit a crime and is thinking clearly and deliberately about doing so with a view to success (i.e., stealing the purse or car without getting caught), then they are likely going to move their activities to a place where they can operate beyond the gaze of the camera. In other words, deterrence presupposes the sort of person who would prey upon the limitations that are built into a CCTV system, that is, upon the space that exists beyond the scope of the camera's gaze. Therefore, CCTV systems cannot function as deterrents because those who are most likely to be deterred are not going to commit their crimes in the view of the cameras.[2]

The claim that surveillance cameras will deter crime has deeper problems, however. Much has been written about what philosophers call human existing, and the nature of choice and rationality upon which our existing rests.[3] We are always finding ourselves encountering specific situations already interpreted on the basis of the cultural tools and symbolic meaning systems we learn primarily from our families and other socializing groups, and as interpreted in the context of the projects, goals, and ambitions we have adopted. When something happens, it happens not in a way that we can objectively interpret, but already "makes sense" in terms of the cognitive schemas that have been shaped by experience, by means of which we anticipate and make ourselves at home in the world. When we hear a truly foreign language being spoken, we encounter a breach in our experience precisely because it is an event that doesn't help us in our project of getting to know and find our way around our world.

Our normal experience, on the contrary, is of things making sense, of things fitting our way of sorting the world. We do not calmly and rationally, let alone objectively and neutrally, hold objects or events up for decision and analysis, as if meaning or sense is something still to be determined. We are always constructing our experience (and ourselves and our identities) in relation to the objectives and meaning systems we have unwittingly adopted from a time before we knew the implications of adopting them. In ways most of us never fully reckon with, our ways of making sense of our experience have been operating inconspicuously, influenced by a variety of local factors, including our family and friends, but increasingly as well through the communications media we consume. The ideal of "passive neutrality" in how we interpret the world is clearly at odds with what is a robustly creative and active process of meaning and identity construction.

According to this way of looking at things, we are not purely rational and dispassionate creatures for whom the logic of deterrence can apply absolutely. Consider again the serious crime I described above involving the severe beating of the young man with the billiards cue. The evidence read into the court transcript by participants and eyewitnesses to the crime (remember the cameras did not capture the beating) suggested that the victim had made disparaging remarks about a young woman to some people on the street outside a local bar. Both the remark and the reason behind it were in dispute. However, what was not disputed was the fact that two young men interpreted (by the codes of masculinity generated by the culture with which they had come to identify) his remarks as a call to violence, a reading that was no doubt facilitated by their alcohol consumption. The billiards cue was a handy and opportune weapon, and they began to beat the young man mercilessly, stopping only when others intervened.

On the basis of the sort of person presupposed by the logic of deterrence, the two young men ought to have reflectively and neutrally weighed the seriousness of the remark. Then, upon calculating the gravity of the offence and the likelihood of it being captured on at least one of the surveillance cameras in the area, they should have stopped themselves from commencing with the brutality they were about to inflict. Rather, the young men's interpretations and behaviour lend credence to the sort of view of human experiencing I have described above—we experience an inherently contingent world within the flawed and limited terms of our immediate projects. In this case, the "weights" of alcohol, erotic energy (recall the presence of the girlfriend), and all the hardship of a life of frustration and want no doubt ensured the commission of a crime that no number of cameras could have prevented.

The point is not to excuse the beating in any way. Rather, my objective is to describe the futility of using surveillance cameras as instruments of deterrence. Here, as in cases of "captured" events like an aggressive panhandler harassing a senior citizen going into a bank, the cameras look away from what would otherwise be real deterrents to crime and social disorder: education, economic opportunities, and some form of vital social space.

In a collection of his early essays, David Foster Wallace (1997) defined addiction as entailing a relationship to something that poses as a solution to a felt problem, but in fact only worsens the problem.[4] Drawing on Wallace's terms, I take CCTV systems and surveillance cameras in general to be a crippling form of technological addiction. In using machines to make the social space apparently more humane, we only heighten the sense of social alienation and disconnection the machines are purportedly designed to correct. This, if you like, is the ultimate example of *looking away* from both the social and political causes of crime and urban decay and the possible solutions that involve promoting more authentic forms of human interaction as a means to revitalize social space.

The reasons that drive people to commit violence of any kind are complex, and their causes and solutions are deeply rooted in elaborate social networks. Supporters of CCTV surveillance often implore critics to come up with better solutions for addressing or resolving crime, or appeal to surveillance cameras as "just another" crime-fighting tool that should be acceptable on the grounds of common sense. I would argue, however, that this demand is disingenuous, and that even in sincere efforts to battle social disorder, surveillance cameras do little more than erase or obscure the complexity of the underlying problems, and ignore and suppress the real causes and solutions of crime. CCTV systems look away from causality, in all its details, toward an indifferent and impersonal recording of what can be captured and stored on film (or digitally, in the case of more sophisticated technologies).

Surveillance cameras fail to deliver on the promises of their supporters because they concede the very thing they seek to prevent—the criminalization of social space—and rely on a sense of decision making that is at odds with the nature of human experiencing. Further, this failure takes the form of exacerbating the very insecurities they hope to remedy by creating a culture of fear, suspicion, and social anxiety. In the end, unless we commit ourselves to seeing, recording, and addressing the true problems posed by the competing demands of social space, we will never be able to create safer and more secure communities.

References

Hay, C. (1995). Mobilization through interpellation: James Bulger, juvenile crime and the construction of a moral panic. *Social and Legal Studies, 4*(2), 197–223.

Wallace, D. F. (1997). *A supposedly fun thing I'll never do again: Essays and arguments.* Boston: Little, Brown & Co.

Notes

[1] A consequence of the indiscriminate gaze of the cameras is that it allows those monitoring them to more or less independently decide what is and is not actionable. In summary reports carried by the local Sudbury newspapers on the week's surveillance activities, the most common form of police intervention was to disrupt panhandlers. This is an interesting way in which something like the redistribution of private property becomes criminalized by virtue of the absence of specificity in the location and gaze of the cameras.

[2] I am not arguing that CCTV cameras do not deter crimes anywhere or at any time. Indeed, they do have some demonstrated efficacy as deterrents in closed spaces such as parking garages, where crimes are committed purely on the basis of rational decision making. Crimes like terrorism, violence, or those that occur as the result of drunken and disorderly behaviour (e.g., public urination) in city centres are highly unlikely to be prevented by the presence of a camera. The July 2005 subway bombings in London demonstrate this fact well.

[3] The most compelling of these is John Russon's *Human Experience* (State University of New York Press, 2003). It is a clear and forceful indictment of the fixation on abstract rational selfhood as the ordinary model of being a person and experiencing the world. Russon draws on various thinkers, from Aristotle to R.D. Laing, to argue that we are instead creatures shaped in vital ways to be open to specific opportunities, which we have selectively interpreted in ways learned and adopted from the demands of family life.

[4] Wallace is describing television, but the broader application of this definition is also apparent in his novel *Infinite Jest* (Little, Brown & Co., 1996).

Discussion Questions

1. What is your first reaction when you notice that you are in an area covered by CCTV surveillance?

2. How intrusive can something that poses as a deterrent be to your individual sense of privacy and security? Do you think that some people are more likely to have their privacy rights violated than others? If so, do you think this is just?

3. What are the broader societal effects of increasing surveillance in public space?

4. In what ways do technological solutions like surveillance systems, which claim to look more closely at social problems, actually look away from them?

5. If, as this chapter suggests, the British public accepts CCTV, does that make it right?

6. Who should decide what is proper in terms of privacy?

7. Does the fact that England has been subject to continual attacks by terrorists justify extraordinary measures?

8. What types of CCTV cameras are in use where you live, work, and/or go school? How often are you aware of being under surveillance? What do you think about being watched by monitors whom you do not know and cannot see? How does this make you feel?

ISSUE 4

Technological fixes: Can new communications technology save democracy?

✔ YES

Participatory Democracy Thriving on the Internet: A Modern Town Hall Meeting Occurs as Citizens Have Their Say—Electronically
Mary Gooderham (The Globe and Mail)

Nigel Blumenthal is not what you would call a political activist.

The Toronto consultant and software designer rarely attends public meetings. He can't vote because he's a British citizen, but said he wouldn't anyway. For years he has felt disillusioned with the ability of people to influence the political process.

But since he signed on to a computer forum on the amalgamation of Metropolitan Toronto two months ago, Mr. Blumenthal, 48, has renewed his faith in participatory democracy. Several times a day he joins the on-line discussion, throwing in comments about public policy or politicians' records and reading what others say about the issue.

"It's a reincarnation of the town hall meeting," Mr. Blumenthal said. "We may be seeing the birth of a whole new political medium here."

It's a feeling shared by people logging on to a rash of interactive political discussion groups around the world. Citizens are having their say—electronically—and hope they are being heard.

"These are places for people to participate," said Liz Rykert, a social worker and community organizer who runs the Website and Internet forum for the anti-amalgamation group Citizens for Local Democracy (C4LD). "The political process is about building positions and developing ways for people to get involved in civil society. For the last few years that's been relegated to the vote."

Ms. Rykert, who created an electronic network for eight community agencies involved in a health program for inner-city children, started the service in January. It quickly grew and was split into two different subscribed e-mail lists, one for discussion and another for notices, presentations, and background information.

One of the biggest topics of discussion these days is what will happen to the service now that the referendum is over. Most people would like to see it continue, both to pursue the amalgamation legislation and other "mega" moves by the province as well as to become a general discussion of political issues.

It will join a number of other such services. The oldest and most successful is the Minnesota Politics On-line Discussion Forum, or E-Democracy, which started in 1994 as a place for electronic debates on election issues and has grown to include a regular audience of 1,000 people.

"It is bringing citizens with diverse viewpoints together to talk about politics that are local and relevant," said Steven Clift, 27, the chairman and founder of E-Democracy. "The people who participate really own that space."

The discussions, which have 400 regular contributors, have ranged recently from the politics of snow removal to an announcement by a St. Paul city councillor that he would not run for mayor.

Mr. Clift said although the Internet reaches throughout the world, the key to such forums is that they unite a core of participants based on their topical, community or geographical interests. He would like to see a global grid of such groups pulled together by the Internet, calling the result "glocalization."

The most extreme example of the phenomenon is in computer networks that link rural organizations and human-rights groups in developing countries.

Sam Lanfranco, a development economist and associate professor of economics at York University, has been responsible for setting up dozens of such groups in the past 15 years, from "untouchables" in India and dock workers in Britain to toy-factory workers in China.

He is a senior program specialist at the Bellanet International Secretariat, an agency run by the International Development Research Centre in Ottawa to help developing countries make use of information and telecommunications technology.

Mr. Lanfranco said all different types of communities can share the "virtual workspace" provided by a computer network. The boundaries of time and distance are eliminated. People actively participate in the space and have incredible access to information.

He is most frequently asked whether information technology is appropriate for poor, already disenfranchised and seemingly technologically backward people. But he said it is just these people who are getting on computer networks because they realize the potential of the technology more than the rich and powerful. The equipment is increasingly inexpensive and simple to use and women and old people especially are embracing it, he said.

Ms. Rykert rankles at suggestions her C4LD service is biased against amalgamation and unrepresentative because people require computers and modems in order to participate.

"We have definitely taken a side here," she said. "But we're about citizen participation and public accountability and public participation in policy making."

She said people on the Yes side of the debate are welcome to join in the computer discussion and people do not have to be on the Internet to contribute because C4LD takes in material by disk, fax, telephone and even written in longhand.

There are currently 254 subscribers to the service and 145 people participating in the forum, she said, but those numbers are not necessarily representative because the material is passed along to others.

Ironically, while electronic mail has a reputation for being fleeting, Ms. Rykert said the best thing about the C4LD forum is that it has become an archive of statements by politicians and citizens that will stand for years to come.

"We're building a public record that's going to be here for the next election," she said, suggesting such a wealth of material about past issues, such as the opposition to the building of the Spadina Expressway in Toronto, would have been invaluable.

Getting all of that information on-line is not always easy. Paul Nielson, the head of technical services for the Manitoba Legislative Library and president of the Manitoba Library Organization, said he has had a hard time since he set up his first political discussion group on a community network in 1995. Politicians and governments either don't want to participate or want to control the forum, he said, while citizens are apathetic or aren't plugged in.

"You want to have a marketplace of ideas," he said. "It's a very slow, frustrating process."

The most optimistic Web aficionados, on the other hand, suggest the Internet will be used to cast electronic ballots, maybe to the exclusion of paper ballots in the not-too-distant future.

Mr. Clift said he hopes computer networks will "make society more democratic" by encouraging discussions and debates about issues, not bring in a system of direct democracy.

"Personally, I really believe in representative democracy," he said. "The problem is that people aren't talking to each other and the politicians can't represent people who aren't democratic in their own lives."

Mr. Blumenthal, meanwhile, is impressed with the quality and the level of the commentary on services such as C4LD, compared with Internet discussion groups on more general topics, where the discourse is often juvenile and unfocused.

He said such participation, "if it's used properly, could make life tougher for politicians but we might get better government." At least it has revitalized his own interest in the political system.

"Democracy seems to be that you get a vote every four years and then shut up and go away," he said. "There's no forum for discussion. This is a forum for discussion."

ISSUE 4

Technological fixes: Can new communications technology save democracy?

✘ NO

Deserving Democracy: Technology Was Never the Problem, and It Won't Be the Solution
Catherine Frost

Catherine Frost is a professor at McMaster University in Hamilton, Ontario. She earned her Ph.D. from the University of Toronto in 2000 and held research fellowships at the Hebrew University in Jerusalem and McGill University in Montreal. Frost publishes on the political and moral implications of the Internet revolution as well as on issues in contemporary normative theory, including nationalism, multiculturalism, and representation. Her work appears in the *Journal of Political Philosophy*, the *Review of Politics*, the *Information Society*, the *Canadian Journal of Communication*, and *Irish Political Studies*. Her book *Morality and Nationalism* was published in 2006.

Democracy is a device that ensures we shall be governed no better than we deserve.

—George Bernard Shaw

INTRODUCTION

Democracy can mean all things to all people. For some it's about self-government and community bonds, for others it's about civic virtue and the public good, and for others it revolves around social equality or human rights. Yet as Robert Dahl put it, "a term that means anything, means nothing" (1989, p. 2). So what *is* democracy that new communication technologies—and the Internet in particular—should save it? There is one view that sees **procedural** democracy as a process for making binding decisions in the public realm (Dahl, 1989, p. 5). Because this is a more modest understanding of democracy, it should be the easiest to salvage. This means that if the Internet can't enable democracy as decision making, there's little reason to think it will save it in any of its more ambitious versions.

When it comes to democracy as decision making, the process can be viewed in quantitative terms, whereby it is at its best when *all* speak, listen, and evaluate relevant decisions in an informed way. It may also be evaluated qualitatively, in which the focus is not just on full, informed participation, but also on *how* we speak, listen, and decide. If the Internet is going to help drive democratic renewal, it will have to contribute to improving one or both of these aspects.

QUANTITATIVE DEMOCRACY

The most straightforward way that the Internet can improve democracy is through e-voting. If instead of casting ballots the old-fashioned way we could vote on civic and political issues electronically, wouldn't this boost accessibility, turnout, and participation, and ultimately foster democratic renewal? In theory yes, but in practice no because where e-voting has been introduced it has not transformed democracy, but merely automated it with little to no impact on voter turnout (Norris, 2002, p. 2). For example, registering as a voter online or casting an e-ballot does mean we do all the usual stuff of voting electronically instead of mechanically—and this is generally what e-voting amounts to—but these measures do not significantly improve participation levels (Norris, 2002, p. 12). Moreover, automation raises problems that did not affect old-fashioned voting. Aside from the increased potential for processing error, vote tampering, and data loss, it's a lot harder to verify voter identity or to validate results, and the critical democratic option of a recount is all but ruled out. The problems are serious enough that legal challenges have been launched in several U.S. states on the grounds that e-voting undermines voters' rights (Goldfarb, 2006).

But since technologies are improving every day, maybe these are simply technical difficulties that can be resolved through better design. As Dimitris A. Gritzalis (2002) argues, a sound design approach to both constitutional and technical issues can mitigate some if not all of the concerns about how e-voting works. Still, there's a further problem. We known the Internet is plagued with significant inequalities in access based on race, disability, age, income, location, and so forth. This means Internet-based e-voting makes an inequitably distributed resource the basis for democratic participation. If it was to have any significant impact on participation, then we should expect it to deepen the disenfranchisement of already vulnerable groups (Norris, 2002, p. 7).

Perhaps e-voting won't save democracy, but the Internet could provide ways to make government more accessible and accountable by keeping people informed and involved. We could, for instance, hold virtual town hall meetings or seek public feedback on civic proposals early in the policy process. There are few if any technical obstacles here, but it doesn't make the outcome any more promising than in the e-voting scenario. Despite its technical possibilities, studies confirm that government websites are rarely interactive and engaging (Hale, Musso, & Weare, 1999), and instead the Internet is used largely as a *one-way* means of communication. Even where websites are interactive, user access remains a problem and well-prepared issue information is sparse. One study of Swedish municipal websites, for example, found that only 2 percent provided background material on civic issues (Wiklund, 2005, p. 257). So far the Internet does not show great promise for the democratization of government information.

But are governments even the best ones to lead democratic transformation? Would democratic renewal and regeneration not be better achieved through the rapid growth of blogs and alternative media that are more accessible to all people? Chris Atton argues that the "Indymedia" movement, because it overturns the "hierarchy of access to the media," (2003, p. 14) can serve as a democratic information alternative by presenting perspectives that may otherwise go unheard (p. 10). This means we will no longer be solely dependent on the elite media to filter our news.

Now anyone anywhere with access to an Internet connection can speak her piece and reach a potentially limitless audience, whether it's Tibet's government in exile or just some guy blogging from a wartorn capital. And even with the digital divide, that's still a lot more participation than we've seen before. Although the lowest income brackets continue to be the least likely to be online in Canada, middle-income groups are gradually catching up with the more affluent, closing the divide and bringing ever more people within the reach of Internet communications (Sciadas, 2002, p. 3).

Granted, while the Internet appears to do a spectacular end run around traditional media monopolies, it would be foolhardy to think it doesn't have monopolies of its own. Blogs may be splendid examples of personal expression, but on an overcrowded Internet, some blogs will get more attention than others. In particular, we are more likely to see blog-celebrity come from this new revolution than we are blog-democracy, and the cause célèbre blogs like the Drudge Report (http://www.drudgereport.com) only confirm this phenomenon.

But another and more serious monopoly than the celebrity factor is at work in the Internet—one that is more serious because most users have no idea of how much information access they are regularly denied. Indeed, most are blithely unaware that they are daily enabling systems that filter and limit their information experience. But we couldn't make the Internet work any other way at this stage, because these filtering systems are in fact the search engines that navigate the gigantic unorganized mass that is the World Wide Web. Even the best search engines index little more than 16 percent of the data on the Internet. Add the top ones together and you still cover less than half of the available information (Introna & Nissenbaum, 2000). So how do they select the content they will include? Most search engines won't tell you, but generally the selection criteria are based on some combination of secret algorithms, corporate judgments, and for-profit listings (Introna & Nissenbaum, 2000, pp. 171–173). And as if this wasn't enough, you need to factor into this process the active blocking of sites at the request of political powers, such as the Google China decision to block sites that include dissident terms like "democracy," "human rights," and "justice." So it's pretty clear at this stage that the Internet in its current manifestation provides access to vast amounts of information, but it also does so in a way that can restrict as well as promote democracy.

QUALITATIVE DEMOCRACY

If the Internet is going to save democracy it doesn't look like it will do it through e-voting, government accessibility, or information democratization. But these approaches look for an increase in the volume of participation or democratic exchange, and there are many that argue the problem lies not in the quantity but the quality of today's democracy (Barber, 1984). Can the Internet turn this process around? Could it reinvigorate public discourse, reconstitute the public sphere, and renew citizen engagement in their communities, all civic virtues that many observers agree are in short supply?

Key to the qualitative democratic renewal we're talking about is a change in how people approach public debates over political issues. Under this concept of democracy, people are supposed to make their decisions based on sound information, after listening with an open mind to all reasonable points of view and carefully weighing these arguments in light of what is in the public—as opposed to their own private—interest. Finally, they are expected to accept the legitimacy of the outcome even if it doesn't reflect their personal preferences. The Internet could boost this process at a number of points. It might provide better information. It might encourage better discussion or encourage open mindedness. It might support the bonds of civic community over individualism. Or it may simply represent a new public sphere where we could learn to do democracy better.

We've already learned we should be cautious about our expectations of the Internet as an information resource for democracy. But it might be countered that the Internet has one capacity that could still be critical to democratic renewal, because it's one of the few media that is organized on a truly global scale. This means it can connect us to the implications and impacts of our decisions like few media before. The environmental consequences of everyday choices about food and transportation, for instance, can be linked directly and vividly to melting in the high Arctic or desertification in Africa. It also means that today's democracies are under the watchful eye of not just domestic populations but also the international community. Surely this is cause for some optimism.

The global reach of the Internet is indeed a remarkable thing. But what's equally remarkable is that we put it to such poor use. While the technology is no respecter of national borders, usage patterns have a decidedly national footprint. One multination study (Halavais, 1999) found that hyperlinks are predominantly to other sites in the same country, or else to sites in the United States. The only exception was Canada, which linked so heavily to the United States that it surpassed in-country links. Add to that the fact that the vast majority of Internet content is in English (Castells, 2001, p. 253), a language spoken by at most 25 percent of the world's population, and there seems little reason to assume that the Internet's global reach will reinvigorate global democracy.

What if we're aiming too high, though? What if the Internet's role is not to forge new democratic communities (local and global), but to teach us how to talk and listen better to one another with that kind of open-minded reasonableness that democratic discourse needs? But it's not clear why the Internet would deliver a level of discourse that we haven't managed through any other media. In fact, indications are that if the Internet has any impact on the quality of discourse, it may be to lower it. Instead of heralding a new age of democratic deliberation, studies find that not only are there issues around access and participation (Albrecht, 2006), but online user behaviour also can be decidedly uncivil. People generally talk more than they listen, talk mostly to people who already think like themselves, don't respond to others, don't sustain long discussions, often don't give reasons for their viewpoints, and don't feel responsible to one another (Wilhelm, 2000, pp. 86–104).

Indeed, early optimism around online engagement projects like the Santa Monica Public Electronic Network (PEN), for instance, proved short-lived. PEN was conceived of as an "electronic city hall," and the system allowed registered users to access municipal information and services, contact city officials, and participate in online conferences and discussions. While it showed some early success, the service eventually degenerated into a level of bickering and abuse that drove away most citizens and city representatives (Dutton, 1996; Wilson, 2002).

Why does the Internet lead people to behave in ways they would never in real life? The answer is something that psychologists have known for a long time. It's called the deindividuation effect, and it holds that when people think they can't be seen, inner restraints are lost and people act in ways that are more selfish, less altruistic, and more aggressive (Demetriou & Silke, 2003, p. 214).

An example of this kind of effect is seen when people get behind the wheel of their car, because when drivers feel less visible and more anonymous in their vehicles, they are more likely to drive aggressively and less likely to show restraint. Of course, one of the great charms of the Internet is its supposed anonymity, which disinhibits people and lets them try out new roles, personalities, and conduct. While the Internet is eminently liberating in one sense, it has also often meant the end of accountability. When one study found that well over half of randomly selected users were ready to commit criminal acts online (accessing hardcore porn, stealing passwords or game software), the authors concluded that deviant behaviour on the Internet is not just common, "it's the norm" (Demetriou & Silke, 2003, p. 220). We just don't seem to expect people (including ourselves) to live up to the same moral and social standards online.

Nevertheless, it might be argued that the Internet is having a democratizing effect because more people are having their say online, and perhaps all these new voices clamouring for attention will yield greater awareness and openness to the ideas of others. It's hard to not be seduced by such optimism, but it's important to be skeptical as well. As noted above, banks of search engines that limit our informational possibilities filter the Internet. Moreover, as Cass Sunstein (2001) argues, we can now pick and choose the sites and content that will receive our attention, meaning that rather than exposing us to others, the Internet has helped to create the "daily me." Unlike a newspaper, which will present a standard range of information, the Internet can be set to exclude information that doesn't meet your fancy. Depending on how their Internet experience is personalized, users no longer have to encounter opinions they don't like, topics that don't appeal to them, or issues that don't concern them (Sunstein, 2001, pp. 3–23). Democracy is unlikely to thrive in the context of such narrowed social and political awareness.

Granted, we aren't all engaging in the kind of mind-expanding encounters that democracy calls for, but at least people who lacked the power or influence to get on the agenda in other media can now find new audiences. The Internet undeniably offers great advantages to marginalized groups. Consider, for example, the boost given to the Zapatista movement in Mexico by their successful Internet campaign, or the antiglobalization movement that relied on the Internet to rally and organize support for the 1999 protests against the World Trade Organization in Seattle. But giving all marginalized groups a platform is not necessarily good for democracy. Some groups are marginalized for a reason. White supremacists don't get equal time in the popular media, and our democracy is all the better for it. Yet the Internet gives new resources not only to the good causes but also to the bad ones. It provides just as much organizational and promotional boost for right-wing groups as for any beloved grassroots cause (Adams & Roscigno, 2005). If the Internet means more of us can get behind little-known social initiatives, it also means we can sign up with racist, sexist, or other movements with antidemocratic tendencies.

One final possibility remains. Perhaps there is some intangible way in which the Internet will constitute a new public sphere. Perhaps because of the kinds of encounters it makes possible, because of its naturally open and inclusive structure, we'll learn to use it in new and better ways to make a new style of democracy possible. That is, of course, assuming that the Internet has a nature and that its nature is one of openness and inclusivity. But this is far from proven. Lawrence Lessig (2000) argues that the Internet has no nature, as its nature comes from the code we write into its architecture, and that it will as easily support an architecture of surveillance and control as it will of openness and empowerment. How this code and architecture evolve is crucial because these will set the terms for the kinds of democratic possibilities we might envision (p. 25). But while he is optimistic about the Internet's democratic potential, Lessig detects a growing trend toward commercialization and control (p. 99). The difficulty is that democracy requires a level of equality and trust that is anathema to the free market that drives changes in communications technologies, and government regulation requires a level of surveillance that can undermine civil rights.

If things didn't look promising for the Internet to save **quantitative democracy**, they look even grimmer for its **qualitative** version. Particularistic interests can undermine global awareness, Internet communities are selective, thin, and short-lived, and Internet discourse is narrow and self-absorbed. While it no doubt has democratizing potential, the Internet also provides a platform for extremism, supports solipsistic information habits, and liberates antisocial behaviour. And to cap it off, it may be enabling a system of control and surveillance for either market or government purposes the likes of which has never been seen before.

CONCLUSION

It is said that when NASA decided to send a man to the moon, thousands of dollars were invested to develop a pen that could write in space, while the Russians used a pencil. In fact, it's an urban myth. Both space programs started out using pencils and ended using ballpoints for safety reasons, and NASA never paid a dime for the development of the "space pen." But like most urban myths, it's also a cautionary tale because it warns against investing time and effort into developing a needlessly elaborate technological solution when a simple answer is already right under our noses.

So could the Internet help save democracy? Yes, in part it could. But so could old technologies like pencil and paper, correctly used. That's because democracy is not a product of technology, it's a product of personal and collective choices. If we want a better democracy we had better earn it, because no technology is going to serve it to us on a silver circuit board. While each medium has its own characteristics or bias, this factor is dwarfed by the role of personal and political commitment in how we shape a society (Frost, 2000). It is the commitment to use media in particular ways that makes change possible, which means we can neither hang our hopes on technology to save us from ourselves, nor scapegoat it as the roots of our downfall.

In sum, if we have a poor democracy it's not because we lack the technology, it's because our practices have been poor and the Internet gives scope for them to get worse. The expectation that technology can lift us from this morass is a symptom of how bad things have gotten, because it looks for solutions in the wrong place. Instead, we must give up dreams of technological salvation and assume full responsibility for our social and political choices and for the kinds of public life they make possible. Until then, Internet or no Internet, we'll get the democracy we deserve.

References

Adams, J., & Roscigno, V. J. (2005). White supremacists, oppositional culture and the World Wide Web. *Social Forces, 84*(2), 759–778.

Albrecht, S. (2006). Whose voice is heard in online deliberation? A study of participation and representation in political debates on the Internet. *Information, Communication & Society, 9*(1), 62–82.

Atton, C. (2003). Reshaping social movement media for a new millennium. *Social Movement Studies, 2*(1), 3–15.

Barber, B. (1984). *Strong democracy: Participatory politics for a new age.* Berkeley: University of California Press.

Castells, M. (2001). *The Internet galaxy.* Oxford: Oxford University Press.

Dahl, R. A. (1989). *Democracy and its critics.* New Haven, CT: Yale University Press.

Demetriou, C., & Silke, A. (2003). A criminological Internet "sting." *British Journal of Criminology, 43,* 213–222.

Dutton, W. H. (1996). Network rules of order: Regulating speech in public electronic fora. *Media, Culture & Society, 18,* 269–290.

Frost, C. (2000). How Prometheus is bound: The Innisian method of communications analysis and its application to Internet technology. *The Canadian Journal of Communication, 28,* 9–24.

Goldfarb, Z. A. (2006, May 30). Debating the bugs of high-tech voting. *The Washington Post,* p. A15.

Gritzalis, D. A. (2002). Principles and requirements for a secure e-voting system. *Computers and Society, 21*(6), 539–556.

Halavais, A. (1999). National borders on the World Wide Web. *New Media and Society, 1*(3), 7–28.

Hale, M., Musso, J., & Weare, C. (1999). Developing digital democracy: Evidence from Californian municipal web pages. In B. N. Hague & B. D. Loader (Eds.), *Digital democracy: Discourse and decision-making in the information age* (pp. 96–115). New York: Routledge.

Introna, L. D., & Nissenbaum, H. (2000). Shaping the Web: Why the politics of search engines matter. *The Information Society, 16,* 169–186.

Lessig, L. (2000). *Code and other laws of cyberspace.* New York: Basic Books.

Norris, P. (2002, May 10–11). *E-voting as the magic ballot?* Paper presented at the workshop "E-voting and the European Parliamentary Elections," Robert Schuman Centre for Advanced Studies, European University Institute, Villa La Fonte, San Domenico di Fiesole, Italy.

Sciadas, G. (2002). *The digital divide in Canada* (Cat. No. 56F0009XIE). Ottawa: Statistics Canada.

Sunstein, C. (2001). *Republic.com.* Princeton, NJ: Princeton University Press.

Wiklund, H. (2005). A Habermasian analysis of the deliberative democratic potential of ICT-enabled services in Swedish municipalities. *New Media and Society, 7*(2), 247–270.

Wilhelm, A. G. (2000). *Democracy in the digital age.* New York: Routledge.

Wilson, M. (2002). Does a networked society foster participatory democracy or is commitment to place-based community still a necessity for civic engagement? In M. Pendakur & R. Harris (Eds.), *Citizenship and participation in the information age* (pp. 372–387). Aurora, ON: Garamond Press.

Discussion Questions

1. What are the possible problems associated with e-voting? Is e-voting worth the risk?

2. In what ways might the Internet be making equality in democratic decision making more difficult to achieve?

3. Why does online discourse so often bring out the worst in people? Can anything be done to improve it?

PART 4 Regulation and Cultural Industries

Radio, music, drugs, and intellectual property: all of these "products" influence Canadian culture in significant ways, and all are subject to various forms of regulation. But how much regulation should exist—and to what extent should it influence the Canadian marketplace and, by extension, the lives of everyday Canadians?

This section begins with a debate over the issue of free speech on the radio, focusing specifically on whether Canada should censor "shock jocks"—radio personalities who seek to entertain audiences often with offensive jokes, comments, and commentary. Ronald Cohen argues that shock jocks should, unquestionably, be censored when their speech violates Canadian public rights, such as the right to be free from inappropriate comment, excessively vulgar language, and unduly sexually explicit or violent programming. **Freedom of speech**, which shock jocks and their supporters draw upon to support their "right" to communicate, is not the *only* right of importance in Canada, Cohen argues. While freedom of speech is indeed a "precious right, it does not mean that Canadian audiences should be subject to any form of speech." Other societal rights matter: Canadian values and concerns must also be given respect.

Josh Paterson, on the other hand, argues that freedom of expression constitutes an essential feature of democratic society. Canada should not censor shock jocks, he insists, because censorship is "a clumsy tool" that can cause much more harm than good. Censorship can actually work to "hide prejudicial views and ensure that nobody is able to challenge them—because nobody is allowed to hear them." To make his argument, Paterson examines the Canadian Radio-Television and Telecommunications Commission (CRTC) licensing regulations and outlines how the justifications for regulation are inappropriately suited to Canada's current media environment.

The second issue under consideration shifts focus from radio's personalities to its music. The debate grapples with whether Canadian content (CanCon) regulations are necessary to promote Canadian music. David Young states that CanCon's 35-year-old regulations remain essential because they help to support Canadian recording artists, studios, and producers. There is a public interest at stake in radio broadcasts, Young argues, and regulations ensure that Canadian talent actually gets heard on the radio. Furthermore, CanCon regulations work to protect Canadian culture from globalizing and Americanizing cultural influences—something that is still of great concern in today's marketplace.

Ira Wagman dismisses the arguments in favour of CanCon regulations as mere myths. He claims that CanCon regulations, in fact, "have very little to do with music." They have more to do with supporting the Canadian music *industry*. Wagman observes that the criteria for determining Canadian content might actually work against the efforts of Canadian musicians, allowing certain songs to qualify while rejecting others. Perhaps the greatest difficulty with the CanCon system, states Wagman, is that it "overlooks the numerous venues in which Canadians experience music in the course of their daily lives." Local music festivals, Internet radio, websites, and various other channels for music distribution also factor strongly in the ways that Canadians access and experience music.

The third debate follows the thread of regulation, but in a much different context (and with much different content). Moving from music to drugs, the issue is whether direct-to-consumer (DTC) prescription drug advertising should be limited in Canada. Josh Greenberg opens the discussion by asserting that it should. His analysis is situated in the context of a recent court challenge by the CanWest media corporation, Canada's largest media conglomerate, to pry open the debate about how prescription drug advertising is regulated. This campaign, he argues, is fundamentally about profit and not free speech or consumer empowerment, as CanWest claims. Through a critical analysis of the social effects of advertising, Greenberg argues that a more liberalized approach to drug advertising will ultimately lead to more, not less, social control and intensify the medicalization of everyday life. Both outcomes, Greenberg's essay suggests, are incompatible with the objectives of informing and empowering patients.

Kelley Main presents the opposing stance in the DTC drug advertising debate. Main argues that Canadians should not be reticent about swallowing DTC advertising. Why? Because DTC advertising brings both *individual* and *relational* benefits.

That is, DTC advertising allows patients to actively participate in their own health care by educating consumers and providing information on various treatment options (individual benefits). DTC advertising, furthermore, allows patients to better communicate with their physicians (relational benefits). Doctors actually welcome patients' questions regarding advertised pharmaceutical drugs, Main argues, as it allows patients to take a more active—and empowered—role in their own health care.

The final debate deals with the state of intellectual property rights in Canada. Intellectual property (IP) pertains to creations of the mind, and IP rights work to protect those who have created inventions, literary works, and symbols/designs used in commerce. Recently, questions have been raised regarding the extent of such rights; put bluntly, the question addressed is whether intellectual property rights have run amok.

Sheryl Hamilton opens the discussion by stating that intellectual property rights have gone too far. Things previously understood as unownable or as shared cultural resources (from colours to mice) are being claimed as property by businesses in a process known as "propertization." And the result is that shared myths, scientific facts, names, organisms, and elements of nature are increasingly framed as off limits to people. One disturbing consequence is that "our everyday cultural activity is increasingly controlled, censored, and criminalized."

Graham Henderson views intellectual property rights in a completely different light. Focusing primarily on copyright, Henderson argues that Canada's IP regulations are not stringent enough. Canada lags behind the rest of the international community with regards to IP, argues Henderson, which puts "our cultural fabric at risk." The consequences of this lax approach to IP will play out in both the economy and society. For Henderson, the "if it's there, it's free" ethos (which characterizes much thinking around entertainment, such as music downloading) actually harms artists, "reduces Canada's tax base, increases Canadian unemployment, and undermines Canada's ability to remain competitive in the IP-based economy."

ISSUE 1

Speakers cornered: Should Canada censor shock jocks?

✔ YES

Speakers cornered: Should Canada censor shock jocks?
Ronald Cohen

Ronald Cohen is the national chair of the Canadian Broadcast Standards Council (CBSC) and the author of numerous articles on the subject of the CBSC and broadcast standards. He is also the founding chair and a current board member of the Academy of Canadian Cinema and Television, the president of the Friends of Library and Archives Canada, and the author of the following books: *Quebec Votes: An Analysis of Quebec Voting Patterns in Federal Elections*; *The Regulation of Misleading Advertising: A Comparative Approach*; *The Constitutional Validity of a Trade Practices Law for Canada*; and *A Bibliography of the Writings of Sir Winston Churchill.*

Censor? The word begins in such a dialogue on the negative side of the ledger. It implies restriction, not restraint. Imposition rather than self-control. "Big Brother" rather than self-imposed judgment. It is a provocative term to describe what might reasonably be characterized as the societal comfort of the preservation of values and order on the airwaves. Could the question not equally have been framed "Should shock jocks be free to say whatever they wish on Canadian airwaves?"

Using such an unpalatable word as "censor" implies that, in the competition between an offending speaker and the "offendee," the former ought always to win. Should that be the case? I know of no reason why it should. In the clash of societal values in the 21st century, it cannot make sense that freedom of expression is the *only* value worth preserving, the one that *must* trump all others.

The point is that freedom of expression must take its place with other societal rights, those that, essentially, entitle audiences to be free from certain broadcast matter. If freedom of expression is not the ace of trumps, someone must decide which rights will triumph in the event of a conflict. Someone must, in other words, take the measure of the conflict. Who that is, which rules are to be applied, and when are all relevant issues. What one calls the process is of minor import. Whatever it is called, as this chapter will argue, we need to balance society's rights, values, and concerns, which will invariably lead to restrictions on broadcast fare.

AN AGE OF ACCESS

We live in an age of access. It is very much an issue of two-way access. There is, of course, access *by* us to content, but there is also access *to* us by content providers. Our ability to pick and choose the speech, information, or expression we will ingest differs significantly from that available to individuals when the fundamental principle protecting the right of the speaker was enshrined. In those early days, when suppression by authority put the speaker's right to expound at risk, it was critical to ensure the preservation of that right. Moreover, the concern was greatest where it was uncertain that the expression of political perspectives, particularly policy dissidence, might not otherwise be assured.

Today, the access issue is different, at least in the normal broadcast environment. When we turn on our radios or televisions, they exude the published offerings of all stations, networks, and services licensed by the regulator. These offerings cover the content gamut: news and public affairs, including information, magazine format, documentary, political commentary, and other forms; drama in its manifold guises, including weekly series of many genres, soap operas, and movies, whether created for the cinema or television, live action or animation; children's programming; comedy, whether stand-up, sketch, or fictional; talk or call-in programs; music from classical, jazz, and oldies to rap and hip-hop; reality programming; sports; and so on.

And almost any of those genres may include content that is potentially offensive to someone, whether on the basis of coarse language, abusive comment, violence, nudity, sexual content, other adult themes, bad taste, political point of view, or religious righteousness. The question is, should any of those categories of content be overseen by anyone other than the individual viewer or listener?

Some might argue that it is enough that all broadcasting, like all other activities in Canada, is subject to the public laws enacted by the federal and provincial legislatures. Surely, in this age of access, though, those rules, designed for other purposes, cannot suffice in this environment. In the first place, the airwaves are publicly owned. Second, important spectrum remains scarce. Third, the industry is regulated; it makes no sense that simply anyone should be able to access a licence without regard to rules and conditions of relevance to the state. And the state and its inhabitants have values and concerns. Are those values and concerns not entitled to respect?

SOME CONSTITUTIONAL COMPARISONS

What we in Canada refer to as "freedom of expression" is termed "free speech" in the United States. It may indeed be that the root of that right in the United States, known by its shorthand title, the First Amendment, is the best-known legislative provision in the world. It is old legislation, dating from 1792, while its Canadian equivalent, found in the *Canadian Charter of Rights and Freedoms*, dates from 1982. One might say that Canada went to school on its American statutory forebear.

The First Amendment provides that "Congress shall make no law ... abridging the freedom of speech, or of the press." Section 2(b) of the Canadian Charter is framed differently. It protects "freedom of thought, belief, opinion and expression, including freedom of the press and other media of communication."

More to the point, though, the American principle sounds and feels more absolute— "Congress *shall* make *no* law"—while the Canadian equivalent appears far more, well, Canadian. It does not even *appear* absolute. It feels balanced. Canada's freedom of opinion and expression is subject "to such reasonable limits ... as can be demonstrably justified in a free and democratic society." It feels like it can and should be weighed against something else. It generally is, at least insofar as the Canadian Broadcast Standards Council (CBSC) is concerned and, it would appear, the Canadian Radio-television and Telecommunications Commission (CRTC), as well as, to some extent at least, the Federal Court of Appeal, speaking recently in the CHOI-FM/Genex licensing appeal. Indeed, in that decision, Mr. Justice Létourneau was quite explicit on the boundaries of freedom of expression.

> The appellant makes much of the guarantee of freedom of expression in paragraph 2(*b*) of the *Charter* and seems to want to treat it as unqualified, something that the courts have never recognized. I do not think I am mistaken in saying that freedom of expression, freedom of opinion, and freedom of speech do not mean freedom of defamation, freedom of oppression, and freedom of opprobrium. Nor do I think I am mistaken in saying that the right to freedom of expression under the *Charter* does not require that the State or the CRTC become accomplices in or promoters of defamatory language or violations of the rights to privacy, integrity, human dignity and reputation by forcing them to issue a broadcasting licence used for those purposes. To accept the appellant's proposition would mean using the *Charter* to make the State or its agencies an instrument of oppression or violation of the individual rights to human dignity, privacy and integrity on behalf of the commercial profitability of a business. (*Genex Communications v. Canada,* 2005)

The point really is that, whatever either constitutional provision sounds like, free speech is not totally free in either the United States or Canada. "Free" is in the end a relative term, reflecting the values of each country, and that is as it should be.

SPEECH WORTH PROTECTING

The CBSC draws a clear line between comments dealing with political issues, government policies, politicians, and the like, on the one hand, and all other comment, on the other hand. Thus, on a delicate issue of government policy with linguistic and ethnic overtones, the CBSC's Ontario Regional Panel (1993) observed

> that an opinion on the government *policy* of bilingualism constituted an *opinion* on that issue and was not *racially* driven. Nothing can be more fundamental to the principle of freedom of speech enshrined in the *Charter* than the entitlement of an individual to express a differing view on a matter of public concern, including government policy.[1]

That principle also was supported by the Ontario panel in 1994 in the defence of satirical comments directed toward a sitting member of Parliament in the following terms:

> Indeed, it is the most essential component of the principle of free speech that the fullest criticism of political figures and political positions be permitted in a free society. Provided that the satire or criticism is levelled at political persons on the basis of their actions as public figures *and not on the basis of their national or ethnic origin*, it must be permitted, if not encouraged.

The consistent application of the principle was tested in the first of the Howard Stern decisions, tested in the sense that the challenged comments were largely racist, sexist, sexual, and inappropriate for children. Nonetheless, among the standard-violating chaff there were comments of a political and historical nature. In their joint ruling, the Quebec and Ontario panels (1997) defended the latter category of commentary, noting

> the importance of differentiating between insults aimed at identifiable groups and comments related to the political or historical environment in Canada and in France.... Those comments relating to the state of radio in Canada, the use of English in Quebec, the value of French culture, Canada as an appendage of the United States, the role of the vanquished French in Vichy France, the issues relating to separatism, and so on, are the host's opinions and, unless utterly and irresponsibly uninformed,... they are his to espouse.

SPEECH WORTH PROTECTING?

Where, however, the expression has no such *inherent* redeeming value as that described in the preceding section, the CBSC panels will not stretch to defend it. Consider, for example, the nonhistorical/nonpolitical comments Howard Stern made in the challenged episodes of his program in 1997. In addition to the juvenile locker-room banter about women's breasts and sexual activities, there was, in one of the broadcast bits, a dash of violence added.

> **Howard Stern**: [Referring to Kim Basinger] Oh, I just wanna take that piece of ass body, put tape over her mouth, and do things to her. [Playing sound effects of a woman in a sexual encounter throughout the following passage.] And have her lay by my pool in a bikini and have her come out and service me. And I'm laying by my pool, in comes that nude with just a pair of heels. And then like, I reach in, I yank out her vocal chords and then she just orally satisfies me by the pool. Oh, she's totally a mute Kim. And she's totally nude.... Oh. And then I break her legs and position them in the back of her head so that she's sitting, and they're permanently fixed like that. We let them knit and mend.[2]

All in all, the panels found the comments to be sexist and in breach of the broadcasting code of ethics. They expressed their position in the following terms:

> Stern consistently uses degrading and irrelevant commentary in dealing either with guests or callers. The CBSC understands, by his demeanour and laughter, that he and, presumably, [co-host Robin] Quivers and others on his show find such comments amusing. It may well be the case that many in his audience find such comments entertaining. This sort of adolescent humour may work for some in private venues but it is thoroughly in breach of Canadian codified broadcast standards. Women in this country are entitled to the respect which their intellectual, emotional, personal and artistic qualities merit. No more than men. No less than men. But every bit as much as men.

> There may be broadcast circumstances, say in a dramatic or informational context, in which the physical attributes of either men or women may be relevant. There may be corresponding circumstances in which sexual experiences of either men

or women may be relevant. The CBSC has not seen the relevance of any of these, as spoken by Stern, in any of the tapes or transcripts it has reviewed. Moreover, their use seems almost exclusively reserved for Stern's dealings with women. The CBSC does not, however, consider that their regular application to men would be an improvement in any way, except in the balance of insults and irrelevancies. Such comments are constantly present and reflect a fundamental attitude of the Show's host and his self-granted entitlement to say whatever crosses his mind at any time.

Since the World Trade Center attack, the Muslim community has more often been the subject of discussion and even humour than before September 2001. One example of offending humour ran on a Calgary station as a parody "quiz" segment, during which callers were asked a few multiple-choice questions that they had to answer with the third choice, "c," which was predictably the most provocative of all three possible choices. One segment went as follows:

Forbes: Okay. Muslims around the world continue to travel to Mecca on the weekend to celebrate: a) a celebration of forgiveness; b) homage to Allah; or c) just a way to build up some frequent flyer miles so you don't have to pay the next time you want to ram an airplane in the stronghold of the Western civilization.

Pat: I'll take C.

Forbes: Absolutely right there.[3]

The Prairie Regional Panel (2003) concluded,

There are times in the life of a society when it is far too easy to single out an identifiable group as a recipient of harsh discriminatory comment. Society is frequently ready to find a scapegoat for segments of its ills, perhaps as a catharsis for their resolution. It is perhaps when such solutions come most easily that society ought to be most vigilant. Since the shocking events that have come to be known simply as "9/11" and the proliferation of incidents of terrorism both before and after that date, it has been all too easy to target the Muslim communities with comments that are generalizations which are negative, hurtful and utterly unjustified.

That was the case with the challenged program. The humour in this broadcast was singularly unacceptable. The implication that all Muslims (how else could one interpret the words "Muslims around the world"?) might travel to their *holiest* city in order to fund terrorist activities is outrageous. To put it in perspective, the failure to distinguish between the Muslim community and terrorists is no more acceptable or justifiable than a failure to distinguish between (to choose one of many possible examples) white persons and the Ku Klux Klan. The Muslim community bears no more responsibility for persons within its ranks who break the laws than all white persons bear responsibility for the illegal actions of Klan members.[5]

COMMENTARY ON THE CUSP

There are also the quasi-religious observations of commentators like Laura Schlessinger, Jimmy Swaggart, R. W. Schambach, John Hagee, James Dobson, and others opposed to homosexuality and same-sex marriage. Should there, for example, be a distinction made between Laura

Schlessinger's comments characterizing the sexuality of gays and lesbians as "abnormal," "aberrant," "deviant," "disordered," "dysfunctional," and "an error," and dialogue between politicians on the policy of same-sex marriage? For that matter, do the following comments of televangelist Jimmy Swaggart on that subject deserve protection or condemnation?

> This utter, absolute, asinine, idiotic stupidity … of men marrying men [sounds of agreement from audience]. I've never seen a man in my life I wanted to marry [Swaggart laughs; audience applauds]. And I'm gonna be blunt and plain; if one ever looks at me like that, I'm gonna kill him and tell God he died.[4]

The various CBSC panels called upon to deal with aggressive comments by the above individuals have been careful to distinguish the nature and extent of the comments. The more extreme comments, such as those of Jimmy Swaggart, have been found in breach of the human rights clause of the Canadian Association of Broadcasters (CAB) code of ethics (CBSC, Ontario Regional Panel, 2005). More balanced comments, such as those of James Dobson in *Focus on the Family*, have been protected, the distinction being drawn as follows:

> Where, in other words, the challenged comments are "not directed to the *group* of persons *on the basis of* their sexual orientation," where there is no offending characterization of the group, where the comments are limited to a moral or religious assessment of *practices* alone, the comments will be unlikely to be viewed as abusively or unduly discriminatory. (CBSC, Ontario Regional Panel, 2001)

THE CANADIAN SOLUTION

There are other examples of programming that has interfered with different kinds of public rights, including the right to be free from gratuitously violent programming, misleading news, improper comment, unduly coarse language, and unduly sexually explicit programming (these relate to time of broadcast), and so on. Canada's private broadcasters, however, have applied a common solution to these public rights and to human rights . In these and other areas, they have codified the standards by which they consider they and the public would be well served. Those standards make up the CAB Code of Ethics, the Sex-Role Portrayal Code (soon, likely in 2007, to be replaced by the Equitable Portrayal Code), and the Violence Code. They also apply the Radio and Television News Directors Code of (Journalistic) Ethics to their news and public affairs programming. And all of these are administered by the CBSC.

It goes without saying that the CRTC is the regulatory authority with ultimate jurisdiction in all aspects of broadcasting, but, as a general rule, it limits its interventions in content issues to public broadcasters and those few private broadcasters that are not members of the CBSC.

It is worth noting, on a comparative basis, that the United States limits its content differently. Its Federal Communications Commission is immensely concerned with indecency. Bare breasts, bare butts, a two-second glimpse of a penis contorted into a bizarre shape (in the Australian minstrel show *Puppetry of the Penis*), the f-word or its derivatives, sexual commentary—*these* are the American issues. The fleeting glimpse of Janet Jackson's right breast cost the CBS affiliates who ran the 2004 Super Bowl US$550,000. In Canada, we received fewer than two hundred complaints on the matter and, it should be added, found no breach. When *NYPD Blue* first ran years ago, David Caruso's bare bottom attracted American audience anger, but it was the violence in that show that troubled Canadian viewers. Ironically, though, the organized-crime series *The Sopranos* runs only on pay cable, HBO, south of the border, while in Canada, the series runs on both pay and conventional television, although only after the watershed, 9 p.m.

CONCLUSION

The bottom line is that both Canada and the United States feel compelled to restrict broadcast content, whether of the "shock jock" variety or otherwise, although the substance of the impositions on freedom of expression differ in both jurisdictions. While, in an age of access, it is clear that freedom of speech is a precious right, this does not mean that Canadian audiences should be subject to absolutely *any* form of speech. Because the Canadian system does not permit excessive violence during children's programming, because it does not allow abusive comments on the basis of people's religion, sexual orientation, or skin colour, because it does not allow imbalance in the portrayal of men and women does not mean that our free speech is unduly restrained or that the Canadian social and political fabric is weakened.

References

CBSC, Ontario Regional Council. (1993). *CKTB-AM re the John Gilbert Show* (CBSC Decision 92/93-0179). Decided October 26, 1993.

CBSC, Ontario Regional Council. (1994). *CHOG-AM re the Jessie and Gene Show* (CBSC Decision 93/94-0242). Decided November 15, 1994.

CBSC, Ontario Regional Panel. (2001). CFYI-AM re *Focus on the Family.* (CBSC Decision 99/00-0724). Decided June 28, 2001.

CBSC, Ontario Regional Panel.(2005). *OMNI.1 re an episode of the* Jimmy Swaggart Telecast (CBSC Decision 04/05-0097). Decided April 19, 2005.

CBSC, Prairie Regional Panel. (2003).*CJAY-FM re Forbes and Friends (multiple choice "quiz")* (CBSC Decision 02/03-0638). Decided December 15, 2003.

CBSC, Quebec Regional Council & Ontario Regional Council. (1997). *CHOM-FM re Howard Stern Show* (CBSC Decision 97/98-0001+). Decided October 17, 1997; *CILQ-FM re Howard Stern Show* (CBSC Decision 97/98-0015+). Decided October 18, 1997.

Genex Communications v. Canada (A.G.), [2005] 283 F.C. at para. 221.

Notes

[1] All CBSC decisions can be searched on its website, at http://www.cbsc.ca/english/decisions/about.htm.

[2] Transcript provided in Appendix B of CBSC decisions 97/98-0001+ and 97/98-0015+ (see http://www .cbsc.ca/english/decisions/about.htm).

[3] Transcript provided in CBSC Decision 02/03-0638, "The Facts" (see http://www.cbsc.ca/english/decisions/ about.htm).

[4] Transcript provided in CBSC Decision 04/05-0097, "The Facts" (see http://www.cbsc.ca/english/decisions/ about.htm).

ISSUE 1

Speakers cornered: Should Canada censor shock jocks?

✗ NO

Free Expression and Censorship of Shock Jocks in Canada
Josh Paterson

Josh Paterson is a lawyer who, at the time of writing in 2006, was acting director of the Freedom of Expression Project at the Canadian Civil Liberties Association in Toronto, advocating and coordinating litigation on free speech and human rights issues. After graduating from the University of Toronto in 2004 with a law degree and a master's degree in international relations, he served as a judicial clerk at Ontario's Superior Court of Justice in Toronto. During law school he worked at a poverty law clinic in Toronto and interned at a human rights legal organization in Mumbai, India. He now lives in Vancouver, where he practises law and continues to be active in the area of civil liberties, human rights, and urban issues. He continues to represent the Canadian Civil Liberties Association on a *pro bono* basis.

On a radio talk show, the host is discussing psychiatric hospitals. Discussing a particular patient, the host asks, "Why don't they just pull the plug on him? He doesn't deserve to live. The guy's a freaking burden on society. What I think they should do in [the psychiatric wing of the hospital] is fill up the rooms, and then there'd be a switch, and once every four months, they press the button and just a little bit of gas comes out, and then you go in and pick it all up and put it in bags" (*Broadcasting Decision CRTC 2004-271*, 2004, para. 49). When listeners complained, the radio station said that the comments were just a joke during a debate on the controversial social issue of euthanasia. Most people would probably find these remarks offensive. Plenty of people, disabled and able alike, might find this "joke" to be hurtful. Yet, this is an actual example of something said by a shock jock on a Canadian radio station.

For a number of years in Canada, controversy has simmered about whether shock jocks should be allowed on the airwaves. Shock jocks are radio personalities whose shows aim to entertain—often by saying offensive things. Many people, even some who are periodically offended, think that shock jock radio shows are funny, entertaining, and even politically subversive. The shows' huge audiences attest to that. Sometimes shock jocks' remarks come across as racist. Often they are perceived as sexist and as disrespectful of women. Almost always, they are controversial. Should something be done about them? Should this expression be censored?

Attempts to regulate what people are allowed to say on air may be well intentioned; usually, regulation is aimed at promoting equality by banning statements that offend, poke fun at, or attack people based on their race, culture, religion, or gender. While the promotion of equality is an important goal in a democracy, censorship is a clumsy tool that can do a lot more harm than good. It restricts freedom of expression, a vital feature of democratic society. Furthermore, censoring offensive opinions and humour has not been shown to help promote understanding and equality. There is no evidence that censoring such messages leads to less discrimination and greater intercultural understanding. It can, however, hide prejudicial views and ensure that nobody is able to challenge them—because nobody is allowed to hear them.

Radio stations operate under licences from the federal government. The CRTC decides who is allowed to operate a radio or television station in Canada. Its mission is to regulate radio, television, and telecommunications in the public interest. Its powers apply only to radio and television media, and not to other media such as print or the Internet.[1] The CRTC doesn't have the power to tell broadcasters what they can and cannot put on the air, other than specifying Canadian content regulations.[2] The CRTC requires broadcasters to comply with its regulations. Since the broadcast licences aren't permanent and need to be renewed every few years, the CRTC can rescind a radio station's permission to be on the air when it breaches these standards. The CRTC is not meant to act as a board of censors with a power of **prior restraint**, which prohibits material from being heard or seen at all. Prior restraint censorship is ordinarily not permitted in Canadian law. The Supreme Court of Canada has stated that censoring material before the fact is a severe restriction on freedom of expression (*Little Sisters Book & Art Emporium v. Canada*, 2000, p. 1154).

The refusal to renew a licence can be based on the broadcaster's failure to comply with the broadcasting industry's self-imposed code of ethics or with the CRTC's morality-based regulations. This is what happened to Quebec City's CHOI-FM, the radio station that carried the comments about psychiatric patients by host Jeff Fillion in May 2003. The CRTC received numerous complaints about the station's "shock jock" broadcasts from listeners who felt that the material they heard was sexist, racist, and otherwise offensive. These included Fillion's numerous remarks about a female television host's sexual attributes, in particular, the size of her breasts, and host André Arthur's criticism of the number of African and Muslim foreign students at Laval University. In November 2003, Arthur claimed the students were mostly the "children of the most disgusting political leaders in the world, people who are sucking their countries dry, people who kill to gain power and torture to keep it. People we call cannibals, people who are extremely cruel." CHOI-FM argued that the comments were in the public interest and were meant as an exaggeration so listeners would think about whether the children of dictators were attending Quebec universities. The CRTC disagreed, and in 2004, because of repeated complaints (and in spite of the public demonstrations of thousands of the station's supporters), the CRTC refused to renew the station's licence. It found that the broadcasts violated the law because they "did not constitute programming that reflects Canadian values" and did not reflect the right to equality (*Broadcasting Decision CRTC 2004-271*, 2004, para. 54). Instead, it concluded that the broadcasts were likely to expose persons with mental disabilities, and Black or Muslim students at Laval, to hatred or contempt. The CRTC also found that the remarks about the female television host were abusive and exposed her, and women in general, to contempt on the basis of sex. Moreover, it concluded that the remarks did not "safeguard, enrich or strengthen the social fabric of Canada, nor do they reflect the status and aspirations of women." It stated that programming that substantially undermines the value of equality between women and men "runs counter to the objectives of broadcasting policy for Canada and is not worthy of broadcast on the public airwaves." As a result, the CRTC ordered CHOI-FM to shut down. That unprecedented decision is, at the time of this writing, being challenged at the Supreme Court of Canada. Jeff Fillion has since left broadcasting, and André Arthur was elected as an independent member of Parliament in the January 2006 federal election.

In effect, the CRTC's power to revoke a broadcast licence because of program content that is being aired by a radio station amounts to a power of prior restraint. While the CRTC wasn't able to preempt the broadcast of the offensive material that precipitated the refusal to renew, it made sure that the station will never again broadcast offensive material—or any material at all. The station is permanently shut down.

Even when the CRTC does not go so far as to actually refuse a licence renewal, it can threaten to do so, or issue fines, if stations continue to broadcast objectionable material. The threat to cancel a licence, in effect, is a form of prior restraint in disguise. It can impose a chilling effect on expression that is much broader than the censorship of a particular segment of a particular broadcast. It can stop the broadcaster from putting *anything* on the air that could even come close to violating CRTC rules. A wide range of speech that doesn't violate the rules can effectively be prevented from getting to air simply by the CRTC's threatening termination.

What rules does the CRTC use in making these kinds of determinations? The *Radio Regulations* of 1986 state that "a licensee shall not broadcast … any abusive comment that, when taken in context, tends to or is likely to expose an individual or a group or class of individuals to hatred or contempt on the basis of race, national or ethnic origin, colour, religion, sex, sexual orientation, age or mental or physical disability" (s. 3). The *Broadcasting Act* sets out that the Canadian broadcasting system should "safeguard, enrich and strengthen the cultural, political, social and economic fabric of Canada" and requires programming to be "of high standard" (s. 3). The CRTC also bases its decisions on the code of ethics of the Canadian Association of Broadcasters, which prohibits the broadcast on radio of all content that is "unduly sexually explicit."[3] The CRTC has agreed on standards in cooperation with the broadcasting industry, which is largely responsible for self-regulation. However, when a radio station does not appear to be adequately regulating its content, the CRTC is able to warn and to shut down the station. This is what happened in the CHOI-FM case.

Let's look at the government's rationale for the CRTC's powers over broadcasting content. The four basic reasons are the scarcity of the broadcast spectrum, the "public trust" of the airwaves, the desire to protect children, and the pervasive and inescapable nature of the broadcast media.

1. Scarcity of the radio broadcast spectrum

The principal justification for government regulation of the airwaves relates to two propositions: that the bandwidth available for broadcast media is limited, or scarce, and that the few available frequencies should be used in the public interest (Antonoff, 2005, p. 273). Radio spectrum scarcity implies that there is competition for free-to-air broadcasting. This means that if one station is using a particular frequency, another station is deprived of the ability to use the same frequency. If any broadcaster were free to use any frequency that it chose, then in most crowded urban markets it would be impossible to listen to the radio at all—there would be too much interference caused by overlapping frequencies. This is why radio and television broadcasters require licences, while other media such as newspapers do not. Anyone who wishes to print a newspaper or start a webpage may do so, assuming they have the necessary financial resources, as there is currently no effective limit on the amount of newsprint or Web space available (Varona, 2006, pp. 167–168).

Some commentators, and notably, some judges in the United States, reject the scarcity argument. They respond that the supply of resources used in other kinds of media, such as newsprint, is also limited. They note that scarcity is an obsolete idea in the era of six hundred–channel cable subscriptions, satellite television, the Internet, and the ability to cram more signals onto the broadcast spectrum than ever before (Varona, 2006, p. 153).

Because technology has provided a great abundance of ways for media messages to be disseminated, the idea that broadcast resources are scarce is simply outdated. However, the fact is that many more potential broadcasters apply for radio licences in major markets than there are frequencies to allot to them. This is not the case for websites, newspapers, and many other media. It remains the case that television and radio are still, by far, the media that most consumers use to get their information and entertainment (Varona, 2006, p. 153).

Scarcity, then, is a notion that effectively applies uniquely to those media using the airwaves, not to the media across the board. However, even if we accept that a limited number of signals are available, does this necessarily justify content regulation and censorship? Does it make any difference? Scarcity alone doesn't seem to be enough to justify censorship.

2. "Public trust" of the airwaves

Closely connected to the idea of scarcity is the idea that the airwaves are publicly owned. Since signals are limited in number, and since it is in the public interest that broadcast signals be used clearly, without interference, for public communication, the government created the legal fiction that the airwaves are a public trust. It is a fiction because it is impossible for anyone to have *actual* possession of the broadcast spectrum; it is difficult to possess something that cannot be seen or touched. Nonetheless, the concept of public ownership of the airwaves allows the government to set up a system in which it grants a licence to a broadcaster in exchange for a promise that the broadcaster will act as a trustee over the public resource of broadcast bandwidth, using it in the public interest (Brown & Candeub, 2005, p. 1479). The broadcaster, of course, stands to profit a great deal from the revenues that a radio or television station can bring.

The new broadcast technologies are not regulated in the same way. In both the United States and Canada, broadcast regulators have decided against regulating the Internet.[4] The U.S. regulator, the FCC, decided that there should be no Internet regulation, even for the purpose of protecting children, if this would place an "undue burden" on the communication of material between adults (Antonoff, 2005, p. 272). The CRTC's 1999 *New Media* decision not to regulate the Internet cited the fact that technologies now develop so quickly that the lag time for the CRTC to develop regulations and a licensing scheme for new media might effectively stifle the industry's growth. As a result of this decision, different broadcasting standards are being applied, depending on which form of media is used to communicate a message. This double standard is hard to justify and will only become more problematic as technologies advance and other media proliferate (see Antonoff, 2005, p. 274).

Given that the government must have a very compelling reason to justify a restriction on free expression under Canada's *Charter of Rights and Freedoms*, the seeming arbitrariness of the distinction between radio and other media puts the CRTC's content regulation on a shaky footing.

3. Protection of children

Most people agree that the government has an important responsibility to ensure the protection of children. Supporters of broadcast censorship, not least lawmakers and courts, often justify censorship by saying that it is needed to protect children from hearing age-inappropriate things on the radio, or seeing them on television. They argue that the broadcast media are uniquely accessible to children, and that children are not as likely to gain access to inappropriate material (either accidentally or on purpose) through other media. The U.S. Supreme Court has even said that it is less likely that children will encounter this material on the Internet than in broadcast media, because they have to take more affirmative steps to see sexually explicit or indecent content on the unregulated Internet than they do in the broadcast media (Rooder, 2005, p. 896).

Anyone who knows a 12-year-old knows that this view is out of touch with reality. If one were to imagine that there was no regulation of content on the radio or TV at all, then it is easy to picture children accidentally stumbling across inappropriate material in their channel surfing. But while children might be marginally less likely to *accidentally* run across explicit content on the Internet than on unregulated broadcasting, it is clearly very easy for them to gain access to a world of sexual material on the Internet never contemplated on TV or the radio. The child who seeks it out will be exposed to reams of sexual material in seconds, and even children who don't seek it out may accidentally happen across it with some frequency, depending on the terms they use in their Internet searching.

A justification for censorship that is based on broadcasting's easy accessibility by children is fairly shaky, because in reality, broadcasting is not significantly more accessible by children than are other forms of media. It also has the problematic result of preventing adults from hearing the material deemed to be unfit for children (Rooder, 2005, p. 895). Some believe that, in fact, this is exactly the point. A famous U.S. court decision involving indecency in broadcasting stemmed from a comedy routine by George Carlin in which he used a great number of "swear words." The case, *FCC v. Pacifica Foundation* (1977), generated a list of seven words that the court decided should be illegal to say in broadcasting. While protecting children was a major theme in the decision, some think that this might be, in part, a cover for the fact that the court actually wanted to protect unwilling *adults* from hearing such material, even for the few seconds that it would take to change the channel (Greene et al., 2005, pp. 1127–1128).

The right of adults to listen to a wide range of material, part of *their* freedom of expression, is constricted by protections ostensibly aimed at children. These rules might be worthwhile if children were actually protected by the censorship. But technology and indeed popular culture have progressed to the point that, in spite of government regulations, children can gain access to inappropriate content with unprecedented freedom. Not only the Internet, but also movies and music (granted, with the ratings system and parental advisory labels) contain all sorts of material that was relatively unknown in popular media 30 years ago, before some of the major court decisions (Marino, 2005, pp. 160–161). As much as it may be a worthy goal, censoring broadcast media does not effectively protect children from undesirable influences (Rooder, 2005, p. 906). In light of this, the cost of radio censorship in terms of freedom of expression, and the freedom to listen, is too great to justify. We are paying a high price in freedom for very feeble, even nonexistent results.

4. Pervasiveness of broadcast media

The concern about the risk of coming across inappropriate content is not limited to children. In the debate over shock jocks, the concern has been less about what children might hear than about what adults will be exposed to, and the harm that the messages could create. Some of the discussion about shock jocks has suggested that you could come across Howard Stern, the most well-known American shock jock, doing a monologue on anal sex just by using the seek key on your radio (Garry, 2005, p. 554). There is disagreement over whether the strategy of just hitting the seek key again, changing the channel, or averting one's eyes is an adequate solution to the problem of offensive content in broadcasting (Garry, 2005, pp. 557–558).

Many, including some court decisions, support a "marketplace" model in which content will be regulated simply by whether or not people choose to listen. If too many people are offended, they will stop listening and even complain to advertisers. Advertisers will pull their support from stations and shows that have smaller audiences, and eventually broadcasters will be forced to switch to content that is in line with community standards.

Others argue that the broadcast media work hard to ensure that viewers and listeners become habituated to their programming, and that they shape people's media consumption tastes deliberately to support that programming which will generate the most revenue. According to this view, individual agency and choice by rational consumers are, in effect, supplanted by the seduction of the media. Here, broadcasting is unlike the speaker on the street or the pamphleteer; the aim is not to persuade but to hook the listener (Garry, 2005, pp. 557–560). As a result, it may make less sense to rely on the individual choices of media consumers to regulate the industry. Collective action through government regulation is seen as necessary to balance the relationship between broadcasters and the public (see Garry, 2005, pp. 560–561). This argument supposes that because the media work hard to shape individual consumers' choices, consumer choice ought to be taken away by the government. This idea can also be framed in terms of listeners' rights: consumers shouldn't need to spend the effort to change the channel or turn off their TVs in order to avoid sexual or violent content (Garry, 2005, p. 560). This view sees controversial content as an imposition or an invasion on consumers' private enjoyment of broadcasting.

To stave off the risk of such brief exposures of the unwilling listener to unwanted material, the law has created a remedy that dramatically constrains freedom of expression. The fines imposed on broadcasters in the United States are problematic enough, but in Canada, the CRTC goes so far as to completely pull the plug on a radio station. Although Canada already has laws against the promotion of hatred against identifiable groups, the Canadian government has additionally reserved for itself the power to silence voices that simply offend rather than break the law. In the American *Pacifica* case, one of the justices of the Supreme Court wrote in dissent that "whatever the minimal discomfort suffered by a listener who inadvertently tunes into a program he finds offensive during the brief interval before he can simply extend his arm and switch stations, or flick the "off" button, it surely is worth [it] to preserve the broadcaster's right to send, and the right of those interested to receive, a message entitled" to full constitutional protection (*FCC v. Pacifica*, 1977, p. 766).

Arguably, the criminal law's prohibitions against **hate speech** and obscenity that are already in place, and the anti-hate provision of the *Canadian Human Rights Act*, are enough to deal with expression that is thought to be truly harmful. While these laws are themselves the subject of much debate, and are opposed by many proponents of civil liberties as excessive and dangerous to free speech, there is certainly no need to supplement them with CRTC censorship.

CONCLUSION

In spite of the waning relevance of the CRTC and FCC brought about by technological developments, or perhaps because of it, content regulators have stepped up their enforcement of obscenity rules. In the United States, President George W. Bush signed an Act that sees a tenfold increase in fines for radio and television content that violates decency standards, including extensive profanity or sexual conduct.[5] This has been seen as a move by Congress to shore up ebbing support in the conservative Republican base. Even before this new law, the FCC had been stepping up its enforcement, sending a shockwave of self-censorship through the industry. CBS Radio announced a zero tolerance policy for indecency on the air, and Clear Channel fired its shock jocks, including Howard Stern, who has moved to satellite radio, which is unregulated in the United States. In April 2007, long-time shock jock Don Imus had his show cancelled by CBS for negative remarks he made about Black women athletes on a university basketball team, prompting a firestorm of debate over free speech and the airwaves in the United States.[6] When Bono used the "f-word" in excitement at receiving a Golden Globe Award on NBC in 2003, the FCC ruled in March 2004 that his statements were indecent and profane. After the Super Bowl halftime show featuring Janet Jackson's "wardrobe malfunction" on February 1, 2004,[7] there was a political firestorm in the United States and a push to "clean up the airwaves" (Fallow, 2004, p. 25). The same month, the Grammys on CBS aired with a five-second delay for the first time in history and removed Janet Jackson from its roster of presenters (although not Justin Timberlake, who was the other performer involved in the incident). The Oscars on ABC followed with a five-second delay, also for the first time in its history (Fallow, 2004, p. 26). Two years after the Janet Jackson incident, ABC adopted a five-second delay for the Super Bowl itself (CBC, 2006). Many broadcasters may even curtail live broadcasting segments, including news, because of the difficulty in predicting whether or not the program will violate the rules (see Cohen, 2005, p. 138). The FCC is using a vague standard for indecency that says, essentially, they can't tell you in advance what is indecent, but they'll know it when they see it. But how can such a body truly determine what is offensive and what is not for 300 million Americans? How can the CRTC do it for Canada?

If you ask a hundred different people what is offensive, you are liable to get a hundred different answers (Patel, 2004, p. 12). Does this mean that people should be able to say anything they want on the air? Maybe not, but the restrictions on freedom of expression (on air and elsewhere) have to be both narrowly defined and constitutionally justifiable. The CRTC's overly broad and nebulous prohibition of "abusive" language on air cuts a wide swath through freedom of expression, and imposes a chill on free speech that is out of proportion to any public interest that the government relies on to justify it.

References
Cases

Broadcasting Decision CRTC 2004-271. (2004, July 13). Retrieved June 12, 2007, from http://www.crtc.gc.ca/archive/eng/decisions/2004/db2004-271.htm

FCC Forfeiture Order—Complaints against various television licensees concerning their February 1, 2004, broadcast of the Super Bowl XXXVIII halftime show (FCC 06-19). (2006, March 15). Retrieved June 12, 2007, from http://www.fcc.gov/eb/Orders/2006/FCC-06-19A1.html

FCC v. Pacifica Foundation (1977), 438 U.S. 726.

Little Sisters Book & Art Emporium v. Canada, [2000] 2 S.C.R. 1120.

Legislation

Broadcasting Act, 1991. c. B-9.01. Available from http://www.crtc.gc.ca/eng/LEGAL/BROAD.htm

Radio Regulations, 1986, S.O.R./86 - 982. Available from http://www.crtc.gc.ca/eng/LEGAL/Radioreg.htm

Secondary Sources

Antonoff, Ian J. 2005. "You don't like it… change the (expletive deleted) channel!: an analysis of the constitutional issues that plague FCC enforcement actions and a proposal for deregulation in favor of direct consumer control." *Seton Hall Journal of Sports and Entertainment Law* 15: 253-274.

Brown, K., & Candeub, A. (2005). The law and economics of wardrobe malfunction. *Brigham Young University Law Review, 2005*(6), 1463–1513.

CBC. (2006, February 4). Nervous ABC keeps delay on Super Bowl signal. Retrieved June 12, 2007, from http://www.cbc.ca/arts/story/2006/02/04/abc-delay.html

Canadian Association of Broadcasters. (2002). *Code of Ethics*. Retrieved June 12, 2007, from http://www.cab-acr.ca/english/social/codes/ethics.shtm

Canadian Radio-television and Telecommunications Commission. (1999). *Broadcasting Public Notice CRTC 1999-84/Telecom Public Notice CRTC 99-14—New Media*. Retrieved June 12, 2007, from http://www.crtc.gc.ca/archive/ENG/Notices/1999/PB99-84.htm

Cohen, M. J. (2005). Have you no sense of decency? An examination of the effect of traditional values and family-oriented organizations on twenty-first century broadcast indecency standards. *Seton Hall Legislative Journal, 20*, 113–143.

Fallow, K. A. (2004). The Big Chill? Congress and the FCC crack down on indecency. *Communications Lawyer, 22*(1), 25–32.

Garry, P. M. (2005). Confronting the changed circumstances of free speech in a media society. *Capital University Law Review, 33*, 551–565.

Greene, A., Davenport, W., Hoeh, J., Baker, E. E., McGeady, P. J., & Fiorini III, J. (2005). Panel III: Indecent exposure? The FCC's recent enforcement of obscenity laws. *Fordham Intellectual Property, Media and Entertainment Law Journal, 15*, 1087–1142.

Marino, J. L. (2005). More "filthy words" but no "free passes" for the "cost of doing business": New legislation is the best regulation for broadcast indecency. *Seton Hall Journal of Sports and Entertainment Law, 15*, 135–172.

Patel, S. I. (2004). An indecent proposal. *New Jersey Lawyer, 231*, 10–14.

Rooder, B. J. (2005). Broadcast indecency regulation in the era of the "wardrobe malfunction": Has the FCC grown too big for its britches? *Fordham Law Review, 74*, 871–907.

Varona, A. E. (2006). Out of thin air: Using First Amendment public forum analysis to redeem American broadcasting regulation. *University of Michigan Journal of Law Reform, 39*, 149–198.

Notes

[1] The CRTC also regulates telecommunications and telephone services, in addition to all forms of broadcasting, including radio and television (free-to-air, cable, and satellite).

[2] Forcing radio stations to broadcast certain material, such as Canadian musical content, also has implications on freedom of expression. I am unable to address the issue of Canadian content within this chapter, but it has been noted that while the government's public ownership of the airwaves may not justify censorship, it probably justifies government regulations that force broadcasters to carry certain material. The government can require the addition of content on air, but it cannot prohibit content from being broadcast (see Greene, 2005, pp. 1127–1128).

[3] The "Human Rights" clause of the Canadian Association of Broadcasters' code of ethics states, "Recognizing that every person has the right to full and equal recognition and to enjoy certain fundamental rights and freedoms, broadcasters shall ensure that their programming contains no abusive or unduly discriminatory material or comment which is based on matters of race, national or ethnic origin, colour, religion, age, sex, sexual orientation, marital status or physical or mental disability."

[4] In the United States, the FCC does not regulate the content of any fee-based media, including satellite radio and cable television, although it does issue broadcast licences and has allocated satellite bandwidth between different service providers. There is currently some pressure in Congress to extend the FCC's content oversight to pay television and radio services. See PBS, "Revolutions in Radio," at http://www.pbs.org/newshour/media/radio/comparison.html.

[5] President Bush signed the *Broadcast Decency Enforcement Act* on June 15, 2006.

[6] These events were unfolding at the time this chapter went to print.

[7] The "wardrobe malfunction" occurred when Janet Jackson's breast was exposed during a live television performance with Justin Timberlake for the Super Bowl halftime show in 2004. The FCC fined CBS $550,000.00 on February 21, 2006 for broadcasting indecent material (See FCC Forfeiture Order, 2006).

Discussion Questions

1. Should offensive speech on radio programs be censored? If so, whose determination of offensiveness should be used for this purpose (radio station management, government, etc.)?

2. Should there be government guidelines for public expression?

3. Should broadcasters be required to have a government-issued licence? If so, for what purpose, and will licensing broadcasters achieve this purpose? What are some other effects you can think of that might result from a licensing requirement?

4. Aside from government directives, how can we protect children from seeing or hearing inappropriate expressions of opinions, ideas, arguments, and values on public media?

Music matters: Are CanCon regulations necessary to promote Canadian music?

✔ YES

Why Canadian Content Regulations Are Needed to Support Canadian Music

David Young

David Young is an assistant professor in the Department of Sociology at McMaster University. He specializes in media sociology and political sociology. His areas of research include awards shows, the political economy of Canadian cultural industries, media policy, and media history. He is the author of several journal articles, including three that report research on the Juno Awards for the Canadian music industry. The latter articles are "The Promotional State and Canada's Juno Awards" (in *Popular Music*), "The CBC and the Juno Awards" (in the *Canadian Journal of Communication*), and "Ethno-racial Minorities and the Juno Awards" (in the *Canadian Journal of Sociology*). Young is currently researching the Genie Awards for the Canadian film industry.

INTRODUCTION

After decades in which Canadian music was rarely heard on the radio, 1971 marked a turning point. "Signs" by the Five Man Electrical Band, "Sweet City Woman" by the Stampeders, and "Put Your Hand in the Hand" by Ocean are just a few of the many now-classic Canadian songs that dominated the airwaves that year. The success of these songs and acts has a lot to do with the Canadian content (CanCon) regulations for Canadian radio stations that came into effect in 1971 (Breithaupt, 1999, p. 5). CanCon regulations have been controversial ever since they were implemented, and they have increasingly come under attack in recent years. In this chapter, we will examine three key arguments in defence of the regulations. First, CanCon regulations were crucial in light of conditions that largely precluded music by Canadians. Second, the regulations have supported various components of the Canadian music industry. Third, while the doctrine of neoliberalism has generated pressure to eliminate CanCon, the regulations are still needed because prevailing economic interests threaten to undermine the achievements and further development of Canadian musical artists.

THE EMERGENCE OF CANCON REGULATIONS

From the 1950s to the end of the 1960s, there was little production and airplay of Canadian music. To the extent that they existed, Canadian-owned record companies (such as Quality) made profits by pressing foreign master tapes into records. The profits would sometimes be used to finance the production of recordings by Canadian-based performers (Straw, 1993, pp. 56–57). It is also important to note that recordings by Canadian artists were not the primary fare of the private radio industry; in 1968, it was estimated that only between 4 and 7 percent of the music on private stations was Canadian (Audley, 1983, p. 8). Although some Canadian acts received airplay, including Gordon Lightfoot and the Guess Who, American or other foreign music was emphasized on Canadian commercial radio (Haysom, 1996, p. F1). The popularity of this music drew listeners, which in turn generated high advertising rates and therefore profit for private radio stations.

The concept of a promotional state helps to shed light on developments in Canadian music from the 1970s onward. Reacting to the dominant presence of foreign music, a promotional state attempts to support domestic music through a number of interventionist strategies (Cloonan, 1999, p. 204). Public broadcasting and government funding are key aspects of Canada's promotional state, but another important factor is CanCon regulations (Young, 2004, p. 272). The CRTC, which is the federal government agency that sets rules for broadcasting, announced in 1970 its proposal to establish Canadian content regulations for music on Canadian radio stations. The CRTC's public hearings on the issue revealed sharp divisions between various groups. Represented by the Canadian Association of Broadcasters, private radio stations opposed the idea of CanCon because they did not want further regulation. However, the CRTC's proposal was strongly supported by Canadian record companies, music publishers, and trade unions, which included Canadian musicians (CRTC, 1971, pp. 19–20).

On the basis of the public hearings, the CRTC proceeded with CanCon regulations. Starting in January 1971, a minimum of 30 percent of musical compositions over the entire broadcast day on AM stations had to meet at least one of the following criteria: the music had to be written by a Canadian; the playing or singing (or both) had to be principally by a Canadian; the performance must have been recorded in Canada; and the lyrics had to be written by a Canadian. After one year, a minimum of 30 percent of the musical selections needed to satisfy at least two of these criteria (CRTC, 1971, pp. 16–17, 20). The CRTC later applied lower minimum levels of CanCon to FM stations because less of the material aired on these stations qualified as Canadian under the guidelines. The agency also required substantial amounts of French-language CanCon to be played on radio stations in Quebec. With minor definitional modifications, the four criteria of what became known as the MAPL system (music, artist, production, and lyrics) have continued to provide the basis for determining what constitutes Canadian content. The CRTC has stated that the *cultural objective* of CanCon regulations is "to encourage increased exposure of Canadian musical performers, lyricists, and composers to Canadian audiences," while the *industrial objective* is "to strengthen the Canadian music industry, including both the creative and production components" (CRTC, 2001).

THE EFFECTIVENESS OF CANCON REGULATIONS

When considered in relation to these cultural and industrial objectives, CanCon regulations have been effective. Wright notes that the emergence of CanCon "opened the recording industry to Canadian talent as nothing had done previously, and a great scramble to build record companies and to sign artists followed" (1987–88, p. 30). By encouraging Canadian artists to record in Canada, the regulations helped to support Canadian recording studios and producers (Dafoe,

1991, p. C1). As a result of radio airplay in the first half of the 1970s, the copyright royalties paid to Canadian composers and lyricists more than tripled (Spurgeon, 1992, p. 2). Of course, recording artists also received airplay as a result of CanCon. For instance, Randy Bachman (of Bachman-Turner Overdrive) and Rich Dodson (of the Stampeders) have stated that CanCon regulations helped their bands to get on the radio during the 1970s. Similarly, *Canadian Idol* judge Sass Jordan noted that the airplay she enjoyed in the 1980s and 1990s can partially be attributed to the regulations (Breithaupt, 1999, p. 5; Leary, 2003).

Although CanCon regulations have been effective, some Canadian recording artists and private radio broadcasters have attacked the regulations or attempted to undermine them. Bryan Adams criticized the CRTC in 1992 after songs from his latest album failed to qualify as CanCon because the music and lyrics were cowritten with a foreigner. However, Adams also conceded in a column he wrote for the *Toronto Star* that CanCon has assisted many Canadian artists by giving them exposure (1992, p. J1). Representatives of the private radio industry have made similar admissions (McCabe, 2001, p. R1). Nevertheless, because private stations still wanted to emphasize foreign music, a "CanCon ghetto" had emerged at a number of stations by the 1980s. Even though the CRTC required CanCon selections to be played throughout the entire broadcast day, some stations were not playing them during peak listening periods (the morning and afternoon hours). Instead, regarding the CRTC's figure of 30 percent CanCon as the *maximum* requirement rather than the intended *minimum*, the stations attempted to meet the requirement by playing Canadian music during low-listening times (Lanthier, 1989, pp. 2–3). According to a study conducted by the Canadian Independent Record Production Association (CIRPA) and the Society of Composers, Authors and Music Publishers of Canada (SOCAN), this ghettoization of Canadian content continued into the 1990s (Jones, 1996, p. 16). Under its 1998 Commercial Radio Policy, the CRTC attempted to deal with the problem by establishing tighter rules regarding the hours for playing CanCon during the day while also increasing the minimum level of CanCon for popular music stations from 30 percent to 35 percent (CRTC, 1998).

THE CONTINUING NEED FOR CANCON REGULATIONS

The practices of private radio broadcasters demonstrate that CanCon regulations are needed and must be enforced, but the rise of neoliberalism presents challenges to the regulations. Neoliberalism is a philosophical and economic doctrine that has been influential since the late 1970s. It advocates a minimalist role for the state, the centrality of the individual, and the importance of a free market (Naiman, 2000, p. 337). Neoliberalism holds that government is an ineffective provider of social welfare and that individuals should assume responsibility for their own well-being. When applied to the music industry, neoliberalism suggests that Canadian music is a commodity that should be developed and sold by competing performers in an unfettered marketplace. These elements of the neoliberal paradigm provide the basis for three key arguments against CanCon regulations, and all three must be critically interrogated.

To begin with, while neoliberalism favours a significantly limited role for the state, private radio broadcasters have not offered compelling reasons for reducing or eliminating CanCon. Believing that they should be able to play whatever music their listeners want, these broadcasters have long complained that the regulations are an "assault on broadcast freedom" (Hoy, 1998). However, since the Canadian airwaves are seen as public property that is subject to the *Broadcasting Act* (the legal foundation for CanCon regulations), the public interest overrides the freedom of individual broadcasters (McPhail, 1986, pp. 46–48). A more recent argument is even less convincing. In 2006, as the CRTC prepared to revise its Commercial Radio Policy, private stations contended that CanCon requirements should be reduced because of the competition they face from music sources such as the Internet (Shecter, 2006, p. FP4). However, as Sutherland noted in 2002, "it will be some time before the Internet becomes as ubiquitous as radio and even then there is no guarantee that it will displace it in terms of its importance for music" (p. 13).

The continuing influence of radio is suggested by a national survey that Decima Research (2005) conducted for the Department of Canadian Heritage in May 2005. Survey respondents indicated that they spent considerably more hours per week listening to music on the radio compared to (in descending order of usage) the three categories of CDs, MP3s, or cassettes; television; and the Internet (p. 68). Radio was also the most frequently cited means through which respondents as a whole discovered new music (followed by word-of-mouth, television, the Internet, print/advertising, concerts, stores, and movies). Respondents in the 15–20 age category most often cited word-of-mouth, but even this group placed radio over television and the Internet as a source of exposure to new music (p. 90). The survey also found that in 2005, music by Canadian artists accounted for about 40 percent of the CDs that respondents purchased and roughly 30 percent of the songs they acquired online through either free or purchased music downloads (p. 83, 88). These data imply that radio still has a more prevalent role than the Internet with regard to music, and it has probably influenced the decisions of consumers to acquire music by Canadian artists. Even if the Internet eventually surpasses the dominant position of radio, the development of new media has not meant the disappearance of the old media; the old media like radio and television "almost inevitably find new niches, new methods, new audiences and new leases on life" (Taras, 2001, p. 66). There is no reason, then, to loosen the obligations imposed on private radio broadcasters for using the public airwaves.

Some arguments against CanCon reflect a view of the individual that is associated with neoliberalism, and they consequently ignore conditions in capitalist society that make the regulations essential. Liberal ideology subscribes to the notion of a meritocracy and engages in blaming the victim (Naiman, 2000, p. 233). If people do not succeed, they must lack ability or a willingness to work hard enough. Such thinking is often applied to people who are unemployed or on welfare (even though capitalism generates the elimination of jobs and other conditions that are the real source of their misfortune), and this becomes a justification for cutting employment insurance or social assistance. The same reasoning is used to call for the elimination of CanCon regulations. In the above-mentioned column he wrote for the *Toronto Star*, Bryan Adams argued that "real talent will always win out whether or not it is supported by the government. It's time to shut off the government tap as it relates to music" (1992, p. J1). Adams's arguments are problematic since they focus on the individual rather than considering larger organizational barriers to artistic (e.g., musical) production. Talent alone is not necessarily going to get Canadian performers on the radio. Many private radio stations ignore Canadian artists who are not signed to (or least distributed by) one of the multinational conglomerates that dominate the music industry. As a result, Canadian acts that are associated with independent record companies face obstacles at commercial radio (Everett-Green, 2001, p. R3; McLean, 1996, p. 1). An online petition initiated in May 2005 by Indie Pool, a group representing independent artists, has been directed toward correcting this problem. The group's aim is to lobby policymakers to strengthen CanCon regulations so that radio stations will be encouraged to play developing (independent or unsigned) Canadian performers (Terrance, 2005). Especially since it appears that radio will still be a considerable force in relation to music for some time to come, CanCon regulations are needed to help these artists.

Finally, while neoliberalism advocates free trade and global competition, CanCon regulations are a crucial aspect of the fight to protect Canadian culture from globalizing (and Americanizing) cultural influences. Some opponents of the regulations suggest that they are inconsistent with globalization and run counter to Canada's support for international free trade agreements (Stanbury, 1998, pp. 67–68). Although there is a contradiction between free trade and the continuing existence of CanCon, this is arguably positive because it shows that Canada has been willing to put limits on free trade. The United States has long seen music, television programs, films, and so on, as products for trade rather than reflections of culture. Because American entertainment industries have economic interests in accessing foreign markets, the United States has objected to domestic content regulations (quotas) and other protective measures on the ideological grounds that they restrict the free flow of information. However, in the view of less powerful countries, such measures are needed to ensure space for media expressing their own culture (Smythe, 1981, pp. 233–242). Among these countries, Canada has played an influential role. Nations trying to protect their own domestic music have studied CanCon regulations for radio (Straw, 2000, p. 176). After Canada managed to secure a cultural exemption during negotiations for the 1988 Free Trade Agreement with the United States, France and the European Union tried but failed to secure a cultural exemption under the General Agreement on Trade in Services.

Along with France, Canada has also led the attempt to establish an international agreement upholding the right of governments to support and promote the diversity of cultural expression (Azzi, 2005, pp. 766–768). This agreement on cultural diversity was drafted as a formal convention through the United Nations Educational, Scientific and Cultural Organization (UNESCO). In a vote held by UNESCO members during October 2005, 148 countries approved the convention, while 2 countries opposed it (including the United States) and 4 countries abstained from voting (Coalition for Cultural Diversity, 2005a). The convention must be ratified by at least 30 countries within a few years and preferably by as many countries as possible if it is to become an effective counterweight against U.S. pressure for free trade in culture. In November 2005, Canada became the first country to ratify the convention (Coalition for Cultural Diversity, 2005b).

These developments have been supported by the Canadian Coalition for Cultural Diversity, which includes the CIRPA and SOCAN, additional bodies connected to Canadian music, and various cultural organizations and unions. The coalition noted that the massive vote in favour of the convention shows that "the right to have cultural policies (domestic content quotas, subsidies, tax credits, foreign ownership rules, etc.) is now recognized as a priority by countries all over the world" (Coalition for Cultural Diversity, 2005a). Since many countries are engaged in a struggle to protect their culture, and since Canada has taken a leadership role in this struggle, any movement toward reducing or abandoning CanCon regulations will be a step in the wrong direction.

CONCLUSION

CanCon regulations have been fundamental to the promotion and support of Canadian music. The regulations emerged with the industrial objective of developing Canadian music production, but CanCon also had the cultural objective of opening up space for Canadian musical talent and music with a Canadian flavour. Evidence suggests that CanCon has been effective in many ways, despite the efforts of private radio broadcasters to undermine the regulations. The economic interests of these broadcasters, combined with the worrying implications of neoliberalism, demonstrate a need to maintain and strengthen existing Canadian content requirements. CanCon regulations are an example of what the eminent Canadian communications scholar Dallas Smythe (1981) referred to as "cultural screens." Smythe warned that if the notion of cultural screens and the need for them ever seemed "novel or strange," this would indicate how successfully the screens had been dismantled by "modern capitalism" in "its ceaseless quest for profits" (p. 232). Such a situation should not be allowed to exist, and it is up to Canadian citizens to ensure that this does not happen.

References

Adams, B. (1992, February 8). "Real talent will always win out," Adams says. *Toronto Star*, p. J1.

Audley, P. (1983). *Canada's cultural industries: Broadcasting, publishing, records and film*. Ottawa: Canadian Institute for Economic Policy.

Azzi, S. (2005). Negotiating cultural space in the global economy: The United States, UNESCO, and the Convention on Cultural Diversity. *International Journal, 60*(3), 765–784.

Breithaupt, D. (1999, May 8). Second-class stars no more. *National Post*, p. 5.

Canadian Radio-Television and Telecommunications Commission. (2001, May 31). *The MAPL system*. Retrieved May 17, 2006, from http://www.crtc.gc.ca/eng/INFO_SHT/R1.htm

Canadian Radio-Television and Telecommunications Commission. (1998, April 30). *Public Notice CRTC 1998-41 (Commercial Radio Policy 1998)*. Retrieved May 22, 2006, from http://www.crtc.gc.ca/archive/ENG/Notices/1998/PB98-41.HTM

Canadian Radio-Television Commission. (1971). *Annual report, '70–'71*. Ottawa: Information Canada.

Cloonan, M. (1999). Pop and the nation-state: Towards a theorisation. *Popular Music, 18*(2), 193–207.

Coalition for Cultural Diversity. (2005a, October 21). Coalitions for Cultural Diversity hail adoption of UNESCO Convention on Cultural Diversity; urge countries to ratify on urgent basis [News release]. Retrieved May 23, 2006, from http://www.cdc-ccd.org/Anglais/Liensenanglais/nouveautes_eng/framenouveautes_eng.htm

Coalition for Cultural Diversity. (2005b, November 23). Canada's action to become first country to ratify UNESCO Convention on Cultural Diversity applauded by Canada's cultural sector [News release]. Retrieved May 23, 2006, from http://www.cdc-ccd.org/Anglais/Liensenanglais/nouveautes_eng/framenouveautes_eng.htm

Dafoe, C. (1991, September 24). It's time to fine tune a sound principle, Chris Dafoe argues. *The Globe and Mail*, p. C1.

Decima Research. (2005, July). *Canadian film and music opinion study* [Prepared for the Department of Canadian Heritage]. Retrieved May 8, 2006, from http://www.pch.gc.ca/pc-ch/sujets-subjects/arts-culture/film-video/pubs/07-005/film_sondage-study_2005_e.pdf

Everett-Green, R. (2001, March 1). Why Nelly became a radio star. *The Globe and Mail*, pp. R1, R3.

Haysom, I. (1996, March 8). Do we still need CanCon after 25 years? *The Hamilton Spectator*, pp. F1, F4.

Hoy, C. (1998, May 11). Media applauds CRTC's assault on broadcast freedom. *The Hill Times*. Retrieved April 21, 2006, from Proquest, McMaster University, Hamilton, ON: http://proquest.umi.com.libaccess .lib.mcmaster.ca

Jones, C. (1996, April). Review of CanCon regs urged. *Words & Music*, 16.

Lanthier, N. (1989, May–June). The CanCon ghetto. *The Music Scene*, 2–3.

Leary, J. (2003, July 7). Bachman: Rocker says increase in Canadian content good for radio. *The Vancouver Sun*. Retrieved April 27, 2006, from Friends of Canadian Broadcasting: http://www.friends.ca/News/ Friends_News/archives/articles07070303.asp

McCabe, M. (2001, March 29). Our stars in their stripes. *The Globe and Mail*, pp. R1, R11.

McLean, S. (1996, March 11). Indies getting skinned on CanCon spins. *The Record*, 1, 13, 14.

McPhail, B. M. (1986). Canadian content regulations and the Canadian Charter of Rights and Freedoms. *Canadian Journal of Communication, 12*(1), 41–53.

Naiman, J. (2000). *How societies work: Class, power, and change in a Canadian context* (2nd ed.). Toronto: Irwin.

Shecter, B. (2006, March 16). Ease content rules, CRTC told. *National Post*, p. FP4.

Smythe, D. W. (1981). *Dependency road: Communications, capitalism, consciousness, and Canada*. Norwood, NJ: Ablex.

Spurgeon, P. (1992, May). Why we need Canadian content regulations. *SOCAN Probe*, 2.

Stanbury, W. T. (1998, August). Canadian Content regulations: The intrusive state at work. *Fraser Forum*, 5–90.

Straw, W. (1993). The English Canadian recording industry since 1970. In T. Bennett, S. Frith, L. Grossberg, J. Shepherd, & G. Turner (Eds.), *Rock and popular music: Politics, policies, institutions* (pp. 52–65). London: Routledge.

Straw, W. (2000). In and around Canadian music. *Journal of Canadian Studies, 35*(3), 173–183.

Sutherland, R. (2002, June). Canadian content at 32. *Canadian Issues*, 13.

Taras, D. (2001). *Power and betrayal in the Canadian media* (updated ed.). Peterborough, ON: Broadview.

Terrance, G. (2005). Let's fix CANCON. Retrieved April 27, 2006, from http://www.letsfixcancon.ca/

Wright, R. A. (1987–88). "Dream, comfort, memory, despair": Canadian popular musicians and the dilemma of nationalism, 1968–1972. *Journal of Canadian Studies, 22*(4), 27–43.

Young, D. (2004). The promotional state and Canada's Juno Awards. *Popular Music, 23*(3), 271–289.

ISSUE 2

Music matters: Are CanCon regulations necessary to promote Canadian music?

✗ NO

The B Side: Why Canadian Content Isn't Necessary for the Survival of Canadian Music
Ira Wagman

Ira Wagman is an assistant professor of mass communication in the School of Journalism and Communication at Carleton University.

There is something dramatic about the idea that Canadian content regulations, or CanCon, are necessary for the survival of Canadian music. It conjures up images of innocent victims, nefarious characters, and superheroes arriving just in time to save the day. Here, the innocent victims are Canadian musicians struggling to eke out a living, while the nefarious characters are money-hungry commercial radio broadcasters playing the stylized music produced by multinational corporations over the airwaves. These forces conspire to divert the aural attention of Canadians away from the music of their fellow citizens, slowly corroding the nation's cultural fabric. As for the superheroes? They are officials from the CRTC, Canada's broadcast regulator. Their main weapon against the villains of Canadian music, the content regulation, ensures the survival of an entire nation's musical expression by forcing broadcasters to play a certain amount of material certified as "Canadian."

For a country not known for its heroic narratives, the story of how CanCon protects Canadian culture is a notable exception. In fact, it is repeated so often that it seems commonsensical. One can find it in newspaper columns, like that of *Ottawa Citizen* columnist Charles Gordon, which argue that Canadian content rules are necessary because "no one else in the world is going to protect and encourage our artists" (Gordon, 1998, p. A13). One can also find it in the rhetoric used by music industry associations, like the Canadian Music Publishers Association, which states that their members "would be mortally handicapped" without content regulations (CMPA, 2005). Everywhere one looks, it is easy to find examples of arguments articulating how Canadian content saved Canadian music.

However simply repeating a story doesn't make it true. By relying on a simplistic explanation about the role of government regulations on Canada's music sector, we continue to lack a solid understanding of the relationships among Canadian musicians, record companies, and listening audiences. Indeed, to believe the story about CanCon saving Canadian music, one needs to accept that Canadian music was on the brink of extinction and that an artist's citizenship is more important than musical skill or talent. There is little evidence to suggest that Canadians were on the verge of losing their abilities to express themselves musically, and there is even less evidence that an artist's passport determines listening behaviour.

Once we set aside these myths, what can be said about Canadian content regulations? First, CanCon regulations have very little to do with music. There are examples of Canadian content regulations in a number of industrial sectors; this model has been transposed onto the sound recording industry. As a number of case studies will illustrate, CanCon regulations actually worked against some of the country's most successful artists. Second, the argument for Canadian content saving Canadian music stands only if we fail to examine the elaborate networks, agencies, institutions, and social formations that play a key role in the ways Canadians experience and engage with music. Studying these "pathways of cultural movement" (Straw, 2005) shows that musical success or failure has little to do with content regulations.

ANYTHING BUT MUSIC: CANADIAN CONTENT AS INDUSTRIAL DEVELOPMENT STRATEGY

The most popular component of the triumphalist narrative about CanCon equates the invention of content regulations with the development of Canada's music industry. As the story goes, Canada's music industry barely existed before 1970. During this time, one rarely heard Canadian acts on domestic radio stations. In addition to the relative silence over the air, few federal initiatives were offered to support the development of the Canadian sound recording industry (Audley, 1983, p. 236). Then, thanks to the lobbying efforts of music industry representatives, the CRTC instituted CanCon regulations requiring Canadian radio broadcasters to air specific amounts of Canadian music. This was a measure that had already been applied to television a decade earlier, and it offered to stimulate the development of Canada's sound recording industry. To determine exactly what constitutes a "Canadian song," the CRTC created the MAPL system. If two of the following components of a song—musician, lyricists, producer, and label—are Canadian or if the piece of music has been performed or recorded in Canada, it is considered to be Canadian.

The impact of these regulations on the music industry is easy to grasp. A rule that required radio stations to air specific types of material produced by specific categories of people naturally resulted in the creation of an industry able to satisfy these rules. This would happen in any industry. If the government required the Banana Republic chain of stores to ensure that 35 percent of its inventory came from Canadian clothing manufacturers, or if it required Starbucks to ensure that 40 percent of its coffee sales came from beans produced by Canadian roasters, then producers would spring forth to satisfy these regulations. This is precisely what happened in the music industry, with independent record labels and the Canadian arms of multinational corporations being created, producing content to meet the new demand.

As an industrial strategy offering protection and market stability, Canadian content regulations didn't actually begin in the cultural sector, but existed in a variety of industrial sectors before they were applied to solve the problems of the music industry. One of the first to get CanCon regulations was the country's automotive sector. As a way of fending off the effects of the Great Depression in the 1930s, the government of the day proposed to stimulate automobile production in Canada by dropping high tariffs on the import of American engines if the final automobile contained a certain percentage of "Canadian content," measured parts and labour.

This arrangement existed well into the 20th century as part of the Canada-U.S. Auto Pact (see Anastakis, 2005). A similar dynamic occurs in the Canadian Football League, where an "import quota" exists preventing teams from stocking their lineups with too many "foreign" players.

For a music industry whose size and shape is directly related to CanCon regulations, satisfying these criteria is serious business. Even the slightest alteration to the rules—raising or lowering Canadian content regulations by 5 percent, for example—prompts both excitement and hand-wringing not about the future of *Canadian music*, but about the future of the *Canadian music industry*. Michel Filion reveals this reaction when he explains that, in Canada, "cultural and industrial objectives are closely interrelated." (1996, p. 112).

Since the 1980s, the government has unveiled several measures to assist Canada's sound recording industry. For example, the Canadian Music Fund and the Radio Starmaker Fund assist musicians to develop their musical and entrepreneurial skills and assist record companies to produce music from Canadian artists. VideoFact is a program that gives grants to artists to produce music videos, while PromoFact helps record companies develop promotional materials. Seeing that CanCon is just one of many measures targeting the sound recording industry, it is unreasonable to conclude that its elimination would contribute to the disappearance of Canadian music.

Considering both its history and the affinities it has developed over time, CanCon carries important and deep-seated consequences. The first is the issue of regulatory compliance; just because the government requires an industry to act in a certain way does not mean either that it will fully cooperate or that customers of that industry will adopt the appropriate behaviour pattern. In the music industry, radio stations may be expected to play 35 percent Canadian content, but radio listeners may prefer to listen to non-Canadian acts, to purchase non-Canadian CDs, to see non-Canadian musicians in concert, and so on. In other words, while governments can manage industry behaviour, they cannot manage audience tastes.

It is also unclear whether they are able to manage the behaviour of radio stations themselves, who have viewed CanCon regulations as obstacles to achieving their commercial objectives. For many years, critics of CanCon have pointed to the fact that in response to the CRTC's regulations, radio stations have come up with constructive ways to keep the Canadian material from interfering with their primary musical content, such as by playing a small number of Canadian artists repeatedly over the course of the broadcast day (Belanger, 2006, pp. 134–135).

There are also a number of well-known examples in which content regulations appear to work against the efforts of Canadian musicians. Consider the case of Bryan Adams, widely acknowledged to be a Canadian performer. In 1992 his song "Everything I Do (I Do for You)" failed to qualify as Canadian because it was recorded in another country and co-written with a non-Canadian. At around the same time, however, songs by American singer Bonnie Raitt and British rocker Rod Stewart *did* qualify as Canadian because they had been written and composed by Canadians.

By now you might be asking, what separates Bryan Adams from Rod Stewart? The answer to that question is that in using a Canadian writer and composer, Rod Stewart worked with more Canadians than Bryan Adams. Therefore, in the eyes of those enforcing Canadian content regulations, Rod Stewart is "more Canadian" than Bryan Adams. Here one sees how Canadian content regulations privilege quantitative, industrial factors over qualitative, individual, or artistic factors. Should it matter if Adams decides that the best way to enact his artistic vision is to work with non-Canadians? Is the artistic vision more important than the extent to which the artist contributes to larger job creation? While such a question may apply when talking about the automotive industry, the **cultural industries** are supposed to operate according to a logic that is different than that applied to the mass production of cars.

This makes claims about Canadian content's cultural components highly questionable. If Canadian content regulations were about Canadian musicians, Adams and others like him would not have been punished for their individual artistic achievements. However, since Canadian content regulations are about industrial development, those who do not put enough Canadians to work on their songs don't count. If one argued, on the other hand, that artists who work with record labels in Britain or prominent American performers do not need CanCon regulations to get their material on the air, the result is the further stigmatization of Canadian music as forced upon Canadian citizens by the state, devoid of any artistic merit because of its function as "content."

Two recent examples involving the American band the Black Eyed Peas serve as contemporary cases of Canadian content's ugly side. Over the last few years, the band performed in the Grey Cup's halftime show and during the Juno Awards honouring Canada's music industry. The presence of the Peas during these events attracted editorials in some newspapers wondering why an American band was appearing at a venue honouring Canadians. The editors of the Regina *Leader Post* put it this way: "At the risk of seeming chauvinistic, this is Canada's biggest sporting event, why not feature Canadians?" ("Who Gives a Rap?" 2005, p. B7). For the editors of the *Globe and Mail*, a similar theme emerged: "You don't have to be a wild-eyed cultural nationalist to wonder why the Canadian Football League could not have found a Canadian group for this all-Canadian event" ("Imported Peas," 2006, p. A20). Similar language followed the band in the lead-up to their next major performance at the Juno Awards. An article in the *Edmonton Journal* focused on the fact that many industry representatives were "uncomfortable with the international line-up, arguing that home-grown artists should be the focus" (Pacienza, 2006, p. C3).

The backlash over the Black Eyed Peas reveals once again that the industrial components of CanCon appear even in places where content regulations do not apply. First, the notion that only someone approved by the Canadian music industry, or someone who "qualifies" as a Canadian musician, should perform at "real Canadian" events like the Grey Cup and the Juno Awards is the extension of an industrial argument to other zones of cultural activity. Since there are so few major "Canadian" events, allowing the Black Eyed Peas to perform squeezes out opportunities for Canadian musicians. If the Americans dominate the rest of the airwaves and awards shows, the critics maintain, why should they also be present on *our stages*?

The answer to that question is that, like most concerts, the musical act was booked based on the idea that the audience would enjoy the performance, not as an extension of citizenship or as sponsorship of Canada's music industry. The unease over the Black Eyed Peas expresses the long-standing discomfort with the impact of American culture on Canada, and assumes that the audience's musical preferences should always be calculated based on how their enjoyment contributes to industrial development. Having the Black Eyed Peas at the Junos alongside Canadian artists actually demonstrates that Canadians possess musical tastes that are both sophisticated in nature and international in scope. This is a compliment. Since CanCon regulations do not to recognize audience behaviour except to frame it around nationalist themes, commentaries on the Black Eyed Peas are oblivious to this fact.

The point of these examples is to show that CanCon has very little to do with music. Instead, CanCon measures are part of an *industrial* strategy that can be applied to any economic activity. A specifically *cultural* strategy might look very different but would also require that we ask some very clear-minded—and not romantic—questions about the place of music in Canadian society and how those components operate in an industrial context.

EVERYWHERE BUT RADIO: THE OTHER SPACES OF CANADIAN MUSIC

Perhaps the most compelling argument against CanCon regulations is that the overwhelming focus on the effectiveness of these regulations overlooks the numerous venues in which Canadians experience music in the course of their daily lives. Radio has always been only one venue for musical exposure; it has always offered a limited number of formats to listeners, based primarily on the different ways in which stations cut up their local advertising market. The proliferation of stations offering "Jack" or "easy listening" formats is just the latest in a long line of formats stretching back to the invention of top-40 that have effectively limited musical diversity on the radio dial. As a result, many musical styles, ranging from punk to opera, have found it difficult to gain airplay on Canadian radio, particularly on stations located outside big cities.

Since many types of music do not receive regular airplay, the question that remains is exactly what the relationship is between radio exposure and the purchase of Canadian recordings. For Richard Sutherland, radio airplay has an "intrinsic impact on record sales" (2002, p. 15). However, a report submitted by the Canadian Association of Broadcasters (CAB) to the CRTC argued—with citations from record company executives—that radio airplay had a "waning impact" on overall sales (Leblanc, 2006). Some have observed that radio has exercised a declining influence on record sales, particularly for younger listeners, for some time, owing largely to the fact that station playlists became more and more conservative by the end of the 1970s (Lopes, 1992, pp. 67–69). The emergence of music video channels like MTV and MuchMusic have offered artists new opportunities for exposure beyond radio and have captured the interest of younger music fans (Wagman, 2001). In addition, the proliferation of technologies to make recorded works portable, from the tape deck in cars to the Walkman, and from MP3 players to iPods, has served as effective competition to radio for the listening time of many Canadians.

What neither Sutherland nor the CAB recognized is that understanding why Canadians consume the music they do is complicated. Many Canadians learn about domestic musical acts by seeing them in local surroundings, such as in bars or at events like Ottawa's Blues Festival or the Montreal Jazz Festival. Bands also emerge out of local music scenes in which there happens to be an explosion of new musical talent, abundant performance spaces, and local support from fans who buy CDs, attend concerts, and tell friends in other cities about their favourite bands or DJs. This is a major reason for the success of Montreal's music scene, which has produced acts such as Wolf Parade, the Stills, and Arcade Fire.

In some measure, the popularity of these bands took off through exposure in American media circles, articles in U.S. magazines, Internet radio stations, websites such as pitchforkmedia.com or popmatters.com, and social networking sites like MySpace that provide music samples, band information, and fan feedback. Services from Amazon to iTunes offer people the chance to sample music before paying to download it and provide examples of user playlists built around themes such as "I Love Canadian Music," available on amazon.ca and "Canada Now" or "Toronto 20," available on iTunes. Sites such as YouTube and Google Video now allow people to stream music videos and concert footage. Finally, there are numerous websites and now blogs offering reviews of music and featuring sound clips.

These relatively new musical spaces are significant for a couple of reasons. First, they provide effective means of reaching audiences both domestically and internationally in ways that were previously restricted to musical acts signed to major record labels. Second, they fall outside the CRTC's jurisdiction, as the regulator has chosen wisely not to regulate Internet activity. By the time bands like Arcade Fire began appearing on mainstream Canadian radio stations, they had already achieved a significant level of success. In other words, for many Canadian acts, content regulations serve as the last link in the promotional chain, if they serve any purpose at all, after the band has been exposed in these other windows. We must therefore remember that Canadians experience music in a variety of ways and through an elaborate web of social networks, media forms, and, government policy measures. As Will Straw explains, "Cultural citizenship is less about residing in culture than about the necessity of moving within it, and the negotiations and transformations which that movement entails" (2005, p. 183). The interpretation that equates Canadian content with the survival of Canadian music only perpetuates our romance with CanCon, and it simply cannot capture the complexity that lies at the heart of the Canadian cultural experience.

CONCLUSION

When Canadian content regulations appeared over 35 years ago, issues surrounding the success or failure of the cultural industries dealt with ensuring place over scarce airwaves. Radio frequencies were in short supply, and concerns were raised that without various forms of government intervention, Canadians would be denied access to their own performers, and Canada's sound recording industry would never leave the ground. Even if we accept the argument that Canadian content regulations have assisted in developing the sound recording industry, it is extremely unlikely that Canadian music would have died out if the measures had never been put in place. While the industry would look significantly different than it does today, that does not mean that Canadians would have been unable to carve out their own musical niches in other ways, with music reaching local and national audiences through different distribution pathways.

If scarcity served as the prominent feature driving cultural policies such as Canadian content for the better half of the 20th century, abundance is now the dominant motif for the digital age. While conventional radio and television frequencies are limited, channels for music distribution are numerous. While a number of broadcasters can determine what is and isn't heard on AM and FM stations, such an argument is impotent in a world where musical materials flow through the

Internet relatively effortlessly. It is in this environment that Canadian music is thriving, in a zone of cultural activity free of content regulations. While CanCon rules represent a handy resource for some musical acts and serves as a powerful form of nationalist rhetoric, they are hardly necessary for Canadian music to succeed, in spite of the stories we tell.

References

Anastakis, D. (2005). *Auto pact: Creating a borderless North American auto industry, 1960–1971.* Toronto: University of Toronto Press.

Audley, P. (1983). *Canada's cultural industries.* Toronto: James Lorimer & Co.

Belanger, P. (2006). Radio in Canada: An industry in transition. In P. Attallah & L. R. Shade (Eds.), *Mediascapes: New patterns in Canadian communication* (2nd ed., pp. 130–147). Toronto: Thomson Nelson.

Canadian Music Publishers Association. (2005, March 1). Position paper. Retrieved August 12, 2006, from http://www.musicpublishercanada.ca/userUploads/industry.CMPA-Position-CanCon.pdf

Filion, M. (1996). Radio. In M. Dorland (Ed.), *The cultural industries in Canada* (pp. 118–141). Toronto: James Lorimer & Co.

Gordon, C. (1998, May 7). A home grown philosophy of Canadian content. *Ottawa Citizen,* p. A13.

Imported Peas [Editorial]. (2005, November 29). *The Globe and Mail,* p. A20.

Leblanc, L. (2006). *Music distribution in Canada.* Report prepared for the Canadian Association of Broadcasters. Retrieved August 15, 2006, from http://www.cab-acr.ca/english/research/06/sub_mar1506_app_h.pdf

Lopes, P. (1992). Innovation and diversity in the popular music industry, 1969–1990. *American Sociological Review, 57,* 56–71.

Pacienza, A. (2006, March 21). Homegrown acts miffed at Junos' international line-up. *Edmonton Journal,* p. C3.

Straw, W. (2005). Pathways of cultural movement. In C. Andrew, M. Gattinger, S. Jeannotte, & W. Straw (Eds.), *Accounting for culture: Thinking through cultural citizenship* (pp. 183–197). Ottawa: University of Ottawa Press.

Sutherland, R. (2002, June). Canadian content at 32. *Canadian Issues/Thèmes canadiens,* 13–17.

Wagman, I. (2001). Rock the nation: MuchMusic, cultural policy and the development of English-language music video programming. *Canadian Journal of Communication, 26*(4), 503–518.

Who gives a rap? (2005, November 29). *Regina Leader Post,* p. B7.

Discussion Questions

1. In addition to radio airplay, where else do you consume music?

2. In your opinion, what would happen if Canadian content rules were somehow phased out of existence?

3. If we live in an environment of "media abundance," what is the purpose of cultural policy in the 21st century?

4. Review the findings of the Decima Research survey conducted for the Department of Canadian Heritage. How do your preferences compare to those of the survey respondents? Through what media do you spend most of your time listening to music? How do you typically discover new music?

5. What do you think about Bryan Adams's controversial position on CanCon regulations? Do you agree or disagree with him?

6. Is it important to protect Canada from globalizing and Americanizing cultural influences? Why or why not?

ISSUE 3

Pharmacare: Should direct-to-consumer advertising be limited?

✔ YES

This Ad May Be Bad for Your Health
Josh Greenberg

Josh Greenberg is an assistant professor in the School of Journalism and Communication at Carleton University in Ottawa, where he teaches courses on communication and community-based research, critical public relations, and qualitative methods. His substantive areas of research and publication are political communication, communication and social justice, media representations of social issues, and surveillance. He is the author of numerous journal articles and book chapters on these topics, and is coeditor of *Communications in Question, The Surveillance Studies Reader*, and *Surveillance and Social Problems in Canada*.

INTRODUCTION

I enjoy fatty foods. Actually, I more than enjoy them—I revel in them, particularly the cheesy, meaty, pie-shaped variety that gets delivered to my door in under 30 minutes, or the warm, singed-with-the-scent-of-the-grill sort you find smothered in ketchup and with a side of fries. But these culinary choices are getting a lot of bad press these days. Indeed, something approaching a moral panic has engulfed the fast-food industry and fast-food eating, and while for many years I stubbornly refused to be mobilized by this discourse, I've lately grown more anxious, fearful even about the possible consequences of my indulgences.

My partner always scorned my weakness for greasy spoons, warning me about the dangers of high blood pressure and cholesterol. And now it seems that wherever I turn, from television to the Internet to the city-centre billboard, it's all cholesterol all the time. *High cholesterol isn't just a number, it's a warning*, proclaims one recent ad for Bristol-Myers Squibb's superdrug Pravachol. *What would you rather have, a cholesterol test or a final exam?* Pfizer, the maker of the top-selling cholesterol-fighting drug, Lipitor, brings you this question headlining an image of a toe-tagged corpse. And my favourite is the recent all-media (TV, print, billboard, Internet) ad campaign, also paid for by Pfizer, featuring an "everyday man" walking along a sidewalk where a rhinoceros lurks just beyond reach, the tagline menacingly forewarning that *when you live with high cholesterol you never know what's around the corner*. While not promoting Lipitor directly, Pfizer's scary rhino ad orients readers toward defining the problem of high cholesterol as a disease in a way that almost guarantees the resonance of the more direct ad campaign, and the sale of its wonder drug.

In light of this explosion of disease-and-drug discourse, I began to ponder whether my feelings of drug-ad bombardment reflected an empirically observable change in the mediascape, or whether they simply stemmed from a growing self-awareness about the importance of personal health management. In other words, maybe it's that I'm simply becoming more health-conscious and taking notice of ads that speak to my angst as a 30-something engaged in early rounds of a battle with the bulge.

Or maybe it's not. Analyzing the hard copy and online sites of some leading current events, entertainment, and health and lifestyle magazines, I began to notice that prescription drug ads were both highly visible and conspicuous in their proximity to editorial content. Take, for example, *Prevention* magazine. A scan of the December 2006 issue reveals that 19 of the first 50 pages (almost 40 percent) are devoted to promoting prescription drugs for all kinds of health and lifestyle ailments: acid reflux, constipation, rheumatoid arthritis, cholesterol, and sleeping diffi-culties. Looking to impress your friends with your culinary skills at your next dinner party? Check out *Prevention*'s simple-to-use recipes for delectable dining—and if you suffer from heartburn or an overactive bladder, ask your doctor about the potential benefits of Nexium and Enablex. Want flat and toned abs, super-sexy shoulders, a no-jiggle butt, and thighs like Eva Longoria? Let the experts at *Shape* magazine show you how to get chiselled in only three hours per week—and then ensure your skin matches your body by asking your doctor about Botox Cosmetic.

THE DRUG ADVERTISING BUSINESS

Drug advertising is huge business. The global pharmaceutical industry is the world's most profitable stock market sector, with annual revenues exceeding US$600 billion (Rosen, 2006). Pharmaceutical sales in North America topped a staggering US$265 billion in 2005, and in the United States, where 90 percent of the continental market is located, big pharma spent close to US$5 billion that year on advertising alone (Agovino, 2006; Edwards, 2006; Thomaselli, 2006b). Given Canada's significantly smaller population and a proclivity for state regulation, our market is meagre by comparison. Unlike in the United States, where advertisers have practically unlim-ited rein to promote diseases and treatments directly to consumers through paid television, print, and online advertising, so-called direct-to-consumer (DTC) prescription drug advertising in Canada is technically prohibited under the *Food and Drugs Act* administered by Health Canada.[1] In practice, however, while Health Canada adjudicates complaints about misleading DTC adver-tising, the job of regulating these ads falls to voluntary codes of conduct established, not surpris-ingly, by pharmaceutical and advertising industry associations interested in protecting profit.[2] While millions of dollars can be made providing valuable treatment for genuinely sick people, *billions* more can be made by convincing healthy people they're sick.

The upshot of the regulatory environment for drug advertising is that the big drug and media companies in the United States not only have far more opportunity to promote disease and treat-ment, but also have clearer policies and guidelines about what is (and is not) permissible than is the case in Canada. In the United States, advertisers can promote the name of the drug and the condition it's intended to treat provided the ad also lists possible risks or side effects. These "full-product ads" are distinguished from "disease-oriented ads," which, like the Pfizer-sponsored rhino spot, promote awareness about the condition but not a particular drug per se, and "reminder ads," which include only the brand name but no health claims or hints about the product's use.

At first blush the rules in Canada appear to protect us from being persuaded into believ-ing we're sick and in need of pharmacological intervention. However, a recent report by the

Parliamentary Standing Committee on Health revealed several loopholes that allow advertisers to influence how Canadians make sense of both disease and treatment (Mintzes, 2006). For starters, prohibitions on industry-sponsored advertisements are poorly enforced, and there is a dearth of independent, unbiased, and publicly financed information on prescription drugs available to Canadians. Moreover, active surveillance and identification of regulatory infractions require more financial investment and political will than currently exists. Although all political parties represented on the committee supported these findings and their calls for action, implementation of the report's recommendations has been relegated to the political backburner. In other words, while the U.S. system appears to make Americans more vulnerable than Canadians to drug ad persuasion, this is a conclusion not necessarily borne out by the available evidence (Mintzes, 2006).

CANADIAN MEDIA GO COURTING FOR DRUG MONEY

These loopholes and putative political consensus notwithstanding, a massive public relations campaign by media corporations, advertisers, and pharmaceutical corporations is challenging whether the aforementioned DTC drug ad restrictions should be eliminated altogether. This country's largest media conglomerate, CanWest MediaWorks,[3] recently launched a court appeal claiming that its right of free expression, guaranteed by the *Charter of Rights and Freedoms*, was being infringed upon. In a press release from December 2005, CanWest argued, "the current advertising restrictions are unfair and discriminatory" because different rules apply in the United States, and Canadian viewers regularly see full-product drug ads on the Internet and on American television and in American magazines, both of which are in steady supply in Canada. In short, CanWest argues that in a global media environment where citizens can access any kind of information they want, policies designed to limit what viewers can see, read about, and hear are not only paternalistic but ineffective as public policy. If the horse and carriage have already left the barn, their protest suggests, what's the point of locking the door behind them?

On the surface, CanWest presents an interesting and compelling argument. Its position will likely appeal to those who believe that capital markets should operate unfettered from government regulation and that drug corporations should be permitted to sell pills just like the makers of cars, cookies, or computers. It's a matter of free speech for the corporations and access to information by consumers, they proclaim. CanWest's submission will also be likely to resonate with people who endorse the notion of "active" media audiences as impervious to the attempts of advertisers to mystify and manipulate them into buying products they don't want or need.[4]

However, there are also several reasons to oppose these arguments. First, increasing the promotion and sale of prescription medications will lead to overuse and raise the potential of drug misuse.[5] Researchers at the University of Southern California showed that among patients who visited their doctors to report signs of major depression, 53 percent who specifically asked for a particular prescription drug were granted their request, and in cases of less serious adjustment disorder, the prescription rate was 55 percent (Kravitz et al., 2005). This finding was particularly startling "because there is little evidence that patients with adjustment disorder will benefit from antidepressants," the study's lead investigator argued. Indeed, the pressure DTC advertising places on the physician-patient relationship is well known not only by researchers but also by representatives of the drug companies themselves. A sales rep with a major drug firm explained to me in a September 2006 interview,

> Many of the doctors I work with tell me their patients come into their office with an ad from a magazine, or they mention a specific commercial and say "this is what my friend/aunt/neighbour is on, put me on this too because I have the same symptoms." The doctors get frustrated and time is wasted having to explain to the patient that this is probably not the right drug for them or that they don't even need to be on this drug.... You remember what happened with Vioxx? Everyone and their dog wanted to be on it because it was thought to be such a powerful pain reliever … when patients are in severe pain they will do almost anything, including take the claims of an ad at face value.[6]

A second reason to oppose the CanWest argument is that when more people start asking for more drugs they don't need, the costs on public and private drug insurance rates rise (affecting everyone's fees). In fact, a recent report in the *Wall Street Journal* showed that with drug costs skyrocketing, insurance companies and employers are aggressively promoting generic (i.e., nonbranded) drugs to employees, even when the brand-name drug a patient is using doesn't have a generic equivalent (Fuhrmans, 2006). Third, although drug companies, advertisers, and media corporations promote DTC drug advertising as a form of patient empowerment, there is no empirically verifiable evidence that these ads facilitate diagnosis, improve drug use, reduce hospitalization rates, or encourage more responsible decision making by consumers (Mintzes, 2006).

Beyond these counterpoints, there are more important reasons for students of communication to think critically about drug advertising and to resist appeals to change the regulations governing prescription drug promotion in Canada. We will investigate this issue by first examining the nature of advertising and then exploring its relationship to the strategies of social control we exercise over our bodies and minds. Advertising is about much more than just the promotion of consumer goods designed to inform, educate, and satisfy a corporation's bottom-line objectives. It is primarily a cultural technology that incorporates images, persons, and commodities into a seamless discourse that blurs the distinction between products and people. The rhetoric of drug advertising, which encourages individuals to focus increasingly on their minds and bodies as sites of disease requiring attention and administration, serves as an effective tool of governance and a potential strategy for social control. If this is the objective of drug advertising, it suggests the need for consumers to become more vigilant in resisting the promotional efforts of drug companies and advertisers, but it also requires that the state implement more robust regulation to protect citizens.

ADVERTISING AND ITS DISCONTENTS: MAGIC AND THE MECHANISM OF CONFORMITY

> I am Julie. Last night I did a striptease for my husband. What would you do with a few pounds less?
>
> Ask your doctor about Julie's story. Medical options are available.
>
> —Print advertisement for Xenical

Stomach pain, oily farts, slimy stool, and unexpected bouts of anal seepage—this partial list of side effects for Hoffman-LaRoche's obesity superdrug Xenical are painful, uncomfortable, and, frankly, embarrassing. But you certainly wouldn't know it by the ad campaign titled "Julie's story." In contrast to the thin and beautiful model portrayed in the "striptease ad" described above who is looking to lose just "a few pounds," this is a serious medication for treatment of obesity and chronic weight problems. Although the makers of Xenical acknowledge on the drug's website that the product is "no magic pill," the narrative and visual imagery used in this campaign suggest otherwise.

The Xenical ad illustrates some of the characteristics of what Raymond Williams (1960) describes as "the magic system" of advertising. In what is now a classic essay, Williams argues that advertising proves fundamental to the social and political structure of society because it is "the source of finance for a whole range of general communication" (p. 27). In other words, television, newspapers, magazines, radio programs, and, nowadays, online news and information cannot exist without advertisers underwriting at least some of the production costs. For Williams, advertising resolves the problem of overproduction because the capitalist system produces more goods and products than are required to serve the functional needs of citizens. Thus, advertising helps to manufacture needs where they may not otherwise exist.

Williams suggests that the significance of advertising extends beyond the "use value" of products alone—advertising "has become involved with the teaching of social and personal values" (p. 27). In a period of overproduction, goods and services must be made desirable for consumers. For instance, a bottle of Gatorade is not consumed simply because it quenches thirst (since water would arguably be just as effective) but because it signifies the importance of sport and competition as dominant cultural values and inscribes in the user the "competitive edge" needed to succeed. The purchase of an IBM computer, likewise, stems not from the functional utility of the machine per se but because it demonstrates the reach and expansion of technology from the workplace into the home as the capitalist economy has become more flexible. Extending this argument, the use of Xenical, then, teaches individuals about cultural norms and values of beauty and desirability. The drug product becomes associated with a belief that the failure of obese people to practise self-control and self-discipline is linked to broader historical processes of disciplining the body to be more efficient and productive.

Beyond suturing the cultural with the economic and technological dimensions of everyday life, advertising also creates "false needs" and unscrupulously exploits "true needs." In his book *Eros and Civilization* (1955), Herbert Marcuse wished to understand how the individual comes to be dominated by society through ideological conformity and the internalization of social control. Cultural development, Marcuse argues, is shaped by human beings' pursuit of pleasure. "This striving becomes an 'aim' in human existence: the erotic impulse to combine living substance into ever larger and more durable units is the instinctual source of civilization ... 'the struggle for existence' is originally a struggle for pleasure" (pp. 113–114). But rather than seeking emancipation and liberation from an oppressive society through collective class-consciousness, Marcuse suggests that humanity may also be freed through fantasy and pleasure. Fantasy, in Marcuse's account, has a "truth-value" of its own, and it is in fantasy that reconciliation between desire/reality or happiness/reason can be found. For Marcuse, our hopes and daydreams (which are the stuff of modern advertising) enable us to anticipate a better, more gratifying life that is free of societal domination.

This theme of hope and anticipation, of preserving what Marcuse calls "the repressed harmony of sensuousness and reason" (p. 130), is particularly evident in DTC drug ads for depression. Advertisements for Prozac commonly use visual metaphors associated with seasonal changes to symbolize the transition from pain (sensuousness) to recovery (reason) (Grow, Park, & Han, 2006). These ads contrast visual signifiers such as clouds, shattered eggs, or wilting trees that articulate weakness and incompleteness with images of sunshine, budding flowers, and decorated trees that connote strength and wholeness. Colour, which can be an effective communicator independent of textual content (Elliott, 2005), is also prominently used in Prozac advertisements to fuse sensuousness with reason, as dark blues, greys, and reds symbolize depression, as opposed to yellows, bright blues, and greens, which symbolize recovery (Grow et al., 2006). To use a different example, a recent cartoon ad for Pfizer's antidepressant superdrug, Zoloft, tells the story of Kathy, a 41-year-old mother depicted as a bean-shaped character. Kathy watches unhappily as her bean-shaped child plays on the swing, the caption explains, then tells us, "When my daughter said, 'Mommy, you're no fun anymore' it hit me. It was time to get help."[7] DTC advertisements for antidepressants like Prozac and Zoloft commonly de-emphasize any psychosocial causes of depression in favour of individualized (i.e., biological) causes that demand individualized (i.e., biochemical) solutions. More importantly, they demonstrate that something approaching salvation can be directly linked to the purchase of a pill (Grow et al., 2006).

The Xenical, Prozac, and Zoloft ads described above also illustrate Marcuse's argument that domination is best understood as a mode of social control characterized by "voluntary servitude" and "happy submission." Marcuse argues that as capitalism and technology developed over the twentieth century, advanced industrial society demanded that individuals accommodate themselves (i.e., conform) to the dominant economic and social apparatuses. In this context, marketing, public relations, and other promotional sciences helped create a one-dimensional society comprising one-dimensional citizens whose capacity to envision an alternative way of life is virtually obliterated by the "mechanics of conformity."

> The people recognize themselves in their commodities; they find their soul in their automobile, hi-fi set, split-level home, kitchen equipment. The very mechanism which ties the individual to his society has changed, and social control is anchored in the new needs it has produced.... The products indoctrinate and manipulate; they promote a false consciousness.... And as these beneficial products become available to more individuals in more social classes, the indoctrination they carry ceases to be publicity; it becomes a way of life. (Marcuse, 1964, p. 9)

Of course, prescription drugs are not like cars or stereo systems. Yet, the scientific and technological processes of our times have transformed these "fruits of pharmacological research" in a way that affects not only how we perceive drugs, but also the very meanings we ascribe to health and disease (Tracy, 2004). Through the process of **commodity fetishism**, the most banal experiences of everyday life (e.g., hair loss, constipation, heartburn) have been *commodified* and *fetishized*—that is, inscribed with mysterious powers and inherent value we believe to be a part of their nature.[8] In other words, these otherwise normal occurrences have been transformed into diseases that require an assemblage of medico-scientific solutions in the form of pink or purple pills that get assigned extraordinary powers to transform how we think and feel.

Marcuse, writing in the 1960s, was not attendant to the explosion of drug advertising. His argument that "technology has become the great vehicle of **reification**" (1964, p. 169) is useful, however, to understanding these processes of pharmaceutical fetishism and commodification.[9] The explosion of a disease-and-drug discourse feeds a harmful obsession with health that obscures the sociological and political explanations for what we perceive to be "health problems" (Moynihan, Heath, & Henry, 2002). The best way to overcome this crisis, Marcuse suggests, is to distinguish *true needs*, which are crucial to human survival, from *false needs*, which are ideological and exploitative and only bind individuals to a repressive social order. The problem, however, is that advertising in general, and prescription ads in particular, blurs the distinction between true and false needs by exploiting fundamental human desires (for love, affection, social acceptance, etc.) and inscribing these into the products themselves.

CONCLUDING REMARKS: DRUG ADVERTISING AND THE MEDICALIZATION OF BODIES

To understand the implications of DTC drug advertising, it's important to situate its growth in relation to broader political and economic changes that have been occurring in medical and health care systems. Across Canada, the United States, most of Western Europe, and Australasia, there has emerged a privileging of the market in the regulation of medical practice and an emphasis on individual and commercial actors as agents primarily responsible for health and well-being. As governments and public institutions come under attack (for being too interventionist, wasteful, inefficient, etc.), individuals are increasingly called upon to monitor, manage, and plan their lives in a way that minimizes risk and maximizes pleasure. Pharmaceutical drugs, or so the advertisements promise, offer us a quicker route to becoming a more desirable wife (Xenical), a more potent lover (Viagra), and a better mother (Zoloft). But they do so in a way that causes us to look at our own personal failings rather than at the failings of the social environment in which we live. The obsession we have with being healthy has reached arguably unhealthy proportions, and the increased prevalence of drug advertising has played a major role in this cultural shift of medicalizing everyday life.

Some may criticize my argument for being overly pessimistic and for not giving media audiences enough credit to negotiate, resist, or oppose the rhetorical appeals of drug advertising. But citizens can do only so much on their own. Indeed, it is they who must become more critical in their engagement with drug advertising by understanding the persuasive appeals of its sponsors. However, it is also the responsibility of governments to regulate and protect the public interest by creating effective and binding policies. Creating a Wild West of drug advertising in Canada that resembles the U.S. model is the wrong way to go. Our health very much depends on it.

References

Agovino, T. (2006, October 5). Pharmaceutical advertising rose 9% in first half, with magazines grabbing a bigger share. *Associated Press*.

Burnside, J. (2005, March 19). Would you run "Julie Ad" campaign? *Toronto Star*, p. F6.

CanWest MediaWorks. (2005, December 23). *DTCA legal challenge*. Retrieved November 16, 2006, from http://www.canwestmediaworks.com/newsroom/viewNews.asp?NewsroomID=596

Consumer drug ads drive up employer drug costs. (2005, May 1). *Employee Benefit News Canada*. Retrieved November 1, 2006, from http://ebnc.benefitnews.com/

Edwards, J. (2006, May 8). New Pharma ad results in … more ads. *Brandweek*. Retrieved July 11, 2006, from http://www.brandweek.com/

Elliott, C. (2005). Colour™: Law and the sensory scan. *Media/Culture, 8*(4). Retrieved September 15, 2006, from http://journal.media-culture.org.au/0508/06-elliott.php

Fuhrmans, V. (2006, October 31). Employers, insurers push generics harder. *The Wall Street Journal*, p. D1.

Grow, J. M., Park, J. S., & Han, X. (2006). "Your life is waiting!" Symbolic meanings in direct-to-consumer antidepressant advertising, *Journal of Communication Inquiry, 30*(2), 163–188.

Kravitz, R. L., Epstein, R. M., Feldman, M. D., Franz, C. E., Azari, R., Wilkes, M. S., et al. (2005). Influence of patients' requests for direct-to-consumer advertised antidepressants: A randomized controlled trial. *Journal of the American Medical Association, 293*(16), 1995–2002.

Marcuse, H. (1955). *Eros and civilization: An inquiry into Freud*. Boston: Beacon Press.

Marcuse, H. (1964). *One dimensional man*. Boston: Beacon Press.

Marx, K. (1976). *Capital: A critique of political economy* (Vol. 1). Middlesex, England: Penguin. (Original work published 1867).

Mintzes, B. (2006, January). *Direct-to-consumer advertising of prescription drugs in Canada: What are the public health implications?* Toronto: Health Council of Canada. Available from http://www.healthcouncilcanada.ca

Moynihan, R., Heath, I., & Henry, D. (2002). Selling sickness: The pharmaceutical industry and disease mongering. *British Medical Journal, 321*, 886–891.

Prescription drug ads. (2006, March 31). *Talk of the Nation* [Radio broadcast]. National Public Radio. Audio streamed at http://www.npr.org

Rosen, M. (2006, May 22). Big Pharma's continued hunger and search for new products. *Wisconsin Technology Network*. Retrieved November 11, 2006, from http://wistechnology.com/article.php?id=2986

Thomaselli, R. (2006a, May 8). DTC ads prompt consumers to see physicians … interest in advertised drugs continues to rise. *Advertising Age*, 30.

Thomaselli, R. (2006b, May 29). Gov't pushes for greater power over pharma ads. *Advertising Age*, 3.

Tracy, J. F. (2004). Between discourse and being: The commodification of pharmaceuticals in late capitalism. *The Communication Review, 7*, 15–34.

Williams, R. (1960). Advertising: The magic system. *New Left Review, 1*(4), 27–32.

Notes

[1] The first direct-to-consumer drug ad appeared in the early 1980s. The pharmaceutical industry's traditional drug marketing strategy was geared toward influencing physician decisions. The industry bills DTC advertising as a way of informing consumers, empowering them to self-diagnose, and encouraging them to engage their physicians in dialogue about real or prospective health problems.

[2] These include the research-based prescription drug pharmaceutical industry association, Rx&D; Advertising Standards Canada (ASC), also an industry-based association; and the Pharmaceutical Advertising Advisory Board. See Mintzes, 2006.

[3] The parent company, CanWest Global Communications, owns the *National Post*; the Global Television and CH broadcast networks; specialty media stations such as TVtropolis, DejaView, and CoolTV; and numerous regional and community papers, radio stations, and television stations across Canada. In the newspaper business alone, CanWest owns or controls approximately one-third of the national daily market.

[4] CanWest is not alone here. Most major news media in Canada support the appeal. *Toronto Star* publisher Michael Goldbloom, for example, argues that the current rules for prescription drug ads "treat Canadians as if they need to be coddled" and that his paper's readers are discerning enough to know when an advertiser is trying to trick them. See Burnside, 2005.

[5] See "Consumer drug ads," 2005. In another study of 78 primary care physicians in the United States and Canada, patients who specifically requested an advertised drug were 17 times more likely to be given a prescription than patients who did not. See also Thomaselli, 2006a, p. 30; "Prescription Drug Ads," 2006.

[6] The interviewee and the company he or she works for are unnamed to protect their identity.

[7] This ad "works" on a variety of levels. First, that Kathy is a 40-something mom of a young child speaks to a whole generation of "echo boom" women who chose to have successful careers first and a family second. Second, the cartoonish presentation of the characters is abstract enough to invite almost anyone (though especially the intended 40-plus female audience) to identify with the mom and child depicted in the ad. And finally, the ads interpellate the viewer as someone familiar with and believing in the cultural values of family and motherhood.

[8] The notion of "commodity fetishism" derives from Karl Marx's critique of capitalism. See Marx, 1867/1976.

[9] Like the notion of commodity fetishism, the term "reification" also derives from Marx and denotes a stage of social and economic development at which human beings experience society as though it existed beyond their actions. Reification takes place, in other words, when individuals attach to economic forces purposes and functions (e.g., the "needs" of the market) while objectifying and rendering real human needs invisible.

ISSUE 3

Pharmacare: Should direct-to-consumer advertising be limited?

✗ NO

The Transforming Health Care Landscape: The Case for Direct-to-Consumer Pharmaceutical Advertising
Kelley Main

Kelley Main received her Ph.D. at the University of British Columbia and is currently an assistant professor of marketing at the Asper School of Business at the University of Manitoba. Her research focuses on issues related to consumer behaviour, such as the effectiveness of warning labels, what makes consumers suspicious, and why people don't use coupons. Her work has been published in the *Journal of Public Policy and Marketing*, the *Journal of Consumer Psychology*, and the *Journal of Personality and Social Psychology*.

On June 28, 2005, the pharmaceutical industry was thrown into the media spotlight in an unprecedented way by a rather unusual source. In the now-infamous *Today Show* interview with Matt Lauer, Hollywood leading man and Scientology advocate Tom Cruise launched into a tirade about over prescription of Ritalin, following discussion of his criticism of actor Brooke Shields's use of psychotropic drugs to treat postpartum depression. As a follower of Scientology, Cruise does not believe in the use of prescription drugs, and in subsequent remarks during the interview he denounced the psychiatric establishment's heavy reliance on pharmaceuticals (MSNBC News Services, 2005). This event ignited a firestorm of controversy about Americans' dependence on prescription drugs, and, indirectly, it problematized the pharmaceutical industry's promotional practices.

Pharmaceutical companies have historically promoted drugs to consumers by influencing the prescription choices of their doctors (Menon, Deshpande, Perri, & Zinkhan, 2003, p. 181). In the last few decades, however, the medical profession's monopoly on expert information has begun to change owing to broader cultural shifts that have legitimized lay knowledge and empowered patients to play a leading role in their own health care. Recognizing this transformation, while also seeking to capitalize on it, pharmaceutical companies have expanded the scope of their marketing by promoting prescription drug information direct to the public through print, television, and new media like the Internet in a practice known as direct-to-consumer (DTC) advertising (Finlayson & Mullner, 2005, p. 429; Shin &Moon, 2005, p. 397). From serious medical conditions like depression to so-called lifestyle ailments like hair loss or erectile dysfunction, pharmaceutical advertisements promising to make consumers look and feel better are now a ubiquitous feature of the modern mediascape.

Despite its popularity and increased proliferation, DTC drug advertising is a subject of considerable controversy and debate within Canada and abroad. Noted critics of the practice, such as the American and Canadian medical associations, the Canadian Pharmacists Association, the New Zealand Consumers' Institute, and the European Union, as well as a large number of academics, argue against DTC advertising for numerous reasons. Some of the most common are that patients will misunderstand the risk and benefit information (Beltramini, 2006, p. 334; Singh & Smith, 2005, p. 372); the practice challenges physician expertise (Shin & Moon, 2005, p. 398); it perpetuates the medicalization of illness (Auton, 2004, p. 29); and it will strain the medical system's already diminishing resources (Herzenstein, Misra, & Posavac, 2004, p. 203; Richardson & Luchsinger, 2005, p. 102; Shin & Moon, 2005, p. 399).

These arguments resonate strongly in a country like Canada because of prevailing views toward health care as a public resource that should be available to all regardless of income, class status, or other indicators and social categories. The increased proliferation of DTC advertising also highlights the difficulties that modern societies such as Canada face in balancing the rights of corporations to advertise their products and the rights of patients to receive reliable information. In a broader historical context in which scandals involving corporate malfeasance (e.g., Enron, WorldCom) have become easy fodder for the mass media, debates involving the "rights" of corporations to communicate as they wish are controversial. The debate about DTC advertising also stems from the recognition of the nature of advertising itself. Most people recognize that the generally accepted purpose of advertising is to inform and persuade. Given this, critics tend to argue that advertising creates "false consciousness" in consumers by manipulating them into believing that they can become healthy, wealthy, and wise by taking the path of conspicuous consumption rather than simply modifying how they think and act in the world.

Seductive as these criticisms may be, they are misplaced because they fail to consider the broader context in which prescription drug advertising occurs. In particular, whether they are talking about the more generalized effects of advertising or the so-called rights of corporations to communicate, critics of DTC advertising base their arguments on three potentially problematic assumptions, which this chapter will critique while advocating for a more liberalized approach to regulating DTC advertising. First, critics assume a pervasive susceptibility of individuals to advertising that is based on a crude understanding of what people actually "do" with advertising. In reality, evidence suggests that consumers are becoming more suspicious and skeptical of advertising in general (e.g., Darke & Ritchie, 2007). Second, critics seem to assume that patients are passive in decision making about their health and believe that following exposure to DTC ads, patients immediately run to their doctors to demand a prescription. It seems much more likely that being exposed to new information motivates patients to seek out additional information from trusted sources (such as by talking to their doctors or pharmacists, researching certain conditions or treatments, discussing issues with friends/family). And third, there seems to be an idea that we live in an information vacuum where health information comes only from our physicians. However, this is far from the case, as global access to all forms of media means that patients around the world have access to health information regardless of legislation regarding DTC advertising in their country of origin (Wielondek, 2005, p. 266). Consumers are frequently exposed to health information from all over the world in a variety of sources, including magazines, television, and, increasingly, the Internet. After providing some context for the emergence of DTC advertising, I will address these points in turn and hope to persuade the reader that the benefits of DTC ads can outweigh its problems and when used responsibly can actually serve a positive function.

A BRIEF HISTORY OF DTCA

The history of DTC advertising begins in the United States in 1963 when the Federal Drug Administration (FDA) proposed the first regulations for prescription drug advertising. The first DTC ad appeared in 1981 promoting a prescription painkiller called Rufen, and shortly after its appearance the FDA requested that the industry refrain from directly marketing drugs to consumers until the issue could be thoroughly investigated (Richardson & Luchsinger, 2005, p. 100). By 1985 the FDA mandated that DTC advertising could proceed only if the ads contained risk information including any contraindications, warnings, precautions, and side effects. In 1997 the FDA relaxed the rules for DTC television advertising of drugs by requiring pharmaceutical companies to include four types of information in their ads: a toll-free phone number, a website, a concurrent drug ad in a similarly disseminated print media outlet, and a statement directing consumers to consult their doctor or pharmacist for additional information (Menon et al., 2003, p. 182).

New Zealand provides another example that is instructive for the Canadian context. In New Zealand, DTC advertising increased throughout the mid-1990s, particularly following the passage of the country's bill of rights in 1990. This was a significant policy achievement because it essentially guaranteed pharmaceutical companies (and other corporations) the right to advertise their products under the auspices of free speech (Hoek & Gendall, 2002, p. 203). As DTC advertising proliferated in New Zealand, questions began to emerge about how to regulate it given that New Zealand did not have an established regulatory body such as the FDA, whose foremost responsibility is to protect the public. There were two options for the New Zealand government: either give the responsibility to a government agency such as MedSafe, a division of the Ministry of Health, or continue the industry-based self-regulation used in other advertising sectors. The decision was made to let the industry self-regulate. In November 2000, the Therapeutic Advertising Prevetting System (TAPS) was introduced, which required a mandatory evaluation of all ads making a therapeutic claim prior to their release to the public.

Although the United States has a greater direct influence on Canada in terms of cross-border media exposure to DTC ads, there are more similarities between Canada and New Zealand's regulatory frameworks and health care systems (Mintzes, 2006, p. 12). In Canada, DTC drug advertising is prohibited under two provisions in the *Food and Drugs Act*, a part of the federal *Criminal Code* (Mintzes, 2006, p. 6). Currently, Health Canada allows two forms of DTC advertising: reminder and disease-oriented ads (Mintzes, 2006, p. 8). Reminder ads include only the brand name with no other health claims and do not require the inclusion of risk information, while disease-oriented or help-seeking ads do not mention a specific brand but talk about a particular condition and suggest patients talk to their physician. To illustrate, while it is entirely permissible to run an ad for Viagra, that advertisement cannot indicate the condition (i.e., erectile dysfunction) that the drug is designed to treat (i.e., a reminder ad). Alternatively, an advertisement that raises awareness about erectile dysfunction is perfectly allowable provided there is no mention of Viagra (i.e., a disease oriented or help-seeking ad).

In terms of regulation, Canada is also more like New Zealand in that it relies on industry self-regulation rather than following the U.S. model of direct regulation by the FDA (Mintzes, 2006, p. 18). Although Health Canada is ultimately accountable for enforcement, responsibility has been delegated to three organizations: the Code of Marketing Practices Committee of Rx&D (an association of individuals working for research-based pharmaceutical companies); Advertising Standards Canada (an advertising industry association); and the Pharmaceutical Advertising Advisory Board (an independent review agency composed of a number of stakeholders, such as the pharmaceutical industry and various consumer associations) (Mintzes, 2006, p. 9). Critics of industry self-regulation point to problems with potential conflicts of interest in the review of DTC ads as a result of the participation of advertisers on the boards, lax enforcement, and insufficient transparency and accountability (Working Group on Women and Health Protection, 2006–2007). One of the major benefits of self-regulation is thought to be the preclearance required of new drug ads; however, there are some concerns about the strength of the standards (Health Canada, 2003). It is not enough to argue that the current system of self-regulation fails; instead, these problems need to be addressed through increased fines, transparency in proceedings, and accountability.

Current estimates have spending in the pharmaceutical industry at almost US$4 billion per year, more than combined advertising spending by Pepsi, Coca-Cola, and Cadbury Schweppes (Richardson & Luchsinger, 2005, p. 100). Given the enormity of industry spending and potential for profit, debate about the merits and problems of DTC advertising is divisive. Proponents and opponents of this practice have staked out their positions with remarkable consistency. Although the rhetoric against DTC advertising is compelling, it does not take into account the larger environment in which it occurs. The following section reviews the major supporting factors for DTC advertising and considers both individual benefits (increasing patient and public awareness and education) and relational factors (such as improving the relationship between patients and doctors).

INDIVIDUAL FACTORS
Patient Awareness and Education

Historically, physicians have been the exclusive authority on patients' needs, and little thought has been given to allowing patients to actively participate in their own health care (Pinto, Pinto, & Barber, 1998, p. 91). Over time, that view has changed and DTC ads have helped facilitate that change by educating consumers and making them more aware of their treatment choices. Proponents maintain that the goal of DTC advertising is to inform consumers about important health issues (e.g., Hoek & Gendall, 2002, p. 202), while opponents claim the ads persuade patients to purchase specific branded medications that are more costly (e.g. Richardson & Luchsinger, 2005, p. 102). Notwithstanding that pharmaceutical companies are in the business of making money and that advertising helps them achieve this goal, more importantly we need to recognize the difficulty of applying the same evaluative standards for commodities such as cars or clothing to pharmaceutical drugs. While the financial bottom line to earn a profit is the same across product types, prescription drug advertising is quite different from other types of advertising in two respects. First, DTC ads are designed to target only a narrow segment of the population (e.g., those with erectile dysfunction, those suffering from high cholesterol, or with depression), while ads for running shoes, for example, are designed to appeal to the athlete (real or imagined) in all of us. While there is a side-benefit that DTC drug advertising will increase overall societal awareness of certain health conditions (particularly those conditions that are subject to negative stigmas such as obesity or mental illness), DTC ads are not intended for all consumers. Second, and more importantly, whereas in regular purchasing contexts consumers are the sole or final decision makers, this is not the case with pharmaceutical drugs. While we may be able to run to the mall for that cool pair of GAP jeans after watching a television ad, to get the latest treatment for our hair loss we must still see our physician for a proper diagnosis and prescription. If the medication is deemed unsuitable, the physician is not going to give patients a prescription just because the ad promised they could look more youthful and vibrant!

DTC advertising also serves a social function because it helps to create greater overall awareness of health conditions and can lead to earlier detection of diseases and increased compliance with treatment protocol (Hoek & Gendall, 2002, p. 202). In fact, a recent FDA survey of physicians shows that 73 percent believe that advertising geared directly toward consumers can increase awareness about potential treatments when practised responsibly (Vogt, 2005, p. 12). The ads facilitate earlier awareness of important health conditions and prompt intervention that can decrease the need for more expensive treatments required at later stages of diagnosis (Hoek & Gendall, 2002, p. 202). Data from the Centers for Disease Control, Vital and Health Statistics suggest that from 1980 to 2001, rates of hospitalization in the United States declined by 40 percent; it has been suggested that new medicines have helped to shift health spending from institutional care to outpatient care (Ward Health Strategies, 2005). In other words, DTC advertising may help to reduce future pressures upon the health care system.

Huh, Delorme, and Reid (2004, p. 797) also argue that DTC advertising plays an important educational role for consumers. In a mail survey of adults living in the southern United States, respondents indicated that the perceived information value of these ads was positively associated with health care decisions. Huh and Becker (2004, p. 462) show that exposure to DTC ads is strongly predictive of further information seeking behaviour. Specifically, the researchers used secondary data from an FDA telephone survey to show that exposure to DTC ads predicted consumer intentions to seek more information about the advertised drug or general health concerns, and prompted patients to communicate more directly with their doctors about a specific health condition or treatment. Such information-seeking behaviours are important because they can help patients learn more about the diseases or conditions that affect them or their family and friends *before* deciding whether to take it. The importance of patient self-awareness is particularly acute at a time when governments are less willing or able to meet all of the health care needs of its citizens.

Facilitated Health Care Decision Making

Another benefit of DTC advertising is the increasingly active role it enables patients to take in decisions regarding their health care. The importance of participative medical decision making is rooted in the psychology literature on perceived control and self-efficacy. Perceived control refers to one's perception of the availability of a solution to a particular threat (i.e., the availability of treatment for a health condition), whereas self-efficacy refers to one's confidence in the ability to engage in that response (i.e., to follow a particular treatment regime) (Litt, 1988, p. 149). A great deal of research supports the importance of control and efficacy in promoting health and wellness, such as aiding in smoking cessation, recovery from heart attacks, physical endurance, and sports performance (Litt, 1988, p. 149). Baukus (2004, p. 564) suggests that this participatory decision making can make patients more amenable to the outcome of their health care decisions.

In addition to the potential for DTC advertising to foster feelings of control over one's health and increasing compliance with medical treatment, another benefit is enhanced communication with physicians. Huh and Becker (2004, p. 462) find that exposure to DTC advertising is strongly predictive of a patients' intention to communicate with their physicians about new or existing health concerns. More specifically, DTC advertising has been found to lead patients to discuss a previously unreported condition with their doctors after seeing information about their symptoms from a DTC ad (Aikin, 2003, p. 11). For example, one study showed 27 percent of respondents in 1999 and 18 percent in 2002 attributed their decision to ask their doctors about a new condition to a DTC advertisement. Similarly, 20 percent who saw a DTC ad discussed a new concern with their physicians, and approximately 30 percent talked about potential treatment changes for ongoing conditions (Weissman et al., 2003, p. W3-85). Of the patients who reported visiting their physicians after exposure to a DTC ad, nearly 25 percent were given new diagnoses (Weissman et al., 2003, p. W3-85). The ability of DTC advertising to contribute to individuals being more attentive to their health and wellness and to enhance the flow of information between patient and physician is a benefit that cannot and should not be ignored.

RELATIONAL FACTOR
Improving the Physician-Patient Relationship

Some critics argue that DTC drug advertising is dangerous because the advertisements can trick or persuade consumers into believing that an ailment afflicts them and that the problem can be solved through a simple exchange of money for drugs. Others claim that DTC advertising will encourage the public to seek drugs for all ailments and that this will overwhelm their already overworked doctors, who, to stem their workloads, will comply with patient demands. Although DTC ads are becoming a more common form of advertising and are increasing awareness about various conditions, they are not the primary source of medical information for patients. The majority of patients still rely on their doctors (89 percent) or pharmacists (51 percent) as the primary sources of information about new drugs (Aikin, 2003, p. 9). Critics worry that the increasing access to information through DTC advertising and other sources (e.g., the Internet) will adversely influence the physician-patient relationship by usurping the authority and expertise of the physician (Shin & Moon, 2005, p. 398). However, Gonul, Carter, and Wind (2000, p. 222) demonstrate that the more experienced physicians actually value this form of advertising and are less likely to feel threatened by it. Rather, increasing exposure to DTC ads brought in by patients over time positively and significantly contributes to the value physicians see in using the mass media to make patients more aware of their treatment options (Gonul et al., 2000, p. 222).

Indeed, other research shows that patients report improved relationships with their physicians when they have the opportunity to discuss the DTC ads they see in the media. An FDA survey revealed that 93 percent of patients reported that their doctors welcomed their questions regarding advertised treatment options, 86 percent of doctors discussed the drug with patients, and 76 percent of the patients were pleased with the reaction they received from their doctors (Aikin, 2003, p. 36). Reports on the physicians' actions illustrate that while close to half of patients received the drug they sought more information about, 34 percent of physicians recommended another drug as more suitable, and 41 percent recommended that patients pursue a lifestyle or behaviour change instead (Aikin, 2003, p. 38). Overall, for doctors who are not threatened by patients taking a more active role in their medical decisions, DTC advertising contributed to a more open and respectful relationship between patients and physicians that can have nothing but benefits for both parties.

CONCLUSION

The debate concerning DTC drug advertising is far from over, but the benefits for patients must not be overlooked. Many of the criticisms of DTC advertising take on a limited and rather paternalistic view of patients as easily manipulated by advertising, as passive recipients of medical information, and as irresponsible managers of their own health care who never seek the advice of their physicians. It is unfortunate that these criticisms fail to take into account the overall context in which individuals use DTC ads, and they overlook the prospect for empowering patients' involvement in their own health care. In addition to increasing patient awareness of existing health conditions and treatment options, DTC advertising can facilitate and foster a more open flow of communication between patients and their physicians; this can only benefit each party and enhance the relationship between them.

Staunch critics of DTC drug advertising such as the American and Canadian medical associations acknowledge that this approach to drug promotion is likely here to stay and suggest that the debate begin to focus on how to improve the *effectiveness* of DTC advertising for patient education and welfare (Paul, Handlin, & Stanton, 2002, p. 566). We should, by now, have moved beyond the impasse imposed by simplistic theories of media effects and patient-physician relationships, and begin to reflect seriously on the potential of this promotional practice for enhancing health care. The goal now should be to optimize the positive influence that DTC advertising can have for health and wellness by developing consumer education programs and giving more authority and resources to the regulatory bodies charged with overseeing drug advertising.

The issues surrounding DTC advertising incite vigorous debate because they touch on broader societal issues such as the role of advertising in contemporary society. The very nature of advertising as a source of information and persuasion has long been cause for concern, and in a mediascape defined by some as oversaturated by media messages, this concern is particularly acute. As a society, we have a long love/hate relationship with advertising. As Pollay poignantly argues,

> Advertising is without a doubt a formative influence within our culture, even though we do not yet know its exact effects. Given its pervasive and persuasive character, it is hard to argue otherwise. The proliferation and the intrusion of various media into the everyday lives of the citizenry make advertising environmental in nature, persistently encountered and involuntarily experienced by the entire population. It is designed to attract our attention, to be readily intelligible, to change attitudes, and to command our behavior. (1986, p. 1)

Given the persuasiveness and proliferation of advertising in contemporary society, it is time for not just regulatory bodies but citizens as well to demand that advertisers recognize their social responsibility and seek to exceed current efforts in making advertising a powerful educational tool. When this happens, the possible benefits of DTC drug advertising should be a pill that all of us will feel much less reticent about swallowing.

References

Aikin, K. J. (2003). The impact of direct-to-consumer prescription drug advertising on the physician-patient relationship: Patient survey results. U.S. Food and Drug Administration Center for Drug Evaluation and Research. Retrieved July 5, 2006, from http://www.fda.gov/cder/ddmac/aikin/sld002.htm

Auton, F. (2004). The advertising of pharmaceuticals direct to consumers: A critical review of the literature and debate. *International Journal of Advertising, 23*, 5–52.

Baukus, R. (2004). DTC advertising: Commentary. *Journal of Health Communication, 9*, 563–564.

Beltramini, Richard F. Consumer believability of information in direct-to-consumer advertising of prescription drugs. *Journal of Business Ethics, 63*, 333–343.

Darke, P. R., & Ritchie, R. B. (2007). The defensive consumer: Advertising deception, defensive processing, and distrust. *Journal of Marketing Research, 44*, 14–21.

Finlayson, G., & Mullner, R. (2005). Direct-to-consumer advertising of prescription drugs: Help or hindrance to the public's health. *Journal of Consumer Marketing, 22*, 429–431.

Gonul, F., Carter, F., & Wind, J. (2000). What kind of patients and physicians value direct-to-consumer advertising of prescription drugs. *Health Care Management Science, 3*, 215–226.

Health Canada. (2003, August 11). Direct to consumer advertising (DTCA) of prescription drugs. Retrieved September 21, 2006, from http://www.hc-sc.gc.ca/ahc-asc/pubs/legren/consumer-consommateur_e.html

Herzenstein, M., Misra, S., & Posavac, S. S. (2004). How consumers' attitudes towards direct-to-consumer advertising of prescription drugs influence ad effectiveness and consumer and physician behavior. *Marketing Letters, 15*, 201–212.

Hoek, J., & Gendall, P. (2002). Direct-to-consumer advertising down under: An alternative perspective and regulatory framework. *Journal of Public Policy and Marketing, 21*, 202–212.

Huh, J., & Becker, L. B. (2004). Direct-to-consumer prescription drug advertising: Understanding its consequences. *International Journal of Advertising, 24*, 441–466.

Huh, J., Delorme, D. L., & Reid, L. N. (2004). The information utility of DTC prescription drug advertising. *Journalism and Mass Communication Quarterly, 81*, 788–806.

Litt, M. (1988). Self-efficacy and perceived control: Cognitive mediators of pain tolerance. *Journal of Personality and Social Psychology, 54*(1), 149–160.

Menon, A. M., Deshpande, A. D., Perri, M., III, & Zinkhan, G. M. (2003). Consumers' attention to the brief summary in print direct-to-consumer advertisements: Perceived usefulness in patient-physician discussions. *Journal of Public Policy and Marketing, 22*, 181–191.

Mintzes, B. (2006, January). *Direct-to-consumer advertising of prescription drugs in Canada: What are the public health implications?* Toronto: Health Council of Canada.

MSNBC News Services. (2005, June 18). In a tense moment, Cruise calls Lauer glib. Retrieved August 29, 2006, from http://www.msnbc.msn.com/id/8344309

Paul, D. P., Handlin, A., & D'Auria Stanton, A. (2002). Primary care physicians' attitudes toward direct-to-consumer advertising of prescription drugs: Still crazy after all these years. *The Journal of Consumer Marketing, 19*, 564–574.

Pinto, M. B., Pinto, J. K., & Barber, J. C. (1998). The impact of pharmaceutical direct advertising: opportunities and obstructions. *Health Marketing Quarterly, 15*, 89–101.

Pollay, R. W. (1986). The distorted mirror: Reflections on the unintended consequences of advertising. *Journal of Marketing, 50*, 18–36.

Richardson, L., & Luchsinger, V. (2005). Direct-to-consumer advertising of pharmaceutical products: Issue analysis and direct-to-consumer promotion. *Journal of American Academy of Business, 7*, 100–104.

Shin, J., & Moon, S. (2005). Direct-to-consumer prescription drug advertising: Consumers and evidence on consumers benefit. *Journal of Consumer Marketing, 22*, 397–403.

Singh, T., & Smith, D. (2005). Direct-to-consumer prescription drug print advertising: A study of consumer attitudes and behavioral intentions. *Journal of Consumer Marketing, 22*, 369–378.

Vogt, D. U. (2005, March 25). Direct-to-Consumer Advertising of Prescription Drugs. CRS Report for Congress, received through the CRS Web. Congressional Research Service. The Library of Congress. Retrieved April 24, 2006, from http://www.law.umaryland.edu/marshall/crsreports/crsdocuments/RL3285303252005.pdf

Ward Health Strategies. (2005, March 22). Efforts to make pharmaceutical industry "profits" the scapegoat for rising health costs ignore economic reality. *Drug Policy Monitor*. Retrieved September 21, 2006, from http://www.wardhealth.com/index.php/en/newsletters/drug_policy_monitor

Weissman, J. S., Blumenthal, D. Silk, A. J., Zapert, K., Newman, M., & Leitman, R. (2003). The effects of direct-to-consumer drug advertising. *Health Affairs, 22*(2), W3-82–87.

Wielondek, M. (2005). Can direct-to-consumer advertising help in re-inventing the mage of the pharmaceutical industry instead of eroding its credibility? *Journal of Medical Marketing, 5*, 264–273.

Working Group on Women and Health Protection. (2006–2007). Direct-to-consumer advertising of prescription drugs. Retrieved September 21, 2006, from http://www.whp-apsf.ca/en/documents/dtca.html

Discussion Questions

1. Discuss the contradictions present in direct-to-consumer advertising of prescription drugs in Canada that do not exist elsewhere.

2. What are the advantages and disadvantages of industry self-regulation in this context?

3. If you were appointed to a government advisory panel that would make suggestions to industry on current drug advertising practice, what changes would you suggest with respect to direct-to-consumer advertising of prescription drugs?

4. What is problematic about the argument that advertising is primarily designed to inform consumers about the attributes and functionality of commodities and services?

5. Why should we make distinctions between pharmaceutical products and other consumer products, like cars or computers? What are the implications of this distinction for how these goods are advertised?

6. Raymond Williams argues that the significance of advertising extends beyond the "use value" of products alone such that advertising "has become involved with the teaching of social and personal values." Thinking about your own experience and habits, how are your favourite products and services advertised to you and with what effects on your identity and values?

Not so intellectual: Have intellectual property rights run amok?

✔ YES

Trademarking the Moon: Losing Control of Our Culture
Sheryl N. Hamilton

Sheryl N. Hamilton is the Canada Research Chair in Communication, Law, and Governance at Carleton University. She works in the area of cultural studies of law, intellectual property, media studies, gender and technology, and cyberculture studies. Her coauthored book, *Becoming Biosubjects: Public Cultures of Biotechnology*, is under consideration at University of Toronto Press and she currently has a monograph under contract with UTP entitled *From Person to Persona: Law, Culture and Personality*, also with UTP. She has published in journals such as *Communication Theory*, *Journal of Communication Inquiry*, *Convergence*, *Canadian Review of American Studies*, and *Science Fiction Studies*.

In a 1948 article exploring the relationship between advertising, trademarks, and the public interest, Ralph S. Brown Jr. suggests, "In an acquisitive society, the drive for monopoly advantage is a very powerful pressure. Unchecked, it would no doubt patent the wheel, copyright the alphabet, and register the sun and moon as exclusive trade-marks" (p. 1206). Brown's examples of intellectual property rights run amok are meant to be ludicrous—how could anyone possibly patent the wheel, copyright the alphabet, or trademark the moon? However, we could equally well ask, how could anyone possibly patent an entire population's genetic makeup, copyright the most popular children's song in English, or trademark a common, everyday smell? And yet, Iceland sold its gene pool to Swiss pharmaceutical giant Roche; AOL/Time-Warner owns (and polices the use of) the song "Happy Birthday"; and Dutch marketing company Senta obtained a Europe-wide trademark to infuse its tennis balls with the odour of freshly cut grass.

James Boyle (2003) suggests that we are currently experiencing a **second enclosure movement**. The first enclosure movement was a series of moves in England from the 15th to 19th centuries to fence off common lands, transforming them into private property. Boyle argues that the second enclosure movement is enclosing the "intangible commons of the mind," where things that were formerly thought of either as unable to be commodified or as shared resources are becoming subject to new or expanded private property rights through intellectual property. Boyle is right: intellectual property law has gone too far in enforcing private property rights in our culture, and the result is that our everyday cultural activity is increasingly controlled, censored, and criminalized.

WHAT IS INTELLECTUAL PROPERTY?

Intellectual property (IP) is distinguished from real property (land and buildings) and personal property (movable objects) as the intangible property that is the product of the mind. There are two major reasons why we protect creative production as property. First, it is a fair reward for the labour the creator puts into a work. Second, it stimulates a healthy market; property rights provide economic incentives to encourage more and better creation. Yet, in our educational, professional, and public domains and in our entertainment activities, virtually every text or object is subject to a battery of intellectual property rights, from our refrigerators and drugs to our music and clothing. And frequently, the money we pay to access our culture goes not to the creators, but rather to the corporate owners of the intellectual property rights.

Copyrights, patents, and trademarks are the most common forms of intellectual property.[1] Copyright means, literally, the right to copy, and copyright legislation in Canada grants to owners the sole and exclusive right to copy, perform, or publish a work.[2] Rights are extended to literary, dramatic, photographic, musical, and artistic creations; broadcasts; and performances, including graffiti, pornography, plays, novels, paintings, computer programs, databases, and greeting cards. The copyright owner holds the rights for the life of the author plus 50 years in Canada and life of the author plus 70 years in the United States.[3] After this period, the work enters the public domain.

A patent is a monopoly right granted to an inventor for an invention, preventing anyone else from making, using, or selling that invention during the 20-year period of the patent. Inventions include useful processes, machines, compounds, and manufactured items; patents have been granted for inventions as diverse as Viagra, the Phillips screwdriver, and the combustion engine. The logic behind patents is that the period of monopoly permits inventors to exploit their inventions, free from competition, in order to recoup their investment and make an appropriate profit. After that, the useful knowledge enters the public domain.

Finally, a trademark is a mark that distinguishes the products or services of one business from those of another. Many different signs can be trademarks: words, logos, designs, letters, numerals, colours, figurative elements, slogans, or shapes. Examples include words like IBM, Wal-Mart, Braun, or Harvey's; phrases such as "If life were like this, you wouldn't need a VISA card" or "I'm lovin' it"; shapes such as that of the Absolut vodka bottle or Toblerone chocolate bar; and logos like the apple on Mac computers and the red, white, and blue flag of Tommy Hilfiger. Trademarks last indefinitely, provided that the particular mark continues to distinguish the owner's goods in the marketplace.[4]

While applying to very different areas of human creativity—artistic, scientific, and commercial—copyright, patents, and trademarks have all been at the heart of heated debates in recent years as more and more of our shared cultural domain is enclosed as the private property of large corporations. Two major developments have hastened this process. First, we have seen the dramatic impact of digital technology on intellectual property rights in general, and on copyright in particular. Being able to digitize, reproduce, and distribute cultural content at a very low cost is arguably the biggest threat that copyright has ever faced, as millions of music file sharers around the world have proved. Yet we too often forget that technology cuts both ways; technological protection measures and digital rights management are being deployed by owners to combat the anarchic effects of technology.[5]

Second, intellectual property rights have become increasingly globalized. The World Trade Organization's *Trade-Related Aspects of Intellectual Property* and the various treaties signed under the auspices of the World Intellectual Property Organization are at the forefront of these international agreements responsible for regulating intellectual property. Dominated by the United States' strong pro-property, pro-owner perspective, these treaties have led to the international homogenization of the law, an expansion of what qualifies as intellectual property, and an intensification of owners' rights and protections.[6]

Against this backdrop, the enclosure of the cultural commons is being mobilized through two key processes: propertization and brand-name bullying. **Propertization** is the increasing reinterpretation of what used to be thought of as shared cultural resources, or at least as unownable—language, names, scientific facts, organisms, elements of nature, shared myths—as property that can be owned, bought, and sold (Rose, 2003, p. 94). **Brand-name bullying** is David Bollier's (2005) term to describe the intimidation tactics of intellectual property rights owners, which succeed in silencing us because of our lack of legal and financial resources.

ENCLOSING OUR CULTURE

From Smuckers defending their patented no-leak Peanut Butter and Jelly Sandwich, to Meatloaf disputing a trademark for the phrase "bat out of hell," to Disney enforcing its rights in Hercules, Aladdin, Pocahontas, Cinderella, Snow White, and other classic tales that have been part of cultures around the world for hundreds and even thousands of years, intellectual property rights can seem ridiculous. But neither propertization nor brand-name bullying is a benign practice. The implications for ordinary citizens are troubling.

The Motion Picture Association of America (MPAA) recently filed hundreds of lawsuits against people it accuses of file sharing movies. The MPAA is following in the footsteps of the Recording Industry of America Association, which has brought over 6,000 lawsuits against file sharers since 2003. And while the industry effectively destroyed Napster in the mid-1990s and more recently took some of the stuffing out of Kazaa, file sharing continues undaunted.[7] Lawsuits have been only one attempt at bullying, however.

The U.S. entertainment industry successfully lobbied for the *Digital Millennium Copyright Act* in 1998 in response to the explosion of file sharing.[8] The legislation dramatically increased the remedies available to owners and has come under much criticism for its draconian measures, such as empowering copyright owners to police Web content with its "notice and take down" provisions. While the legislation has not perceptibly curbed file sharing, it has resulted in public domain material, uncopyrightable facts, and valid social criticism being removed from public circulation (Ahlert, Marsden, & Young, 2004; Electronic Frontier Foundation [EFF], 2003; Katyal, 1999; Yu, 2004). The *Sonny Bono Copyright Extension Act* of 1998 extended the term of copyright in the United States by 20 years. Not coincidentally, Disney Corporation was its biggest advocate; some its early footage of Mickey Mouse was set to enter the public domain in 2004.[9] An estimated 400,000 American books, movies, and songs that were about to enter the public domain in 2004 will now be controlled by private owners until at least 2018 (Bollier, 2005, p. 148).

But the movement to expand, overvalue, and overpolice copyrights is not limited to file sharing. Copyrights are holding our culture hostage. The American Society of Composers, Authors and Publishers informed hundreds of American summer camps in 1996 that their campers could not sing copyrighted songs around the campfire without paying a licence fee of US$1200. A filmmaker had to pay US$10,000 for a four-and-a half-second clip of *The Simpsons* playing in the background of his film, and the makers of *Mad Hot Ballroom* had to pay the same amount to EMI because a cellphone rings in the background in one of the scenes and the ringtone is the theme from *Rocky*. Once we accept that cultural products have single authors, that they can have unlimited value in the marketplace, and that we, as audience members, have no inherent rights to them, the conditions are ripe for censorship. Something is wrong in a society where Adobe's e-version of *Alice's Adventures in Wonderland* can't be copied, read aloud, or shared, though the original book is already in the public domain, or when the estate of Margaret Mitchell tries to block publication of *The Wind Done Gone*, a book by Alice Randall that dares to retell *Gone with the Wind* from the slave's perspective.

The implications of propertization and corporate bullying in the areas of patents are equally troubling. Typically applied to chemical compounds, objects, and mechanical inventions, patents now apply to plant and animal life forms, including human genetic material. While micro-organisms had been patentable since the 1960s, in 1988 the United States became the first nation to permit a patent on an entire mammal, in that case a mouse with a cancer gene inserted into it (see Haraway, 1997). This meant that the corporation backing the research owned not just the individual oncomice, but the entire species line of all nonhuman mammals with that gene. While that decision was very controversial, once the line had been crossed that higher life forms could be someone's property, biopatents exploded.[10] By mid-2000, the United States had granted more than 6000 patents on genes isolated from living organisms and were considering 20,000 gene-related patent applications (Safrin, 2005, p. 641).

Researchers in the West quickly realized that life form patents were a potential cash cow and began "bioprospecting," mining less-developed countries for their biodiversity, looking for anything that might have exploitable medical or commercial benefits. As a result, the University of Colorado has a patent on the grain quinoa, the University of Mississippi owns the medicinal plant turmeric, Pfizer owns carnations, and the University of Florida owns several strains of jasmine rice. The indigenous populations who have used these plants for centuries received nothing.

Human genes have more biological potential, however, and biopiracy soon moved to new targets. Canadian researchers obtained a patent on the gene pool of the people who live on the island of Tristan da Cunha, and American researchers patented a cell line from a Guayami woman's blood after taking blood samples from her tribe on the pretext of testing for leukemia. These were not isolated incidents. The political organization of countries in the south has forced researchers to move toward profit-sharing models, but often this substitutes national for international ownership, continuing to leave indigenous peoples themselves out in the cold.[11]

People in the West have not been immune either. The University of Missouri holds the U.S. patent on the process of human reproductive cloning (although current legislation prohibits it from actually producing a clone). Companies now own property rights in much of the human genome, many human proteins, and countless cell lines. In the famous *Moore* case (1990), an American court held that while John Moore did not own his body parts as property, the doctors who had removed his cancerous spleen did own the cell line they developed and patented from his body parts (without his knowledge or consent). The patent was worth US$3.01 billion, and Moore was entitled to none of that money, even though he offered up the raw biological material without which the cell line could not have been produced. Once again the boundaries of property have been expanded. Even the human body is property—it just doesn't belong to us.

Finally, propertization and brand-name bullying are also at the heart of trademarks. What is more shared than our everyday language and the sensory perceptions we have of the world around us? And yet, in our brand society, human language and the sensorium are being staked out by owners seeking to expand their repertoire of culturally valuable signs. Recently, a rash of celebrities has rushed to trademark characteristic phrases: Donald Trump trademarked "You're fired!"; Verizon trademarked "Can you hear me now?"; and Paris Hilton owns "That's hot!" Britney Spears even trademarked her baby's name, Sean Preston, so that she can use it for a line of children's clothing. And of course, it is not only celebrities. McDonald's has trademarked at least 131 ordinary words and phrases in the English language; television network Fox owns the rights (ironically, some suggest) to "fair and balanced"; and MasterCard owns "priceless." Pending legislation in the United States will give further resources to the powerful, eliminating the fair use defence for the noncommercial use of a trademark.[12] Everyone from bloggers to social commentators could face legal challenges for using those trademarked phrases and names, even when not using them to sell products.

In the past, courts have been somewhat reluctant to permit sensorium trademarks, but as corporations aggressively pursue them, the realm of human experience, too, is being propertized. Owens-Corning owns the colour pink for its fibreglass insulation; British oil company BP owns its shade of green; Europe's Deutsche Telekom has rights in magenta; and Cadbury trademarked its famous shade of purple for boxes and wraps. It doesn't stop with colours. A California company has a trademark for a floral scent for knitting yarn, NBC has a trademark on the sound of a chime used to identify a station break, and JR Freeman and Son have registered the first six bars of Bach's Air on a G String for their cigars. Recently, a Paris-based company, Eden Sarl, sought a trademark on the scent of fresh strawberries. It lost, but only because strawberries were determined by experts to have up to five distinct scents, not because there was anything wrong with trademarking a smell.

It is important to remember that a trademark is not a form of absolute ownership; it merely protects the use of that mark to designate goods in that particular marketplace. If the use of even identical marks would not be confusing to the consumer, there is no problem. However, the courts seem to be adopting what Jessica Litman has called the "extraordinarily gullible consumer" test (1999, p. 1722). For example, MGM Studios went after a gay-rights group for their street safety patrol called the Pink Panther Patrol. The court found that it was likely that gay men calling the street patrol would think that the service emanated from the movie studio!

Arguably, an even bigger problem than the cases that go to court are those that do not. Corporations are becoming famous for their aggressive "cease and desist" letters, which, while not necessarily grounded in a valid legal claim, intimidate small businesses and individuals into silence. Most of us don't have the time and financial resources to take on a McDonald's, a

Coca-Cola, or a Nissan. This is where the brand-name bully is most dangerous (see Bollier, 2005; Coombe, 1998, p. 78).

Warner Brothers earned international approbation when it went after two 15-year-old girls for registering homemade Harry Potter fansites. The ever-vigilant McDonald's even stooped so low as to pursue McSushi, a small Japanese take-out in San Francisco, and Disney lawyers advised a daycare to remove the paintings of its animated characters from its walls. A group of senior citizens trading vintage Coca-Cola bottles and cans was shut down by Coca-Cola Company in 2000, even though nothing was being sold and the site clearly stated that all trademarks belonged to Coke. Many have fallen afoul of Mattel's vigorous defence of Barbie, including American artist Paul Hanson, who created "Barbie art" by making a Tonya Harding Barbie and a Drag Queen Barbie. Mattel sued him for US$1.2 billion in damages, and although the case never went to court, eventually Hanson was forced to stop making the dolls.[13]

Even more troubling, it seems that American brand-name bullying is getting legal endorsement. The *Trademark Dilution Act* of 1995 and its pending amendments protect "famous" trademarks against use that might dilute their value, even if there is no possibility of customer confusion. Essentially, this gags cultural commentators. Parody, satire, and legitimate social critique are silenced—the trademark owner can freeze and sanitize the meaning of the mark in perpetuity. Trademark, designed to regulate competition between businesses in the same market, becomes a means to censor and censure all of us.

CONCLUSION

The shape of a society's property relations tells us much about the shape of that society. Ours is a society where all forms of knowledge and cultural production are becoming someone's private property.[14] We are witnessing the radical expansion of what is subject to intellectual property rights—from facts to millennia-old myths to the sensorium to our genetic essence. We see legislatures bowing to corporate pressure to provide stronger and stronger means to enforce ownership rights, while removing the mechanisms through which we have traditionally had access to intellectual property. Finally, in most instances, the rights owners are not the creators of the work; they are corporations poised to make even greater profits if they can convince (or bully) us into treating us as thieves. Culture is an inherently shared undertaking in which we all participate; art and science have always been built on what has gone before. The second enclosure movement is an attempt by corporate owners to impose increasingly total control over our shared expression, an attempt made ever more likely to succeed as our intellectual property rights are running amok.

References
Cases

BMG Canada Inc. et al. v. John Doe et al., [2004] F.C. 488 (F.C.T.D.).

BMG Canada Inc. et al. v. John Doe et al., 39, [2005] C.P.R. (4th) 97, 252 D.L.R. (4th) 342 (F.C.A.).

CCH Canadian Ltd. v. Law Society of Upper Canada, [2004] 1 S.C.R. 339 (S.C.C.).

Harvard College v. Canada (Commissioner of Patents) (2002), 21 C.P.R. (4th) 417 (S.C.C.).

Mattel, Inc. v. 3894207 Canada Inc., [2006] S.C.J. No. 23 (S.C.C.).

Monsanto Canada Inc. v. Schmeiser (2004), 31 C.P.R. (4th) 161 (S.C.C.).

Moore v. The Regents of The University of California et al. (1990), 51 Cal. Rptr. (3d) 120 (S.C. of Cal.).

Society of Composers, Authors and Music Publishers of Canada v. Canadian Association of Internet Providers, [2004] S.C.C. 45 (S.C.C.).

Veuve Clicquot Ponsardin v. Boutique Cliquot Ltée, [2006] S.C.J. No. 22.

Canadian Legislation

An Act to Amend the Copyright Act, 1st Sess., 38th Parl., 2005, available from http://www.parl.gc.ca/PDF/38/1/parlbus/chambus/house/bills/government/C-60_1.PDF

The Copyright Act, R.S.C. 1985, c. C-30.

The Patent Act, R.S.C. 1985, c. P-4.

The Trade-marks Act, R.S.C. 1985, c. T-13.

U.S. Legislation

Digital Millennium Copyright Act, Pub. L. No. 105-304, 112 Stat. 2860 (1998).

Federal Trademark Dilution Act of 1995, Pub. L. No. 104-98, 109 Stat. 985.

The Sonny Bono Copyright Term Extension Act, S505 (1998).

Trademark Dilution Revision Act, H.R. 683 (2005).

Secondary Sources

Ahlert, C., Marsden, C., & Yung, C. (2004, May 1). *How "liberty" disappeared from cyberspace: The mystery shopper tests Internet content self-regulation.* Retrieved February 2006 from http://pcmlp.socleg.ox.ac.uk/text/liberty.pdf

Bollier, D. (2005). *Brand name bullies: The quest to own and control cultures.* Hoboken, NJ: John Wiley & Sons.

Boyle, J. (2003). The second enclosure movement and the construction of the public domain. *Law and Contemporary Social Problems, 66,* 33–74.

Brown, R. S., Jr. (1948). Advertising and the public interest: Legal protection of trade symbols. *Yale Law Journal, 57,* 1165.

Coombe, R. J. (1998). *The cultural life of intellectual properties: Authorship, appropriation and the law.* Durham, NC: Duke University Press.

Coombe, R. J., & Herman, A. (2001). Culture wars on the Net: Trademarks, consumer politics and corporate accountability on the World Wide Web. *South Atlantic Quarterly, 100,* 919–947.

Coombe, R. J., & Herman, A. (2004). Rhetorical virtues: Property, speech, and the commons on the World-Wide Web. *Anthropological Quarterly, 77*(3), 559–574.

Cyranowski, D. (2002). Microbe hunt raises doubts over local benefits of bioprospecting. *Nature, 420,* 109.

Electronic Frontier Foundation. (2003). *Unsafe harbors: Abusive DMCA subpoenas and takedown demands.* Retrieved February 2006 from http://www.eff.org/IP/P2P/20030926_unsafe_harbors.php

Haraway, D. J. (1997). *Modest_witness@second_millennium. FemaleMan©_meets_OncoMouse™: Feminism and technoscience.* New York: Routledge.

Katyal, S. K. (2003). The new surveillance. *Case Western Reserve Law Review, 54,* 297–385.

Litman, J. (1999). Breakfast with Batman: The public interest in the advertising age. *The Yale Law Journal, 108*(7), 1717–1735.

McLeod, K. (2001). *Owning culture: Authorship, ownership, & intellectual property law.* New York: Peter Lang.

Rose, C. M. (2003). Romans, roads, and romantic creators: Traditions of public property in the information age. *Law and Contemporary Problems, 66,* 89–110.

Safrin, S. (2005). Hyperownership in a time of biotechnological promise: The international conflict to control the building blocks of life. *The American Journal of International Law, 98,* 641–685.

Yu, P. (2004). P2P and the future of private copying. *University of Colorado Law Review, 76,* 653–765.

Notes

[1] Other types of intellectual property protected by statute and common law in the West include publicity rights, trade secrets, industrial designs, integrated circuit topographies , and plant breeders rights.

[2] While there are some differences across jurisdictions, of course, many of the basic principles of copyright, patent, and trademark laws are similar across Western nations. They participate in mutual enforcement of their laws, and as a result of a series of international agreements, their legislation is becoming more and more similar.

[3] The author of the work is the creator and usually also the first owner of copyright. However, in most commercial contexts, the *author* of the work sells the copyrights to an *owner* in exchange for publication, production, or distribution. For example, many musical artists no longer own copyrights in their songs; instead, the major labels own and enforce the copyrights.

[4] Interestingly, being successful can be one of the ways that a trademark can cease to be distinctive. Band-aid ceased to be a trademark because it became a generic reference to a small self-adhesive bandage. Now the company always refers to their product as "Band-Aid brand." Over the years Nylon, Gramophone, Shredded Wheat, Xerox, and Hoover also lost their trademark status.

[5] For example, certain CDs cannot be played on a computer, music purchased from iTunes can be copied only a limited number of times, and broadcast flags in some American television programs do not permit their copying. Obviously, these measures contain illegal copying, but they quash legal copying as well.

[6] Legislation has been the approach taken with respect to copyright and trademarks, whereas with patents, most nations have relied on their existing legislation, merely reading new "inventions" into the existing terms. For example, the *TRIPS* agreement requires parties to recognize patents in bioengineered goods, and the *WIPO Copyright Treaty* requires that parties recognize the "making available right," or the right upon which the pursuit of file- sharers is based.

[7] The Canadian Recording Industry Association has deployed similar tactics in Canada, but with less success. Canadian legislation does not currently contain the making available right, and courts have made it clear they will not read it in (see the *BMG* decisions). Further, in its recent cases on copyrights (*CCH* and *SOCAN* in particular), the Supreme Court of Canada has been a defender of balance between the interests of consumers and owners, going so far as to talk about "user's rights."

[8] Interestingly, Canada remains a bit of an exception to this trend toward intensified legislative powers for intellectual property rights owners. For example, after a protracted policy review process, the Canadian government finally proposed legislation in 2005 to bring Canada into line with its international commitments and closer to the United States. However, that legislation died on the order paper when the Liberal government fell in late 2005. It is likely that legislation will be re-proposed that will include the making available right, effectively ending the legality of file sharing in Canada.

[9] Disney donated funds to 18 of the 25 sponsors of the Bono Act in the House of Representatives and Senate, lobbying extensively. Lawrence Lessig, a Stanford University law professor and copyright activist, challenged the U.S. Congress's right to extend copyright and lost in 2002. The American Congress has extended copyright 11 times in the past 40 years.

[10] Interestingly, the Supreme Court of Canada broke with the rest of the Western world in 2002 in holding that higher life forms could not be patented in Canada when it considered the Oncomouse (see *Harvard College v. Canada*, 2002). However, two years later, in a case between agribusiness giant Monsanto and a Saskatchewan farmer (see *Monsanto v. Schmeiser*, 2004), the court found a de facto patent in a different higher life form—this time a canola plant. Experts suggest that the current membership of the Supreme Court is more likely to find the patent of nonhuman mammals to be valid if faced with the question again. The federal government's advisory body on biotechnology has recommended that all nonhuman animals, all plants, and all parts of the human being except whole humans (at any stage of development) be patentable.

[11] In 2002 the Chinese government approved a bioprospecting project to locate microbes in Tibet with proceeds to go to the Chinese government and not to Tibetans, who also were not consulted (see Cyranowski, 2002).

[12] The *Trademark Dilution Revision Act* has passed both the House of Representatives and the Senate and is at the committee stage.

[13] Refreshingly, the Supreme Court of Canada took a stand against Mattel's antics and would not force a restaurant in Montreal called Barbie's, specializing in barbecued food, to change its name (see the *Mattel* case, 2006). It also took the wind out of the sails of bubbly-maker Veuve Clicquot when they pursued a Montreal clothing boutique called Cliquot (see the *Veuve Clicquot Ponsardin* case, 2006).

[14] It is important to note that organizations like the Electronic Frontier Foundation, individual activists like Lawrence Lessig and Vandana Shiva, and everyday consumers are resisting both propertization and brand-name bullying; however, their resistance is sporadic, isolated, and unorganized. As a result, it is unlikely to stop the overwhelming force of the second enclosure movement. For examples of resistance see Bollier, 2005; Coombe, 1998; Coombe and Herman, 2001, 2004, EFF, 2003; McLeod, 2001.

ISSUE 4

Not so intellectual: Have intellectual property rights run amok?

✗ NO

It's a [VERY] Long Way to the Top (If You Wanna Rock 'n' Roll)
Graham Henderson

Graham Henderson is president of the Canadian Recording Industry Association (CRIA). Prior to joining the CRIA, he was senior vice-president of business affairs and e-commerce at Universal Music Canada, where he managed Universal's e-commerce strategy and was instrumental in the launch of Puretracks.com, Canada's first legal digital music download service. Graham began his legal career in 1987 at McCarthy Tétrault, where he became a partner, and in 1993 he founded his own practice. His clients included a veritable who's who of Canadian music at the time (among them Alannah Myles, Crash Test Dummies, Loreena McKennitt, and Randy Bachman). Graham lives in Toronto with his wife, Margo Timmins of Cowboy Junkies, and their son, Ed.

To many observers around the world, the fact that Canadians are today debating whether or not intellectual property rights in this country have run amok will seem perplexing, even startling.

Most nations see IP rights as the foundation of a sophisticated, innovative, modern economy, and they have acted expeditiously to safeguard those assets. Canada, on the other hand, has fallen behind its major trading partners. Despite the advantages of a high bandwidth penetration rate and an active online community, Canada's progress in the digital marketplace has waned. Under the shadow of governmental dalliance with ideas that have been discarded in the rest of the world, Canada lags badly in investment, sales, and innovation in this sphere. And our cultural fabric is at risk.

All of this has and will continue to have serious consequences for our economy and society. The fault lies not with IP rights that have run amok, but with the cavalier, irresponsible behaviour of many Canadians. Canada has the highest per capita incidence of online file-swapping in the world, according to the Organization for Economic Cooperation and Development (OECD, 2005, p. 75). Hand in hand with this problem—driving it, in fact—is a simple fact: Canadians' understanding of intellectual property is poor, and all too many of us do not respect the rights of others. Sadly, if it isn't bolted down—if it's in digital format—many Canadians will just take it.

The foundation of this troubling state of affairs is an antiquated *Copyright Act* that provides inadequate legal protection for intellectual property, undermining Canada's social and economic progress in the digital era. In the absence of modern safeguards, the creative people who generate

The title of this chapter is taken from an AC/DC song on the album *High Voltage,* 1976 "products of the mind"—music, books, movies, software, and more—are themselves under-mined, robbing us all of the benefits of their work.

If, on the other hand, IP is given appropriate legislative protection, Canada can forge a path to a new era of innovation, cultural advancement, and economic growth that will ensure the future prosperity of Canadians in a global, knowledge (i.e., intellectual property) based economy.

THE IMPACT OF CANADA'S FAILURE TO PROTECT IP RIGHTS

Canada's failure to properly protect its IP assets is applauded by some academics and lawyers, especially those who seek to cynically exploit the availability of "free" downloads over the Internet. Teenagers, not surprisingly, have raced to the banner of "free." But the rest of the world (for the most part) has turned its back on this model. Sadly, the academics and theoreticians have been enormously influential in counselling Canadian governments to ignore international treaty obliga-tions and societal norms. Instead, they wish us to embrace a "made-in-Canada" solution that has resulted in our isolation as the only major, industrialized Western country that has failed to update its copyright laws. This has landed Canada, embarrassingly, on international piracy watch lists.

Should this perspective continue to shape Canada's policies, the cultural and economic beacons of the software, music, film, and other IP-based industries will inevitably grow dimmer. Already, economists in Canada are taking note of a growing prosperity gap between Canada and the United States (Milway & Poole, 2006). This gap translates directly into fewer jobs and slower economic growth. It also threatens a loss of the cultural vitality that has become a source of great pride to Canadians through the strong presence of our writers, filmmakers, and music artists on the world stage. A recent article in *Strut* magazine surveyed the dismal economic prospects of some of Canada's best-known new bands. Artists who 10 years ago would have turned their fame into comfortable homes find themselves living hand-to-mouth ("Poor Little Rock Star," 2006, p. 113).

Perhaps even more troubling, this perspective has a corrosive effect on values at the core of our society. The "if it's there, it's free" thinking extends far beyond entertainment products and software to ideas themselves. It's no great leap for those who believe it's OK to steal a song over the Internet to think it's OK to grab the original thinking of others and present it as their own. Witness the rampant plagiarism in our schools and universities, an epidemic that mirrors the rise of unauthorized music file swapping.

The evidence backs this up. According to a recent University of Guelph study, cheating is rampant in our high schools and universities, a phenomenon made easier by digital access to the ideas and work of others.[1] A 2005 Pollara study found that the vast majority of music file swapping is concentrated in Canada's younger generation. Composing just 21 percent of the population, Canadians between 12 and 24 years are responsible for 78 percent of illegal music downloading (Pollara, 2005b).

This coincides with a study by Environics Research Group (2005), which found that, compared with the general population, Canadians aged 18 to 29 are much more willing to engage in unethical or illegal activities such as making illicit copies of software programs (35 percent versus 19 percent for the general population), cheating on a test or exam (27 percent versus 10 percent), or leaving a store without paying for a piece of clothing (6 percent versus 2 percent).

Environics' findings illustrate diminished concern with personal ethics among Canadian youth today compared with previous generations. David MacDonald, a vice president at Environics, concludes, "This values shift, coupled with advances in technology, is creating a new landscape in which intellectual property is under unprecedented threat" (CRIA, 2005a).

What about jobs and the economy? The importance of the IP industries to this country's future prosperity is well documented. The Government of Canada, in its 2001 study *A Framework for Copyright Reform*, estimated that the copyright-related sectors accounted for 7.4 percent of Canada's GDP, or $65.9 billion, in 2000. These sectors were growing at an average annual rate of 6.6 percent—double that of the rest of the Canadian economy.

Such growth has been undermined by unauthorized file swapping, an activity that is actually *encouraged* by the ambiguity and uncertainty that arise from Canada's archaic copyright regime. The impact of such blatant disregard for IP is on open display in Canada

- A recent study conducted by international technology research firm IDC for the Business Software Alliance found that decreasing Canada's piracy rate from 36 percent to 26 percent would add more than $7 billion to the economy and create 14,000 new jobs between 2004 and 2009 (Canadian Alliance Against Software Theft, 2005).

- With the advent of widespread unauthorized file swapping, the Canadian recording industry has experienced its most dramatic downturn in history. Since 1999, the industry has lost $558 million in annual retail sales and 20 percent of its workforce (see Figure 4.1).

The digital black market measurably harms not just businesses, but people who seek to earn a living through the sale of movies, books, software, music, and other IP products.

Take, for example, the case of Jully Black, a critically acclaimed new voice on the Canadian music scene. After a lifetime of work, Black finally released her debut album last year—only to have it immediately stolen and distributed over unauthorized file-swapping networks. Putative fans swapped her tracks at a ferocious rate, making 2.8 million requests within two weeks. Meanwhile, her CD struggled to attain sales of 18,000 units.

Inevitably, young people considering a career in music take heed of stories like this. Even those who beat the odds to achieve popular success can face tougher challenges covering the rent. The dream of a music career is as intoxicating as ever, but how many young people today are forgoing that dream, knowing that their work—and their livelihood—will be stolen by Internet piracy? What about *their* rights? Years ago AC/DC penned and made famous the lyric "It's a long way to the top if you wanna rock 'n' roll." For new musicians, the road just got longer, and tougher, and a whole lot less financially rewarding ("Poor Little Rock Star," 2006, p. 113).

Last year, Gwen Stefani became the first artist to sell a million downloads in the United States with the song "Hollaback Girl." In Canada, by comparison, "Hollaback Girl" has barely surpassed 20,000 legal downloads, according to Nielsen SoundScan. Based on population size, CD sales on both sides of the border, and Canada's relatively high broadband penetration rate, Canadian sales should have been more than seven times that amount.

Arguments in some quarters that file swapping drives music sales by exposing albums to a wider audience are countered by the facts. According to Pollara's research, there is a direct inverse relationship between illegal downloading and purchasing music. Furthermore, the younger the age

FIGURE 4.1 Decline in Canadian Recording Sales Since the Advent of File Swapping

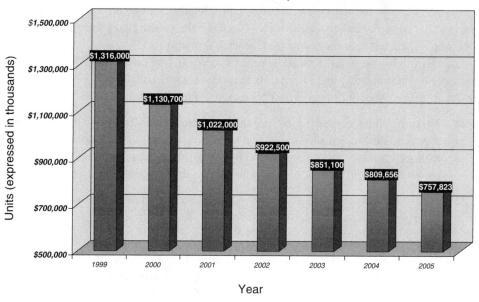

Retail Sales of Prerecorded Audio Products in Canada, 1999 to 2005

Source: Canadian Recording Industry Association

group, the higher the proportion that is downloading and the less music they buy. The price paid by Canadian artists looking to get a start is huge: as a result of lost revenues, the member companies of the Canadian Recording Industry Association (EMI, Sony, Universal, and Warner) reduced budgets to promote Canadian artists from $321 million in 2001 to only $214 million in 2005.

By squeezing out the legal market, the black market not only harms artists and the people who support them, but it also reduces Canada's tax base, increases Canadian unemployment, and undermines Canada's ability to remain competitive in the IP-based economy. Investors here are unwilling to back innovative digital businesses or even traditional copyright industries such as startup music companies (Henderson, 2005).[2]

Even in the United States, where piracy rates are much lower, the impacts are deeply felt. A new study commissioned by the Motion Picture Association of America found that motion picture piracy costs U.S. workers US$5.5 billion annually in lost earnings, and that without piracy, more than 141,000 new jobs would have been added to the U.S. economy (Institute for Policy Innovation, 2006).

CANADA: ADRIFT IN A WORLD OF MODERNIZED IP RIGHTS

Canada's failure to develop a robust, legitimate online marketplace for music and other IP products is surprising in light of our highly developed digital infrastructure and Canadians' almost religious devotion to the Internet. According to market research firm Ipsos Reid, 77 percent of Canadians had access to broadband Internet in 2005 , far more than in almost any other country (WebSiteOptimization.com, 2005). Averaging 12.7 hours per week on the Internet, Canadians spend more time surfing online than they do listening to the radio and nearly as much time as they spend watching television (Ipsos Reid, 2005).

Similarly, changes in the popularity of music cannot explain the sharp drop in sales. These days, music can be found almost everywhere—on cellphones and PDAs, on home stereos and laptops, on portable CD and MP3 players. The ageless appeal of music is as strong as ever.

Despite these fertile conditions, Canada has fallen sharply behind its main trading partners in developing a legitimate digital marketplace. The statistics tell a clear story

- Canadians with Internet access at home are far more likely to have used a peer-to-peer network than a paid service to download a music or movie file—25 percent as opposed to 9 percent (Environics, 2005). By comparison, American teenagers are using legal music downloading services at the same rate as peer-to-peer sites (Pew Internet & American Life Project, 2005), and in Europe, only 11 percent of Internet users swap files on peer-to-peer networks (International Federation of the Phonographic Industry [IFPI] & Jupiter/IPSOS, 2006).

- A study conducted for the Canadian Alliance Against Software Theft (CAAST), an industry alliance of software publishers, found that software piracy rates in Canada are significantly higher (33 percent) than in the United States (21 percent) (CAAST, 2006a).

- The Canadian online music market, which generated US$15 million in sales during 2005 compared with US$636 million in the United States (IFPI, 2006b), is far smaller than it should be after adjusting for population differences (see Table 4.1).

The fact is, Canadians with Internet access rarely download from legal sources. Their appetite for pirated music is voracious, with more than a billion tracks downloaded in 2005 alone (IFPI, 2006c).

Understandably, the international community perceives Canada as a backward nation that doesn't respect or protect one of its most precious resources—intellectual property.[3] The remarkably cavalier attitude of Canadians to intellectual property was captured in a recent CAAST poll (2006b). The research found that software piracy ranked near the bottom of a list of perceived serious offences and trailed *stealing office supplies* by a substantial margin.

Piracy can thrive only in an environment that tacitly condones such activity—and in which there is a willing market. What, then, has caused this troubling state of affairs? How have Canadians developed these attitudes to IP when the cost to our social values, jobs, and the economy is so enormous? The answer can be found in Canada's lax and outdated copyright laws, in their slack enforcement, and in the chronic failure by our government to place a high priority on IP.

TABLE 4.1	Top 10 Digital Markets in 2005 (trade revenues in millions)		
COUNTRY	DIGITAL REVENUES IN MILLIONS (EQUIVALENT IN US$)	PERCENTAGE OF DIGITAL SALES ONLINE	PERCENTAGE OF DIGITAL SALES MOBILE
USA	636	68%	32%
Japan	278	9%	91%
United Kingdom	69	62%	38%
Germany	39	66%	34%
France	28	47%	53%
Italy	16	31%	69%
Canada	15	71%	29%
South Korea	12	42%	58%
Australia	7	41%	59%
Netherlands	5	82%	18%

Source: International Federation of the Phonographic Industry (IFPI). (2006, March 1), World sales 2005: Key facts and figures. Available at http://www.ifpi.com/site-content/library/worldsales2005-ff.pdf. Copyright © International Federation of the Phonographic Industry (IFPI). Reprinted with permission.

THE WIPO TREATIES: A PROVEN, READY-MADE SOLUTION IS CLOSE AT HAND

In contrast with Canada's inaction, an international consensus has developed on the need to safeguard IP in the digital sphere. For example, the European Copyright Directive (2001) notes the importance of digital copyright protection to ensure continued creative production and to protect creators (paras. 10–11).

With the exception of Canada, every leading Western industrialized nation has embraced this consensus by implementing the World Intellectual Property Organization (WIPO) Treaties on digital copyright (see Figure 4.2). Canada, which is a signatory to these treaties, now lags behind virtually all of its major trading partners in fulfilling its obligations. The WIPO Treaties protect creators such as writers, software makers, filmmakers, artists, and musicians, as well as online business models based on their creations and those who invest in them.

In countries that have modernized their copyright laws, online businesses have the legal certainty they need to flourish. In the United Kingdom and Germany, which have both implemented the WIPO Treaties, the number of individuals purchasing legal downloads now equals the number of individuals engaging in file swapping (IFPI, 2006a, p. 15). In Canada, by comparison, illegitimate file swapping swamps legal sales by a ratio of 14 to 1 (Pollara, 2005a).

The treaties lay the groundwork for a legitimate online marketplace without compromising the freedom of rights holders to choose how their work is used and disseminated on the Internet. If artists want to give away their music for free and earn a living in some other way—say, through live performances—nothing prevents them from exercising that choice.

FIGURE 4.2	Leading Canadian Export Markets That Have Implemented the WIPO Treaties		
COUNTRY	**IMPLEMENTED WIPO TREATIES**	**COUNTRY**	**IMPLEMENTED WIPO TREATIES**
United States	✓	Czech Republic	✓
Japan	✓	Denmark	✓
United Kingdom	✓	Finland	✓
Germany	✓	Greece	✓
Mexico	✓	Hungary	✓
South Korea	✓	Ireland	✓
France	✓	Italy	✓
Australia	✓	Poland	✓
Belgium	✓	Portugal	✓
Netherlands	✓	Sweden	✓
Austria	✓		
Canada	✗		

Source: World Intellectual Property Organisation. (WIPO). Treaties and contracting parties/WIPO Copyright Treaty. Available from http://www.wipo.int/treaties/en/ip/wct/index.html; WIPO. Treaties and contracting parties/WIPO Performances and Phonograms Treaty. Available from http://www.wipo.int/treaties/en/ip/wppt/index.html

Compare that with the current scenario in Canada, where honest citizens who want their private property protected and their wishes respected are out of luck. It is not their rights but their *lack of rights* that has run amok.

In many ways, Canada's situation is foreseen by the economic observations of Harvard Business School professor Debora Spar in her book *Ruling the Waves* (2001). Spar observes that all capitalist developments—from the emergence of the British East India Company in the 17th century to the Internet in the last two decades—are based on an evolution of several key economic phases: inno-vation, commercialization, creative anarchy, and, finally, rule making. In the case of the Internet, the world rapidly progressed through Spar's initial phases of innovation, where the technology was available to an elite few, and commercialization, which saw it introduced to the world at large. But as throughout history, these introductory phases were followed by a chaotic period of "creative anarchy" in which it was difficult to distinguish the good guys from the bad guys.

When it comes to the Internet, governments around the world had anticipated this phase. In a remarkably prescient action, they moved to enact the WIPO Treaties with the goal of harnessing the Web to develop digital economies and restrict IP theft.

Almost inexplicably, rather than fulfill our treaty obligations in step with our international partners, Canada has become mired in a decade-long debate on how best to create new laws. (In 2005, the Liberal Government tabled Bill C-60 to amend the *Copyright Act*, but the legislation died on the order paper when an election was called.)

The Supreme Court of Canada, in its landmark online music decision in 2004, recognized the legal challenges this inaction has imposed. According to the decision, while other countries around the world have enacted the WIPO Treaties, Canadian "courts must struggle to transpose a Copyright Act designed to implement [19th century treaties] to the information age, and to technologies undreamt of by those early legislators" (*Society of Composers, Authors and Music Publishers of Canada v. Canadian Assn. of Internet Providers*, 2004).

As Spar points out in *Ruling the Waves*, technological innovations often leave governments and lawmakers confused about how to respond,

> When a technology is new, it usually looks so radical, so untamable, that those closest to its creation can't conceive of it being governed. This is particularly true— as with oceanic trade, radio, or cyberspace—when the technology reveals a space that, for practical purpose at least, hadn't been there before. (2001, p. 19)

But that time has long since passed, and today Canada is almost in a category of its own. Not only have *all* our leading trading partners enacted the WIPO Treaties, but many of them have implemented supplementary rules.

Countries that have taken these steps to encourage investment and innovation in the digital environment are already seeing the payoff. For example, the global mobile entertainment market is projected to grow to US$42 billion by 2010, according to forecasts cited at the 2006 3GSM World Congress in Barcelona (Hendery, 2006).

Opportunities like this are possible only in countries where IP is valued and protected, and where innovative digital delivery models are secure. In the absence of modern rules, values that define our society, such as respect for other people's property and the right to earn a living from one's own labour, will become further obscured in the haze of outdated laws.

Canadians understand this. Recent polls indicate clearly that they are willing to accept new legislation that would more carefully protect digital marketplaces for intellectual property. According to Pollara, the vast majority of Canadians—91 percent—agree that the work of musicians, artists, composers, authors, and others should be protected by copyright to ensure they get paid for copies of their work (CRIA, 2005b). Even among young people between the ages of 15 and 24, more than two-thirds agree that people who use and enjoy the works of artists, musicians, and writers should pay for them.

This broad agreement begs the question, what is it about copyright that gets so many people riled up? In part, the answer can be found in Canadians' poor understanding of copyright and the legislation that has been adopted in other countries. Or perhaps they have been influenced by the common straw men arguments, such as "innovation will suffer and privacy will be threatened." The idea that innovation will suffer in Canada is belied by the fact that our largest trading partner, the United States, has lived with digital copyright legislation for almost 10 years—and they are still a world leader in technological and cultural innovation. As for privacy, Canada right now has some of toughest privacy legislation in the world; to pretend that this protection would be swept aside is intellectually dishonest.

IT IS TIME CANADA'S RULES CAUGHT UP TO THE INFORMATION AGE

There are hopeful signs the current federal government will fulfill the wishes of Canadians, as identified above, and introduce changes to the *Copyright Act* in late 2006 (The details of this new law were unavailable at the time of writing). Parliament must send clear signals about what constitutes acceptable behaviour in a civil digital society. The WIPO Treaties—co-written by Canada, signed by Canada, but not yet honoured by this country—provide the roadmap.

Once Canadian laws are updated, it will be up to Canada's copyright industries to catch up with other countries that have already established Internet markets for their products. In today's digital marketplace, they must introduce technological solutions to make it more difficult for people to take others' property without authorization. Parents and educators can also play an important role by engaging children on the ethics of the Internet and theft of intellectual property.

The international consensus on the WIPO Treaties should provide comfort to a government poised to enact legislation, as should the legislative and market experience of our trading partners. The treaties' rules are by their nature measured, balanced, and flexible.

With this framework in place, we can get Canadians to respect the rights of others in the digital environment and we can, in Spar's terms, rule the waves—waves we once thought could not be ruled but we now know to be merely unruly.

References

Canadian Alliance Against Software Theft. 2005, December 8). *A lower software piracy rate in Canada could yield $8 billion in economic gains, according to new CAAST study* [News release].

Canadian Alliance Against Software Theft. (2006a, May 23). *Canada shows progress in reducing software piracy.*

Canadian Alliance Against Software Theft. (2006b, September 14). *Canadians find falsified resumes a bigger offence than using pirated software.*

Canadian Recording Industry Association. (2005a, September 29). *Recording industry launches campaign to protect and promote products of the mind, citing the results of two new national polls* [News release].

Canadian Recording Industry Association. (2005b, December 28). *New election poll: Two-thirds of Canadians want commitment from parties for stronger laws protecting Canadian musicians from unauthorized downloading.* Available at http://www. cria.ca/news/281205_n.php

Environics Research Group. (2005, June). *Survey: Usage and attitudes of illegal downloading.*

European Parliament and Council of the European Union. (2001, May 22). *Directive 2001/29/ECon the harmonisation of certain aspects of copyright and related rights in the information society.* Available at http://europa.eu.int/information_society/eeurope/2005/all_about/digital_rights_man/doc/directive_copyright_en.pdf#search=%22EU%20Copyright%20Directive%22

Henderson, G. (2005, September 29). A national dialogue on the need to safeguard and promote products of the mind. Speech to the National Press Club, Ottawa. Available from http://cria.ca/news/290905_n.php

Hendery, S. (2006, February 21). The next big things—mobile TV and porn. *New Zealand Herald.*

IFPI (Jupiter/IPSOS). (2006, August). *IFPI European digital music survey.*

Institute for Policy Innovation. (2006, September). *The true cost of motion picture piracy to the US economy.*

Intellectual Property Policy Directorate, Industry Canada, & Copyright Policy Branch, Canadian Heritage. (2001, June 22). *A framework for copyright reform.* Available at http://strategis.ic.gc.ca/pics/rp/framework .pdf#search=%22A%20Framework%20for%20Copyright%20Reform%22

International Federation of the Phonographic Industry. (2006a, January). *IFPI:06 digital music report.* Available at http://www.ifpi.org/site-content/library/digital-music-report-2006.pdf

International Federation of the Phonographic Industry. (2006b, March 1). *World sales 2005: Key facts & figures.* Available at http://www.ifpi.com/site-content/library/worldsales2005-ff.pdf

International Federation of the Phonographic Industry. (2006c, July). *The recording industry 2006 piracy report.*

Ipsos Reid. (2005, August 9). *The Internet continues to impact consumers' usage of other media.* Available at http://www.ipsos-na.com/news/pressrelease.cfm?id=2749

Milway, J., & Poole, C. (2006). Realizing Canada's prosperity potential. *EcDevJournal.com.* Available at http:// ecdevjournal.com

Organization for Economic Cooperation and Development. (2005, December 13). *Digital broadband content: Music.* Available at http://www.oecd.org/dataoecd/13/2/34995041.pdf

Pew Internet & American Life Project. (2005, November). *Teen content creators and consumers.* Available at http://www.pewinternet.org/pdfs/PIP_Teens_Content_Creation.pdf

Pollara. (2005a, May). *Survey: Music in Canada wave V.*

Pollara. (2005b, spring). *Survey: Music Canada wave VI.*

Poor little rock star . (2006, spring).*Strut Magazine, 12,* p. 113.

Schmidt, S. (2006, September 30). Most undergrads admit to cheating, study finds. *Victoria Times-Colonist.* Available at http://www.canada.com/victoriatimescolonist/news/story.html?id=12ff17c0-815d-499e-b3d5-5e54b889f0cb&k=18245

Society of Composers, Authors and Music Publishers of Canada v. Canadian Assn. of Internet Providers, [2004] 2 S.C.R. 427, 2004 S.C.C. 45. Available at http://scc.lexum.umontreal.ca/en/2004/2004scc45/ 2004scc45.html

Spar, D. (2001). *Ruling the waves: Cycles of discovery, chaos, and wealth from the compass to the Internet* (1st ed.). New York: Harcourt.

WebSiteOptimization.com. (2005, June). *US–Canadian broadband penetration gap at 20 points—US broadband penetration crawls to 58.8% in May–June 2005 bandwidth report.* Available at http://www .websiteoptimization.com/bw/0506/

Notes

[1] "Seventy-three per cent of first-year university students reported instances of serious cheating on written work while in high school. More than half of undergrads—53 per cent—admitted to continuing this practice at university in the last year, according to the survey of 14,913 undergrad students from 11 institutions across five provinces" (Schmidt, 2006).

[2] Grant Dexter, President of Maple Music had this to say,

> We recently launched our music label. It was a labour of love that was not made any easier by the fact that it was damn near impossible to raise money from the typical sources that entrepreneurs like us look to. We live in a country in which copyright laws do not protect businesses like mine and in which courts and Copyright Boards support the proposition that downloading and uploading of music is legal. This isn't legal anywhere else. But they say it is here. That makes no sense to me, as a businessperson, at all. As a result of this, raising capital to grow our business was almost impossible. Prospective investors view the music industry as a no-fly zone. And they will continue to until we get the proper laws to protect developing businesses like mine. Maple has been a success; but it sure as hell hasn't been easy. We make it work because we have to.

[3] In 2006, the Office of the U.S. Trade Representative named Canada to an international watch list and initiated an out-of-cycle review of Canada, and the U.S. Congressional International Anti-Piracy Caucus also placed Canada on its watch list.

Discussion Questions

1. Why do we offer legal protection to creation in the form of intellectual property, and do our rationales for doing so hold up in our current economic and social context?

2. What have been some of the impacts of digital technologies on patents and copyright?

3. Do increased propertization and brand-name bullying lead to increased censorship of ordinary citizens, and if so, how?

PART 5 Entertainment and Popular Culture

ISSUE 1	Extremely "real": Has reality TV gone too far?
ISSUE 2	The *CSI* Effect: Is popular television transforming Canadian society?
ISSUE 3	The self-help society: Has pop psychology gone too far?
ISSUE 4	Entertaining politics: Is it all about image?

Entertainment is a substantial component of both interpersonal and mass communication. Popular entertainment, in many respects, operates as the lingua franca of contemporary society—we connect with others through a shared interest in (or dislike of) musical genres, popular television shows, movies, Internet sites, and celebrity fandom. But the question arises: what is the relationship between popular entertainment and personal perspective? How does what we consume for entertainment influence our broader understanding and view of the world?

Such queries are particularly relevant to our personal, political, and social world. This section explores how popular television genres—from reality television and self-help programming to crime shows—have implications that extend beyond the 60-minute time slot. Sometimes these implications have to do with degree—that is, exploring the extent to which crime shows influence popular perceptions on forensics or the extent to which entertainment has infiltrated the world of politics. All of the debates in this section speak to the question of whether such "entertainment" has gone too far.

The section opens with a focus on reality television. Fiona Whittington-Walsh presents the "spectacle of physical makeover shows" as

evidence that reality television has, indeed, gone too far. Such programs as *Extreme Makeover, The Swan*, and *Nip/Tuck* work to normalize the idea of invasive cosmetic surgery, she argues, while fashion-inspired shows like *Style by Jury* are similarly problematic in advocating an idealized beauty type. The side effects of such messages are extensive, fostering low self-esteem in girls and women while fuelling the demand for liposuction, breast enhancement, and face-lifts. Reality television shows also normalize surveillance and work to implicate viewers in the control of others and themselves. In viewing physical makeover shows, Whittington-Walsh claims we are "participating in our own destruction, which we are consuming as entertainment."

Derek Foster disagrees with the view of reality television as destructive. Reality TV, he argues, does not deliver "reality per se"; the shows merely offer predictable narratives that viewers know to be constructed, just like any other television genre. To view these shows as realistic is to take them too seriously. Certain reality television shows have the positive benefit of allowing audiences to become more engaged: audiences can phone or text in votes for favourite contestants. Critics of the genre, then, should recognize that all reality TV shows are not created equal. Just like other televised

NEL

genres, there is good programming and not-so-good programming, which audiences consciously consume to meet various needs.

Reality television is not the only genre embroiled in controversy. The second debate pivots on whether popular crime dramas such as *CSI: Crime Scene Investigation* are transforming Canadian society. News media have reported on a *CSI* effect, whereby the television show is specifically affecting the Canadian legal system and generally influencing perceptions about crime investigation. Marc Patry, Veronica Stinson, and Steven M. Smith, drawing on several of their own studies, affirm that "substantive evidence" points to a *CSI* effect in Canada. Patry, Stinson, and Smith document, among other things, that, first, Canadian media reports frequently assume that juror expectations are being influenced by the dramatized portrayals of crime scene investigation, and second, experienced Canadian defence lawyers find their clients hold "distorted views on legal processes and timelines" as a result of watching television crime dramas. As a consequence, legal professionals are changing their behaviour to *anticipate* a potential bias that jurors and clients might bring as a consequence of watching *CSI*-styled shows. While the authors note that the full extent and implications of the *CSI* effect remain to be determined, evidence does suggest that these shows tend to create more positive opinions about scientific evidence in the eyes of the viewers.

Michael Mopas looks at these same "whodunit crime mysteries" and suggests that finding any credible *CSI* effect proves equally mysterious. It is challenging to disentangle the *CSI* effect from a host of other factors, Mopas argues, and we need to carefully scrutinize these factors before any "effect" can be reasonably affirmed. Political, technological, and cultural trends must also be considered in light of the so-called *CSI* phenomenon.

Moving from crime to therapy, Graham Knight examines the "therapeutic advice" that steadily flows from television talk shows, self-help books, and advice columns. He argues that such therapy functions as a form of powerful social control that

also shapes our self-identity. The key message emerging from this voluminous quantity of advice, Knight argues, is that "your life is problematic, and you need to take charge to help yourself change." But this message is fraught with difficulties because it suggests that the answer to all problems (structural, institutional, interpersonal) lies within oneself.

Michel Dorland views therapeutic advice from a different angle. He examines the historical underpinnings of psychology (and its project to understand the science of the mind) and then outlines how the popularization of therapeutic culture has actually worked to distort the intention behind psychology. While Freud's psychology was developed to be psychologically and socially liberating, popular psychology actually "advises" a type of social conformity. In light of this, Dorland argues that pop psychology has not gone far enough in terms of its overall social project.

The final debate moves from the personal to the political, tackling the question of whether contemporary Canadian politics is "all about image." Bernie Gauthier argues that it is, but also that image can provide critical insight into the person making the promises. Image is about appearance, articulation, and actions, which Canadians observe and "actively use" to decide whether or not to support a politician. Image, in brief, provides an efficient snapshot for voters who are striving to assess a politician's potential effectiveness, morality, and competency.

Echoing Gauthier, Denise Rudnicki asserts that "it would be folly to argue that image doesn't matter" in politics. However, she equally affirms that image is not "all it's cracked up to be"—particularly in Canada, where the political climate is not as receptive to "market-tested messages" and where journalists often resist governmental attempts to set the news agenda. Image without ideas simply does not work, Rudnicki argues, and even the best tailored suit or most polished speech cannot prevent reality—wars, scandals, floods—from "getting in the way." Image, therefore, is simply that; Canadians still seek out the ideas behind the spin and are not seduced by style in place of substance.

ISSUE 1

Extremely "real": Has reality TV gone too far?

✔ YES

Guilty by Assumption: *Style by Jury* and Makeover Reality TV

Fiona Whittington-Walsh

Fiona Whittington-Walsh is a Ph.D. candidate in sociology at York University, Toronto. She is also an instructor in the Department of Sociology at Ryerson University, Toronto, where she teaches courses in popular culture, fashion and society, media and images of inequality, and gender. She works on community-academic research partnerships as well as the life experiences of women with facial/physical differences and has published in both of these areas, as well as in disability and cinematic representation. Her current research examines cosmetic surgery and the production of beauty consumption. She would like to thank Murray Pomerance for his enduring mentorship and in particular his editorial assistance with this article.

[Humankind's] self-alienation has reached such a degree that it can experience its own destruction as an aesthetic pleasure of the first order.

—Walter Benjamin, *Work of Art in the Age of Mechanical Reproduction*, 1968, p. 242

INTRODUCTION

Imagine, for a minute, you're approaching your favourite drive-through coffee spot at lunchtime. You place your order for a decaf soy latte, and when the garbled voice asks if you would like anything else, you quickly scan the menu and respond, "Yes. I'll take café deal number 4: three orders of injectables."[1] This includes Restylane instant wrinkle filler for the deeper lines around your mouth and eyes, as well as upper and lower lip enlargement, and Botox injectable for the finer facial lines you noticed as you surveyed your reflection in the rearview mirror. You approach the pick-up window and tilt your seat back, and the mechanical arm manoeuvres in and begins shooting you up. By the time the shaved chocolate is sprinkled over the steamed soymilk, your latte and your face are done. Rest assured with Restylane injectables, when you return to work you will have been transformed into a younger-looking "you," at an approximate price of $500 per injection[2] (PURE Med Spa, 2006). The irony, of course, is that you are unable to drink your latte until the bruising and swelling of your lips wear off. But then again, a cold latte is a small price to pay for "beauty."

While this futuristic vision of the evolution of both the drive-through and cosmetic surgery may seem "out there," we are in fact not too far away from its materialization. Take, for example, Dr. M. Kara of the Scollard Clinic in downtown Toronto, who boasts of being the first surgeon in Canada to offer a 24-hour breast augmentation recovery procedure, while in England the MediSpa Clinic has just announced a "lunchtime boob job," stating that women can walk away with new breasts in under four hours for £4500 (Tither, 2006).

THE PRODUCTION OF BEAUTY

Pursuing ideal beauty is not a recent phenomenon. Berger (1972) connects questions of power and the history of the objectification of women with the concept of the **male gaze**, which situates men in the active social world and women in the nonactive world, positioned as mere objects on display for the pleasure of men. Further, the solitary practice of beautification not only removes women from the public realm but also minimizes their political agency (Bordo, 1993; Gilman, 1999; Peiss, 1996). Supporting this ideology is the mediated spectacle of physical makeover shows, where reality television has clearly gone too far by normalizing not only the consumption of beauty production but also the beauty ideal, creating the illusion that "it," the perfectly beautiful body, actually exists while simultaneously fuelling the economy.[3]

Attempting to attain the beauty ideal through cosmetic procedures is also not a recent phenomenon. However, never before has the process been so popular,[4] so accessible (with on-site financing offered by most surgeons and clinics), and, because of a remarkable increase in television coverage, so visible. With the introduction of *Extreme Makeover* in the fall of 2002, the spectacle of bodily transformation through cosmetic makeovers (both invasive and noninvasive surgical and nonsurgical procedures) reached a fever pitch (Whittington-Walsh, 2007). Currently, audiences can watch dozens of shows that focus on the production and consumption of beauty through cosmetic procedures. Some of these shows include *Extreme Makeover, Fakeovers, I Want a Famous Face, Nip/Tuck, The Swan, Plastic Surgery: Before and After, Dr. 90210*, and Britain's *Plastic Surgery Live*. Canadian audiences can add two new shows from the W Network[5]: *Style by Jury* and the not yet released *Make Me Over*.[6]

Many of these shows offer a titillating peek into the world of surgical "enhancements." *Dr. 90210* offers a "unique glimpse into the elite world of cosmetic surgery," focusing on the surgeons, who reside and work in Beverley Hills (the most competitive place for cosmetic surgery), rather than the patients.[7] Graphic body-contouring procedures are interspersed with snippets of the surgeons' personal "real" lives. This infusion of "reality" adds to the normalization of the transformations, and is, in my opinion, one of the more dangerous implications of reality television makeover shows. The invasiveness of the surgeries disappears into the background. What we become transfixed by is the personal lives of the real stars of the show, the surgeons and their glamorous lifestyles. This focus helps to solidify the belief in the link between "beauty" and the world of glamour. As Berger (1972) argues, this notion of glamour creates not only envy of those who we believe possess "it" but also shame for those of us who do not enjoy "it."

GUILTY BY APPEARANCE: *STYLE BY JURY*

Other shows, like the Canadian contingents, offer cheaper, noninvasive makeovers. *Style by Jury* is a Toronto-based[8] reality makeover show with candidates between the ages of 25 and 55. Although the websites' preamble states they are both women and men, the transformation photos offered on the website that documents all four seasons to date make it clear that all 53 candidates are women. Women are the main targets for the ideology behind the consumption of beauty. Within modern Western capitalist society, idealized notions of beauty subjugate and control women to the point where we become consumed by consuming and cease to have political agency in the social world (Bordo, 1993; Gilman, 1999; Whittington-Walsh, 2007). All of this consumption is geared toward achieving a homogeneous "beauty" that is utterly unattainable (Davis, 1997; Etcoff, 1999; Gilman, 1999; Whittington-Walsh, 2007; Wolf, 1997) and is believed to reside primarily in white bodies[9] (Gilman, 1999; hooks, 1997; Whittington-Walsh, 2007).

Style by Jury[10] offers the unique twist that the candidate is not fully in on the premise of the show.

> A woman stands before a two-way mirror. She thinks she's auditioning for a makeover show. What she doesn't know is the show has already begun. The cameras are rolling and behind the two-way mirror 12 strangers wait to offer their honest, sometimes brutal first impressions. (Jacoby-Smith, 2005)

In Season 4, Episode 55, which aired August 2005, we meet Vesna, a 49-year-old travel agent who is also a newlywed. Her husband lives in Cuba and is 15 years younger than she. Vesna, a self-professed cougar,[11] wants to look younger. After the scheme of the show is revealed to her she listens to the jury as they cast their opinion on her appearance.[12]

The audition call sheet for jury members for the show requests non-union people who consider themselves to be animated and unafraid to speak their minds. *Style by Jury* uses a judicial system premise. The notion of a jury conveys that whatever "verdict" they arrive at is somehow based on an absolute truth that has been proved beyond a reasonable doubt. However, this form of justice is not based on the assumption of innocent until guilt is proven. Rather, *Style by Jury* asserts that Vesna, and all contestants, are automatically guilty of not possessing the beauty ideal. There is no trial, just the verdict.

Within the private sanctity of the jury room it's no holds bared. Vesna, like all contestants, is finally upset by some of the comments made there:

> "If she were my mom I would be embarrassed to walk beside her."

> "Ouch—her jeans are restricting her from full movement."

> "A little too much cleavage there."

> "I think she needs a bra."

> "A sturdier one!"

> "She's old and she's trying to look young."

> "She's fighting against her age."

What is interesting about the jury's comments is that they are primarily directed at the way she is dressed, rather than at her actual organic body. The jurors are sitting behind a two-way mirror, which is positioned at the other side of the room where Vesna and the show's host, Bruce Turner, are seated. From that distance it would be impossible to pick up detailed nuances in Vesna's appearance, such as her teeth and skin condition. Despite this, bodily transformation is what she will receive, and the primary area will be her face, where alterations and, according to the beauty ideology, *improvements* will be made to the very nuances that make Vesna who she is as a unique individual.

Interestingly, Vesna does in fact want a full face-lift but time restrictions won't allow for this—the show's transformation, shown in brief vignettes, can take only one week (a half-hour in TV time). This rules out her desired face-lift but puts her in a growing population of women turning to nonsurgical cosmetic procedures. According to recent reports, the number of nonsurgical cosmetic procedures is on the rise (increasing by 54 percent since 2000), while facial surgical cosmetic procedures have declined by 8 percent (American Society of Plastic Surgeons [ASPS], 2006). The move toward nonsurgical procedures is attributed to new injectable wrinkle fillers, such as Botox, Restylane, and Hylaform.[13]

Vesna is whisked off for a transformation that will include a chemical peel to make age spots caused by sun damage lighter; Botox injections to get rid of "sunken lines caused by facial expressions such as smiling or frowning"; Restylane to "lighten deeper lines"; laser eye surgery; a new hair style and tinting so her "unimpressive, limp hair" will become "fun and flirty"; and a new stylish wardrobe including a new bra because, as the style guru tells us, "nobody wants droopy boobies." She also gets an enhanced smile that has the promise of taking 15 years off her looks. We are told she has basically everything you could imagine wrong with her teeth, including receding gums and discoloured teeth that are cracked and aging. She receives 18 porcelain veneers ("Cuba Bound," 2005).

For Vesna's final reveal (Bruce tells us that she is radiant), she is informed that an entirely new jury is waiting to cast their first impressions of her. Of course, the show wouldn't be able to fulfill the mandate of the beauty ideal if she did not receive rave reviews after her transformation. As a result of her participation in the production and consumption of beauty, Vesna is finally acquitted of all guilty charges.

"Wow—I really like that look."

"The hair, the earrings, makeup, the whole package—very dateable in a way."

"She's in charge of her life. She's in charge of herself. I get the feeling she's in charge of other people sometimes."

Vesna has achieved the ultimate transformation by situating herself closer to the elusive and unattainable beauty ideal, which is strongly linked to the notion of being desirable for the male gaze as well as being in control. Those who do not fit the ideal are therefore undesirable and out of control, somehow lacking discipline. We are constantly bombarded with images representing the ideal beauty, so much so that we are reduced to shame about our real organic bodies and will go to any lengths to attain "it." Bruce's comments at the end of the episode attest to this: Vesna now feels good about how she looks and, perhaps for the first time, is actually starting to feel shame for how she looked before.

COSMETIC "REALITY"

Shame is a key mechanism that keeps women and young girls consuming beauty products. Adolescent women and young girls are particularly affected by body image concerns, puberty being one of the most serious developmental stages for body image dissatisfaction to occur. Statistics Canada (2002) found that girls as young as 5 are conscious about their weight and are considering dieting (Eating Disorders Review, 2004), while a recent British magazine survey revealed that 40 percent of teenage girls (average age 14) want plastic surgery ("40% of Teens," 2005). A nationwide Canadian survey (Boyce, 2004) found that a greater proportion of girls than boys had very low self-esteem regarding their appearance. The study reported that 21 percent of female grade ten students feel they are "not good looking," while Statistics Canada (2002) reported that 40 percent of grade three girls are dissatisfied with their appearance. This figure increases to 80 percent by the time young girls reach grade eight.

The most disturbing statistics in the rise of cosmetic procedures is the increase for the age group 18 and under, with a total of 333,363 procedures performed in the United States in 2005, accounting for 3 percent of the total. Rhinoplasty is documented as the most popular procedure for this age group. Breast augmentation was performed on 3581 patients in this age group, accounting for 1 percent of the total. Nonsurgical procedures are also ranked high, with Botox eclipsing over 11,900 procedures, a 357 percent increase since 2000 and 33 percent increase from 2004 (ASPS, 2006).

Psychotherapist Andrea Scherzer, who specializes in eating disorders, laments,

> Teenage girls are acutely aware of and influenced by the lengths adult women are prepared to risk their physical health in pursuit of a "perfect" body. And every year the pressure to be perfect increases.... Modern reality TV shows which focus on plastic surgery may seem laughable and grotesque to older people, but they have a worrying impact on teenage girls in the throes of puberty. ("40% of Teens," 2005)

Adam Searle, consultant plastic surgeon and president of the British Association of Aesthetic Plastic Surgeons (BAAPS), states that the increased rates of cosmetic surgery can be attributed to "the increasing media coverage that provides the public with ever more information on what surgical procedures might achieve" (BAAPS, 2006). The American Society for Aesthetic and Plastic Surgery (2006) concurs, attributing the increase in both surgical procedures (mainly body contouring, including liposuction and breast enhancements) and nonsurgical ones to the increased media coverage of such ones (Warner, 2005). Not all physicians, however, find this form of entertainment positive. Diana Zuckerman states, "As long as programs like *The Swan* and *Extreme Makeover* glamorize surgery as the answer to all problems, there will be a lot of women and teens trying that strategy" (quoted in Boodman, 2004).

Most critics focus on the fact that the shows minimize the risks involved in the surgeries and the recovery period. On FOX's highly criticized *The Swan*, each contestant underwent, on average, between 10 (minimum) and 14 (maximum) cosmetic procedures, far eclipsing what is considered "normal" and safe within the industry (Harvey, 2004). Further, more visibility within the media translates into higher patient expectations. "Instead of wanting to do 'something' about drooping eyelids, a patient may very well insist on a blepharoplasty, plus a checklist of other well-enunciated procedures—all in one operating period" (Bryant, 2004, p. 1).

Despite the warnings, this cheap form of programming remains one of the most popular. According to the Culture Statistics Television Program Project, on average Canadians spent more time watching reality television in 2004, at 15 percent of total television programming compared to 13 percent from the previous year (Statistics Canada, 2006). The four main U.S. television networks, CBS, NBC, ABC, and FOX, all added an average of 5.1 additional hours per week to reality television programming ("Reality TV," 2005). Further, according to employment statistics released by the Screen Actors Guild (SAG, 2004), reality TV has caused a dramatic decrease in the quantity of new scripted roles for its members, resulting in 3500 fewer roles in 2003, while the percentage of reality television shows rose by 46 percent. In May 2006, the CBC announced its plans to increase reality programming, taking a cue from its British counterparts and referring to it as "factual entertainment" programming. Kirstine Layfield, the public broadcaster's executive in charge of programming, stated, "We've already done reality shows, from *Making the Cut* to *The Greatest Canadian*. We think it's a great way to tell Canadian stories. But we're not talking about *Extreme Makeover* or *The Swan*" (quoted in Gill, 2006). Time will ultimately tell if the CBC holds true to its word and ignores the high revenues these cosmetic reality shows generate.

INTERACTIVE SURVEILLANCE

It is in the mediated spectacle of physical makeover shows, however, where reality television normalizes not only the consumption of beauty production but also surveillance, which keeps the male gaze firmly placed on, for the most part, the female body. Some media critics (Andrejevic, 2004; Bazalgette, 2000) commend the introduction of reality television as a chance for the audience to become participants, thus facilitating an "interactive revolution" in television watching (Andrejevic, 2004, p. 2).

Further, this notion of participation can be found on W Network's website, where a sidebar entitled "Be on TV" describes each show and details what kind of people they are looking for.[14] The casting call sheet for the not yet released *Make Me Over* states the following:

> A new Toronto PERSONAL MAKEOVER TV SHOW wants you!
>
> Stuck in the 80s and need help? Looking for a promotion but don't have the right look? Is your look NOT working for you?
>
> Seeking women 20–55 with a great story for a new W-Network TV Makeover Series.
>
> Makeover includes a $500 wardrobe, cosmetic dentistry and non-evasive cosmetic work such as chemical peels, botox and laser hair removal as well as professional make-up and hair.
>
> Please send your photo with age, phone number, profession, and a description of why you need a makeover to or nominate a friend! If we choose someone you nominate, you'll get $300.

The idea embedded here is a fundamental ideology infiltrating all aspects of our daily lives today, in the post-9/11 world. While it can be argued that the promise of reality television programming was originally seen to offer a mediated form of Bertolt Brecht's populist interactivity[15] (Ouellette & Murray, 2004), it has in fact materialized in a medium where, as Andrejevic argues, *surveillance* has become the "mediated spectacle" (2004, p. 2). My analysis of *Style by Jury* adds to this argument the fact that not only has surveillance become the norm, but we are also encouraged to nominate offenders, thus solidifying our interactivity within the process even if we can't be the candidate. Further, this feeling of participation extends to those of us who are merely involved in surveillance—those who are just watching. We are also participating in the "reality" because most of us are actively participating in the production of beauty consumption in our everyday lives, through the areas of dress, makeup, diet, exercise, and so forth.

While some critics (Andrejevic, 2004; Lewis, 2004; Wilson, 2004) have referred to Orwell's *1984* in considering the surveillance characteristics of reality television, I would like to add another dimension from the classic and the reason why Big Brother's system of control and domination was so effective. In Oceana, comrades are encouraged to turn those responsible for thoughtcrimes over to the Thought Police. Similarly, *Style by Jury* encourages us to turn in our family and friends who are guilty of not possessing the beauty ideal; thus, those informants are participating in keeping the beauty ideal alive and the population "beautiful" and are therefore in control and easily controlled.

Further, once our bodies have undergone a cosmetic surgical transformation, we symbolically and physically no longer exist. We are replacing our real organic bodies with inorganic material and vaporizing our real selves. In a far from democratic process, Vesna, just like Winston in Orwell's *1984*, received no trial, just a sentence brought down on her by strangers who judged her by her body alone. All the personal nuances of Vesna's appearance that make her a unique individual were ultimately condemned as guilty and have since been vaporized. In *1984*, Orwell writes,

> In the vast majority of cases there was no trial, no report of the arrest. People simply disappeared, always during the night. Your name was removed from the registers, every record of everything you had ever done was wiped out, your one-time existence was denied and then forgotten. You were abolished, annihilated: *vaporized* was the usual word. (1949/1989, p. 21)

CONCLUSION

Cosmetic surgery reality shows are just another of the constant daily reminders that we are not good enough, our bodies are fundamentally flawed, and only participation in the production of beauty consumption can cure us. These shows make the ideal beauty real by showing us a finished product that is so removed from our organic, living body that it is no different from a painted picture. Ironically, it is finally the real body and not the made-over body that we are shown in the show's finale, the blood and tissue stuck to pieces of gauze and tossed aside on the operating tray or on the floor. The real involvement we are experiencing is far from Brecht's populist interactivity. We are, as Benjamin warned so long ago, participating in our own destruction by consuming it as entertainment.

References

American Society for Aesthetic Plastic Surgery. (2006). *Cosmetic surgery statistics.* Retrieved July 16, 2006, from http://www.surgery.org/press/statistics.php

American Society of Plastic Surgeons. (2006). *National clearinghouse of plastic surgery statistics.* Retrieved July 16, 2006, from http://www.plasticsurgery.org/public_education/Statistical-Trends.cfm

Andrejevic, M. (2004). *Reality TV: The work of being watched.* Lanham, MD: Rowan & Littlefield.

Bazalgette, P. (2001, November 19). *Golden Age? Is this It?* (Part 2). *The Guardian,* pp. 10–11.

Benjamin, W. (1968). Work of art in the age of mechanical reproduction. In H. Arendt (Ed.), *Illuminations: Essays and reflections* (pp. 217–252). New York: Schocken Books.

Be on TV: Apply to be on a W Network show. (2006). *W Network*. Available from http://www.wnetwork .com/corporate/participants.asp

Berger, J. (1972). *Ways of seeing*. London: Penguin Books & British Broadcasting Corporation.

Boodman, S. (2004, October 26). For more teenage girls, adult plastic surgery: Rise in breast implants, other procedures raise doubts about long-term effects. [Health feature]. *The Washington Post*. Available from www.washingtonpost.com, p. A01.

Bordo, S. (1993). *Unbearable weight: Feminism, western culture, and the body*. Los Angeles: University of California Press.

Boyce, W., Craig, W., Freeman, J., King, M., Klinger, D., Lee, M., Pickett, W., and Saab, H. (2004). *Young people in Canada: Their health and well-being*. Ottawa: Health Canada.

Brecht, B. (1964). *Brecht on theatre*. London: Methuen.

British Association of Aesthetic Plastic Surgeons. (2006, January 16). *Over 22,000 surgical procedures in the UK in 2005: British association of aesthetic plastic surgeons report 35% increase*.

Bryant, R. (2004, June 1). Reality television: Are makeover shows changing perception of cosmetic surgery? *Cosmetic surgery times*. Available from_http://www.modernmedicine.com/modernmedicine/article/ articleDetail.jsp?id=102225

Cuba bound (Vesna) [Season 4, Episode 55]. (2005, August). *Style by Jury*. Toronto: WTN.

Davis, L. (1997). *Constructing normalcy: The bell curve, the novel, and the invention of the disabled body in the nineteenth century*. In L. Davis (Ed.), *The disability studies reader* (pp. 9–28). New York: Routledge.

Eating Disorders Review. (2004, July/August). *Panel examines risk for eating disorders throughout the life cycle, 15*(4). Available from http://www.gurze.net/site12_5_00/newsletter25.htm

Etcoff, N. (1999). *Survival of the prettiest: The science of "beauty."* New York: Anchor Books.

40% of teens want plastic surgery. (2005, January 5). *BBC News*. Available from http://news.bbc.co.uk/go/pr/ fr/-/2/hi/health/4147961.stm

George, L. (2004, April 26). Presto chango. *Maclean's*. Available from http://www.psurg .com/macleans-2004-04-26.htm

Gibson, V. (2001). *Cougar: A guide for older women dating younger men*. Toronto: Key Porter Books.

Gill, A. (2006, May 10). CBC adding to reality TV onslaught. *The Globe and Mail*. Available from http://www .theglobeandmail.com

Gilman, S. (1999). *Making the body beautiful: A cultural history of aesthetic surgery*. Princeton, NJ: Princeton University Press.

Harvey, R. (2004, April 23). Plastic surgery shows denounced as perverse. *Toronto Star*. Available from http:// www.thestar.com/NASApp/cs/ContentServer?pagename=thestar

hooks, b. (1997). *Selling hot pussy: Representations of Black female sexuality in the cultural marketplace*. In K. Conboy, N. Medina, & S. Stanbury (Eds.), *Writing on the body: Female embodiment and feminist theory* (pp. 113–128). New York: Columbia University Press.

Jacoby-Smith, J. (2005). *Style by Jury. Green and White: University of Saskatchewan Alumni Magazine*. Available from http://www.usask.ca/alumni/alumnisite/publications/green_white/issues/spring2005/feature

Lewis, J. (2004). The meaning of real life. In S. Murray & L. Ouellette (Eds.), *Reality TV: Remaking television culture* (pp. 288–302). New York: New York University Press.

Medicard Finance. (2003). Cosmetic surgery quick facts. *PlasticSurgeryStatistics.com*. Available from http:// plasticsurgerystatistics.com/quick_facts.html

Medicard Finance. (2005). *Canadian cosmetic surgery statistics, 2004*. Medicard & the Rotman School of Business, University of Toronto. Available from http://www.medicard.com/canadian_stats.php

Orwell, G. (1989). *1984*. London: Penguin Books. (Original work published 1949).

Ouellette, L., & Murray, S. (2004). Introduction. In S. Murray & L. Ouellette (Eds.), *Reality TV: Remaking television culture* (pp. 1–15). New York: New York University Press.

Peiss, K. (1996). Feminism and the history of the face. In T. R. Schatzki & W. Natter (Eds.), *The social and political body* (pp. 161–180). New York: The Guildford Press.

PURE Med Spa. (2006). Available from http://www.purelaserspa.com/home.htm

Reality TV "dents" acting roles. (2005, October 7). *BBC News*. Available from http://newsvote.bbc.co.uk/1/hi/emtertainment/tv_an... 2005/10/07

Scollard Clinic. (2006). Available from http://www.scollardclinic.com/plastic_surgery_body.htm

Screen Actors Guild. (2004). Performers bear brunt of reality TV and runaway production trends, 2003 casting data shows. *SAG 24/7: Screen Actors Guild—home*. Available from http://www.sag.org

Statistics Canada. (2003). Adolescent self-concept and health into adulthood. *The Daily*. Wednesday November 19. Available from http://www.statcan.ca/Daily/English/031119/d031119b.htm

Statistics Canada. (2006, March 31). Television viewing. *The Daily*. Available from http://www.statcan.ca/Daily/English/060331/d060331b.htm

Tither, H. (2006, February 10). Quick-fix boob jobs over lunch. *Manchester Evening News*. Available from http://www.manchestereveningnews.co.uk/ news/health/s/204/204033_quickfix_boob_jobs_over_lunch.html

Warner, J. (2005). Cosmetic procedures become even more popular. *FOX News*. Available from http://foxnews.webmd.com/content/article/102/106655.htm

Whittington-Walsh, F. (2007). Beautiful ever after: Extreme makeover and the spectacle of rebirth. In *Popping culture* (4th ed.). Toronto: Pearson.

Wilson, P. (2004). Jamming Big Brother: Webcasting, audience intervention, and narrative activism. In S. Murray & L. Ouellette (Eds.), *Reality TV: Remaking television culture* (pp. 323–343). New York: New York University Press.

Wolf, N. (1990). *The beauty myth: How images of beauty are used against women*. Toronto: Vintage Canada.

Notes

[1] Robert Thomson, director of the Centre for the Study of Popular Television at Syracuse University, refers to the acceptance of injectables as "drive-in cosmetic techniques" (quoted in George, 2004). I came across the article after completing this current work, but because of the similarity with my idea of a drive-through service, I felt it should be sourced.

[2] Further, these are high-end prices, perhaps at Starbucks. I predict that once Tim Hortons catches on and offers a similar, low-cost, Canadian alternative, we will see a competitive injectable war and prices will be lowered, as well as standards. One can only hope Wal-Mart doesn't start offering drive through services.

[3] Statistics for 2005 saw a staggering gross of over $9 billion in the United States (American Society of Plastic Surgeons, 2006) and $500 million in Canada in 2003 (Medicard, 2004).

[4] According to the American Society of Plastic Surgeons, in 2005 there were over 10 million procedures, an increase of 11 percent from 2004 and a 35 percent increase since 2000 (ASPS, 2006; Medicard Finance, 2004). The British Association of Aesthetic Plastic Surgeons (2006) reported a 35 percent increase from 2004, while the first and only Canadian statistics show an increase of 24.6 percent for 2003 (Canadian Statistics, Medicard, 2003).

[5] Formerly the Women's Television Network (WTN).

[6] The W Network denies the existence of such a show. However, I auditioned to be a candidate on *Make Me Over* at the International Anti-Aging Show in Toronto on March 24, 2006. On the casting info sheet, I was asked a series of questions, including "Why do you NEED a makeover?" "Are your looks holding you back? If yes, from doing or being what?" "How do you think a makeover will change your life? What will it help you to do or inspire you to accomplish?" I also signed a release form allowing them to take my picture, including a close-up of my teeth. I was told that they were looking for compelling stories from women between the ages of 20 and 55. My story and my own issues concerning body image and appearance anxiety were not found compelling enough for the show. For a thorough discussion of my own methodological ethics involving researcher as subject, see Whittington-Walsh, 2006.

[7] Some examples of the procedures performed on the first season are breast augmentations, face-lifts, tummy tucks, rhinoplasty on a 15-year-old girl, and perhaps the most titillating, hymen reconstruction on a "Middle Eastern" young woman who feared for her life because she was no longer a virgin as a result of date rape. Rather than exploring the patriarchal, misogynist ideology of most fundamentalist religions and the sanctity of virginity, this episode leaves us fearful of the "primitive" culture of the Middle East and, by suggestion, Iran. For a more thorough discussion of extreme makeover reality TV and the link to the American war on terrorism, see Whittington-Walsh, 2007.

[8] Ontario has the highest number of cosmetic procedures performed in Canada, at 42 percent, followed by British Columbia at 26 percent, Alberta at 11 percent, and the rest of Canada at 20 percent (Medicard Finance, 2003).

[9] For a more detailed examination of makeover reality TV shows and the racialization of the beauty ideal, see Whittington-Walsh, 2007.

[10] The W Network has denied me permission to quote from their website and television show. I have paraphrased actual comments from the television show.

[11] A cougar is a woman whose "social and emotional life just happens to match up with what many young men want—hot, satisfying sex with someone"(Gibson, 2001: page 18). The show arranged for Vesna to meet Valerie Gibson, a columnist for the *Toronto Sun*, who autographed a copy of her book for her. The idea of a cougar creeping along the mountaintop looking down and tracking its unsuspecting prey for hours is what comes to my mind.

[12] "Reveals" are central to all makeover shows. They deny us the opportunity to actually see the finished product until the highly staged final reveal. *Style by Jury* offers a double reveal: the reveal of the finished product as well as of the contestant learning the truth about the show. For more on the politics of reveals, see Whittington-Walsh, 2006.

[13] It is ironic that injectables are highly popular and profitable in the attainment of the beauty ideal at a time when "injectables" are being criticized as the method of execution used in the State of California, especially as Botox is from Botulin toxin and is a neurotoxic protein produced by the bacterium closterium botulinum, and although highly toxic is sold commercially.

[14] The W Network denied me the right to quote from their website. Therefore, I am quoting from *Make Me Over* casting info sheet, which is similar to *Style by Jury*'s call for participants. The *Style by Jury* material is available at http://www.wnetwork.com/corporate/participants.asp#style.

[15] German playwright Bertolt Brecht (1989–1956) was interested in using technology, such as film and television, to facilitate a democratic medium that would replace the one-way transmission of performance with audience participation. His aim was to create a forum documenting real people's lives without corporate, commercial media filters. See Brecht, 1964.

ISSUE 1

Extremely "real": Has reality TV gone too far?

✗ NO

Extremely Real: How We Can Learn from Reality Television?
Derek Foster

Derek Foster is an assistant professor in the Department of Communications, Popular Culture, and Film at Brock University in St. Catharines, Ontario. His research interests focus on rhetorical analyses of diverse forms of media, from mass media to new media to unconventional media such as architecture and public art. His research into visual rhetoric attempts to mine the gap between mass communication and speech communication. To this end, he has published in the areas of television studies (with an emphasis on reality TV and Canadian variants), discourse analysis of public and popular culture(s), and the construction of social issues.

For some, reality television has taken an extreme turn—they criticize the "unreality" and sheer ludicrousness of shows such as *Extreme Makeover* and *The Swan*. However, even with such representations, we should not be fearful of the consequences of reality TV going "too far." Some reality TV may indeed be controversial. But to understand television, we ought to take seriously its most popular and even its most outlandish variants, including reality television. Through an understanding of reality television, we learn things about the medium and about ourselves as we consume it. The central argument of this article, therefore, is that reality TV has not, in fact, gone too far. This is a sensible conclusion if we approach reality TV with an open mind as a potential object of analysis instead of opposing it as an object of derision. It should become obvious that reality TV has not gone too far at all as we explore the following five arguments in greater depth:

1. We ought to focus on the context of viewing reality TV, rather than getting incensed over its content.

2. Reality TV does not deliver "reality" per se.

3. We must examine our own viewing practices before condemning what we watch.

4. Audiences for reality TV can be truly active participants in the reception and the production of television.

5. We must step out of an effects-based mindset.

To learn anything from reality television we must first understand the dangers of immediately dismissing reality TV for having gone too far. As one critic announced, "this may as well be network crack: reality TV is fast, cheap and totally addictive.... The shows are weapons of mass distraction ... causing us to become dumber, fatter, and more disengaged from ourselves and society" (quoted in Hill, 2005, p. 7). For the most part, this seems to be the dominant frame for discussing reality TV, one that is reinforced with such evidence as *Fear Factor*'s gross-out eating challenges, the worst of which may have been the January 6, 2003, episode that featured contestants consuming large pieces of horse rectum. Outlandish, for sure, this segment was offensive for many. One NBC affiliate pre-empted the episode, acknowledging, "the stunt show regularly pushes the envelope of good taste, but the horse-rectum stunt seemed over the line" (Porter, 2003).

Indeed, it is easy to suggest that reality TV has gone too far if one focuses on specific instances of outrageous content. But the answer to the question "Has reality TV gone too far?" changes if we focus on the larger context of this programming. After all, admitting that one's own taste is offended is quite different from suggesting that reality TV has gone too far in lowering wider cultural standards. Still, a culture of complaint surrounds reality TV, placing it in the shadow of the tradition of documentary that has long been associated with a broader set of **discourses of sobriety**—representations that claim to tell the truth and clearly separate fact from fiction and entertainment from knowledge (Nichols, 1991, p. 3). We might be better served, however, if we viewed reality TV as a contribution to public culture that does not just dumb it down but actually performs a public service. Rather than being exploitative, uninteresting, and indulgent, the genre can teach us something about television in general.

Reality TV can be useful if we first dispose of the misapprehension that it represents reality. As Johnathan Fiske noted in the 1980s, television "is 'realistic' not because it reproduces reality, which it clearly does not, but because it reproduces the dominant sense of reality.... Realism is not a matter of fidelity to an empirical reality, but of the discursive conventions by which and for which a sense of reality is constructed" (1987, p. 21). In other words, it is fake. But it knows it is and doesn't try to obscure that fact, unlike other more "serious" and "legitimate" forms of informational and entertainment programming. Thus, those who suggest reality TV goes too far tend to focus on the fact that it is not their preferred reality that is depicted. Reality TV has gone too far if it tries to convince people that it's selling reality, but most shows offer no such pretence. In fact, reality TV producers such as *Survivor*'s Mark Burnett have tried to distance themselves from the reality TV "brand" (see Foster, 2004).

The loosely structured genre is now saddled with the popular and unfortunate moniker of "reality TV," but this is more of a marketing label than a helpful label outlining its content. Not all dramas are equally dramatic and not all sitcoms are equally funny. The same generic constraints apply to "reality" shows. To place something within a genre is to try to classify its general identifying factors—but it is not a scientific designation that everyone can objectively agree on. The same is true of the claim to "reality" with reality TV. The label connotes reality but does not confer any privileged status or uniform meaning. Instead, reality TV offers nothing more than the pretence of realism since it depends on "real" people (compared to the actors who populate other genres). These series typically depend on stock character types (involving careful casting decisions) inserted into prefabricated situations to ensure requisite amounts of drama and conflict, but they are still largely unscripted programming in which the outcome is not entirely preordained. Of course, this description refers strictly to the contest-style show (*Amazing Race*, *Canadian Idol*, etc.). Other reality series (such as *Extreme Makeover: Home Edition*, *The Nanny*, *Wife Swap*) still depend on the "shock of the real" and the unpredictable nature of people's untrained, impromptu reactions. However, even as these series rely on the compelling nature of capturing supposedly unvarnished human nature, the narratives of individual episodes tend to follow a predictable structure and, like many a sitcom, typically are resolved in neat 30-minute vignettes.

Thus, in all variants of the reality TV formula, shows present highly nuanced representations of events, people, places, and things. Reality TV is not TV that is meant to be about reality, per se. It is about the televising of reality, which is something completely different. It is about reality as we see it on TV, which is never a clear-cut translation. Consequently, it is a particular kind of TV representation that tells us more about TV itself rather than one that presents the truth about people and places it portrays. And, ultimately, what it tells us about TV is that all representations are constructed and that reality TV shares many of the same characteristics as other genres on TV. The simplicity of this statement belies its importance. It does not suggest that nothing is real on television; instead, reality TV is as real as anything else on TV. With dramatic TV, documentary TV, news and current events on TV, or reality TV, the operative term is not "drama" or "documentary" or "news" or "reality," but "TV"!

It is also difficult to substantiate the claim that reality TV has gone too far in its celebration of celebrity (e.g., *Newlyweds: Nick and Jessica*, *The Osbournes*, *The Surreal Life*). From its earliest days, television has always exhibited a fascination with celebrities and offered people at home a voyeuristic relationship with them. In the 1970s, Lasch noted how "mass media, with their cult of celebrity and their attempt to surround it with glamour and excitement, have made Americans a nation of fans.... The media give substance to and thus intensify narcissistic dreams of fame and glory" (1979, p. 21). Reality TV simply offers us further permutations of the formula.

Obviously, then, reality TV does not seek to "better" us through stimulating dialogue but hails us through the dissemination of images and through the appeal of distraction and dissent. These are characteristics of what DeLuca and Peeples term the **public screen** (2002). Today, with the supposedly lowest common denominator fare of reality TV overtaking the airwaves and audiences showing no signs of stopping their flock toward these programs, many observers are critical of what they see as a trend away from the hopeful conditions of the ideal public sphere: productive exchange, dialogue, rationality, and civility/decorum. Yet, instead of lamenting the rise of barbarian-themed content and morally deprived programmers, perhaps we ought to suggest that reality TV is symptomatic of the public screen. Through the public screening of contemporary life, skewed though it may be, reality TV does not reveal the world but rather displays mediated images of it. Like all TV (indeed, all media), these are partial and subjective representations.

Those who would suggest that reality TV has gone too far in these representations seem to be troubled by the privileging of "images over words, emotions over rationality, speed over reflection, distraction over deliberation, slogans over arguments, the glance over the gaze, appearance over truth, the present over the past" (DeLuca & Peeples, 2002, p. 133). But instead of falling into the trap of critiquing this spectacle for having gone too far, perhaps we should examine our own viewing practices first. We are not forced to watch reality TV. And yet, millions of viewers make shows such as *American Idol* and *Survivor* top network draws. Interestingly, though, the way in which many respond to reality television programs counteracts some of what DeLuca and Peeples characterize as contemporary culture's engagement with the public screen. They cite Walter Benjamin's concept of the flâneur and use this idea of a carefree individual strolling through crowds and taking in the spectacle of the urban experience as a metaphor for the modern-day screen-based viewing experience. They suggest that the "focused gaze has been displaced by the ... glance of habit ... in the sense that one is not an observer gazing from a critical distance, but an actor immersed in a sea of imagery, a self pressed upon by the play of images and driven to distraction to survive" (2002, p. 135).

While this is obviously true of some examples of the genre, some of the most popular serialized reality TV shows have become must-see TV just like top-ranked dramas such as *Lost* or *24*—series whose success depends on constant engagement with the major characters and a tightly knit story that suffers if you miss one week's installment. Far from causing us to become lost in a sea of images, reality TV provides the fodder for many of today's TV audiences to survive—not just through distraction but through prolonged engagement with shows, with the reality that is depicted in them, and with others who are preoccupied with similar content.

Indeed, reality TV is potentially innovative in terms of its reliance on an active audience. There is no reason to assume that people will sit dazed and distracted before the spectacle of reality TV, at least, not any more so than other "nonreality" products. Viewers are not simply active as meaning-makers or even as contestants on these shows (applying and being part of the production process). Some of the most popular examples of reality TV depend on viewers' active involvement in determining the outcome of the show. Through phoning or texting in votes on contest-based series, they partake of this reality. In fact, the potential that reality TV offers for crossovers between online presence and loyal online audiences prompted David Kronke's observation that *Big Brother* "changed the way television and new media can interact" (quoted in Wilson, 2004, p. 324). Perhaps reality TV has not gone far enough in exploring the relationships between producers and consumers.

It should be obvious, then, that in addition to the relation of producer and viewer, relationships between viewers and the relationships between viewers and what they view depend on how television is viewed. The context of television viewing is very important. "As technology and programming change, so too does watching television.... Rather than essentializing television and its watching, one should treat both the medium and its uses as open-ended, multiple, and capable of transformation" (Best & Kellner, 1988, p. 69). So, instead of suggesting that reality television has gone too far, we ought to confront the multiple encodings and decodings of its content and recognize that reality television keeps on going and it is up to us to make sense of this evolution. As consumers of popular culture and participants in public cultures that depend on televisual discourses, we must neither suspend our critical perspective nor apply it like a hammer, flattening any potential meanings that can emerge from the frequently banal but occasionally intoxicating rhythms of reality television.

Certainly, audiences can exercise judgment, whether they compare "reality" offerings to "traditional" choices or whether they choose between reality variants. A clear example of this freedom of choice was the decision by viewers to reject, en masse, CBC's bumping of the flagship news show *The National* in the summer of 2006 to make room in the schedule for *The One* (a U.S. import with a similar formula to *American Idol* or *Rock Star*). Quite separate from the nationalistic furor that this programming choice caused, people didn't watch because the show was simply bad. In its debut week, concurrent music-themed reality programming in Canada (*Canadian Idol* and *Rock Star: Supernova*) attracted significantly more viewers (1.2 million and 938,000, respectively, compared with 236,000 for *The One*) (CBC News, 2006). Thus, even when confronted by questionable judgment by networks, viewers can clearly discriminate among their offerings.

No matter one's opinion of the genre, reality TV is part of a radically different television landscape than that which existed a generation ago. New viewing technologies have brought a wider choice and range of viewing options. With the explosion of cable, digital, and satellite television offerings, reality TV fills a need for programming and, yes, some of this will be puerile and offensive. But for many viewers, a lot of the dramatic programming that exists alongside reality TV is similarly distasteful. Even if you don't like reality TV, you have to admit that there is a lot of trashiness outside of the flexible contours of the genre. *South Park* and *Da Ali G Show*, lionized by some, are immediately recognized as vulgar. Why should we focus on reality TV when other forms of programming have also gone too far in pushing boundaries? For instance, *Starved* makes comedic storylines out of eating disorders, "a conceit that would have been unfathomable a decade ago. One by one, social issues that were once too controversial for television have become rather pedestrian. *Degrassi* has tackled abortion. *24* has turned torture into a spectator sport" (Menon, 2006, p. G5).

Yes, horse rectum or not, some reality TV content is tough to swallow. But to suggest that reality TV goes too far in presenting such material invokes calcified notions of right and wrong instead of asking what the consequences of such content might be, and it also sidesteps the possibility that audiences can ignore it or productively question and critique it. Many viewers realize that reality TV is not "good" for them, even as they enjoy watching it. To say that it has gone too far is to engage in an abstraction that ignores the different viewing responses it engenders and glosses over differences within the genre. Consequently, this approach tends to carry inductive logic to its illogical extremes. It ignores potentially educational products such as PBS's *Frontier House* and BBC's *Amazon*. Reality TV is far from a stable, coherent, and self-contained object lending itself to broad generalizations informed from specific observations. Instead, we ought to view reality TV as a shifting terrain composed of a constantly updated supply of new shows, each one attempting to appeal to the widest possible audience, each one with its own particular appeal. With each iteration, there are new opportunities to make sense of the genre and new judgments to be made about what reality TV has to offer, both to us as particular viewers and to the wider society. Yes, we watch reality TV. But we also use it. When we laugh at it or reject it, reality TV's programming is like that of television in general: "We should not think of these meanings as *affecting* everyday life, as if they entered a causal relationship with it; rather they are *part* of everyday life" (Fiske, 1991, p. 64). Reality television does not automatically cause people to become subordinated. It does not have some special power over audiences that causes them to stop thinking (nor does it have some special stimulating power that encourages productive engagement with characters or storylines). There is not one grand narrative that structures all of the genre's stories or an overarching experience that characterizes viewers' consumption of these shows.

Of course, reality television carries with it the potential for debasement of our culture, just as it can promote passivity and the consumption of vicarious spectacles in the privacy of our own homes. Yet the widespread nature of criticism (both professional and quotidian commentaries) indicates that reality television has not seduced the masses. Nor are we addicted to these images. Ratings for reality television series fluctuate wildly. And not all viewers are ultimately passive, either. Some shows have cultivated a thriving online subculture of reality television fans who participate in and extend the narrative of these shows. In this capacity, it is no different from the wider television industry that spawned it. TV is "the dominant mode of relaxation, diversion, and entertainment—as well as a central vehicle of ideology and socialization, where values and lifestyles are learned" (Best & Kellner, 1988, p. 45). Reality television is but a recent variation that is neither wholly manipulative propaganda nor wholly innocuous content. Consequently, as observers of it, we must occupy a careful position between condemning it and being apologists for its ideological and socializing potential.

Reality TV is not the spectre of a wholly hedonistic or debased public sphere, but even in its excess and in its impropriety, in its public screening of material that some find tedious or offensive, it offers us the chance to reevaluate how we come to form such distinctions in the first place. Germaine Greer suggested that "reality TV is not the end of civilisation as we know it: it is civilisation as we know it. It is popular culture at its most popular, soap opera come to life" (quoted in Biressi & Nunn, 2005, p. 146). There must be a middle ground between condemning it for going too far and ignoring what it has done. But Greer's statement is instructive. If reality TV has gone too far, then so have we as a culture. And we ought not to slay the messenger, even if we are unimpressed with the message.

In the end, we should recognize that reality TV is both a product and a constituent part of wider industrial and cultural practices. It offers yet another opportunity for scholars of television, popular culture, and mass communication to come to grips with their shifting object of study. To suggest that reality TV has gone too far implies a preconceived opinion of this type of television. It devalues a very popular form of television programming and discounts it as a legitimate object of inquiry for those who ask questions about the medium, text, and various contexts of consumption. Reality TV has not gone too far—in fact, we ought to encourage its continued development and not bemoan its direction in order that we can continue to learn about both television and how we relate to it.

References

Best, S., & Kellner, D. (1988). Watching television: Limitations of post-modernism. *Science as Culture, 4*(1), 44–70.

Biressi, A., & Nunn, H. (2005). *Reality TV: Realism and revelation.* London: Wallflower Press.

CBC News. (2006, July 26). Canadian version of *The One* still possible: CBC executive. Available from http://friends.ca/News/Friends_News/archives/articles07280608.asp

DeLuca, K. M., & Peeples, J. (2002). From public sphere to public screen: Democracy, activism, and the "violence" of Seattle. *Critical Studies in Media Communication, 19*(2), 125–151.

Fiske, J. (1987). *Television culture.* London: Routledge.

Fiske, J. (1991). Postmodernism and television. In J. Curran & M. Gurevitch (Eds.), *Mass media and society* (pp. 55–67). London: Edward Arnold.

Foster, D. (2004). Jump in the pool: The competitive and collegial culture of *Survivor* fan communities. In S. Holmes & D. Jermyn (Eds.), *Understanding reality television* (pp. 270–289). London: Routledge.

Hill, A. (2005). *Reality TV: Audiences and popular factual television.* London: Routledge.

Lasch, C. (1979). *The culture of narcissism: American life in an age of diminishing expectations.* New York: W. W. Norton & Co.

Menon, V. (2006, March 9). Sensitive subjects. *Toronto Star.* p. G5.

Nichols, B. (1991). *Representing reality: Issues and concepts in documentary.* Bloomington: Indiana University Press.

Porter, R. (2003, January 7). Missouri NBC affiliate pulls "Fear Factor." Available from http://tv.zap2it.com/tveditorial/tve_main/1,1002,271|79578|1|,00.html

Wilson, P. (2004). Jamming Big Brother: Webcasting, audience intervention, and narrative activism. In S. Murray & L. Ouellette (Eds.), Reality TV: Remaking television culture (pp. 323–343). New York: New York University.

Discussion Questions

1. Can "reality" ever be truly represented on television (in reality television or other genres, such as documentary shows, news reports, and dramatic programming)? If not, is there a better label for this type of programming, or is any generic label destined to be frustratingly inadequate?

2. Is reality TV any more damaging than other genres on television?

3. If reality TV can have bad effects on viewers, can it also have good effects? If so, what are they?

4. What do you think are some of the most significant social consequences of not being considered beautiful in Western capitalist society?

5. Why do you think reality makeover television is so popular with both audiences and producers?

6. Discuss your own position regarding the production and consumption of the beauty ideal. How does this system of objectification affect you in your daily life?

ISSUE 2

The *CSI* Effect: Is popular television transforming Canadian society?

✔ YES

The Reality of the *CSI* Effect
Marc Patry, Steven M. Smith, and Veronica Stinson

Marc W. Patry is an assistant professor of psychology at Saint Mary's University in Halifax, Nova Scotia. He received a bachelor of arts from Castleton State College in Vermont in 1997 and went on to pursue doctoral work in psychology and law at the University of Nebraska-Lincoln. He was awarded a master of legal studies and a Ph.D. in social psychology in 2001. He was an assistant professor at his undergraduate alma mater, Castleton College, for four years before accepting a position at Saint Mary's University. His research interests include correctional psychology, media and the law, and jury decision making.

Steven M. Smith, Ph.D. is associate professor of psychology at Saint Mary's University. He completed his B.A. at Bishop's University in 1995 and his M.A. and Ph.D. in social psychology at Queen's University, graduating in 2000. His current research program involves a number of topics, including attitude measurement and change, the effectiveness of health promotion and communication, and the investigation and evaluation of eyewitness identification procedures. He has conducted and published research on these topics in peer-reviewed journals and books, and has presented his findings at local, national, and international conferences. In the past his research has been supported by grants from the Social Sciences and Humanities Research Council of Canada, the Canadian Institutes of Health Research, and the Nova Scotia Health Research Foundation, among other organizations.

Veronica Stinson is associate professor of psychology at Saint Mary's University. Her primary research interests are in the area of social cognitive processes involved in memory and decision making. She has consulted widely with government agencies and corporations both in the United States and in Canada on matters involving the intersection of psychology and law.

INTRODUCTION

Television is a ubiquitous force in our society. But can it be said that popular television is transforming Canadian society? In this chapter, we will address the potential impact of one form of television media, the crime drama, on the legal system in Canada. In recent years, the news media has dubbed this potential influence the **CSI effect**. In the first part of this chapter we will consider an overview of the *CSI* effect and its potential influences. Next, we will examine some recent research on the *CSI* effect in the United States, followed by recent and ongoing Canadian research. Finally, we will consider some preliminary conclusions about the potential impact of the *CSI* effect.

OVERVIEW OF THE *CSI* EFFECT

Long-running television programs such as *CSI: Crime Scene Investigation*, *Law & Order*, and their numerous spin-offs are topping television viewer ratings in North America and internationally. For the 2005–2006 television season, these shows have ranked among the Nielsen top ten shows in the United States, and *CSI* is consistently among the top five shows (usually number one or two) in Canada.

Each episode of these crime dramas tells the story of a sensational criminal case (often "ripped from the headlines"), which investigators solve using state-of-the-art **forensic science**. Television crime dramas tend to blur the line between reality and fiction. The techniques presented on these shows are usually plausible, but they are often inaccurately depicted and far from common. Millions of viewers may be "learning" (incorrectly) how forensic evidence is gathered, processed, and analyzed. One recurring theme in these shows is that the quality of scientific evidence (such as DNA, fingerprint, and other evidence) is far superior to nonscientific evidence (such as confessions or eyewitness evidence). Moreover, these shows inculcate viewers with the notion that "science will lead us to the truth" and that "the evidence is there and is speaking to us." What impact, if any, might this have on the Canadian viewing public?

The *CSI* effect is typically described in four different ways: (1) jurors are more likely to acquit defendants if they are fans of *CSI*, (2) legal professionals have changed their behaviour in order to deal with these perceived changes in juror behaviour, (3) television crime dramas have peaked student interest in topics related to forensic science, and (4) criminals are learning ways to avoid capture by watching these shows (Patry, Smith, Stinson, Head, & Hole, 2006). In this chapter, we focus on presenting the research evidence for the first two premises.

Most references to the *CSI* effect present it as an undesirable effect exhibited by jurors which results from their perceived expertise about forensic techniques and police investigations (see Podlas, 2006; Tyler, 2006). These reports suggest that watching *CSI* gives jurors unrealistic expectations about the quantity, quality, and availability of scientific evidence. Essentially, the argument is that owing to their perceived expertise on all matters forensic, *CSI*-educated jurors are expecting to see more scientific evidence and more compelling evidence than they have in the past. When the scientific evidence presented at trial fails to meet jurors' expectations, they are presumably more likely to acquit the defendant. Believing this scenario to be true, legal professionals are changing their behaviour to address these apparent changes in juror expectations.

RECENT U.S. RESEARCH ON THE *CSI* EFFECT

Although many news reports have documented the perceptions of legal professionals with regard to the *CSI* effect, there is little empirical research about this topic. One notable exception is an analysis of the perceptions and behaviours of members of the prosecuting attorney's office in Maricopa County, Arizona. The prosecuting attorney's office conducted a survey of 102 prosecutors to assess the perceived impact of the *CSI* effect and how these lawyers are responding to this issue (Maricopa County, 2005).

The report showed that prosecutors believe there is a *CSI* effect: 38 percent of attorneys reported they had lost a case because of the *CSI* effect; 45 percent contended that jurors relied on scientific evidence more than they should; and 72 percent maintained that *CSI* fans exerted undue influence on other jurors. The prosecutors also cited striking examples of acquittals. In one case a man was acquitted of drug possession after the jury apparently ignored a police officer's eyewitness account of the suspect tossing a packet of drugs. Jurors reasoned that the package should have been fingerprinted. In another acquittal, corrections officers had removed drugs from a body cavity of a prisoner. Jurors stated that residue on the baggie should have been subjected to DNA analysis. The Maricopa county report also documented the approaches prosecutors had taken to reduce the *CSI* effect: 70 percent asked jurors about television-viewing habits; 90 percent took the time to explain police procedures to jurors; 52 percent plea-bargained cases when they anticipated their evidence was insufficient to overcome the *CSI* effect; and 83 percent felt judicial instructions (i.e., instructions provided by the judge to the jury before deliberations take place) would be appropriate.

Despite the beliefs of legal professionals, the extent to which trial outcomes can be directly attributed to the effect of television crime dramas remains unclear. To date, three studies have assessed the *CSI* effect in a legal context. Podlas (2006) reasoned that frequent viewers of *CSI* should hold specific beliefs consistent with the image of forensic science portrayed in the shows. In that study, participants read a scenario of an alleged rape that was based entirely on the credibility of witnesses (no forensic evidence was presented), then rendered a verdict and reported on the basis for their decision. Although the lack of forensic evidence was the reason most often provided for mock jurors' decisions, frequent viewers of *CSI* were not more likely than infrequent viewers of *CSI* to cite the lack of forensic evidence for their not-guilty verdicts. Podlas concluded that the data did not support the idea of an anti-prosecution *CSI* effect.

In another set of studies, O'Neil and his colleagues found limited support for a relationship between viewing *CSI* and mock juror decision making. They conducted two mock juror studies in which they examined self-reported viewing of crime dramas to test for relationships between viewing habits, perceptions of evidence, and verdicts. In one study the data showed relationships between crime drama TV viewing and perceptions of evidence and the defendant, but viewing habits had no impact on mock juror verdicts (Reardon, Cooper, Morales, & O'Neil, 2006). A second study also showed no relationship between self-reported viewing of crime dramas and mock juror verdicts (York, O'Neil, & Evans, 2006). These studies suggest that watching *CSI* and other law-related programs may influence mock jurors' perceptions of evidence and may play a role in decision processes. However, there is no overwhelming empirical evidence that viewing these programs directly influences jurors or jury verdicts.

Given this inconsistent evidence, perhaps it is not surprising that some scholars have argued that there is no *CSI* effect, or that if one exists at all it probably favours the prosecution. Tyler (2006) argued that although evidence on television violence, juror decision making, and pretrial publicity suggests that a pro-defence *CSI* effect could exist, there are equally compelling arguments that the *CSI* effect could be working in the prosecution's favour. For example, in almost all the storylines on *CSI*, the criminal is caught and convicted. Indeed, in our content analysis of the first season of *CSI* and *CSI: Miami*, almost 100 percent of the storylines ended in the criminal being caught (Patry et al., 2006). Tyler speculated that this consistent conclusive ending may give people unrealistic expectations for real-life cases. Therefore, complaints of a pro-defence bias may be erroneous, and may be the result of disgruntled prosecutors trying to find alternative explanations for their failure to win more cases. Tyler highlighted the need for empirical investigations of the *CSI* effect to determine what influence (if any) shows like *CSI* and *Law & Order* have on the general public. To address these and other issues, we have begun to conduct some empirical research along these lines.

RECENT AND ONGOING CANADIAN RESEARCH ON THE *CSI* EFFECT

To address the critique that research on the CSI effect has been merely anecdotal and lacking in scientific rigour, we conducted seven studies, briefly summarized below. Taken together, this research provides substantive evidence for a *CSI* effect in Canada (see Table 2.1 for a summary of the studies).

In conducting our research, we first wanted to understand how the *CSI* effect was described in the media (see Table 2.1 for a description of the Patry et al., 2006, study, hereafter referred to as Study 1). Examples of some of the headlines from articles about the *CSI* effect include "'CSI effect' has juries wanting more evidence" (Willing, 2006) and "'The CSI Effect': Does the TV crime drama influence how jurors think?" (2005). The results of Study 1 suggested that the news media reports frequently characterized the *CSI* effect as negative and assumed that juror expectations were being affected by the unrealistic portrayals of crime scene investigation on television crime dramas. Thus, our second goal was to explore the extent to which *CSI* accurately portrays crime scene investigations and scientific analysis of evidence.

In Study 2, we conducted a content analysis of the first seasons of *CSI* and *CSI: Miami* (see Patry et al., 2006). We sought to document the types of forensic procedures portrayed, the frequency of errors, and the types of sentiments expressed by characters on the show, such as the theme that scientific evidence, when properly gathered, leads to the truth. We identified over 75 forensic evidence techniques portrayed on the shows. The two most common types were DNA evidence, which was present in 18.9 percent of the main storylines, and fingerprint evidence, which appeared 12 percent of the time. There was a consistent theme that science is the only truth. Finally, the perpetrator of the crime was successfully identified in 98 percent of the storylines, since on *CSI*, evidence that conclusively points to the guilt of one suspect is almost always available at the crime scene, a condition that is far less common in real life. Importantly, on the *CSI* episodes we examined, forensic investigators conducted scientific tests of evidence 72 percent of the time, whereas in real life, it is specialized laboratory technicians who conduct these tests (T. McCullough, personal communication, 2005). Thus, there is a clear difference between how actual forensic investigations work and the way they are portrayed on *CSI* shows.

In Studies 3 and 4 (Stinson, Smith, & Patry, 2006), we surveyed legal professionals to determine the extent to which they perceive that crime dramas are influencing the public and whether or not their professional roles are affected by these programs. Study 3 was a Web-based survey of nine experienced Canadian defence lawyers. The lawyers generally did not see the *CSI* effect as a problem, though two-thirds said their clients had distorted views of legal processes and timelines

TABLE 2.1 Summary of Our Empirical Research on the *CSI* Effect

STUDY	TOPIC AND CITATION	METHODOLOGY	PARTICIPANTS	MAJOR FINDINGS
1	Content analysis of news coverage (Patry et al., 2006)	Content coding of over 200 news articles	N/A	Fourfold news media conception of *CSI* effect
2	Content analysis of shows (Patry et al., 2006)	Content coding of first season of the original *CSI* show	N/A	DNA and fingerprint evidence are most commonly portrayed forensic techniques
3	Defence lawyer perspectives (Stinson, Smith, & Patry, 2006)	Web-based survey	N = 9 experienced Canadian defence lawyers	*CSI* and other crime dramas influence perceptions of the legal system
4	Death investigator perspectives (Stinson et al., 2006)	Paper-and-pencil survey	N = 127 Canadian professional death investigators (e.g. police, fire, emergency workers)	Crime dramas influence public expectations of professionals, who have altered the way they interact with the public
5	Perceptions of forensic techniques (Smith, Patry, & Stinson, 2006, study 1)	Paper-and-pencil survey, snowball sampling	N = 320 Canadians	Scientific evidence seen as more reliable than nonscientific evidence
6	How *CSI* relates to attitudes (Smith et al., 2006, study 2)	Paper-and-pencil survey, snowball sampling	N = 148 Canadians	Self-reported viewing of crime dramas correlated with high expectations of forensic science
7	Causality and *CSI* exposure (Smith et al., 2006, study 3)	Experiment: random assignment to watch zero, four, or eight episodes of *CSI*	N = 190 Canadian university students	Exposure to *CSI* causes higher expectations of DNA and fingerprint evidence

as a result of television crime dramas. Most lawyers thought that judicial instructions regarding *CSI* would be useful.

In Study 4, we conducted a paper-and-pencil survey of 124 Canadian death investigators (83 police investigators, 28 medical examiners, 7 fire/arson investigators, and 6 others) attending a regional training seminar. These professionals overwhelmingly confirmed that crime dramas are less than accurate, and over half of the participants reported that these programs have changed the way in which they practise and/or investigate. For example, one participant remarked, "I am more careful to explain concepts to juries, understanding that they may think they know more than they do" because of the *CSI* effect. Another respondent said, "I watch the episodes so I will be aware of what kind of questions to expect." One participant noted that his/her behaviour in court had changed as a result of the *CSI* effect: "[You] have to explain why you did or did not do certain procedures." Almost all respondents (94 percent) indicated that television crime dramas have changed the Canadian public's expectations of their profession, and almost two-thirds of participants indicated that television crime dramas have influenced the way in which they interact with the public.

Thus, it is clear that legal professionals believe in the existence of the *CSI* effect, and they are changing their behaviour as a result. However, it is possible that legal professionals are overreacting to media hype about the *CSI* effect, a finding that has yet to be substantiated with empirical evidence. Therefore, in another series of studies we explored the extent to which shows such as *CSI* and *Law & Order* influence public perceptions of forensic evidence.

In Study 5 (see Smith, Stinson, & Patry, 2006), we surveyed a sample of 320 jury-eligible adults (e.g., students, military personnel, medical professionals, teachers, construction workers, banking professionals, and retired individuals) to obtain their opinions about several types of scientific and nonscientific evidence. The data clearly indicated that the Canadian public has a strong preference for scientific evidence over more traditional forms. Perhaps not surprisingly, DNA and fingerprint evidence were consistently rated as the most reliable and useful types for criminal investigations. Nonscientific forms of evidence (e.g., confession, motive and alibi evidence) were consistently rated as less useful and reliable. What is still unresolved is the origin of people's opinions about these forensic techniques. There are numerous potential sources for people's schemas and opinions about forensic techniques (e.g., other people, books, television, newspapers), but we suspect that television crime dramas such as *CSI* may be an important factor in this equation.

In our next study (Study 6; see Smith et al., 2006), we explored how people's television-viewing habits related to their beliefs about forensic evidence. Data from 148 participants showed that self-reported viewing of *CSI* and *Law & Order* shows was related to favourable views regarding a number of types of scientific evidence, but it was unrelated to ratings of nonscientific evidence. However, that study did not address the issue of causality, the question about whether viewing crime dramas is the *cause* of changes in people's expectations and perceptions of law enforcement and the legal system, or whether these changes may be due to some other factor. While a causal effect is plausible, the relationships we observed between viewing habits and opinions about forensic evidence may be due to the fact that people who are interested in forensic evidence, or science in general, may be more likely to watch the show. Thus, our objective for Study 7 was to test for a causal relationship between exposure to *CSI* and participant attitudes about forensic evidence.

In Study 7 (see Smith et al., 2006), we randomly assigned 190 Canadian undergraduates to watch zero, four, or eight episodes of *CSI*. To maximize external validity, we instructed participants to view the episodes in the comfort of their own homes or wherever they normally watch television. Participants assigned to view episodes of *CSI* took DVDs home with them and returned to the lab when they had completed their viewing assignments. Compared to those who did not view *CSI*, participants who watched four to eight episodes had higher estimates of the reliability of DNA evidence, both accuracy and reliability of DNA and fingerprint analysis, and had more confidence in their judgments about the reliability of DNA analysis. It is quite possible that this effect occurs because these two types of evidence, DNA and fingerprint analysis, are also the techniques most commonly portrayed on the show (see Study 2). To our knowledge, this study is the first to demonstrate that watching crime dramas influences how people perceive different types of forensic evidence.

SUMMARY AND CONCLUSIONS

At the beginning of this paper, we asked the question of whether or not the *CSI* effect actually exists. It appears the answer to this question is a *qualified* yes. Taken together, the evidence summarized above points to the clear presence of a *CSI* effect in Canada, specifically with regard to public perceptions of forensic evidence and public perceptions of professionals working in areas related to criminal law. Further, the evidence suggests that changes in public expectations stemming from television crime dramas are having an impact on how these professionals perform their day-to-day tasks. However, more research is needed to determine the breadth of the *CSI* effect and its potential implications for Canadian society.

To return to the title of this chapter, is popular television transforming Canadian society? Based on the available data, we argue that, to some degree, programs such as *CSI* and *CSI: Miami* are influencing Canadian society. However, the full extent, nature, and implications of this effect are yet to be determined. One important issue that is not yet clear is whether the *CSI* effect is likely to influence trial proceedings. Indeed, current evidence suggests that it may not (see Podlas, 2006; Reardon et al., 2006; York et al., 2006). Nonetheless, legal professionals seem to be changing their behaviour in response to the *CSI* effect, which could be unwise in the absence of conclusive evidence about the exact nature and consequences of this effect. It is important to understand the nature of any potential bias at the jury level before undertaking any intervention (see Wegener, Kerr, Fleming, & Petty, 2000). If the strength of the bias is underestimated, the intervention will be ineffective in eliminating the bias. Alternatively, if the bias is overestimated, any correction applied may have a boomerang effect, resulting in further unfair outcomes. Thus, additional research in this area is required before meaningful policy changes or other major reform efforts can be developed (see also Tyler, 2006).

If it is indeed the case that television crime dramas influence jury decisions, there are a number of ways in which this bias might manifest itself. However, based on the research to date, it seems unlikely that crime dramas will generally *cause* jurors to acquit in criminal trials (the conclusion so often reported in the news media). Indeed, our research suggests that people who watch *CSI* judge forensic evidence to be *more* reliable and accurate, and therefore they may be *more* likely to convict if that evidence is present. We have shown that people who watch *CSI* have significantly more positive views of forensic evidence. In other words, the *CSI* effect may result in a pro-prosecution bias when the expected evidence is presented at trial, and a pro-defence bias if the expected evidence is not available.

In closing, the research evidence suggests that the *CSI* effect may exhibit itself in somewhat different forms than what is typically discussed in the media. The results of the studies we presented here indicate that shows like *CSI* and *Law & Order* are related to people's judgments of forensic evidence. Specifically, watching these shows tends to produce more positive opinions about scientific evidence but not more traditional types of evidence (such as eyewitness and confession evidence). It is clear that more research is needed in order to fully understand the extent to which television crime dramas such as *CSI* are influencing public expectations about the legal system, the police and their investigative procedures, trial outcomes, and, by extension, Canadian society.

References

"The CSI Effect": Does the TV crime drama influence how jurors think? (2005, March 21). *CBS News*. Retrieved August 25, 2006, from http://www.cbsnews.com/stories/2005/03/21/earlyshow/main681949.shtml

Maricopa County. (2005, June 30). *The* CSI *effect and its real-life impact on justice: A study by the Maricopa County Attorney's Office*. Retrieved September 20, 2005, from http://www.maricopacountyattorney.org/Press/PDF/CSIReport.pdf

Patry, M. W., Smith, S. M., Stinson, V., Head, N., & Hole, C. (2006). *Forensic techniques in television crime dramas and newspaper media*. Unpublished manuscript.

Podlas, K. (2006). "The CSI Effect": Exposing the media myth. *Fordham Intellectual Property, Media and Entertainment Law Journal, 16*, 429–465.

Reardon, M., Cooper, M., Morales, G., & O'Neil, K. (2006, March). *Examining criminal and evidence expectancies with the use of profile evidence*. Paper presented at the American Psychology-Law Society Annual Conference, St. Petersburg, FL.

Smith, S. M., Patry, M. W., & Stinson, V. (2006). *Is there a* CSI *effect? Exploring the effects of television crime dramas on opinions and expectations concerning forensic science*. Unpublished manuscript.

Stinson, V., Smith, S. M., & Patry, M. W. (2006). *Perspectives of lawyers and police professionals on the* CSI *effect*. Unpublished manuscript.

Tyler, T. R. (2006). Viewing *CSI* and the threshold of guilt: Managing truth and justice in reality and fiction. *The Yale Law Journal, 115*, 1050–1085.

Wegener, D. T., Kerr, N. L., Fleming, M. A., & Petty, R. E. (2000). Flexible correction of juror judgments. *Psychology, Public Policy, and Law, 6*, 629–654.

Willing, R. (2006, August 5). "CSI effect" has juries wanting more evidence. *USA Today*, Retrieved August 10, 2006, from http://www.usatoday.com/news/nation/2004-08-05-csi-effect_x.htm

York, R. M., O'Neil, K., & Evans, J. (2006, March). *The "CSI effect:" Presentation style, evidence quality, and a possible remedy*. Paper presented at the American Psychology-Law Society Annual Conference, St. Petersburg, FL.

ISSUE 2

The *CSI* Effect: Is popular television transforming Canadian society?

✗ NO

Cross-Examining the Evidence: Does the *CSI* Effect Really Exist?

Michael Mopas

Michael Mopas is a lecturer in the Department of Sociology and Anthropology at Carleton University and a doctoral candidate at the Centre of Criminology, University of Toronto. His research interests are in the areas of policing, the regulation of cyberspace, and the use of science and technology in criminal justice.

INTRODUCTION

C SI: Crime Scene Investigation and its spin-offs, *CSI: Miami* and *CSI: NY*, are part of a new generation of "whodunit" crime mysteries where science and technology play a central role in catching criminals. Although very few would mistake it for educational programming, the show appears to be having an influence on how its audience comes to think about forensics and the work of forensic investigators. According to various news reports (see Cole & Dioso, 2005; "Lamer Assails," 2005; Lovgren, 2004; Stockwell, 2005; Willing, 2004), *CSI* is greatly misinforming viewers about the "realities" of forensic science and its place within criminal justice.

Critics warn that many viewers are now under the impression that the use of forensics in criminal investigations is not only common but quick, easy, and without budgetary constraints. The term "*CSI* effect" is being used to describe these distorted perceptions of forensics that the show has produced. However, the concern is not so much about people being misled, but about the larger impact this effect is supposedly having in other areas. Numerous writers have blamed *CSI* for a variety of recent trends, ranging from the rising number of "science-savvy" jurors to the increase in student enrolment in forensic science programs. Watching *CSI* has even been connected to the proliferation of cases where suspects burn or otherwise tamper with evidence to cover their tracks (see Milicia, 2006).

But despite all of the hype, there is still a dearth of reliable empirical evidence that demonstrates a correlation between watching *CSI* and the several outcomes described by the media. The only data we have are the personal accounts given by lawyers who tell us about an increase in the number of jurors demanding forensic evidence at trial, or police officers who assert that there are now more instances in which evidence is messed with or destroyed. And, while we may accept these claims as being true because of their basis in firsthand knowledge, the inferences such experts make that these trends are linked to *CSI* are speculative, at best. In the end, we are left wondering whether or not *CSI* is really distorting public understanding of forensics, and, if so, what effect this misperception is causing.

Nonetheless, we can rest assured that social scientists from various disciplines are on the case. In the not-so-distant future, we can expect to find a plethora of "scientific" studies, employing an array of research designs, methodologies, and theoretical frameworks, which speak to this question of whether or not there is such a thing as a *CSI* effect. Still, even with the availability of empirical data, it may be unwise to simply accept or reject at face value findings that either support or refute the idea that watching *CSI* is producing certain outcomes by perverting people's opinions of forensics. Quite the opposite—as social scientists, it is imperative that we remain skeptical and pose questions that will not only help to reveal the many limitations of research, but force us to think about these studies and their results within the contexts in which they are undertaken.

The aim of this chapter is to question and critically interrogate our understandings of the *CSI* effect and to assess the prospects of social science research offering definitive "truths" about the nature of the relationship between the media and audiences. More specifically, I present a number of methodological and conceptual issues that need to be raised in assessing the validity of any claim made about the *CSI* effect and the different outcomes it is said to be producing. In doing so, I illustrate how any type of *CSI* effect that one happens to "discover" can never be completely disentangled from a host of other factors. I argue that the relationship between television and its viewers is a complex one that cannot be easily understood without carefully considering the larger social, political, technological, and cultural landscape in which it exists.

THE CSI EFFECT: SCIENCE FACT OR SCIENCE FICTION?

Although it may be easy to dismiss it as just another TV show that romanticizes the work of those in law enforcement, many critics are claiming that *CSI* is having a profound effect on its audience by misinforming them about what forensics can truly deliver (Cole & Dioso, 2005). This distortion of public understanding, in turn, has had a major impact in both the classroom and the courtroom: The show is being blamed for everything from the spike in applications to forensic science programs to the acquittal of a former Hollywood celebrity on trial for the murder of his wife.[1]

In the United States, various news outlets have reported a growing anxiety among legal analysts about the impact *CSI* is having on criminal cases. A number of defence lawyers are claiming that *CSI* is creating jurors who rely too heavily on scientific findings and, conversely, are less skeptical about the potential for human or technical error or fraud (Cole & Dioso, 2005; Willing, 2004). Likewise, the show is said to be turning jurors into science sleuths who demand that the prosecution provide the same type of irrefutable evidence they see on TV (Lovgren, 2004).

But can these programs have such an impact on criminal justice and really influence the outcome of a trial? Not everyone is convinced. Simon Cole and Rachel Dioso (2005) argue that there is "not a shred of evidence" to substantiate the claim that shows like *CSI* are raising the number of acquittals. Whatever evidence does exist, they suggest, is purely anecdotal. Cole and Dioso assert that "there is a robust field of research on jury decision-making but no study finding any 'CSI effect' " (p. W13). Like others engaged in this debate, they argue that the various "truths" about the *CSI* effect can be revealed only through proper scientific inquiry, and that what is needed are empirical studies and hard evidence.

This turn toward social science as a way of understanding the impact of media on society is nothing new. Scholars from a variety of disciplines have all contributed to a long tradition of "media effects" research that investigates how exposure to different forms of media (television, video games, music, etc.) can influence the attitudes and behaviours of its audience. Many of these studies are based on self-report survey data that allow researchers to examine how consumers and nonconsumers of certain media differ on what are thought to be related measures, such as aggression or fear of crime.

These media effects studies could easily be adopted to examine the various outcomes of watching *CSI*. If we wanted to know whether or not the show is changing the way viewers think about forensics, we could administer a survey to a random sample of people and ask them about the amount of exposure they have to *CSI* and their general attitudes toward forensic science and technology. For example, we could ask participants how often they think forensic evidence is used in real criminal cases, or to rate, on a scale of 1 to 5, the likelihood that certain forensic tools could generate false results. Then, controlling for other factors that may explain our findings (e.g., gender, age, race, education), we could see how viewers of *CSI* compare with nonviewers on these indicators. If the difference between the two groups is "statistically-significant," we could reject the "null hypothesis" that watching *CSI* has no effect on people's attitudes toward forensics and, instead, accept the premise that a *CSI* effect is taking place.

Of even greater interest would be assessing what these images of forensics mean for various aspects of criminal justice. Given our present concern that the show is producing science-savvy jurors, we could conduct a study that examines how exposure to *CSI* can influence jury decision making. Like much of the research being done within the field of law and psychology (e.g., Ogloff & Vidmar, 1994), we could run a mock trial that would allow us to compare the ways in which viewers differ from nonviewers in regards to how they may act as jurors in a courtroom.

THE PROBLEMS WITH EFFECTS RESEARCH

Still, it may be unwise for us to believe that empirical studies can end this debate by giving us definitive answers about whether *CSI* is distorting how viewers understand forensics. Instead, it is important that we remain cautious of social scientists' findings that "prove" that a *CSI* effect exists. Social science research is always limited, and, as such, it is imperative that we consider these limitations when assessing the validity of a study's results.

One of the major problems with social science research is the tendency to confuse correlation with causation. To say that two variables are correlated means that an observed change in X occurs *simultaneously* and is *associated* with an observed change in Y. Causation, on the other hand, implies a very different type of relationship in which some change in X has *caused* a change in Y. However, critics often fail to make this distinction when they talk about a *CSI* effect. In fact, the very use of the term "effect" connotes a causal relationship.

This assumption of causality is problematic for several reasons. On a methodological level, it is impossible to infer causality on the basis of correlation alone (McCall, 1994, p. 155). Consequently, we should never accept a researcher's proposition that *CSI* watching is what *causes* individuals to have greater faith in the capabilities of forensics or that this relationship *produces* more findings of guilt when such evidence is produced at trial. While it is tempting to assume that media consumption can generate these outcomes, it is important to recognize that this is only one possible causal relationship. An equally valid way of explaining this correlation would be to suggest that the strong belief in forensics is what *drives* these individuals to watch *CSI*. So, rather than being the cause, watching programs like *CSI* may actually be the effect.

Another plausible explanation is that a third variable has produced the *CSI* effects we are presently witnessing. For example, one could argue that the need to generate forensic evidence at trial and the sudden outbreak of science-savvy jurors are not caused by watching *CSI*, but can be directly attributed to criminal defence lawyers and their legal strategizing. Indeed, defence attorneys are using the popularity of *CSI* to gain a legal advantage for their clients in a number of ways. For instance, jury consultants are now being hired by the defence to help select jurors who watch shows like *CSI* and are therefore assumed to be more likely to spot the absence of forensic evidence in the prosecution's case (Willing, 2004). At trial, these lawyers are also beginning to exploit the lack of scientific proof to plant doubt in the jury's mind, even when there are eyewitness accounts, confessions, or other forms of compelling evidence (Stockwell, 2005). Thus, by using *CSI* watching as a point of reference for jury selection and trial preparation, it may be cunning lawyers and not naïve TV viewers who are transporting the distorted pictures of forensics into the courtroom and transforming the *CSI* effect into a legal reality.

The argument presented here is not solely a methodological one, however. In addition, this critique points to more conceptual and theoretical problems that underlie the assumption that *CSI* is the cause of current criminal justice. The notion that media shape how individuals think and act paints a fairly determinist picture of human action. Human beings, unable to separate fact from fiction and void of free will, are therefore viewed by advocates of the *CSI* effect as automatons whose behaviour is dictated by what they see on TV.

Again, it is important that we consider others ways of thinking about our connection to media. Rather than seeing ourselves as cultural dupes and the *passive* recipients of the messages presented on television, we need to look at how various actors are *actively* taking up these representations for different purposes. As I have already argued, the *CSI* effect that is happening in the courtroom may be the result of lawyers who purposely draw upon the show's popularity when building their cases. Criminal attorneys, however, are not the only ones who may be "riding the *CSI* bandwagon" in pursuing their own interests. It is possible that various forensic science and criminology departments are also reinventing themselves in light of *CSI* to attract prospective students.[2] So, while the popularity of the show may have a lot to do with the increasing number of people enrolling in these programs, we cannot ignore what schools are doing to help fuel this demand.

WHAT EXACTLY ARE WE MEASURING?

It is hard to deny that the current trends in criminal justice have coincided with the rising popularity of forensic crime dramas. Yet, the ways in which this relationship between audience and media operates may not be as one-sided or deterministic as some commentators claim. As I have suggested, the connections we are seeing may be attributed to other intervening variables that we have not previously considered. It may also be that what we are witnessing and calling a *CSI* effect is something larger and beyond the purview of any single media effects study. In particular, it is possible that other "rival plausible explanations" (Palys, 2004) account for both the popularity of *CSI* as well as the recent trends in crime and justice.

The inability to see these broader factors is an inherent limitation in effects research and the attempt to purify the relationship between media and audience. These studies try control for all other explanatory factors, so that any changes in our variable of interest (e.g., aggression, fear of crime) can be solely attached to media exposure. However, in trying to isolate media effects in this way, we often overlook the larger context that frames our exposure to media. Indeed, we need to consider a variety of social, political, technological, and cultural trends that contextualize the *CSI* phenomenon. Specifically, we must view the *CSI* effect in relation to the larger shifts occurring in criminal justice.

THE BROADER CHANGES IN CRIMINAL JUSTICE

Since the late 1960s, critics in North America have questioned the state's ability to deal with crime. Despite the vast amounts of public spending on policing and corrections, crime rates continued to increase over the last 40 years (see Garland, 2001). Various studies also revealed that police were far less capable of preventing, deterring, and apprehending criminals than was previously assumed, and that rehabilitation and treatment programs offered in prisons had little to no effect on rates of recidivism (Garland, 2001).

This same period also saw greater attention paid to the systemic and overt forms of racism that permeated the criminal justice system. In both Canada and the United States, critics began pointing to the overrepresentation of visible minorities in prison as evidence that criminal law was being unequally applied to certain segments of the population. This claim was in addition to the serious charges of police brutality and misconduct made by different minority groups. Certainly, within the last 20 years a number of high-profile cases have kept these issues of racism and abuse in the media spotlight.

In addition, we have also begun to witness a greater reliance on forensic science within criminal justice. While it is not used to the same extent as on TV, forensics has become more common in criminal investigations. Yet, prior to *CSI*, the value of forensics was not so much in its ability to identify suspects, but in how it could be used to vindicate the wrongfully convicted. In Canada, for instance, the wrongful convictions of Donald Marshall Jr., David Milgaard, and Guy Paul Morin were all overturned with the use of DNA evidence.

A recent judicial inquiry led by former Supreme Court of Canada justice Antonio Lamer was conducted into how the criminal justice system in Newfoundland and Labrador failed Greg Parsons, Randy Druken, and Ronald Dalton. All three were convicted of murder but later exonerated or found not guilty after appeal with the help of DNA testing. In his report, Lamer accused both the police and the prosecution of "fostering a culture of tunnel vision in its investigations" ("Lamer Assails," 2006). Lamer's claim that a "culture" of tunnel vision was at the heart of these miscarriages of justice speaks to the human side of the judicial system. More troubling is the fact that without the aid of forensic science, these wrongs might have never been corrected.

We therefore find ourselves in an interesting era for criminal justice, one in which our faith in the efficacy and fairness of the system is being seriously tested. At the same time, we have started to put more trust in the infallibility of forensics and the neutrality and proficiency of forensic experts. Aware that our search for justice remains a predominantly social endeavour that is always subject to human error, we now appear to be looking to scientists as the final arbiters of "truth."

This reliance on science is not limited to crime and justice. From testing unborn babies for potential birth defects to using home drug kits to determine drug use by a child, we have looked toward science and technology for answers to a variety of questions. Within popular culture, our fascination with science and technology as a way of arriving at the truth is not restricted to TV crime dramas. The talk show *Maury*, for example, has become infamous for its episodes that reveal the results of DNA paternity tests on the air.

To summarize, by looking at the *CSI* effect within the broader social, cultural, political, and technological landscape, we are presented with very different ways of understanding our relationship with media. Rather than being caused by *CSI*, , recent trends in criminal justice could be symptomatic of much larger changes. The growing number of jurors demanding forensic evidence at trial may have more to do with a lack of public confidence or general mistrust of those who work within the criminal justice system than with the popularity of a TV show. Conversely, this dependence on forensic evidence may be attributed to our faith in science and the ability of scientists to reveal certain "truths" about the world. Either way, we are left with a set of rival plausible explanations that cannot be easily ignored.

WHERE DO WE GO FROM HERE?

Instead of trying to present evidence that can somehow "prove" that the *CSI* effect does not exist, this chapter has pointed to the dangers of studying the connection between media and audiences as a simple matter of "cause and effect." I have tried to demonstrate that approaching the *CSI* phenomenon in this way, and trying to purify the links between exposure to media and a variety of outcomes, blinds us from thinking about these issues within the broader contexts in which they take place. If our goal is to better understand our relationship with media, then we need to avoid this oversimplification and stop thinking about media exposure as if it takes place within an experimental vacuum removed from the larger social world. Rather than asking about *what effects* the popularity of *CSI* has produced, we need to pose more fruitful questions for discussion that explore *how* these representations of forensic science and technology are being used to *effect* certain changes and, more importantly, *where* this *CSI* phenomenon fits within our society.

References

Cole, S., & Dioso, R. (2005, May 13). Law and the lab. *The Wall Street Journal*, p. W13.

The CSI Effect. (2005, March 21). *CBS News*. Retrieved May 25, 2005, from http://www.cbsnews.com/stories/2005/03/21/earlyshow/main681949.shtml

Garland, D. (2001). *The culture of control: Crime and social order in contemporary society*. Chicago: University of Chicago Press.

Lamer assails "tunnel vision" in justice system. (2006, June 21). *CBC News*. Retrieved June 21, 2006, from http://www.cbc.ca/canada/newfoundland-labrador/story/2006/06/21/nf-lamer-marshall-20060621.html

Lovgren, S. (2004, September 23). "CSI effect" is mixed blessing for real crime labs. *National Geographic News*. Retrieved May 24, 2005, from http://news.nationalgeographic.com/news/2004/09/0923_040923_csi.html

McCall, R. (1994). *Fundamental statistics for behavioral sciences* (6th ed.). Toronto: Harcourt Brace College.

Milicia, J. (2006, January 31). "CSI effect" provides criminals help in cover ups. *Iowa State Daily*. Retrieved May 15, 2006, from http://www.iowastatedaily.com/media/storage/paper818/news/2006/01/31/Pulse/csi-Effect.Provides.Criminals.Help.In.Cover.Ups-1544826.shtml?norewrite200606261126&sourcedomain=www.iowastatedaily.com

Ogloff, J., & Vidmar, N. (1994). The impact of pretrial publicity on jurors: A study to compare the relative effects of television and print media in a child sex abuse case. *Law and Human Behavior, 18*(5), 507–525.

Palys, T. (2004). *Research decision: Quantitative and qualitative perspectives*. Toronto: Thomson Nelson.

Stockwell, J. (2005, May 29). Jurors want CSI-quality forensic evidence. *San Francisco Chronicle*. Retrieved May 29, 2005, from http://www.sfgate.com/cgi-bin/article.cgi?file=/c/a/2005/05/29/MNGTTCSVTD10.DTL

Willing, R. (2004, August 5). "CSI effect" has juries wanting more evidence. *USA Today*. Retrieved May 24, 2005, from http://www.usatoday.com/news/nation/2004-08-05-csi-effect_x.htm

Notes

[1] Legal commentators cite the Robert Blake murder trial as a prime example of how the *CSI* effect has entered the courtroom. One analyst claims that, despite more than one witness testifying that Blake had asked him to kill his wife, the defendant was found not guilty because the prosecution could not show the jury blood evidence or conclusive gunshot residue ("The CSI Effect," 2005). As jury foreperson Thomas Nicholson said after the trial, "[The prosecution] couldn't put the gun in his hand.… There was no blood splatter. They had nothing." Coincidentally, it was reported that at least half of the jurors selected for this case said they regularly watched shows like *CSI* ("The CSI Effect," 2005).

[2] At Carleton University, a new ArtsOne Program has been created to provide first-year B.A. students with a more intimate learning environment. Students who register in this program must apply to one of six different "clusters," which revolve around different academic themes. One of these clusters, aimed at students intending to pursue a major in law and/or criminology, is called "Beyond *CSI*: Perspectives on Criminology and Criminal Justice."

Discussion Questions

1. How is forensic science and technology typically represented in popular media? Are forensic experts on fictional crime dramas like *CSI* usually right or wrong in their analysis of evidence? What are the possible implications of these sorts of portrayals?

2. Can media effects research tell us for certain that the *CSI* effect truly exists? Why or why not?

3. Are there dangers in thinking about media exposure and the potential impact it may have on audiences as simply a matter of cause and effect? What are the possible limitations in viewing the relationship between media and audience in this way? Why is it necessary to think about this relationship between media and audience within the larger social, political, and cultural contexts in which they exist?

4. How would you define the *CSI* effect?

5. Do you think there is sufficient evidence to conclude that there is a *CSI* effect in Canada?

6. Do you think the *CSI* effect is a pressing issue for the Canadian legal system? Why or why not?

ISSUE 3

The self-help society: Has pop psychology gone too far?

✔ YES

The Detachable Self: Media Advice Giving and Social Control
Graham Knight

Graham Knight is Chair of the Department of Communication Studies & Multimedia at McMaster University in Hamilton, Ontario. His research interests include political communication, media activism, and media representations of social problems. Among other venues, his published work on these topics has appeared in the *Australian Journal of Communication*, *Social Movement Studies*, *Communication and Critical/Cultural Studies*, *Management Communication Quarterly*, *European Journal of Communication*, and *Canadian Journal of Communication*.

Wherever you look in the media you find an extensive and diverse array of advice. Some of this advice takes the form of generalized information and instruction, such as how to save and invest for a secure retirement or "street-proof" your children. Some of this advice is specific, a response to those with particular personal problems that nonetheless have broad social resonance and relevance. This is the kind of therapeutic advice that emanates from TV talk shows, self-help books, and advice columns in newspapers, in magazines, and on the Internet. This type of advice is geared to assisting those who have suffered harm, loss, or some other kind of personal difficulty to come to terms with their experiences and repair the damage these experiences have left. Sometimes advice is directed to problems that individuals bring on themselves as a result of risky lifestyles and behaviours. And sometimes advice is addressed to issues that people face as a result of the behaviour or choices of others around them.

What does all this advice giving tell us about ourselves and our society, and what does it indicate about the role and impact of communications media in our lives? To address these questions, this chapter will begin by outlining the salient features of media advice giving. The discussion will then focus on the ways that advice giving reinforces social control and how, in turn, it contributes to significant changes in the ways that **social control** functions as contemporary society becomes more individualistic. Media advice giving reflects the fact that social control does not simply restrain us from the outside, but reaches inside us, shaping our self-identity, motivation, and understanding. Through advice giving, social control is internalized: it becomes self-control. This is not simply a rational process based on the calculation of self-interest or social obligation. It is also an emotional process that involves how we feel about ourselves and our actions. Social control mobilizes certain emotions as the means to control other emotions and shape the way we behave. These changes, in turn, point to the growing importance of communications media as a vehicle of social control that conveys a socially idealized view of how modern individuals should conduct themselves, relate to one another, and take charge of who they are.

THE SOCIAL IMPLICATIONS OF MEDIA ADVICE GIVING

Despite its extensiveness and diversity, advice giving in the media has several common character-istics. First, advice implies that life is problematic. Social theorists have long characterized modern society as one in which people generally act in rational, calculating ways. We constantly see things as problematic, in need of improvement or repair, and this view predisposes us to seeking out knowledge and information that will help us make the necessary changes. Second, media advice giving is usually directed at individuals rather than groups, organizations, or other collective actors. Advice giving tends to adopt a personalized approach to understanding and addressing problems; as a result, the central condition for resolving problems is that the individual become self-reliant and self-activating. Third, successful advice giving entails the internalization of social control. By acting on the recommendations, suggestions, proposals, and step-by-step programs through which the media promise a better life, we not only transform our actions to conform with prevailing social values, but we also come to identify with and believe in those values and exercise self-restraint on their terms. The values inherent in advice give us a way to legitimate, justify, and explain ourselves and our actions, and accounting is the fundamental premise of control.

At first sight the relationship between these three characteristics of media advice giving—problematization, individualism, and social control—seems to be paradoxical. If we think of social control as the way society ensures conformity with institutionalized expectations of behav-iour, then the restlessness and discontent that come from constantly problematizing the world would seem to undermine rather than reinforce this process. Similarly, by promoting an indi-vidualistic attitude to resolving problems, advice giving may subvert social control by encourag-ing the priority of personal needs and self-interest over social conformity. In practice, however, advice giving enhances social control rather than weakening it. To understand how this process occurs, we need to recognize that the relationship between problematization, individualism, and social control reflects important changes in how social life is defined and structured and how it functions. As social life changes, so too does the nature and functioning of social control.

In the last 25 years or so the growing use of terms such as "postindustrial society," "postmodernism," "late modernity," and "reflexive modernity" indicates that modern society is changing in significant ways. The image of society as a stable set of institutions; mutually compatible, shared values and norms; and reliable, familiar roles, identities, opportunities, and biographies has been increasingly been brought into question. Modern society is now widely seen as becoming more fluid, institutions less stable, and identities and life experiences less routine. Social life is becoming more individualized, traditional patterns of behaviour and expectation are being eroded or modified, and the social contexts where we enact our roles and establish our identities are becoming more contingent—open to new possibilities and challenges, whose value or direction may be unclear. These changes do not make life any less social, but they do open up social life to negotiation and reconstruction. This openness stimulates the growing supply of and demand for advice and makes the process of self-improvement and self-help increasingly dependent on communication generally and the media in particular. The media have become an especially significant vehicle for popularizing advice giving on the part of professional experts (e.g., Dr. Phil) whose influence has become more far reaching as the authority of traditional sources of advice giving, institutions such as the family and religion, has waned. At the same time, media such as the Internet have also become a forum for criticizing and challenging the authority of experts, as well as a source of alternative advice giving derived from experience and based on commonsense knowledge.

As a result of these changes in social life, social control functions more and more through individuals rather than imposing itself on them or against them. The assumption that there is tension or conflict between the individual and society has always been misplaced, but even more so in contemporary society where **individualization** is a prominent feature of social change. The individual is the agent rather than merely the target of social control, and advice giving becomes an important part of how this agency is enacted. Social control functions by inducing individuals to reflect on themselves and their problems, to take responsibility for themselves and their lives, and to work out socially acceptable courses of action to resolve these problems and enhance or improve their mental, physical, and social well-being. This process whereby individuals internalize the gaze of others and assume responsibility for their own social control can be illustrated best by looking more closely at the kind of advice giving directed at self-help, advice that responds to those who have specific personal problems such as addiction, abusive relationships, body image issues, or psychosomatic disorders. These are the kinds of problems and advice giving that figure centrally in TV talk shows like *Dr. Phil* and *Oprah*; radio and television advice shows such as *Dr. Ruth* that deal with sexual, health, family, and other lifestyle matters; self-help books like the Chicken Soup series; and even themes in fictional media such as soap operas and crime dramas.

MAKE A SCENE: THE CONFESSIONAL-THERAPEUTIC NATURE OF MEDIA ADVICE GIVING

A system of social control that operates through rather than on or against individuals has two important implications for understanding how advice giving works. The first is that social control is best seen as a circular rather than linear process. It is not unusual to think of social control as a top-down process of constraint in which social institutions like governments or corporations use their power to promote and enforce socially acceptable standards of behaviour. It is certainly true that the content of these standards tends to represent the interests and values of dominant classes and other privileged groups, and that top-down control does occur. The heavy hand of the law has far from disappeared altogether. Most of the time and for the majority of people, however, social control functions as a circular process, passing continuously through individuals, groups, organizations, and institutions without any definite or fixed point of origin or destination. Individuals are themselves as much the agents of social control as institutions are, and institutions are as much the object of control as individuals—each is both a recipient and a donor. Control is not a relation of confrontation but one of partnership; control does not stand outside individuals but implicates itself in them, in their thoughts, identities, and lives. For control to be successful and continuous, individuals must not only conform with accepted standards, they must identify with them as their own. Individuals have to know what is legitimate and to believe in it and feel it too.

The second implication, therefore, is that individual psychology—the individual's cognitive, emotional, and evaluative capacities—is assumed to be the wellspring of behaviour. If the object of social control is to manage problems that threaten or disrupt accepted standards or norms, then these problems are assumed to be ultimately a matter of individual psychology. This does not mean that social forces such as poverty, social insecurity, or racism are ignored as contributing causal factors, but it does mean that individual psychology tends to be seen as the primary locus for resolving or remedying these problems. Social control that works through individuals lends itself to a primarily **therapeutic model** of problem resolution: problems are resolved by curing troubled and/or troubling individuals at the psychological level. Much of the media advice giving directed at self-help is therapeutic in effect. Its aim is to encourage and enable individuals to help themselves by recognizing their true inner self; how their current self is flawed or vulnerable; how their problems have arisen as a result of these flaws or vulnerabilities; and how they can begin to take the necessary steps to resolve these problems by strengthening themselves psychologically. Advice giving is directed at revealing to individuals what they are capable of becoming based on who they already are. It works to create a self that will no longer be susceptible, dependent, fragile, erratic, gullible, and so on—in other words, a self that will be in control.

Some form of psychotherapy, then, is central to advice giving directed at specific problems that are the staple diet of media forums like TV talk shows (cf. Cloud, 1998; Lowney, 1999; Shattuc, 1997; White 1990). And as the talk show label itself makes clear, a major part of the therapeutic process is talk itself. Therapy is first and foremost about communication. It is not incidental that psychoanalysis, one of the main branches of the "psy" complex of psychologically oriented therapies, was known as the "talking cure." The significance of communication is that it is the principal link between problem and resolution or remedy. In one sense this is obvious, as advice giving is a purely discursive process. Advice giving provides people with information, instructing them, admonishing them, encouraging them, directing them, and so on. But the primary act of communication is not through the advice giver (whether a professional expert, program host, or audience member), but the individual to whom advice is directed. For the therapeutic process to work, individuals must reveal themselves, talk about who they are, confess their problems or sins, and explain why they act in the ways they do. Individuals must be able to identify their thoughts and feelings about themselves and others, explain what they hope to achieve, and understand why they have come forward to make their private lives public.

Advice giving, then, entails a therapeutic model of remedy and also rests on a **confessional model** of problem identification. The therapeutic form of advice giving can begin only once the individual engages in a public act of self-admission. Self-admission concerns matters that are not only troubling or problematic, but also transgressive or in some way morally dubious. Even though the recipient of advice is often a victim of some kind, victimhood is itself a morally suspect condition. Victims may evoke public sympathy to some extent, but the assumption is that victimhood should not become a permanent identity. There is a stigma that quickly attaches to victimhood if the victim does not take appropriate action to rectify the situation, and the prospect of this stigma becomes a powerful incentive to act. Overcoming victimhood, therefore, is one of the central goals of therapeutic advice; admitting that one is a victim—if only a self-inflicted one—is the first step toward recovery and the development of a normal self and life. Confessing one's true self in the present is the key to becoming a better self in the future.

This transgressive dimension makes public confession difficult to some extent, particularly in a culture that values the distinction between private life and public knowledge. A large part of this difficulty relates to the way that the internalization of social control has depended on our ability to learn how to restrain the open display of feelings and emotionally charged behaviour we might otherwise exhibit. Problems are experienced emotionally, but the unrestrained expression of emotion is itself problematic because it threatens to disrupt behavioural expectations. In his theory of the "civilizing process," sociologist Norbert Elias (1978) argued that a central feature of the development of modern society that began in Europe at the end of the Middle Ages was growing social pressure on individuals to exercise emotional self-restraint in their interactions with others. This was particularly so in the case of negative emotions such as anger, fear, or hatred, which give rise to displays of violence; but it also applied to expressions of positive emotions such as joy or affection. For Elias this change came about as society became more differentiated, diverse, and complex. The result, Elias argued, was that the consequences of people's actions travelled further, touching the lives of others outside the immediate circle of those familiar and close to them. Therefore, actions charged with strong emotions became potentially more disruptive and threatening.

This finding led Elias to note that one emotion could control all others: shame. Social control was thus internalized and inculcated through shame. When we begin to give in to our emotions, shame intercedes to activate self-restraint and allow cooler heads to prevail. "Don't make a scene" was the motto of the shameful self. Shame became the hinge that joined normative standards of social behaviour on the one hand and the social control of personal emotions on the other. However, confession, the precondition for successful advice giving, means that the individual must overcome feelings of shame that public disclosure of personal problems might entail. "Make a scene" is the message that advice-giving media now communicate, a message that can easily result in outlandish, carnival-like behaviour, as talk shows like *Jerry Springer* illustrate.

Feeling reserved, reticent, or ashamed impedes the need to confess that is the initial step to self-help and a better life. In this respect, the confessional-therapeutic model of media advice giving would seem to contradict one of the basic premises on which the internalization of social control in modern society has been based. What has happened, however, is not that self-restraint has been significantly undermined, but rather that shame has been supplemented or even replaced by another meta-emotion as the internal regulator of feelings and behaviour: anxiety. Rather than control ourselves out of shame, we increasingly control ourselves out of anxiety. Shame and anxiety differ, however, in how they function. Shame implies a clear understanding of what norms, standards, and expectations are. We can feel ashamed only if we are aware that what we have done, or the situation we find ourselves in, involves some element of transgression and the stigma that attaches to this. Shame can work only in a context of shared certainty. Anxiety, on the other hand, implies uncertainty and what this suggests in terms of insecurity, ambiguity, and ambivalence. We feel anxious when we are unsure of our actions and the situations in which we act, when the expectations or consequences are unclear and subject to change, when we are faced with difficult choices. Anxiety, therefore, is likely to become more prominent as the social world is opened up to negotiation and reconstruction, and social life becomes more uncertain. Faced with a growing array of possibilities, anxiety plays a greater role than shame as an emotional agent of self-restraint.

THE DETACHABLE SELF: THE SOCIAL IMPLICATIONS OF CONFESSIONAL-THERAPEUTIC ADVICE

One of the factors that feeds into the creation of anxiety is not only the constant reminder that our selves and lives need improvement, but also the endless stream of corrective advice on offer in the media from different experts, each of whom has a particular perspective or theory and, as often as not, a book, course, or some kind of plan to market. This advice is often inconsistent if not contradictory, and this has certainly led to the backlash against professional experts and the development of alternative sources of advice giving, especially via the Internet. But the overall effect is simply to add to the total volume of advice that is available. While this diversity of advice may be confusing and only serve to compound anxiety about what should be done, the central (albeit implicit) message remains fairly constant: you need to think about how your life is problematic, and you need to take charge to help yourself change. Don't be satisfied with who you already are.

The self is seen from this perspective as an endless project on the rocky road to improvement, but the motor force of this movement lies within the self and not within society. While your problems may result in part from the actions (or inactions) of others, you can find and implement the solutions to these problems only from within. Dr. Phil's advice about "discovering your life chain" to "make your self matter" is suggestive here.

> Just think about where you were born, what family you were born into, and who you grew up around. You simply became part of a long chain—its links consisting of your parents, your grandparents and your siblings. Consider the momentum that this chain created—the messages and expectations that passed from one link to the next, through generations. That chain sealed much of the fate that was to be yours. You did not have the slightest choice about the links in your life chain, but you do have a choice in what you do now! ("Self Matters," 2006)

As Dr. Phil's advice suggests, you may feel aggrieved by society—and blaming others can be temporarily therapeutic—but dwelling on grievances only solidifies a victim identity that will not get you very far and will serve in the long run to reinforce psychological weakness, dependency, or vulnerability. Individuals have only themselves to rely on, and the goal of self-help and self-improvement is to strengthen the self to the point where it is effectively self-sustaining, well armoured, and independent. It is only on the basis of psychological self-reliance that people can enter into relationships with others, since self-reliant individuals can easily detach themselves once there is a hint the relationship might go awry.

The detachable self is one that depoliticizes the resolution of problems through a process of deep individualization. From the confessional-therapeutic perspective, society comprises little more than simply other individuals with their own troubles, difficulties, and flaws, who should, if they follow advice, be likewise engaged in their own projects of self-help and self-improvement. Looking to others to assist with problem resolution is futile; they are chiefly a mirror of what shouldn't be done. Any view of society as a system of institutions with resources such as power and money that can be mobilized to address the structural causes of social problems—racism, sexism, inequality, social exclusion—effectively goes missing from the hyperindividualism of the confessional-therapeutic view of the world. Making collective demands on society—adopting a political stance, in other words—falls far off the radar screen of media advice giving. If you have a difficult relationship with your boss, then look to yourself, your own attitude and personality, your way of relating to authority figures, your emotional tendencies, but don't join a labour union—that's the advice the "psy" expert will likely give. By the same token, what is also largely absent from this worldview is any recognition of society as a community in which individuality is sustained through relationships of mutuality, commitment, and solidarity with others. Don't join a labour union, but also don't talk to your co-workers about the need for a collective response to offset the power of those who are in charge.

The conception of sociality at the heart of media advice giving is best described in terms of networks rather than institutions or communities. Like the detachable selves that advice giving implies, networks are flexible, mobile, and light; they are based on rational or instrumental calculations of benefit and cost. Networks come and go, they form, reform, and deform without significant difficulty and leave little trace of their past presence. Institutions and communities, on the other hand, are heavy, ponderous, and slow to change. They entail enduring structures, identities, relationships, and commitments, and this does not make them conducive to individualized problem solving. In a society of networks, the ideal individual serves the interests of social control by making personal problems and grievances public, solutions individualized and personal, and affiliation with others flexible, mobile, and detachable. For now, though, this ideal remains a fiction, the imaginary construct of the media's confessional-therapeutic advice giving. Individuals continue to look to institutional and communal means to resolve their problems collectively, make collective demands, take collective action, develop collective identities, and engage in social relations that entail more than the calculus of self-benefit or cost. For all that the media are omnipresent, they are not yet omnipotent.

References

Cloud, D. (1998). *Control and consolation in American culture and politics: Rhetoric of therapy*. London: Sage.

Elias, N. (1978). *The history of manners: The civilizing process* (Vol. I, E. Jephcott, Trans.). New York: Urizen Books.

Lowney, K. (1999). *Baring our souls: TV talk shows and the religion of recovery*. New York: Aldine de Gruyter.

Self matters: Discover your life chain. (2006). *DrPhil.com*. Retrieved November 10, 2006, from http://www.drphil.com/articles/article/86

Shattuc, J. (1997). *The talking cure: TV talk shows and women*. New York: Routledge.

White, M. (1990). *Tele-advising: Therapeutic discourse in American television*. Chapel Hill & London: University of North Carolina Press.

ISSUE 3

The Self-help society: Has pop psychology gone too far?

✗ NO

The snap, crackle, and pop in pop psychology
Michael Dorland

Michael Dorland is professor of communication in the School of Journalism and Communication at Carleton University. Author of many books and articles, for the past five years he has done research in and taught the history of psychoanalysis.

Has pop psychology gone too far?

No, it hasn't, for reasons that will become clear below. But first, let's establish what we're talking about here. What do we mean by "pop psychology"? By pop psychology, we mean people like Oprah, Dr. Phil, the shelves of self-help books you can find at your local Chapters; these are people watched by and read by millions to learn how to deal with their life problems. You could call them shrinks for those who can't afford to pay for "real" ones. How such people came to command the respect they do is the subject of this chapter. And what's "too far"? If we are referring to such phenomena as the rash of so-called demonic child abuse cases in U.S. daycares some years ago, in which adults were imprisoned on the say-so of utterly improbable stories by young children who were coached by "caregivers," this points to problems that need to be better understood. Same with so-called false memory syndrome, in which countless women, also coached by "caregivers," suddenly seem to remember being raped as small children by their fathers, uncles, etc. You might think that these two examples prove that pop psychology has *not* gone too far. But they don't. On the contrary, they speak eloquently to the degree to which the psychological actions of human beings remain a mystery. Why people claim to think or recall what they imagine might have once happened to them—in other words, what goes on in people's heads or minds—is why what we loosely call "psychology" emerged as a science some hundred-plus years ago.

To speak, then, of a science of the mind or soul (which is what the "psych" part—from the Greek word "psyche"—of such concepts as psychology or psychoanalysis refers to) implies several things. For one, the problem of the "psyche" has been a puzzle for human beings for millennia, and such things as religion and literature have been ways of understanding the psyche for about as long. But we live, and have done so for several centuries now, in a time defined by the term "science," or a form of knowledge that is believed to be more accurate than any other form of knowledge. Science, or so the story goes, is reliable. It is not "made up" like literature. It has rules or methods that serve to guarantee its accuracy, if often in a statistical sense: under certain conditions, this will be considered "true" within a margin of error of x or y percent. Or until such time as we get a different result.

That said, however, one of the big differences between sciences is that some are considered to be more scientific than others. It's one thing to deal with physical things, like rocks or planets, or even less obviously physical things, like chemical processes. It's rather different when what a science claims to study involves human beings. Here again, it depends a lot on what part of the human being is being studied. If it's a matter of human anatomy, that's one thing: a broken leg can be fixed, an organ removed. One can even peer inside the human body with remarkable sophistication, and in there do some pretty extraordinary repairing. But it becomes a lot trickier when dealing with those less visible parts of human beings, such as emotions, feelings, what makes us happy or unhappy. We can't see an emotion, but we can see the physical results of an emotion: a sad person looks sad or cries. Why that person is sad or crying is harder to say. An adult or at least a human with speech can say why they think they are sad; it's harder with children and even more so with people who are in such a state of agitation or distress that either they can no longer explain what's wrong or they are hurting themselves as a substitute for voicing pain. And while it's hard enough to deal with just one adult person, it gets even more complicated with the groups that people tend to come in—families, tribes, social classes, nationalities, and so on. Each of group leaves a psychic imprint of some kind on the individuals that make up the group, and each in different ways. Why, within the same family, do siblings manifest different personality traits?

Questions such as these, and others, led to the rise of the human or social sciences, especially sociology and psychology, in the course of the 19th century. These are the bodies of knowledge that attempt to explain human actions and motivations either individually or in the many groups and subgroups that make up what we call "society." This is an extremely vague word, since its covers all types of social organization, from families to kinship groups, corporations, cities, and everything in between, up to such vast social processes we blithely refer to as "globalization." In the course of time, the human sciences, despite their many continuing problems, have also developed sophisticated, specialized ways—called "expertise"—in dealing with what they do. You don't become an expert overnight, except maybe on TV. It requires long years of study to master often very specialized ways to talk about things—think of medical doctors as portrayed on TV with their " 6ccs of epi, IV push" and batteries of complicated tests.

Two other aspects are worth noting about living in a predominantly scientific culture. The first is that science is, as sociologist Max Weber put it, "disenchanting" (1904/1958). Scientific explanations of things are often so complicated that only another scientist can understand them—which leaves everybody else feeling like dummies. You don't know what they are talking about, and it's even more unnerving if they are talking about you! Second, because each science has its own specialized language or jargon, you need someone who knows both the jargon and ordinary language to explain it to you. Think of all the "For Dummies" books. This process of "translating" a specialized language into language more people can understand is called scientific vulgarization, or popularization, from which we get the word "pop," as in pop psychology. It's got nothing to do with music and much more to do with a term like "pop culture," which is another way of asking what happens to the general culture when what sits atop it and basically defines the language is a specialized culture of expertise jargon.

So the next obvious question is this: if we live in a culture of expertise that only the experts themselves understand properly (and often even they don't), what if these expert cultures filter down into the more general or popular culture? Since what is involved is a process of translation, how accurate is it? And what happens if it's a really bad translation? And how to know? Basically, you can't. You have to take somebody's word for it. Or just believe what you read, which is always risky. A further problem is the rise of subexperts (journalists and the like) who try to translate what they think the expert-experts are saying into ordinary language. But how reliable are they? Some certainly can become very popular and widely read. Think of someone like "Dear Abby," whose newspaper column of advice about marriage, relationships, and sex was translated into over 50 languages throughout the world. What she did to make sure she wasn't talking through her hat was first consult other experts. It's the same with people like Oprah or Dr. Phil on TV today. It becomes a form of vicious circle, and the problem as always is how to know if you are getting reliable information. Since this flood of expertise also began to take place with the rise of the modern media of newspaper journalism, then radio and TV, and now the Internet, we're basically drowning in information whose reliability is uncertain. And who has the time to check it all out to make sure? When an Internet search gives you a million hits on a topic, how much of that will you actually look at? So it becomes not only a knowledge problem but a communication problem as well.

Ultimately, the real issue here concerns the sources of moral authority. Who do we turn to not just for "information" but for answers to questions of right and wrong actions? Let's say you're "depressed" (we all know vaguely what that means), and let's say that part of your depression involves the idea of killing yourself, and this idea won't go away. What do you do, or what's the right thing to do? Some people might say, so you want to kill yourself, go ahead. Others might say, no, you can't, it's a sin (depending on your beliefs). On one level, this is a moral question. The likelihood, however, is that you won't go see a priest or a philosopher of ethics, both of whom claim expertise on these questions. Chances are you'll go see your doctor, who may try to help or refer you to a psychiatrist. Or if it's really bad, you'll go to the hospital. How did we come to a situation where for the answer to what is a moral dilemma, we turn to medical authority, a category that includes shrinks, psychologists, etc.?

Once upon a time, the moral experts were clearly defined. Priests, rabbis, or imams were who you saw on moral matters, on matters of conscience. And they gave you spiritual advice or absolution, but they didn't often tell you to take an aspirin because they weren't medical experts. Somewhere within the past 150 years, and especially in the West, these distinctions of authority got confused as medical authority substituted itself for what used to be moral authority, and matters of conscience became the purely psychological idea of consciousness. The culture became, as another famous sociologist, Philip Reiff, first put it, a therapeutic culture (1966). If something is ailing you (either in the body or soul), there's a therapy—whether Dr. Quack's little pills, Dr. Silas Weir Mitchell's rest therapy for poor nerves, or Christian Science. The lines between what used to be religion and medical science became blurred. The kind of society and culture we live in changed, roughly, from one of "You can't do this or that" (usually because it was considered a sin) to one of "Just do it!" and especially if there is a product or service that will help you do it, whatever it is.

This change was one of great significance, and so many other factors were involved, but basically what it represented was a change in the fundamental understanding of the human "psyche" and the emergence of the "psychological" type. According to Reiff, who was one of the first to analyze this change, there have been four predominant personality types in history. The first was the political type of classical Greece that invented a way of living together we call "politics" and with this, the idea of democracy. The second type, often associated with the rise of Christendom and the other two monotheisms, Judaism and Islam, was the religious. From about the 16th to the mid-19th century, there was a third type, the rational economic type and the "invisible hand" of the market. The fourth type emerged in the time frame I've been discussing, more or less mid-19th century into the present, and is the psychological type, that is, an organization of personality driven less by moral imperatives ("Thou shalt not") than by impulses, drives, and instincts—all psychological ideas—that all loudly scream, "Thou shalt!"

Reiff was not the first to understand these changes. His work was highly influenced by lengthy study of that of Sigmund Freud (1856–1939), who was the greatest revolutionary of psychological thought of modern times, and I should briefly explain why. Freud liked to say that human consciousness over time had received three tremendous slaps to its own self-admiration. The first was when Copernicus overturned the Ptolemaic idea that "man" was at the centre of the universe, and that the planets and sun revolved around man and God's earth. The second was Darwin with his theory of evolution; the idea that we're basically evolved apes, an idea that is still immensely controversial in the United States. The third was Freud's own idea that our much-admired consciousness was only a very small part of our minds, which were largely made up of what he called "the unconscious." The unconscious was actually the source of all our secret wishes and repressed desires; the source of all our motivations and actions, most of which we were not conscious. Freud also believed that these unconscious desires manifested in coded ways in dreams and in neurotic symptoms that could be decoded through the talking cure he invented and called "psychoanalysis." That is to say, aspects of our unconscious could be brought into consciousness by the analyst, and also the patient, by careful listening to the many bizarre stories we tell ourselves as we try to explain who we are and why we do what we do. For example, "I'm fat and overeat because my mommy didn't love me," already presumes some idea of the workings of the psyche.

The thing about human beings is that we can scarcely remember the most important years of our lives—namely, those early years before we could speak or do anything much other than scream and poop our diapers, and were totally helpless little creatures, utterly dependent for all our needs on our parents. Yet even then, the infant has some consciousness, a capacity to make up stories to explain what's happening: "Wow, I'm pretty cool; I scream and Mommy comes and breastfeeds me; it's tasty plus it feels good," or words to that effect if the child could speak. We just don't remember all this information processing and mastery of motor skills, the biggest learning curve we ever experience; it all pretty much goes into the unconscious and seemingly disappears, only to return in bizarre ways such as thumb sucking.

For Freud, the child was not an innocent babe, but a bundle of desires, feelings, emotions, most of them sexual since the child's body is one vast erogenous zone. Tiny baby boys get erections, for instance. All of this, of course, was deeply shocking, and Freud was decried as a monster. What! Our children are nothing but little perverts? What! Everything we do, think, and feel is all about sex? This Freud is nothing but a quack! And yet the biggest irony of all is that Freud's ideas and often a pop version of them found their biggest reception in the United States, the first foreign country to invite him over to lecture at a university. Freud's ideas soon spread like wildfire, initially among mental health professionals; then in the growing business of advertising, always very attuned to any idea about what makes people tick; and eventually to the culture at large, in cartoons, in movies, in jokes, you name it. Freud's ideas, or some version of them, became American pop culture from the 1920s on. And soon there were more psychologists, psychiatrists, and psychoanalysts in America than anywhere in the world. America itself became the world's most advanced psychiatric society.

There was, of course, a big price to pay for all this success, not least being that Freud despised America for its vulgarity; but he needed American patients, as they paid well.

By 1975 a very smart journalist, Richard Rosen, coined a word to describe the psychologization of American society. That year, he published a book called *Psychobabble*, his term for the proliferation of once Freudian-inspired language and the many, many kinds of therapies that had popped up by then (and have only increased since), offering, as his subtitle made clear, "fast talk and quick cure in the age of feeling." For Rosen, the problem with psychobabble was not only that it had been embraced by mass-circulation magazines, novelists, and the middle class, but that it had become "an all-purpose linguistic atmosphere … that reduces psychological insight to a collection of standardized observations … a frozen lexicon to deal with an infinite variety of problems." In short, it had become part of popular language (and music). So a person was no longer just fearful, but "paranoid," a clinical term but now loosened from its context and free-floating throughout the society, turning up at parties, in conversations in subways, or in Black Sabbath hits. As Rosen put it, "confession [of whatever your emotional state or relationship problems] is the new handshake."

Rosen got many of his ideas in *Psychobabble* from a more academic book by a social historian named Russell Jacoby. In his *Social Amnesia* (1975), Jacoby offered a blistering examination of the following paradox: why had Freud's ideas, developed to free human consciousness from the shackles of the unconscious, to change the education of children to be less repressive, to understand better the miseries that marriage imposed upon women, and ultimately to liberate human sexuality from its multiple dysfunctions, been turned into their complete opposite, or what Jacoby called "conformist psychology," one of the most powerful tools ever developed to keep people "normal"?

It's a tough question, but a short answer is that when a culture becomes mainly one of feeling, fast talk, and quick cures, that is, when "it's all about me," what gets forgotten is everybody else. What gets forgotten is the social context in which ideas circulate and are communicated. Which is why pop psychology still has a long, long way to go.

References

Hale, N. G. (1971). *Freud and the Americans: The beginnings of psychoanalysis in the United States, 1876–1917.* New York: Oxford University Press.

Jacoby, R. (1975). *Social amnesia: A critique of contemporary psychology from Adler to Laing.* Boston: Beacon Press.

Reiff, P. (1966). *The triumph of the therapeutic: Uses of faith after Freud.* New York: Harper & Row.

Rosen, R. D. (1975). *Psychobabble: Fast talk and quick cure in the age of feeling.* New York: Avon Books.

Weber, M. (1958). *The Protestant ethic and the rise of capitalism* (T. Parsons, Trans.). New York: Charles Scribner's Sons. (Original work published 1904).

Discussion Questions

1. What does it mean to inhabit a "psychological" culture?

2. Science is said to be "disenchanting." How do you understand this idea?

3. If we live in a "culture of experts," who polices the experts?

4. Compare how two TV talk shows deal with a social problem that interests you. Do the two shows vary in the extent to which they rely on the confessional and therapeutic models to represent the problem and how it should be resolved?

5. How has the Internet changed the role of media advice giving? Has the Internet made people more skeptical of professional advice by giving ordinary people the opportunity to share their personal experiences and rely more on common sense as the way to solve their problems?

6. Are people controlled more by shame or anxiety when it comes to seeking out advice about how to deal with their problems?

ISSUE 4

Entertaining politics: Is it all about image?

✔ YES

More than Words: Why image matters so much in politics
Bernard Gauthier

Bernard Gauthier is a consultant and partner in a leading public relations agency in Ottawa. With more than 20 years of experience, he has counselled and trained dozens of leaders in business, the not-for-profit sector, and government on how to communicate more effectively using words, voice, body language, and clothing. He is a regular commentator on political communication and image with some of the country's leading media outlets, including CTV, CBC Radio, the *Globe and Mail*, and Global News. He has also lectured in advertising and public relations at the Carleton School of Journalism and Communication since 1998. Bernard is currently completing a Ph.D. in communication at Carleton University. His principal areas of interest include advertising history and theory, event sponsorship, the culture of professionalism, and political communication and image.

If, in the era of FDR, or even Kennedy, economists, intellectuals and engineers constituted the requisite "brain trust," today's inner circle is made up of pollsters and image consultants.... Advertising and public relations experts, pollsters and spin doctors, political consultants and cosmeticians were now beginning to script the political process itself. (Ewen & Ewen, 1992, p. 212)

Stuart and Elizabeth Ewen are only two of the many scholars who have noted and criticized the growing role of image in politics.[1] They and many others lament the work of PR professionals, spin doctors, and image consultants (I've been labelled as each of those at some point or another) and, in particular, efforts to create an ideal image for politicians by carefully managing their speeches, appearance, body language, and speaking style in an effort to win the support of the public. If politics is all about image, so the argument goes, then democracy is weakened because voters are no longer assessing policies and debating issues. Rather, we're comparing suits and falling for carefully rehearsed speeches and photo opportunities. Television, being a popular and effective way to transmit images, often gets much of the blame.[2]

This chapter will argue that modern politics is indeed largely about image. Unlike many critics, however, I won't point a finger at PR professionals, nor sound the alarm bells for the political process. Rather, I'll argue that image matters so much in politics because it's much more than surface appearances and first impressions. Rather than being overwhelmed or duped, voters make full use of what they learn by assessing a politician's image. They base their support not only on promises and policies, but also on an assessment of the person behind the promises and policies, based on qualities like body movement, clothing, speaking style, and more.

Before moving to the argument, however, it's important to define exactly what is meant by "image" in politics. Focusing on the role of image in elections, Dan Nimmo and Robert Savage (1976) offer up a concise definition that suggests a central role for communication by candidates in shaping their image. Their definition stresses that a **candidate's image** is subjective; it resides in each individual voter's mind: "the candidate's image consists of how he is perceived by voters, based on both the subjective knowledge possessed by voters and the messages projected by the candidate" (p. 9).

Image is the summary of what an individual knows and feels about a politician. That image is constantly being reshaped by new information about the politician; at the same time, the politician's image helps shape the way voters receive and interpret new messages. Lynda Lee Kaid and Mike Chanslor (2004) have a similar definition that puts more emphasis on the role of a politician's appearance. For them, image is composed of a combination of "appearance dimensions and candidate characteristics" (p. 134). Image, then, is based partly on what politicians say and do during an election campaign, and partly on how they look in the process. Kaid and Chanslor argue that by considering both what is said and how, voters construct a politician's image that includes their assessment of the politician's competence, integrity, reliability, charisma, physical attractiveness, and communication skills.

So does image—charisma, physical attractiveness, communication skills—matter all that much in politics? Do voters really assess politicians' competence, integrity, and reliability on the basis of appearance and how they speak?

MORE THAN JUST IMAGE

I would argue yes on the basis of the rich information about politicians contained in their appearance and speaking style. What many are quick to dismiss as just image is a complex system of communication we use to send messages out to others and to interpret the messages people send us. Ray L. Birdwhistell, a pioneering communications scholar[3] in the field of body motion and meaning, felt strongly that the communication that happens when one person utters words and others listen is important but is only part of a complex system. He wrote in the introduction to his book *Kinesics and Context* (1970) that "whatever 'meaning' is, it is not merely conventional understandings boxed in *words* [italics added]" (p. xii). For Birdwhistell, communication[4] between people is made possible by a layered and continuous system that includes numerous channels operating at once: an "audio" channel that transmits the words, a "kinesthetic" channel, and a "tactile" or touch channel among others (1970, p. 70).

The audio channel carries the words and sentences we speak, the tone of voice and silences we create. This complete package of sounds and silences (what Birdwhistell calls the "speech behaviour") works to create meaning (p. 27). This is why, for example, finishing a sentence (e.g., The country's economy is strong) with a rising voice changes it from a declarative statement to a question.

Kathleen Hall Jamieson studied the speech behaviour of politicians and explored how modern communication technology has profoundly changed this channel in her book *Eloquence in an Electronic Age: The Transformation of Political Speechmaking* (1988). Jamieson laments the passing of traditional speech behaviour or rhetoric from political speechmaking and describes the new qualities that ensure the success of modern politicians who use the audio channel. In particular, she notes how successful politicians now use a more conversational style of delivery more suitable for the close up and intimate space of the radio or television in the home. She also suggests that success comes with a speaking style that is intimate and reveals the autobiographical details of the individual. Jamieson demonstrates how the use of memorable phrases (e.g., George W. Bush's "Axis of Evil") is essential if a politician wants to be seen, heard, and remembered. These phrases become "capsules in which television viewers store the event" (p. 91).

Timothy Stephen, Teresa M. Harrison, William Husson, and David Albert (2004) also studied how modern politicians use the audio channel and reached many of the same conclusions as Jamieson. Using statistics rather than historical analysis, they studied the impact of voters' perceptions of the interpersonal communications styles of candidates. The authors found that the winning candidates in each of three U.S. presidential elections (1984, 1988, and 1992) were more likely to be described as "self-contained, secure, relaxed and interpersonally functional" (p. 185) in their speaking style. On the other hand, the losing candidates in each election were more likely to be described by survey respondents as "overbearing, tense, contentious, histrionic and serious" (p. 185).[5] Their analysis of the survey and election results was so compelling that the authors described the audience's perception of a candidate's speaking style as "the elemental building materials for the construction of more detailed accounts of candidates" (p. 194)—as they see it, the audio channel is where candidate images are made.

The second channel Birdwhistell describes—**kinesics**—carries all the body movements we use to express ourselves, from head movements to hand gestures and the way we plant our feet. For Birdwhistell, a seemingly simple gesture like a smile is actually a complex combination of movement in the lips, the cheeks, the muscles around the eyes, the forehead, the head, the shoulders, arms, hips, legs, and feet. Here again, the complete package on the kinesthetic channel is what helps us determine the meaning of the original movement of the lips—whether the politician's smile for the cameras signals happiness, embarrassment, or fear. Subtle differences in the kinesthetic channel can be magnified by TV cameras, making this a very powerful channel in modern politics. For example, pointing a finger at an opponent during a televised debate contributes to an angry and aggressive image. The very same gesture done holding a pen softens the image considerably.

Birdwhistell's third channel—the tactile channel—is both powerful and delicate. Edward T. Hall studied this tactile channel closely and expanded the concept to include not only touch but the distance people keep between them when they communicate—what he dubbed "proxemics." In *The Silent Language* (1959), Hall wrote that "space communicates" (p. 190) and showed how the meaning created by standing very close and touching or standing far apart varies greatly from one culture to another. Politicians want to demonstrate that they are warm and approachable, which is why they never miss an opportunity to hug babies, for example. There are risks to communicating using the tactile channel, however. Standing too close and touching can make people in North America uncomfortable; this was captured by the media and public reaction to the image of President George W. Bush holding the hand of Saudi Crown Prince Abdullah as the two walked around Bush's Crawford, Texas, ranch. On the other hand, standing too far apart can create an image of a cold and distant politician, which is why so many were struck by Prime Minister Stephen Harper shaking hands with his son as he dropped him off at school.[6]

To Birdwhistell's audio, kinesthetic, and tactile channels, I propose that we could also add a clothing channel. In his book *Fashion, Culture and Identity* (1992), Fred Davis argues that clothes speak by allowing people to communicate some things about themselves, their status, and their lifestyle, as well as their "attributes and attitudes about themselves" (p. 16). Unlike spoken language, the meanings evoked by combinations of fabric, texture, colour, pattern, volume, and silhouette are forever shifting and "in process" (p. 5). The codes are clearer when it comes to formal uniforms, of course, but the meaning of the blue business suit or a cowboy hat can vary widely based on the occasion (a speech to the United Nations or a pancake breakfast at the Calgary Stampede) and the social group in whose midst the politician is (banking executives or university students).

The importance of the clothing channel in politics is evidenced by the work of the *Washington Post*'s Pulitzer Prize–winning fashion columnist, Robin Givhan. Givhan regularly writes about the clothing worn by politicians and whether it sends the right message to American voters. In an interview on CBS News show *Sunday Morning*,[7] she commented on the symbolism of U.S. Vice President Dick Cheney's choice of a bulky parka to wear to a ceremony marking the 60th anniversary of the liberation of Auschwitz: "Here he was wearing something that visually didn't symbolize to me the level of solemnity and respect that I thought a service like this demanded."

INFORMATION PUT TO WORK

So far, I've argued that politics is all about image because image is more than just window dressing—it's communication. Of course, if none of us paid any attention to speaking style, body language, and clothing, then politics would not be all about image. We do, however, pay attention and actively use what we learn to decide whether or not to support a politician.

Samuel Popkin argued in his book *The Reasoning Voter: Communication and Persuasion in Presidential Campaigns* (1991) that voters who are increasingly busy and deluged with information need to be very strategic in how they gather and use information during an election. Far from a pessimist who sees modern voters as overwhelmed, Popkin writes that voters find efficient ways to arrive at reasoned choices—what he calls, "**low information rationality**" (p. 41). Popkin describes many shortcuts to reasoned choices, such as seeking the opinions of others around us and taking cues from the political party to which the politician belongs. Voters also base their choice of candidates on their assessment of overall competence, rather than trying learn the candidate's specific position on a long list of issues. We save time and effort by seeking "a measure of ability to handle a job, an assessment of how effective the candidate will be in office, of whether he or she can 'get things done'" (p. 61). And where do voters get the information with which they can assess the candidate's competence? They look to those qualities that critics are quick to dismiss as mere image. Consider, for example, Popkin's description of how voters assess a candidate's competence during a political convention,

> The campaign exposes the candidate to voters in complex and fast-breaking situations. As they watch the candidate handle crowds, speeches, press conferences, reporters and squabbles, they can obtain information with which they imagine how he or she would be likely to behave in office. (p. 62)

As we watch candidates in these moments, the audio, kinesthetic, tactile, and clothing channels are operating fully. This is precisely when image can be assessed and judgments made.

Popkin also draws attention to how voters focus on assessing the personal qualities of candidates. Rather than trying to assess the candidates' positions on every issue that may or may not come up during their term in office, we assess their overall values, empathy, caring, and morality. Popkin writes, "We care more about sincerity and character when we are uncertain what someone will do" (p. 65). While words on the audio channel may be well suited to communicating a position on a specific issue, it seems to me that voters look more to speaking style, body movement, proxemics, and clothing when assessing politicians' personal qualities.

WHY THE SPIN?

So if we agree that modern politics is all about image, the next question is, why does it have to be "managed" so carefully? To go back to the analysis of Birdwhistell (1970), it has much to do with the way these more subtle communication channels work. Birdwhistell argues that, unlike the words and sentences we use, we are often not aware of the meaning of the messages we send through the nonverbal channels. The language of speaking style, kinesics, and proxemics is not as precise, and we haven't all been formally schooled in these since the age of five. Similarly, Fred Davis describes how we give meaning to clothing "allusively, ambiguously and inchoately" (1992, p. 5). Sending the right message with these channels is difficult, and the risk of inadvertently sending the wrong message is high.

Adding to the importance of managing what is said through these channels is the fact that the flow of messages through them is continuous. All of these channels are not always operating simultaneously, but Birdwhistell argues that one or more of them are always working to allow us to communicate. The audio channel matters most whenever politicians step up to the microphone, of course, but the other channels do most of the communicating whenever the candidate is seen but not heard. Kathleen Hall Jamieson (1988) argued that in the age of television, candidates are seen more often and heard less, as speeches are reduced to sound bites and 60-second advertisements. In the 16 years since she made her observation, the visual impact of television has been supplanted by photos and video on the Internet (computers, cellphones, handheld MP3 players) and ever more colourful newspapers and glossy magazines.

Of course, adding to the need for careful attention to the messages sent through all channels is the very nature of election campaigns. Politicians, like most of us, simply change when they're under pressure. They stiffen up, their eyes dart nervously, their skin pales, and their brows sweat—with disastrous results, as Richard Nixon found out in his first televised debate against a tanned, properly made up, and more relaxed John F. Kennedy. The glare of camera lights and the threat of every mistake being broadcast to millions and aired dozens of times only add to the tension. In these conditions, the risk of inadvertently sending the wrong message is high. The decision to hire people who can help a politician communicate effectively using all channels makes sense.

CONCLUSION

So where does this leave us? Is politics all about image? Should it be? I would argue the answer is yes to the first question and no to the second.

Yes, image matters a great deal in politics. Speaking style, body movement, use of personal space, and choice of clothing all communicate a great deal and help voters better understand the meaning of what politicians say. What's more, voters actively use what they learn from this communication to assess the overall competence of candidates and determine their personal qualities. For voters who feel the issues of an election are not pertinent to them, the candidate's image becomes all the more essential.[8]

That being said, there is also and should also be an important place for genuine discussion of important issues in modern politics. Many Canadian federal elections, for example, have been focused on important issues (e.g., free trade in 1988, accountability in 2006), and, at the end of the day, the choices we make as a country on those important issues will in large part determine the kind of future we have collectively. Even the most focused discussion of issues, however, can be rendered moot if matters of image are ignored and voters are left to misunderstand, distrust, forget, or ignore the debate. Image helps voters connect with candidates and connect to the issues those candidates are discussing. While I don't believe the debate about image versus issues in politics is simply an either/or proposition,[9] I do think that in an environment where we face so many competing messages, and in a situation in which communicating effectively through all channels is so complex, image plays a determining role.

The lesson for voters here is to make the effort to get beyond negative candidate images and pay attention to the debate on important issues. Democracy needs engaged voters who make the effort to listen actively, even when much of what is coming across on various nonverbal channels is distracting or confusing. The lesson for candidates is to work hard to meet voter expectations of image and get their message across. Voters need candidates who reach out, communicate effectively through multiple channels, and provide information voters can use to engage in the political process and make informed decisions.

References

Birdwhistell, R. L. (1970). *Kinesics and context: Essays on body motion communication*. Philadelphia: University of Pennsylvania Press.

Davis, F. (1992). *Fashion, culture and identity*. Chicago: The University of Chicago Press.

Ewen, S., & Ewen, E. (1992). *Channels of desire: Mass images and the shaping of American consciousness*. Minneapolis: University of Minnesota Press.

Hacker, K. L. (2004). A dual processing perspective of candidate image formation. In K. L. Hacker (Ed.), *Presidential candidate images* (pp. 105–132). Toronto: Rowan & Littlefield.

Hall, E. T. (1959). *The silent language*. Garden City, NY: Doubleday & Co.

Jamieson, K. H. (1988). *Eloquence in an electronic age: The transformation of political speechmaking*. New York: Oxford University Press.

Kaid, L. L., & Chanslor, M. (2004). The effects of political advertising on candidate images. In K. L. Hacker (Ed.), *Presidential candidate images* (pp. 133–150). Toronto: Rowan & Littlefield.

Nimmo, D., & Savage, R. (1976). *Candidates and their images*. Pacific Palisades, CA: Goodyear.

Popkin, S. L. (1991). *The reasoning voter: Communication and persuasion in presidential campaigns*. Chicago: The University of Chicago Press.

Stephen, T., Harrison, T. M., Husson, W., & Albert, D. (2004). Interpersonal communication styles of political candidates: Predicting winning and losing candidates in three U.S. presidential elections. In K. L. Hacker (Ed.), *Presidential candidate images* (pp. 177–196). Toronto: Rowan & Littlefield.

Turner, G. (2004). *Understanding celebrity*. Thousand Oaks, CA: Sage.

Notes

[1] See also the conclusion to Graeme Turner's *Understanding Celebrity* for a critique of "celebrity, politics and spin" (2004, p. 130).

[2] Though she longs for the logic and clarity of classical rhetoric, Kathleen Hall Jamieson recognizes the essential role that image necessarily plays in "this age of electronic advocacy … when you must get your message across in twenty-eight-second cellular morsels" (1988, p. 248).

[3] Though Birdwhistell is among the first communications scholars to look seriously at the meaning we create with our bodies, he is by no means the first to explore the topic. As early as 1873, Charles Darwin wrote *The Expressions of the Emotions in Man and Animals* and explored the links between verbal and visible behaviour of different mammals and certain emotional states.

[4] Birdwhistell later offers a very concise yet broad definition of communication that is helpful to remember as you consider image in politics: "a structural system of significant symbols (from all the sensorily based modalities) which permit ordered human interaction" (1970, p. 95).

[5] Further analysis by the authors revealed five qualities or "factors" of interpersonal communication style that are particularly effective in predicting the outcome of elections. Winners are more likely to be those rated highly by voters for the five following factors: (1) attentive, thoughtful, considerate, egalitarian; (2) good natured, convivial, laughing, smiling; (3) self-confident, assertive; (4) able to mount aggressive verbal attacks; and (5) speaking with great volume, force, compelling gestures (2004, p. 187).

[6] In Harper's defence, I suspect he was merely protecting his children from the embarrassment of being hugged by their father not only in front of news cameras but, worse still, in front of classmates. I'm sure my own kids would have preferred it that way too.

[7] The interview originally aired on May 14, 2006. An article based on the interview is published on the CBS News website at http://www.cbsnews.com/stories/2006/05/14/sunday/main1616585.shtml.

[8] Samuel Popkin argues that busy voters are increasingly selective about the issues to which they pay attention, favouring those that are personally relevant and visible. For each issue, a community of concerned voters will emerge; the rest of the public will pay only limited attention. The result, according to Popkin, is that "there are few, if any, national policy debates that the mass public can follow in their entirety" (1991, p. 35).

[9] Indeed, Kenneth L. Hacker, editor of *Presidential Candidate Images* (2004), argues that the hard line between image and issues is artificial and overemphasized by both those who feel elections are all about issues and those who feel elections are all about image. Instead of this artificial duality, Hacker calls for a "consolidative dual processing model" (2004, p. 124) by which information on issues and information on candidate character traits are processed at the same time, as each influences the other. Hacker describes his model as "a complex process involving many possible causal directions among many cognitive elements" (2004, p. 129).

ISSUE 4

Entertaining politics: Is it all about image?

✗ NO

All the Pretty Baubles
Denise Rudnicki

Denise Rudnicki brings more than two decades' experience as a journalist and communications executive to the Journalism Program. She was a national affairs correspondent, host, producer, and reporter for both CBC Radio and TV in newsrooms across Canada. She has reported for all the CBC's flagship news programs and has been host of *The House* and cohost of *The Journal* and *Midday*. She created and hosted *Ottawa Inside Out* for Newsworld. Denise has also been a communications consultant and most recently served as director of communications for the federal minister of justice. Much of her career was spent on Parliament Hill, as a journalist and then in government communications. Her research area is the growth of government communications and its impact on political journalism.

It was a triumph of image making. A victorious president, in a fly-boy's uniform, lands in a jet on an aircraft carrier in the Pacific. The leader of the free world has come to celebrate the overthrow of a tyrannical despot. Lit by the setting sun and hanging behind him as he speaks to the exuberant sailors is a sign that reads "Mission Accomplished." The scene fairly throbs with patriotism and triumph. A beleaguered and post-9/11 nation, suffering from the worst trouncing it had ever taken on its own soil, feels the pulse of pride and victory, led to this glorious state by its masterful war leader.

Wow. In the face of such potent image making and the subsequent pay off—meaning a spike in the president's public approval ratings—it would be folly to argue that image doesn't matter. In the American context particularly, modern presidential image management has been crucial to a successful administration.

There's a reason why presidents devote so much time and resources to cultivating a winning image. Presidents don't have any real legislative power. They must bargain with Congress to get anything done. This means modern presidents have learned the art of persuasion to propel their policies. Public opinion is a critical bargaining tool to persuade Congress that what the president wishes to be done ought to be done. Crafting an image of President George W. Bush as a war leader and popularizing that image with a public that was in a rally-around-the-flag mood helped persuade Congress to support the war in Iraq.

Does this mean that substance no longer matters? It's true that we live in an era of hypercompetition for the public's ever-shrinking attention span, and while I may be a voice in the wilderness, I'll argue that image, though key to the engineering of consent and the art of persuasion, is not the sole definer of political success. Indeed, substance does matter and it can matter a lot more than image—image or spin, in other words, isn't all it's cracked up to be.

America is a place in which image consultants dominate, as do advertisers, pollsters, spin doctors, and political operatives, all working to package the president as a commodity and market him as a brand (Ewen, 1988). The White House choreographs every public appearance of the president, knowing that what the people see has a profound impact on what they think, and that what the people think has an equally profound influence on what Congress will or will not support.

Americans have taken image management to new heights. Political marketers now regularly strap pulse-o-meters onto citizens to see what political messages hit the so-called voter g-spot (Luntz, 2006). Messages are thoroughly market tested before they cross the lips of any candidate. So can we be faulted for thinking that image management is all about winning and keeping power, and not at all about communicating public policy? My two decades in the Parliamentary Press Gallery taught me that we barely ever remember what any politician actually says. This would suggest that the point of image management is to induce a coma of indifference to public policy in particular, and to politics generally. The question is, does it really work?

Emphasizing style over substance has certainly worked in the past. In 1984 Ronald Reagan was considerably more popular than his policies. His campaign manager Ed Rollins developed a strategy to market Reagan's personality and downplay the issues. Rollins admits it was a feel-good campaign, "short on specifics and long on fuzzy thematics" (quoted in Stahl, 1999). The president was reelected and the media took a hit for focusing on style over substance.

It's always useful for students of political communication to look to the Americans for lessons on image management. This is the country, after all, that turned marketing and branding into a virtual art form. Yet while it may seem like a self-evident statement, Canada isn't the United States. For one thing, the prime minister doesn't need to persuade a body such as Congress to support his or her policy agenda. A PM with a majority government has virtually a free rein to define and drive policy. The obstacles in Canada are the bureaucracy, which has a glacial reaction to change, and, of course, the Cabinet, which is generally filled with people who want to advance their own agendas as much as their government's. Public opinion campaigns and market-tested messages don't hold much sway with bureaucrats and cabinet ministers. That isn't what persuades them to get on board with a prime minister's policy agenda. In Canada, a prime minister uses the power of appointment, the bait of advancement, and deputy minister and Cabinet shuffles to maintain loyalties.

Canadian journalists do not have a built-in deference to the office of the prime minister, unlike their American counterparts, who exhibit an almost breathless reverence to the president as figurehead. Canadian journalists can, over time, grudgingly come to respect the particular individual who happens to have been elected prime minister, but you won't see them stand up when the prime minister enters the room, as they do in the United States. In fact, members of the Parliamentary Press Gallery refused to stand up at a news conference when a member of the newly elected Stephen Harper government suggested they do so.[1] The media's furious resistance to Harper's early efforts to maintain message control—limiting access to Cabinet ministers, vetting all public comments, refusing to recognize certain reporters' questions—provide ample proof of our less than submissive media culture. So right from the get go, a prime minister does not enjoy the same ability to put a subservient media in their place, to set the news agenda, and to control his or her image.

The Canadian public, thanks in large part to our media culture, is hyper-alert to any effort by the Prime Minister's Office to snow them, unlike in the United States, where the administration boasts of its ability to manipulate public opinion. Ari Fleischer was press secretary to President George W. Bush during his first term, from January 2001 to July 2003. He was cinematically dubbed the Flak from Hell by the White House press corps for his robust media handling and message control. In 2003 he spoke to the Council of Public Relations Firms, the national trade association for the American public relations industry, in New York. He told them that their jobs were really no different from his; it was just a matter of the size of the audience (Council of Public Relations Firms, 2003). Imagine how Canadians would react to someone from the Prime Minister's Office publicly bragging that the goal of the sophisticated government PR machine is to market public policies to a pliable "buyer."

This is the real problem with the argument that image is everything. It assumes that the poor unsuspecting public can be tricked into voting for someone by clever branding and packaging, and that they haven't the wherewithal to distinguish market-tested language from the real thing. It also assumes that the media are the hapless victims of the pretty ornaments dangled by political public relations peddlers. And of course it assumes that politicians have no substance, and that policies are just props in the pursuit of power by image management.

Jim Armour was director of communications for Reform Party leader Preston Manning between 1997 and 2000. He likes to tell the story of Genghis Khan to illustrate his view of image politics. Khan is usually portrayed as a Mongol thug who murdered and pillaged his way through Asia and parts of Europe. In actual fact, says Armour, once he conquered a place he set about implementing some real reforms. He abolished torture, he instituted universal religious freedom, and he encouraged cultural pursuits—not our familiar image of Khan as a marauding killer. Armour proposes that while Genghis Khan was a great doer and an enlightened ruler, he was a lousy self-promoter. He refused to allow people to chronicle his accomplishments and banned all portraits. As a result, it was left to his enemies to define him and his image. As Armour says, "Genghis had great ideas and lousy PR."

Armour isn't comparing Preston Manning to Genghis Khan, but he does point out that the same could be said about Manning in the early days. Manning was more concerned with ideas than he was with image. And so he allowed his political opponents to define him as a wild-eyed, moralizing, Prairie radical. After-the-fact attempts to modify his image—the haircuts, contact lenses, and new suits—were seen as insincere and superficial. For his part, Manning believed that changing his haircut and getting rid of the glasses were ways to remove obstacles to the effective communication of his ideas. TV hosts can have a makeover and we're all relieved they've made themselves more attractive. Politicians do it and the media tell us it's a manipulative voter-getting manoeuvre.

It is a simple fact that a good image will help a candidate. The surest route to political obscurity is ideas without image. Politicians need a sophisticated set of positive attention-getting skills to get the notice of an overloaded public in a pick-and-choose media environment. The whole idea, though, of image consultants, pollsters, and media coaches constructing the perfect candidate on the basis of sound bites and photo ops is, not to put too fine a point on it, ridiculous. Image without ideas doesn't work—just look at Stockwell Day, whose brief tenure as leader of the Canadian Alliance Party was embarrassingly marred by clumsy image management, including the decision to arrive at his first news conference on a Jet Ski and sporting a wet suit.

Veteran political journalist Susan Riley has been around long enough to recognize baloney when she smells it frying, "I don't think we are particularly successful in Canada at building politicians out of constituent parts like lego blocks, adding a little homespun humour here, a bit of stout resolve there, appropriate compassion when needed, with a flawless and picturesque family in the background. Voters see through these disguises to the real person beneath, for better or for worse."

So the best image for politicians is the one that suits their personality as well as their political needs. People will sniff out a phony, and if image isn't plumb and level to the real world, then people won't buy it. As Jim Armour says, "No one would buy George W. Bush giving an economics lecture at an Ivy League school even though he has a Master of Business Administration from Harvard—just as there would be few takers for Stephen Harper at a New Age Meditation Centre. It's got to have a ring of truth to it."

When Paul Martin was finance minister, he projected an image of a deficit-slashing, budget-balancing man on a horse, a pinstriped saviour of the federal books. He was competent, focused, decent—a man with ideas. This image was entirely suitable to who Martin was as a successful finance minister with ambitions to become prime minister. He was also helped along the way by the talented PR professionals at Earnscliffe who wisely used Martin's measurable accomplishments as finance minister to create the Martin brand. Image *and* ideas converged to create a winning candidate.

Campbell Clark has been a parliamentary reporter for the *Globe and Mail* since 2000. He notes that as finance minister, Paul Martin was seen as someone who could focus on the most important priorities and effectively attack them. Here was a man who stuck to his convictions. But Clark saw a change after Martin became prime minister. "His image became that of someone who was scurrying from issue to issue in a panic, and obsessed with tactical manoeuvres for political gain." Maybe he was a good finance minister because he really only had one thing to do. Maybe multitasking wasn't his strength. Maybe he was called Mr. Dithers because, well, he dithered ("Mr. Dithers," 2005). This is a case of image being undone by an absence of ideas and a transparently self-serving focus on keeping power by trying to please everyone while pleasing no one. And let's not forget the sponsorship scandal. That debacle only served to highlight the arrogance of what Canadians came to view as a government bereft of both ideas and integrity. No pulse-o-meter was going to turn this one around.

This is something else those with a morbid fascination for image politics often don't consider. Shit happens. And when it does, even the best image makers on the planet can't control the outcome. Look again to the United States. The war in Iraq is outlasting the American public's tolerance for the conflict. Too many American soldiers are dying. The media have lost the early complaisance they showed following 9/11, when journalists were reluctant to criticize a president who was on the verge of leading his nation to war. And domestic urgencies—the flooding of New Orleans, the gas crisis—are taking the bloom off the president's image. Reality is getting in the way. It's the same on the Canadian political scene. Prime ministers traditionally enjoy a honeymoon period with the media, which inevitability ends because, as *Globe and Mail* columnist John Ibbitson puts it, "something always happens to slap a government upside the head."

Interestingly, both politicians and journalists—precisely those who participate most vigorously in the creation of image politics—claim to loathe the trend. Politicians blame the media's focus on image, trivia, and hype for a public that is increasingly cynical about politics.[2] Journalists argue they are only exposing the increasingly sophisticated tools politicians use to craft image. Politicians respond by going to even greater lengths to regain control of their image and the political agenda, and journalists push back even harder. Round and round we go, on an endless treadmill of charge and countercharge, all playing out in the media and, some say, ruining politics (see Lloyd, 2004).

Here again is where we can look to the Americans for a lesson in what to do when people get wise to image politics. Al Gore provides a handy example. He had an appalling image when he ran for the presidency in 2000. He was wooden, stage managed, so chilly ice wouldn't melt in his mouth. He lost to George W. Bush, who looked positively cuddly by comparison.

So why is Al Gore now considered to have a decent run at the presidential race of 2008? Surely it's not because Americans have decided that cold beats warm. The answer is subtler. It's because stuffed shirt has been rebranded as strong character. This is so clever it really is worth noting. The American PR talents have realized that people are fed up with what they view as cynical and manipulative attempts to create a winning image. When image becomes a bad word, a new mantra is needed. The new mantra is anti-image. Image is out. Character is in.

Pan across the 49th parallel to Stephen Harper. His image in the early days of his new government has been fascinating to watch. He rebuffs media attempts to get close to him and his ministers. He tells journalists that he's available to answer questions if there are questions of substance, a condemnation of what he clearly views as a wrong-headed journalistic obsession with trivial matters such as image. He projects an image of someone who doesn't care what the media think. He also seems not to care about his looks, which is, for most of us, what image is really all about. He wears brown pants with a fishing vest on an official visit to Mexico. He dresses like a member of the Village People at the Calgary Stampede. His shirt comes out of his trousers when he's throwing a ball around on Parliament Hill, showing his rather worldly paunch. Commentators write about his lousy media relations and even lousier sartorial skills and he seems not to care. Judging by opinion polls, neither do a substantial number of Canadians. In a Decima poll taken in April 2006, the Tories were enjoying 41 percent support; up from the 36 percent of the popular vote they took on election day. Interestingly, however, by August 2006, another poll by Decima was showing that support had dropped to 32 percent. The shift was blamed on discomfort with Harper's policies on Afghanistan and the Middle East. So on the one hand, Canadians like a leader who seems not to care about image, but on the other, they will slap his government upside the head when his policies grate.

A friend of Harper's, John Weissenberger, suggests that image management is never going to matter to the prime minister. "He's not there to build an image. He's there to run a government." We know that image and government are inseparable, and cynics would say Harper is building an image of someone who doesn't care about image. I can imagine the breathless PR types around the table, latching onto Harper's anti-image image and crying out, "We can sell that!"

Journalist Susan Riley has noted the new trend. "Stephen Harper is making his lack of charisma—his anti-image, if you want—into a virtue. He looks stolid, deliberate and serious when he isn't looking petulant, immature and vindictive. In other words, he is who he is."

Conservative Senator Marjory LeBreton has been a long-time supporter of Brian Mulroney, who was prime minister from 1983 to 1993, and she worked on Harper's 2006 election campaign. She believes that Canadians have grown tired of political spin, phony stunts, and staged photo ops. Her experience travelling on the Harper campaign led her to credit Harper's "unphonyness" for a big part of their electoral success. People "just wanted politicians to get to work and get out of their faces. This benefited Stephen Harper because it suited his personality." It also suits his political needs. Projecting disdain for mere image shows Harper to be just that type of old-fashioned politician whose vision entails not just winning but governing, and that will certainly support his long-term goal of winning a majority government.

Arguing that image in politics doesn't matter is ultimately quite impossible. But there are lessons we should learn from the ongoing debate. While image in politics matters, image politics is, in fact, largely fiction. Good image management is simply necessary to propel policies onto the public agenda. The purpose of image management, and of government communications more broadly, is to get your political boss prominently featured in a positive way, to be the primary definer of media discussions of policy, and to sideline dissenting voices (Franklin, 2003).

What lessons, then, can be learned about image and politics by the student of communication? First, don't be seduced by the cellophane packaging of the "image is everything" argument. Think of all those examples where the almost blind focus on image seemed to backfire in the face of substantive criticism. In Canadian politics, the sponsorship scandal resulted in large part because the obsession with marketing the image of Canada met head on the expectation of parliamentarians and Canadians that ethics and a commitment to due process be respected.[3] Outside of institutional politics, the global athletics corporation Nike became a target of a massive anti-sweatshop campaign in the mid-1990s when students, human rights organizations, religious groups, and other activist groups began calling media and public attention to the contradiction between the *image* Nike crafted of itself as a responsible corporation and its transgressions of international labour standards (Greenberg & Knight, 2004).

Second, what goes on in the United States doesn't always occur in Canada. Differences between the nature of the two countries' political systems have important implications for the differences in how politics is reported, on the one hand, and how politicians attempt to manage coverage about themselves and their policy agendas, on the other.

Third, the corollary of this argument is that the media systems in Canada and the United States are also very different. Canadian reporters have considerably greater access to parliamentarians and the prime minister than their colleagues at the White House, who are far more reliant on officials for information, and thus more vulnerable to being hoodwinked or misled by the package that information comes in.

In other words, image management is a tool but it isn't everything. Ideas matter too, and often a lot more than the journalists, media critics, and PR flacks (many of whom are also former journalists) would suggest. We recognize an empty vessel and a phony when we see one. We also recognize staged photo ops, whether they use daycare kids or sailors as props. The world of celebrity journalism may offer a cautionary tale. Tabloids, magazines, and entertainment shows have tired of the official "star" photos that agents and PR professionals provide. They want candid shots of celebrities—shopping, sun tanning, and behaving badly in public places. As a result, celebrities are losing control of their manufactured images. I'm not making a prediction that politicians will soon suffer a similar fate at the hands of a new breed of political paparazzi, but it does show what can happen when image control becomes too controlling. People demand reality. And journalists are happy to oblige.

References

Council of Public Relations Firms. (2003, November 6). Ari Fleischer shares White House experiences with Council of Public Relations Firms' luncheon. Available from http://www.prfirms.org/news_center/in_the_news/2003/AF110603.asp

Ewen, S. (1988). *All consuming images.* New York: Basic Books.

Franklin, B. (2003). A good day to bury bad news? Journalists, sources and the packaging of politics. In S. Cottle (Ed.), *News, public relations and power* (pp. 45–61). London: Sage.

Greenberg, J., & Knight, G. (2004). Framing sweatshops: Nike, global production and the American news media. *Communication & Critical/Cultural Studies, 1*(2), 151–175.

Kozolanka, K. (2006). The sponsorship scandal as communication: The rise of politicized and strategic communications in the federal government. *Canadian Journal of Communication, 31*(2) 343–366.

Lloyd, J. (2004). *What the media are doing to our politics.* London: Constable.

Luntz, F. (2006, May 5). Communicating conservative messages. Speech at the 2006 Ottawa Roundtable on Democratic Infrastructure.

Mr. Dithers and his distracting fiscal cafeteria. (2005, February 19). *The Economist.*

Mulroney, B. (1998). Images that injure. In E. E. Dennis & R. W. Snyder (Eds.), *Media and democracy.* New Brunswick and London: Transaction.

Stahl, L/ (1999). *Reporting live.* New York: Simon & Schuster.

Notes

[1] Stephen Harper joked about the Canadian media's lack of deference at a joint news conference with President Bush in Washington on July 6, 2006.

[2] Brian Mulroney complained that he endured "the malice of an incorrigibly hostile media" and blamed journalists for subverting legitimate public policy with "mountains of trivia and drivel and trash" (1998, p. 108).

[3] On the sponsorship scandal and its broader political and communicative underpinnings, see Kozolanka, 2006.

Discussion Questions

1. Think about what impressions you have formed about the image of a prominent Canadian politician. Describe instances where image and substance have clashed, and discuss whether image always triumphs.

2. How sophisticated do you believe Canadians are about image management? If you agree that it means more than hair and clothes, discuss the subtle ways politicians control their images.

3. What impact will the Internet have on a politician's ability to control his or her image? Do sites such as YouTube have the ability to threaten the control of political image managers? How do you think the politicians might respond?

4. Was democracy better off before politicians began to surround themselves with pollsters and image consultants? Why or why not?

5. Are image consultants able to deceive voters when they "make over" a politician, or does the public see through these efforts?

6. What role do you think the Internet will play in terms of influencing how little or how much image matters in politics? Why?

POSTSCRIPT

Focus on the field: A look at the historiography and role of media in Communication Studies

Reconsidering the future of the field: Cognitive science and the future of Communication Studies in Canada

Focus on the Field: A Look at the Historiography and Role of Media in Communication Studies

Leslie Regan Shade

Leslie Regan Shade is an associate professor at Concordia University in the Department of Communication Studies. Her research focus since the mid-1990s has been on the social, policy, and ethical aspects of information and communication technologies (ICTs), particularly issues of gender, globalization, and political economy.

A book that intends to put Canadian communications in question would not be complete without a focus on the field of communication studies in Canada. This essay provides such a focus. Since many key controversies discussed in this book relate to communication and media, this essay seeks to provide a background and contemporary look at communications and media studies in Canada from a social sciences and humanities perspective. Its focus on communication studies scholarship from a media-centric perspective is not to discount or distract from an important body of work in communication studies that is interdisciplinary, catching within its net the fields of psychology (interpersonal, organizational), linguistics, cognitive science, and computer sciences (human-computer interaction, computer-supported cooperative work). Nor is its focus meant to detract from functionalist and positivistic approaches toward communication studies, wherein the strain encompasses the media effects tradition and measurable and highly quantitative behavioural "evidence." Certainly these types of communication research, including other applied communication approaches (public relations, government communications, etc.), have made an impact in Canadian academia. However, in this essay I focus on critical communication studies from political-economic and cultural studies perspectives, arguing that this critical sensibility focuses on communications media as a social process and that questions and issues of power remain central to, and grounded in, the wider social, economic, and cultural realities of Canada.

The chapter thus argues that innovations accompanying media technologies, media practices, and media policy have made communication studies exciting and credible within and outside of the academic community. Communication studies in Canada, I argue, *is* about the media—whether it is old media or new media—and it embraces analyses of media institutions, media policies, media genres, and media uses.

In the historiography of communication studies in Canada, we cannot escape the crucial role that communication technologies and media policies have played in forging a distinct scholarship. In contrast to the development of communication studies as a discipline in the United States, many argue that Canadian communication studies arose as a need to respond to various royal commissions studying media—in particular, the role of Canadian media in cementing a distinct Canadian identity counter to the powerful influence of American media (Robinson, 2000).

This essay will first consider what we mean by media, and how digitization and its attendant convergence across diverse media platforms have created multiple technological, political-economic, and cultural and social changes. Second, it will consider the historical role that communication technologies have played in discourses about nationhood and identity in Canada, and argue that it is the important role of the media that has characterized Canadian communication studies as a unique and vital academic discipline, through its use of political-economic and cultural studies perspectives. Third, the essay will highlight how recent Canadian scholarship reinforces the dominant role that media assumes in Canadian communication studies. During the mid-1990s, the Internet began to be popularly diffused among Canadians and integrated into the management and servicing of public and private sector institutions, as well as playing a key role as an enabler of personalized and alternative information and communication services. Internet studies has thus become an engaged domain of research in Canadian communication studies, alongside nascent studies of other evolving converged media, notably video-gaming and mobile technologies.

WHAT'S THE MEDIA, ANYWAY?

Canada is one of the most connected and wired nations in the world. According to Statistics Canada (2005), basic telephone service and cable services are among the highest in the world. Data from 2003 indicate that over 20 million Canadians had access to fixed telephone lines, 13 million to mobile telephony, 7 million to residential Internet access, 2.5 million to dial-up Internet access, 4.5 million to high-speed Internet access, 7.5 million to cable television, and 2.2 million to satellite and wireless cable TV. Taken as a composite, these figures indicate that all of these network connections totalled 153.8 per 100 people, a 24.4 percent increase from 1999.

Given these figures, it is not surprising that young Canadians are cognizant of the conventions and practices of the media, and are thus increasingly attracted to studying the media in college and university. Ask students to define communication studies and most will reply, "the study of the media." Ask them to be more specific about what "the media" is and they will likely respond with a list of communication technologies, media genres, or media practices: the television, radio, newspapers, magazines, the Internet, film, computers, cellphones, music, popular culture, Hollywood, cartoons, soap operas, video games, iPods, instant messaging (IM), downloading, webcasting, and social networking spaces such as MySpace or Facebook.

"Media" is the plural of "medium," which refers to a means of transmitting or communicating information. What young people now refer to as "the media" encompasses a traditional definition of "mass media"—that is, media designed to reach as large an audience as possible—coupled with what some refer to as "new media,"—a more personalized, interactive, and digitized media environment integrating many forms of converged media. "Convergence" refers to how digital technologies complicate the traditional distinctions between print and broadcasting media; it became a common technique of media industries in the 1990s, when the ownership of cross-media platforms and assets, coupled with the integration of digital technologies, produced vertically and horizontally integrated conglomerates. Promoted as one-stop shopping for consumers, media corporations envisioned themselves not only as providers of information and entertainment, but as content distributors through telephone and cable systems, new forms of subscription services, and new trends in advertising. This new communications environment has led to the creation of what Valerie Scatamburlo-D'Annibale and Paul Boin call media telecommunications and electronic companies (MTE's): "MTE's are horizontally and vertically integrated companies that control information (content), the channels within which information passes (carriage), and the electronic devices (platforms) from which content is viewed" (2006, p. 239).

We now commonly refer to "media" as the institutions of electronic broadcasting, printed matter of newspapers and magazines, and new media forms encompassing digital media such as the Internet, video games, and the "third screen" of mobile technologies—from cellphones to personal digital assistants (PDAs) such as BlackBerries. For the purpose of this essay, then, "media" encompasses both traditional mass media and new media, also referred to as information and communication technologies (ICTs).

COMMUNICATION TECHNOLOGY, NATIONHOOD, AND IDENTITY

Twenty years ago, Maurice Charland wrote an influential essay that examined the history and development of Canadian technologies, from the Canadian Pacific Railway to the Canadian Broadcasting Corporation, and argued that technology is constitutive of and a manifestation of Canada's ethos. Technological nation building is imbued in Canadian policy, and according to Charland, is "insidious, for it ties a Canadian identity, not to its people, but to their mediation through technology" (1986, p. 197). This rhetoric, prevalent in English Canadian discourse, has been responsible for creating and sustaining state-sponsored public broadcasting, and it can be argued, has contributed to further state-supported developments in communication technology, from Telesat Canada and the Anik A1 satellite[1] to current federal government programs promoting broadband Internet access in rural and remote Canada.

Communications technology and theory are important to Canada and Canadians because of the importance of our vast geography, our geographical proximity to the United States, our official bilingualism, and our multicultural diversity. Communication technologies—broadcasting and telecommunications—are seen as a viable and vital tool to ensure universal access and affirm freedom of knowledge and information. Such intrinsic communication rights are highly valued in democratic societies such as Canada.

Indeed, communication studies in Canada has constantly grappled with issues of culture and identity. Media have played a fundamental role in nourishing and sustaining Canadian identity and culture. The involvement of the Canadian federal government in cultural matters through policy legislation and the creation of programs and funding designed to encourage cultural production, from films to book publishing, has provided a fertile ground for scholars to study media. Cultural sovereignty—the ability of a country to enact laws and policies that protect and promote its culture and cultural industries—has been a fixation in scholarship, both in critical communication studies (Hamilton, 2006) and in cultural studies (Kinahan, 2006).

Critical communication studies focuses on the political economy of media industries—media ownership and media concentration, power dynamics in media practices, and alternative media practices toward social justice. Political economy examines the relationship between media and communication systems and the broader social structures of society, asking questions about how media systems reinforce, challenge, or influence existing class and social relations. It interrogates the interrelationship between media ownership, government policies, and various support mechanisms in terms of influencing media content and behaviour. It asks questions about structural and labour practices in the production, distribution, and consumption of media.

Cultural studies is concerned with analyzing the myriad ways that various media construct meaning, in how audiences engage with media, and the social role of the media. Canadian cultural studies tends to focus on the role of the state in developing cultural policy and specifically the interplay of Canadian cultural industries within a globalizing mediascape, as well as analyses of popular culture within Canada. Important as well are analyses of the ideological content of media and a theoretical approach that "illustrates the ways in which Canadian audiences are active producers of meaning, and active participants in the creation of culture" (Kinahan, 2006, p. 40).

Canadian communication studies scholarship can thus be characterized by its insertion of both political economic and cultural studies analyses into the study of various media institutions, media genres, and media uses, and as Sheryl Hamilton argues, this "critical-ness of Canadian communication studies has been mapped onto discourses of the ongoing search for a unique Canadian national identity" (2006, p. 22).

So far this essay has discussed the very important role that studies of communication media have played in forging distinctly Canadian communication studies. Now this claim will be used to show how recent English Canadian scholarship has investigated digital media. This brief overview of scholarship, which embraces political-economic and cultural studies analyses, highlights the multifaceted and engaged dimensions that a focus on media in communication studies assumes.

THE INTERNET AS A LOCUS OF STUDY

Research on the Internet in Canada emerged in the early 1990s, documenting the development of the high-speed backbone network CA*net in the late 1980s, network upgrading through CANARIE (the Canadian Network for the Advancement of Research, Industry and Education), and the implementation of various federal policy initiatives to assess Internet initiatives (Barney, 2000; Gutstein, 2000; Menzies, 1996; Moll & Shade, 2001; Shade, 1994; Winseck, 1998). Much of this research can be deemed critical in that it provides a political-economic analysis of the ownership of the Internet (from a public to a private infrastructure), documents the encroaching commercialization of the Internet by private interests and the concomitant erosion of the public interest, assesses the various convergence strategies of large media companies through new cross-media ownership initiatives designed to leverage innovative digital opportunities, and highlights the role of citizen-based alternative media as a counter to corporate media.

Political-economic perspectives are also evident in scholarship that examines labour issues, policy, feminist orientations, and alternative media practices. "Digital restructuring" is Barbara Crow and Graham Longford's term (2000) to highlight how digital technologies have been intrinsic to the scope and speed of global economic and political restructuring. In particular, they stress the impact of labour through digital restructuring, via heightened precarious and contract work, telework, telecommuting, and outsourcing. Applying a gendered lens to these new forms of work reveals the many ways that ICTs in work practices perpetuate gendered and racialized patterns of inequities (see also Scott-Dixon, 2004).

Notions of technological nationalism have certainly played themselves out in the creation of policies and programs promoting the Internet. The creation of federal taskforces (the Information Highway Advisory Council, 1994–1997 and the Broadband Task Force, 2001) and CRTC policy decisions[2] have focused on the use of the Internet for encouraging Canadian global and national economic competitiveness, creating and nurturing "made in Canada" content and culture, fostering education and lifelong learning, and enhancing democratic participation.

Ensuring equitable access to the Internet for all Canadians has been a priority for governments and community groups across Canada, and many programs with the objective of ameliorating the "digital divide"[3] sprung up in the 1990s. Federal government support for public Internet access coalesced around Industry Canada's suite of programs under the "Connecting Canadians" umbrella; these included SchoolNet, the Community Access Program, Volnet, Library Online, Smart Communities, and Government Online. Canada boasts that it is one of the most connected nations in the world, but as Catherine Middleton and Christine Sorensen argue, in a quantitative analysis of Statistics Canada data, this claim

> masks unequal Internet adoption patterns … households headed by lower-income, less-educated, or older Canadians have Internet adoption rates well below the Canadian average. In contrast, households with heads who are highly educated, earn above-average incomes, or are younger than 55 are adopting the Internet at rates well above the average. (2005, pp. 463–464)

Quantitative measurements of Internet access in Canada and comparative measurements across nations have been conducted by several initiatives involving academic partnerships, including the Statistics Canada Connectedness Series and their Household Internet Use Survey 2001 and 2003[4]; the World Internet Project, an international collaborative project with a strong Canadian presence through the Canadian Internet Project[5]; and Orbicom's series of digital indicators, conducted collaboratively with many entities, including the Canadian International Development Agency (CIDA) and the International Telecommunications Union (ITU), as part of the World Summit on the Information Society (WSIS).[6]

Criticism of Canadian ICT policy has concentrated on the shift from the objective of citizen-based universality to a regime of market-generated rules (Moll & Shade, 2001). The emphasis has been on developing programs and policies that fixate on the technical, rather than the social infrastructure. Darin Barney chastises Canadian ICT policymaking, arguing that it suffers from a democratic deficit, "policy in this area has reflected the priority of unfettered technological innovation and growth, and a complementary determination to develop these technologies in ways that maximize their potential as media of industry, commerce, and economic accumulation" (2004, p. 104; 2005). These policies run counter to citizen-centric initiatives, which have also been a priority of recent Canadian Internet scholarship (Moll & Shade, 2004; Skinner, Compton, & Gasher, 2005).

Canadian feminist perspectives on digital media have focused not only on labour and new economy issues, but also on the themes of gendered space and language, everyday uses, advocacy and activism, and relations of technology and art. Canadian feminist research continues the tradition of Canadian media scholarship that integrates political-economic perspectives and enquiries into the relationship of technology and nationalism (Shade & Crow, 2004).

Alternative media can be defined as media that provide a range of perspectives and stories not covered in the profit-oriented corporate mainstream media. Alternative media encompass local, community-based, and citizens' media, and as David Skinner (2005) documents, within Canada, the development of alternative media has been viable since the mid-1960s, although periodically fraught with sustainability issues. The Internet has facilitated new forms of alternative media, with many Canadian scholars focusing on the activist uses and policies of independent media centres, or Indymedia (Langlois, 2005; Scatamburlo-D'Annibale & Chehade, 2004; Sénécal & Dubois, 2005).

Cultural studies perspectives are reflected in qualitative enquiries on everyday uses of the Internet, and include Maria Bakardjieva's study of Vancouver-area household Internet users (2005); Andrew Clement's Everyday Experiences of Networked Services study (Viseu, Clement, & Aspinall, 2004); Barry Wellman's Connected Lives project; Tracy Kennedy's research on gender and the domestic Internet; Leslie Shade's work on domestic use of the Internet by children and young people (Shade, Porter, & Sanchez, 2005); and Sandra Weber's Digital Girls project. These studies seek out the voices of citizens as active users, producers, and negotiators of Internet technologies, and aim to situate their knowledge and expertise within the context of Canadian ICT policy.

Much of this research has been funded through the Social Sciences and Humanities Research Council of Canada (SSHRC) via their Initiative on the New Economy program. These include multiyear intra-university and community-based collaborative projects examining community networking, surveillance practices, ICT use within education, use of the Internet by children and young girls, and privacy and anonymity in networked environments.[7] These funded projects emphasize conducting research that can have a direct impact on media policy formulation, and that serve the needs of diverse audiences, from academics to community members to governments.

Early Canadian communication scholarship was influenced by the priorities of governmental commissions and mandates related to communication and cultural policies, including the Massey Commission (1951), the Fowler Commission (1957), the *Broadcasting Act* (1958, 1991), and the *Telecommunications Act* (1993).[8] More recent commissions include the Canadian Heritage Standing Committee on Broadcasting (2003), the Telecommunications Policy Review Panel (2006), and the Standing Senate Committee on Transport and Communications related to news media (2006). These commissions, detailing issues of corporate concentration, cross-media ownership, and the challenges of digitization, will undoubtedly be the focus of renewed scholarly attention.[9]

Characteristic of this recent scholarship is attention to the nuances of power within the prevailing political economy of the ICT industry, consideration of the development of communication structures that work toward increasing Canadians' access and indigenous content, reaffirming the moral obligation of the government to provide universality to enrich the public good through policy and cultural industry legislation, research on media for social justice purposes, and an awareness of innovative uses of new forms of ICTs for independent voices and alternative communication flows. This scholarship seeks an audience within and outside of the university, and has an overriding purpose not just to critique, but also to stimulate change and provoke dialogue and debate.

Media is integral to Canadian communication studies. As Canadian consumers and citizens, we are highly dependent on various media in our everyday lives—from e-mail, IM, and googling to cellphones, cable television, and our daily newspapers. Because we rely on various media for sustaining our social and work lives, we also need engaged scholarship that addresses the multifarious media institutions and policies, media forms, and media uses prevalent in our local and global communities. Canadian communication studies scholarship, in its allegiance to political economy and cultural studies, has proven to be abundant and provocative in responding to the needs and controversies of Canadian identity and Canadian issues.

References

Bakardjieva, M. (2005). *Internet society: The internet in everyday life.* London: Sage.

Barney, D. (2000). *Prometheus wired: The hope for democracy in the age of network technology.* Vancouver & Chicago: UBC Press/University of Chicago Press.

Barney, D. (2004). The democratic deficit in Canadian ICT policy and regulation. In M. Moll & L. R. Shade (Eds.), *Seeking convergence in policy and practice: Communications in the public interest* (Vol. 2, pp. 91–108). Ottawa: Canadian Centre for Policy Alternatives.

Barney, D. (2005). *Communication technology.* Vancouver: UBC Press.

Canadian Radio-television and Telecommunications Commission. (1999, May 17). *CRTC won't regulate the Internet* [News release]. Available at http://www.crtc.gc.ca/ENG/NEWS/RELEASES/1999/R990517.htm

Charland, M. (1986). Technological nationalism. *Canadian Journal of Political and Social Theory/Revue canadienne de théorie politique et sociale, X*(1–2), 196–220.

Crow, B., & Longford, G. (2000). Digital restructuring, gender, class, and citizenship in the information society in Canada. *Citizenship Studies, 4*(2), 207–230.

Gutstein, D. (2000). E.con: *How the internet undermines democracy*. Toronto: Stoddart.

Hamilton, S. (2006). Considering critical communication studies in Canada. In P. Attallah & L. R. Shade (Eds.), *Mediascapes: New patterns in Canadian communication* (2nd ed., pp. 9–27). Toronto: Thomson Nelson.

Kinahan, A.-M. (2006). From British invasions to American influences: Cultural studies in Canada. In P. Attallah & L. R. Shade (Eds.), *Mediascapes: New patterns in Canadian communication* (2nd ed., pp. 28–43). Toronto: Thomson Nelson.

Langlois, A. (2005). How open is open? The politics of open publishing. In A. Langlois & F. Dubois (Eds.), *Autonomous media: Activating resistance & dissent*. Montreal: Cumulus Press.

Menzies, H. (1996). Whose brave new world? *The information highway and the new economy*. Toronto: Between the Lines.

Middleton, C. A., & Sorensen, C. (2005). How connected are Canadians? Inequities in Canadian households' internet access. *Canadian Journal of Communication, 30*(4), 463–483.

Moll, M., & Shade, L R. (Eds.). (2001). *E-commerce vs. e-commons: Communications in the public interest*. Ottawa: Canadian Centre for Policy Alternatives.

Moll, M., & Shade, L R. (Eds.). (2004). *Seeking convergence in policy and practice: Communications in the public interest* (Vol. 2). Ottawa: Canadian Centre for Policy Alternatives.

Robinson, G. J. (2000). Remembering our past: Reconstructing the field of Canadian communication studies. *Canadian Journal of Communication, 25*(1). Available at http://www.cjc-online.ca/viewarticle.php?id=568&layout=html

Scatamburlo-D'Annibale, V., & Boin, P. (2006). New media. In P. Attallah & L. R. Shade (Eds.), *Mediascapes: New patterns in Canadian communication* (2nd ed., pp. 235–249). Toronto: Thomson Nelson.

Scatamburlo-D'Annibale, V., & Chehade, G. (2004). The revolution will not be televised, but it might be uploaded: The Indymedia phenomenon. In M. Moll & L. R. Shade (Eds.), *Seeking convergence in policy and practice: Communications in the public interest* (Vol. 2, pp. 363–379). Ottawa: Canadian Centre for Policy Alternatives.

Scott-Dixon, K. (2004). *Doing IT: Women working in information technology*. Toronto: Sumach Press.

Sénécal, M., & Dubois, F. (2005). The alternative communication movement in Quebec's mediascape. In D. Skinner, J. R. Compton, & M. Gasher (Eds.), *Converging media, diverging politics: A political economy of news media in the United States and Canada* (pp. 249–266). Lanham, MD: Lexington Books.

Shade, L. R. (1994). Computer networking in Canada: From CA*net to CANARIE. *Canadian Journal of Communication, 19*(1). Available from http://www.cjc-online.ca/viewarticle.php?id=217&layout=html

Shade, L. R., & Crow, B. (2004, spring). Canadian feminist perspectives on digital technology. *Topia: Canadian Journal of Cultural Studies*, 161–176.

Shade, L. R., Porter, N., & Sanchez, W. (2005). "You can see anything on the internet, you can do anything on the internet!": Young Canadians talk about the internet. *Canadian Journal of Communication, 30*(4), 503–526.

Skinner, D. (2005). Alternative media. In P. Attallah & L. R. Shade (Eds.), *Mediascapes: New patterns in Canadian communication* (2nd ed., pp. 213–229). Toronto: Thomson Nelson.

Skinner, D., Compton, J. R., & Gasher, M. (Eds.). (2005). *Converging media, diverging politics: A political economy of news media in the United States and Canada*. Lanham, MD: Lexington Books.

Statistics Canada. (2005, June). *Canadians connected in many ways. Innovation Analysis Bulletin, 7*(2), Cat. No. 88-003-XIE, p. 13.

Viseu, A., Clement, A., & Aspinall, J. (2004, March). Situating privacy online. *Information, Communication & Society, 7*(1), 92–114.

Winseck, D. (1998). *Reconvergence: A political economy of telecommunications in Canada*. Cresskill, NJ: Hampton Press.

Notes

[1] Anik A 1 was the first commercial, domestic communications satellite in geostationary orbit, deployed in 1973 by the CBC to provide live television for the first time to the Canadian North.

[2] Notably, the CRTC's 1999 decision on new media, which stated that the CRTC will not regulate new media under the *Broadcasting Act*, that existing Canadian law already covers issues of illegal and offensive content, and that there is no shortage of Canadian content on the Internet. See CRTC, 1999.

[3] The "digital divide" is a term widely used by journalists, advocacy groups, and academics to describe the disparity between those who have access to the Internet and those who don't. A variety of sociodemographic characteristics are recognized as increasing (or inhibiting) access, including income, education, gender, race, ethnicity, age, linguistic background, and geographic location (rural vs. urban).

[4] The Statistics Canada Connectedness Series is a periodic reporting of various statistics on telecommunications and Internet indicators—access in schools, broadband in Canada, etc. —and can be found online at http://www.statcan.ca/bsolc/english/bsolc?catno=56F0004M. The 2003 Household Internet Use Survey can be found online at http://www.statcan.ca/bsolc/english/bsolc?catno=88-003-X20040037429.

[5] The Canadian Internet Project website is at http://www.cipic.ca. The World Internet Project website is at http://www.worldinternetproject.net/.

[6] Orbicom—the international network of UNESCO chairs in communication—is at the Université du Québec à Montréal (UQAM). *From the Digital Divide to Digital Opportunities: Measuring Infostates for Development* (2005) can be found on the Orbicom site at http://www.orbicom.uqam.ca

[7] The SSHRC website is at http://www.sshrc.ca. For specific SSHRC-funded projects see the Canadian Research Alliance for Community Innovation and Networking (http://.cracin.ca); Everyday Experiences of Networked Services (http:///www3.fis.utoronto.ca/research/iprp/ee/index.html); the Surveillance Project (http://www.queensu.ca/sociology/Surveillance/); On the Identity Trail (http://idrail.org/); Teaching and Learning Technology: Enhancing Equity for Canadian Youth (http://ace.acadiau.ca/research/techequity/general_information.html); Children, Young People and New Media (http://artsandscience1.concordia.ca/comm/shade/);and Digital Girls (http://www.digitalgirls.org/). Wellman's many research projects can be found on his webpage at http://www.chass.utoronto.ca/~wellman/netlab/PUBLICATIONS/_frames.html, and Tracy Kennedy's ongoing research is at http://www.chass.utoronto.ca/~tkennedy/outline.htm.

[8] An excellent overview of Canadian communication and cultural policy can be found at the Media Awareness Network, at http://www.media-awareness.ca/english/issues/cultural_policies/cultural_policy_chronology.cfm.

[9] See the Canadian Heritage Standing Committee report, *Our Cultural Sovereignty: The Second Century of Canadian Broadcasting* (2003), at http://www.parl.gc.ca/InfoComDoc/37/2/HERI/Studies/Reports/herirp02-e.htm; *The Telecommunications Policy Review Panel Final Report* at http://www.telecomreview.ca/epic/internet/intprp-gecrt.nsf/en/h_rx00054e.html; and the *Final Report on the Canadian News Media*, Vol. I and II, from the Senate Committee on Transport and Communications (June 2006), at http://www.parl.gc.ca/Common/Committee_SenRecentReps.asp?Language=E&Parl=39&Ses=1.

Reconsidering the Future of the Field: Cognitive Science and Communication Studies in Canada

Alexandre Sévigny and Karin R. Humphreys

Alexandre Sévigny is an associate professor jointly appointed to the Department of Communication Studies & Multimedia and the Department of French at McMaster University in Hamilton, Ontario. He is also an associate member of the Department of Psychology, Neuroscience & Behaviour and the Department of Linguistics & Languages. He is a founding member of McMaster's Communication Studies Program, Cognitive Science of Language M.Sc./Ph.D. Program, Digital Society M.A. Program, and Communication and New Media M.A. program. In 2006 he was the recipient of the Petro-Canada Young Innovator Award, which recognizes excellence in research and teaching. He is also an active consultant in political communication. He received his Ph.D. in computational linguistics from the University of Toronto. His research specialization is in artificial intelligence and social discourse analysis, with a particular emphasis on the processes that underlie language comprehension in humans.

Karin R. Humphreys is an assistant professor in the Department of Psychology, Neuroscience & Behaviour at McMaster University in Hamilton, Ontario. She is also associate member of the Department of Linguistics & Languages. She is a cofounder of both McMaster's Linguistic Cognitive Science B.A. and its Cognitive Science of Language M.Sc./Ph.D., which are interdisciplinary, interfaculty enterprises that bring together researchers and students who study language from many different perspectives. She received her Ph.D. in cognitive psychology from the University of Illinois at Urbana-Champaign in 2002. Her research specialization is in psycholinguistics. She is especially interested in the processes that underlie speaking. She has also worked on social discourse analysis, from an empirical and quantitative perspective.

INTRODUCTION

What is communication studies, where has it been, and where is it headed in the future? These are important questions for communication students to consider because they provide a better understanding of the context in which the field of communication studies has developed, and also because the answers they provoke signal possibilities for future options in professional practice and scholarship. Some scholars advance a historiography of Canadian communication studies that is steeped in the critical tradition. They articulate a vision of the field that is circumscribed by concerns about political economy, an approach that privileges theoretical pursuits over empirical ones, and one that is founded in the humanities and social sciences (e.g., Babe, 2000). This vision explains why the field of Canadian communication studies is considered by definition to be inherently critical (for a discussion see Hamilton, 2006). Yet while there have been many advances in the study of communication within Canada from other disciplinary traditions, these fields do not seem to have as privileged a place in scholars' discussion of the discipline's past and future. Fields such as commerce, political science, sociology, health studies, and economics have all contributed tremendously to research in communication, often taking an empirical approach to areas such as market research, attitude formation, health communication, institutional economics, and decision making. One area perhaps less well known to communication studies departments is cognitive science, which examines empirically how human minds process information. We believe that cognitive science is truly a cognate field to communication studies, and its contributions have the potential of opening up the field of enquiry in new directions.

The social world is undergoing rapid change as science and technology continue to alter the nature of human life and communication processes at accelerated rates. In just a short time, computers have radically transformed how students communicate with their professors, with one another, and with the institutions where they study. Everyday activities such as shopping, banking, and purchasing airline tickets have also been altered in ways that transform the nature and processes of conventional forms of communication. Rarely, if ever these days, do we accomplish such mundane tasks with the assistance and participation of another human being; increasingly, we do so by engaging with machines that possess humanlike interfaces (i.e., they are not human but have been programmed to talk and operate as if they were). In this essay we argue that to fully comprehend and explain these changes, communication studies should embrace more systematically the contributions of the sciences. We believe cognitive science in particular offers exciting opportunities for Canadian communication scholarship—opportunities that permit access to cutting-edge research and produce valuable training for students who want new perspectives on emerging research fields that are radically altering our contemporary definitions of what it means to be human, human consciousness, human identity, and culture. Such an approach can only serve to strengthen, orient, and broaden the field of communication in the contemporary era of information and bioscience.

COGNITIVE SCIENCE AND EMPIRICAL METHODS IN COMMUNICATION STUDIES

There are several cognitive scientific/empirical disciplines, including cognitive and social psychology and linguistics, whose research methods and findings inform communication studies in productive and meaningful ways. A major theme that emerges from all of these approaches is the use of rigorous cognitive scientific methodology in order to uncover patterns and systematicities in human thoughts, feelings, and behaviour, in part by looking at the complex representations and computational processes that make up the mind. Some may be concerned that the idea of adopting a cognitive scientific approach will reduce our understanding of human nature to a normative set of laws and principles that set human nature in stone or establish a concept of an ideal or norm that will then limit the free development of human identity. We wish to suggest that cognitive scientific methodology can help us to understand the complexity of the human condition, and in fact help us explore the very same set of questions that humanists have been grappling with, such as questions about the mind, the self, and the other, and about communication and society, while providing the valuable addition of a different perspective. Rather than taking the perspective of power relationships and their effects on social groups, expressed through history and language, cognitive science explores mental processes and the networks of knowledge that lie within an individual, and how these relate not only to the behaviour of those individuals, but also to that of groups, societies, and organizations. As we illustrate below, these approaches can usefully inform the future of communication studies in a way that will not only provide fertile ground for new study, but also open up new professional possibilities for students who are entering careers in communication.

Psychology

Cognitive psychology is the study of how the mind works, and it has given rise to a great many research findings and methodologies that can be applied to questions of interest to communication researchers. In terms of methodology, cognitive psychology employs a range of measures, such as looking at the accuracy of memories or decisions; the time taken to process information; the pattern of eye movements while reading (using **eyetracking**); or a pattern of brain activity as seen on electroencephalography (EEG), event-related electroencephalography (ERP), or functional magnetic resonance imaging (fMRI). These, when employed in conjunction with well-controlled experimental designs, can help one discover information about even highly sophisticated cognitive processes. Many of these kinds of techniques (and others discussed in this chapter) are useful and feasible from both a technical and financial standpoint for communication studies researchers.

Cognitive psychology has made considerable progress, for example, in understanding how people learn information, how they remember it, and how they later recall it. This information is useful for students of communication studies because it offers much insight into the effects on individuals of all kinds of media representations, such as advertisements, political speeches, and television newscasts. Empirical results about issues such as the efficacy of a particular advertising campaign clearly have practical implications for media professionals. Moreover, specific knowledge about how people tend to engage with media provides a strong basis for new kinds of critical analysis. As one example of the relevance of memory research to communication studies, Lewandowsky, Stritzke, Oberauer, and Morales (2005) looked at people's memory for information presented in the news about the war in Iraq. One aspect of these reports that is particularly interesting from a communication studies perspective is the fact that a great deal of misleading or false information was reported in the media in the early stages of the war, much of which was later retracted, corrected, or disconfirmed. Lewandowsky and coauthors asked people in the United States, Australia, and Germany about the accuracy of various statements, including items that had been correctly reported by the media, items that had been subsequently corrected, and fictional events. People in the United States, where support for the war was high, were not sensitive to corrections. That is, they recalled as true news reports that had been subsequently corrected, even when it could be shown that they had some memory of the correction. However, in Australia and Germany, where suspicion about the motives for the war was higher, respondents were sensitive to whether information had been retracted or not. The fallibility of human memory has been a particularly productive vein of research in cognitive psychology, which has clear implications for communication research.

There is also a great deal of research on how people read, from the lowest levels of visual letter identification up to how large texts are read and integrated into people's prior knowledge. The study of how people create mental representations while reading, going beyond the literal text and using inferences based on their world knowledge, has been a mainstay of reading research within cognitive psychology (e.g., Kintsch, 1998). This sort of scholarship has been instrumental in fields such as Web design and textbook design. It is also relevant to news media studies conducted in the framework of critical discourse analysis. Underlying many critical theories are unexamined assumptions about how people understand and learn from media, in relation to themselves and to the world. Cognitive psychology allows us to actually examine (rather than merely speculate about) those underlying assumptions. For example, while critical theory holds that a reader or viewer might make certain inferences about race, class, or gender from a news report, cognitive psychology provides ways of testing whether those inferences are actually made and also enables us to build empirically based models that allow us to predict what inferences will be made, and when.

The field of decision-making science has also been extremely informative about how people take in information and base their (frequently non-rational) judgments and decisions on that information combined with their preexisting biases. Any kind of persuasive communication, (e.g., advertising, marketing, public relations, political communication) has the ultimate goal of influencing a person's decisions, whether that involves encouraging them to vote in a particular way or to choose one type of consumer product over another. An understanding of the processes that people use to make their decisions has been of great importance to corporate and other powerful interests. While critical theorists have effectively established the underlying political and economic interests that may animate or structure these processes, they have often neglected the processes themselves. We suggest that an understanding of this field should be of near paramount importance to both audiences and producers of persuasive communication, and thus should be addressed by communication researchers and examined by their students.

The field of social psychology also employs rigorous empirical methodology in order to discover how people's thoughts, feelings, and behaviours are affected by other people and by culture. It includes how people make judgments about other people, how they behave with other individuals or in groups, and how they create understandings of self. Social psychology has provided insights that are particularly relevant and useful to communication researchers on attitude formation, persuasion, cognitive dissonance, and the creation of social identities. For example, Julian Roberts and Anthony Doob, researchers from Ottawa University and the University of Toronto, showed that people's attitudes toward criminal sentences were strongly influenced by newspaper accounts, which led people to support harsher sentences (1990). **Cognitive dissonance theory** (Festinger, 1957), on the other hand, which is concerned with explaining the process of tension and psychological discomfort that occurs when individuals realize they are experiencing conflicting beliefs about an issue, has been actively used by political actors during election time to influence uncertain voters. For example, citizens who are torn about how to vote the day before an election may seek to reduce dissonance by voting for the candidate who opinion polls tell them is likely to win and who they already think stands a good chance of winning (Morwitz & Pluzinski, 1996). In an effort to limit their feelings of psychological discomfort, voters seek to bring their beliefs and behaviour in line with that of the presumed majority.

Linguistics

Language is the most human of all communication forms and is a central part of our ability to interact with other people and to create culture. An understanding of the fundamental nature of this code must lie at the heart of all forms of communication studies. Approaches from syntax, semantics, pragmatics, sociolinguistics, computational linguistics, and, of course, critical discourse analysis have been adopted by linguists and many communication theorists interested in social discourse analysis in order to study the human communication process, as well as the nature of language in news reporting (e.g., Fairclough, 1989). This work has also led to major advances in the field of gender, identity, and language, such as Susan Ehrlich's work (2001) on the representation of rape, which investigates the "institutional language" of sexual assault trials in the courts and concludes that courtroom discourse about rape and sexual assault disadvantages complainants and reinforces rape myths. Any work in linguistics relies, to some degree, on cognitive models of how language works in the mind. While communication studies has benefited from much of this research, we argue that it has ignored the *cognitive elements* of linguistic theory and has instead tended to espouse the *ideological analysis* of texts and cultural objects as its main theoretical thrust.

A particularly important contribution that linguistics can make to communication studies comes from cognitive pragmatics, or relevance theory. Relevance theory seeks to understand how individuals (as comprehenders) go beyond the literal (and thus limited) meaning of a text or utterance. In order for communication to be optimally efficient, one cannot use literal meanings alone. Instead, any utterance conveys a host of ideas that are not explicitly stated. The critical question is, how does the listener make these inferences? The guiding principle behind relevance theory is that people's inferences are highly constrained by a tendency to search for ways to make the text "maximally relevant" to the comprehender, and that the inferences people make will be those that allow the text to make the most sense and produce the most communicative value (Sperber & Wilson, 1995). For example, on August 28, 2006, the U.S. Vice President Dick Cheney made the following literally true statement: "We were not in Iraq on September 11, 2001, but the terrorists hit us anyway." If a listener were searching for a way for the sentence to make the most sense and have the greatest relevance, one would expect that listener to conclude that Vice President Cheney is claiming that "if we were in Iraq on September 11, 2001, the terrorists would not have hit us," which might reduce to "Iraq = terrorists." If one does not make these assumptions, the statement is a fairly vacuous one. While the principle of relevance may seem simple enough to be almost trivial, it has permitted cognitive scientists interested in culture to hypothesize that a single cognitive mechanism accounts for how human beings interpret any meaningful cultural, linguistic, or semiotic signal. This hypothesis has allowed for great insight into artificial intelligence, translation studies, and communication disorders, among other concerns.

Applications

All of these disciplines have either been studying communication phenomena directly or developing knowledge and methodologies that are potentially applicable to the questions communication studies researchers pose. Communication studies departments should be able to take advantage of these advances and adapt them to further their research agendas, even if it means simply being better able to critique them. Here, we present just a few examples of exciting new applications of cognitive science to communication studies that have come directly from the interdisciplinary cross-pollinations we have discussed above. The examples include communication with intelligent systems, interpersonal communication as mediated by technology, health communication, and audience research.

A new and increasingly significant form of communication is occurring between humans and "intelligent systems." Canadian communication studies departments are in a good position to contribute to our knowledge about these systems, both to help develop greater critical awareness about their potential dangers and implications as well as to facilitate design improvements to enhance rather than diminish communication among individuals, groups, and institutions. A wide variety of tools, from the refrigerator to the automobile, smart houses to e-commerce websites, use intelligent systems that we communicate with almost every day. While these models are limited in their scope and relatively unsophisticated for the moment, they are created to facilitate communication between humans and machines. As they grow in sophistication, these machines could fundamentally change the way we perceive our concepts of humanness and sociality. Already, we interact with avatars in video games and virtual realms such as Second Life, not to mention Emily, the automated help desk assistant on Bell Canada's phone system. The creation of intelligent systems relies on sophisticated models of the self and the symbolic structure of social interaction that are the result of cognitive scientific observation, mathematical modelling, and behavioural testing. Communication researchers and students should have a strong hand in these developments, as they are reshaping our sense of self and other in dramatic ways.

Interpersonal communication as mediated by information technology is also a hot topic for linguists and cognitive scientists, as well as communication scholars, marketing executives, and nonprofit organizations. Web 2.0 offers a plethora of communication media options for people to communicate through: Facebook and MySpace have altered our sense of participation in the lives of our friends and strangers, while instant messaging and podcasting have, in many ways, retrieved a strong sense of oral culture. This oral culture allows for peer-to-peer communication that can be informal and extemporaneous in a way that cannot be achieved through more conventional modes of communication (e.g., telephone conversations, formal lectures). Marshall McLuhan, a communication theorist strongly influenced by cognitive psychology, predicted this advance when he spoke of the "global village" and the "retribalizing" power of the digital society (McLuhan & Zingrone, 1995).

The study of the links between human health, cognition, and communication is a topic that has been receiving more and more interest recently. For example, sociolinguist Anna Moro, pediatrician Irene Turpie, and cognitive scientist Ellen Ryan, all of McMaster University, examine the effectiveness of clinician-patient communication in second-language speakers. This is a topic of increasing importance in our era of culturally diverse, multilingual, and differently abled people all expressing themselves differently to physicians, speech and language pathologists, psychiatrists, nurses, and therapists. Effectively and respectfully serving such a population requires a deep and empirical understanding of how and why communication works. What do people from diverse communities pay attention to? What are expressible topics? What is the impact of religious belief on how a patient will communicate with a health practitioner? How do elderly people, especially elderly members of diverse communities, deal with the natural decay of their second language? By understanding these issues, we can then start to devise practical ways to improve people's lives. Given Canada's aging and ever more diverse population, these areas of research should be part of the agenda for communication studies departments.

Audience research—which involves diverse ways of understanding how people receive and interpret information—is one of the most widely used communication applications and has always been a core area of attention for communication scholars. Audience research has traditionally been concerned with questions of how individuals receive and process information; much of this research has concluded that individuals are vulnerable to powerful mass media influence (Dill & Dill, 1998). More contemporary approaches to media audiences note that audiences are socially structured and that their "readings" of "texts" stem from the consequences of social context, in which your relationships with your family, peers, and the media inform how you make sense of and derive meaning from the media you watch, read, and listen to. For example, Scheel and Westefeld (1999) found that young women and men who listened to heavy metal music had a higher level of suicidal ideation than young people who did not. Nabi and Sullivan (2001) found that the amount of television viewing influenced judgments of violence prevalence, and consequently the self-protective measures viewers intended to take. Underlying some of the more normative approaches to audience research is the question of information efficacy: how effective is the source? Of course, different cultural producers will have different definitions of effectiveness. Educators might care to evaluate how effective online course materials are in imparting knowledge to students. On the other hand, advertisers or political sources may be more concerned with how memorable and persuasive their content is with consumers and voters. Entertainment providers want to know what makes for compelling viewing. Public health officials might wish to know how effective public education campaigns are in terms of altering certain kinds of behaviour (e.g., what will compel teens to stop smoking or engaging in unsafe sex). Alternatively, citizens may wish to know what the unintended effects are of exposure to violence on television or in video games.

CONCLUSION

It is clear that a considerable body of cognitive scientific research developed outside of communication studies departments holds great promise for advancing the discipline of communication studies. In providing new insights and new methodologies, cognitive science is now a driving force in the revolutionary changes occurring in areas that used to be dominated by critical cultural scholarship. Given its historic links with psychology, philosophy, linguistics, and information science, communication studies is a natural point of contact between these differing approaches. It could serve as a model for a renewed humanism that incorporates, challenges, and reimagines how the sciences are approaching questions of the human being. We do not in any way suggest that these cognitive scientific approaches should supplant humanist ones in communication studies departments, since questions of power remain relevant; rather, we argue that the two should be able to inform and challenge the assumptions of each other and form true collaborative links, lending an extraordinary breadth and depth to the state of scholarship in the field. Cognitive science can provide a way for Canadian communication studies departments to stay current in the digital era, where communication studies scholarship should be more relevant than ever in understanding what it means to be a thinking, feeling, and social human being.

References

Babe, R. E. (2000). *Canadian communication thought: Ten foundational writers.* Toronto: University of Toronto Press.

Dill, K. E., & Dill, J. C. (1998). Video games violence: A review of the empirical literature. *Aggression and Violent Behaviour: A Review Journal, 3,* 407–428.

Ehrlich, S. (2001). *Representing rape: Language and sexual consent.* New York: Routledge.

Fairclough, N. (1989). *Language and power.* New York: Longman.

Festinger, L. (1957). *A theory of cognitive dissonance.* Stanford, CA: Stanford University Press.

Hamilton, S. (2006). Considering critical communication studies in Canada. In P. Attallah & L. Shade (Eds.), *Mediascapes: New patterns in Canadian communication* (2nd ed., pp. 9–27). Toronto: Thomson Nelson.

Kintsch, W. (1998). *Comprehension: A paradigm for cognition.* Cambridge: Cambridge University Press.

Lewandowsky, S., Stritzke, W. G. K., Oberauer, K., & Morales, M. (2005). Memory for fact, fiction, and misinformation: The Iraq War 2003. *Psychological Science, 16,* 190–195.

McLuhan, E., & Zingrone, F. (Eds.). (1995). *Essential McLuhan.* Concord, ON: House of Anansi Press.

Morwitz, V. G., &. Pluzinski, C. (1996). Do polls reflect opinions or do opinions reflect polls? The impact of political polling on voters' expectations, preferences, and behavior. *Journal of Consumer Research, 23*(1), 53–67.

Nabi, R. L., & Sullivan, J. L. (2001). Does television viewing relate to engagement in protective action against crime? *Communication Research, 28,* 802–825.

Roberts, J. V., & Doob, A. N. (1990). News media influences on public views of sentencing. *Law and Human Behavior, 14,* 451–468.

Scheel, K. R., & Westefeld, J. S. (1999). Heavy metal music and adolescent suicidality: An empirical investigation. *Adolescence, 34,* 253–273.

Sperber, D., & Wilson, D. (1995). *Relevance: Communication and cognition* (2nd ed.). Oxford: Blackwell.

Discussion Questions

1. What are the differences between critical humanist and cognitive scientific approaches to communication studies? In what ways do they complement each other?

2. How can Canadian communication studies incorporate cognitive science approaches?

3. What should the future directions of Canadian communication studies be? What are some of the questions that researchers should be pursuing, and how should these questions be approached?

GLOSSARY

AGENCY: The ability of human beings to make choices and have an impact on the world around them.

ALTERNATIVE MEDIA: Media that provide a range of perspectives and stories not covered in the profit-oriented corporate mainstream media and that are not owned or operated in the same manner as corporate mainstream media.

BIAS: An unfounded preference for or against an idea or concept. Bias is an opinion, preference, prejudice, or inclination formed without reasonable justification that then influences an individual's or a group's ability to evaluate a particular situation objectively or fairly.

BLOG: Derived from "weblogs," blogs are websites that resemble personal diaries where the author posts thoughts, opinions, and comments. Often, blogs are arranged in reverse chronological order and link to other websites.

BLOGOSPHERE: The online community that is created via the interconnected, hyperlinked nature of blogs.

BRAND-NAME BULLYING: David Bollier's term to describe the increasingly aggressive intimidation tactics employed by corporations to enforce their intellectual property rights as absolute property. Often, the legal foundation for their actions is not solid, but their greater resources and expertise allow them to "bully" ordinary people and small organizations into accepting their position.

CANDIDATE IMAGE: A subjective summary of what an individual knows and feels about a politician, based on both the knowledge possessed by voters and the messages projected by the candidate. Candidate image is constantly being reshaped by new information about the politician; at the same time, the politician's image helps shape the way voters receive and interpret new messages.

CIVIC ENGAGEMENT: How individuals as members of communities become interested and meaningfully participate in the issues and events of public interest.

CIVIL SOCIETY: Refers to all social relations that spring spontaneously from interpersonal contact and are not governed or managed by the state or political authority. Such relations can range from family picnics to bowling leagues to social protest movements. Civil society is the source of public opinion to which the state and political authorities must usually respond.

COGNITIVE DISSONANCE THEORY: A theory used to explain how individuals seek to deal with the psychological tension that can exist when they hold incompatible beliefs or opinions. For example, students may be conflicted when they are unable to find employment in their field after investing four years in a highly specialized undergraduate program—they experience dissonance because they undertook this field of study thinking it would lead to a productive career. Dissonance could be eliminated by deciding that it doesn't matter since they weren't really ready for a career anyway (reducing the importance of the dissonant belief), or focusing on the value of the experience of having learned something new in and of itself (thereby adding more consonant beliefs).

COMMERCIAL VALUES: Qualities and techniques used to construct the news which serve the interests of profit over citizen education and which valorizes consumerism.

COMMODITY FETISHISM: Refers to the notion that while commodities appear to be trivial things, they have a mysterious nature that manifests powers we believe are part of their nature. When commodities are believed to have value in and of themselves (i.e., as distinct from the labouring process that creates them), we mistakenly assign powers to them which they do not actually possess.

CONFESSIONAL MODEL: Encourages individuals to admit to themselves and others their problems, flaws, and vulnerabilities. The act of confession can be an important and effective technology of self-government and social control.

CONVERGENCE: The integration of digital technologies into print and broadcasting media, producing vertically and horizontally integrated conglomerates.

CRITICAL DISCOURSE ANALYSIS (CDA): A research method that primarily explores the way social power, dominance, and inequality are produced, reproduced, and resisted in our everyday text and talk in the media and in other social and political arenas of society. It not only attempts to reveal or deconstruct the ideological messages contained in discourse, but it also emphasizes the specific linguistic techniques writers use to help make their case.

***CSI* EFFECT:** The distorted perceptions produced by popular TV crime shows like *CSI*, *Law & Order*, and *Crossing Jordan* that many in the general public hold about the infallibility and reliability of forensic science and technology. The *CSI* effect is being blamed for a variety of recent trends, ranging from the rising number of science-savvy jurors to the increase in student enrollment in forensic science programs.

CULTURAL IMPERIALISM: The idea that the United States advances its interests, not simply militarily and economically, but through colonizing other nations' channels of communication and entertainment. Cultural imperialism is considered to be a way that American society works to infiltrate and dominate other cultures. Power, in this view, flows not so much from the barrel of a gun as from the laugh track of a situation comedy taped in California.

CULTURAL INDUSTRIES: A phrase used to describe the industries that have a cultural role—such as creating, producing, and commercializing contents. The cultural industries include advertising, architecture, crafts, fashion clothing, film, printing, publishing and multimedia, audiovisual and cinematic productions, and so forth. The contents produced can take the form of goods or services.

CULTURAL SOVEREIGNTY: The flip side to cultural imperialism. Cultural sovereignty insists that, in order to protect national self-identity, channels of communication and the media require a measure of protectionism that would be illogical in other areas (such as automobile manufacture or potash mining). Canada, for instance, may apply domestic laws and policies to protect its unique national, regional, and local culture(s) and its cultural industries from the powerful economic forces of both transnational media corporations and neoliberal policies.

DISCOURSE: The individual social networks of communication that are transmitted through language and nonverbal signs. Discourse consists of words, spoken and written, but also images, symbols, expressions, and gestures. When we speak of media discourse, we mean the signs and symbols that give rise to cultural meaning.

DISCOURSES OF SOBRIETY: Discourses that claim to tell the truth. Typically associated with documentary, these representations purport to reference the real and clearly separate fact from fiction and entertainment from knowledge.

ETHICAL MARKETING: A type of marketing that communicates information about goods that will be "best" for customers in terms of appeasing their moral imperatives, instead of persuading in light of short-term profits.

EYETRACKING: A method, using a specialized apparatus, to investigate how a reader or viewer looks at a text or other visual stimulus. Point of gaze and eye movements are measured in real time as the person looks at the stimulus. Eyetracking permits the researcher to construct a map of a person's looking patterns.

FORENSIC SCIENCE: Any aspect of science that relates to law. Forensic science is typically used in the gathering of evidence that can help prove that a crime has occurred and/or identify the person(s) who committed the crime.

FREEDOM OF SPEECH: The right to voice opinions and communicate messages publicly, without fear of repercussions from the government in the form of censorship or persecution. This right is one part of freedom of expression, which includes other methods of communication besides speech (e.g., artistic expression such as dance, music, film, and visual arts). Many countries guarantee this freedom, which is entrenched in the Universal Declaration of Human Rights. In Canada, as in numerous other countries, this freedom is not unlimited; there are restrictions on freedom of speech in relation to hate speech, obscenity, and defamation.

FUN FOOD: Fun food is a burgeoning category of food that is targeted and marketed to children (and their parents) by emphasizing the food's play factor, interactivity, and artificiality. Fun food is not necessarily junk food or food that is bad for you—rather, it is premised on the idea of food as entertainment.

HATE SPEECH: A contested term that can mean any expression that denigrates persons on the basis of their race or ethnic origin, religion, gender, age, physical condition, disability, or sexual orientation. It could also be more narrowly defined as persecutory, hateful, or degrading speech communicating messages of inferiority directed at historically oppressed groups.

INDIVIDUALIZATION: The idea that as social life becomes more contingent, flexible, and complex, identities and actions become increasingly a function of personal choice and risk.

INTELLECTUAL PROPERTY: Distinguished from real property (land and buildings) and personal property (movable objects) as the intangible property that is the product of the mind. The most common kinds of intellectual property are copyrights, patents, and trademarks. There are two major reasons why we protect creative production as property. First, it is a fair reward for the labour the creator puts into a work. Second, it stimulates a healthy market; property rights provide economic incentives to encourage more and better creation.

KINESICS: Coined by Ray Birdwhistell, a language-like system of meaning we use when we move our body to communicate, including facial gestures, how we move our head, how we move our hand, and how we plant our feet.

LOW INFORMATION RATIONALITY: A term used by Samuel Popkin to describe the many shortcuts people use to make reasoned choices in a limited amount of time. In an election, these could include asking the opinions of others around us, taking the advice of the news media or other opinion leaders, and taking cues from the political party to which the politician belongs. Assessing a candidate's image during an election to draw assumptions about how that candidate will perform once in power is also a form of low information rationality.

MAINSTREAM MEDIA: Often used to describe larger established news outlets, such as television networks and newspapers, with a defined organizational structure and professional staff.

MALE GAZE: The idea that men are represented in the public active world, while women are represented as objects of desire on display to be owned and controlled by men.

MANUFACTURING OF CONSENT: A process by which governments try to generate public support for a political or military initiative that the public might normally be inclined to oppose.

MEDIA CONCENTRATION: The degree of concentrated ownership both within and across various media sectors. Critics fear that more heavily concentrated ownership reduces diversity of information, limits access to marginalized groups, and reduces accountability of media owners to the public. Others argue that increased capital of media owners increases competitiveness and allows for more differentiated products that will appeal to niche audiences.

MEDIA EFFECTS RESEARCH: The body of research that investigates how exposure to different forms of media (television, video games, music, etc.) can directly influence the attitudes and behaviours of its audience.

NEOLIBERALISM: An economic and political ideology, typically espoused by corporate elites and international trade organizations, which suggests social well-being can be achieved through unfettered "free markets" with minimal governmental intervention. In the communication/media sector, neoliberalism is characterized by the relaxation of rules that constrain concentrated ownership (deregulation) and the privileging of corporate interests over public interests (privatization, hypercommercialism).

NEW MEDIA: The Internet, blogs, chat rooms, iPods, and cellular phones, which individuals can access as both users/consumers and producers of content.

NEW MEDIA DISPOSITION: Changes in broadcasting technology and audiences associated with the shift from the classical period (1950s–1980s), when a few large networks dominated the airwaves and manufactured content in their own studios for widespread dissemination according to fixed schedules, to a newer period (1970s–present). This period is marked by the introduction of cable and then VCRs, DVDs, videogames, the Internet, etc., which allow audiences to watch what they want when they want and to even produce or distribute content.

THE NEW WORLD INFORMATION AND COMMUNICATION ORDER (NWICO): An initiative spearheaded by UNESCO in the 1980s, first to draw attention to U.S. domination of the global information flow, and second to redress this imbalance. Fiercely resisted by U.S. and allied interests, the initiative faltered. Elements of the argument have recently been revived on the international stage, but on economic rather than cultural grounds. The new objection to U.S. media exports is not that they threaten national identities but that they unfairly inhibit the development of profitable national media production, especially in the film and television industries.

OLD MEDIA: The daily press, private and public broadcasters, and 24-hour cable television networks (e.g., CBC Newsworld), which individuals access merely as audiences/consumers of content.

PESTER POWER: The term marketers use to describe the influence children can have on family purchases and purchasing patterns. (Also known as the "nag factor.")

POSTFEMINISM: A term used to describe a range of theories that express dissatisfaction with traditional feminist arguments for collective political and economic struggle, arguing they are often irrelevant in today's society. Many postfeminist arguments posit, instead, an individual path to liberation premised on personal choice, pleasure, and consumption.

POSTMATERIALISM: The shifting of core social values away from material well-being to more ethically oriented concerns such as human rights and environmentalism.

PRIOR RESTRAINT CENSORSHIP: A particularly severe form of restriction on freedom of expression that requires government approval before material can be published, broadcast, or exhibited. Courts in Canada, the United Kingdom, and the United States have been historically reluctant to approve of prior restraints on speech, although they have been tolerated in a number of situations—publication bans on court proceedings and prohibition of certain "obscene" materials are forms of prior restraint censorship.

PROCEDURAL DEMOCRACY: An understanding of democracy that sees it as a process for making binding decisions in the public realm.

PROPERTIZATION: The increasing reinterpretation of what used to be thought of as shared cultural resources, or at least as unownable—language, names, scientific facts, organisms, elements of nature, shared myths—as property that can be owned, bought, and sold.

PUBLIC BROADCASTING: A way of organizing the production and distribution of radio and television content without attempting to generate profit and without direct state control. Examples of public broadcasters include the CBC in Canada, the BBC in Great Britain, NHK in Japan, and PBS in the United States. Public broadcasting tries to provide content that reflects the public interest.

PUBLIC SCREEN: The idea that the most important public discussions today take place via screens (computers and televisions, in particular). This implies that politics and citizenship can take place via spectatorship and not just through embodied speech making and reading.

PUBLIC SPHERE: A central feature of modern society. The concept, particularly associated with the work of Jürgen Habermas, refers to a space where individuals engage in discussions and debate relating to the issues of the day and participate in defining meaning in our society in a way that should be unaffected by relations of power.

QUALITATIVE DEMOCRACY: The idea that democracy should transform how we relate to fellow-citizens in public decision-making processes, and that it should require us to shift from self-interested calculation to focus on the collective good as the main principle of such processes.

QUANTITATIVE DEMOCRACY: The idea that democracy should maximize the number of participants and/or their level of information about, and involvement in, public decision-making processes.

RACIALIZED/RACIALIZATION: The process by which people, places, discourses, and behaviours are understood, classified, and controlled through race-based ideas and beliefs. Racialization refers to the process of being racially marked and can influence individuals' access to opportunities and resources by attributing race to particular social practices, marginalizing and demonizing particular ethno-racial groups.

RACISM: An ideological phenomenon that involves a negative representation whereby cultural and/or biological human characteristics are attributed to a real or perceived ancestral population on the basis of somatic, physical, or sociocultural features. These representational processes take place in the context of material struggle and are formed through the process of defining self and other, to the extent that evaluations of inferiority and superiority are produced and reproduced.

REIFICATION: A stage of social and economic development when human beings experience the world as though it exists beyond their actions. Reification takes place when individuals attach to economic forces objective purposes and functions (e.g., the "needs" of the market) while rendering human needs invisible.

RELEVANCE THEORY: A theory that explains, in cognitively realistic and empirically testable terms, how a hearer infers a speaker's meaning on the basis of the evidence provided. (Also referred to as "cognitive pragmatics.")

SECOND ENCLOSURE MOVEMENT: James Boyle's suggestion that we are seeing a radical shift to new and expanded intellectual property rights in realms of culture previously not subject to private ownership. He argues this parallels the enclosure of land movement that took place in England between the 15th and 19th centuries, where common lands were fenced off and became private property.

SOCIAL CONTROL: The processes through which behaviour is shaped and patterned by the interaction of social constraints and socially internalized values, ideals, desires, and emotions.

THERAPEUTIC MODEL: The idea that individuals should be urged to take personal responsibility to change themselves psychologically and emotionally as the way to remedy social problems.

VIDEO NEWS RELEASES (VNRS): Reports prepared on video by public relations firms representing self-interested sources designed to disguise propaganda as news. TV news operations use them to lower the costs of producing the news.